D. H. LAWRENCE:

A COMPOSITE BIOGRAPHY

Gathered, arranged, and edited

by Edward Nehls

Volume Three, 1925-1930

THE UNIVERSITY OF WISCONSIN PRESS

Published 1959
The University of Wisconsin Press
Box 1379, Madison, Wisconsin 53701

Printings 1959, 1977

Printed in the United States of America
ISBN 0-299-81503-X; LC 57-9817

D. H. LAWRENCE:

A COMPOSITE BIOGRAPHY

Assemble, first, all casual bits and scraps
That may shake down into a world perhaps. . . .
Sigh then, or frown, but leave (as in despair)
Motive and end and moral in the air;
Nice contradiction between fact and fact
Will make the whole read human and exact.

—Robert Graves, "The Devil's
Advice to Story-Tellers"

D. H. LAWRENCE:

A COMPOSITE BIOGRAPHY

D. H. Lawrence, Florence, 1928.
From a photograph taken by Robert H. Davis.
Reproduced by courtesy of the Davart Company, New York.

TO GRACE MARY, PETER, TINA,

and the lost world of Bourne Mill

FOREWORD

Lodovico Ariosto opens the last *canto* of his *Orlando Furioso* with a pleasant fancy. The years of concentrated work needed to bring his poem to completion are likened to a long ocean voyage, and when at last he sees land and his port ahead he gladdens himself by imagining how friends and colleagues will press to greet and to congratulate him when they hear of his successful arrival. It is true that in the contemporary literary dogfight any such generous approval of a living writer seems unlikely, but in studying Mr. Edward Nehls's monumental "composite biography" of D. H. Lawrence, which now fills three large volumes, the parallel often came to my mind. During the years of work on his book Mr. Nehls has made many new friends and acquaintances, who will be happy to welcome him as he brings his literary ship triumphantly into port after the long and arduous voyage.

By skill, enterprise, intelligence, and much hard work Mr. Nehls has made himself one of the leading American authorities on the life and works of D. H. Lawrence. One might re-quote the old Oxford joke, and say that what he doesn't know about the subject "isn't knowledge." At a time when literature is being more and more forced relentlessly into journalism, when in so-called "creative writing" the applause and the rewards so often go to mere entertainment, which is often unworthy and sometimes downright depraved, it is a pleasure as well as a welcome duty to give all due praise to a work of conscientious and disinterested scholarship such as Mr. Nehls's *Composite Biography of D. H. Lawrence*. It is only fair to include in this praise the University of Wisconsin Press, which has made the achievement possible.

Biography is "the history of the lives of individual men" according to the dictionary—to which I should add the words "and women." Like most definitions this admits, and has admitted, of different interpretations. If in England you raise the subject of biography, almost certainly you will be referred to Boswell's *Johnson*. But in that work the last twenty-one years of Johnson's life receive between four and five times as much space as the fifty-four which passed before Boswell met him. The proportions are all wrong, and Boswell was not so much a biographer as the supreme genius among literary reporters. His book would have been as valuable— perhaps more so—if he had limited it to *Conversations with Johnson*. It is obviously in the same class as Eckermann's *Conversations with Goethe* and Stanhope's *Conversations with Wellington*.

Is biography an art or a science? An excellent topic for a prize essay! Roughly speaking I should say that the French tend to treat it as an art and the Germans as a science, as we might expect. Both conceptions, valid in themselves, tend to fall into excess. In France we have had the deplorable *vies romancées* (recently revived as *vies passionées*), which attempt to turn biographies into novels, and too often only succeed in combining the defects of both forms. In the solemn pursuit of minute and complete *"data"* the Germans fell into such absurdities as the thesis on Dickens (reported and probably invented by Ford Madox Hueffer) amazingly entitled *Die Schwester von Mealy Potatoes*. Mealy Potatoes was one of the boys who worked with David Copperfield at the factory, and since he had already been the victim of a Ph.D. thesis, this one was devoted to his little sister who "did imps in the Pantomime."

We must not forget the nineteenth century British *Life,* which often burgeoned into a *Life and Times of . . .* , the strange composition too advantageously spoken of as "the standard biography," which Lytton Strachey has mocked so wittily and cogently:

"Those two fat volumes, with which it is our custom to commemorate the dead—who does not know them, with their ill-digested masses of material, their slipshod style, their tone of tedious panegyric, their lamentable lack of selection, of detachment, or design? They are as familiar as the *cortège* of the undertaker, and wear the same air of slow, funereal barbarism."

To crown all, we have among us some who would discourage all biography as "trash," above all in the case of writers. "You can always tell a bad critic," they assert, "because he begins with life." Even more easily can one "tell" a pedant, who begins with words and ends with words and never touches life at all. And yet these would-be disparagers cannot deny that biography has had an immense influence on the Western world for nearly two millennia. I will give you, not one example, but four— Matthew, Mark, Luke, John.

And then came Mr. Nehls with *une idée geniale*, a biographical idea of genius to deal with a genius. Why not? yes, why not re-create the strange, fascinating saga of Lawrence by bringing together in chronological order the relevant available evidence, not only from others but from Lawrence himself, and allowing it to speak for itself, with no narrative and strictly "factual" notes. An excellent idea. The work of "bringing together" the material from which to select what is essential must indeed have been arduous, since it included a search through all Lawrence's voluminous works and the many books and studies and reminiscences about him, with the addition of a further search for new material which involved much correspondence, and a considerable period in England to collect personal testimonies. The achievement is of permanent value, and all thorough students of Lawrence in the future will be indebted to Mr. Nehls.

No doubt this method would not be equally successful for all lives. Applied, let us say, to Jane Austen, a satirical, intelligent maiden lady, whose life, however, was not only blameless but circumscribed, the method would very likely bring only limited results. On the other hand if it had been applied to Queen Victoria, hundreds of volumes would not contain the results. But in the case of Lawrence this method has proved most successful in bringing out the varying aspects of a tempestuous and adventurous life, of a vehement and contradictory character, as well as the occasions for writings which are among the most remarkable of our century.

True, the available material is so abundant that Mr. Nehls has been compelled to select carefully, in order to keep his book within reasonable limits. Inexorable limits of space have forced him to draw but sparingly on the Lawrence Letters and writings generally. I know Mr. Nehls regrets this and share his feelings, for the books and letters bring us most interesting information about the "inner man" when the testimonies of witnesses and similar evidence tend inevitably to tell us most about the "outer man." Moreover in the nature of things such testimonies must be read with critical care, since in some cases they tell us far more about the writer than about Lawrence, and in still others are obviously inaccurate or prejudiced. On the other hand it is illuminating (and sometimes funny) to see the results produced by the impact of Lawrence's personality on other people, even if they go no further than the resentment of wounded vanity, the blunders of misunderstanding, or the fussing of local patriotisms. All were worth recording, and all have their value. Not the least valuable is the hagiography of faithful females. If a man finds only one woman to take him seriously until he dies, he is lucky; and Lawrence found more than one.

Socrates in the Platonic dialogue prays that "the inner and the outer man may be at peace." It seems unlikely that Lawrence ever made the same prayer, but he certainly should have done so. Was there ever a man so often at loggerheads with himself, or with the world about him and his few devoted friends in particular? His mother once told him his life was "battle, battle, battle," and years afterwards he announced that his future life-programme would be "retire to the desert and fight." (Of course, he and she meant Blake's "mental strife," for he was not interested in the strife which results when the guns begin to roll.)

There was a strange perversity in the man, apparently noticeable in his father too, which impelled him to insult and to wound those who could harm him as well as those who tried to help him, and at times a species of megalomania under the influence of which he conceited himself the judge and master, not only of those he knew, but even of the world in general. And yet at those moments when the inner man and the outer man were at peace, he was the most affectionate, charming, amusing, fascinating, and inspired of beings. Katherine Mansfield has fortunately left a record of one such happy moment of time:

"He was just his old, merry, rich self, laughing, describing things, giving you pictures, full of enthusiasm and joy in a future where we become all 'vagabonds'. . . . Oh, there is something so lovable about him and his eagerness, his passionate eagerness for life—that is what one loves so."

Yet, yet and yet . . . only sixteen months later that same "merry, rich self" could find it in his heart to send her that dreadful unpardonable letter which she mentions:

"Lawrence sent me a letter to-day. He spat in my face and threw filth at me and said: 'I loathe you. You revolt me stewing in your consumption. . . . The Italians were quite right to have nothing to do with you,' and a great deal more."

Three years later she was dead of consumption, just as he tried to renew a friendship whose loss he must have regretted by—sending her a postcard from her native city of Wellington, New Zealand!

Other ugly incidents, which Mr. Nehls most rightly has not tried to conceal or to gloss over, are recorded of Lawrence, but few quite so gratuitous and "repulsive" as that letter to Katherine Mansfield. After his death, when Frieda published her naïve but honest and very valuable book about Lawrence she related the incident of his throwing a glass of wine in her face because he was jealous—and how absurdly and irrelevantly jealous he could sometimes be!—of her love for her daughter. With that courteous chivalry which marks the modern "press," the London journalists made banner headlines of it, and disregarded all the good she had to tell—so true it is that we get from life and books what we bring to them.

Lawrence appears as a character in several contemporary novels, which is not to be wondered at, seeing how freely he made use of his friends for satirical fiction. To my mind the best of them are Aldous Huxley's, the Rampion of *Point Counter Point,* and better still the Kingham of *Two or Three Graces.* This is a vivid but good-natured skit on the irritating side of Lawrence as it affected those of his men friends who did not lend themselves to the semi-homosexual relationship he tried unsuccessfully to set up with Murry and others. "I exasperated him," says the 'I' of the story, "but he continued to frequent my company—chiefly to abuse me, to tell me passionately how hopeless I was. . . . I winced, but all the same I delighted in his company. We irritated one another profoundly; but we were friends."

And again later on in the same story: ". . . what in other men would have been a passing irritation held in check by self-control, to be modified very likely by subsequent impressions, was converted by Kingham, almost deliberately, into a wild fury which no second thoughts were allowed to assuage. . . ."

Traces of this violent habit may be found throughout Lawrence's life story, and Mr. Nehls most rightly has allowed them to be recorded by the victims, who have not all been "assuaged" by the passage of thirty or forty years. But this is not all—in addition, there was Lawrence's extraordinary faith that by writing and publishing his books he would immediately have a decisive influence on human society and the course of history. When Frieda, in Bavaria, in 1912, had a fit of acute "miserables" at the enforced separation from her young children, he told her vehemently: "Don't be sad. I'll make a new heaven and earth for them, don't cry, you see if I don't." And two years later his country was at war with hers.

Even after the war he retained this unfounded belief. In that wonderful Introduction to the Maurice Magnus *Memoirs of the Foreign Legion,* he brings up the topic of war in this outburst: ". . . never again shall you fight with the foul, base, fearful monstrous machines of war which man invented for the last war. You shall not. The diabolical mechanisms are man's and I am a man. Therefore they are mine. And I smash them into oblivion."

As we all saw in 1939–45. True, he goes on to say that "many, most" men are with him, but the delusion of immense personal power is none the less present and deplorable. The War of 1914–18 raised Lawrence's inner conflict to a state of frenzy, which may be studied in his letters to Bertrand Russell, the publication of which was the most severe blow Lawrence's reputation ever suffered. They are not only absurd, but even ignominious when he drops to the point of asking Lord Russell to bequeath him money! Frieda's attempted get-out—that Lawrence knew Russell had no money—is very feeble. If he knew that, why did he ask for it? And, then at another time he wrote to ask Lady Ottoline Morrell to subsidise his artists' colony of "Rananim," which is at best a reflection of the "Pantisocracy" of the youthful Coleridge and Southey.

These are undeniable facts. The mistake (which Mr. Nehls has entirely avoided) is either to ignore them as some books on Lawrence have done, or else never to get beyond them, as the case is with other books or statements about him. Certainly it is absurd to represent him as a kind of "messiah," blameless and crucified, but it is equally absurd to see him as a little Satan, "a force for evil," or as a person with a hatred for all mankind, and still more absurdly as a Nazi!

That such resentment against Lawrence can still flare nearly thirty years after his death gives one a most favourable idea of the force and influence of his character. Lawrence can only be estimated fairly by those who have rid themselves of uncritical hero-worship and prejudiced resentment, whether personal or otherwise. It seems to me that the Danish artist, K. Gótzsche, expressed a good deal of the truth about Lawrence as a person in a few colloquial sentences:

"He seems to be absolutely nuts at times, and to have a hard time with himself. He over-estimates himself. He thinks he can show by his feelings what people think and do. At other times he is so reasonable and so overwhelmingly good that there is no end to it."

I should say myself that the third sentence is rather off the mark. I should prefer to say: "He thinks that by writing and publishing his feelings about what people think and do he can influence their lives and even change the world."

Unfortunately, the "overwhelmingly good" side of Lawrence has been far less amply recorded than the disagreeable and hysterical side, perhaps because human vanity is so easily offended and so implacably resentful. Well, he is not the first of whom it might be said:

> The evil that men do lives after them;
> The good is oft interred with their bones.

But in Lawrence's case the best of the "good" has not been lost, and lives on, in writing which taken as a whole forms so original and beautiful a contribution to English literature in this century. How regrettable it is that many of his books are out of print, even in his native country, where some of his finest work must even now be sought for in the second-hand book market. Thus are great writers honoured! And let us always keep in mind, that if Lawrence had not been a great literary artist we should not still be talking about him.

Lawrence's "proletarian origin" has been held to explain some of the disagreeable traits in his character, such as his ingratitude (as if he gave nothing!), his censorious attitude, his intense class-consciousness, his endless abuse and wrangling. But others cannot be so easily brushed off. How, for instance, do we explain the undoubted homosexual streak in him which combines unpleasingly with his vehement and obsolete assertions on the necessity for a woman's "submission"—and that, absurdly enough, in an epoch and country where the "Suffragette" movement for the emancipation of women was becoming irresistible? (By the way, he took that particular pig to the wrong market when he married Frieda.) How can we explain his strange Power delusions? So far, the professional psychologists do not seem to have found any very valid explanations of these or other traits in him. One doctor is said to have found tell-tale symbols of Lawrence's horrid impulses in the various dishes forming a meal eaten by Birkin and Ursula in *Women in Love*. I cannot be positive, but my impression is that, as so often in his novels, Lawrence did not invent the meal but simply remembered it—and hence it can have no psychological significance whatsoever.

Even more interesting, and so far as I know almost ignored as well as unexplained, is the remarkable "moon madness" which sometimes possessed Lawrence during a full moon. The synchronisation with the full moon may be a coincidence, but the seizures certainly happened. They are reported from his point of view in *The Trespasser* and *Women in Love* (see the very odd chapter called "Moony") and from the point of view of a distressed and unwilling witness by his first sweetheart, Jessie Chambers, who reports two or three such occasions. It is interesting, if only as one more instance of that extreme sensibility which brought

Lawrence so much suffering as well as so much joy and beauty.

Among all the writers and painters of his time Lawrence was pre-eminently one "for whom the visible world existed." The tag is musty, but nothing else so well expresses him. Not even Théophile Gautier who invented it, nor Goethe its greatest exponent before it was invented, deserved the phrase more than Lawrence. Oscar Wilde, who was fond of applying it to himself, was a *poseur* compared with Lawrence who was as alert and sensitive to every changing aspect of the living world about him as Walter Pater claimed to be. Norman Douglas—sometimes obtuse about Lawrence, and often hostile—speaks approvingly of "his blithe and childlike curiosity." The phrase is true so far as it goes, but it does not go nearly far enough. It is not enough to explain how it was that for twenty years Lawrence continually renewed himself and poured out so vivid and original a stream of experiences.

It is not a question of "descriptions of scenery," as one writer dispar-agingly puts the matter, not even of "giving pictures" as Katherine Mans-field wrote—it *is* the living world, that vivid moment of transitory but intense awareness which Goethe thought the real inspiration of poetry. And, apropos that, how strange it is that Lawrence claimed he detested Goethe so much. Perhaps it was because in some of the innumerable striking phrases Goethe hit out we detect something like a prophecy of Lawrence. Deploring the fashionable art of his old age Goethe said it lacked "mind, *naiveté* and sensuousness" and though some might question Lawrence's full right to the first, few will deny the other two qualities. Goethe spoke of the English as "practical and pedantic," and it was against an excess of their practicality and pedantry that Lawrence reacted so strenuously and bitterly. "Freedom," said Goethe, "consists not in re-fusing to recognise anything which is above us, but in respecting some-thing which is above us; for by respecting it, we raise ourselves to it"— which protests against the ignominy of "democracy" Lawrence sedu-lously inculcated, though prone perhaps to imply that he was the "some-thing above." Goethe pre-figured Lawrence's contempt for petty critics, and his determination to go his own way in spite of them—"we will keep to the right way, and let others go as they choose." Lawrence may not have known of it, but he certainly seemed to believe wholeheartedly Goethe's assertion: "What we agree with leaves us inactive, but contra-diction makes us productive." Most striking is Goethe's insistence on the "value of the present moment," that "representative of a whole eternity" and true inspiration of poems. "The world is so great and rich, and life so full of variety, that you can never want themes for poems. But they must be 'occasional' (*Gelegenheitsgedicht*), that is to say, reality must give both impulse and material for their production." There Goethe expresses in aphorism very much what Lawrence said in his preface to the American edition (1920) of *New Poems*.

Pondering over Lawrence's contradictions and perpetual self-contradictions one is inclined to say in despair that it is virtually impossible to generalise about him. Still, one aspect much in his favour seems beyond dispute. He was not mealy-mouthed, he was not a timeserver or a flatterer, and he was not a careerist. He lived and died poor, the more honour to him. If he had cringed and conformed, if he had climbed the social ladder prudently, if he had used others for his advancement and then dropped them when they ceased to be of service, there is no saying how high he might have risen in the magazine and high royalties world. His awkward efforts "to cultivate the right people" always ended in mutual explosions of bad temper. There was no taming him. The Sun-God, Lord of Song, uses such devices to protect his few favourites from the contaminations of conformity, respectability, and success.

RICHARD ALDINGTON

PREFACE

The three volumes constituting this present composite biography of D. H. Lawrence were conceived as a single unit several years ago, and brought to completion by plans worked out in advance by the Director and Editorial Staff of the University of Wisconsin Press and myself. The principles laid down in the preface to the first volume, therefore, have remained constant, and I repeat them here for the last time.

I have continued to be guided by the single desire to collect and preserve as much trustworthy material concerning D. H. Lawrence as I could locate, and to give each contribution its full significance by proper placement in a context. The work is intended to be both autobiography and biography, a blend of Lawrence's life as he himself and others saw it.

I have furnished the full text of all unpublished letters to which I have had access, but have not thought it necessary to employ an irksome editorial apparatus to flag up occasional lapses in punctuation and spelling.

To enable the reader to identify Lawrence's own voice, I have employed a distinguishing type face. And to keep the chronology of the Lawrence story clearly before the reader, I have supplied the dates of all letters whenever possible, but standardized the addresses from which they were written. The dates plus the pertinent passages from the letters have thus been arranged to give the effect of a journal; but in "Notes and Sources" I have supplied the name of the addressee and the form of the address given in the original letter, as well as the source from which the excerpt was taken.

Again I have been obliged to cut full-length memoirs, but have in each case tried to include as much as I could, and within the necessary limitations to choose those passages which seemed especially relevant to any consideration of Lawrence the artist and the man, which provided source material for his writing, which explicitly amplified or contradicted another memoir. Whenever possible, I have submitted my own tentative selections from book-length memoirs to the authors concerned. I have used material from the late Mrs. Frieda Lawrence Ravagli only when she alone could tell the story; whenever a third person is on record, I have chosen to use the outsider's point of view. I have often been obliged to break the reminiscences into short sections in order that the over-all chronology might be preserved. But I have never deliberately omitted ill-tempered or damaging portraits of Lawrence. I have sincerely tried to include all valid reminiscences, whether they fitted my own preconceived notions of Lawrence or not.

By the use of ellipsis points I have tried to indicate that a cut has been made in a Lawrence letter or a published memoir, and in my "Notes and Sources," to be precise in supplying the exact pages on which the material was originally printed.

To facilitate reference, I have placed the pertinent biographical data for the memoir-writers in an appendix, "The Lawrence Circle." On occasion, I have supplied more detailed biographical data in "Notes and Sources," following the initial source identifications.

I have provided the reader with two bibliographies: one, a list of the sources used in the compilation of this final volume; the other, a list of the major first editions of Lawrence.

I have tried to be alert to errors in the memoirs when I found them, and to supply corrections when I could. But the reader must make his own allowances for differences in observations, lapses in memory, variations in spellings. When the memoirs have been published in both the United States and England, I have given the American source whenever the American copyright is still valid; in certain instances when an English source has been cited, I have done so either because the English is the only source, or because the American copyright is no longer in force. All material published for the first time is so indicated. Subject to the demands of space, I have tried to the best of my ability to identify various people the memoir-writers mention in passing, but chiefly those not readily found in standard works of reference. Because it is unlikely that the reader would have available to him the periodicals and newspapers in which Lawrence's short stories, articles, and poems first appeared, I have usually cited the titles of collections in which they were published.

Again, I have been allowed to print almost everything I asked for. The single exception is a sequence of three letters written by the solicitors acting for the Commissioner of Metropolitan Police, London, relating to the Lawrence Exhibition case. The present Commissioner is not prepared to authorize their publication.

Unable to establish an authoritative date for it, I have chosen not to include a brief glimpse of Lawrence recorded in the late H. M. Tomlinson's *Norman Douglas* (1931, rev., 1952). Nor have I reprinted the correspondence, occasioned by his death, between a number of Lawrence's admirers and detractors printed in *The Nation and Athenaeum,* partly because the sequence is concerned primarily with the merits of Lawrence as an artist, chiefly because of the limitations of space.

In the compilation of this final volume I have encountered a number of new problems.

One was the placement of hitherto unpublished letters written *to* Lawrence. I decided to adhere strictly to the established chronology, and the reader is asked to recognize and allow for the time interval between the posting and receipt of these letters.

Another problem resulted from the fact that here for the first time the Lawrence story was being enacted upon two fronts. The Exhibition case unfolded in London, while Lawrence himself was in Italy and Germany. My dilemma, therefore, lay in keeping *two* facets of the narrative before the reader, while maintaining the over-all chronology.

The publication (June, 1957) of Mrs. Brigit Patmore's memoirs of Lawrence came too late for their incorporation in Vols. I *and* III, but, fortunately, in time for reprinting in the latter. The recovery in late 1957 of the W. Siebenhaar memoir has enabled me to print it in Vol. III, although the greater portion belonged in the Australian chapter of Vol. II. And the discovery of the Chambers Papers at Christmas, 1956, was made after Vol. I was in proof. I have placed the Patmore and Siebenhaar memoirs at the most reasonable points in the chronology of Vol. III, allowing the portions more suitably pertaining to earlier periods to stand as backgrounds, and have made a chapter of the Chambers Papers. The latter serve to complete a circle I had not anticipated.

I encountered a final problem in authenticating all sources cited in reference to the Lawrence Exhibition case. Mr. Philip Trotter used for his basic authority an album belonging to the Warren Gallery and containing the findings of a professional clipping service. Both he and I have checked and rechecked newspapers for dates and, in the case of magazines, for volumes, issues, pages. But some of these newspapers and periodicals have long since ceased publication, and it has not been possible for us to locate runs of the period in other collections and libraries. In a very few cases, therefore, we have been obliged to rely solely upon the dates supplied by the scrapbook. If there are errors in our citations, these facts must explain them.

A word must be said concerning the conclusion of the Lawrence story. I have attempted to bring it to the point where biography fades into legend, where, in the 1930's, the artist is all but forgotten. The resurgence of interest in Lawrence in the late 1940's, as evidenced by the White bibliography, is for another to explore and explain. I am aware that some readers may be disappointed in the fact that I have made little attempt to trace the story and legends of Frieda between Lawrence's death in 1930 and her own in 1956. But a man's life must be concluded at some point, and Frieda's warrants someone else's researches.

My own feelings, as I conclude this experiment in composite biography, might be compared with those of a film editor who, with yards of exposed but unused film coiled about his feet, wonders whether his cutting and splicing have preserved the best possible scenes and resulted in the best possible whole. No doubt he also laments the sequences never shot, the occasional poor lighting or inadequate sound, the failure of sharp focus in certain crucial episodes. Perhaps he too regrets the limitations of his medium, and the necessity to remain voiceless.

E. N.

Urbana, Illinois
Spring, 1958

ACKNOWLEDGMENTS

I

I wish to thank the following publishers for permission to make use of the materials from the books indicated. Detailed acknowledgment is made in the bibliographical citations accompanying the text.

Brandt and Brandt, for permission to quote from "Two Houses, Two Ways: The Florentine Villas of Lewis and Lawrence, Respectively," in *New World Writing* (Fourth Mentor Selection), by Mark Schorer. Copyright, 1953, by The New American Library of World Literature, Inc.

Jonathan Cape, Ltd., for permission to quote from *Reminscences of D. H. Lawrence,* by John Middleton Murry.

Chatto and Windus, Ltd., for permission to quote from *Looking Back,* by Norman Douglas.

Collins, Sons and Company, Ltd., for permission to quote from *More Than I Should,* by Faith Compton Mackenzie.

The John Day Company, Inc., for permission to quote from *Journey with Genius,* by Witter Bynner.

J. M. Dent and Sons, Ltd., for permission to reprint from *Everyman* "D. H. Lawrence," by Richard Aldington.

The Dial Press, Inc., for permission to quote from *The Passionate Years,* by Caresse Crosby; and *Between Sittings: An Informal Autobiography,* by Jo Davidson.

Duell, Sloan and Pearce, Inc., for permission to quote from *D. H. Lawrence: Portrait of a Genius But . . . ,* by Richard Aldington.

E. P. Dutton and Company, for permission to quote from *The Nets*, by Brewster Ghiselin.

Harcourt, Brace and Company, for permission to quote from *From Another World*, by Louis Untermeyer.

William Heinemann, Ltd., for permission to make use of hitherto unpublished letters of D. H. Lawrence; and the memoir by William Siebenhaar.

Her Majesty's Stationery Office, for permission to quote from *Parliamentary Debates* (House of Commons).

The Humanities Research Center, University of Texas, for permission to quote from *D. H. Lawrence: Reminiscences and Correspondence*, by Earl and Achsah Brewster.

Alfred A. Knopf, Inc., for permission to quote from "Seized Pictures," by D. H. Lawrence (originally printed in *The Nottingham Evening Post*).

J. B. Lippincott Company, for permission to quote from *Lawrence and Brett: A Friendship*, by Dorothy Brett.

MacDonald and Company, Ltd., for permission to quote from *Life Interests*, by Douglas Goldring.

The Macmillan Company, for permission to quote from *The English Past*, by A. L. Rowse; and *Confessions of a European Intellectual*, by Franz Schoenberner.

St. Martin's Press, for permission to quote from *Penny Foolish*, by Osbert Sitwell.

Secker and Warburg, Ltd., for permission to quote from *The Savage Pilgrimage*, by Catherine Carswell.

Stackpole Sons, for permission to quote from *Time of Our Lives*, by Orrick Johns.

Stanford University Press, for permission to quote from *Imagism and Imagists*, by Glenn Hughes.

The Viking Press, Inc., for permission to quote from *"Not I, But the Wind . . . ,"* by Frieda Lawrence Ravagli. Copyright 1934 by Frieda Lawrence. Reprinted by permission of The Viking Press, Inc., New York; *The Letters of D. H. Lawrence*, edited by Aldous Huxley. Copyright 1932 by the Estate of D. H. Lawrence, 1934, 1936 by Frieda Lawrence; *Phoenix: The Posthumous Papers*, by D. H. Lawrence. Copyright 1936 by Frieda Lawrence; and for permission to make use of hitherto unpublished letters of D. H. Lawrence.

II

For permission to reprint, in whole or in part, contributions to periodical publications, I wish to thank the following.

The Bulletin [Sydney], for permission to quote from "D. H. Lawrence in Australia," by Roland E. Robinson.

The Daily Express [London], for permission to quote from "D. H. Lawrence as Painter."

Horizon, for permission to quote from "Lawrence in Bandol," by Rhys Davies.

John Bull, for permission to quote from "Famous Novelist's Shameful Book: A Landmark in Evil."

The London Magazine, for permission to quote from "Conversations with D. H. Lawrence," by Brigit Patmore.

The New Mexico Quarterly, for permission to quote from "A Visit to Kiowa Ranch," by John C. Neff.

The New York Times Book Review, for permission to quote from "D. H. Lawrence, Shy Genius, Sits for Two Camera Studies," by Robert H. Davis.

The Pine Cone, for permission to quote from "The Lawrence I Knew . . . ," by Mabel Dodge Luhan.

The Saturday Review, for permission to quote from "Trade Winds," by Bennett Cerf.

The Star [London], for permission to quote from "A Talk with Lawrence's 'Princess'. . . ."

The Times [London], for permission to quote from "Mr. D. H. Lawrence's Lost Will"; and "Seized Pictures . . . ," by D. H. Lawrence.

III

For permission to use the works indicated, I wish to thank the following authors, literary agents, and executors.

Richard Aldington, for permission to quote from "D. H. Lawrence."

Curtis Brown, Ltd., for permission to quote from *Contacts,* by Curtis Brown; *Memoirs of a Polyglot,* by William Gerhardi; and "D. H. Lawrence in Bandol," by Rhys Davies.

Rosica Colin, agent for Richard Aldington, for permission to quote from *Life for Life's Sake.*

Rhys Davies, for permission to quote from "D. H. Lawrence in Bandol."
William Gerhardi, for permission to quote from *Memoirs of a Polyglot.*
Mrs. Gladys Holden, for permission to quote from the letters of Ralph A. Holden.
The Countess Iris Origo, for permission to quote from Geoffrey Scott's letter to Arnold Bennett.
Laurence Pollinger, literary executor of the Estate of D. H. Lawrence, for permission to make use of hitherto unpublished letters of D. H. Lawrence.
Joyce Weiner, literary agent for Faith Compton Mackenzie, for permission to quote from *More Than I Should.*

IV

As in Volumes I and II, my debt continues to the following: the late Mrs. Frieda Lawrence Ravagli; Mr. Laurence Pollinger, literary executor of the D. H. Lawrence estate; the Viking Press; Mr. Richard Aldington; Professor Harry T. Moore; and many others mentioned in the Acknowledgments of the two earlier volumes.

For patiently and courteously answering my many questions either in person or by correspondence, I am indebted to these people of England and Scotland: Mr. Colin Agnew, Mrs. Barbara Weekley Barr, Mr. Spencer Curtis Brown, Mr. John Carswell, Mr. Frederick Carter, Dr. J. D. Chambers, Mr. Hubert Cole, Miss Helen Corke, Mr. Rhys Davies, Mr. Rolf Gardiner, Mrs. Margaret Gardiner-Bernal, Mr. William Gerhardi, Mr. Douglas Goldring, Mr. Raymond V. Hewett, Mr. and Mrs. F. J. Hill, Mrs. Gladys Holden, Mrs. Olive L. Hopkin, Miss Margaret Kennedy, Prince Leopold of Loewenstein-Wertheim, Mr. Jack Lindsay, Miss Rose Macaulay, Lady Compton Mackenzie, the late Dr. Andrew Morland, the late Mr. John Middleton Murry, Mrs. Brigit Patmore, Mr. Randolph Quirk, Mr. A. L. Rowse, Mr. Hardiman Scott, Mr. Martin Secker, Sir Osbert Sitwell, Mr. Philip Trotter, Mr. Montague Weekley, Miss Rebecca West, Mr. Walter Wilkinson, and Mr. John R. Wood.

To these of the United States: the Hon. Dorothy E. Brett, Mr. Witter Bynner, Mr. Bennett Cerf, Mr. Alan C. Collins, Mr. Edward Dahlberg, Mrs. Robert H. Davis, Mrs. Ida Rauh Eastman, Mrs. Mary Freeman, Professor Brewster Ghiselin, Miss Marjorie Griesser, Miss Aimée Guggenheimer, Professor Bruce Harkness, Professor Frederick J. Hoffman, Professor Glenn Hughes, Mr. Willard Johnson, Mrs. Mabel Dodge Luhan, Dr. Louis A. Muinzer, Mr. John C. Neff, Professor T. M. Pearce, Dean

H. H. Ransom, Capt. Angelo Ravagli, Mr. Franz Schoenberner, Professor Mark Schorer, Dr. Hans Syz, Professor E. W. Tedlock, Jr., Mrs. Jean Starr Untermeyer, Mr. Louis Untermeyer, Mr. Edward Weeks, and Miss Dorothy Yorke.

To these of various countries: Mr. Harold Acton, Signor Raul Mirenda, and the Countess Iris Origo of Italy; Mr. Earl H. Brewster of India; the late Mrs. William Holbrook, and Mr. William Holbrook of Canada; Professor R. G. Howarth of South Africa; Dr. Else Jaffe-Richthofen of Germany; Mr. Roland E. Robinson of Australia; Mr. Philippe Soupault of France; and Signor Carlo Zanotti of Portugal.

I wish to thank the following for enabling me to copy and use hitherto unpublished Lawrence letters: Mr. William Gerhardi, Professor Brewster Ghiselin, Mr. William Holbrook, Mr. Philip Trotter, and Mrs. Jean Starr Untermeyer.

To all individuals and publishing firms who have allowed me to reprint here selections from their printed works, and to those many friends of Lawrence who have written original memoirs for use in this book, I extend my thanks. It has been impossible for me to acknowledge by name all of those to whom I am indebted for assistance, but to them as well I offer my gratitude.

CONTENTS

Contents

LIST OF ILLUSTRATIONS

D. H. LAWRENCE:

A COMPOSITE BIOGRAPHY

CHAPTER ONE

1925–1926: England, Italy, Capri

[A] man must be more than nice and good, and . . . heroes are worth more than saints . . . . I do not come for peace. The devil, the holy devil, has peace round his neck . . . .

. . . I don't want peace. I go around the world fighting . . . . In the grave I find my peace. First let me fight and win through.

—Frieda Lawrence, pp. 142–43

ENGLAND

1 October 1925   *Garland's Hotel, Suffolk Street, Pall Mall, London, S.W. 1*

❡[*Frieda and I landed [at Southampton] last night—Brett stayed be-hind in America—I suppose we shall be here a week—then go to my sister's [Ada's], and perhaps take a house by the sea in Lincolnshire for a month—after that, the Mediterranean.*[1]

Catherine Carswell

The Lawrences arrived as planned, and went first to Garland's Hotel for a couple of days. Coming up for a half-day from the country, I saw them there, and arranged that they should have the loan of my younger brother's flat—then unoccupied—in [73] Gower Street. Leaving their luggage at the flat, they would pay a visit to the Midlands, and would return to see a few friends before going to Italy by November. Lawrence did not speak of his health, and, as usual, there was nothing of the invalid about him; but under his big-brimmed Mexican hat his face looked pinched and small, and one easily guessed that he could not face a London winter. Neither could he yet afford the sort of comfortable house somewhere on the South Coast where he might have stayed safely if there had been enough interest or friendship to make England attractive to him. On this occasion he seemed very solitary in London.

This particular solitude was of his own making, as he had told only a few people of his arrival. He came alone, however, to spend the first week-end with us in the country. He said he would spend a day and night with us.[2]

We both met him at High Wycombe [Bucks.] station and travelled uphill in the country bus. Why he was by himself I don't remember. Either Frieda had gone before him to the Midlands or—more likely— she was visiting alone elsewhere. But here he was, and not in a cheerful mood, though as always well-disposed towards me. I was not, just then, very cheerful myself. Things had not gone as well as we could wish, and we were poor and anxious.

He was disappointed with the look of the immediate country, which is not particularly attractive, and on Sunday we all four [3] walked under grey skies in the beech woods, while I thought how poor and tame it must seem to him after the pine slopes at Taos. Then, as we sat over a log fire and were near getting to some real talk, unexpected visitors came from London and robbed the occasion of its intimacy.

What with these visitors, my own domestic cares (which just then were pressing), and the sadness I divined in Lawrence, I was in a distracted state, and only two incidents of the visit stand out clearly now in memory. One was pleasant, the other the reverse. While we stood by the garden gate to see the London people off, John Patrick, then aged seven, made some sudden and unsolicited gesture of love towards me, and as quickly broke away again to his play. We continued with our adieux, paying no attention to the child, but I noticed Lawrence looking keenly at him, and later he referred to the boy in a letter in a special way, which I took to be connected with that remembered glance. "Wait and see," he wrote, "this will be *ein seltsamer Mensch.*"

By the other incident I felt wounded and taken aback. But, as it shows once more how scrupulously Lawrence insisted on paying his way through life, I give it also. As we sat round the tea-table he produced a five-pound note, and in a manner half shy, half careless, threw it across to John Patrick. The child had never seen such a thing before, and did not know what to make of it. Neither did I. I remembered unhappily that it was precisely the sum I had given to Frieda for a travelling coat once when they were leaving England and she badly needed such a thing. Possibly I was wrong, but I don't think so, when, with a pang, I felt that this symbolized the sort of squaring up of accounts that goes with a long

6

farewell. True, we were now rather poorer than Lawrence and with less prospect of growing richer, which he knew. But equally well I knew that he had not any spare five-pound notes to throw across tea-tables. Though he was now fixed up with a new American publisher he was still mainly dependent upon what could be "squeezed out of" the first unlucky one.[4] However, there was nothing for it but to take it, as he would have it so.

From Derbyshire he sent us one of the famous Midland pork pies, with apologies for its not being so big as Midland pies—according to him— ought to be.[5]

Barbara Weekley Barr

By the time Lawrence and Frieda had returned from America the second time, I had become engaged. I took the man to dine with them at Garland's Hotel, where they sometimes stayed. He was considerably older than I was . . . a lazy, philandering sort.

In a black suit, looking frail and distinguished, Lawrence talked politely to the man. So did my mother. Afterwards we went to see *The Gold Rush*.

It did not take Lawrence long to make up his mind about the engagement.

"We shall have to laugh her out of this," he told Frieda. "Where is Barby's *instinct?*" [6]

7 October 1925 Garland's Hotel, Suffolk Street, Pall Mall, London, S.W. 1

⟪ *I've been in my native land eight days now, and it's not very cheering: rather foggy, with very feeble attempts at sun: and the people very depressed. There's a million and a quarter unemployed, receiving that wretched dole: and you can't get a man to do an odd job, anywhere . . . .*

We are going today up to the Midlands, to stay with my sisters. I don't suppose we shall be in England more than another fortnight—then we go to Germany, to my wife's mother, and on to Italy.

It's a pity, really, to leave the peaceful ranch, and the horses, and the sun. But there, one's native land has a sort of hopeless attraction, when one is away.[7]

13 October 1925   *Eastwood, Notts. ?*

❴ *We are going to Ripley tomorrow . . . . The weather's awful, and we simply hate it up here.*[8]

16 October 1925   *c/o Mrs. Clarke, Gee Street, Ripley, Nr. Derby*

❴ *Oh, dear! The next to the last galley of* Quetzalcoatl *is missing: galley 156 . . . . I think we shall stay here till next Wednesday [21 October 1925].*

I still say, this is the most important of all my novels. But I hate sending it out into the world.

Been motoring all over my well-known Derbyshire. One of the most interesting counties in England. But I can't look at the body of my past, the spirit seems to have flown.[9]

Barbara Weekley Barr

A little while after our meeting in London, I saw Lawrence at his sister Ada's house at Ripley, just outside Nottingham. This was the first time Lawrence had had a chance to talk to me about my "young man."

I met both his sisters there. Emily, older than he, was a fair, stolid-looking Midlands type. Her husband, Sam, and she had not been getting on since he had been through the war, though at first they had been a devoted pair. Lawrence had been lecturing Emily in an effort to act as peacemaker.

Ada, the other sister, was two or three years younger than Lawrence. She was a handsome, dark version of Lawrence and had a rather unhappy adoration for him.

When I saw my mother in this house, I thought she seemed a little out of place. I do not think Ada ever liked her, or forgave her for going off with her favourite brother.

Lawrence had a cold. Sitting up in bed in Ada's spotless room, he talked to me about my "young man."

"You see," he explained patiently, "he hasn't enough *life*. Your father with his books and so on has some life; this man hasn't *any*. The fight that every man knows he has to make against the world . . . he just shirks, using you as an escape from his life responsibility. He's a cadging dog, and he'll be much happier, really, if you kick him off . . . they always are. He's a bit inferior somehow. One feels a bit shamed of him sneaking up the street. No, don't marry him, unless you feel divorce is a light business. Just shake him off, like a dog shakes off his fleas."

I sat feeling woebegone during all this. To defend a weak position, I said:

"Well, he seems *stronger*, somehow, than I am."

It was a lie, and Lawrence looked mystified.

" 'Stronger?' I simply don't see it," he remarked, "unless it is in being outside the pale . . . alien to society. Maybe he is in that way."

I began to be won over at this point.

"You can't play with life," Lawrence told me. "The only thing worth having, anyhow, is courage."

Lawrence then came downstairs. We had a pleasant meal at Ada's. It was suggested that I should spend the night.

I telephoned my hostess, wife of a Nottingham professor. When she told her husband, he was very much alarmed. The idea of my spending a night under the same roof as Lawrence horrified him. Supposing he should happen to meet my father, who was in Nottingham, too? Presently his wife telephoned, imploring me to go back to their house. I reluctantly agreed and then went to tell the others.

Lawrence sprang to his feet, white with rage.

"These mean, dirty little insults your mother has had to put up with all these years!" he spat out, gasping for breath.

I was dismayed, not knowing how to act. The others were silent, Ada looking a little scornful.

Feeling something like a criminal, I crept dejectedly back to my Nottingham friends in the dark.

Lawrence and Frieda went abroad again a few days later, first to Baden, then on to Spotorno, in Italy.[10]

Catherine Carswell

[Lawrence] had intended to stay a week at home and then to go with his sisters to the Lincolnshire coast for a few weeks. But instead he remained ten days at home and fled again south. He would always be fond of Ada, and would feel kindly towards his "own people." He was pleased, he wrote to me, to find them in "comparative opulence—*com-*

parative, of course—judging by old home standards." But he hated more than ever "past things like one's home regions," and when I saw him soon after his arrival in London he told me how, especially on that visit, the horrors of his childhood had come up over him like a smothering flood. Glad he would have been if the place thereof "were puffed off the face of the earth." The weather too had been atrocious and continued so. He must get away or a "cold" would lay him low.[11]

26 October 1925   73, Gower St., London, W.C. 1

⟦ I met the Constant Nymph [12] and Rose Macaulay [13] on Friday [23 October 1925], also Wm. Gerhardi: he's nice: said he was coming here tomorrow afternoon.[14]

William Gerhardi

At a literary tea party, where the most strenuously besieged person was Margaret Kennedy, just then resting on the laurels she had won with *The Constant Nymph,* a curiously untidy person in a morning-coat, which bore evidence that he had put it on under protest, came up to me, with a very fetching grin on his face and a curiously girlish, hysterical voice. I guessed immediately that he was D. H. Lawrence. He at once conveyed to me his disapproval of nearly everybody else in the room, and this, coupled with his jolly sort of approval of my *Polyglots* and a lot of advice as to what I should avoid as a writer, all proffered in the most cheerful way, surprised me agreeably, since I had imagined Lawrence to be a disgruntled individual. He told me I had an absolutely original humour; that I should eschew sentimentality like poison; and that he thought I displayed an uncalled-for fear of death. Though feeling that nothing could be more baleful for the natural development of my own talent than the influence of that great rough force contorted into soured rhetoric, I nevertheless said to him at once, feeling that the occasion demanded it: "You're the only one we younger men can now look up to." He lapped it up, grinning with an air which suggested that he agreed with me, and later remarked to someone how pleasant it was at last to have met an intelligent man.

Lawrence took me across the room to introduce me to his wife, who, interrupting her conversation with another woman, beamed at me very largely and said: "What do you make of life?"

"Come, come," said her husband.

Mrs. Lawrence told me how intensely her husband admired my books. Lawrence qualified this. "I liked the humour," he said. He scribbled down his address on the back of a cigarette box. I was to come to tea the next day.

When I called, Lawrence himself opened the door. His satanic look was absent. In the sunlight his red-bearded face looked harrowed and full of suffering, almost Christ-like. There were a couple of women at tea who seemed to resent a little our man-to-man conversation. One woman even went so far as to show impatience at the dryness, to her, of our subject, when finally she rose to leave. This roused Lawrence's fury. He imitated her inflexions. "The insolence of the bitch!" he said when she was gone. "Imagining we're here to entertain her!" And he once more imitated her unmercifully; after which he relapsed again into a serene tone of voice appropriate to our subject-matter—immortality. I mentioned Tolstoy saying life was a dream, death the awakening. Lawrence shook his head. "No," he said, "I don't see it like that." And he explained, very gently, looking at me very kindly with a sort of Christ-like expression. "You see," he said, "it's like this: in your inside. . . ." And I looked very attentive, very coy.

Our discussion continued for several hours. Lawrence's idea of immortal life was not something which would start after death, but a living reality within us going on even now, all the time, though intermittently clouded over by the illusion of time. He grew enthusiastic. Anything true to its own nature, he declared, was immortal. And his eyes expressed a gleam of self-satisfaction, certainly not immortal. A cat bristling his fur, a tiger in his fierceness . . . . He stopped, a little troubled. I nodded comprehendingly.

We talked of Katherine Mansfield and Middleton Murry, whom, Mrs. Lawrence told me, they regarded as children to be helped out of their troubles. I regretted that Middleton Murry, so sensitive and outstanding a critic, should be himself devoid of any talent whatever; and D. H. Lawrence sneered: "I should have thought it was the only thing he had."

It was now dinner time, and Lawrence asked me to stay. Mrs. D. H. Lawrence, when you first set eyes on her, is the type of woman to gladden your heart. A real German Hausfrau, you say to yourself, suits him down to the ground, the intellectual, incompetent husband! The reality, however, is the reverse of this. Mrs. Lawrence dislikes housework; her husband excels in it. Lawrence, a beam on his face, which was like a halo, brought in the dishes out of the kitchen, with the pride of a first-class chef in his unrivalled creations: no, as if cooking and serving your guests were a sacrament, a holy rite. When I told Lawrence of my friendship with Beaverbrook,[15] he astonished me by the intensity of his deprecation. Why should I allow myself to be patronized? Why should I, a messenger of the spirit, acknowledge Caesar? I, on the other hand, urged that the Holy Ghost in me prompted me to treat Caesar with that extra grace which the spirit can so easily lavish on the flesh—providing always that Caesar does not take unto himself that which is not Caesar's. But Lawrence demurred. If I wanted money, why not write articles for the magazines? He sat down and there and then wrote me a letter to Lengel of the *Cosmopolitan*. Authors, he implied, had been known to get on without the boosting of newspaper proprietors. "And even with it," I said. "But why see any harm in the genuine interest in me of a charming newspaper proprietor, himself half a genius, who obviously cannot cherish an ulterior motive in regard to me?"

"Because," Lawrence insisted, "he hates you."

"Come, come," I said.

"I don't say he hates you personally," Lawrence contended. "But these men, they're like vampires. When they see an immortal soul they hate it instinctively." His eyes gleamed. "With a terrible black hatred, and instinctively try to annihilate what is immortal in you."

At which remark Mrs. Lawrence trembled with rage and expressed her agreement with some violence, which seemed to me a waste of effort, since if she had met Lord Beaverbrook she would undoubtedly have bowed to the man's extraordinary charm. D. H. Lawrence, wincing at this display of superfluous emotion, said quietly: "Not so much intensity, Frieda."

Mrs. Lawrence, perhaps living up to the elemental naturalness of her husband's heroines, replied: "If I want to be intense I'll be intense, and you go to hell!"

"I'm ashamed of you, Frieda," he said. Whereupon Frieda's hatred for Lord Beaverbrook transformed itself into hatred for her husband, and was soon a spent cartridge.

I told Lawrence of some scientific difficulty I had about my plot for *Jazz and Jasper*. I wanted a handful of people left on a mountain top with the rest of the world disintegrated to nothing. The problem had defeated H. G. Wells, who told me that the only plausible thing I could do was to make it a dream. D. H. Lawrence brushed aside the suggestion as unworthy and mapped the whole thing out for me in five minutes, breaking into ripples of girlish giggles at the ingenuity of his solution.

Lawrence said that the cells of Tchehov's writing were disintegrating cells, emitting, as they burst, a doleful twang which remained with us. Tolstoy's, on the contrary, were reintegrating cells, which gladdened the heart and tightened the nerves. When I told this to Middleton Murry, he sighed and said Lawrence never understood Tchehov. And I would add that, in my experience, I have never known anywhere, Russia not excepted, two souls more sensitively appreciative of Tchehov's work than Katherine Mansfield and Middleton Murry, though both could read him only in translation.

There was something so genuine and attractive about Lawrence, in spite of his curiously adolescent habit of derisive generalities, deploring the trend of his time, and other ballast of this kind, which he could have chucked overboard with advantage. Pointing to a crowd in the street, "These London girls," he said to me. "I would as soon sleep with them as with a water closet." And I pictured a number of attractive young girls, for no crowd is without them, mortified at the refusal of a sickly, red-bearded, untidy individual of middle-age to meet their advances, which in fact had not been forthcoming. "I am fleeing again from my native country," in a letter. Sad, bad stuff! His being capable of it explains perhaps his readiness to surround himself with the most inconceivable mutts, patient listeners, haggard women, towards whom he no doubt conceived it his duty, at great effort—no wonder—to inculcate in himself a feeling of sex. And though he preached the gospel of the "complete man," harmoniously attuned, Lawrence wore his red hair brushed down over the forehead, as if to conceal it—possibly to identify himself with the lowbrow primitive, whose centre of gravity is below the belt.

There was in Lawrence a real passion, a real longing to adjust his feelings about things to the enduring, the immortal side of life, intimated to us in fitful glimpses of Nature. Lawrence's revelation of animal life, his landscapes, and his human portraits are nearly always beautiful, original, powerful and moving. They are spoilt sometimes by needless reiteration prompted, one suspects, by a sort of gauche adolescent vanity —"I'll do it again, I will, if only to annoy you." He is like a man who wants to show off his strength with a great big hammer and proceeds to drive the nails too far, and spoils the woodwork somewhat. Then testing it: "It's strong," he says, and walks away swinging the hammer. Lawrence told me he liked his books while he wrote them, but hated them the moment he saw them in print. I am not surprised. His bitterness is the reaction of a proud spirit subjected from an early age to social and bodily humiliations. His inauspicious birth caused him to exert his strength fully as a rebel with little humour left to dispose of as a free man. Hence his hatreds, his insistence on his needs of "blood contact" with the lower classes, as if it were not the inadequacy of all human contacts which throws one back on oneself, and makes the artist. Social self-consciousness, when it becomes articulate and tries to explain and justify itself, is a nuisance.

Everything I told Lawrence about the writers I had met seemed to provoke a kind of savage satisfaction in him, a grunt confirming his worst suspicions about the man. But when I mentioned Shaw, the passion and indignation which inspired his remarks evaporated completely. He said, with a disdain which did not pay Mr. Shaw the compliment of being positive, a mere absence of interest, a mere negative: "Are you interested in sociology? I'm not!"

With all his cheerful simplicity, his strength, his instinctive preoccupation with the real meaning of life (which is to "evade," as Tchehov says, "to circumvent, the unreal, the shallow, gratuitous, phantom-like which prevents us from being happy") there was withal something superfluous, something gawky and left-handed about Lawrence. His humour was defective. Yet, like so many people whose humour is poor, he prided himself on his tremendous sense of fun. "I wish," he wrote to me [14 November 1928], "*we* created a *Monthly Express,* out of our various anatomies, to laugh at it all. Just a little magazine to laugh a few things to death. 'The Big Toe Points out the Point or Points in Point Counter Point'—and so on. Let's make a little magazine, where even the liver can laugh." [16] Hardly first-rate.

It is not perhaps what a writer sees that matters in the end, but the "smell" he exudes. Zola also thought he saw the truth and that it needed saying. Where is Zola's "truth" to-day? Where Lawrence's "truth" will be to-morrow. One writer's "truth" is in the end as problematic as another's. It's the taste, the smell of his writing, which matter. And I cannot help thinking that D. H. Lawrence has a "smell" about him which is unsatisfactory. [17]

26 October 1925   73, Gower St., London, W.C. 1

❡ We gave up the idea of staying in England—we leave for Baden-Baden on Thursday [29 October 1925].

Could you [Murry] come up on Wednesday?—come here, we'll see

14

about a room for you. And I'll make no arrangements with anybody for Wednesday.[18]

John Middleton Murry

[On] 1st October [1925] I was surprised to have a postcard from [Lawrence] saying that he had arrived in London the night before.[19] He was going to the seaside in Lincolnshire for a month, then to the Mediterranean. In between, he was coming, as he had promised, to stay with me at Abbotsbury [Dorset]. It was clear, though he said nothing about this, that he had said a final farewell to America. A day or two later [26 October 1925], he wrote to say he had given up the idea of staying in England: he was leaving for Baden-Baden in two days' time. Would I come up and stay the night with him at 73 Gower Street? I did. Our meeting was a little sad and ghostly; and I could not help thinking in what a hopeless position I should have been at that moment, if I had really gone with him to New Mexico eighteen months before. The American adventure was over for good and all. We forbore to speak of that. Instead, we disputed about Jesus. He had liked my books on Keats, he said; but why must I write about Jesus? The older he got, the more unsympathetic Jesus became to him. Now Judas—that was a different matter. If only one knew a little more about him!

I felt strongly then, as I have come to feel even more strongly since, that Lawrence's vehemence against Jesus was simply the measure of his identification with him. It was the hatred of an intense love. But I didn't say so; it wouldn't have been any use. I simply said, what indeed was true, that I had had to make up my mind about Jesus, and the only way I could afford to make up my mind about anybody important was to write a book about him. This I had done; I had made up my mind in the essential: and the result was that Jesus had become my greatest hero. If my attitude looked sentimental and sloppy, well, it couldn't be helped; it was *my* attitude. It was no use my pretending to be something other than I was. It was, indeed, a great relief to me to have burned my boats.[20]

So we left it. *J'avais pris mon assiette.* But at that moment, when the issue was more clearly defined between us than it ever had been before, we felt the pain of the old affection more deeply. But manifestly there was nothing to be done. Still, when he asked me to come with my wife to stay with him in Italy—he was then attracted by the notion

15

of going to Ragusa—I wanted to go, and I said we would come.[21] The end of our meeting, on the next morning, was characteristic. Ten minutes before it was time for me to go, Lawrence ran out to buy a big bag of fruit for me to take home. If he wasn't back in time, I was to drive in the taxi by way of the shop, and meet him. He was not back in time. There were two ways of getting to the shop and the taxi-driver chose the wrong one. When we got to the shop, Yes, they said, a slim gentleman with a beard had been there and just left. If I went after him, I was bound to lose my train, and would not be home that night. I caught my train.

That was the end of my last meeting with Lawrence. I never saw him again, except in a dream shortly after his death.[22]

31 October 1925 ·   Hotel Eden, Baden-Baden, Germany

⟨ *I'm sorry I missed you [Murry]—I hurried straight to the house, on the obvious way. I had such a nice bag of fruit for you to take home, with fresh figs and dates and Carlsbad plums. But perhaps you'd have hated carrying it, so heavy.*

Just the same here—very quiet and unemerged: my mother-in-law older, noticeably.

I make my bows and play whist with old Excellenzen: Aber Excellenzchen! cries my mother-in-law. Titles still in full swing here, but nothing else. No foreigners. Shades of Edward VII and Russian princes. The Rhine villages untouched and lovely: we had to motor from Strasburg: and the peasants still peasants, with a bit of that eternal earth-to-earth quality that is so lost in England. Rather like a still sleep, with frail dreams.[23]

S P O T O R N O , R I V I E R A P O N E N T E , I T A L Y

16 November 1925   Villa Maria, Spotorno, Italy

⟨ *We got here yesterday—it's lovely and sunny, with a blue sea, and I'm sitting out on the balcony just above the sands, to write. Switzerland was horrid—I don't like Switzerland anyhow—in slow rain and snow. We shall find ourselves a villa here, I think, for the time.*[24]

Frieda Lawrence Ravagli

[On] the coast, not far from Genoa, we found Spotorno, that Martin Secker had told us was not overrun with foreigners. Under the ruined castle I saw a pink villa that had a friendly look and I wondered if we could have it. We found the peasant Giovanni who looked after it. Yes, he thought we could. It belonged to a Tenente dei Bersaglieri in Savona. We were staying at the little inn by the sea, when the bersaglieri asked for us. Lawrence went and returned. "You must come and look at him, he is so smart." So I went and found a figure in uniform with gay plumes and blue sash, as it was the Queen's birthday. We took the Bernarda and the tenente became a friend of ours. Lawrence taught him English on Sundays, but they never got very far.[25]

Capt. Angelo Ravagli

To be honest, I did not know Lawrence very well. I met him and Frieda in Spotorno, Italy, in the way that Frieda describes in her book, "*Not I, But the Wind.* . . ." This happened in the winter of 1925. The Lawrences were in Spotorno in order to meet Martin Secker, Lawrence's English publisher, who was spending a vacation there, visiting his wife's parents. Frieda saw a pink house on the hill above the village and asked if it could be rented. The house belonged to my wife. Frieda got in touch with the caretaker, who phoned me. I was on duty at the time and unable to meet them. The first opportunity I had to meet with them was on the Queen's birthday, which was a holiday. As I was an officer in the Italian Army I had to wear my dress uniform for the occasion. I met the Lawrences at the Hotel Ligure and we walked up to the Villa Bernarda, which was about three hundred feet above sea level, on quite a steep dirt road. They saw it, they liked it, and in no time, with a few English pounds, the deal was made for a rental of four months.

During their stay I went to see them very often, almost every week end. Lawrence was always busy, mostly doing housework. I never saw him writing. At that time there was no gas, and the kitchen range was heated by wood or coal. He always had a hard time to make it go. One day the kitchen was full of smoke. Lawrence was furious. Frieda tried to calm him down, but he was swearing about the smoke which almost choked him. I took off my uniform, put on overalls, and helped him to

17

clean the pipe. I disconnected it behind the stove and took off the elbow, which was full of dirt. And to be sure that there was nothing else to stop the draft, I climbed on top of the roof. There I pulled out the cap of the chimney. With a small stone enveloped in a rag tied to a rope, I rubbed it up and down several times inside the pipe, while Lawrence was keeping a bucket under the pipe in the kitchen to collect the dirt.

He was very grateful, for one thing, I am sure, because he would never dare to climb on the roof because it was terribly steep, and Frieda told me afterwards that he had said to her, "That is a man who would be useful to have at the Kiowa Ranch in San Cristobal, New Mexico."

Sometimes I found Lawrence busy painting decorative designs on silk material or on handkerchiefs, in indelible inks, extremely well executed, one of which he gave as a present to my wife. He got along very well with my wife because they had more in common. She was a Professor of Italian Literature and History, and also spoke French. We spoke to each other in broken Italian, but succeeded in understanding each other. In the winter, every regiment, in order to keep the officers busy, offered courses in foreign languages. Previously I had studied French, but now I studied English, and every time I visited the Lawrences at the Villa I took my lesson book with me. Lawrence was very patient in helping me with my pronunciation, but, as Frieda said in her book, we did not get very far.

On other occasions we would go for long walks. I remember Lawrence liked the way I could walk, and told me so. This was no surprise to me, as I had done nothing but walk for the past ten or fifteen years. The Bersaglieri are the fastest walkers of any Infantry regiment in the world.[26]

19 November 1925   Villa Bernarda, Spotorno, Italy

❲ We've taken a house here till April—above the village and the sea—big vineyard garden, and castle ruins—nice—you know the kind of thing. The village isn't anything to stare at, but there's the sea, and good walks in the hills.

I heard from Brett. She has got to Capri.[27]

❲ [The Villa Bernarda is] on the sea, on the Riviera, about three miles from Monte Carlo. The village is just a quiet Italian village, but we have friends here. The house is nice, just under the Castle, in a big vineyard garden, with terrace over the roofs of the village, the sea beyond. We do the housework ourselves: Frieda obstinately refused a maid. But there's a gardener lives downstairs, he does all the fetching and carrying, goes shopping every morning at 7.30, pumps the water, and is there when we want him. We've got three floors: we live mostly on the top floor, high up, where there's a kitchen and bedroom and sitting-room, and a big terrace from the sitting-room: we sleep on the middle floor: the bottom floor we store things in. It's real Italian country style—a pleasant sort of life, easier than America. The weather is on the whole sunny and dry, but we've had bitter cold winds. We go for walks in the hills—there are snow mountains behind—and do bits of things. Yesterday we got oranges from the trees and made marmelade, which I burnt a bit. But it's good . . . . There are no horses to ride, no spring to fetch water from. The pine-trees are those puffs of umbrella pines, all scattered separate on the stony slopes to the sea.[28]

7 December 1925   Villa Bernarda, Spotorno, Italy

(Here it freezes, but is sunny. In France 14 degrees below zero. What price the ranch! Went to Alassio yesterday, to see F.'s daughter Barby. Alassio well begins: Alas! for it's a chronic hole, awful.[29]

16 December 1925   Villa Bernarda, Spotorno, Italy

(We are having lovely weather here again. Yesterday it wanted to snow, but this morning no such thing, only beautiful sunshine. My publisher Martin Secker is here, went to Savona with me [today]. He is nice but not sparkling.

Now it is evening: we are sitting in the kitchen high under the roof. The evening star is white over the hill opposite, underneath the lights of the village lie like oranges and tangerines, little and shining. Frieda has devoured her whipped cream from Savona at one gulp, and now she moans that she hasn't kept any to eat with coffee and cake after supper. Now she sits by the stove and reads. The soup is boiling. In a moment we call down into the depth: "Vieni, Giovanni, é pronto il mangiare." Then the old man runs up the stairs like an unhappy frog, with his nose in the air,

sniffing and smelling. It is nice for him to know that there is always something good for him to eat.[30]

29 December 1925   Villa Bernarda, Spotorno, Italy

⟨ Barby ——— is here since Christmas Day, nicer this time. She's busy
painting, has faint hopes of one day selling something. But the Slade
took all the life out of her. That Slade is a criminal institution, and gets
worse.[31]

Barbara Weekley Barr

In 1926, I spent a very happy Spring with Lawrence and Frieda on
the Italian Riviera.

This visit caused a certain amount of fuss and trouble at home,
but eventually I reached Alassio, a few miles from the village of Spotorno,
where they had rented the Villa Bernarda.

For reasons of family decorum, I was to stay at Alassio in a *pensione*,
excellently managed by a Miss Hill and a Miss Gould. Miss Hill, a
colonial and the niece of an archbishop, was romantic and ethereal.
Miss Gould, a chubby Englishwoman doggedly devoted to Miss Hill, was
a feminine replica of a vicar uncle of mine.

Lawrence came over with Frieda to lunch and made himself very
agreeable to the two spinsters. He rather liked taking a look at new
people. "One of those women's marriages," he remarked amusedly afterwards.

Italy seemed a kind of paradise to me, though Alassio, once just a
fishing village, had now become a sort of retreat for English gentlefolk
living there to benefit from the favourable exchange rate. Many of them
were Anglo-Indians—army people or civil servants—who looked on
the Italians as a slightly improved kind of "native."

I tried to paint at Alassio and once when I was working out of
doors, an English admiral came up, admired my painting, and took me
out to tea.

Lawrence disapproved of this escapade. There was a curious streak of
conventionality in him which cropped up now and then and which he
no doubt inherited from his hard-working, puritanical mother. "You

want to be very careful of that kind of man," he warned me severely.

He was also shocked to hear that I travelled third class in Italy, and said, "An English girl doing that here gives the impression that she is looking for an 'adventure.'" Fortunately, I was able to assure him that my worst experience had been drinking out of a bottle which was handed round a compartment by Italians with the friendly invitation "Come on, don't be fussy."

Before long I went to stay at the Villa Bernarda at Spotorno.

I remember so well walking in darkness up the narrow streets of the village, enthralled by its romantic ancient feeling and the wonderful foreign smell.

From the villa, a little way up the hill, I saw the light of an upstairs balcony window shine out towards the sea. The house was in two stories, connected by an outside stone staircase. Built on a slope, the villa had a still lower part, intended for storing wine and oil.

When I knocked, Frieda flung the door open joyfully. I saw Lawrence sitting up in bed against the sitting room wall.

"Why did you come so late?" he asked, crossly.

Talking endlessly over the chicken, which she had cooked on the charcoal fire, and the red wine, Frieda and I were very happy. Lawrence, in his nearby bed, took in every word. I went to bed in one of the downstairs rooms.

The next morning I was awakened by loud bumping noises overhead. I was half prepared for this, as I had heard that the Lawrences threw saucepans or plates at each other. However, I hurried upstairs to intervene.

Frieda, her neck scratched, was in tears. "He has been horrid," she said with a glare at the glum, pale man sitting on the edge of his bed. She had told him that, now I was with her at last, he was to keep out of our relationship and not interfere. This had infuriated Lawrence. I was exhilarated, rather than shocked.

It soon blew over, but a few days later the sparks flew again when Lawrence, after inveighing bitterly against Frieda, flung his wine in her face. This time I joined in, shouting, "She's too good for you; it's casting pearls before swine!"

After Frieda had gone out of the room in anger, I asked Lawrence, "Do you care for her?"

"It's indecent to ask," he replied. "Look what I've done for your mother! Haven't I just helped her with her rotten painting?" [32]

In spite of his independent mind, Lawrence felt the need of sympathy. He was trying to sort out his feelings and values, and find a balance. He wanted Frieda to do the same, but she resisted him, somehow.

"Why does your mother want to be so *important?*" he demanded. "Why can't she be simple and talk to me naturally, as you do, like a woman?"

I listened to his complainings. The incident was trivial, but his feelings seemed really shattered.

Afterwards when someone told me that he had said, "Frieda's daughter tried to flirt with me," I thought it mean of him.

He and I liked to go for long walks. At Spotorno, and afterwards at Scandicci, we often went off in the afternoons and walked up the mountains. We talked a lot, mostly about people. Then we would forget about them, and just enjoy looking at the lovely Italian scene.

I began to paint the landscape. Lawrence, who had learned how to paint in oils, perhaps from Dorothy Brett in New Mexico, was a discerning critic. At first he was disparaging about my "studio stuff." "*Play* with the paint," he urged me. "Forget all you learned at the art school."

One day, after spending the morning up the mountain, I came in and flung down a canvas despondently. "It's good . . . there's air in it," said Lawrence, jumping up. His judgment was sound, for this was the first picture I sold when I got back to London.

"Screw the tops on your paint-tubes afterwards," Lawrence said. "It just takes courage. You'll never get a husband if you are too untidy."

Sometimes he took a hand in my painting, putting figures of peasants in the landscape, saying that it needed them to give it life. A picture of mine called *Peasants Building a House* was the most successful of these. Lawrence put in a black-haired young man drinking out of a Chianti bottle, and an old man holding a trowel, standing up in the half-built house.

The creative atmosphere of the Lawrence household was like a draught of life to me. I painted away assiduously at Spotorno.

"She might be an artist if she finds herself," Lawrence told Frieda.

Sometimes he talked of his childhood, proudly saying that there had been more life and richness in it than in any middleclass child's home. Ada was his favourite sister. When they had been youngsters, he had once said to her, "Let's go away, and find a better life together somewhere." But Ada had been too timid; not having his gifts, she had perforce to stay where she was.

Lawrence had formerly hated his drunken father, but at this time had swung in sympathy towards him, away from his mother. She had been a sensitive woman, who, added to her hard lot, had endured the extra strain of having a self-indulgent, violent man as her husband.

When Lawrence was sixteen, he had a serious illness. His mother could not afford the medicines he needed, or good food even. This illness probably sowed the seed of the tuberculosis which killed him.

His mother died in her fifties of cancer . . . a disease Lawrence told me was "usually caused by fret."

I believe the Lawrences had some Irish blood in them. There was a story, too, that as a child his great-grandfather had been found wandering on the field of Waterloo after the battle, and brought home by English soldiers.[33]

His elder sister Emily would recite sentimental poetry at great length to Lawrence when he was small. "I used to pull her hair till she cried, but she went on and on, the tears streaming down her face." He chuckled. So did I. I could just picture the plain Midlands face of the persistent, weeping Emily.

In the grounds of the Villa Bernarda were the ruins of an old castle. The villa itself was a haphazard sort of house. You could sit upstairs or downstairs and do as you pleased.

One afternoon, Lawrence was downstairs reading the autobiography of Mabel Dodge Luhan.[34]

"It's terrible, the will to power of this kind of woman," he exclaimed. "She destroys everybody, herself included, with her really frightful kind of will." The manuscript seemed to fascinate him with horror. "Read it, and let it be a lesson to you!" he said.

Lawrence must have read a great deal, though I did not often see him with a book. The only serious writer I heard him speak of with respect was Hardy. He didn't like Dickens, and said his people were "frowsty." Charlotte Brontë repelled him. He thought *Jane Eyre* should have been called *Everybody's Governess*. At that time he had just read *Gentlemen Prefer Blondes* with amusement. The part about Germans and eating reminded him of my German grandmother.

"Two hours after supper she has a few snails. Then at bedtime some honey-cake, with Schnapps. Really, I don't know *how* she can do it," he told us, laughing.

Lawrence had been learning Russian, and would often turn up with a Russian dictionary. For some time he had wanted to visit Russia, believing there was a spark there which had been quenched in the rest of Europe. "It seems to sink into a soupy state—Europe today," he said. "That's why I would like to be back at the ranch."

Lawrence detested Bolshevism. Fascism was not to his taste either. While we were at Spotorno, an Englishwoman, Violet Gibson, shot at Mussolini.[35] The Italians referred politely to the incident to us, and seemed almost sympathetic to the "poor mad lady," whose bullet had passed through the cartilage of their bovine dictator's nose.

"Put a ring through it," Lawrence advised a lieutenant of the Bersaglieri who happened to visit us the next day.

Some of *Mornings in Mexico* was written at the Villa Bernarda.[36] In it he mentions Giovanni, the gardener who lived in the lower part among his chickens and wine bottles. Lawrence was indulgent towards the old man, but Frieda and I didn't care for him, because he would get drunk and frighten us.

Lawrence hardly ever wrote for more than four or five hours a day. His writing flowed off the end of his pen. "If it doesn't, my writing is no good," he said. He never discussed his writings with me, and advised me not to read his books till I was older. "By the time you are forty, you will be able to understand them." After Lawrence had finished a novel, he seldom wanted to look at it again.

Lawrence was quite clever with his hands. He could cook, sew, and was even good at embroidery.[37]

9 January 1926   Villa Bernarda, Spotorno, Italy

〔 I'm still struggling with my Glad Ghosts.[38] Alas, and a thousand times alack, it's growing long—too long, damn it! Even Sun [39] is a bit too long.

Am in bed for two days with that cold on the chest. But it's dissolving satisfactorily. Here, it's cloudy, but not cold any more.[40]

9 January 1926   Villa Bernarda, Spotorno, Italy

〔 Now let's make some sort of a plan. Do you think we could manage a boat? Why couldn't we possibly hire a little lugger just for two months, and do the Isles of Greece that way? Surely it would be possible!—and it would be lovely. Start towards end of March, when it would be warm on the sea. I'd like that best.

Alternatives?—perhaps a little flight to Spain. It wouldn't cost more than a trip in Italy. But I do hanker after a boat.[41]

25 January 1926   Villa Bernarda, Spotorno, Italy

⟨ At present I'm not doing anything.[42] January is always a hard month to climb through: it was at this time last year I got ill. This year I'm doing my best to avoid it, and I really feel much better. I think Italy really agrees with me better than America does; I feel sounder, solider. My sister [Ada] arrives on Feb. 9th—for two weeks. Frieda's daughter Elsa on Feb. 12th. Barby is here since last Wed., and we're settling down better—do paintings. I wish we could really make some nice trip, when our visitors have left.[43]

29 January 1926   Villa Bernarda, Spotorno, Italy

⟨ I shall send you next week a long story, The Virgin and the Gipsy,[44] about 25,000 or 30,000 words. Secker wants me to make another three-story book like The Ladybird, and he rather fancies Glad Ghosts and The Virgin for two of them.[45]

11 February 1926   Villa Bernarda, Spotorno, Italy

⟨ I'm in bed these six days with 'flu—don't see daylight yet. It gave me bronchial haemorrhage like at the ranch, only worse. The doctor says, just keep still. My sister [Ada] came yesterday with a friend—Mrs. Booth —so they, too, are here in the fireless house. It pours with rain, is very cold, and has been like this, the weather, for nearly three weeks. My sister left Dover in bright sunshine, and a fine clear evening in Paris—no snow till Italy! F.'s daughter Elsa arrives in Ventimiglia tonight, Barby has gone to meet her. They come back tomorrow, stay in the little Hôtel Ligure here till my sister has gone—she leaves on the 25th.—then they two move up here. But I like Barby.[46]

Barbara Weekley Barr

In early February [1926], my sister Elsa came for a brief visit. She flew to Paris . . . then still quite an enterprising thing to do. Lawrence was surprised that anyone should want to fly. "I hate those artificial sensations," he commented.

Elsa was better disciplined. Unlike me, she hated "rows." At the Bernarda she lectured Frieda about them, being concerned to see, after one of their quarrels, that Lawrence had tears in his eyes . . . a rare thing for him.

Elsa liked Spotorno, and joined in our afternoon walks, but more in disagreement with us than in accord. "You and Lawrence encourage each other to be spiteful about everyone," she said. There was some truth in this, though Lawrence thought that I was much worse than he was.

"You always have a vendetta against someone," he exclaimed one day. "I wouldn't marry you, Barby, if you had a million pounds."

"You'll never care about anybody," he told me another time. "You with your everlasting criticisms! If the Archangel Gabriel came down from Heaven and asked you to marry him, you'd find fault." The idea seemed to amuse him.

One day he talked to Elsa about the stars, the millions of other universes, and the endlessness of space, saying, "So you see our little lives aren't so very important after all."

This reminder of human insignificance must have made Elsa reckless, because that evening she drank too much wine at supper, and talked wildly.

Seeing her tipsy, and listening to her haranguing Lawrence, I laughed hilariously, as did Frieda. Lawrence was amused too, but with reservations. "The contrast from her usual self is too sharp, it frightens me," he observed fastidiously.

Also in February, Lawrence's sister Ada came with a friend to stay at the Bernarda, so Elsa and I moved to the tiny Hotel Ligure. As we breakfasted on the balcony over the sea, Frieda appeared looking angry and upset. Ada and the friend had been "bossy," she said. They had tried to oust her from her kitchen, where she managed so well.

Elsa and I both gave her advice. The situation disturbed us. When I went up to the Villa, I was very chilly to Ada.

"I don't trust Barby; she's too clever," Lawrence told my mother resentfully. His feelings were hurt as well. The atmosphere was unpleasant for a few days until Lawrence went off to Monte Carlo with Ada, later going on alone to Capri where he stayed with the Earl Brewsters.[47]

Capt. Angelo Ravagli

One day I found that the Lawrences had company. Frieda's two beautiful daughters had arrived from England. Elsa aged twenty-one, and Barbara aged nineteen. Not knowing the language I could not understand what went on between Frieda and Lawrence, but I sensed that Lawrence did not share Frieda's happiness in having her daughters with her for the first time since she had married him.

On my next visit, I found Frieda and the two girls alone. Lawrence had gone to Monte Carlo with his sister [Ada], whom I never met. He had sent for her to come from London to balance the show. It didn't work, so they both went away.[48]

19 February 1926   Villa Bernarda, Spotorno, Italy

❨ I'm going away with my sister [Ada] on Monday [22 February 1926], to Monte Carlo for a few days: then probably on to Spain, alone. Frieda has her two daughters here, two great tall girls, 21 and 23 years old. I feel absolutely swamped out, must go away by myself for a bit, or I shall give up the ghost . . . . Somehow everything feels in a great muddle, with daughters that are by no means mine, and a sister who doesn't see eye to eye with F. What a trial families are![49]

24 February 1926   Monte Carlo

❨ Staying here a few days, with my sister [Ada]—very sunny and bright, but as far as life goes, come-down, and boring—no temptation to gamble.[50]

C A P R I

4 March 1926   *Torre dei Quattro Venti, Capri*

❨ I am actually in Capri for the time. Frieda is at Spotorno with her two daughters.[51]

The Hon. Dorothy Brett

I am on the steamer, crossing the bay of Naples. Vesuvius is smoking dreamily in a hazy sky; the sea is hazy; everything is languid. Ahead is little Capri, pale and tiny, sitting on the sea. Capri! I hold my letter of introduction to the Brewsters firmly; [52] they expect me; will be on the quay to meet me. The island grows in size and clearness, and soon, as we draw in to the harbor, I can see three white figures standing in a row. That surely must be the Brewsters.

The steamer stops, whistling loudly. A swarm of boats gathers round and the passengers are lowered carefully into them. The three white figures scan the boats eagerly as they are rowed in. Mine is almost the last, but they have decided that I look more English than the other passengers and are waving. I wave back and, as my boat rows up to the landing stage, I take a look at them.

Achsah Brewster, all in white, with a long floating veil draped over her hat and a long white cape that hangs loosely from her shoulders, has a pale face and white-gray hair parted in the middle, which sweeps down on each side of her oval face. Her eyes are gray, too. How lovely she looks! The long skirts swing as she moves forward. She is entirely unexpected—of no race and of no time. Earl Brewster is small, has gray hair, almost white, a sharp, pointed nose, and dark, dark eyes, with a strange, hidden look. And the girl, Harwood (twelve or thirteen, I can't tell) is gay, smiling, robust. Her queer uneven eyes and upward-curling mouth, is very like her mother's. And yet in every other way she is entirely unlike either of them.

I feel warmed and heartened at sight of them. I am greeted eagerly and quickly hustled into a carriage. I turn to Achsah and say:

"How splendid my horse, Prince, would look with such a plume on his head!" The long plumes of the horse and the ribbons and bells fascinate me as we gallop up the hill.

The Hotel Internazional has only one empty room. The German *femme de chambre* takes me along passages and stops at a door. I look at the door number and a chill goes over me—a fleeting apprehension: the number is thirteen. The maid is quick to notice; she tries to reassure me.

"In Italy," she says, "thirteen is a lucky number. It is Italy's lucky number." I am not convinced, but I engage the room temporarily, telling her to give me another the moment there is one vacant.

The Brewsters are waiting for me in the hall. I join them and they take me to their villa on the hill, Quattro Venti. It is white with a red-tiled roof and a small, square tower. It faces all ways and catches all the winds. The rooms are dark, tiled and cool, almost too cold. The sitting-room has a small stove that I am told is called a "pig," and how I came to hate that smoky pig! The furniture is simple. In the window there is a piano. Outside, there are lovely patios, in which we have meals.

Here, with the Brewsters as my constant companions, I spend five months. I make many friends among their friends, but it is their friendship which counts most—theirs and a poet called Branford and his golden-haired wife.[53]

Christmas has come and gone. You [54] are writing from Spotorno. You hope to be able to come over for a short trip. Then you have the flu—badly. I hear nothing for many days, when suddenly the hoped-for happens: a telegram from you to say that you are arriving from Nice the very next day.

.   .   .

Harwood and I are running down the road. The steamer is in sight, whistling for the boats. The electric launch is just skimming in, too.

"He may come on the launch," I say, panting.

"Mother says he is sure to come by the steamer," returns the blithe, unpuffing Harwood. We reach the beach; the electric launch is already tied to the landing-stage; the rowboats from the steamer are rowing in. I scan them anxiously: I can see no sign of you in them.

Suddenly a man bending over a suitcase on the landing-stage, straightens up and looks round. It is you. You had, after all, come by the launch. Harwood and I rush forward. How pleased you are to see us. A new brown overcoat, a new gray suit, a brown Homburg hat, brown shoes—heavens! no wonder I did not recognize you. But once again how frail, how delicate and collapsed you look. We hail a carriage, your suitcases are piled on the small seat, and we three squeeze into the back seat, facing the driver.

"I asked Achsah to put you up, knowing you hate hotels," I explain. "I thought you would like that better than the Internazional."

"I only want to be quiet," you say, "quiet and peaceful." We all talk at once as the horse gallops up the hill. The little carriage rattles and sways, the horse's plumes and ribbons fly out in the wind, the bells jingle.

"Think," you say, "of Prince and Azul and Aaron [55] with plumes on their heads—how surprised they would be!" You are excited and gay at this arrival. Harwood and I carry your suitcases up the many, many steps to Quattro Venti. Achsah has tea ready and we sit and talk. You tell us how the electric launch refused to start.

"It turned in circles on its rope. I was sitting in it. It whirled round and round like a top and no one knew what to do. The sailors shouted and gesticulated. Then, for no reason at all, as far as I could see, it stopped; then restarted with such a jerk that I nearly fell into the sea. They had forgotten to unfasten the ropes!" The tears are running down your face from laughing.

We talk until dinner. We talk for hours after dinner: all my adventures from Del Monte to Capri and some of yours, though you seem reluctant to tell much of yourself. It gets late—much too late. You begin to look very white and tired. I get up, telling you that I will come up early in the morning; and I go back to my hotel to bed.

.   .   .

I hurry to Quattro Venti early, to see how you have borne your long journey. The living-room feels chilly after the warm sun, but you are looking rested.

"Let's get away; let's go out somewhere," you say.

"I know all the walks, now," I reply; and we take a small path that leads to terraces of olive trees and vines. You are not yet fit for a long or arduous walk. We sit down with our backs against some rocks, under the trees. The sea is a deep ultramarine blue, the olive trees a waving mist of silvery green. We watch the sea and the olive trees for awhile in silence, then you slowly begin telling me the events that led to your coming here. You sigh, wearily.

"I am so tired of it all, Brett," you say. "Oh, so tired!"

"I know," I say, "it's terrible. But what of the flu? How did you get that on top of it all?" You throw your hat on the ground and stretch out on the grass.

"I don't know," you reply, "I got it soon after my sister [Ada] came. I was pretty bad, too. Directly I could crawl, I crawled away with my sister; but I am tired to death of the whole business." There is such a depth of weariness in your voice, so hurt a look in your eyes, that nothing I can say seems adequate. I look at the bright sea, the faintly smoking mountain; I can hardly bear to look at the weary man beside me—pale, fragile, hopeless.

"Why not go right away, for a long trip?" I suggest.

"Sometimes," you say, "I think I must. My life is unbearable. I feel

I cannot stand it any longer. Chopping and changing is not my way, as you know; but I get so tired of it all. It makes me ill, too. I don't know what to do. I just don't know what will happen." The only thing I can think of is for you to keep away. I look at you and wonder if you have the courage, the strength to break away.

"If only I had enough money," you continue. "But I never do have enough. Then I could go away for a time. But it would mean letters and telegrams all the time. I would like to buy a sailing ship and sail among the Greek Islands and be free . . . free! Just to be free for a little while of it all!" I smile at you and say, cheerfully:

"Well, you are free now for the time being, so make hay while the sun shines." A faint smile flits over your face, followed by a look of bitterness. A strange severity hardens you.

"I won't stand it!" you say bitterly. "I won't! My life is my own, after all." Alertness seems to flow into you. You sit up and look around you —at the sea, the trees, the ships. Then you sink back wearily again, and you answer me sadly:

"You have no idea, Brett, how humiliating it is to beat a woman; afterwards one feels simply humiliated." There seems to be no way out. My mind becomes blank with the endeavor to find some solution for you. You look at your watch.

"Time to start back for lunch," you remark. "I am having a fish today. I hope it will be a big one. I am no Buddhist and I long for chops."

.   .   .

We arrive back at Quattro Venti a few minutes late. A long, strange-looking fish is lying in a dish in front of your place.

"Whatever is it?" you ask.

"It's a devil fish," Achsah replies. There seems to be no other fish in the town today. You settle down and eat it, nearly bones and all, you are so hungry.

.   .   .

How lovely a day it is. The sea is so clear, that I can see the shells and stones and glistening sea-weed at the bottom. And what a blue! You and I are sitting on the sands of the Piccola Marina. The walk down the narrow, stony path, down the endless uneven stone steps, tired you a little; but lying full-length on the hot sand, relaxed, peaceful and quiet, brings your strength back again.

"I am beginning to feel better," you say. "I am getting stronger." We talk at intervals, lazily.

"I must show you my picture, it's nearly finished," I murmur, almost to the sea.

"Your primrose Christ?" you answer, laughing. "I am longing to see what kind of a Christ you have made. Not my idea of a Christ, I bet." I smile to myself. I also am longing for the moment when you see my picture, but I will not give my secret away. Bathers have appeared out of the wooden sheds. We watch them. There are not many, but the few are varied.

"Self-discipline," I say, "is perhaps the most important thing of all."

"Yes," you agree, "one should always discipline oneself. People don't discipline themselves enough."

"And again," I continue, "there is pride of body. One should feel and keep a pride in one's limbs." I look at your slim length on the sand: the neat suit, the neat shoes, the massed hair narrowing down to the carefully clipped, pointed beard; the sensitive body, alert and aware —an aristocrat from head to foot. I look at a very fat man and woman in their tightly strained bathing-suits, the enormous bare legs and arms. You laugh and say, emphatically:

"People never will discipline themselves enough; and they have absolutely no pride. Their legs mean nothing to them. Think what a beautiful, alive thing a leg is—so narrow and strong, with the sensitive sole of the foot at the end of it. That is why I like to wear thin shoes; I like to feel the earth; I like my feet to be as close to the earth as possible. I used to love to feel the water in the irrigation ditch at the ranch, running over my sandals, round my feet. Sometimes I wish I had never left the ranch, the horses, the ditch. I envy you going back there."

"Why don't you go back," I say. "Why don't you get put on the quota as I am. Any moment, now, I may hear from the Consul. It makes it so much easier."

"Perhaps I will," you reply, "but just now I don't feel strong enough to cope with Consuls or anyone."

"I would like to call on the Branfords on the way back," I say. "They have been so kind to me. He is ill—has to lie out in the sun in bathing-pants all day. She has the bluest of blue eyes, and red-gold hair. She has been thinking of nothing else but your visit for days." You look intrigued and suggest that we start. We climb slowly up the steps and path, with many pauses to sit and rest. The Branfords are out. I leave a message with little Dot, their child, that we will come again in the afternoon.

Lunch is ready at Quattro Venti. Afterwards you rest for a couple of hours and sleep. We return to the Branfords' house. As we near it, I can see Martha through the window. She is coiling her long, red-gold hair round her head in a plait. She sees me and sends me a flashing blue glance. How marvellously blue her eyes are! She knows that I know she thinks she looks her best with her hair plaited and bound round her head like a wreath. Dot has evidently given our message.

Branford meets us at the door: tall, dark, nervous, a big hooked nose, and dark caverns of eyes. How dark and different from her. He welcomes us cheerfully.

"Dot said you had called with Father Christmas," he tells me. You are immensely tickled at that. Dot is peeping round the corner of the door at you, very shy, a bit scared; but too fascinated to move.

It has turned a bit chilly and so the fire is lit and the kettle put on to boil. Branford gives us each a generous supply of rum in our tea. Martha hovers round you, excited and flushed. The warmth of the fire, the warmth of the rum, loosens your tongue, and you give many and amusing descriptions of old times in England, of old English friends.

But Dot remains near the door, a fixed, fascinated stare fastened on you. She tells her mother, later, that she thinks it wicked that Father Christmas should come any other day but Christmas Day.

It begins to get late, so we leave, hilarious and flushed, and return to Quattro Venti.

.   .   .

It is very cold on the Piazza. I have been waiting for half an hour for you. At last you come. You have been looking at Achsah's paintings, you explain. I have a parcel of sandwiches from the hotel. We start off for the Tragara on an easy, winding path along the cliff, through olive woods, along the terraces of vines and trees. We walk slowly. The sea is almost too bright to look at. At intervals, we sit and rest.

"Let's call on Faith," you say. "We have to pass her house. What a pity she had to leave her old villa with the dark cypress trees." Faith Mackenzie's new villa is tucked in among other villas. We knock loudly on the door. For a while no one comes, but at last the Italian servant opens the door. You enquire for Faith and we go in—to find a completely dumbfounded woman. Faith is astounded and stares at you amazed. She can hardly believe her eyes. We sit and talk with her awhile and drink some excellent wine and listen to her beautiful gramophone. She asks you to supper with her one evening. Her husband, Compton Mackenzie, is away on one of the Channel Islands. They have a new home there. Then we stroll on, along the Tragara, past Faith's old lovely villa.[56]

Lady (Faith) Compton Mackenzie

[Lawrence] came again [to Capri] in 1926, and Dorothy Brett, the late Lord Esher's daughter, in *Lawrence and Brett*, tells how he said one day, "Let's call on Faith," and they came to the little place where I picnicked with the furniture from Solitaria, and Brett says that I was dumbfounded, that I stared at him and could hardly believe my eyes. I don't remember that, but I do remember sitting round a table with them and being more than usually amused by his conversation, which was mostly about women, while Brett's ear-trumpet waved to and fro, her cheeks flushed and her eyes sparkling under an unruly fringe of straight dark hair.

"The longer I live," he said, "the more breathless I become."

Women had been more than usually breath-taking and exasperating just lately, and that was why he had fled to Capri. It must have been heavenly for Brett to have him to herself, far away from that maddening household in New Mexico, with its emotional squalor and spiritual discomfort. For Lawrence to allow himself to be surrounded by a corps of infatuated women was perfectly natural. It is the sport of genius; their antics have a tonic effect, and even the exasperation to which Lawrence was occasionally driven, and of which we read in the copious reminiscences that his death produced, was stimulating enough to be worth while. . . .

Now in Capri he is a little tired of sport, and needs a rest. Brett was the least exacting of his satellites, the best behaved, perhaps the most unselfishly devoted, and certainly the least critical. He was right to turn to her, and he suggested going off in a sailing ship to the Greek Islands to get away from everything. That was his mood and she was content, though that voyage never happened.

I saw them often, and Brett used to come to my little parties, and dance with Italians and Russians to my noisy gramophone in her red Mexican coat and hair flopping wildly. In her heart was a world of which we knew nothing, a world where mountains shook, Indians danced, and a horse could be your best friend. When she went back to the ranch she used to write me long and fascinating letters about her life there. She was then alone, as the Lawrences were absent, but it had become her whole life, and a full one.

When Lawrence asked me to dine alone with him at a little restaurant called Esposito, I went gladly, because I enjoyed his company. And when we discussed Monty [Compton Mackenzie] I let him talk more frankly than I would have allowed any one else to do, "because," I wrote in my diary, "I know he loves him." And, of course, I talked myself, warmed by Capri wine, and his sensitive understanding and the glow of kindness in his deep eyes. To me that night he seemed an angel, and I gave him some of the secrets of my heart which hitherto had never been let loose. Unfortunately some months later a short story[57] appeared in one of the popular magazines which he could not have written if I had not dined with him that night in Capri. A malicious caricature of Monty, and a monstrous perversion of facts, yet the source of it clearly recognisable. "He was an angel; and he was a devil."[58] I think John Middleton Murry is right there. He did great harm to the people who adored him. I suppose no genius has left such a trail of malice in the hearts of those who professed to love him. In their bitterness against each other they do him violence. Who that truly loved him would have made public the tragically futile party in a plush room at the Café Royal?[59] The pathos of that lonely figure, overcome by the fumes of unaccustomed wine, carried out unconscious by his none too sober guests after he had asked what for most of them was the impossible: to leave all and follow him—to New Mexico! If it had been a great historic occasion; if with one accord they had said "yes," and the nucleus of a new cult had been formed and become a force in the world, then there would have been justification for recalling it. There was none; it fizzled out as flatly as an unsuccessful cocktail party, and that was the tragedy of it. And that was why it should have been forgotten, buried—buried deep.[60]

The Hon. Dorothy Brett

"Let us go round by the cave," I suggest.

"All right," you reply, "we will lunch on those rocks over there." When we reach the rocks, we settle down and eat our sandwiches and drink our bottle of wine. We have a small bottle each of light red wine. We are sheltered from the wind and the sun is hot, but you look somewhat tired. You reach out and pick a flower, holding it tenderly in your hands.

"Do you know what this is, Brett?"

"No," I answer, "I don't."

"Good Lord, Brett, what an ignoramus you are! Did you never study botany? It is the old Greek asphodel. Asphodel is so lovely a name, and the flower is lovely, too. One of the things I enjoyed most as a boy at school, besides drawing, was botany; and later, as a schoolmaster, the two things I liked teaching best were drawing and botany; and I had very good classes in both. You are lucky, Brett, in the things you have not had to do to earn your living." Certain chapters in *The Rainbow* rushed into my mind. "Yes," you say, "It can be very bad; but I never had much trouble. The boys, I think, liked me. But even when a boy, I always felt there was something so mean in tormenting one's teacher."

The old cave is dark. I hate caves: I hurry through it. I won't even go to the blue grotto. You poke about in it, then follow me up the path. The climb up out of the cave is steep: you are puffing and look white.

"You should not have brought me such a long walk," you say testily. "I am not fit enough yet." I feel terribly distressed. I insist on your sitting down. Then I suggest our calling on Mr. Brooks,[61] another old friend of yours whose villa we are bound to pass. This you think an excellent idea.

Mr. Brooks is as surprised to see you as Faith [Compton Mackenzie] was. He is a handsome, white-haired old man. We settle down comfortably in his large leather chairs in the cool room with its big window. He gives us some wine and we sit sipping it and talking. You ask him about ships.

"I want to buy a sailing ship and sail among the Greek islands. With a captain and a couple of sailors, we could do the rest." Mr. Brooks looks doubtful. Ships are cheaper, but still very expensive. He says he can inquire; he will do what he can to find out for you.

"I will come along to Quattro Venti and let you know about them," he says. And we start on our way back.

While Achsah, you and I sit in the living room, waiting for supper, you talk of marriage quietly. There is something even more gentle and sensitive than usual about you this evening.

"Women," you say, "are hardly ever true to themselves: that is why they are not true to others; that is what makes most of the tragedies of married life. Also women destroy themselves by their obsession to have their own way." And you sigh, heavily, while Achsah and I look at each other over your head.

.   .   .

An old friend of yours and Achsah's [62] has now joined the party. With my usual love of nicknames, I have named her "The Gadfly." Once, a few years ago, she was able, as she occupied a post of social importance, to help you. Now you feel you must return the kindness. Achsah also wishes to repay past kindnesses, and we are burdened with the Gadfly.

Lying out on the grass in the garden after lunch, she lies with her head in my lap. I say nothing, but I look cautiously at you. A very grim smile, with the usual pull down of the corner of your mouth, answers my look. I never once saw you wink, never. The Gadfly is small, vivacious. Some years beyond middle age, she chatters like a magpie and has a strong desire for eternal youth.

As she takes herself off to her hotel, the Reynolds' children arrive, looking for Harwood. You have read the poetry of the youngest child, and are somewhat appalled at her precocious talent. In spite of all argument to the contrary, you will not believe it is not all trained and forced and a great mistake. The mail is brought in by Harwood. There is a letter for you. You read it quickly, stuff it angrily into your pocket, and a weary look of annoyance passes over your face.

At supper, we talk of our various childhoods. You give a vivid and very terrible picture of your early life. "It was terrible," you say. "Terrible, with the constant struggle, the lack, nearly, of the bare necessities of life. To be sick meant the doctor; that meant any extra shillings went for the doctor's fee and medicine; and usually we had only one shilling extra every week—only one. Think of that, Brett. Boots and clothes had to be saved up for slowly, week by week. Every little thing we needed extra, meant saving and scraping for, and not having enough to eat. And the wages varied—never more than twenty-five shillings a week, sometimes much less.

"At times my mother hardly knew what to do, how to manage. You do not know, Brett; you have never experienced certain things owing to your up-bringing; you never can know. My eldest brother [63] died, I believe, because of those early days of semi-starvation, of never having enough clothes, enough warmth, enough to eat. He died of pneumonia, while overworking, and he was, I always think, even more brilliant than I am."

We none of us say anything—we are too horrified. Then to some query of Earl's about Buddhism, about Oriental teaching, you reply:

"Eternity. My idea of Eternity, I can best illustrate by the rainbow: it is the meeting half way of two elements. The meeting of the sun and of the water produce, at exactly the right place and moment, the rainbow. So it is in everything, and that is eternal . . . the Nirvana . . . just that moment of the meeting of two elements. No one person could reach it alone without that meeting." And you lapse into a long silence.

. . .

Achsah has begged me to light the pig for her. With extreme difficulty I get a wretched fire going. You come in to find Achsah and I crouching over it. You look a bit chilled and white. We all three crouch round it and talk of the lugger.

"If only," you say, "I could sail off to the Greek Islands and leave everything for awhile—forever!" I look up from poking a stick of damp cedar wood into the fire.

"Think," I say, "how lovely to hang the colored lights on the masts in the evening."

"Yes," you reply, "we would do most of our own work. Just a captain and a couple of sailors to navigate the ship—the rest we could do. They tell me the Greek Islands are so lovely, but that the coast is tricky, a bit dangerous for sailing. But to be free of everything for awhile . . . I wish I could. How I wish I could!" Achsah and I glance at each other. There is a depth of yearning in your voice, in your white face, in your whole tired figure as you sit crouched over the stove.

"Sometimes," you say, giggling a little, "I feel so weak. I feel like a white geranium in a pot." I look up and say grimly:

"More like a cactus in a pot." You dart a surprised look at me, so rarely do I scratch you. Then I know by the expression on your face, that you are only biding your time until you can get even with me. "I was only pulling your leg," I say.

"You had better be careful, or I'll pull yours right off," you reply.

Later on in the day, you do get magnificently even with me. But all the morning we crouch over the smoky, miserable pig and talk of the lugger.

. . .

The Gadfly is chattering, chattering. Even the sandwiches can't quell her perpetual garrulousness. You listen patiently and answer "yes" and "no," and giggle occasionally. I get stonier and stonier. Our days are ruined: we always have to trail her along with us. I sit and throw stones at the nearest tree-trunk. The olives are just as silvery as ever, as feathery in the wind, the sea as deep a blue; but the peace and the silence has gone—it has vanished in this constant babble.

. . .

You are talking to Earl about the solar plexus, sitting in their living-room.

"It is perfectly hopeless to abuse the solar plexus," you say. "If the solar plexus is outraged, it is going to get back at you. Oh, yes, it will take its revenge. You cannot disregard it absolutely, you just can't. That is what has happened to your friend: he outraged the solar plexus, forced himself to do things in spite of it. And now see what has happened. It will take years and years to repair—has taken years, as far as I understand."

The return of Achsah and the Gadfly breaks up the conversation, and we all start for Annacapri to visit the Brett Youngs.[64] You are to lunch with them, the Brewsters are going somewhere else in Annacapri, and the Gadfly and I have sandwiches. We sit under a wall, and the talk trails on and on like a noisy stream.

We are to meet you at the Brett Youngs, so at about two-thirty we go up to the house. The Gadfly is so trivial, so irritating with her craving to be young, that you and I get angry. On the way home in the carriage, with the rain dripping down our necks, the Gadfly is so flirty with you, so arch and coy, so utterly silly, that you are maddened as if a mosquito were buzzing round you, stinging you. You sit more and more upright; your face hardens into a cold, unseeing mask; you look straight in front of you and answer in short monosyllables.

What an agonizing drive! I want to laugh, I want to curse—I do neither. Why add to your embarrassment? By the time we reach Quattro Venti, you are seething with rage; and only the long, exhausting flight of steps saves the Gadfly from an explosion of the kind she least expects.

That evening, after she is gone, we celebrate with wine and great joyousness, the anniversary of our first start to America two years ago [5 March 1924]. You give amusing descriptions of the horses, of Susan [the cow], of our ranch life. Harwood is allowed to sit up, and we sing, all of us, the old songs and ballads. You sing your favorite, *Mary and Joseph,* and many other old English songs. The wind is blowing big guns outside, the tower is shaking; but the wind fits into our singing, fits into our mood of lovely gayety, of laughter, and of those wearisome things you are wishing to forget.

At last I go out into the howling wind to fight my way down the steps and along the road, dashing round corners as the wind beats me back, and finally arriving at the hotel.

.   .   .

This afternoon Achsah, Harwood, you and I are playing dumbcrambo. Singly, each in turn, we act a word. Sometimes two of us together, but mostly we act alone. Into this fun comes the Gadfly. Her voice precedes her like a cyclone blowing into the room, and we subside; the acting withers and dies out. But we decide to dress up for dinner, and later in the evening, you and I and Harwood disappear into her little room.

There is no make-up. We ransack the whole house for clothes and paint. You are to be a schoolmaster. You turn your soft collar up, tie a broad pink ribbon round your neck, and the ends of the collar stick out like little wings. You put on a black coat of Earl's. (It is much too small for you.) Then you paint your face with lip-salve, powder it, blacken round your eyes, and part your hair in the middle.

Harwood, in one of her mother's dresses, with one of her mother's large hats balanced on her head, and with flowing veils around her, is like a Romney. She twirls a little parasol over her head and swings her long skirts in a swaying walk.

I powder my face a dead white, sleek back my hair with water, paint my eyebrows a deep black, blue my eyes, and paint my lips the brightest scarlet I can find.

Then, arm in arm, the three of us walk in to dinner. Achsah and Earl are scandalized. They look askance at you, and wonder whether it is not a bit undignified. You are the prim schoolmaster, precise, priggish. I am a hard-boiled "know all" kind of woman. And Harwood is charmingly flirty, still twirling her little parasol over her head.

Into this comes the Gadfly, dressed as a child of five; a large bow on her hair, socks, a frock down to her bare knees, looking so grotesque that not one of us is amused. She plays the buffoon all through dinner, while you remain oblivious of her, still the mincing, priggish schoolmaster. I also remain the cold, relentless woman of the world. And Harwood, smirking under her big hat and parasol, flirts delightfully with you. You ask her if you may kiss her. She refuses, politely but firmly. You are not allowed to kiss her, though you ask her continually, all through dinner. Achsah and Earl are just nonplussed.

After dinner we act charades. I become, somehow or other, your daughter; and as your daughter, I flirt outrageously. You are the brutal father, but your brutality fades before my bewildering onslaught. Never have you seen me act like this before, and never have I acted like that since. What with the wine, the disguise of paint, the presence of the Gadfly—that grotesque old child of five—I am drawn out of my usual shyness and my self-consciousness vanishes. I charm you into embarrassment. The austere father turns into the responsive male.

At eleven o'clock, still painted, I run down to the hotel.

.　　　.　　　.

Today, you and I are going up to the Tiberio rock to picnic. The hotel provides us with huge sandwiches. What a day it is, too, lovely and hot, the white clouds like long slices of thin ice in the blue sky. It is a long pull up; we walk slowly, with many pauses.

I tell you of my early years, of things that I experienced round about the age of eighteen to twenty. You turn on me, angrily; you are indignant, hurt; something in your manhood flames angrily, fiercely outraged. I stand for a moment, helpless, at a loss what to say. You turn away with a heavy sigh.

"It's not fair, Brett," you say. "You have never had any luck—never a decent chance!"

We scramble up a ragged path to the Tiberio Inn, and sit and rest in the niche from where the unfortunates were thrown down the sheer rock to the sea below. The woman of the Inn brings us glasses of cold, delicious beer. Then we wander on to the extreme edge of the cliff. Here, against an old ruined wall, we settle down. The dark blue sea is shadowy far away below us, like a blue haze; across the bay, the long rugged line of the coast of Sorrento fades into a point, to the Siren Islands, mere hazy specks. We eat our sandwiches and talk of the feeling of unreality, of the old days of glory, that Italy gives us.

"I only see people in togas," I say.

"Think," you reply, "of Pan, of the mythical Gods; think of all that old mythology; of Lorenzo the Magnificent. That is what Italy and Greece mean to me."

"You remember," I say, "how I wrote you that I found Pan on the cliff road down to the Piccola Marina?"

"Yes. What of the picture?" you ask.

"I will show it you tomorrow," I reply. Our bottles of beer foam over onto the grass.

"In the old days, Brett, the sailing ships had sails of crimson silk. Think of that in the sunlight: crimson silk on a blue sea, with the sunlight and the white waves."

We are silent. You lie watching the sky; I sit looking down at the hazy sea far below me. Round the sharp corner of the precipice, comes a sailing ship, mysterious, shadowy; it sails towards us; it glides like a ghost beneath us, two-masted, with curved, billowing sails. It floats past like a dream, floats on, and fades into the mist.

"Look, Lawrence!" I cry, "Look! Our lugger!" But you are fast asleep, curled up with your head on your arm.

I sit and watch you. The sun pours down relentlessly on your head; a heavy lock of hair falls over your face; your beard glitters red in the sun. As I watch you, the meaningless modern suit seems to drop away. A leopard skin, a mass of flowers and leaves wrap themselves round you. Out of your thick hair, two small horns poke their sharp points; the slender, cloven hoofs lie entangled in weeds. The flute slips from your hand. I stare at you in a kind of trance. Your eyes open suddenly, a gleam of blue. Nothing moves, nothing stirs; but your eyes are looking at me, looking at me. . . .

.   .   .

What a terrible wind! It is cold as well as hard. Earl has persuaded you to remain indoors and I come up after lunch to Quattro Venti to find you low-spirited. We spend a quiet afternoon sitting round the smoky stove—the pig. (It is certainly much the shape of one!) The Gadfly has gone back home, thank God, and our peace has been restored to us.

We sit quietly round the stove while you read out to us some of your most recent poems in a quiet, low voice. A letter is sticking out of your pocket. I look across at Achsah. She shakes her head, sadly, and afterwards tells me that you have received a cruel, hard letter, which has upset you very much. Before I return to the hotel, I ask you whether you do not think it best for me to delay my return to America; not to go too far away, for fear of more trouble.

"I would be nearer at hand, in case of trouble. I would feel uneasy in my mind, if I went so far. What do you think?" I say.

"Yes," you reply, with so much weariness mixed with boredom, that I feel nothing on earth matters very much to you. "It would be best. I don't know what to do. We must wait and see." Thus we settle it, and I struggle through the wind to the hotel.

.   .   .

The Brewsters are packing for India, box after box. Earl is tired out. You have come down to the hotel to see my picture. I have perched it on the bed, in the best light available. You look at it in astonishment; then you laugh and say quickly:

"It's a good idea, but it's much too like me—much too like."

"I know," I reply, "but I took the heads half from you and half from John the Baptist."

"It's too like me," you repeat abruptly. "You will have to change it. Also put a little more pink in the sunset: it's too golden. Just a touch of pink would help. But wherever did you get the idea from?"

"I don't know—it just came. It seemed to come from you, to be you."

The picture is of a crucifixion. The pale yellow Christ hangs on the Cross, against an orange sunset. With that final spurt of strength before death, he is staring at the vision of the figure in front of him. His eyes are visionary, his figure tense and aware. Before him, straddled across a rock, half curious, half smiling, is the figure of Pan, holding up a bunch of grapes to the dying Christ: a dark, reddish-gold figure with horns and hoofs. The heads of Pan and of Christ are both your head. Behind lies the sea. A deep curve of rocks brings the sea-line low in the middle of the picture; and below Pan's rock is just visible the tower of Quattro Venti. Alas, that the laughter and criticism of others made me cut the picture up in a rage! I have only the heads that I rescued. But some day I will paint it again.

"It is you," I say.

"Perhaps," you answer grimly.[65]

Achsah Barlow Brewster

After leaving Ceylon [1922] we eventually returned to our old haunts, Torre dei Quattro Venti, Capri, where we remained during the next four years. In March, 1926, we were again preparing to go East. During this interval the Lawrences had travelled much—to New Mexico, Old Mexico, to Europe, back to America, and now they had returned again recently to Europe.

On the eve of our departure for India everything at Quattro Venti was being packed, when Lawrence had appeared, asking if it would be inconvenient to put him up. He was keener than ever about our getting a lugger and all of us going to the East by way of it; he recalled someone who had purchased an old freighter and when finally arriving in China had sold the boat at a profit. The lugger was postponed; but Lawrence promised to join us in India in the autumn if we advised it.

Out on the terrace of Quattro Venti, sitting in the spring sunshine, we were talking about the curse of money. He related his story of "The

Rocking-Horse Winner," [66] bringing money, but the little boy's death. The tale was told of a woman's inheriting a fortune, whereupon she bought herself a close collar of pearls; soon afterward a bee stung her on the throat, which swelled before the collar could be removed, choking her to death. Someone else recounted that a poor farmer inherited forest land which he sold for ten thousand dollars. When he was told it should have brought twenty thousand, he was so chagrined that he hanged himself on one of the trees. There seemed no end of such tales. Lawrence decided at once to write a volume of them under the title of *Tales of the Four Winds* from which the proceeds should be divided equally among us, that the curse of the riches should be shared by us all. We might invest them in a lugger.

I was remonstrating with the child [Harwood] over some trifle when Lawrence said: "That is like my mother, who would look at me reproachfully, and say: 'You used to be such a dear good boy, Bertie.'" His eyes looked blue and innocent, and his mouth turned up so demurely that the child burst into laughter.

With red hair like his, of course, he would have a temper, I remarked. To this he took exception, announcing that his hair was not red, that it used to be pure yellow gold and now was brown; his beard might be red, but his hair was golden brown! Looking again, I could see that he was right, but it seemed surprising, and still does.

One radiant morning Lawrence, Brett and I were rattling down in a little carriage from Anacapri; Lawrence was sitting on the seat with the driver, facing us, swaying with each lurch of the carriage; Brett was expostulating with me against fear and my dread of going to India. I replied that anything could be faced when need be, but there were many things not to be chosen recklessly. We were rumbling past the madonna in her grotto where blue lithospermum and narcissus were blossoming in every crevice. Lawrence pointed at the masses of bloom, saying that if you pulled the flowers up and put them in the wrong place they would die. He said decisively: "It's not fair. She knows her own life current."

In the dismantled library we were playing charades one evening. With his hair plastered down into bangs, a red bow tie under his chin, he was a clerk in a shoe-shop—the empty library shelves stocked with all the stray shoes the house had. The skill with which he argued his customers into buying what they did not want would have been the envy of any salesman.

The packing had continued throughout his visit. Bit by bit was stowed away until there was left the last tattered sheet, and no table linen. A stream of people came to see him—newspaper correspondents and photographers. Lawrence stayed on to the end, closing the garden gate as we drove down to the boat in the harbour.[67]

Earl H. Brewster

In the spring of 1926 Lawrence visited us in Capri just before our second journey to the East. Once again "our lugger" had to be postponed!

We showed him our paintings. He never left us in doubt regarding his reaction from a picture: for he was as strong in his disapproval of some as he was warm in his appreciation of others. But I never felt that I understood the basis of his taste in pictures. Some of my more abstract ones he declared were inspired by bitterness and hatred: I did not understand. He disapproved of the abstract in painting, he hated the theory which led the artist to abstract forms: he hated the very word *abstract*. Perhaps he felt that such work implied too great a dislike of concreteness and reality. I thought then that his judgements sprang too much from his literary predispositions. Now I perceive that the concrete and abstract are not opposing elements, but that a work of art should be created in the fullest possible awareness of both. I do not remember that we ever argued about Art or Aesthetic theories.

At this time Lawrence had not made any of the pictures which he later exhibited, but he frequently painted. As we were dismantling our studio he enthusiastically carried away all the left-over materials.

Lawrence stood at the gateway of Quattro Venti waving us a good-bye as our small carriages, piled high with luggage, bore us down the road for our departure to India.[68]

The Hon. Dorothy Brett

The Brewsters started early this morning for India. Quattro Venti is empty and desolate. You and I are going to Amalfi, to join Miss [Millicent] Beveridge and Miss [Mabel] Harrison,[69] old friends of yours that you are anxious to see.

You come down to the Hotel and we take the funicular down to the boat. It is again horribly windy. The sea is rough. The sailors seize us and drag us from the little boat onto the ladder of the steamer. Our suitcases follow—and a new adventure begins.

The steamer tosses heavily. It ploughs its way to Sorrento. It is cold and we creep into the bows for shelter. I feel wretched, a bit sick. Suddenly a steward appears and suggests our going down to the cabin and having some brandy and food. We slide along the wet deck and sit in the stuffy little cabin. I drink as much brandy as I can and begin to feel alive. Fried eggs and bacon then appear; and by some miracle I am able to eat them. You are feeling perfectly all right; the rough sea does not trouble you; you are pleased to be on the move again. Once past the Siren Islands, in the gulf of Salerno, the sea becomes smooth, the sun comes out, and it is lovely on deck. We stand and watch the rough coast, bare and bleak, until we draw near Amalfi.

"We will go up to the hotel first and find out if my friends are there, or whether they are up at Ravello," you say. In the last earthquake, one hotel had slid into the sea and vanished; but the hotel we drive up to is an old monastery, built into the rock. We look into the tiny cell rooms: it is attractive. But as your friends are not there, we decide to drive on up to Ravello.

"Look at the macaroni," you say; and there, lying out in the sun, are masses and masses of macaroni, laid over wires or strings stretched from posts. Also the fishing nets are hanging out drying; and there are many fishermen sitting mending their nets. Our driver hurries his wretched little ponies up the hill. It is a long, steep, twisting climb. Half way up, the driver, who is keeping up a running conversation with you, sitting sideways on the box-seat, pulls up sharply. Then, in a loud voice, he bellows across the valley.

"What is he doing?" I ask you.

"There is a famous echo here," you reply. "Can you hear it?" I put up [my ear-trumpet] Toby, but I can hear nothing, not a sound. You lean forward and explain to the driver that I am deaf. He beams at me, and in a stentorian voice he bellows again and again across the valley. I hear nothing; but the man is purple in the face. At last you interrupt his fearful efforts and explain that I still cannot hear. The driver speaks to me. You tell him I cannot speak Italian. He shrugs his shoulders contemptuously, gives me a disgusted look, turns round on his seat and gallops his ponies up the hill. You are laughing, highly amused at the man's contemptuous back as he swings round the corners until his poor little horses stop in spite of him, to breathe. We go up more slowly, now. The road is steeper than ever. We come to some stone walls.

"This is Ravello," you say. "We will go to the Palumo and take rooms there. Then we will look for Miss Beveridge." But there are no rooms anywhere, in any of the hotels. The Palumo has an annex, but the annex is full, too. The good woman of the hotel is full of concern; she has the use of some rooms in a very nice cottage—would we like to see them? Off we go. They are very nice and clean. We take them until the hotel has some free rooms. Our bags are deposited and we renew the hunt for Miss Beveridge.

We cannot find her. So we return to their hotel and sit in the hall and wait. At last Miss Beveridge and Miss Harrison appear. They are very delighted to see you, and give us tea. Then we go for a walk along the rambling little paths on the top of the rock that is Ravello.

The Hotel Palumo is so full that you and I have a table in a glassed-in porch, all by ourselves. You are tremendously hungry. You tell me that your vegetarian diet with the Brewsters has given you a huge appetite. It has! The large steak, with onions and potatoes, seems all too little for you.

After dinner, we sit in one of the public drawing-rooms and solemnly play bezique. We are watched with curiosity. I feel eyes piercing my back, and you become fidgety. Some people sitting near, ask us why we play so old-fashioned a game. We don't know, except that you are so slow at learning games that I have not struggled to teach you another; and, as we are only two, we can't play bridge. Anyhow, we like our bezique, and in spite of the smiles, we continue to play. After a few games, we get up and saunter out. It is late and we are tired.

"I wonder," you say, "if I can find my way to the cottage. What a perfect nuisance the hotels are full. And look! Just look at the key!" You haul an immense old iron key out of your pocket. It is at least eight inches long; a huge, medieval key.

"I wonder if it will open the door," I say, hopefully. We stroll on in the moonlight. The little tortuous path winds round old walls, through hedges. There are little lights bobbing on the sea, and a faint wind is blowing.

We come to the old wooden door in the stone archway. You fit the key in the lock and turn and twist. Only a rusty squeaking. You turn and twist more angrily, swearing and cursing. Suddenly, for no apparent reason, the lock turns. We push the heavy door open, feel our way in, relock the door, and climb up the pitch-dark stone staircase. You turn into your room with a cheery good-night. I fumble my way into mine, find the matches and the tallow candle, and jump into the hard, relentless bed.

.   .   .

"Let us explore," you say to me next morning as we sit breakfasting in the hotel sun-porch. So off we go. We stroll through the gardens of Cimbrone, and come suddenly on a blue Venus. You are immensely amused by her. "We will bring our paints and sketch her this afternoon," you say. We follow the narrow paths until we come to the edge of the rock. There we sit and watch the sea and the sailing ships. You give a heavy sigh.

"We are the only two left," you say sadly to me. "Only you and I. Everyone else has gone over to the enemy." I am appalled at the depth of despair in your voice. What can I do? What can I say?

"I think it will come all right for you in a little time," I reply. "Surely it must. If not, why not break free?"

"I wish we could get a lugger," you say. "I would so like to sail among the Greek Islands. They say they are so lovely! It would be so restful, too."

"Can't we buy one?" I suggest. "If we could get one or two others to help, we could buy a lugger and sail off in it." We look longingly at the two-masted schooners drifting along below us, so white and radiant on the brilliant sea.

"Why," you say petulantly, "have we never enough money, never? And it would not take much, really."

After lunch we collect our paints and return to the Blue Venus. Miss Beveridge has given us out of her paint-box a marvelous blue—a blue I have longed for since and never traced. With this precious color, we settle down to the Venus. It is piping hot, and we choose shady spots. The Venus is, I suppose, copper, colored by the sun. She is life-size, cut off just above the knees. I am feeling very pleased with mine until you come and look at it.

"Oh, Brett," you exclaim, "how lady-like you have made her; how elegant and slim. Come and look at mine." I get up and look: a large, florid blue lady, among vague trees. Certainly there is nothing wishy-washy about your Venus. She is so flamboyant that mine has no chance against her.

"She is splendid," I agree, "and I like the way you have done the trees."

"So do I," you say, proudly. "I think mine is much the better!" As you always do think so, I never argue. The only remark I venture is that I like my blue the best.

"Color is not everything," you reply, tartly. "Tomorrow," you add, "I have asked Miss Beveridge and Miss Harrison to walk down to Amalfi with us. My throat feels a little sore, and I want to buy some mustard plasters. Just in case, that's all; I'm all right, really."

.   .   .

Next day we start off with your friends and walk down the lovely path to Amalfi. It is stony and steep, and very, very hot. We pass through a strange village of stone, under great archways, through narrow, dark passages—and arrive, hot and exhausted, in Amalfi.

The chemist has mustard plasters and cough mixture: you buy sufficient of both. Your friends take you to the bank: they have some kind of money trouble. Then we have lunch and hire a two-horse carriage to carry us up the hill again.

.   .   .

We take many, many walks along the paths of Ravello. Your two friends are kind and amusing and gay. The people in the hotel question me; they recognize you from photographs in the papers. But we lead a quiet, simple life there, undisturbed by the other guests; mostly walking into the mountains, to avoid the steep climb back up to Ravello. We lie on the grass in the gardens, and you sleep a lot and rest.

Then one day I come back to the hotel to find a letter from the English Consulate in Naples. My quota papers have arrived, and I have to see about them. I am disappointed and furious. How tiresome! What can I do? I am advised to go back and see about them.

"It's all right, Brett. You can come back," you say. "I will see you onto the boat, and it won't take long." I feel desperate; it seems so silly to have to go all that way back to Naples.

"But you may not stay here!" I protest.

"I think I will," you reply. "Anyhow, if I leave, you can always join me in Florence. I might try Tuscany. I have some tales I want to write in Tuscany. Let's sit here for a bit."

We sit down. A black beetle is rolling a small ball of dirt laboriously up the path. With a twig, you roll the ball back down the path again. The beetle hurries after it. No sooner has it pushed the ball back again, than you roll it down hill once more. What patience! Heavens, what patience and perseverance that beetle has! A little black snake coiled up on a rock, suddenly sees us, lifts a wicked-looking head, flickers its fangs at us, and glides swiftly into a hole in the rock.

"Cheer up, Brett," you say. "Why can't you learn to accept? You want the quota number; now is your chance to get it. There is nothing to fuss about. I am so much better, too. I really am much stronger. Let me be the judge of this. I am sure I am right."

"Maybe," I reply, "but something in my bones tells me I am making a mistake. I will join you in Florence, anyhow, if you go there." The beetle has at last pushed the ball over the edge of the path. We get up, and walk slowly back to the hotel.

.   .   .

The sun pours into my little room. I can hear you moving about in yours across the way. We are going for a walk in the gardens. With immense difficulty, you lock the great wooden outer door of the cottage, sunk deep in the arch of the wall. The huge key still turns heavily; the lock needs about a ton of oil.

We find a warm corner in the gardens, on smooth grass. The sea is pale gold, unbearably bright. I am wretched and glum; my coming departure fills me with dread. You look at me and laugh. We have been talking about love—you with your usual jeer.

"Every rose has its thorn, Brett. You know I don't believe in love or friendship." But there is no answering smile in me. "Cut out the ecstasy," you continue. "Oh, I know; I know the ecstasy. Cut it out, Brett. Cut it out. Think of the Beyond." I am not thinking at all; I am too filled with dread, with apprehension.

"The Beyond," I murmur.

"Yes," you reply, "Think of the Beyond!" Power and pride sweep over you; I am carried away for the moment, by the force in you. The frail body becomes tense and aware, the forehead seems a glow of power, the eyes large and dark.

My eye catches sight of a white violet. I pick it and hand it to you. You hold it with that strange tenderness that flowers bring to your hands. I smile back at you; the despair for the moment has gone, and there is a radiance everywhere. The white violet shines in your hands; the power has given place to peace—and for a timeless moment, I am carried beyond the future.[70]

18 March 1926   Ravello, Província di Salerno, Italy

〖 *I have been moving around a bit, while Frieda stays in Spotorno with her two daughters. . . . The plans for the summer are vague. Frieda talks of leaving Spotorno for good on April 10th and going to Germany. . . . Brett may be coming to America quite soon.*[71]

The Hon. Dorothy Brett

I am packed and ready, but bewildered. Something seems to be happening all around me. Why, I wonder, oh, why cannot he free himself? Free himself from everything! Why does he wrap these old beliefs, old prejudices, old laws so tightly round himself? You do not believe in them, I know; and yet you have not the courage. Is it courage? No, maybe you have the courage in one way. I don't know. My mind whirls round all the trouble. I am exhausted by my doubts and torments. I feel tired, useless, tormented. Inwardly, I curse the quota. You are nervous, excited, a queer tormented look in your face, too.

"I don't know, Brett," you say to me, "I don't know what I will do. I may go back to Frieda soon; she is quieter, now, more friendly. I can't tell. Her last letter was so much better. But please don't fuss. Behave yourself. There is nothing to fuss about."

"I just don't like leaving you," I repeat.

"It's all right," you reply, tersely. "I must be the judge of this; and we must leave our next meeting on the knees of the Gods!"

I pick up my suitcase and follow you down the stairs, out into the chill morning air. The little two-horse carriage is waiting for us. It is so early in the morning that no one is about; and no one seems to know just when the boat starts. We decide to start thus early in the morning and wait at Amalfi. How dark the winding road is, as the horses trot briskly down the hill: dank and chilly and dark. You pull your light overcoat round you. I seem, in my white serge coat, to gleam like a ghost. I am glum and depressed.

"It's all right, Brett," you keep on saying, "You needn't fuss. You can come right back directly you are through with the Consul." But I am filled with doubts and forebodings. I laugh miserably. This moment seems more precious to me than all the quota numbers in the world! "You never can tell, Brett," you say, consolingly, "it may prove more worthwhile in the end; and I do need someone to look after the ranch for me. And I never know: I may return quite soon—I never can tell how I am going to feel." But I am not convinced.

"Let's go back," I urge. "Hang the quota!" But you laugh at my fears and on we rattle. The road turns into the sunlight; for a moment the sea swings into view, then is gone again as we plunge back into shadow once more.

At Amalfi, we find that the steamer does not start back until after lunch. We stroll through the town, and climb up to the hotel to order lunch. In the hotel, everyone stares at us. We are given a small table and we eat uncomfortably with all the eyes watching us. I am still filled with reluctance to go.

"It's a mistake," I keep on murmuring.

"Don't be so superstitious, Brett," you reply. "Believe me, I am right. I will let you know my plans. And if I leave here before you return, I will let you know; and maybe you could pick me up in Florence or wherever I go. But don't lose the coveted quota number!" The same power rises in you again; in that dark room, the light glows on your white forehead, your eyes widen and darken, your head is suddenly powerful and overwhelming.

Then you become fidgety and restless under the constant glances in the dining room. We hurry our meal and go out and sit on one of the terraces until it draws near the time for the boat to go. You cannot shake me out of depression and reluctance to go. At the last minute I still want to return to Ravello, while you still point out the wisdom of my making sure of my number.

We walk down to the beach, collect my suitcase, and hail a rowboat. The steamer is whistling: I have to go. I step reluctantly into the boat. You give me a warm clasp of the hand, smiling gently and whimsically at me.

"*Hasta la vista!*" you say. "Let me know if you arrive safely, and when you can return."

You stand on the little stone pier and watch the rowboat until it reaches the steamer. I scramble up the ladder onto the deck, then walk to the stern. The whistle is blowing, shrilly. You get into your carriage; the driver whips up his horses. I can see you the whole way along, as the carriage threads its way through the town and out onto the Amalfi road.

You wave to me. I stand there in my white coat, waving back to you. Something—God knows what—tells me I will never see you again. I am filled with this dread apprehension, as I stand and wave and wave. You lean out of the open carriage, a small figure, waving the blue and green silk scarf I have given you.

And, still waving, you are borne round the bend of the road, and are gone . . . gone forever. . . .[72]

❨ *I stayed ten days or so in Ravello—very nice. Brett liked it too. Then with my friends [Millicent Beveridge and Mabel Harrison] I came slowly north, staying in Rome, Perugia, Assisi, Florence, Ravenna . . . .*[73]

4 April 1926 (Easter)   Villa Bernarda, Spotorno, Italy

❨ *I am back. The three women were down at the station when I arrived yesterday, all dressed up festively, the women, not I. For the moment I am the Easter-lamb. When I went away, I was very cross, but one must be able to forget a lot and go on.*

Frieda has a cold but Elsa and Barby have grown much stronger and Barby has painted one or two quite good pictures. I also feel much better, almost like in the past, only a little bronchitis. But they say, an Englishman at forty is almost always bronchial.

We don't know yet what we want to do. We leave this house on the twentieth and perhaps we'll go to Perugia between Florence and Rome, for six or eight weeks. I think I would like to write a book about Umbria and the Etruscans, half travel-book, also scientific. Perhaps I'll do this.[74]

7 April 1926   Villa Bernarda, Spotorno, Italy

❨ *Frieda has a bad cold, but the two girls are very well. They are nice girls really, it is Frieda, who, in a sense, has made a bad use of them, as far as I am concerned.*[75]

Barbara Weekley Barr

When he returned from his journey, Lawrence told me: "Ada depresses me; I have to get away. She doesn't *believe* in me. She loves me. . . . Oh, yes!"

Young then, and enthusiastic, I believed in him.

Lawrence thought that Elsa had more sense than I had. "She is wise, and will make the best of life," he wrote to me once. "You are too inclined to throw everything away because of one irritating factor. There's been too much of that in all lives. You throw your soup at the waiter because it's too hot, or set fire to your bed, because there's a flea in it. Well, then you can lie on the ground."

There was a quality in Elsa that he liked. Beyond her conventional autocratic exterior, he found a wistfulness.

"She rather makes a man feel he would like to put her in his pocket. Your pathos is unreal," he said to me, discouragingly. "Your troubles are all your own fault." [76]

19 March 1926   Villa Bernarda, Spotorno, Italy

❲ *I am very much better in health—getting on my own real feet again and then one can stand firm. We leave for Florence tomorrow—address Pensione Lucchesi, Lungarno Zecca. Frieda will probably go to Baden after a week, with her daughters, but I think of staying on in Italy till July.*[77]

Capt. Angelo Ravagli

A few weeks later Lawrence came back. I remember, as Frieda has described it,[78] how Elsa and Barby were after her to look nice and be nicer to him and forget all about the quarrel. I suppose that harmony in the family was re-established. At that time I had to rush to my mother's bedside, but I was too late, she was dead. I had to remain for a week or so in Tredozio, to calm my two unhappy sisters. When I returned the Lawrences told me that they had decided to go to Florence.

On the day of their departure I tried my best to be there to say goodbye in a very friendly manner.[79]

CHAPTER TWO

1926–1928: Italy, England, Austria, Germany, Switzerland

For the creative soul is for ever charged with the potency of still unborn speech, still unknown thoughts. It is the everlasting source which surges everlastingly with the massive, subterranean fires of creation, new creative being: and whose fires find issue in pure jets and bubblings of unthinkable newness only here and there, in a few, or comparatively few, individuals.

—"Education of the People," in Phoenix, pp. 608–9

24 April 1926   *Pensione Lucchesi, Lungarno Zecca, Florence, Italy*

❡ [We] *left Spotorno last Tuesday [20 April 1926], for good. Frieda's two daughters are leaving next Tuesday [27 April 1926] for London, and we are either staying on in Tuscany or Umbria a couple of months, or else we shall go to Germany. I'm not sure yet. But we shall be here another ten days or so.*

.   .   .   .

Italy doesn't seem to me so jolly as it used to be: Very little fun going. But Frieda rather wants to take a house—a villino—in the country here, till July: myself, I am doubtful. However, I don't care very much.[1]

Barbara Weekley Barr

Towards the latter part of April [1926], Elsa and I were returning to England. Before we left Italy, Lawrence and Frieda took us to see Florence where we stayed at the Pensione Lucchesi, on the Arno. Lawrence showed us round Florence. At the Uffizi we stood in front of Botticelli's *Venus Rising from the Sea,* which he said was full of air. It was true: the figure seemed to float in sea air.

We met Norman Douglas, Pino Orioli, and many of the Florentine

57

eccentrics, too, all of whom were very friendly to "Frieda's daughters."

I saw the *Misericordia* go to the scene of an accident. This is the voluntary ambulance service for which young men are chosen from noted Florence families. It was begun in the Middle Ages, and it has always been the tradition that the men who serve it wear masks, so that their charity has no personal significance. Florence did not cast its spell over me on this first visit, perhaps because it rained, and we were going back to England.

That spring in Florence, Lawrence met the Aldous Huxleys again. They became great friends. Sometime after my return to England, I had a letter from Aldous Huxley's Belgian wife, Maria, asking me to go and see her at the flat where they were staying in London. Lawrence and Huxley had first met in 1915,[2] but they did not form a friendship until after their third meeting in Florence in that year, 1926.

Maria, with her charming face and large blue eyes, interested me very much, but we were both a little shy of each other.

The Lawrences' relationship had been an enigma to me, but Maria made me see its significance. "A great passion" was how she described it. "Frieda is silly. She is like a child, but Lawrence likes her *because* she is a child," she said.[3]

25 April 1926   Pensione Lucchesi, Lungarno Zecca, Florence, Italy

❨ [I] really don't want to go to America: and I am getting weary, and wearier, of the outside world. I want the world from the inside, not from the outside. Which doesn't mean, for me, killing desire and anger. Greed, lust, yes! But desire and anger are from God. Give me anything which is from God, desire or anger or communion of saints, or even hurts. But nothing any more of the dreariness and the mechanism of man.

Brett sails for Boston on May 2nd. She wants to go, and I feel it is her direction. But in myself, every week seems to alienate my soul further from America. I don't want to go west.[4]

15 May 1926   Villa Mirenda, Scandicci, Florence, Italy

❨ We've taken the top half of this old villa out in the country about seven miles from Florence—crowning a little hilltop in the Tuscan style. Since the rent is only 3,000 liras for a year—which is twenty-five pounds—I took

*the place for a year. Even if we go away, we can always keep it as a pied à
terre and let friends live in it. It is nice—looking far out over the Arno
valley, and very nice country, real country, pine woods, around. I am
reading up my Etruscans, and if I get along with them shall go round
to Perugia and Volterra, Chiusi, Orvieto, Tarquinia. Meanwhile we can
sit still and spend little. There's only one family of foreigners near—
Wilkinsons—sort of village arty people who went round with a puppet
show, quite nice, and not at all intrusive. Then the tram is only 1½ miles,
at Vingone, and takes us into Florence in ½-hour. This is a region of no
foreigners. The only thing to do is to sit still and let events work out. I
count this as a sort of interval.[5]*

Raul Mirenda

In April, 1926, through the agency of the Messrs. Wilkinson, who lived
in a villa [6] a short distance from that of my family, I became acquainted
with David Herbert Lawrence, who was then staying in Florence at
the Pensione Lucchesi on the Lungarno. Lawrence was thinking of rent-
ing an apartment or a villa on the hills which crown Florence, possibly
to the south of the Arno, to reside there with his wife, Frieda von
Richthofen. Lawrence's personality made a favourable impression upon
me. Rather tall, slim, with a lively, penetrating eye, a good-humoured
smile, hair and moustache blond, tending to red, his parting on the left,
at ease in conversation—he expressed himself clearly in Italian. On his
temples were a few threads of white hair, which engraved on his frank,
intelligent features a peculiar aspect of interior torment. His beard was
like that of the Nazarene.

He told me at once that the situation of the Villa di S. Polo a Mosciano
(Comune di Scandicci) on a hill [7] of some two hundred acres between
the Vingone-Casa Scotti and Vingone-Casignano roads pleased him infinitely, and that if I could let him a comfortable apartment there, he
would be delighted to stay there for some time, with his wife.[8] I offered
him the suite on the second floor of the villa, furnished. It comprised an
apartment of six rooms, with service. Three rooms, facing south, looked
over a small park, three, facing north-north-west, over a grass-covered
court. From each side one enjoys a splendid view: to the north-north-
west the eye ranges over a wide tract of the valley of the Greve and the
Arno, the suburbs of Florence, the Cascine, and the Campi plain as far
as Prato; to the south lie the magnificent pine and fir woods of Valicaia,

Poggio Brandi, and la Poggiona. On either side the foothills of the Apennines are apparent, and, on clear days, the eye reaches as far as the magnificent chain of the Apennines themselves.

The apartment met with the full approval of Mr. Lawrence, who lost no time in occupying it with his wife, choosing as the bedroom one of the rooms facing south. To please them, I gave Mr. Lawrence permission for them to enter the little park to the south of the villa, and pass their time there as often as they wished to do so.

Lawrence delighted in the Tuscan countryside, with its wealth of colours, especially in the spring, and for the variety of its cultivation, and he devoted his whole being to the country life, following with interest and a warm, friendly familiarity the farm workers in their daily occupation.

One cannot speak easily of the wide range of activities to which Lawrence devoted himself in the restful peace of the Tuscan countryside, for, shy in speaking of himself, he avoided reference to them in any form whatsoever.

Both my wife and I had established cordial relationships with the Lawrences, exchanging friendly visits, especially in the summer, when my wife used to stay in the country for several months without a break.

On various occasions I invited the Lawrences to tea in our apartment, for they showed themselves particularly appreciative of the very beautiful view which one enjoyed from a broad terrace to the east of the villa. They had wished to rent this terrace together with their apartment, but I could not grant them this since the terrace formed part of the apartment remaining for the use of my family. I assured him, however, that they would have access to the terrace to see the view whenever they wished to do so.

Sometimes I took tea with them. Conversation with Mr. Lawrence was intensely interesting, for with his profound literary erudition he combined a wealth of varied experience gained in extensive travels (he had recently returned from Mexico). Frieda Lawrence, the gracious and charming lady of the house, was a woman of wide education and endearing warm-heartedness.

The writer's day began quite early: in the morning it was his custom to go on foot to Scandicci, with a little basket to fetch the provisions necessary for his table. When no shopping was required he used to go into the Poggiona woods to breathe the balsam-laden air of the pine trees, and to read and think.

Sometimes he would remain sitting in a stretch of wood to the north of the country lane which runs beside the Solia torrent, contemplating the panorama spread out before his eyes, oblivious of all that was going on around him. He used to return to the house before mid-day, and, a little later, the sound of his little typewriter could be heard, as he fixed on paper his impressions and memories.

After lunch—he usually took the first meal of the day towards 1 p.m. —he would rest for a short time, and then return to his work: he was occupied for the most part with what came to be adjudged his best work, and was translated into very many languages: *Lady Chatterley's Lover,*[9] but he also worked at other novels, poems, and stories.

One often heard him walking and whistling some vague little tune, always the same, perhaps to distract himself and focus his thoughts the better. Among his intellectual occupations he interposed tasks of a domestic nature: he used to repair the collars of his own shirts, ironed them, wove straw hats, and sometimes devoted himself very capably to the culinary art, preparing dishes for the table with his own hands. In this connection I remember an incident which, at the time, had its amusing side. Lawrence had prepared a leg of lamb for roasting, and, waiting to put it in the oven, had set it, ready larded, on a small table in the dining room, which adjoined the kitchen; then he had gone to a little balcony, perhaps in search of a moment's distraction.

Profiting by Lawrence's preoccupation, a peasant's dog made its way into the house, took the shoulder of lamb, and fled to eat the delicious morsel in some secluded place. Lawrence, after trying in vain to catch the dog, smiled and said good-humouredly, "Today Geppurillo" (that was the name of the dog) "will eat better than we."

Sometimes he amused himself by painting the furniture in the apartment which he occupied, choosing lively colours, yet always ones which harmonised with the walls of the rooms. I remember an old chest of drawers, worn out long ago, on which Lawrence had painted particularly realistically a bunch of red and white roses.

His versatility was such that to his talents as writer, poet, and thinker, he added those of a painter.

He reproduced on canvas, among other subjects, a young farmer, one Piero Pini, half-brother of the Giulia Pini of whom I shall come to speak later, showing him in the act of leading his oxen to work. To have a model true to life, he made Pini pose beside his oxen, for which he had obtained two fine red muzzles, against the background of a farm threshing-floor. This work—assuredly deserving praise—was, I remember, exhibited in London, with others.[10]

Besides this, he sketched out, in oils, a nude male figure, for which he made the same farmer, Piero Pini, pose; but I do not know whether the work was brought to completion.[11] At that time, it seems, a section of his countrymen were boycotting him, thanks to their puritanical outlook.

Of profound human feeling and generous spirit, he lavished every form of assistance on the families of the peasants of S. Polo.

At the Christmas and New Year festivities he used to prepare in his home a Christmas tree and invite the children of the peasants with their mothers, distributing sweets and presents to all.[12] He used to help the wives of peasants when they had given birth to a child, providing a ration of milk for the mother for a period of two months.

The child of a certain peasant, Dino Bandelli, had been afflicted from birth with a double inguinal hernia. Lawrence made it possible for the child to enter the hospital at Florence, and bore the entire expense of the operation, which was completely successful. Deep indeed was the gratitude felt by the parents of the child towards their benefactor.[13]

Lawrence's sensitivity of feeling was apparent, too, in his kindness and forbearance towards animals. He used to feed the dog of a peasant who lived near the villa, and it sometimes spent whole days in his house. He used to extol the patience and submission of the draught oxen, for which he would have wished greater care and better treatment at the hands of the farmers.

To help his wife, Frieda, in her domestic work he brought in a young girl of about sixteen years of age, the daughter of a peasant, one Giulia Pini, whom he kept in his service throughout his residence in the villa of my family, and to whom both he and his wife came ultimately to be attached by sincere affection and warm friendship. Correspondence between the Lawrences and Giulia Pini continued for some time, even after they had left the villa at S. Polo to go to Florence and on to Switzerland.[14]

One winter he was ill with bronchitis, and confined for some time to his bed, where he was tended by his wife and Giulia Pini, but even at such a time as this he continued to press on with his work. Later his health improved, but for some time he was tortured day and night by an obstinate cough.

An uneasiness, perhaps due to the serious threat of disease of the lungs which brought him to his grave, caused him at times to be assailed by an overwhelming need to move, to change his surroundings, and go and live under distant skies. At such times he would absent himself with Frieda his wife for four or five months, continuing to have the apartment in the villa S. Polo reserved for his use. Then, weary from his travels, he would return to seek, in the peace of the countryside, relief from the afflictions of mind and body. At such times the sound of his typewriter came to the ear more frequently, with greater intensity. Even when they were far distant, both the writer and his wife kept up a correspondence with the little housekeeper, Giulia Pini.

With courteous hospitality he used to entertain at intervals friends and relatives, who realised the demands made on him by his labours as thinker and writer. Lawrence let it be clearly known that he delighted to live in Italy, and in the country, far from the society of his own country, with its excessive love of convention.

In 1928 he left the villa of S. Polo at Florence for Switzerland, perhaps in the hope of finding there relief for the malady which was torturing him. In April, 1929, he went to Majorca; in a letter to Giulia Pini he promised to return to Italy in July of the same year.[15]

Lawrence left to me, and I still have, a little rustic table, at which the writer and his wife used to sit for tea, two armchairs covered in Florentine straw, a small wooden bookcase, painted black, and a wooden pen-rack, the last item left forgotten in a drawer of a chest.[16]

Walter Wilkinson

D. H. Lawrence seems to have lived always against an immense landscape—Mexico, the high plateau of New Mexico, Australia, the Italian lakes and mountains, and it was so when I met him living in the country south of Florence. If I remember, his letters from there were headed Scandicci, but his villa was far removed from that long sordid village on the plain. You took the tramvia from Florence right through Scandicci to the terminus at Ponte Vingone where the low hill country begins across the plain for Florence. You climbed the gently mounting road winding, without hedge or fence, between the orchards of olives and trailing vines and the beautiful cabbages and grains grown under the trees. Where the peasants, like works of art, laboured in the glittering shadow of the fragile olives—men in blue aprons and black hats, women in faded, washed-out colours, and the holy, white oxen, hitched to the rose coloured carts, meditated gently on the ways of peace and the art of slow movement. Rough grass and blue chicory flowers lined the road and as you mounted you began to get that wide flat view over the plain of the Arno, away to Monte Morello, to Prato and Pistoia and

63

the glorious peaks of the Apennines. After a mile or so you mounted an abrupt and sharp hairpin bend (where I remember seeing Aldous Huxley once get stuck in a little car) and you then came out to one of those picturesque groups of Tuscan country buildings—a large cream-washed villa, some peasant houses and a small church all stuck together, clustered over the hilltop under a jumble of crusty roofs. The handsome, antique villa was the Mirenda at the top of which the Lawrences lived. It was not the sordid Scandicci at all. It was one of those large summer villas, rising, with its peasant houses and church, out of a misty grey sea of olive trees. Similar villas and cypress trees on other hilltops posed themselves in simple splendour. There was the large view over the plain and mountains, and a bit of Florence showing seven miles away with the be-villa'd Fiesole rising behind. It was all nature at its loveliest and *compagna cinque cento* where, naturally, Lawrence was re-christened Il Signor Lorenzo.

You entered the Mirenda, which means, more or less, a picnic, between high and splendid gate pillars into a formal Italian garden, all very neglected Boccaccio, and approached a handsome panelled door. In answer to your tug at a long iron bell-pull there was a ghostly rustling behind the door—the belt being withdrawn by a pull upstairs. You pushed open the door, crossed a hall hung with very dull and badly painted Italian family portraits, and after two flights of stone steps you came into the Lawrence flat at the top of the building.

Both Lorenzo and Frieda would be busy about some simple chore—they always seemed to be busy—and either or both as spontaneously as children would begin to talk about anything that happened to be in their minds—no polite gambits, no sparring, no trying to impress the Joneses—they just plunged right in and took you into the prevailing argument, discussion or bright inspiration. It was delightful, whether Lorenzo was railing against the world or not, and an indication of the lively state of mind in which they seemed to live.

The second time I visited Lawrence was immediately after one of his fateful haemorrhages. I walked off the stairs into a bedroom, absolutely bare but for a simple white camp bed, and found Lawrence in his pyjamas, stuffing something into a black leather bag.

"My doctor's bag," he said with a grin. "Everybody laughs at my little black doctor's bag. I don't see why!" he exclaimed in a crescendo of his high voice. "It's very useful. I can put anything into it, and there it is all in!"

He grabbed the bag and led me through the bare white kitchen with a pot or two, and Frieda at a charcoal fire, through a bare white salotta furnished only with a piano, into another white bedroom with another little white camp bed, a small hanging bookshelf standing on the floor, a couple of straw chairs, and some of his own paintings, frameless canvases hanging on the white walls. There were no carpets, no curtains, no ornaments, no bottles, no ashtrays. It was all very clean and bare, like a monastic cell, ascetic and aesthetic. It fulfilled his idea of living completely. "What I like is to get an empty room or two and live in them for a bit—like this—until you're tired of them and then move on." And that is how he lived, skittering about the world, travelling light, camping for a short time in some immense landscape with no dragging social attachments, no conventional routine.

For all his illness and the small pallid face sunk in tawny hair and beard, Lorenzo was very much alive. He began to chatter and grin and told me to get one of his own books from the half-dozen on the bookshelf. Before his illness he had seen a puppet performance of mine at a party. He was amused and interested and sincerely wanted to encourage me. He dashed off an inscription in a copy of *The Lost Girl* and handed it to me.

"But perhaps you don't want it! You may not want to read it! Don't take it if you don't want it. I don't mind. I never read them! Look at those books!" His lean hand waved a dismissal over the six pathetic volumes leaning awry on the shelf. "Books! Book cases! I don't want any books! I don't want any bookcases! Authors, publishers" (immense scorn) —"they send them to me. Why to me? I only spit on them. And look at that—the Oxford Dictionary!" His voice grew shrill with scorn. "Why Oxford? It's atrocious!" he squealed, at the same time grinning at his outrageous audacity.

He went on to throw out some ejaculations on writing as a profession. He knew I had done a little writing, and in his too quick way had erroneously concluded that I was setting up to be a "writer."

"A pound a week job," he said. "That's what we expect—a pound a week. Unless we were lucky and got a book censored—then we got two hundred. But it's really just a pound a week job." I jibbed at that as a generalisation, and he said, yes, of course, you get some luck at times. He instanced selling a short story for seventy pounds which he had written in one evening, and said that he was selling short articles at the moment rather well, and that he thought of giving up the writing of long novels altogether. "Just write round one thing like an olive tree."

I explained that I only wanted to play at writing in the hopes of making a few pennies.

"Well, you ought to be able to do that. Plenty of fools do! Write nothing about nothing and make pots. All of them do! Wells, Bennett, hundreds of them, all of them writing, writing jam puffs without any jam in them."

His white teeth grinned amiably through the tawny beard as he ejaculated jerky insults all round with high-pitched emphasis on the jams, fools and nothing, and an occasional squeal of "atrocious!" He is very like that terra cotta bust of Carlyle in the National Portrait Gallery, I remember thinking—sick-looking, a lot of tough, tawny hair, full of eloquent spleen—but he knows it and enjoys it, like a gamin.

He talked a little about his paintings—about the painting, not the subject. But the bare-faced subjects were more interesting than the technique which was very unpracticed, but for a practically dying man they were an astonishing exhibition of uninhibited energy and brash unconsciousness of what painting a picture entails. Frieda came in and criticized the drawing of the nude man reclining before some passing nuns,[17] as well she might, but Lorenzo only smiled amiably. What he thought of his paintings I could not discover. At some other time, I remember, he remarked to a professional painter that he always got into a mess when he painted. "Yes," remarked the painter, "I suppose you amateurs do." Lawrence only grinned through his beard as if he rather appreciated the "crack."

As Lawrence recovered from that particular haemorrhage his indomitable impatience soon brought him out of doors. He would drift, rather than walk, up to my brother's villa,[18] a bright wisp of a figure in a panama hat and a brilliant blue linen jacket with enormous white buttons, a frail scanty human, dreadfully pale and sick-looking, but, by the school exercise book in his hand, evidently determined to keep on writing. He would rest for a time on the stone bench, analyse with extreme severity the character of a peasant neighbour, or one of the literati in Florence, or announce that he was tired of Florence and was contemplating a change, a visit to Germany, or a tour with a Buddhist friend [Earl H. Brewster] to study the Etruscan civilization; both of which plans he did carry out.

From the villa he would stagger on over the flagstones between the peasant houses into the pine woods, ravishing woods of heaths and rock roses and fragrant herby little plants, and with a stream of pools and runnels and waterfalls struggling over rocks, and where nightingales sang night and day. Presently he would drift back and show, not any writing he might have done, but some wild flower he had discovered, such as cyclamens or primroses.

For all his spleen and rages Lawrence could be extremely kind, quite simply kind. One morning we came on a peasant child sitting on a doorstep, howling his life out and clutching his jaw.

"*Che cosa é?*" asked Lawrence, crouching to the infant's level. "*E il dento? E guasto? Fa noia? Ecco, ecco—tenga*" and he pulled a paper bag of boiled sweets from his pocket with which he always seemed to be provided. "*Tenga—son' dolci,*" and the frightful, howling Gigi was immediately transformed into an angelic *putto*.

And there was the time when some women friends were coming to stay in the neighbourhood for a few weeks. Lawrence not only found a house for them but cleaned the whole place himself—with his own immortal hands, and the help of a pail and a scrubbing brush, Lawrence washed the walls, the paint, the windows and thoroughly scrubbed the floors on his hands and knees.

Lawrence's ideas are, of course, in his books which, he once said, were all autobiographical. His experience of creatures and flowers and landscape is certainly there, and in a lot of his characters, but it is difficult to believe that all those dreary love affairs without babies were autobiographical. He certainly had one great love affair, and that was Frieda, the magnificent, kind-hearted Frieda in whose shelter, rather to the annoyance of his manly pride, I suspect, he found himself forced to live. "What a man wants," he once surprised me by saying, "is a good woman to protect him." And elsewhere he wrote:

> How quaveringly I depend on you, to keep me alive
> Like a flame on a wick!
>
> .   .   .
>
> Suppose you didn't want me! I should sink down
> Like a light that has no sustenance . . . .[19]

---

23 June 1926   *Villa Mirenda, Scandicci, Florence, Italy*

❲ Here it is real Italian summer at last. Everybody sleeps from one till three. Nay, it's quarter to four, and there's not a peasant in sight on all the poderi. But of course they get up at about 4.30 in the morning—we

about six. I'm sitting on the little balcony upstairs—you can so easily imagine this old square, whitish villa on a little hill all of its own, with the peasant houses and cypresses behind, and the vines and olives and corn on all the slopes. It's very picturesque, and many a paintable bit. Away in front lies the Arno valley and mountains beyond. Behind are pine woods. The rooms inside are big and rather bare—with red-brick floors: spacious, rather nice, and very still. Life doesn't cost much here.

. . . .

[One] shouldn't pretend to belong to one place exclusively. Italy is always lovely, and out there at the ranch it is always lovely. I am sure it is right for me to stay this year in the softness of the Mediterranean. But next year, in the spring, I want to come to the ranch, before the leaves come on the aspen trees, and the snow is gone.

. . . .

Does the old tree down at the well, the old fallen aspen, still put out leaves? I often think of it. And has the big greasewood bush grown over the track of the well, so that it pushes your buckets aside?

. . . .

I am very much better in health, now I can go about in shirt and trousers and sandals, and it's hot, and all relaxed. We live very quietly, picnic by the stream sometimes. I have finished typing and revising David [20] in German—he was a job! Did I tell you I had the little typewriter taken to pieces and cleaned? It goes very nicely. But I'm glad it's shut up again, it is an irritable thing, a typewriter.[21]

5 July 1926   Villa Mirenda, Scandicci, Florence, Italy

《 In the hot weather, the days slip by, and one does nothing, and loses count of time. . . .

In the real summer, I always lose interest in literature and publications. The cicadas rattle away all day in the trees, the girls sing, cutting the corn with the sickles, the sheaves of wheat lie all the afternoon like people dead asleep in the heat. E più non si frega. I don't work, except at an occasional scrap of an article. I don't feel much like doing a book, of any sort. Why do any more books? There are so many, and such a small demand for what there are. So why add to the burden, and waste one's vitality over it. Because it costs one a lot of blood. Here we can live very modestly, and husband our resources. It is as good as earning money, to have very small expenses. Dunque—

And then we're silly enough to go away. We leave next Monday, the 12th, for Baden-Baden (c/o Frau von Richthofen, Ludwig-Wilhelmstift), and I expect we shall spend August in England. A friend is finding us a little flat in Chelsea. . . . I want to be back here for September and Vendemmia, because I like it best here. The Tenente [22] still writes occasionally from Porto Maurizio, where he is transferred: rather lachrymose and forlorn.[23]

18 July 1926   Ludwig-Wilhelmstift, Baden-Baden, Germany

⟨ As for literature and publishing, I loathe the thought of it all, and wish I could afford never to appear in print again. Anyhow, I am doing nothing at all now, and have no idea of beginning again. . . . I rather dread the thought of England.[24]

29 July 1926   Ludwig-Wilhelmstift, Baden-Baden, Germany

⟨ Simply pouring with rain! The Rhine valley all in floods. We leave tonight, via Strasburg, Brussels, Ostend, for London: through the night. It makes one shiver.[25]

ENGLAND

Frieda Lawrence Ravagli

8 August 1926: *25 Rossetti Mansions, Flood Street, Chelsea, London.* Always now and then a batch of your past life appears and I devour it. Lawrence is in Scotland, I am glad; London lowers one's vitality. Monty and Lawrence met on the stairs and were all "loving kindness" to each other "all of a heap!" It came so suddenly, it made me gasp. The boy's struggle to get somewhere moves me and interests me and how little use one really is! . . . I don't feel the coal-strike here, but every-

thing seems like only half emerged from the sea and drowsy. The flat is a studio and looks over the roofs. While Lawrence is away I have for each meal an egg, a tomato and a cup of Bovril, to get a little thinner. . . . We have seen Aldous Huxley—charming, cultured, thin, my word, you can get him in half an hour![26] Then a charming youth [Rolf Gardiner] who wants to reform the world by dancing. He was thrilled about the Indian's dancing. Then we went to see the Richard Aldingtons—Arabella comes in Aaron's Rod. She is so like a mixture of Trinidad and Rufina,[27] so black-haired, and Richard is so fair and blue-eyed and Germanic! . . .

Lawrence has had a crisis in health and is better. He does not want to write anything much just now. I am glad. He gave more than he could afford.[28]

Montague Weekley

I saw nothing more of Lawrence until 1926.[29] He and my mother came to London where they took a flat in Chelsea. She asked me to come there at a certain time and when I arrived too punctually she had not yet returned from some expedition. After I had waited on the landing for a few minutes, she emerged on the staircase with Lawrence behind her. I promptly held out my hand to him in order to make the first move toward relieving any embarrassment that might arise. As we got talking in the flat, I noticed that he had retained a markedly Midlands accent, *e.g.:* "Sargent, sooch a bad pëynter." He expressed a very poor opinion of such contemporaries as Wells and Bennett by comparison with nineteenth century giants "or even somebody like George Eliot."

I do not believe that I was unduly influenced by Lawrence's reputation in sensing the personal impact of his genius. He, presumably, was interested to meet his wife's only son, a circumstance that may have enhanced the impression he made on me. Although I have since encountered people who were, at least, very distinguished writers, painters, architects, and sculptors—one of them essentially a man of genius—I have met no one who impressed me to anything like the same extent. The blue eyes in Lawrence's bearded face seemed to be alight with an almost disturbing vitality, as though our meeting had re-kindled all the intensity smouldering within him.[30]

Rolf Gardiner

For a boy growing into manhood in 1919 the world felt like a black night with bright stars blazing high above. After the grey horror of the war years there was hope, impending promise of a new future. So much had been shattered and brought to an end by the internecine strife in Europe; now it was like Christmas presaging a new birth.

It was in this mood of expectancy that I first read *Sons and Lovers*. I read it through enthralled by the feelings of darkness and hope, not perceiving all that it meant, except that the spirit in it was like a torch leading in the darkness.

Lawrence became the torchbearer, the torch leader of my youth. He went ahead exploring the dark, dispelling the limits of our shabby, exhausted vision of things, breaking away from the abstractions of finite ideas, worn-out concepts, barren words and tired symbols. Everything that came from him was quick and fresh, charged with hope and expectancy. It was this grand newness of life and vision which carried one away, challenging not one's intellect but one's soul.

But I was singular in this rapport with my hero-poet. Others thought him a genius, but perverse, morbid, eccentric, obsessed by sex. To me the sex part seemed integrated with something so much greater. It was only one expression of the passionate life, to be sanctified by trueness and honesty, not to be driven into a corner of secretive desires and repressed naturalness.

Lawrence's characters lived from a deeper source of experience than the conventional people of society and the novels of social life. A whole world of energy and consciousness was tapped which other authors slid over in ignorance or fear.

So I instinctively trusted Lawrence. I accepted his veracity without reservation. I was prepared to follow him into the dark, the unknown. Not uncritically but with a warm confidence, a tender trust. Wasn't this natural enough in a very young man who was angry with his time and contemporary society, who was sick of the intellectuals and the sentimentalists alike?

When I went up to Cambridge in 1921 I was chilled by the false gaiety of undergraduate society, by its preciosity and cynicism, by its adulation of brains and cleverness. I was neither brainy nor clever. But I felt powerfully the need to assume responsibility for what was going to happen with my generation in the world.

Europe was in the throes of dissolution. I had seen it during my travels on foot in France and Germany and Italy. I believed that the *Untergang des Abendlandes* was an immediate process. A new Dark Ages was descending on Europe and the world. The English were defying the inevitable with a specious security. The humanism still cherished at our Universities was a withered shred of the great harvest of the Renaissance. When I stammered out my inchoate theories of the need to renew the roots of our culture, to revive religion of the soul through the soil, J. B. Priestley, taking out his pipe, flattered me by saying: "Young man, all ye want is jest a few reforms!"

This was shattering, because Priestley belonged to the generation of men at Cambridge who had just been through the War. And it was the intense disillusioning experience of the war years which, although too young to be a soldier, had brought me to radical reflection. To most of my contemporaries what I was trying to say was bizarre balderdash. I was a romantic, stigmatized by wild pursuits such as folk-dancing and youth movements; even to my fellow Bedalians I was a radical of the spirit.

Cambridge was intellectually as uncongenial to me as it could be. The dons were steeped in scientific humanism and the Bloomsbury elect were the intellectual heroes of the hour. There was not one teacher, not even Goldie Lowes-Dickinson,[31] with whom I could rub my unpolished mind. Years later, speaking to students of the School of Agriculture, I confessed that I had not read their subject when I was up. My reason was that in spite of a galaxy of meritorious technicians there was no chair of agricultural philosophy. And it was a natural philosophy that one wanted if one was to be a farmer. So I clung to Lawrence, Lawrence whose reaction to Cambridge, though I did not know it, had been far bitterer than mine.[32]

The Cambridge attitude to Lawrence was almost wholly that of Bloomsbury and King's. Lawrence, though a genius, must not be allowed to count. A discriminating critic such as I. A. Richards was permitted to admire the technical skill of some of Lawrence's writings.[33] There were a couple of North Country, scholarship-aided, undergraduates who recognised in Lawrence's early novels their own sort of home background and struggles, and with these I had a bond.

But I needed so much a major prophet who could articulate the breathless beliefs which were pulsing through me, and whose thought I could relate to the web of creative activities that I was already trying to spin in England and Europe. Lawrence supplied the need. Here was my hero-poet forging ahead in the contemporary world. Here was an Englishman with roots in the mid-earth of England who yet was at home in Europe, in Germany and Austria and Italy, the lands I had explored as a wanderer and pilgrim as soon as the frontiers had been reopened after the War.

Lawrence's first post-war novel was *Aaron's Rod* (1922) and this and *Twilight in Italy* (1916), which chimed with so many of my own travels on both sides of the Alps, came to my hand as quest-books of the spirit. Here the problems of consciousness, of revelation and balance, of leadership and obedience, seemed wondrously probed and energised. In *Twilight in Italy* the new synthesis, the balance of consciousness and the instinctive life, of Being and Not-being, were suggested by a gospel of the Holy Ghost which re-echoed the prophecy of St. Joachim of Floris [34] that had so powerfully struck me as a boy. The idea that the Persons of the Trinity, although co-eternal, had a special validity at different periods of history, seemed a liberating conception. For two thousand years the figure of the Saviour had dominated the Churches. And this figure of the Redeemer had been overworked and had in our time degenerated into a sickly sentimental Jesus-worship. It was no denigration of the Crucifixion, of the essentially crucial teaching of Christ, to find, in the gospel of the Holy Spirit, the dispensation of divine power in the multitudinous souls of men. Perhaps I did not grasp in detail the arguments which underlay Lawrence's pursuit of the Third way in *Twilight in Italy*,[35] "The Crown" (in *Reflections on the Death of a Porcupine*) and other essays. But I was convinced that Lawrence was somehow on the right track, and I was overwhelmed by "the insight, the wisdom, the revived and re-educated feeling for health," to quote a recent sentence of a later Cambridge don, F. R. Leavis,[36] which Lawrence inevitably brought to bear on almost any subject. And I was baffled by the obtuseness of my Cambridge contemporaries who merely saw in Lawrence a sort of mixture of Carlyle and Nietzsche and Strindberg, a morbid compound of impassioned obsessions.

In 1923 I took over an undergraduate paper called *Youth* and reissued this in an entirely new form as an "international quarterly of young enterprise." The purpose of this journal was to link post-war movements of creative and reconstructive purpose in Europe and England and to relate their activities to whatever new *Weltanschauung* would break down the stale crust of outworn vision and dead dogma. In the first editorial, "Vox Juventatis," I proclaimed Lawrence in a dithyrambic attack on Cambridge intellectualism with a Shelleyan fervour and extravagance that made the suave politicians of Cambridge thought sit up and rub their eyes. It was a reckless call for Courage! courage to be an "axe to fell the thickening trees of sleep, a plough to cleave the hardening crust of life"; courage to reachieve the vision of wholeness, to "experience direct Reality." Science, the neo-humanist religion of Cambridge, was a false creed. It taught us, as Lawrence had written, to see:

> Only a mean arithmetic on the face of things,
> A cunning algebra in the faces of men,
>   And God like geometry
> Completing his circles, and working cleverly.[37]

And I cited Oswald Spengler and Ludwig Wittgenstein [38] as witnesses of the limitations of scientific thinking in relation to dynamic reality.

No doubt in the intemperate rush of words that poured down my youthful pen, the crystals of relevant thought were quite hopelessly dissolved. Cambridge was not used to this sort of lyrical nudity, though, childish as it was, it might conceivably be trying to say something. But the gravamen of the article was an attack on what I termed "the metallist thinkers of Bloomsbury and King's":

You may laugh, you may sneer . . . but I tell and foretell you, that the words of D. H. Lawrence will burn and tingle on the lips of men, when the dingy carpings of men like James Joyce and Marcel Proust, of Lytton Strachey and Sigmund Freud, of Sidney Webb and Maynard Keynes will have long, long been consumed beneath the vanished débris of our potty civilisation.

And the editorial crashed to an end in proclaiming the doom of European culture and the intellectualist consciousness, in demanding the substitution of a romanticism of Action for a romanticism of Words. But it finally came to rest in a few steadying sentences which echoed Plotinus and the mystics, including Lawrence:

Let a man take Courage and go back to the purer sources of himself. Let him come back to himself and possess his soul in patience; let him acquire a real positive quiet, an equilibrium. . . . In these mighty hours of storm and stress, let a man retain the unique quiet oneness of his own being.

I do not think Lawrence ever heard this fanfare for his name and doctrine. But it reached the ears of his chief Cambridge antagonist Maynard Keynes. A few days after the streets of Cambridge were splashed with a specially-designed poster (drawn by Stanley Kennedy-North) advertising *Youth*, I was disarmed by receiving a note which ran as follows:

29 July 1923   46, Gordon Square, Bloomsbury

Dear Gardiner,

Someone was kind enough to send me a copy of '*Youth*'; perhaps it was you. Anyhow let me congratulate you on an excellent number. You don't like my ideas, I gather; but that mustn't prevent me from feeling benevolent towards your venture,—specially if you establish contacts by it with the young men in Europe. Besides, even if intellect does leave some things out, you'll be very incomplete if you leave out intellect!

Yours sincerely
J. M. Keynes

I think your own leader the best thing in the number.

K.

The glinting patronage of this note from Keynes expressed the kindliness of a man who later was great enough to admit the deadness of the set of which he became the illustrious centre, and which led him to write in 1938: "there may have been just a grain of truth when Lawrence said in 1914 that we were 'done for.' " [39]

The theme that appeared to preoccupy Lawrence at this stage also to some extent preoccupied me. It was the idea of leadership, of inspired authority evoking ready obedience and loyalty in the cause of creative change. Lawrence had attacked *en masse* democracy. Like Ludovici [40] he was a believer in aristocracy; he was an aristocrat of the spirit and had married an aristocrat of the blood.

Now in Central Europe, but particularly in Germany, there was not only a surge of semi-Communistic mass movement. There were also the beginnings of a conservative revolution which harked back to earlier forms of non-tyrannic government in which the leaders were acclaimed rather than voted into office, and to whom unbreakable allegiance was given. This habit was adopted in the Buende of the youth movements and some of the ex-Service men's organizations. It opposed the continental interpretation of parliamentary democracy, the system of one man one vote, and the whole paraphernalia of committees and bureaucracy.

In England such ideas were rank heresy. Aristocracy and privilege were on the way out. Democracy was the new godhead of politics. Committees and conferences were the rage. There arose in England for the first time the idea that society could be planned and ordered by experts who were in fact officials.

This increasing slavery to shibboleths which spelt non-freedom was the result of industrialism and the caging of men in cities and suburbs. It was a principle of death, of human paralysis. The individual no longer counted except as a citizen voter or as the member of a union. Government ceased to be personal and direct; it became remote and abstract. Even high civil servants could no longer exercise real initiative. The principle of personal responsibility by the man on the spot, which had created the Empire, was throttled by paper, committees and "safety first."

Lawrence hated this tyranny of the abstract, the impersonal. And I hated it too.

There is no need to delve into the theory of charismatic leadership, the nature of the priest-king, or to distinguish it from the *Führerprinzip* with which the Nazis and Fascists plumed their strutting little heroes. What was at stake was the personal responsibility of the individual as opposed to anonymous, abstract power, the power of institutions, organizations, bureaucracies. It was this depersonalization of initiative and authority which made injustice or mere administrative torpor so difficult to combat. The fatuity with which the highest-ranking ministers sought to erase the persecutions of the system (as in the case of Miss Douglas-Pennant in the first, and of some victims of M.I. 5., in the second, world wars) [41] is a reflection of what I mean.

In England the code of behaviour in permitting change was determined largely by what has been called the "establishment." In no country is real government so subtle a form of taciticity. In the early 'twenties the old men of the late Victorian and Edwardian periods still were in power. They were quite baffled by the winds of change buffeting the coasts of British insularity. Baldwin, by all fair accounts, a sincere and self-dedicated patriot, played the role of cunctator. He seemed to wish to sweeten the bitterness of class-conflict with humane reasonableness. But the real victors of the period were the Fabians, Shaw, Wells, the Sidney Webbs, the middle-class apostles of the Welfare State, of an egalitarian, hygienic and eugenic suburbian England.

The swamping of the traditional England by suburbia was a far more insidious process than the enslavement of the husbandmen and artisans by nineteenth century industrialism. It was this process which had begun like a creeping paralysis to emasculate the England of the 'twenties, to obliterate the Home Counties with a bungaloid octopus, to leach the increasingly untilled fields of workers, to empty, by taxation, the halls and mansions which had for so long been the centres of English rural government and the repositories of English culture. Along the arterial roads leading out of London and cities like Birmingham, an entirely new civilisation began to spread its tentacles.

Against these the Universities in the early 'twenties raised no protest, sought no alternative. Oxford permitted itself to become a vast sub-industrial city, choked with traffic. Cambridge became the centre of scientific research, and the "Labs" of Downing Street produced the new technicians and "backroom boys" of a mechanized age.

Looking around my own generation there seemed to be no foci of creative resistance. Much was nostalgic: such as the movement for the revival of folk dance and song now becoming organised by Cecil Sharp [42] and his lieutenants. A more activist expression were the romantic woodcraft movements which owed their inspiration to Seton-Thompson and Baden-Powell [43] and were breakaways or alternatives to official Scouting for boys. Among these movements, all of them predominantly suburban, John Hargrave's "Kibbo Kift Kindred" seemed the least flimsy in structure and technique. And it was around Hargrave's ideas of leadership and training that I began to correspond with Lawrence.

Hargrave and Oswald Mosley [44] were the only "charismatic" leaders who postured as saviours of suburbia in post-war England, and took their cues from the Fascist model. Less than Mosley even, Hargrave was hardly known to the "establishment." The son of a Cumbrian Quaker and a Hungarian Jewess (who taught him Yoga in his boyhood) Hargrave was predominantly a Jew. He had come into prominence in the Scout movement, as commissioner for camping and woodcraft, and his well-illustrated books such as *The Great War Brings It Home,* had provided manuals for outdoor training of youth which were popular and impressive. He was an empirical pacifist who had served as a stretcher-bearer with the R.A.M.C. in the Dardanelles, and his forthright peace-propaganda linked with a Wellsian conception of World-Unity and -Government attracted the thoughtful ex-Service man in the Scout movement as well as idealists and Utopian reformers. These were mostly clerks, minor civil servants, garage hands and teachers, living in the Home Counties. There was sanity in Hargrave's appeal combined with fantasy, and there was nothing "mushy" or effete about his programme. Attacked for his outspokenness and ambition in official Scout circles, his connection with Scout Headquarters was severed, and his Commissionership terminated.

Hargrave's stand for Woodcraft, Nature Lore and World Friendship against "Patriotic Jingoism based on force," led to the secession of senior scouts and scout leaders who formed with him in 1920 "Kibbo Kift, the Woodcraft Kindred." The Covenant of this body aimed at:

(1) The establishment of Land Reservations and Open Spaces for camp training and Naturecraft; (2) by such training to inculcate pride of body, mental poise and vital spiritual perception; (3) the encouragement of handicraft training and the development of a new interpretation of Craft Guilds, backed by the reorganisation of social economics on the basis of the Just Price; (4) the formation of family groups wherein the children shall be trained by their parents along woodcraft lines; (5) the establishment of regional assemblies to work for the common weal of locality; (6) to stand as a witness for regional, national and world peace based upon the equation of consumption to production; (7) to help to bring about a world educational policy, world freedom of trade, a new world credit system, the abolition of political and financial intrigue and the establishment of a World Council, or Clearing House.

The terms of this far-reaching programme recall the hopefulness which was stirring under the damp blanket of Baldwin's England. The economic-reform clauses were introduced in the mid-twenties after contact with the ideas of Social Credit; and towards the end of this time, and in the 'thirties, Hargrave became the leader of the Green Shirts, a much more Fascist-like movement propagating the tenets of credit reform and control. But in the early stages, though the inevitable incursion of cranks and humanitarians took place, the backbone was composed of sober-minded and earnest ex-Scoutmasters and Rover Scouts who were excellent trainers of young people. These children declared at a ceremony of some solemnity before their clan or tribe:

I wish to be Kibbo Kift and to
1. Camp out and keep fit,
2. Help others,
3. Learn how to make things, and
4. Work for world peace and brotherhood.

Kibbo Kift was, according to Halliwell's *Dictionary of Archaic and Provincial Words*, Old English, meaning "strength or any proof of great strength." Hargrave's intention was honest enough; but the Kibbo Kift Kindred, and the garbing of his followers in jerkins and cowls, inevitably suggested comparison with the Ku Klux Klan.

As the movement sweated out its Utopist fat, it became a lean and hungry creature of Hargrave's ambition. More and more he demanded allegiance to his authority and his solution of the world's ills. Still strongly influenced by H. G. Wells, Hargrave or "White Fox, Headman K. K.," as he was styled, moved along the lines of an Open Conspiracy, to develop "Men like Gods" and establish world peace and economic

78

justice. His analysis was penetrating and incisive. His vision, eclectically fed, was charged with lucid argument. *The Confession of the Kibbo Kift: A Declaration and General Exposition of the Work of the Kindred* (1927) is an astonishing book, and even today is less fantastic than it sounds. It tilts mercilessly at all the muddledom and self-deception of the suburban idealists and faddists, somewhat after the manner of Wyndham Lewis's attacks on intellectual Bohemia. It breathes a certain rigorous sanity and impatience with anything but total solutions. But its lovelessness and lack of gaiety and warmth make it in the end impossible. Hargrave had become more and more isolated on the Everest of his omniscience, more and more of a Hebrew prophet pouring down vials of wrath and disappointment. His following changed continuously. He adopted a lot of the tricks of Fascist propaganda. When, after many years, in the late thirties, I heard him speak at a meeting in the Farringdon Memorial Hall, his face had become more mask-like than ever, his self-dramatisation a pathetic paralysis of inspired purpose. After the outbreak of the Second World War his figure dropped out of even the byways of politics and literature.

But in the decade of the 'twenties Hargrave's was a name to conjure with: his nearness to the Lawrencian hero and yet his essential defects became rather an obsession. Mary Neal, a grand, big-hearted woman of the abbess type, invited me to meet him in 1923, and, considerably against my inner feelings, I joined him, and became one of his leading collaborators for two years. Hargrave was paramount and in every way dialectically ascendant; but I held my own and fought him, using him as a stalking-horse for uniting the continental youth movements by whom his books on open-air training and tribal-organisation were held in respect. By midsummer 1925 I felt sure enough of myself to flout his authority and seek my own following. As Lawrence remarked: Hargrave didn't forgive my leaving him.[45] There was a note of rancour and defensiveness.

All through this period it was Lawrence who remained the touchstone of reality for me. Hargrave's Jewish intellect obtruded abstractions, however practical in manipulation and design he proved himself. As Lawrence finally remarked: "He's overweening and he's cold."[46] Lawrence's judgement (in a letter to me from Villa Mirenda, 17 January 1928) will probably remain the best ever pronounced on Hargrave's attempt:

I read the Kibbo Kift book with a good deal of interest. Of course it won't work: not quite flesh and blood. The ideas are sound, but flesh and blood won't take 'em, till a great deal of flesh and blood have been destroyed. Of course the birthright credit too is sound enough—but to nationalise capital is a good deal harder than to nationalise industries. The man alternates between idealism pure and simple, and a sort of mummery, and then a compromise with practicality. What he wants is all right. I agree with him on the whole, and respect him as a straightforward fighter. But he *knows* there's no hope, his way—en masse. And therefore underneath, he's full of hate. He's ambitious; and his ambition isn't practical: so he's full of hate underneath . . . . But for all that, on the whole he's right, and I respect him for it. I respect his courage and aloneness. If it weren't for his ambition and his lack of warmth, I'd go and kibbo kift along with him. But he'll get no further than holiday camping and mummery. Tho' even that will have *some* effect. All luck to him. —But by wanting to rope in *all* mankind it shows he wants to have his cake and eat it. Mankind is largely bad, just now especially and one must hate the bad, and try to keep what bit of warmth alive one can, among the few decent. But even that's a forlorn hope . . . .[47]

The justness of this tribute by Lawrence to Hargrave was remarkable. It is worth recalling since this careful appraisal was written after Lawrence had turned from his preoccupation with leadership to his central theme of tenderness. In the same letter he says, "The leader today needs tenderness as well as toughness: I need a constructive leader. Otherwise fight!"[48] After I had been to Les Diablerets he wrote again on March 4 [1928]:

I'm afraid the whole business of leaders and followers is somehow wrong, now. . . . [Even] Leadership must die, and be born different, later on. I'm afraid part of what ails you is that you are struggling to enforce an obsolete form of leadership. It is White Fox's calamity. When leadership has died—it is very nearly dead, save for Mussolini and you and White Fox and Annie Besant[49] and Gandhi—then it will be born again, perhaps, new and changed, and based on a reciprocity of tenderness. The reciprocity of power is obsolete. When you get down to the basis of life, to the depth of warm creative stir, there is no power. It is never: There *shall* be light! —only; Let there be light! The same way, not: Thou *shalt* dance to the Mother Earth! only: Let it be danced to the mother earth.[50]

Lawrence's wisdom and insight were telling and true. I knew that he was essentially right.

Over the situation in young Germany Lawrence, without any direct contacts, showed uncanny penetration. In 1927 he had written me:

I don't believe you'll ever get modern Germans free from an acute sense of their nationality—and in contact with foreigners they'll feel political for years to come. They have no self-possession—and they have that naïve feeling that it's somebody else's fault. Apart from that, they *are* lustig, which the English never are. And I think they are capable of mass-movement.[51]

In response to my reports he wrote (7 January 1928):

The German Bünde has the sound of a real thing—but the English side seems not to amount to much. It's very difficult to do anything with the English: they have so little "togetherness," or power of togetherness: like grains of sand that will only fuse if lightning hits it. They will fool about and be bossed about for a time with a man like Hargrave—but there's nothing in it. Think of all the other mountebanking cliques that exist—the Fontainebleau group [52] and the rest. The Germans take their shirts off and work in the hay: they are still physical: the English are so woefully disembodied. God knows what's to do with them. I sometimes think they are too sophisticatedly civilised to have any future at all.

And he went on to criticize my over-striving, my overloaded programmes of activity and effort, quite rightly.

It seems to me a pity you couldn't have made your farm a sort of little shrine or hearth where you kept the central fire of your effort alive: not all this hard work business: not this effort. You ought to have a few, very few, who *are* conscious and willing to be conscious, and who would add together their little flames of consciousness to make a permanent core. That would make a holy centre: whole, heal, hale. Even the German Bünde, I am afraid, will drift into nationalistic, and ultimately, *fighting* bodies: a new, and necessary form of militarism. It may be the right way for them. But not for the English. The English are over-tender. They must have kindled again their religious sense of atoneness. And for that you must have a silent, central flame, a flame of *consciousness* and of warmth which radiates out bit by bit. Keep the core sound, and the rest will look after itself. What we need is reconciliation and atoning. I utterly agree with your song, dance and labour: but the core of atoning in the *few* must be there, if your song, dance and labour are to have a real source. If it is possible.—The German youth is almost ready to fuse into a new sort of fighting unity: us against the world. But the English are older, and weary even of victory. [53]

As, after twenty-eight years, I again copy out these words from Lawrence's splendidly placed handwriting on the authentic page, the wisdom and immediacy of his thought ring out in my mind. I feel his nearness of comment and the privilege of his interest. It was dead true. Every word carried weight and value. And looking back over the span of years I believe my gratitude is best expressed in confessing how loyally Lawrence's injunctions have been obeyed: "keep the core sound . . . the core of atoning in the few must be there." That has been the flesh-blood-and-spirit experience of Springhead. [54] That has been the heart and conscience of our activity, of our dance, song and labour, down the years; and still remains so today: "to make a holy centre, whole, heal, hale."

So in those nineteen letters and two postcards [55] sent me by Lawrence between July, 1924, and December, 1928, a rare comment was breathed on the struggle of the time, on a young man's ardent search for realising wholeness with his fellows, with the soil, with the soul. That Lawrence who was mortally ill, isolated, attacked, had this goodness in him, this generosity of understanding, and sincere concern, was a miraculous gift to a young man's life, a bequest to be recorded and remembered in the history of our times.[56]

Lawrence had written from Baden-Baden [? July 1926] saying that he was coming over to England and would be staying at a little flat (belonging to Mrs. Stanley Fay) [57] at 25 Rossetti Garden Mansions, Flood Street, Chelsea.

I believe [he wrote] we are mutually a bit scared, I of weird movements, and you of me, I don't know why. But if you are in London even for a couple of days after the 30th do come and see us, and we can talk a little, nervously. No, I shall ask you questions like a doctor of a patient he knows nothing about.[58]

So, having got back from my men's Berkshire Hike, and having received another careful little note of direction from Lawrence, I went along the next day at 12.30.

Lawrence opened the door, and I was at once struck by his pale, almost mask-like features, and beautiful, slenderly-proportioned body. I think he was dressed in a rough tweed suit, and remember laughing to myself at his starched collar and knotted rope of a tie—little bits of provincial conventionality which persisted oddly in Lawrence's make-up. I told him about our Hike over the Berkshire Downs and he questioned me closely. I believe that it struck him as a little queer and puzzling, as though England to him were always the England of 1912. Then Frieda came in and was very beaming and affable, and announced lunch which we had in another small back room, sitting by the window which looked out over the housetops and a somewhat dull day. There were chops cooked by Frieda and bottles of ale. I was excited and nervous and ashamed of the self-consciousness with which I stooped to pick up an apple which had rolled off the table on to the floor.

Afterwards Lawrence and I had an animated talk about the approaching doom of civilisation. I told him about the work of the German Buende, about Hargrave's Kibbo Kift. I told him of the political implications in the attempt to get a nucleus in Northern Europe, and he said: yes, such a movement might require a political aspect. The great thing was to get a unit somewhere. He believed that once there had been a sort of world unison, the peoples being in living contact all round the globe. But today this union was mechanical and abstract, one must get a unit first. Then we spoke on the idea of founding centres, "monasteries." And he agreed that we should need to have them, perhaps perambulatory, "flexible monasteries," he said. He asked me if I felt there was a future in England, and I said I thought there was, as a sort of priestly, cultural centre. He said that he himself felt it to be doomed, finished; but that one should believe what one felt. "As long as you feel it, it *is* so." Frieda, stretched out on the sofa smoking a cigarette, said that none the less it was wonderful to be in London; she liked the smooth way things worked, the courtesy of lift- and errand-boys etc.

Then we discussed magic dances, and I told Lawrence about the Morris and the sword dances of the Yorkshire miners, and he described the dances of the Mexican Indians, getting up and showing me the sensuous, birdlike tread of the steps in their round dances. Next he told me of the wild maniacal dances of the Singhalese dervishes or devil-dancers which he had seen in Ceylon, giving an imitation of their frenzy, quite terrifyingly, his piercing blue eyes popping right and left out of his pale face as he twisted like a cobra, shuffling in his carpet slippers like one possessed by demons.

Frieda thought he might be getting tired: "You look so pale, won't you go and lie down, my Lawrence?" But he brushed the suggestion aside, and we talked on for a bit more until I decided that I had better go.

There was something faintly unreal about this first meeting with Lawrence. He had been so overwhelmingly real to me in his books, and now this meeting in the flesh was a nervous, artificial business. I went away musing on the feeling of having met the man three times: once intimately, fundamentally in his books, once in his letters (filled with his temperamental vehemence), and once in the flesh. And these three persons were not yet quite fused together. Before the first I bowed as before a Master, the second I respected sometimes with dislike, and now for the third I felt a kind of winsome affection. Lawrence's voice and features reminded me vaguely of someone else's I knew—the voice was it really like that of Gertrude Bone, Muirhead's wife? [59] There was a far off Atlantean quality about him: his face was like some strange beautiful stone on which the beard and hair grew like tufts of vegetable matter. The new affection and devotion which I felt growing in me for Lawrence-in-the-flesh never quite fused with the dark magic of the man's inspiration until his death. They developed in a new separate existence for me; they were independent of the rapport which I felt with the power which possessed his books.[60]

Richard Aldington

[For] me, the great event of that year [1925] was the return of the Lawrences from America to the European scene. I had not seen them since 1919, and our correspondence had been extremely irregular. At one time Lawrence took a strong dislike to European things and people, and one heard only rumours of his wanderings to Ceylon and Australia and his settling in New Mexico. And now [August, 1926] most surprisingly he wrote from London suggesting a meeting. I promptly wrote and invited the Lawrences for a long week-end, and in accepting Lawrence sent me some of his recent books which I had not read.

I had long admired Lawrence's work and, with sundry disagreements, liked him personally very much. But on reading these books and re-reading some earlier works I had, it seemed to me that I had hitherto underrated him. Seven years' study of literature had sharpened my perceptions or, at least, taught me the rare accomplishment of how to read a book. Seven years of experience had made me more and more discontented with the Olympian, impersonal, and supposedly objective critical attitude adopted by *The Times*. I was more and more inclining to Norman Douglas's opinion that we should take up an author with the implied question: "What has this fellow to say to *me?*" and give him the fairest chance of saying it. Lawrence seemed to have a good deal to say to me, and I liked what he had to say all the more because he went his own way so perkily.

The visit began a little inauspiciously, as Lawrence declared the cottage [Malthouse Cottage, Padworth, near Reading, Berks.] was "sinister." I can't imagine why, as it was sunny and full of books, with bright curtains and a smiling head of Voltaire over the piano; and the garden was brilliant with late summer flowers. And then I had forgotten that in the Midlands you show your respect to a guest by loading the high-tea table with enough provisions to stuff a dozen policemen; so Lawrence was greatly offended by my modest and wineless meal. All this was happily settled by a bottle of whisky for him to have a hot toddy at bedtime, a habit of his which was new to me and had apparently been acquired in America. After that he was in the best of spirits and good humour for the remainder of his stay.

As I knew he was contemplating a book on the Etruscans, I had a dozen standard works on the subject sent down from the London Library; and we spent a good deal of time turning them over and discussing Etruria, which was very important at that time in Lawrence's private mythology. We went for walks, and it was fascinating to see how quick he was in noticing things and making them interesting. Yet he could be devastating in his judgments of human beings. A neighbour of ours, an intellectual climber, had begged to be allowed a glimpse of him, and we contrived some excuse for a brief meeting. After she had gone Lawrence merely said: "Dreary little woman." I liked him for that, for I was sick of the way the London literati would suck up to the humblest of avowed or potential admirers. It would have been just the same if she had been the most potent of salon-rulers.

In private talks Lawrence and I agreed that so far as we were concerned something had gone wrong with England, our England, so that we felt like aliens in our own home. The only thing to do, Lawrence insisted, was to get out and stay out. In Mexico he had felt he ought to make one more attempt to fit into English life, but already he saw it was impossible, and was planning to go away and never return. (He went, and never did return.) He was evidently pining for his New Mexico ranch, for he talked of it constantly and with a nostalgic regret which made me quite unhappy on his behalf. But meanwhile before everything crashed—and he was intuitively certain it would crash sooner or later—we must have just a *little* more of Italy. Soon it would be *vendemmia*. As we talked I saw so vividly the pinewoods and the olive gardens and the vineyards of the Florentine *contrada*, the great cream-white Tuscan oxen, with their wide horns and scarlet muzzle shields against flies, slowly dragging the big tubs of grapes to the press, the men and women singing and laughing and joking as they gathered the big purple clusters, the men and boys dancing on the grapes to crush out the wine, the *vino santo* heating over an open fire, and smelled the air sweet and heavy with the scent of crushed grapes as the vintagers sat down to their evening soup and bread and wine. . . . And yes, I said, I would come to Scandicci for *vendemmia*.

The English, he said, had become half-angels, half-idiots. And he made us laugh with stories of the half-angelic, half-idiotic things they had done to him in the past few days. As David Garnett truly says, Lawrence was a born copy-cat.[61] He amused us by mimicking a dialogue between himself and a woman in the train who tried to lend him her copy of the *Daily Mirror,* and another between himself and an obsequious butcher-boy—"he thanked me for going through the gate." Curious that Lawrence, who was such a good satirist in conversation, was a comparatively poor one in writing. The reason is, I think, that in talk his satire was mostly laughter, whereas in print he scolded.

Best of all perhaps were the evenings when we sang old English and German folk songs, according to the Laurentian custom, and Lorenzo and Frieda talked of their wanderings and adventures. There was a haunted look in Frieda's eyes when she spoke of Lawrence's illness in Mexico City, and of her dreadful experiences in getting him back to the ranch. Lorenzo, it appeared, refused to have a mosquito curtain, maintaining that if you muffled yourself up in the bedclothes, the mosquitoes couldn't get you. But, as thousands of mediaeval angels danced on the point of a needle, thousands of anopheles danced and fed on the tip of Lorenzo's nose; with the natural result of a smart attack of malaria, which in turn aroused his latent T.B. At the height of his illness he insisted on returning to the ranch, and was held up at the frontier by immigration officers, and but for the prompt and humane intervention of the American Consul would probably have died there. I think that was the real reason why Lawrence never went back to the ranch he loved so much; he would not have been allowed to cross the frontier again.

Apart from this unhappy episode, their wandering adventurous life sounded wholly fascinating and rewarding. Most travellers fail to interest me in their experiences, especially if I haven't been to the places they talk about. But Lawrence had the remarkable gift—in his writing and especially in his talk—of evoking his experiences so vividly and accurately that his listeners felt as if they had been present themselves, with the supreme advantage of being gifted with Lawrence's unique perceptions. It would be useless for me to try to reproduce Lawrence's talk; first, because I can't remember his exact words and anything short of that would be a travesty; second, because he has luckily left written accounts of many of these experiences in his books and letters.

He talked of that primitive, ice-cold, remote village of Picinisco where he and Frieda almost froze to death (end of *The Lost Girl*); of their life in Sicily and the trip to Sardinia (*Poems, Letters,* Introduction to *Memoirs of M. M.,* and *Sea and Sardinia*); of Ceylon, with bloodcurdling imitations of night noises from the jungle and satirical acting of an American friend burning joss-sticks to Buddha (*Letters* and *Poems*); of Australia (*The Boy in the Bush, Kangaroo*); and of the ranch (end of *St. Mawr,* last essay in *Mornings in Mexico, Letters*). Some of this was already published and I had read it; but much was either unpublished or unwritten. As he related these things, they became almost epic to his listeners. So might the Ithacans have sat enraptured by the tales of wandering Odysseus. What was remarkable, I reflected, was Lawrence's immense capacity for experience and almost uncanny power of re-living it in words afterwards. Of all human beings I have known he was by far the most continuously and vividly alive and receptive. "What man most wants is to be alive in the flesh," [62] he wrote when almost on his death-bed; and certainly few men and women can have been so much "alive in the flesh" as he was. To say that he enjoyed life intensely would be misleading, because the phrase inevitably suggests all the luxuries and amusements and gratifications Lawrence despised. And, on the other hand, Shelley's "pard-like spirit, beautiful and swift" [63] is too abstract and ethereal. The truth was somewhere in between those extremities.

Soon, too soon, the Lawrences departed; Frieda for Germany (I think) [64] and Lorenzo for Scotland to visit two maiden ladies [65] who misguidedly thought he might like to live in that country. In the intervals between working hours I thought of him a good deal. His talk and personality, the many glimpses of his life, gave point and concentration to the vague rebellious tendencies I have described in myself. It seemed to me that I was being rather cowardly and foolish in allowing so much of life to slip by in mere labour and by allowing my energies to be diverted from writing about what I myself felt and thought to other subjects. I didn't in the least go back on my ambition to know something of European culture, and was grateful to the editors who had given me the opportunity to study it. But in comparison with real writing, all this literary stuff was trivial drudgery. It was respectable and commendable and paid reasonably, but was on the whole parasitic and unadventurous. Lawrence made less money than I did, but he was a free man; whereas I had one leg chained to a library and the other to the London literary press.

The upshot of this was that I wrote a pamphlet [66] about Lawrence and some of his books, in which I abandoned the hocus-pocus of "objective" criticism and the desiccated style it imposes, and wrote entirely from my own feelings and allowed my words to flow spontaneously. I know it is no recommendation to say I greatly enjoyed writing this, because the worst writers take the greatest pleasure in their worst works. The production of it was a catharsis, and it seemed to me the most lively piece of prose I had written. I was confirmed in this favourable opinion by the fact that no London editor or publisher would touch it—until 1930, when Lawrence was news and I was in a position to sell anything I cared to put my name to. As so often happened in my life when I made a step forward, America came to the rescue; and my pamphlet was issued by the University of Washington, Seattle. I think it interesting that what I should now consider my first real poem was published in Chicago, and my first real bit of prose in Seattle.

To my surprise, Lawrence was not displeased with this pamphlet, but in his letter he said: "It's more about you, my dear Richard, than about me." And I dare say he was right.[67]

14 August 1926   "Bailabhadan," Newtonmore, Inverness-shire, Scotland

⟦ I am up here in the north of Scotland for a couple of weeks.[68] It is nice, but rather rainy. The heather is out on the moors: the so-called mountains are dumpy hills, rather sad and northern and forlorn: it is still daylight till about half-past nine in the evening. —But I wouldn't care to live up here. No!

We shall be in England for a week or two. The stage society is giving a couple of performances of the play David in Oct. or Novem. I should like to see the first rehearsals, anyhow. But I don't want to stay long in England. I have said I will go back to Baden Baden and take an inhalation cure, in the Kurhaus, for my bronchials—for twenty days. Then towards the end of Sept. or in October, go back to Florence. That seems to be my programme for the moment.[69]

20 August 1926   "Bailabhadan," Newtonmore, Inverness-shire, Scotland

⟦ Here the weather is mild, mixed rainy and sunny. The heather is out on the moors: the day lasts till nine o'clock: yet there is that dim, twilight feeling of the North. We made an excursion to the west, to Fort William and Mallaig, and sailed up from Mallaig to the Isle of Skye. I liked it very much. It rains and rains, and the white wet clouds blot over the mountains. But we had one perfect day, blue and iridescent, with the bare northern hills sloping green and sad and velvety to the silky blue sea. There is still something of an Odyssey up there, in among the islands and the silent lochs: like the twilight morning of the world, the herons fishing undisturbed by the water, and the sea running far in, for miles, between the wet, trickling hills, where the cottages are low and almost invisible, built in the earth. It is still out of the world, and like the very beginning of Europe: though, of course, in August there are many tourists and motor-cars. But the country is almost uninhabited.[70]

I am going south, tomorrow, to stay with my sisters in Lincolnshire for a little while, by the sea. Then really I should like to come to Bavaria, if only for a fortnight. I have a feeling that I want to come again to Bavaria. I hope I shan't have to stay in England for that play [David]. I would much rather come to Germany at the end of August. And Frieda, I know, has had enough, more than enough, of London. Perhaps after all we can come to Irschenhausen for the first part of September, and let that in-halation wait a while. —I am much better since I am here in Scotland: it suits me here: and probably the altitude of Irschenhausen would suit me too. Anyhow we could go back to Baden to do a bit of inhaling. There is no hurry to get to Italy. —If only I need not stay in London for that play.

I find it most refreshing to get outside the made world, if only for a day—like to Skye. It restores the old Adam in one. The made world is too deadening—and too dead.[71]

26 August 1926   Mablethorpe, Lincs.

⟪ I've been here a few days with my sisters, came on from Scotland. It's rather nice—quite common seaside place, not very big, with great sweep-ing sands that take the light, and little people that somehow seem lost in the light, and green sandhills. I'd paint, if I'd got paints, and could do it. I like it here, for a bit. Frieda is coming up for a fortnight or so. They don't begin rehearsing David till early September; I suppose I'll have to cast an eye on it, though I feel rather reluctant. Somehow, I feel it will be a sham.

.   .   .   .

England seems to suit my health. I feel very well here. But I don't write a line, and don't know when I shall begin again. I shall have to do something or other, soon.[72]

29 August 1926   "Duneville," Trusthorpe Road, Sutton-on-Sea, Lincs.

⟪ I came down to the seaside here to stay with my sisters. Now Frieda has come, my sisters having returned to their homes . . . . I am waiting to hear from the people who are to produce David: they will give two performances at the end of October and are to begin the study and rehearsing any time now. I want to make what suggestions I can, and see them start, before I leave England. It is rather nice here on the Lincolnshire coast—flat country with big sweeps of sand, and a big sky, and low sea. It was here I first knew the sea, on this coast. I rather like being back in my own country, the Midlands. I don't care for London. But I feel my own region gives me something. And I liked Scotland.

I expect by the end of September we shall be going back to the Villa Mirenda, to Tuscany. The thought of the Isles of Greece appeals to me very much . . . .[73]

30 August 1926   "Duneville," Trusthorpe Road, Sutton-on-Sea, Lincs.

❨ I wish you were here—it is so blowy and blustery and sea-foamy and healthy, so very bracing. I like it. . . .

.   .   .   .

Curiously, I like England again, now I am up in my own regions. It braces me up: and there seems a queer, odd sort of potentiality in the people, especially the common people. One feels in them some odd, unaccustomed sort of plasm twinkling and nascent. They are not finished. And they have a funny sort of purity and gentleness, and at the same time, unbreakableness, that attracts one.[74]

12 September 1926   "Duneville," Trusthorpe Road, Sutton-on-Sea, Lincs.

❨ We leave here tomorrow—and by Thursday [16 September 1926] I expect to be in London: at 30, Willoughby Rd., Hampstead, N.W. 3. . . . I expect to stay till towards the end of the month.[75]

❨ I was at my sister's in September, and we drove round—I saw the miners —and pickets—and policemen—it was like a spear through one's heart. I tell you, we'd better buck up and do something for the England to come, for they've pushed the spear through the side of my England.[76]

¶[*It is a soft, hazy October* [September?] *day, with the dark green Midlands field looking somewhat sunken, and the oak trees brownish, the mean houses shabby and scaly, and the whole countryside somewhat dead, expunged, faintly blackened under the haze. It is a queer thing that countries die along with their inhabitants. This countryside is dead: or so inert, it is as good as dead. The old sheep-bridge where I used to swing as a boy is now an iron affair. The brook where we caught minnows now runs on a concrete bed. The old sheep-dip, the dipping-hole, as we called it, where we bathed, has somehow disappeared, so has the mill-dam and the little water-fall. It's all a concrete arrangement now, like a sewer. And the people's lives are the same, all running in concrete channels like a vast cloaca.*

At Engine Lane Crossing, where I used to sit as a tiny child and watch the trucks shunting with a huge grey horse and a man with a pole, there are now no trucks. It is October, and there should be hundreds. But there are no orders. The pits are turning half-time. Today they are not turning at all. The men are all at home: no orders, no work.

And the pit is fuming silently, there is no rattle of screens, and the head-stock wheels are still. That was always an ominous sign, except on Sundays: even when I was a small child. The head-stock wheels twinkling against the sky, that meant work and life, men "earning a living," if living can be earned.

But the pit is foreign to me anyhow, so many new big buildings round it, electric plant and all the rest. It's a wonder even the shafts are the same. But they must be: the shafts where we used to watch the cage-loads of colliers coming up suddenly, with a start: then the men streaming out to turn in their lamps, then trailing off, all grey, along the lane home; while the screens still rattled, and the pony on the sky-line still pulled along the tub of "dirt," to tip over the edge of the pit-bank.

It is different now: all is much more impersonal and mechanical and abstract. I don't suppose the children of today drop "nuts" of coal down the shaft, on Sunday afternoons, to hear them hit, hit with an awful resonance against the sides far down, before there comes the last final plump into the endlessly far-off sump. My father was always so angry if he knew we dropped coals down the shaft: If there was a man at t'bottom, it'd kill 'im straight off. How should you like that? —We didn't quite know how we should have liked it.

But anyhow Moorgreen is no more what it was: or it is too much more. Even the rose-bay willow-herb, which seems to love collieries, no longer showed its hairy autumn thickets and its last few spikes of rose around the pit-pond and on the banks. Only the yellow snapdragon, toad-flax, still was there.

Up from Moorgreen goes a footpath past the quarry and up the fields, out to Renshaw's farm. This was always a favourite walk of mine. Beside the path lies the old quarry, part of it very old and deep and filled in with oak trees and guelder-rose and tangle of briars, the other part open, with square wall neatly built up with dry-stone on the side under the plough-fields, and the bed still fairly level and open. This open part of the quarry was blue with dog-violets in spring, and, on the smallish brambles, the first handsome blackberries came in autumn. Thank heaven, it is late October, and too late for blackberries, or there would still be here some wretched men with baskets, ignominiously combing the brambles for the last berry. When I was a boy, how a man, a full-grown miner, would have been despised for going with a little basket lousing the hedges for a blackberry or two. But the men of my generation put their pride in their pocket, and now their pockets are empty.

The quarry was a haunt of mine, as a boy. I loved it because, in the open part, it seemed so sunny and dry and warm, the pale stone, the pale, slightly sandy bed, the dog-violets and the early daisies. And then the old part, the deep part, was such a fearsome place. It was always dark—you had to crawl under bushes. And you came upon honeysuckle and nightshade, that no one ever looked upon. And at the dark sides were little, awful rocky caves, in which I imagined the adders lived.

There was a legend that these little caves or niches in the rocks were "everlasting wells," like the everlasting wells at Matlock. At Matlock the water drips in caves, and if you put an apple in there, or a bunch of grapes, or even if you cut your hand off and put it in, it won't decay, it will turn everlasting. Even if you put a bunch of violets in, they won't die, they'll turn everlasting.

Later, when I grew up and went to Matlock—only sixteen miles away—and saw the infamous everlasting wells, that the water only made a hoary nasty crust of stone on everything, and the stone hand was only a glove stuffed with sand, being "petrified," I was disgusted. But still, when I see the stone fruits that people have in bowls for decoration, purple, semi-translucent stone grapes, and lemons, I think: these are the real fruits from the everlasting wells.

In the soft, still afternoon I found the quarry not very much changed. The red berries shone quietly on the briars. And in this still, warm, secret place of the earth I felt my old childish longing to pass through a gate, into a deeper, sunnier, more silent world.[77]

William Edward Hopkin

I shall never forget walking with Lawrence over the old ground the last time he was in England. When we reached Felley Dam he stood still and looked across to the Haggs. I went and sat by the pond. After a few minutes I turned and looked at him. He stood as stiffly as a statue, and there was an expression of dreadful pain on his face.

After a while he told me to come along. For ten minutes he never spoke a word, and then he broke out into a lot of brilliant nonsense.

As we neared his old house [in the Breach] he never gave it a glance. I asked when he was coming over again. His reply was "Never! I hate the damned place." [78]

Catherine Carswell

When [Lawrence] came back to London in the middle of September the old weariness was upon him, and he was longing for the rich and glowing autumn of the Mirenda vineyards.

This time they were in rooms in Hampstead [Carlingford House, 30, Willoughby Road], whither even then, we were returning, having taken a studio there. He came with Frieda to lunch, and I was so horrified by his delicate looks that I could think of little else. Our talk, however, so far as I can recall, was chiefly of money—the difficulty of making a living. He had always declared that Donald would never make any money, as money did not enter really into his scheme of things, and that therefore I must. "You should go on a lecture tour in America," he now said, scolding a little. "Now, don't say you can't. That helpless air of yours would just be the very thing. You'd have all the Yanks scrambling about to do things for you." I laughed, partly at this fancy picture and partly relishing his malice. But he insisted, and we argued. "Well," said I after a while, "shall I go on tour and expound D. H. Lawrence and his works?"

He thought this a good plan. Yes, this was what I must do. And immediately he mapped out my tour and gave me all sorts of practical hints about the Americans and how to treat them. Then I would come home with bulging purse and we should all three be able to go and live near the Mirenda or at the ranch, or both. "Have you never thought of lecturing yourself?" I asked. But this he seemed to regard as an unnecessary question. Excellent as Lawrence could be as a fireside or roadside expositor, it was certainly difficult to imagine him as a platform lecturer.[79]

He had brought me a typescript to read, saying that he wanted to know how it struck me. This was a section of Mabel Dodge Luhan's autobiography, beginning with her earliest memories and carrying her well into adult life, which she had sent to Italy for Lawrence's advice about possibilities of publication. His own opinion, as I remember, seemed to be that publication would have to be deferred until after the deaths of all the people who appeared in the narrative.

All autobiographies are interesting, and I found this one especially so. But it was so full of personalities and so unreserved that it struck me as unfit for publication for many years to come. When I told this to Lawrence he agreed. "But I don't care," he added with a grin, "so long as she dies before she gets to Frieda and me!" When he had said a thing like this Lawrence would set his teeth in his lower lip, drop his head and look up at you sideways, his eyes dancing with a special kind of malice. Perhaps he was never more himself than just then, and if you did not like him thus you did not like him at all.

That day, having some other engagement, they had to leave early. I went out to the street to say good-bye, and though I saw that Lawrence sped along as swiftly as ever—not like any town walker—with Frieda careering in full sail beside him, I looked after him with a sinking heart. It was a shivery afternoon. He had told me how depressing and void he found the faded eighteenth-century charm of Hampstead, even at its best. How long ago it seemed since in the summer of 1914 we had all gone for a picnic on the Heath! How far, far beyond our reckoning Lawrence had shot in experience and achievement! Now, by being still in N.W. 3, I felt that somehow I had failed myself and him; that all the while he had sat talking so gently and stimulatingly by the studio fire, he had done so merely out of the kindness that was in him; that really he hated being there. And yet, when I had boasted that John Patrick was "a good traveller," he had shaken his head and said, "Nay, Catherine, but I want to hear of good stayers at home!" All of which contradictory things came with a truth of their own out of Lawrence's richness of spirit, and none of which things would have made my heart sink so badly but for Lawrence's dreadful thinness of body. He had alarmed me by mentioning for the first time that he had had a "bronchial" haemorrhage. But immediately he had brushed my alarm aside. "It's nothing serious," he had assured me, "not lungs, you know, only bronchials—

tiresome enough, but nothing to worry about, except that I *must* try not to catch colds." [80]

Brigit Patmore

It was surprising to hear George Moore say: "I believe there's a man called Lawrence."

As it was in 1926 and D. H. Lawrence had written about twelve novels, several books of travel and volumes of poems, it did seem strange not to have caught up with him—even for a member of the old guard of famous men. George Moore was a man with sympathy for new writers, but I wonder could he have possibly understood the excitement it was for my generation to read Lawrence's novels.

No one has put the effect of Lawrence on us better than Rebecca West when she wrote with penetration and clarity:

"The forces which moved Lawrence seem to us the best part of our human equipment." [81]

A few years before the war of 1914 I met D. H. Lawrence for the first time. Ford Madox Hueffer brought him to have tea with some friends of mine. As usual, Ford talked most of the time in that fluffy, swallowed voice of his, and one strained one's ears to listen, for what he said might be witty, wise, or just nonsense. I do not remember Lawrence saying one word. His face had a square look which vanished completely in later years, and his eyes, that became such an amazing blue, were just greyish; a moustache set up a barrier over his mouth. Frieda, his wife, was not there, so very likely he was absent in heart and mind.

The next time we met was about two years later [1917] when we were all deep in the war hell.

Richard Aldington was in camp near Lichfield and his wife, Hilda, went up there too from time to time; when this happened they lent their flat in Mecklenburgh Square to the Lawrences.

I wrote from the country saying I would be coming to town, would they lunch with me, and suggested calling at the flat for them. When I arrived Frieda had a bad cold and was in bed, but was anxious not to spoil the luncheon. She insisted on Lorenzo (the name she always used for him) and me setting off together. A theory of mine is that most people like contrasts and I asked him should we go to a newish place under the Rialto Cinema. It was rather pretentious but served fairly good food, considering war conditions.

"Yes, let's go and see your world."

"It isn't my world," I protested, rising always to the bait that I was the parasite of a rich useless class. Lorenzo's teasing was his way of touching you with a kind of affection. If he wanted to attack he was quite direct and forthright.

He had been through much suffering and humiliation in Cornwall, but I knew nothing about it, I only saw that he was thinner and seemed taller. He had straightened up the way proud people do under the lash; he had the indifference in look and manner which goes with agony endured, especially cruelty inflicted by one's fellowmen. He had grown a beard and wore a brown velvet coat and fawn corduroy trousers, which made harmony with the deep russet of his uncovered head. His pale skin and the expression of his face showed great sensitivity, but strength was in the slight ruggedness of his features.

We arrived at the restaurant. The waiters were shocked in their vulgar consciousness of Lorenzo's unconventional clothes and they did not disguise it. I refused table after table with the nonchalant impertinence they take for good manners. Lorenzo did not seem to notice their rudeness, but I felt like a watch-dog.

When at last we were settled, he enjoyed advising me about food and wines—very elder-brotherly.

Back in Mecklenburgh Square we found Frieda sitting up in bed by the side of the fire.

"Well, Frieda, are you all right? Do you feel better?"

"Yes. *So* much better, Lorenzo. So lovely and *warm* here. But *such* a stupid book. No *reality,* no *feeling.* How stupid people are! I can't *bear* it." .

"Of course we're never stupid, are we? The woman thinks she's perfect, does she? Well, well." Putting a fresh glass of lemonade on the table by Frieda's pillow. "Brigit took me to the Elysian fields. Think of that. And the waiters didn't approve of Brigit's guest so she turned very haughty and great lady. She wanted to drink claret and I wouldn't let her."

"How *like* you, Lorenzo. Such a *bully.* Poor Brigit, he would go against you just to exercise his power. You *must* not give way."

. The stress Frieda laid on certain syllables was not for intensity. It was a musical call for attention and gave life to whatever she said.

I laughed and Lorenzo brimmed with the inward smile Frieda's mocking love always evoked. Why have people written so much about quarrels between this couple? Could they not see that most of the time he was lashing out at the world, at them? Frieda was the whipping-lass for all society, and she offered herself to his wrath with her gay gibes and wilfulness in the way a tigress draws the play-fight of her cubs. Later, in his pain and weakness he grew bitter, but who would not allow a man rage under torture rather than tears?

We sat in front of the fire. For some reason, Lorenzo never lolled: he sat with knees crossed and body hunched over them and looked like a contemplative bird brooding over a fish about to be caught. He would look at you out of eyes a little closed and ask question after question, which you would answer more in surprise than gratification, for they were searching not flattering.

"So you're married and have two children. Do you like them?"

"Very much."

"Hm, what does your husband say to that?"

"Oh—why—women . . . the home . . . discipline . . . children are company for women. . . ."

"Well, they're quite young yet, aren't they?"

"The elder is about seven."

"A little too young for jealousy. Your husband's rather vain, I suppose? Both boys. Poor Brigit."

"Why? I'd be much more miserable about girls."

"Did you want to have children?"

"Well . . . it's a pretty horrid world, isn't it? Especially for women."

"Didn't you like your father?"

"At first, then afterwards. . . ."

"He treated your mother badly?"

"Yes."

"Is she alive?"

"No." Longish pause.

"What did he do?"

"He drank . . . and then . . . ."

The thought of a son's agony over his mother in *Sons and Lovers* made it easier to allow these probings. After we had absorbed comfort from the flames for a while, I said:

"It's strange, although it was years before I could even mention my mother, and I ran away from my stepmother, I managed to forgive—or rather—to understand my father a little . . . yet somehow I can't get over it."

"No," Lawrence said at once. "One can't. One is cut down to the quick. You know? The quick. There's no more sensitive part of one's life than that. One can't forget that. One is never the same after that."

In those war days at infrequent intervals a telegram came: "Richard is back. Come to-day. We'll have a celebration. Hilda."

And the first train available would slowly take me up to London. In the Aldingtons' room the apricot-coloured walls were lit by candles, dark blue curtains covered the windows. A table had a large red platter heaped with fruit, and a huge plate held whatever could be got of ham and sausages, and there was bread and wine.

Everyone burned with a different incandescence. Frieda in a sun-drenched way, wild, blonde hair waving happily, grey-green eyes raying out laughter, her fair skin an effulgent pale rose. Lorenzo, as if he had drunk fire and was quite used to it. Hilda, a swaying sapling almost destroyed by tempests, all the blueness of flame gone into her large distracted eyes. Cecil Gray was a shaded candle, he held his intelligence watchfully behind spectacles. Arabella, the only dark one amongst us, smouldered under her polished hair. She was cross once because Lorenzo compared her to a lacquer box, but she *was* imprisoned in something and disliked our mental prankishness. Richard flickered with the desperate gaiety of the soldier on leave and unresolved pain. He had the most robust body and therefore its broad strength showed none of our febrile agitations.

After eating our supper we sat round the fire; Lorenzo perched on a chair, most of us squatting on the floor.

Frieda said: "Let's play charades."

"No. We'll act characters and guess who they are."

"Oh *yes*, Lorenzo. Do you remember last summer how you were Adonis and Cecil was the boar?"

"Yes, Frieda, but I'm not going to be Adonis to-night." Frieda's recollections were too fascinating for her to drop them.

"Cecil, do you remember the corn had just been cut and *how* it scratched *just* where Adonis had to lie down and Lorenzo was so *cross* because a harvest bug . . . ."

"Yes," broke in her husband's crisp accent, "and you as Venus, my dear, gave such a squawk of fear because a little—a wee, wee field mouse ran too close to the goddess's ankle."

Richard rolled over in helpless giggles.

"Look, look, Lorenzo. Isn't he like that wonderful tomb of Malatesta in Verona?"

"You're always wrong, Frieda. You mean Gaston La Foix and it's at

Pisa. And anyway Richard's more like one of those Florentine choir-boys of—who's the fellow?—Donatello?"

It was no time to talk of tombs. Richard got up rather hastily.

"Look at Brigit with her hair all round her like a cloak. She's a Madonna. Sit here, Brigit. Here's your baby," handing me a cushion. "Oh! how *tenderly* she holds it!" And Frieda began to sing an old Nativity song. They both had an enormous repertory of songs and could find an appropriate one for almost any event.

"That *reminds* me of the first time we saw the Bambino being carried through the streets that winter in Bressanone."

"We're in England now. Let's be English," Lorenzo said rather impatiently. "Did any of you ever hear Florence Farr do her ping-wanging?" [82]

"At one of Yeats's Celtic Twilight parties in Woburn Place? Yes," said Richard. "But could you call it English?"

"Never mind. Who encourages all those Irish?" Lawrence began chanting monotonously: "You who are bent and bald and blind." Paused, then stretched his thin hands over his knees delicately, as if an instrument lay there, plucked an imaginary string and whined "Pi . . . ing . . . wa . . . ang." Deepening his voice "With heavy heart" staccato ping-wang, "and a wandering mind." And he ping-wanged so violently to show the state of his mind that our hoots of laughter swept him with us and he could not look holy any longer.

.   .   .

During those dislocated days of war, seeing family or friends was a clattering of light and dark shutters—a flashing visit and a sudden vanishing. Frieda and Lawrence moved from place to place as difficulties over lodgings or flats compelled them. I did not see them often enough for my own need: they were the only people I knew who held to the living principle in the human bond. Keats's name for it is "the holiness of the heart's affections." [83] Everyone else's mind was topsy-turvy. Murder was glory, destruction was "living freely," passion was an opiate, tolerance a treachery and hatred the greatest virtue.

I remember going late one afternoon to see them when they were again at the Aldingtons' flat in Mecklenburgh Square. Frieda was standing in the light of one window while Lorenzo pinned and moulded her into a piece of gold and black brocade. She looked very magnificent.

"We've been lent a box for the opera at Covent Garden to-night. Isn't it *Lovely* . . . and Lorenzo says you must come too."

She was wriggling with excitement, enjoying the anticipation and the dressing-up as much as she would enjoy the music and beautiful theatre.

My desire plunged forward in its harness and then fell back, disappointed.

"Oh, I'm afraid I can't. . . ."

"Why *not?*"

"My husband's expecting me back for dinner."

"Well, but ring up and say you're stopping with us and going to Covent Garden."

But somehow not even their company and music would be worth the long explanations, the senseless jealousy of my "writer friends."

"No, truly, I can't."

"Really, it's absurd that you feel you can't do a simple thing like this." Lorenzo paused in his draping of the gold round Frieda. "You shouldn't let *anyone* dictate your actions to you in that way. Have you so little freedom? So weak a character?"

Probably I missed one of the best evenings of my life through this cowardice.

. . .

After the war the Lawrences began their wanderings round the world and were away from England for years. They came home from Mexico in the autumn of 1925 or 1926.[84] Why do I say "home"? For those two made their home wherever they were. As I was working at Wyndham's Theatre they invited me to tea on a Sunday. When I arrived at their lodgings in Hampstead Dorothy Richardson[85] and her husband were there: he was an artist, Alan Odle, who drew with exquisite line and meticulous detail macabre and frightening pictures: his quietude was such that one forgot his presence.

Lorenzo was unchanged save that he looked more fragile and his eyes were more beautiful: However Frieda's gaze appalled me. That unchanging look of horrified pain was all wrong in her easily-laughing green eyes. It haunted me for weeks and was explained by what she told me a year or so later when we were on the island of Port Cros. A doctor in Mexico had told her that Lawrence could not possibly live more than a year—if that.

"He has lived so triumphantly through everything," she said, "I couldn't bear it that he should die now. And I wanted to die and Lorenzo was very angry with me." He was particularly gentle with her that afternoon but she spoke very seldom, only once breaking in suddenly with:

"Yes. You can only be true to the spark that is in you." And she seemed to say it to herself not to us.

During tea Dorothy Richardson asked for news of a friend of ours she had met recently. There had been much gossip about this woman and her husband and Dorothy repeated one of the many stories—an untrue one. Before I could speak Lorenzo banged his hand on the table and cried:

"That's a lie. I can't let that pass."

Then he told the real story, truthfully and kindly—for I knew it well, as fully as an outsider can know the ultimate truth between a man and a woman. One could see that our friend gained more by this pure statement of the truth than by advocacy or an attempt to justify. Dorothy Richardson was given a deeper understanding of a woman who had suffered and liked her the better for it.

Another visitor was admitted, a man whose name escaped me, but a writer obviously, from the conversation which followed. He seemed tormented about his style and spoke of trying to find a new way of writing. Lorenzo looked at him contemplatively; then said:

"It's no use. You're a romantic. Be yourself. You must just sit and re-cover your lost innocence."

The poor romantic hung his head. Strangely enough most people acknowledged Lawrence's right to rebuke them, but to do him justice he was quite pleased if they defended themselves. Hoping perhaps to draw someone else into the culprit's corner with him this writer asked Dorothy if she were publishing any continuation of *Pointed Roofs* and *The Tunnel.*

"Oh, good gracious, no" and she laughed a little like a nice school-mistress. "If I did people would only say 'Here's Miriam waving her old toothbrush again!' No, I'm being paid fifty pounds for correcting the punctuation of H. G.'s novels."

Reluctantly I had to leave early for a Sunday performance at the the-atre. Lorenzo asked me if I liked the job and I said that although in some ways it was a waste of energy, the girls working with me were so inter-esting and human they made up for the late hours and fatigue. At once he said:

"Of course, because they're real people. You've probably never met such reality before."

While he was writing down their future address in Florence I tried to express how great I thought *The Plumed Serpent* was, but he interrupted me with a gentle "Now, now, now." Perhaps, I thought laughing ruefully to myself, I'm not yet intelligent enough! When I sent him later a book of short stories of mine that had just been published he wrote about it with kindness. "You have a curious sixth sense I like," he wrote, "an awareness which takes one to the fine edge of things into another world. The book is very like you." Surely an ambiguous and disturbing thing to say to any author.[86]

23 September 1926
  Carlingford House, 30, Willoughby Rd., Hampstead, London, N.W. 3

⟨ We leave here on Tuesday [28 September 1926], and stay a few days in Paris, on our way to Florence. It is warm and sunny and autumnal, as I remember it in 1915 when we lived for a few months here in Hampstead. I have seen a few of the old people: and yesterday the Louis Untermeyers: extraordinary, the ewige Jude, by virtue of not having a real core to him, he is eternal. Plus ça change, plus c'est la même chose: that is the whole history of the Jew, from Moses to Untermeyer: and all by virtue of having a little pebble at the middle of him, instead of an alive core.

The autumn sounds very lovely in Taos and at the ranch. Part of me wishes I was there—part doesn't. . . .

I suppose we shall be at the Villa Mirenda, Scandicci, Florence, by the first week in October. The grape harvest won't all be over.[87]

Louis Untermeyer

The first time I saw Lawrence in Italy, in a suburb of Florence, we had little to say to each other. The second time I met him in London I talked too much. "H. D." had brought me to Dorothy Richardson's, and the two women had brought Lawrence to the flat in which I was living. Frieda, Lawrence's wife, was also there, an almost theatrical contrast to her husband. Solid, simple, assured, she was health itself: the earth-mother Lawrence was always seeking and escaping, but to which he always returned. She was proud of her rôle and of her past, even of her lineage. She made you know she was a von Richthofen and that Lawrence was a commoner. She refused to be pitied for the hardships she and Lawrence endured during the war when they lived, servantless and unfriended, in a flimsy shack on the coast of England.

"But you mustn't sympathize with me. I didn't do any of the menial work. Lawrence did that. Lawrence scrubbed the floor. He loved it."

Lawrence smiled and went on discussing the scenic designer Robert Edmond Jones and the psychoanalyst C. G. Jung and Mabel Dodge Luhan. He crossed and uncrossed his legs continually while he spoke; his voice, curiously high-pitched, jerked from sentence to sentence; his silky beard was a hank of what, in the artificial light, seemed a bright pink; he had an almost falsetto giggle. Perhaps he was ill at ease. Perhaps I only thought he was. At any rate, I did the wrong thing. I tried to outrace him in conversation.

It was a literature-crammed evening, but I had learned nothing of Lawrence that his books had not continually revealed again and again. What he thought of me was not apparent until Mabel Dodge Luhan published *Lorenzo in Taos* six years later. . . .[88]

I was, I suppose, a little flattered at the association with Moses, for I had told Lawrence that I was planning to write a semi-historical novel, a free fantasia on the Biblical theme of liberty and exile, law and leadership. In the book I drew a new portrait of Moses. I pictured him as part-Jew, part-Egyptian prince, a rebel deeply influenced by Akhnaten's One God—a characterization followed and analyzed by Freud eleven years later in his *Moses and Monotheism*. But what did Lawrence know of me? Or Moses? Or the Jews?

Lawrence would have been the last to see a relation between himself, the eternal artist, and the eternal Jew. But the relation was there.[89]

Jean Starr Untermeyer

In 1926, my husband and myself had rented a small furnished flat in Mayfair and were entertaining our London friends. We had planned a party on a certain evening [22 September 1926]. One of our guests, Dorothy Richardson, the novelist, telephoned us on the day of the party to say that the Lawrences had arrived in London, and asked could they bring them along. Our acquiescence was enthusiastic, for at that time I was reading a great deal of Lawrence, and had been especially moved by the poetry of *The Rainbow*. The room was long and narrow, and when the Lawrences arrived, my husband was at one end of it, and I at the other, near the hearth. As luck would have it, Lawrence went to the end where my husband was presiding and Frieda Lawrence came toward the hearth where I was standing. Our ensuing conversation rather flabbergasted me, but after *"Not I, But the Wind . . ."* appeared, I realized with rueful sympathy that it was a time of trouble for her as it was for me. I was left feeling overwhelmed by a type of arrogance that I was unable to deal with.

Although later I had a couple of letters from Lawrence, I was unable to get to speak to him for more than a word, on this occasion. However I did notice how he sat, his knees pressed close together, his hands tucked under them, and casting tangential glances about the room, his bearded face looking downward. The curious epithet "a sly Christ" flashed through my mind. Some years later when I told this to Alice Corbin Henderson, she replied: "How right! The New Mexican Indians had called him 'Creeping Jesus'!" [90]

W. Siebenhaar

The Literary Institute of Perth, Western Australia, is a very efficiently managed reading centre, with an excellent library and comfortable reading-rooms well stocked with the best English, American, and Australian magazines and newspapers. For years I enjoyed scanning its literary periodicals, and some of its best books. Among the former my favourite one was *The English Review,* then edited by Austin Harrison, since deceased, alas! Among its contributors I especially enjoyed D. H. Lawrence, whose searching essays on some of the most fascinating American novelists of a past period made a considerable impression on me.[91]

It may well be imagined how interested I was one day early in 1922, to hear, from the American proprietress [Mrs. Frances Zabel] [92] of an excellently managed bookstore, "The Booklover's Library," that D. H. L. and his wife had just arrived in Perth [4 May 1922]. They had intended to go straight on to the more populous states of Eastern Australia, but on board ship they had met Mrs. A. L. Jenkins,[93] a distinctly clever Western Australian, and she had persuaded them to put in at any rate a couple of days in Perth. I was asked to meet them at "The Booklover's Library," and after my long years' separation from the great centres of intellectual life in the Old World it may be realised with what alacrity I accepted the invitation to confront the comparatively young champion of the most modern conceptions of novel-writing.

That morning the five of us had a most delightful random chat in the American's bookstore, and I succeeded, backed by my two women-friends, in persuading the affable couple to stay at any rate about a week in the West. I suggested an attractive visit to the beautiful Darling Range of Hills, about twelve miles East of the capital. There, at Darlington, I told them of a splendidly situated *pension* on the eastern slope of its romantic, half-wild valley, subsequently so strikingly described by Lawrence in the earlier pages of his novel *Kangaroo*.[94] I incidentally mentioned that one of the two proprietresses, Miss M. L. Skinner,[95] had written a war book, *Letters of a V.A.D.*

The two travellers promised, before going up there, to pay me a visit in my office the next morning for a good literary chat. How pleased I was, to think that I had never, in the long Australian years, allowed myself to get rusty in the knowledge of literary movements in the Old World!

For an hour and a half, on that Saturday morning [6 May 1922] before my new friends took the train to Darlington, we discussed almost every literary movement of the modern world. I had occasion to point out that Free Verse, although more recently introduced from France into the English-speaking communities, had been long before written in Germany and Holland, and more particularly, with a poetic skill until this day unrivalled, by Heine in his magnificently imaginative *North Sea Pictures*. My statement enthused Mrs. Lawrence, who reminded her husband how they had read them together. I spoke to them of "The Poetry Society" and "The Poetry Bookshop"[96] in London, both of which I had visited in 1913; Lawrence gave me very clearly to understand that, although the members of these movements were his contemporaries, his own literary career had been, and was intended to remain, an entirely individual one. I mentioned that a similar, but greatly more daring movement than the two just referred to, had arisen in Holland, in 1880, possessing all the features of an interesting though more or less wilful attempt at advancement which had grown up in England and America some years before the war. We fairly well agreed about the good as well as the doubtful points in these movements.

Of his novels I had then only read *The White Peacock* and *The Rainbow*. When I mentioned the latter book, I learned from him for the first time that it was banned by the censor, a fact which was wholly unknown in Perth, where it was a quite prominent volume on the Literary Institute shelves. He told me that he himself had not a copy of it left. I promised that I would try and get that copy for him. A few days later I was able to do so. My emphatic statement about the censor's ban so gravely impressed the then Secretary of the Institute, that he gladly, on behalf of the library funds, accepted half a crown for it from me. Some-

what later he even confided to me that there was still another copy of
the book available, but this time, evidently repenting his having let the
other go so cheaply, he asked for 3/6, which I was only too pleased to
pay him to have a copy of my own. D. H. L. told me that he had been
greatly disappointed to find that Bernard Shaw, who had declared that
he thought *The Rainbow* the best book produced by his fellow author,
had not uttered any protest against its being banned.

Towards the end of our conversation I mentioned to him the book that
finally cemented our friendship, the brilliantly impressive Dutch novel
Max Havelaar, which, I told him, stood, in my estimation, immeasurably
above any work of Couperus [97] (an old schoolfellow of mine, by the
way), or of any other Dutch author, and would be difficult to match in
the whole range of literature. I described its author [E. D. Dekker] [98]
as the awakener of Holland from the criminal moral and mental lethargy
of two whole centuries, as I hold, with every truly progressive native of
that country, that "Multatuli," in that and the subsequent works given by
him to the Dutch nation, between the twenty-seven years from 1860 to
1887, reformed its mentality as few nations have ever been reformed. I
gave D. H. L. a typed copy of an English essay I had written on Multatuli's life and works for the occasion of the centenary celebration of his
birth. What I told him on the subject appeared to impress him considerably. Subsequently, in Sydney, he read the essay, which, by the
way, I had offered two years earlier to Mr. Courtney,[99] who kept it a long
time, and then returned it when the immediate occasion for its publication had lapsed. In Lawrence I had been fortunate enough to strike a
man who relied on his own judgement, and did not allow it to be modified by others who probably pretended to possess a knowledge that was
not theirs. His interest was vividly aroused, as some years later was
Bernard Shaw's. But already before leaving Western Australia Lawrence,
whom I told that I should long ago have translated *Max Havelaar* into
English if it had not been for such disappointments as above referred to,
said to me: "I am going to Sydney, where I hope to stay some time. I will
send you my address there, and will also let you know how the essay
impresses me, and whether I ought to encourage you in translating *Max
Havelaar* into English."

That same Saturday, in the early afternoon, I saw my new friends off
in the Darlington train, to receive their first impression of Australia's
nature and life.

I knew well enough that those impressions would be as weird as the
most astounding dream. First there would be the gaunt and unquestion-

ably ragged-looking eucalyptus, not with the dense, soft-green foliage of Europe, but with sparse, hard, glittering green leaves unaffected by the change of seasons; also the spiky green shoots of the uncanny "black-boys" and other star-like shrubs filling the undenuded dells. Then there would be the astonishing fauna: large birds called kookaburras, looking like owls with a wig on, whose only music would sound like a harsh, satirical giggle all along the scales, waking one with strange wonderment quite early in the morning; next, occasionally, in the distance, the Austral cuckoo, perhaps a little less emphatic than its European relative; more prominent and ubiquitous than all, the cheeky, aggressive Austral magpie, whose aggrieved musical yodel is one of the most varied bird-notes I ever heard, capable of imitating almost any sound of material existence, from the soft beginnings of a spring shower to the hard, metallic clanking of iron bars. And finally, not to forget, the realisation of Maeterlinck's magical bluebird, a tiny creature no larger than the colibri, celestial blue without a speck of other colour about it, as I have watched it with its mate nest-building in the creeper-covered trellis outside my window. Again the marsupials: the wallaby that haunts the trees and the roofs, a kind of robust and less shapely, more formidable-looking squirrel; and last but not least, the graceful, gazelle-eyed kangaroo, furtively hopping with giant bounds across the outskirts of the valley. As for the flora, this was not yet the season of the flowers, the multitudes of lovely orchids, the gorgeous scented wattle-blossom, the exotic gigantic "kangaroo-paw" looking luminous against the sunset, the everlastings including an almost imitation of edelweiss. Had it been, our friends would have wondered at the wealth of that great carpeting of strange and varied, multicoloured plant-life that covers the Australian soil in rapid succession during the waning winter and early spring. Also, they saw not yet, nor heard, so shortly after the hot, parching summer, the turbulent waters of the raging brook, hasting headlong through the lower centre of the valley, between rocks and tangled undergrowth, eagerly racing to the meeting with its elder brother, the Helena River, which more impetuously even speeds through the imposing ravine on the other side of the Southern hill-wall. The wonder is that in so short a space of time, and at so unpropitious a stage of the year, Lawrence succeeded in obtaining an estimate of the magic of the scene.

The couple's experiences at Darlington I must leave to be recorded by my friend Miss M. L. Skinner.[100] I do not think they regretted the few days spent there [6–18 May 1922], which, in addition to the first fresh impressions of Australian nature and life, also subsequently led to the partnership production of that forceful novel *The Boy in the Bush*, in reality Miss Skinner's work, but greatly added to and strengthened by D. H. L.[101]

The last meeting in Perth [18 May 1922] [102] I had with Mr. and Mrs. Lawrence was at one of its exceptionally charming luncheon-rooms, where my wife and I had invited them to lunch prior to their departure for Sydney. We had also asked Mrs. Jenkins and the proprietress of "The Booklover's Library." It was to us a delightful hour, even though it naturally did not afford me personally the golden opportunity of another emphatically literary discussion such as I had already so greatly enjoyed in my own office.

One of the things which before his departure D. H. L. mentioned to me as a sight that had particularly struck him was that of one of his two landladies, Miss Skinner, alternately occupied with scrubbing floors and other manual work, and then scribbling most industriously on odd pieces of paper. He had asked her what she was writing, and she had told him. It was the beginning of *The Boy in the Bush.* How he encouraged her with suggestions and courteous criticism, Miss Skinner herself must relate.

From Sydney I soon received a letter, informing me that my "Multatuli" essay had greatly impressed my new friend, and suggesting that I should at once translate the first fifty pages of *Max Havelaar,* to give him some idea of that novel. Needless to say, I, who had sufficiently experienced what more than thirty years before my friend J. T. Grein [103] had prophesied to me about the almost insuperable difficulty of gaining the entry to English literary life from so distant a country as Australia, now set to work with indomitable industry and eagerness, and in a short space of time conquered those first fifty pages of translation. They were at once typed and sent off. In acknowledgment and reply I received a wire: "Greatly impressed. Go on without delay."

Eight months later the work was finished, and I was able to post it to D. H. L. in America. His enthusiasm now extended itself over the whole book, and he promised to make every effort to get it published.[104] Little did I imagine that even with the emphatic recommendation from an artist so deservedly successful, it would take four years to find a publisher sensible enough to accept his advice which by that time had in addition been backed by the opinion of G. B. Stern.[105]

D. H. L. stayed in Sydney long enough to collect impressions and material for his novel *Kangaroo,* which gives an excellent idea of the strangeness of Australia's whole natural aspect. I had the pleasure of reviewing it at length for the Perth *Sunday Times*.

His letters from Sydney, as for that matter most of his correspondence, were brief and pithily descriptive.

The next place after Sydney from which I had word from him was New Mexico.[106] The name brought back to me the novels of my boyhood, the romantic prairie books of the French author Gustave Aimard,[107] at his zenith more than half a century ago. How many boys had they not filled with dreams of romance and stirring adventure! How many boys in Europe had not run away from home to reach that land where life was so wonderful as to be worth living! All my days I had hugged the wish to obtain a truthful, reliable verdict as to whether the Redskins were in reality the poetic race they were so often represented to be. In one of my letters to Lawrence I asked for his impressions on this subject. The answer was brief: "No, they are not as Aimard represented them." It was not sufficiently explicit. I had to wait until he published that brilliantly imaginative book, *The Plumed Serpent*. By then he himself had apparently deepened and widened his knowledge of that remarkable race. He had found the reasons for their insolence to the "Palefaces." He had entered into their dreams of the wild life of old. In the emblem of the Plumed Serpent he has found the secret of their aspirations. The Redskins of Cooper, Mayne Reid,[108] and Zane Grey were only interesting hunters and cruel warriors. Lawrence had found out that after all Aimard was fairly near the truth when he had so persistently hinted at more far-reaching ideals in the strange, stoical mentality of the American Indians!

While I was still in Western Australia, somewhere in 1923, I think, I one day received a visit from Miss M. L. Skinner. She showed me a cable from D. H. L., which briefly stated that he considered *The Boy in the Bush* in the main excellent, but would wish to strengthen it and widen its scope. Would she agree to a partnership publication?[109] Naturally she was delighted, and so, on her behalf, was I. On the other hand she could not help feeling anxious about one aspect of this very generous proposal: would it not be said that D. H. L. was the real author, who had only used some ideas of hers about which to weave a story of his own, and who was generous enough to acknowledge her small share by means of a surface partnership? Although I saw the point, I nevertheless strongly advised her to accept the offer, knowing only too well the difficulty of an unknown author in finding a publisher and in being appreciated even if by some good luck finding one. She took my advice, and in 1924 the book was published in London. I was there at the time, and so was Miss Skinner, and we were both witnesses to the actual realisation of her fears. I think we only met one competent critic who believed in Lawrence's and our own very definite statement of the true position.[110] When I mentioned it to Lawrence, he most emphatically expressed his disgust with the fatuity of the hero-worshippers who did such gross injustice to Miss Skinner. The unfortunate consequence was that her next novel, *Black Swans,* which was not the result of any partnership, but was nevertheless excellent reading, was smothered in obscurity, in spite of some very sympathetic reviews.

This clamouring of an infatuated mob—a mob that has had every opportunity of being educated and yet is not—this clamouring for the accepted stage-hero, this ignorant refusal to see any merit in the other actors on the stage, is one of the most lamentable spectacles in a civilisation allegedly advanced.

Meanwhile Lawrence had had to leave the high altitudes where he had bought a ranch in New Mexico, being seriously affected in health by the there prevailing keen cold winds, which would shortly have cut off his valuable life. Then, in the much lower plains, his delicate constitution was attacked in the opposite direction, *viz.* by a feverish heat. For a considerable time he was very seriously ill, and when at last he recovered, he was compelled to leave a climate of such dangerous extremes, and to return to Europe.

Early in 1926 I was still vainly trying to find a publisher for my translation of *Max Havelaar,* the latest one I had approached, at the suggestion of G. B. Stern, being Alfred Knopf, who was a friend of hers, and to whom she had written on my behalf. I had informed Lawrence of this step, and he had at once strongly urged the matter with Mr. Knopf.

Already repeatedly he had expressed to me his disgust at the inability of many publishers, or their "readers," to recognise exceptionally good work. But fortunately Mr. Knopf yielded to the double persuasion. Quite unexpectedly I received a letter from D. H. L., from his then residence in Italy, to the effect that terms had been offered. He advised me to accept them, although they meant surrender of the copyright. I naturally took his advice, and the publisher was informed accordingly.

The next communication I received (it was still early in 1926) was from Spotorno stating that he would be going to Monte Carlo. It was at the latter place [*ca.* 24 February 1926] that, soon after, I met him for the second time. A sister and a friend[111] were with him; it was easy to see that his health was not what it should be. Yet he displayed the same cheerful and energetic nature as four years earlier. But one evening when he had to stay at home his sister explained to me that he needed a great deal of rest.

During these few days at Monte Carlo the four of us also paid a visit to the celebrated Aquarium at Monaco. During that visit I again had occasion to notice D. H. L.'s vivid interest in every phase of life, shown in the amount of detailed knowledge he possessed of the habits and varied characteristics of a diversity of species of the marine fauna.

As soon as the contract of sale for *Max Havelaar* had been signed, Mr. Knopf asked D. H. L. to write an introduction, and made it a matter of urgency.[112] His urgency, and the fact that by this time we were again a considerable distance apart, prevented, to our mutual regret, a personal consultation on the subject of this introduction. Lawrence had to do the best he could in the face of the handicap, and he did.[113] One or two things I could have advised him to present differently, but in the main it was a very capable statement.

I had asked to see the proofs of *Max Havelaar*, and as I had to go to Holland and England on a lecturing tour towards the end of the summer of 1926, I received them in the latter country, with the request to read them without delay.

In October [27 September 1926] [114] I once more had the good fortune to meet Lawrence, this time in London; but owing to a blunder on the part of his landlady the first meeting arranged for did not take place, and the second one was short and hurried. For the latter he had appointed a meeting at the National Gallery, where we arrived in a pouring rain. He wanted to refresh his memory with regard to a couple of pictures, for some reason he did not explain; and after that he had to go right into the City. On that occasion I had an opportunity of realising the physical energy he was able to display in spite of his very delicate health. The rate at which he raced through the crowded Strand was quite an eye opener to me. It made me think of Shelley and the description given of him to a similar effect. Naturally the conversation under such difficulties in no way approached the interest of the one in Australia, and I cannot even clearly remember the subjects touched upon.

This was the last time I saw him, and the remainder of our intercourse was by fitful correspondence. It included the sending to my wife of a signed presentation copy of that amusing little yarn *Glad Ghosts*.

Like Shelley, Lawrence was a restless wanderer, always looking for some place that might induce him to stay permanently, but never finding such a place.

I never found in him the extraordinarily unreasonable person Mr. Squire has so unkindly made him out to be.[115] When I disagreed with him, I in no way hesitated to tell him so, but he always remained courteous, although we both conveyed our opposing opinions in bantering language. That he could hit hard when unfairly attacked is of course at once admitted; and it would not have been to his credit to act otherwise, even though it is alleged that Christian doctrine admonishes us to turn the other cheek.

His premature death I hold to be a great loss to literature. It is fortunate that, like most men of real genius, he worked with an energy that has bestowed on the world a legacy of striking brilliancy and astonishing volume. Two of his works, in my opinion, stand out above the others for perfection of quality, *viz. Women in Love* and *The Plumed Serpent*.[116]

Catherine Carswell

I next saw [Lawrence] a day or two later [27? September 1926], on what I think was the night before he left for Italy. He had invited us and a few others to his lodgings. Koteliansky was there, and my brother [Gordon Macfarlane] from Gower Street, whose war-novel, *The Natural Man*, had greatly interested Lawrence. It was, for some reason, a harmonious evening with nothing much else to remember it by. Once more we talked of money, Koteliansky maintained that *any* unearned income must alienate the possessor hopelessly from the large portion of mankind who had to earn its bread. I still had £50 a year, and it was discussed whether I was therefore alienated. Kot insisted that I was.[117] Then my brother held forth on the advantages of great wealth, telling us what he would do if only we were "really rich." "Will neither of you people *ever* face reality?" asked Lawrence, shaking his head over my brother and Koteliansky alike. "Of *course* Catherine ought to have her £50, only it ought to be £300 instead. And *of course* Catherine's brother would do none of the things he thinks he would do if he were really rich. Because the moment he was really rich he would be a different person. A lot of money has an influence on the nature of a man that is not to be resisted. I *feel* myself that I, at least, should be able to resist it. But that's just how everybody feels, and I suppose I'd be not so different from the rest of mankind. Money, much money, has a really magical touch to make a man insensitive and so to make him wicked."[118]

I am glad we were all gay and friendly that night. Because I never saw Lawrence again.[119]

Montague Weekley

I think it must have been during this visit of the Lawrences to London that I saw him, for the last time, in rooms that they had afterwards taken at Hampstead. I spent an evening with them. S. S. Koteliansky was there as well, taking Lawrence to task for having made bad terms with a London publisher. I remember that Lawrence described Bernard Shaw as "a very good business man." I also recall his criticism of Shakespeare, countering my bardolatry with a comparison between Shakespeare's and Tolstoy's women which was much in favour of the latter. Lawrence was, however, on that particular evening, less obviously the man who had cast such a spell on me at our first real meeting in the Chelsea flat.[120]

SCANDICCI, FLORENCE, ITALY

5 October 1926   Villa Mirenda, Scandicci, Florence, Italy

It is almost hot here—too hot to sit in the sun. And last night, the rooms being only just opened, it was so hot I could not sleep . . . . These old villas are so massive, made of stone, that after a long spell of sunshine it takes weeks for the walls to cool off, on the south side.

It is very lovely, really—not like autumn, like summer. The peasants are bringing in the grapes, in a big wagon drawn by two big white oxen. Every hour or so they roll up with a load, to go in the big vats in the ground-floor cellars. The grapes are very sweet this year—not very big—little and round and clear, and very sweet. It will be a good wine year, even if the bulk is not enormous. . . . I think to-morrow Richard Aldington and Arabella are coming out to stay a little while here: hope they won't mind the hard beds. One doesn't realise how hard they are till one comes back to them.[121]

Richard Aldington

[*Lady Chatterley's Lover*] was begun at Scandicci in October of 1926, very soon after the Lawrences returned from England. I find that I stayed with them there for a few days, from the 6th October onwards,

113

and thus had the good fortune to be with him at a time when he was at his freshest and most charming after his long rest from hard work, and before his nerves became frayed again by the exacting task of writing this book and all the opposition that came from its publication. In fact, he was so easy and cheerful that I even wonder if in the early half of the month he had yet decided to do the book. Certainly on the 9th he wrote his agent that he intended "just to do short stories and smaller things" and said of the Mirenda that it was "nice to sit in the big empty rooms and be peaceful." [122]

I was fortunate to be with him when he was in a mood "to sit and be perfectly content doing nothing." Not very long afterwards I wrote down my recollections of one such afternoon spent with him at Scandicci. As records of his evil moods are so much more common than of his good moods, that will perhaps serve as my apology for quoting it here. The women had gone into Florence, and he and I sat on deck chairs under the chestnut trees beside the villa.

The October afternoon was very warm and golden, and we talked about this and that, and occasionally a ripe chestnut slipped out of its bulging spiky burr and plopped in the grass. Our real interest was not in talking, but in the children of the *contadini*. Every now and then, a shy little barefoot child would come stealing through the bushes with a bunch of grapes. Lawrence would say: "Look! There's another. Pretend not to see." The child would come very stealthily forward over the grass, like a little animal, and then stop and gaze at him. Finally, Lawrence would look up, and say with a pretence of surprise, "*Che vuoi?*" "*Niente, Signor Lorenzo.*" "*Vieni qui.*" Then the child would come up very shyly, and present the grapes. "*Ma, cosa hai li?*" "*Uva, Signor Lorenzo.*" "*Per me?*" "*Sissignore.*" "*Come ti chiami?*" And then was a grand scene, trying to make out the child's name. We were terribly puzzled by "stasio," until we decided it must be "Anastasio." But every time, Lawrence, ill as he was, went into the house to get the child a piece of chocolate, or some sugar when the chocolate was gone. And each time he apologised to me for the seeming generosity (for at Vendemmia grapes are worth nothing, and chocolate and sugar are always luxuries) by telling me how poor the peasants were, and how the children ought to have sugar for the sake of their health.[123]

18 October 1926   *Villa Mirenda, Scandicci, Florence, Italy*

❴ *We are settling down here, in the big, quiet rooms. It is very nice to be quite still, to let the autumn days go by. It is still quite hot in the middle of the day, only misty in the mornings. But the windows stay open day and night, and we only wear cotton things: hot as summer. In the woods the little wild cyclamens, pink ones, are dotted under the leaves. I am very fond of them. And all the time the famous Italian "hunters" are banging away at the little birds, sparrows, larks, finches, any little bird that flutters. They are awful fools in some respects, these people. To see a middle-aged man stalking a sparrow with as much intensity as if it were a male rhinoceros and letting bang at it with a great gun, is too much for my patience. They will offer you a string of little birds for a shilling—robins, finches, larks, even nightingales. Makes one tired.*

The natives are scared because there is an epidemic of typhoid, from an infected well, two villages away. If it moves nearer, I think we shall leave for a while. No use running risks.

The days pass so quickly. I do very little work—go out for walks by myself in these hills—and talk a bit with our only neighbours—the Wilkinsons. . . . It still seems like summer—I do hope the winter will be a short one. We haven't ordered any wood yet, for firing. We cook on little charcoal fires. (At that very moment the milk boils over!) [124]

Frieda Lawrence Ravagli

[Villa Mirenda, Scandicci, Florence, Late Autumn? 1926]
Dear Monty [Montague Weekley],

It was nice to get your letter, and I'm so glad you are feeling better. From my window I can see a procession of lights going along, some saint's day or other. Lawrence goes into the woods to write, he is writing a short long story, always breaking new ground, the curious class feeling this time or rather the soul against the body, no I don't explain it well, the *animal* part [*ooray!! Eureka*].[125] What are you doing? We are just getting such a jolly room ready, white, and lovely stuffs you get in Florence and the sun shines in all day [*some days*], warm as toast! O dear and you are sitting over horrid gasfires and dark England [*Poverino!!*]. But next spring we'll take a place in England, and you must come for weekends and we'll have a connected life. Lawrence wants it too, wants to see something of the younger generation. . . . Don't be too spartan, but keep a steady core in yourself; but you'll get bored with my preaching. . . . Lawrence says, he'll say a word, *do* come at Xmas if you can?

Your mother [126]

(Dear Monty,

Your Ma is wonderful at giving advice, and even more wonderful at taking it! In which latter, I think you're like her.

115

I haven't heard any more from those Stage Society people, so don't know if we shall come to London in December, for the play [David]. I emphatically don't want to, but "England expects" etc. What about your coming here with Mistress Barby at Christmas time? If we're here, it might be fun. Your Ma is pining for somebody to think the house is grand: she gets no satisfaction out of me, that way. Anyhow it's Sunday evening, we sit in the kitchen with the lamp on the table, your Mother eats a persimmon with a spoon and offers me "the other one"—while I write. So much for grandeur. I have painted windowframes by the mile, doors by the acre, painted a chest of drawers till it turned into a bureau, and am not through, by a long chalk. This is living heroically à la Frieda. Mussolini says vivi pericolosamenta! and then makes millions of laws against anybody who takes a pot shot at him. Siamo cosi. Hope you're well!

D. H. L.[127]

28 October 1926   Villa Mirenda, Scandicci, Florence, Italy

⟨ Aldous Huxley,[128] a writer, and his wife came for the day, in their fine new car. They want me to buy their old car, which is perfectly good. But I won't bother myself learning to drive, and struggling with a machine. I've no desire to scud about the face of the country myself. It is much pleasanter to go quietly into the pinewoods and sit and do there what bit of work I do. Why rush from place to place? [129]

⟨ If Maria Huxley hadn't come rolling up to our house near Florence with four rather large canvases, one of which she had busted, and presented them to me because they had been abandoned in her house, I might never have started in on a real picture in my life. But those nice stretched canvases were too tempting. We had been painting doors and window-frames in the house, so there was a little stock of oil, turps and colour in powder, such as one buys from an Italian drogheria. There were several brushes for house-painting. There was a canvas on which the unknown owner had made a start—mud-grey, with the beginnings of a red-haired man. It was a grimy and ugly beginning, and the young man who had made it had wisely gone no further. He certainly had had no inner compulsion: nothing in him, as far as paint was concerned, or if there was anything in him, it had stayed in, and only a bit of the mud-grey "group" had come out.

So for the sheer fun of covering a surface and obliterating that mud-grey, I sat on the floor with the canvas propped against a chair—and with my house-paint brushes and colours in little casseroles, I disappeared into that canvas.[130]

30 October 1926   Villa Mirenda, Scandicci, Florence, Italy

❲ There are a few aspens on the hill here, and they drizzle slowly away in greeny-yellow. I think of the mountains at Taos and the ranch. No place can ever be more beautiful than that is out there. If only oneself were a bit tougher!

I've been painting pink roses on a dull yellow bureau: doesn't it sound Florentine?

It's a scirocco day, warm, moist, like a hot-house.[131]

11 November 1926   Villa Mirenda, Scandicci, Florence, Italy

❲ I've already painted a picture on one of the canvases. I've hung it up in the new salotto. I call it the "Unholy Family," because the bambino—with a nimbus—is just watching anxiously to see the young man give the semi-nude young woman un gros baiser. Molto moderno! [132]

23 November 1926   Villa Mirenda, Scandicci, Florence, Italy

❲ I'm in bed these two days with a cold. We had such deluges of rain, and I got wet coming up from Scandicci. Everything is steamy, soggy wet, and there are great pale-brown floods out in the Arno valley. We can see them from the window. And still it thunders and lightens at times—and it is warm. We only light the stove in the evening for the damp.

This is the time of the year I dislike most in any country. I wish it would come cold and a bit crisp. The town is no better than the country, and the country isn't much better than the town. One can only grin and abide.

We shan't be coming to England yet. I hear they have postponed the David play until March, and in December are doing my first play that I wrote while I was still in Croydon—The Widowing of Mrs. Holroyd. It is a much simpler thing to produce on the stage than David, so I needn't come home for it, though I should very much like to be there when it is done: about the middle of December.

Only the other day three friends came to lunch, through the downpour. One was a young Russian woman about twenty-five, I suppose. But she had got herself up so exactly like a boy, with her Eton crop and black jacket and narrow skirt, that I gasped, and Giulia, our servant, called her the signorino, the young gentleman. Why ever a pretty girl should want to appear just like a lad from a public school, passes my comprehension. To me it is just repulsive. Why can't women be women—and a bit charming! [133]

Rolf Gardiner

Raven Hall, Ravenscar/Yorkshire/Nov. 28. 1926

My dear Lawrence,

I still have your letter of Oct. 11th [134] unanswered. But this doesn't mean that I wasn't very grateful at receiving it. It arrived almost at the start of our meeting at Rendsburg,[135] when I was feeling rather chilled and disconsolate. I took it with me to the bank of the Kiel canal and rolling my sleeping sack round my middle sat down on the damp turf and read it, while the eternal traffic of steamers churned up the waters below. It gave me no mean measure of comfort; no words could have expressed my fundamental feeling and criticism better than yours. Later I went so far as to read it aloud to my friends at the meeting—or the best part of it; and its burden was comprehended by the people that mattered, especially by my friend Georg Götsch.

Rendsburg, as you will see from the thin and far too rapidly written report, which I enclose, was rather a disappointment from *our* point of view. There were a multiplicity of reasons for this, and I think I have made them clear in the report. To Georg Götsch and myself coming from the blessed fulfillment of the Märkische Spielgemeinde tour in England,[136] the meeting came as a rather prosy anticlimax. The Spielgemeinde tour had lasted three perfect sunny autumn weeks and was one of the most joyful, harmonious and power-giving experiences we have had. It wasn't by any means a concert tour; when we were not singing in one of the big Cathedrals or City Churches, we always insisted on making the "audience" sing as well. It was a revelation to me what power the discipline and restraint of the old music can evoke. The old pre-reformation Canons have the secret of all concerted human activity: the individual is nothing, save in relationship to other individuals; the egotistic will of self-assertion is anathema, and one sings listening with *all* one's senses to the others, but still holding on to one's own part. It is the same principle in the dance: exactly. And then the amazing quiet, the hastelessness of the old music. The old folk knew how to live time.

The Spielgemeinde tour brought a current of new vitality into the sleepy south-west of England. Or rather it was the shock of reminder. As someone—I think C. E. Montague [137] of Burford, said,—it was not a German invasion, but a return of the English 16th century. And singing one evening in the old Chapter house of a Cotswold church, the men in their black velvet doublets with white collars, marching in to an old air by Schlensog,[138] and the room crowded with country folk from the squire to the local hobbledehoys, one could not help being struck by the amazing fitness, naturalness, I should say obviousness, of the scene. It was good from the beginning to the end, from the bright September morning when the company landed at Southampton to go to Bedales to rehearse, to the darkening gusty evening when they left, a blood red sunset, followed by thunder and rain marking their departure and ushering in the fall.

Coming from this, Rendsburg was cold and inhospitable to Götsch and me. Disappointments and faults of organisation gave the meeting a form we did not desire, while unwilling elements, altho' silent, prevented that dynamic circuit which was the object of the gathering, from taking place. Nevertheless I am not dissatisfied. We learnt much, and many really important plans and methods were discerned and accepted. The thing was rather prosy and 'nüchtern'; but far better to begin rather stickily than with meretricious sky-flying kites of self-congratulation. The best of us know what we want and we are going to go on with our work until it is granted us. We have to learn the very A.B.C. of the old magic; for very sooth, the intelligent soul has got to find out the way, and it is not easy. It requires a discipline of self which few modern people are prepared to accept. We have to surrender so much of our *will* and *conceit* and forget so much of our vaunted intellectual superiority. But I am convinced that we must make a start; that now or never, we must act in the quiet, deeply, daringly.

I have had a busy autumn and this winter I am being given no rest: I am kept busy with work and preparation and my calendar is full until this time next year: 1927 is going to be a red-letter year for me, and I am glad. Within me I feel a rich quiet and a ceaseless access of strength. I feel strangely not alone, and although the work is too-often single-handed and lonely, I feel a mere herald among heralds.

No dear Lawrence, I don't merely go out intensely in the spirit. The fighting passionate man in me is very much alive.[139] Only in my letters and the conversation we have had, you have not met him perhaps. I don't know why, but a sort of ague comes over my mind when I have to write to you. I want to communicate in some other way.

At the beginning of the week, I was in Nottingham again. I might have written from there. One afternoon I went out to Hucknall Torkard and watched the colliers return from the pits; sullen, sharp-featured, coal-blackened faces; slaves of the underworld, you once called them. It was a sullen sour afternoon; police from outside the county patrolling two and two like Italian carabinieri, and a sullen hopelessness in the air. Then I took the road into the country, away from the pit-heads and over the girders of railroads that net the country, and I was alone with the sodden dank green fields, and the dark red arable. So strange this section of country wedged between the Mansfield and Alfreton roads; a ploughman driving his coulter into the rich red soil, partridges whirring in drifts from field to field, and the poor black stricken trees raising their blackened limbs in wintry supplication to the darkening sky.

I followed the road in a sort of trance. I came to the next road at Watnall and crossed over into the park behind the Manor. The evening was thickening. From the rising ground under the oaks behind the house, I could see nothing, only hear the unceasing chuff and clank of engines down below. The valleys were cloaked in dark mist, the sky was a purple brown. A great yearning darkness seemed to heave in the bosom of the hill. I stole across the meadow scattering the smutty-faced sheep, and at the top of the rise lay down on a bank. I lay down and let the growing darkness circle round me, felt myself sinking into the embrace of the earth. Such strength and wonder I gained from those minutes of oblivion and yet within me I felt my heart could break. This seemed the centre, the heart of England, and somewhere the fire seemed quenched, put out: and there was no one with sufficient courage to kindle it again. The land seemed doomed and sorrowful, with a yearning doom like sorrow—the end of something; and my heart wanted to break.[140]

Then I shook off my trance and walked sadly down the meadow to the Alfreton road. The night was coming on thick and satisfying. I went down into the valley, blinded, across that blessed country, and so up round Ainsworth and down and up the long hill into Ilkeston. I thought of you vaguely all the time. You were confused for me, with the spirit of the place—Or rather it is that part of you which is rooted in the land, which is fed by the gods of the place, that I knew and felt for. It was the same as before, when I was there eight months ago, before I met you. I cannot explain it, but it is that which touches the vital part of me and makes something passionate within me. Now I am away, having been to Manchester and Leeds and other places and there just remains the strange indefinable nostalgia for the place, like a hurt that one would remember and yet forget. (Aye but I do forget; 'tis so far distant, although it was Tuesday last and today is Sunday.)

When do you come to England? Shall you be back for "The Widowing of Mrs. Holroyd"? I shall come south to London to see the play and meet you, if you wish. This coming week I have to go to Scotland and Newcastle and make preparations for coming activities. Meanwhile I get a short pause here above Robin Hoods Bay, to write and be alone.

My love to you both, and let me know when you come to London.

Rolf Gardiner [141]

6 December 1926   *Villa Mirenda, Scandicci, Florence, Italy*

❰ *It is tramontana here, and quite cold, but rather pleasant. We've got a good warm stove, and a nice room—and the olives and the pine-wood outside. And I've taken to painting for a change: now doing quite a biggish canvas of Boccaccio's story of the nuns who found the gardener asleep.*[142]

Rolf Gardiner

9 Landsdowne Road, London, W. 11/Dec. 13. 1926

Dear Lawrence,

I have just come back from seeing "Mrs. Holroyd." [143] It was a very good performance and Esmé Percy [144] had produced it in the right way. *Mrs. Holroyd* herself was perfect, and *Blackmore* and the *children* and all the subsidiary characters, quite splendid. But the man who played *Holroyd* wasn't fine or big enough, I thought; not that touch of fire and physical splendour that I feel was the hidden ore in the body of him as you meant him perhaps. The atmosphere was right and you were in the play right through; only of course they couldn't talk the Derby vernacular. Bernard Shaw, who was there, said the dialogue was the most magnificent he had ever heard, and his own stuff was "The Barber of Fleet Street" [145] in comparison! The actors loved the play; one felt that. The bulk of the audience? I can't tell. But anyway the audiences at these shows are mostly bloody.

O Lawrence, I'm sick for your country tonight again. Your letter [146] brought it all back to me. Do take me round some day. It means a lot to me, somehow; one of the sacred parts of the earth; but so sad!

Your idea of a *centre* has been in my mind for a long while. We must have dominion with the earth again and woo it truly and masterly. We must get back the real power again; without it all else is futile. I think that all of us are agreed on that. Götsch and I have it ever in our minds; we want farmsteads, and castles and monasteries again, as the Church and the Chivalry had them in the Dark Ages. Many such nuclei, and perhaps a State within the State, growing up like the new burgeon under the rotting fruit. I meant that with the Celto-Germanic-countries business; it must aim as boldly as that, otherwise we shall be crushed. A State within a State from the Adriatic to the Arctic, from the Weichsel to Atlantis. I believe it is possible. That's why I think one must first stir up the people in disciplined activity, getting groups going in every corner of northern Europe. But no hard and fast organisation yet. Only the methods and perhaps the symbol: Yggdrasil. A winter tree with long lusty roots in the dark earth. I take it you meant *The Plumed Serpent* absolutely seriously. For me, it was a most wonderfully courageous essay to think out the course of action that must be taken somewhere. Won't you write us a *Plumed Serpent* for northern Europe, someday? You know, more individuals among my generation are coming to understand, or shall I say accept, your work? Or rather it is for them the most potent agency for breaking down the clogging crust which is imposed by 'modern' knowledge on men, that exists in that form. You have taught me how to feel, I think. And one goes to your books again and again to be warmed and healed by that 'faceless flame' and surging godly rhythm which make all other books seem as dead and dreary as cold mutton in a restaurant window.

I shall build a farmstead in the Cotswolds.[147] I know the spot, and all the land round about belongs to Holland-Martin who was my employer: I tutored one of his sons. It is unspoilt and utterly good: Morris-dance country. I want to get my friends—aye and only the right ones— to join me and help re-energise the district. We must own the countryside between us and keep the defilers out. I shall try and build the farmstead myself together with some of my men, or refurbish an old building as you suggest. It would have to grow slowly; it is often a good thing to begin by planting trees and vegetables; and we might form a sort of guild to do the building and quarry the stone.

I have had all this in my mind ever since I was seventeen. Now I feel

I shall have to begin soon. One must have a centre to which one can return from one's wanderings and travel-work again and again, and where one can forget everything except to work the land and do things with the people. Maybe I shall set to in three or four years time. I shall probably marry then and make my centre. But I can't, won't hurry. In the meantime it is my job to keep on the move, swinging a group here and a group there, and learning to come into manhood. I shan't be ready for another three or four years, but I feel the necessity and I shall keep a look-out all the while. And anything I can do for you or with you, dear Lawrence, will make me proud. I owe you such a lot. But can your lungs stand this climate? That's the problem. It's not much use your coming to England if it is merely going to make you wretched. Perhaps we should do something for you, south of the Alps. But the Mediterranean world seems to be going cold and grey to me; like cypresses that aren't properly dark, or have somehow lost their spear-like, phallic splendour.

I am going back to Yorkshire tomorrow. I want to write the last chapters of a book (*Wisdom and Action in Northern Europe*) [148] before Christmas, and I am wanted by my miners and fishermen. We gave a show at a little village called Upleatham in Cleveland on Friday night. How I love the starry winter-solstice nights. And yesterday I was in Cambridge, seven of us riding on horseback along the old Gogmagog hills through the mist, and singing as we galloped. I've got a chapter on your country in my book, which I wrote seven months ago, before we met. It's terribly personal, so I'd better let you see it, before the publishers print it. I've also recently been working again at my long autobiographical novel *David's Sling* which I began years ago, and dedicated to you in thought years before that. It's good stuff, but the working is very slow, and I'm always being interrupted. However I'll be finished with it soon, I hope.

If you come to England in February, I'll not be here. I leave England immediately after the Midwinter Hike and go to Graz to run a dance and song week with Götsch. Then Berlin for two months. For the rest of the year my programme is as follows:

March 24–30th. National Union of Students Congress, Bristol (to make 'em dance & sing)
Easter. We have four big camps in N.W., central, south and S.W. Germany, lasting three weeks. I expect to be at the northwestern one.
Whitsun. Folk dance week in Yorkshire and men's camp (Boston Spa)
Midsummer. Travelling Morrice tour in South Midlands

July. Anglo-German camp and expedition at Danzig and along Vistula
August Bank holiday. Men's Hike for people from Manchester and Nottingham in Derbyshire.
August. Camp in South Sweden
September. Expedition by Germans with songs, plays and dances to Scotland with Scots through Lowlands and *night foray* against the English on the Roman Wall, during harvest moon. Festival camp and continued expedition to Newcastle.
October. Leaders Mote on Iona or in Northumberland or Yorkshire.[149]

Horrid to be booked up so far ahead, but also rather nice! Do try to come to one of these camps. At Easter to the one in Germany, on your way back, perhaps. You would land right in the heart of things there. I wish you would, for I feel at present that the whole thing is rather remote and cold and therefore repugnant to you. In the warm flesh it isn't. Also if you come to England in mid-February, can't you travel via Germany and look up me and Götsch in Berlin? I shall be at *Dahlem, Unter den Eichen 89a.*

A happy Christmas to you both!

Rolf Gardiner [150]

21 December 1926   Villa Mirenda, Scandicci, Florence, Italy

⟮ We are busy getting ready a Christmas tree for our peasants. There will be about twelve children, and I expect their parents will have to come to look. So many people work on this little estate. And the children are wild little things. They've never seen a Christmas tree, but they heard of some other English people who made one for the peasants, so they all had fits hoping we'd do one. We've got all kinds of little wooden toys from Florence, and with a few glittering things and some sweets and dates, and the candles, it'll do for them. They never get sweets or anything like that from year's end to year's end. They're very much poorer than even the really poor in England. . . .

We shall give them their Christmas tree on Friday evening at sundown. And if the twenty-seven all of them come, it'll be like Ripley fair in this salotto. The men will have to have a glass of sweet wine, and a long cigar called a Toscana, and the women get a glass of wine and a few biscuits. There will be a buzz! [151]

28 December 1926   Villa Mirenda, Scandicci, Florence, Italy

⟨ We had an Xmas tree and all the peasants—27 of them! They liked it, and were nice. Then we had the Wilkinsons out one evening, but have seen nobody else. I find I'm best alone—unless I can choose rather squeamishly, but perhaps it's not really good for one.

We shall stay here if not howked out. I shall probably have to go to London for the play David at end of February. But probably shall come back here. I like it here. I told you we'd fixed up the salotto nice and warm, with matting and stove going and Vallombrosa chairs. . . .

. . . My Boccaccio picture of the nuns and the gardener is finished— very nice and, as Wilkinson says: Well, not exactly nice!—on the long canvas—and the third picture, the "Fight with an Amazon," is nearly done.[152]

10 January 1927   Villa Mirenda, Scandicci, Florence, Italy

⟨ I seem to be losing my will-to-write altogether: in spite of the fact that I am working at an English novel—but so differently from the way I have written before!

I spend much more time painting—have already done three, nearly four, fairly large pictures. . . . Painting is more fun than writing, much more of a game, and costs the soul far, far less.[153]

17 January 1927   Villa Mirenda, Scandicci, Florence, Italy

⟨ . . . Brewster is here for a day or two, looking round for a villa: but Achsah wants to buy one, near Rome—but not more than $6,000. Achsah and Harwood are in Capri.[154]

Earl H. Brewster

In January of 1927, after my return from India (and Greece), I went to visit the Lawrences at Villa Mirenda. I was full of my Indian experiences. Few are the good listeners to one's travels and adventures— but how appreciative were Frieda and Lawrence! The weather was bitter cold: we sat around a roaring fire while I recounted to my heart's content what I had found in India.

Lawrence was always sympathetic regarding Hinduism. He declared: "I have always worshipped Shiva."

"I am glad that at last you have found the many gods, and that you have left the One and the Absolute." When I replied that I believed in both the One and the many, he said: "Oh, I am sorry, it is not as well with you as I had hoped."

We took happy walks over the Tuscan hills. An amusing incident of these comes now to my memory. When we would start forth a neighbour's dog always came eagerly to join us; approaching a farmhouse he usually disappeared for a few minutes, to return proudly carrying in his mouth a freshly laid hen's egg. Wagging his tail he would put it on the ground in front of Lawrence, waiting his permission before he ate it.

Lawrence had painted recently the pictures which were to be exhibited in London [Summer, 1929]. I liked their colour, values and design. He referred often to their tactile qualities. Instead of a brush he frequently painted with his thumb. To me it is a mystery why these paintings caused such a disturbance in London—surely such a reception would not have been given to them in Paris. He declared that after a morning of writing he found more recreation and companionship in his painting than in going out to see people, who generally left him tired and depressed. He communed with his creations.[155]

19 January 1927   Villa Mirenda, Scandicci, Florence, Italy

⟦ We were so pleased to see Earl [Brewster], and though he only stayed two days, it was very nice, and really friendly. I think he's really got a lot out of India this time—the very disillusion is valuable, and then the glimpse of a new reality.[156]

23 January 1927   Villa Mirenda, Scandicci, Florence, Italy

⟦ The days are already beginning to lengthen, and the narcissus flowers are out in the garden already: but the little white wild ones, down by the stream, aren't out yet, nor the wild crocuses. There are lots of Christmas roses wild, but they are greenish, they don't come really white, so they're not so pretty.

We sat in the sun on the edge of the pine wood and listened to a shepherd playing a tin whistle—very badly. They make the weirdest noises, to call the sheep: grunts from the bottom of the stomach, then wildcat hisses. I suppose it takes a peculiar sound to penetrate a sheep's stupid skull. The leading sheep with the bell was called Laura: "Hoy! Laura! Hoy—a—Hoy! Grunt—squish—squee!" so the shepherd kept on at her. And she, like an old maid, munched a bit, and tripped ahead, the rest trailing after her.

The mountains, the Appenines, are covered with deep snow, and they look very beautiful, sweeping away to the north, the furthest up, at Carrara, glimmering faint and pinkish in the far, far distance. And near at hand, the country lies in the sunshine, all open and rolling, with white buildings like dots here and there, and few people. It is very different from England. . . . On a day like to-day an odd butterfly comes flapping out, and there's a bee now and then. The sun is strong enough. I even saw the tail of a little lizard go whisking down a hole in the wall.[157]

6 February 1927   Villa Mirenda, Scandicci, Florence, Italy

⟨ There's no news this end—we go on quietly. I am in the thick of another picture: *Eve Regaining Paradise*. Don't take alarm at a title—that's another bit of modern nervousness. As for mâte surface, I find, for myself, I hate it. I like to paint rather wet, with oil, so the colour slips about and doesn't look like dried bone, as P——'s pictures do. And I'm not so conceited as to think that my marvellous ego and unparalleled technique will make a picture. I like a picture to be a picture to the whole sensual self, and as such it must have a meaning of its own, and concerted action.

.   .   .   .

My new novel is three parts done, and is so absolutely improper in words, and so really good, I hope, in spirit—that I don't know what's going to happen to it.[158]

9 February 1927   Villa Mirenda, Scandicci, Florence, Italy

⟨ I've nearly done my novel—shall let it lie and settle down a bit before I think of having it typed. . . . I'm just finishing a nice big canvas, Eve dodging back into Paradise, between Adam and the Angel at the gate, who are having a fight about it—and leaving the world in flames in the far corner behind her. Great fun, and of course a Capo lavoro! I should like to do a middle picture, inside paradise, just as she bolts in. God Almighty astonished and indignant, and the new young God who is just having a chat with the serpent, pleasantly amused, then the third picture, Adam and Eve under the tree of knowledge, God Almighty disappearing in a dudgeon, and the animals skipping. Probably I shall never get them done. If I say, I'll do a thing, I never do it. But I'll try. . . .

I found the first violet yesterday—and the slope opposite is all bubbled over with little pale-gold bubbles of winter aconites. La Primavera! [159]

16 February 1927   Villa Mirenda, Scandicci, Florence, Italy

❲ It is already beginning to be spring. Under the olive trees the winter aconites, such pretty pale yellow bubbles, are all out, and many daisies: and I found the first purple anemone. . . . The wild tulips are peeping through, though they won't flower till Easter, and the grape hyacinths also are coming. We've had a week of lovely sunshine, and so far have both escaped the 'flu, thank Heaven. There's a good deal about.[160]

27 February 1927   Villa Mirenda, Scandicci, Florence, Italy

❲ Will you [Earl H. Brewster] invite me? Frieda is probably going to Germany about the middle of March. If you and Achsah ask me, I'll come to Ravello for a week or ten days, then we'll go our walking trip. I don't think I shall go to England . . . . let them produce David as they like. Why should I mix myself up with them personally! I hate the very thought of them all.

Or should we meet in Rome and look at those Etruscan tombs? . . .

. . . Outwardly I know I'm in a bad temper, and let it go at that. I stick to what I told you, and put a phallus, a lingam you call it, in each of my pictures somewhere. And I paint no picture that won't shock people's castrated social spirituality. I do this out of positive belief, that the phallus is a great sacred image: it represents a deep, deep life which has been denied in us, and still is denied.[161]

awrence, Frieda, and Pino Orioli at the foot of the Ponte Santa Trinità in Florence
_a._ 1927). In the right background, the balconies of the Berchielli (the "Bertolini's"
Aaron's Rod). From a photograph in the possession of Wm. Heinemann, Ltd.

Barbara Weekley Barr, *ca.* 1922. From a photograph in the possession of Mrs. Barr.

28 February 1927   Villa Mirenda, Scandicci, Florence, Italy

❨ I am sending a "Scrutiny" on John Galsworthy, for a book of "scrutinies" by the younger writers on the elder, which is being published by that Calendar young man Edgell Rickword [sic]. . . .[162]

I'm afraid it is not very nice to Galsworthy—but really, reading one novel after another just nauseated me up to the nose.[163]

8 March 1927   Villa Mirenda, Scandicci, Florence, Italy

❨ Frieda wants to go to Baden-Baden next week—and stay a fortnight and bring her two girls [Barbara and Elsa] back here a month. The Brewsters . . . have moved to Ravello, and are in Cimbrone, Lord Grimthorpe's place . . . . They invited me for a little while. I might go—but I don't know. It depends if I shake off this 'flu. What I've promised to do is to walk with Earl in the first weeks in April. I want to go to the Etruscan places near Rome—Veii and Cervetri—then on the Maremma coast, north of Civita Vecchia and south of Pisa—Corneto, Grosseto, etc.—and Volterra. The Etruscans interest me very much—and there are lovely places, with tombs—a dangerous malaria region in summer.

.   .   .   .

I've done my novel—I like it—but it's so improper, according to the poor conventional fools, that it'll never be printed. And I will not cut it. Even my pictures, which seem to me absolutely innocent, I feel people can't even look at them. They glance, and look quickly away. I wish I could paint a picture that would just kill every cowardly and ill-minded person that looked at it. My word, what a slaughter! . . . Since my "Eve Regaining Paradise" I've not done anything. I began a resurrection, but haven't worked at it. In the spring one slackens off. Then this cursed 'flu.[164]

11 March 1927   Villa Mirenda, Scandicci, Florence, Italy

❨ I am sending today the MSS. of The Lovely Lady, murder story (sic) for Cynthia Asquith. . . .[165]

I've had digs of 'flu—not bad but beastly—this last fortnight. Hope it's about over.

129

I think if I'm well enough I'm going down to Ravello for a change next week . . . .[166]

17 March 1927   Villa Mirenda, Scandicci, Florence, Italy

⟨ *I am going to Rome tomorrow, then south to Ravello.*[167]

Achsah Barlow Brewster

On our return from India . . . we were staying in Ravello. It was early spring and still cold. Close around the hearth where great logs burned we gathered and talked—Lawrence, Earl, the child [Harwood] and I. We were staying on a beautiful estate above Amalfi. Lawrence was visiting us, while Frieda was in Germany with her mother.

In the formal dining-hall the four of us gathered at one end of the enormous refectory table. Lawrence would taste his bouillon and with a sweeping gesture at the child exclaim: "Ah, Jupiter Pluvius!" Bouillon, ever since, has remained for me Jupiter Pluvius. He would pretend surprise at the sight of meat, observing that we were unlike most vegetarians, who would not allow even their dog a bone. After we had dined we would run for our lives up the winding staircases, shivering over the terrace, back to our own special hearth corner. He would turn to the chubby child, whom he called Schwanhild, asking what we should do, to which the invariable response was, that she wanted Uncle David to tell about the people he knew or stories of when he was a little boy.

He would then describe in rich detail some of his friends and acquaintances. I can see the vivid array so clearly. We heard of their longings and successes, their mistakes and tragedies, their shortcomings, their qualities, fine and otherwise—even all their little accessories—their hats and veils, the rows of their tiny shoes, their boot-laces, their ear-rings. Surely they would be amazed if they knew all the details he had remembered and recounted, unless they too have listened amused and charmed by such descriptions. He shared his emotions about his friends as he shared everything he had. He described his own family—his Aunt Pem who baked buns—"Very good they were too, large and full of plums— which she sold six for threepence. My word, I'd like one now!" he laughed. "You went down two steps to enter her shop and a little bell tinkled when she opened the door. She was short and plump, she drove about in a little chaise every bit of which she filled—it was drawn by a small donkey." [168]

"Ever heard of 'Lawrence's Salve'?" he asked, his eyes twinkling. One of his uncles made an ointment prized by the miners. Whenever they had a pain they would come for "Lawrence's Salve." His uncle would heat the plaster before the fire until it was piping hot, and then slap it on to the aching back of the victim. "And then how the miners yelled!"

How gently he described his brother's frail little boy, who lived much of the time in Lawrence's childhood home; how once the child had a terrible abscess on his face, and the agony of waiting for that to burst, then Lawrence had carried him in his arms for days. Lawrence declared that he still had a recurring nightmare in which the child would run to meet him, as he used to do, with his arms outstretched for Lawrence to carry him, but where the child was running was a dangerous precipice.[169]

He became much absorbed when he talked about the miners of his native village. They drank heavily and led free lives. He recounted how the Bethel Chapel engaged a famous Evangelist for a revival meeting —a man of eloquence equipped with personal information about the various delinquents. The revivalist assumed the character of Saint Peter with the book of Judgment Day before him, as he turned over the pages of the large Bible. The audience were electrified as he scrutinized the open book, very carefully searching, it seemed, for the name, as he thundered: "Will *your* name be written there, Richard Smith? What will it say to your having reeled home this morning at 1.30?" Then his fateful finger pointed to Jim Murphy in the middle row. "Will *your* name be written there, James Patrick Murphy? What will the Lord say to your painted Jezebel?" The finger kept on its way prying out each sinner. It felt like the terrible Judgment Day and the effect was tremendous.

Lawrence gave a quiet laugh and continued his story. It needed only a year before it was considered necessary to have another revival meeting. The same evangelist was called again. But he had forgotten the sermon of his last year's visit, so when he began to repeat it word for word, and wagged his accusing finger the sinners nudged each other and cared not a damn whether their names were written there or not!

"Yet, on the walls of our Sunday Schoolroom was written: 'Worship the Lord in the beauty of holiness'—not a bad thing to be brought up on!" Lawrence remarked.

One day he expostulated for long against old paintings: "Why not hang something fresh and new by a living artist? What if the living artist did have the fun of painting the picture, others should have the fun of seeing it too! Even though beauty was in the eye of the beholder and each must create it for himself, we need fresh vision and living beauty from outside too, not dead things encumbering the walls and the mausoleums of museums. Though pictures should die as well as everything else: the shorter lived the better for most, fifty years would be a ripe old age. Perhaps the fulfilment of beauty lies in the joy of creating it. But it must be shared too. The sharing creates another beauty. The real thing is to see beauty and dwell in it continually." [170]

I needed a model for one of the wise men and for Joseph in the canvas I was painting at that time. Lawrence stood still, submitting to a white burnous over his head, and held a soap-dish outstretched in his hand as the wise man's offering. Two pencil notes were made and painted later. He would not keep still, as he maintained that life is motion, and if you could not seize on motion in motion you would not catch a glimpse of life.

Eager as a child with a new toy, singing in bursts of happy excitement, he began to paint a picture. It was going to be a crucifixion with Pan and the nymphs in the foreground. It passed through many metamorphoses and ended by being Pan and the nymphs, without the crucifixion. He was very busy over it, and exuberantly happy while he painted. It was one of his largest pictures (30 x 40 inches or more), and he was greatly pleased with the result.

Lawrence was commiserating over some indisposition, saying how full life was of miserable things. When I rejoined that it also was full of blessings: I could not be euchered out of a happy life, since already I had had one. He admitted that he too had had his fill of joy. He was carrying in his hand a cerise anemone that the March wind had blown open; we agreed that we could depart in peace after beholding so much of the glory of the Lord. Then after a pause Lawrence said: "Such alone can depart in peace!"

We were discussing the quality of *genius*. He assented that his genius was religious, since it was the search for truth which alone freed and vitalized him.

When we were considering the subject of bringing up the young, he maintained that if he had had a son he should have educated him for the highest class of society; the true aristocrat or the proletariat being the only ones who could enjoy life without inhibitions. When they were boys they could do anything, a rich and varied existence. "Imagine being a bourgeois, brought up as a nice, little mardy-boy!" Lawrence complained seriously that he did not feel he belonged to any class of society.

He spoke of human contacts, of the unique beauty possible in relationship, using his favourite symbol: "For me the rainbow interprets this (as well as hope), the glory shining between every two people which can exist only between them. Each human relationship should be a glorious rainbow."

Lawrence was discussing that inexhaustible subject, marriage. He observed that it seemed incidental and accidental in many lives. But perhaps it was only a seeming, and the Hindus were right to believe that the hand of Fate deals out three events—birth, marriage and death—and that no man can escape his fate. He held marriage to be an eternal sacrament which nothing could alter.

Again as we sat around the fire he would turn to the child "Schwanhild," and suggest that we sing an opera as a swan-song. We burst into amazing cadenzas and coloratura passages. Then he would sing *Widdecombe Fair, Polly Oliver* and *Young Herchard of Taunton Dean.* He wrote down the scores, humming out the tunes and putting them down note by note. He knew any number of folk-songs in German, French and English.

The estate had been laid out into splendid gardens adorned by bronze statues, reproductions of Donatello and Verrocchio and the Greek bronzes from Pompeii in the Naples museum. The paths wandered through rose gardens, and past pools where iris grew, under arbours and flowery pergolas on to the belvedere with its marvellous views, and then from terrace to terrace through thick woods.

Lawrence was walking there with Earl, past the Hermes statue and on past the blue-green bronze Venus and on through woods, when they passed a deep grotto where a life-sized white marble statue of mother Eve had been placed. In a whimsical humour, Lawrence said: "She's too bleached out and pale, altogether too demure after her fall. I'll give her a touch of colour," and he snatched up a handful of dark brown earth that lay near, energetically rubbing it on the lady's face.

"There, that's better," he announced, "I'll keep on, I believe," and he gave her a complete mud-bath which transformed the shrinking white marble Eve into a black lady. He stood off to survey his handiwork, saying that it needed only a few leaves to make it perfect, whereupon he put a green cluster in her hair.

Evidently the gardener did not appreciate the effect, for the next morning Eve was as pale as ever! [171]

At the end of his visit we left Ravello together. It was a radiant afternoon as we drove down the winding road, the sun full in our faces, the sea burning blue at our feet. The fig-trees had spurted out two green flames from the tip of each bare twig which delighted Lawrence, as did the cyclamen blossoming on the hills. He espied every new burst of spring. At that time he was writing about the Tuscan wild-flowers, and began to tell us of their beauty.[172]

We changed carriages at Positano, where our drivers laughed and shouted together. Lawrence, white with anger, stopped our man, asking him what he meant by using indecent language before decent people. The driver looked sheepish. Few could understand his dialect or what he was saying, and it did not seem to matter, but to Lawrence it indicated that the whole body politic of Europe had gone rotten. His afternoon was blighted. Such an incident could change his mood suddenly and completely.[173]

22 March 1927   Palazzo Cimbrone, Ravello, Salerno, Italy

⟨ *I shall probably start on a little walking tour next week—on the 28th— walking north.*[174]

Earl H. Brewster

One day, after the promised visit to us in Ravello, Lawrence and I drove out to the end of the Sorrentine Peninsula returning to Sorrento on foot. During that walk he told me the story—*Lady Chatterley's Lover* —which he had recently written. The joy of creation was still upon him: but he was in doubt regarding publication. The manuscript had not yet left his possession. He talked much about the book, saying he did not wish to leave it unpublished: he spoke of its tenderness, and emphatically declared that to his mind it was not an improper book. He reiterated, as in the past, that the only unforgivable sin is to deny life: that there are no words which should not be spoken, no thoughts which should not be expressed: in the darkness of suppression and secrecy poison is engendered: when the hidden words and thoughts are brought into the clear daylight the poison departs: the author renders this service when he writes with reverence for life. I had to agree with him, and to say if he could endure the misunderstandings and censure which the book would cause then he should publish it.

Undoubtedly Lawrence thought of himself as a man with a message. Once I heard him say it would be three hundred years before his writings would be understood. To those who did not know Lawrence personally, and to his readers who may not have discovered the real man in his books, I must bear witness of the Lawrence I knew. He was a Puritan—a term I often heard applied to him in his presence, and one which he accepted and admitted. Those who read praise of licentiousness into his works, should know the disgust with which he regarded that quality. Nature he worshipped, and *natural* impulses he deeply respected, but that pathological condition when the *mind* is absorbed in sex he abhorred. It is true that Lawrence himself was possessed by the subject of sex—but in what a different way! His possession was like that of the doctor who wishes to heal. He deserves our efforts to understand him whether we succeed fully or not, or whether we can agree with him. It is clear that he believed mental life and sex should be more separate —even as our other organic life is more separate from the mental consciousness. To-day most of us deny and repress sex, or indulge ourselves in it without respect for its significance. He did neither, but tried to show that sensuality like sentimentality is false, while sensuousness free of mental tampering—is part of the divine life. Indeed the ancient story of the Garden of Eden seems to tell the same truth—when physical purity vanished with the coming of mental curiosity.

My first impression of Lawrence as the botanist, deeply loving nature, still seems to me to contain the essential truth of his character. I think of him as close to those Hindu worshippers of *Shakti,*—life, vitality, power. In appearance he resembled the slender figure of the Greek Satyr, but curiously at the same time the British Nonconformist—*never* a Don Juan. Delicate and sensuous he was, yet decidedly with the austerity and self-respect of the Puritan.

Never during my years of intimacy with him—gay and free as were our hours together—believing as he did that what a man feels and thinks should be expressed—have I ever known him to tell a vulgar story, nor to joke and speak lightly of sex, never have I known him to treat or regard one human being with less dignity or less delicacy than another. Indeed he was the Puritan.

From Sorrento we started on our Etruscan pilgrimage, beginning with the museum of the Villa di Papa Giulia in Rome. With what lively interest Lawrence studied its treasures! In his writings on the Etruscan cities he has described our visits to Cerveteri, Tarquinia, Grosseto, and Volterra. I have not read all of those articles: I wonder if he describes our long drive from Montalto to Vulci, through the wildest country I have seen in Italy.[175] The road crosses the ancient one-arched Ponte dell' Abbadia. The vast half-ruined abbey beside it, far from any other dwelling, was occupied by a few families who were most hesitant in having anything to do with us, even to selling us candles for the tombs. Yet when we went on to those excavations the whole male population accompanied us and patiently waited for us outside each underground chamber until we emerged.

How happy were our days at Tarquinia! The tombs are on a high plateau back a few miles from the sea. They number about a hundred and cover the area of a small city. We were thrilled by the freshness and beauty of their mural paintings. I felt Lawrence truly maintained Etruscan art has a certain sensitive quality not found in the Greek. The symbolism, as he explained it, seemed so convincing that I could but wonder at the variety of explanations archaeologists give to it. From the jewelled splendour of those dark tombs we came forth into the brightness of an April day and a blue sky, broken by hurrying white clouds: the fields through which we walked were gay with red poppies: our guide unlocked the door leading to another tomb and we would descend again to behold the joyous scenes with which the Etruscans, of such a distant world, chose to decorate the homes of their dead. For hours we continued these alternations between past and present. Late that afternoon we took a long walk, into the valley below the plateau of Tarquinia and climbed to the top of a neighbouring hill. We made bold plans for the future, I at least little suspecting how soon Lawrence would lose even the strength he then possessed. Perhaps those were the last long walks he took.

My memory is that Easter morning [Palm Sunday, 10 April 1927] found us at Grosseto [Volterra]: [176] there we passed a little shop, in the window of which was a toy white rooster escaping from an egg. I remarked that it suggested a title—"The Escaped Cock—a story of the Resurrection." Lawrence replied that he had been thinking about writing a story of the Resurrection: later in the book of that title which he gave me, he has written: "To Earl this story, that began in Volterra, when we were there together." I am inclined to think *The Escaped Cock* the most beautiful writing Lawrence has left us, but I doubt the adequacy of its title, for which I myself might be blamed.[177]

At Volterra our Etruscan pilgrimage ended. Lawrence climbed into the great motor-bus for Florence, and I took the train for southern Italy.[178]

12 April 1927   *Villa Mirenda, Scandicci, Florence, Italy*

(I got back here last night . . . .

.   .   .   .

I am in a quandary about my novel, Lady Chatterley's Lover. It's what the world would call very improper. But you know it's not really improper— I always labour at the same thing, to make the sex relation valid and precious, instead of shameful. And this novel is the furthest I've gone. To me it is beautiful and tender and frail as the naked self is, and I shrink very much even from having it typed. Probably the typist would want to interfere . . . . I think perhaps it's a waste to write any more novels. I could probably live by little things. I mean in magazines.

.   .   .   .

. . . My wife's youngest daughter arrives today from London . . . .[179]

14 April 1927   Villa Mirenda, Scandicci, Florence, Italy

《 *I am home again—I returned Monday evening* [11 April 1927] *from Volterra. I had a very beautiful week with Brewster. We went to Cerveteri, Tarquinia, and Vulci, Grosseto and Volterra, not far from the sea, north of Rome. The Etruscan tombs are very interesting and so nice and lovable. They were a living, fresh, jolly people, lived their own lives without wanting to dominate the lives of others. I am fond of my Etruscans—they had life in themselves, so they had no need to govern others. I want to write some sketches of these Etruscan places, not scientifically, but only as they are now and the impression they make.*

I found Frieda with a cold and a little depressed, but she is well again and herself once more. Barby came Tuesday with Mrs. Seaman [180]—*she is nice, older than last year, not so beautiful, tall as a telegraph pole, quieter, not much life in her. That is London over one. She will stay here three weeks. She works well in her school and really wants to be free, but it will take another year and a half at least. But it is better that she works. . . .*

The weather, thank God, is always lovely. There are still tulips in the corn and apple blossoms. The peasants are faithful and nice. The house is still. It is good to be here. Frieda has gone to Scandicci—Barby and Mrs. Seaman to Florence—so I am alone.[181]

Barbara Weekley Barr

The Villa Mirenda on a hill at Scandicci, a few miles from Florence, was an old white house, more dignified than the Villa Bernarda.

Two large chestnut trees were in flower in front of it when I went there in the spring of 1927. (I also visited the Lawrences at the Villa Mirenda the following spring, 1928.) It had oil lamps, and a stove to light with pine logs in the evenings. There was a piano, hired from Florence, in the big whitewashed sitting room. The floor was covered with fine woven rush. On the wall hung the big *Holy Family* which Lawrence had painted on one of the canvases Maria Huxley had given him. His *Eve Re-entering Paradise* was in another room, as well as the *Nuns with the Gardener* and a picture of naked men among autumn willows.[182] He painted many others as well. Later an exhibition was arranged at the Warren Gallery which so shocked the prigs that the pictures were removed by order of the Home Secretary.

These paintings lacked what is called "technique," but they were alive and mystical. They had a shiny surface like oleographs, caused by Lawrence sometimes smearing on the paint with his hands.

Lawrence was very pleased with his painting, which took less toll of him than writing. He said he was going to give up being an author and paint instead.

Frieda also painted occasionally. Her wonderful colour sense gave her pictures life and gaiety. One of them—of chickens at the ranch—she gave to Elsa, so I put it up on a mantelpiece at home.

"I say, I like that!" exclaimed my father. "Who did it?"

"Oh, someone or other . . . I forget," I replied.

At the Villa Mirenda we sang the Hebridean songs, Frieda accompanying us. Lawrence sang in a high-pitched voice. It gave the songs a weird "other-world" sound, which suited them, although orthodox musicians would no doubt have shuddered. In fact, an elderly friend who was with me on this visit—staying disconsolately at the inn—expressed her disapproval of such amateurish singing.

"What a conceited ass she is," remarked Lawrence's Scots friend, Miss Millicent Beveridge, who was there too.

We also sang *Red, Red Is the Path to Glory*, a tragic border song, and *The Lay of the Imprisoned Huntsman*, which Frieda liked to sing. Aunt Else told me that whenever she heard her sing it she felt sad, because there was a sound in Frieda's voice of a being also imprisoned.

One evening at Scandicci, a family of English puppet makers named Wilkinson invited us to a party, where everyone was asked to do a "turn." The hostess, dressed as William Wordsworth, recited "We Are Seven." Lawrence, who had once seen Miss Florence Farr in London, sat down at an imaginary harp, drew his hands across it, began "I will arise and go now" in a falsetto voice, and ended it with a "ping-a-ling."

This take-off of the high-faluting was over the heads of the company. On the way home Lawrence raved at Frieda for having allowed him to do it.

Lawrence was aloof. He disliked too easy intimacy, or gatherings where people "got together." He said once that the idea of putting his arm around a woman's waist and dancing with her appalled him.

Pretension and commonness upset him. One could sometimes see a glimpse of the working-class Midlander, but he was always remote from vulgarity.

He could be cruel, and even nagging, but never callously indifferent. He did not have the ordinary man's domineering dependence on his womenfolk, but could mend, cook, and find his own possessions.

Lawrence had the clean, fresh look of so many fair people. He liked old clothes, but never looked ill-kempt.

"I don't mind a bit of vanity," he once remarked. He would advise us about our clothes, and was interested in our dressmaking attempts. "Sew it properly," he would implore us. "Things can't keep their shape unless you do."

I remember thinking that his advice about an orange jumper I was knitting at the Mirenda must necessarily be inspired. "The only colour that goes with yellow is pink," he insisted. So Frieda and I finished it off with a strawberry border.

Sometimes she and I sat on one of the little balconies of the upstairs salon, among the white chestnut flowers. There one afternoon we read the MS of another feminine autobiography—an English one this time—with wicked amusement.

"Now I have two women interfering with my papers," protested Lawrence. Things like that did not really annoy him, though.

At this time his illness made further inroads. He was more frail than he had been at Spotorno, and increasingly irritated by the people around him. When Pietro, the young Italian who did the errands with his donkey cart, came into the kitchen of the Mirenda while English friends were there, Lawrence said, "Here he comes, thinking he will give them a chance to see the interesting young peasant."

The two little boys of the Mirenda cottage he really did like. One had large grey eyes. "One sees those eyes like water among the Sicilians," he told me. I longed to see those olive-skinned people with water eyes.

"That boy has a voice like a thrush, Lorenzo," said Frieda delightedly.

"Yes, he has," replied Lawrence in his quick way.

Scandicci was like Paradise in the spring, the Mirenda a house of magic. I loved my big whitewashed room which Frieda had arranged with her wonderful taste. After I had gone back to England, she wrote, "Your ghost still lingers in your room." [183]

14 April 1927   Villa Mirenda, Scandicci, Florence, Italy

❪ When I got back [from the Etruscan tour] I corrected the proofs of the tiny book of essays, Mornings in Mexico. They are essays I like—and they have one basic theme. . . .

.   .   .   .

It is lovely spring here—the red tulips in the corn, and the last of the purple anemones. I have said we will keep this house another year—it doesn't cost much, so is no matter if one abandons it half-way. I feel for the time a sort of soreness, physical, mental, and spiritual, which is no doubt change of life, and I wish it would pass off. I think it is passing off. Meanwhile pazienza! But till it heals up, I don't feel like making much effort in any direction. It is easiest here.[184]

28 April 1927   Villa Mirenda, Scandicci, Florence, Italy

❪ I'm not painting—but wrote a story of the Resurrection . . . .[185]

29 April 1927   Villa Mirenda, Scandicci, Florence, Italy

❪ I've been thinking about Lady Chatterley's Lover and think I'll get him typed in London before long . . . .

It's sunny weather, full summer, and very lovely weather, not a cloudy day these last twenty days. We have come to the lying in the garden stage, and I go off into the woods to work, where the nightingales have a very gay time singing at me. They are inquisitive and come nearer to watch me turn a page. They seem to love to see the pages turned.[186]

3 May 1927   Villa Mirenda, Scandicci, Florence, Italy

❪ I'm supposed to be going to London at the end of the week for at least a month. They are producing David on May 22 and 23. I've promised to go . . . .

Frieda's daughter [Barbara] goes back this afternoon: so of course it's raining for the first time since she has been here. And we'll be going down with Pietro in the baroccino.

.   .   .   .

I wrote a story of the Resurrection, where Jesus gets up and feels very sick about everything, and can't stand the old crowd any more—so cuts out—and as he heals up, he begins to find what an astonishing place the phenomenal world is, far more marvellous than any salvation or heaven—and thanks his stars he needn't have a "mission" any more. It's called The Escaped Cock, from that toy in Volterra.[187]

13 May 1927   Villa Mirenda, Scandicci, Florence, Italy

⟮ I've been malarial and down in the mouth for about ten days, feeling as if I'd never rouse up again. O vita! O mors! I've put off going to London, in spite of a guilty conscience and lamenting letters—but I really wasn't fit.

.   .   .   .

We've had a week's rain, but now it's sunny. The country really is the most flowery I've ever known, and I get a certain consolation out of that. I found a very fine rare white orchid to-day, and a dark purple and yellow wild gladiolus, unknown to me.

    . . . I'm going to try and sit still till July. I did paint a bit of my Resurrection picture—un poco trist, ma mi pare forte. I got him as impersonal as a queer animal! But I can't finish it.[188]

19 May 1927   Villa Mirenda, Scandicci, Florence, Italy

⟮ It's full blazing summer here—some of the hay is already cut and cocked up—the garden fairly blazes with red roses—they smell so sweet—and the fireflies go winking round under the olives and among the flowers at night like lost souls—and by the pools toads croak and bark like dogs. It's really summer—peas and beans and asparagus in full swing, strawberries ripe, and the very first cherries. It's hard to believe it's only the middle of May. There are no gooseberries in Italy—and I like them so much! [189]

141

28 May 1927   Villa Mirenda, Scandicci, Florence, Italy

❨ *They produced David last week. I heard the audience was really rather enthusiastic, but the press notices are very unfavorable. It's those mangy
feeble reviewers; they haven't enough spunk to hear a cow bellow. . . .*[190]
*We had Osbert and Edith Sitwell here to tea the other day. They were very
nice.*[191]

Sir Osbert Sitwell

I only met Lawrence once, when he and his wife were living in Tuscany.
I was staying near by and they asked my sister and myself to have tea
with them; so we drove through the blossoming countryside—for it was
high May—to his farmhouse. This square, blue-painted house stood
among gentle hills, with rather Japanese pines springing from rocks and
brown earth in the distance, and with the foreground sprinkled with
bushes of cistus, flowering in huge yellow, white and purple paper roses.
A few cypresses, the most slender of exclamation-marks—not robust, as
they are further south—orchestrated the landscape. Lawrence opened
the door to us, and it was the first time I had ever realized what a fragile
and goatish little saint he was: a Pan and a Messiah; for in his flattish
face, with its hollow, wan cheeks, and rather red beard, was to be discerned a curious but happy mingling of satyr and ascetic; qualities, too,
which must really have belonged to him, since they are continually to
be found in his work. It was, certainly, a remarkable appearance. Unlike
the faces of most geniuses, it was the face of a genius.

He was extremely courteous, I remember, and prepared the tea
himself, doing all the work: which grieved one, for he looked so ill. The
rooms were charming, simple, Italian-farmhouse rooms, with none of
that broken, gold junk one so frequently encounters in the homes of
the English in Italy; a great relief. On the other hand, they were hung
with large canvases by Lawrence: pictures that he had just at that period
begun to paint. These, though many wise people have since praised
them, I thought then—and still think—crudely hideous and without any
merit save that he painted them and in so doing may have rid himself
of various complexes, which might otherwise have become yet more
firmly rooted in his books; useful, then, but not beautiful.

Two hours, two extremely delightful hours, we spent with them, and

142

then he saw us off at the door, standing with the evening sun pouring down on that extraordinary face: but Lawrence, I am sure, must always have been glad to be alone once more. I left Italy a day or two later, and never saw him again, so that, scarcely knowing him, I am left to fit those two hours and their impressions on to that solitary, delicate and ever so interesting figure. . . . Some of his books bore me profoundly; others seem of an inspired nature that no one can deny. Exasperating is too mild a word to describe some of his repetitive passages. His use of language can be nauseating: viz. his fondness for the words "winsome" and "dainty"; nevertheless, he is a prophet and a poet. And yet even now I think it is less in his novels that he is a great writer than in his miscellaneous books, his *Studies in Classic American Literature* for example, in that wonderful, unpleasant, and even unintelligent preface to *M. M. A Memoir of the Foreign Legion,* in certain of his poems, and, above all, in his short stories.[192]

1 June 1927 Villa Mirenda, Scandicci, Florence, Italy

⟨ *It is very hot here, too hot—to sit in the sun for breakfast, even before seven in the morning. One gets up early, then has a siesta in the afternoon. Frieda is still peacefully slumbering—I have wakened up early from mine—and not a soul is alive on all the poderi—peasants sleeping too. The Arno valley lies hot and still, in the sun, but there is a little breeze, so I shall go down and sit on the grass in a deck chair under the nespole tree. The nespole are just ripe—I shall climb up and get the first today—warm—they are good like that. The big cherries also are ripe—Giulia brings them in—very good. It seems to me always very pleasant when it is full summer and one ceases to bother about anything, goes drowsy, like an insect.*[193]

Capt. Angelo Ravagli

A few months later [after the Lawrences' departure from the Villa Bernarda, Spotorno, April, 1926] I was transferred from Savona to Porto Maurizio, on the Italian Riviera. A year or so later I was promoted to Captain and transferred to Gradisca, Province of Udine. One day I was called as a witness to the Military Tribunal of Florence, to testify at the court martial of a soldier who had abandoned his post. On that occasion I wired to the Lawrences at the Villa Mirenda (Florence) asking if I

143

could pay them a visit. They arranged to meet me at a restaurant in the city where they used to eat with Orioli and other English friends every time they went to the city. We had a very gay lunch and that was that.

For reasons I do not remember, the court martial was not held at that time, and a couple of weeks later I was again sent to Florence for the same purpose. This time, after I had attended to my duties, I went to see the Lawrences, by surprise, at the Villa Mirenda. That was the time Lawrence asked me to show him my military travel documents, and then made his remarks about the "must," as explained by Frieda in "*Not I, But the Wind . . . .*" [194] Thinking back, I am sure he suspected it was just an excuse on my part to go to see Frieda. It could have been, but there was no trick, my papers said "You must go." After that episode the visit was very cordial. I found Lawrence tired but quite well. He showed me all around the place, we had tea together, and we said good-bye. That was the last time I saw him. [195]

9 June 1927 Villa Mirenda, Scandicci, Florence, Italy

❪ *I began the Etruscan essays: have done Cerveteri and Tarquinia so far.* [196] *They interest me very much. . . . Perhaps Frieda and I will do a trip to Cortona, Arezzo, Chiusi, Orvieto, Perugia next week or the week after— before we go to Germany—so I could do enough essays—or sketches— sketches of Etruscan Places—for a book. That would keep us here till end of July—then we'd go to Germany . . . .* [197]

11 June 1927 Villa Mirenda, Scandicci, Florence, Italy

❪ *I am feeling better since the summer is here and one lounges about all day. We get up at six and sleep a bit in the afternoon. It's very quiet and nice. . . . I am writing my essays about the Etruscans, that I've talked about so much, and never got done— Let's hope I have luck with them this time—and painting a small picture—"Finding of Moses"—all ne-gresses. It's amazing, because I don't quite know how to do it.* [198]

13 June 1927 Villa Mirenda, Scandicci, Florence, Italy

❪ *We are going on Wed. [15 June 1927] for a couple of days with Maria [Huxley] to Forte dei Marmi—north of Pisa, not very far from here. . . .*

144

I am working at my Etruscan book—a piece of hopeless unpopularity, as far as I can see. . . .

. . . I dreamed I was made head of a school somewhere, I think, in Canada. I felt so queer about it: such a vivid dream—that I half wonder if it is my destiny! A job! —But I manage to make a living still.[199]

21 June 1927   Villa Mirenda, Scandicci, Florence, Italy

⟨ We've got it really fierce, except that there is a little cool wind from the mountains. I've never known the sun so strong for the time of the year. We too were away at the seaside about a hundred miles from here, not far, a place called Forte dei Marmi. Maria Huxley motored us down. . . . But I am not fond of the flat sandy shores in Italy. The sea is so dead and lifeless and enervating. The rocky shore is best on the Mediterranean. It isn't eight o'clock in the morning, but the sun is already fierce, and the cicalas—big grasshoppers—are singing away in the trees, till you'd think a dozen little people were working little sewing-machines outside. The flowers are over—cherries and strawberries finished—the apricots just coming. Everywhere the peasants are cutting the wheat. It's a fine crop this year, tall and handsome, and a lovely purply brown colour. All the family set out at about four in the morning, and they work one behind the other, women and men and girls, cutting away with the sickles, and laying the armfulls by: just as Ruth did in the Bible. Then they leave off about eleven, and eat, then sleep till four or five in the afternoon, then work again till eight or half-past, when the fireflies are drifting about. But when the corn is cut the fireflies go.

Sometimes I think it would be good to be healthy and limited like the peasants. But then it seems to me they have so little in their lives, one had better just put up with one's own bad health, and have one's own experiences. At least they are more vivid than anything these peasants know.[200]

25 June 1927   Villa Mirenda, Scandicci, Florence, Italy

⟨ Forte dei Marmi was beastly as a place: flat, dead sea, jellyfishy, and millions of villas. But the Huxleys were very nice with us, and they have such a nice little lad. We motored home via Lucca. It is much the best here, where we have space and cool and the woods to go in. We took supper out last night, and from the top of the hill watched the fireworks of San Giovanni day [24 June] in Florence—it was amusing—and man with his fireworks seems curiously silly, in the distance.[201] But up there was almost cold—too cool, anyhow.

.   .   .   .

I wrote my essay on Volterra . . . .[202]

Frieda Lawrence Ravagli

We had a very hot summer that year and we wanted to go to the mountains. One hot afternoon Lawrence had gathered peaches in the garden and came in with a basket full of wonderful fruit—he showed them to me—a very little while after he called from his room in a strange, gurgling voice; I ran and found him lying on his bed; he looked at me with shocked eyes while a slow stream of blood came from his mouth. "Be quiet, be still," I said. I held his head, but slowly and terribly the blood flowed from his mouth. I could do nothing but hold him and try to make him still and calm and send for Doctor Giglioli. He came, and anxious days and nights followed. In this great heat of July nursing was difficult—Giulia, all the peasants—helped in every possible way. The signor was so ill—Giulia got down to Scandicci at four in the morning and brought ice in sawdust in a big handkerchief, and milk, but this, even boiled straightaway, would be sour by midday. The Huxleys came to see him, Maria with a great bunch of fantastically beautiful lotus, and Giglioli every day, and [Pino] Orioli came and helped. But I nursed him alone night and day for six weeks, till he was strong enough to take the night train to the Tyrol.

This was another inroad his illness made. We both fought hard and won.[203]

11 July 1927   Villa Mirenda, Scandicci, Florence, Italy

❨ *Your son-in-law is a poor wretch and is in bed again with bronchitis and haemorrhage. We have the best doctor in Florence, Giglioli—he gives me coagulin but I am still in the corner. It is not dangerous, but . . . but . . . .*

. . . The doctor says my haemorrhage comes from sea-bathing that I took in Forte.

.   .   .   .

Friends are very good. Every day somebody comes from Florence. I've been only five days in bed and in a fortnight I can go away to that Wörtersee, but we don't know where it is yet . . . . The doctor says I ought to go into the pines—eight hundred metres, no higher.

If only once I were well again! [204]

13 July 1927   Villa Mirenda, Scandicci, Florence, Italy

❬ [*Dr. Trigant Burrow is*] *the most amusing person that writes to me. It is really funny—resistances—that we are all of us all the while existing by resisting—and that the p[sycho].-a[nalytic]. doctor and his patient only come to hugs in order to offer a perfect resistance to mother or father or Mrs. Grundy—sublimating one resistance into another resistance—each man his own nonpareil, and spending his life secretly or openly resisting the nonpareil pretensions of all other men—a very true picture of us all, poor dears. All bullies, all being bullied.* [205]

Dr. Trigant Burrow

[It] was never my good fortune to meet Lawrence. What contact we had was restricted to our correspondence and was inspired by a common ground of outlook plus a certain accord in the inner sense of values. [206]

. . . I think it was about the year 1920 that reprints of mine first went to Lawrence. I say 1920 because I incline to think that the most recent of the published papers that went to him at that time was "Psychoanalysis in Theory and in Life" which I read before the International Conference of Women Physicians in New York in the fall of 1919. [207] Whatever other studies went to him at that time were doubtless those that most nearly preceded this address given in 1919. [208]

I doubt if the papers (about seven) published prior to these and beginning in 1911 were sent to Lawrence, although it is possible that all my earlier writings up to 1919 were sent to him. I just cannot be sure as they did not go directly from me. As I recall the circumstance, a student of mine knew Lawrence either personally or through mutual friends. Anyhow he was acquainted with Lawrence's work and much impressed by it and asked if he might have reprints to send him. I no doubt referred him to my secretary and left to him the choice of what papers he might care to have. . . . [209]

"Psychoanalysis in Theory and in Life" was the last paper I wrote preceding the interruption of my practice in order to begin researches in group-analysis. There was an interval of four years before I resumed my writing. It began again with the publication of "Social Images versus Reality" . . . .[210] Thereafter, as I recall, writings of mine went to Lawrence rather regularly. The student to whom I just referred was Mr. Max Rosenberg of San Francisco, now deceased. I remember that he liked especially "Character and the Neuroses" . . . .[211]

The source, or the occasion, of Lawrence's acquaintance with physiology is something I would not know. I take for granted that the terms he used were acquired more from his knowledge of literature than of medicine.[212]

Having hounded Lawrence to death, his persecutors—that is, everybody—are all for making up to him now, so sure are we that his wracked and torn little organism with its feminine soul is too utterly spent and motionless now to make a single further sound in its defense. It is the sentence we shall long continue to pass upon the human anomaly we know as genius—it must burn to death within its own fires. Genius shall not yet be felt and shared as the creative expression of man indivisible and continuous throughout his species. Of course Lawrence had his part in the very persecutions that destroyed him. He was an equal element in the forces that isolated him, for all his outcries and protestations.[213]

Frieda Lawrence Ravagli

21 July 1927: *Villa Mirenda, Scandicci, Florence, Italy.* . . . We had a very nice American here with a wooden leg [Orrick Johns] . . . .[214]

Orrick Johns

On the way to Rimini I went through Forli where Mussolini was born, and where you heard casually at the *trattorìa* the scandalous story that the father of his youngest children was the station master of the town. These travels took me over the trails followed on foot and on horseback and donkey-back by Dante, Byron, Shelley and Keats—all homeless exiles, and the places echoed with their presence. At Volterra and Chiusi I had become interested in the Etruscans, a people whose arts, history and civilization had been completely obliterated by the jealous and militaristic Romans. I heard that D. H. Lawrence was in Italy. I knew that he had studied Etruscan civilization and I wanted to listen to him talk about it.

One day at Doney's, the fashionable place for tea on the Tornabuoni, I saw Lawrence lunching with Michael Arlen.[215] I wrote him asking if I might come to see him.

Lawrence and his wife were living in the Villa Merenda, at Scandicci, southwest of Florence. The Villa Merenda was, I should suppose, a characteristic residence for the Lawrences. It was in the real vineyard country. It was far away from the luxurious life of *pallazzi* and garden estates that surrounds the old city. It was the house of a *podere*, a farm, without conveniences, old. Lawrence and Frieda had the upper story. The farmer, his family, men and beasts, lived below. From the Lawrence terraces the hills of olive and vine could be seen, crowned with other old houses, and cypresses.

It was a rough walk of some two miles from the end of the tramway. Lawrence, ill as he was, went to town rarely. When he did, he walked this distance with his long easy stride. But he kept a boy, Pierino [Pietro?], a two-wheeled cart and a pony for guests. Some days were needed to arrange for meeting guests with the *barroccino* and the boy. Finally my letter arrived. Two visitors could crowd in with the boy on the level grade. All three got out going up.

On this, my first visit in the summer of 1927, Lawrence was doing little writing. He had been painting diligently for some months, and the paintings were to be seen on the walls of the Villa Merenda. These were the nucleus of an exhibition which made a stir in London a year or so later. I remember three quite well.

The Holy Family—a humble interior, a workman, his wife, his son. They are posed in stiff, uncomfortable attitudes. They are on show. They have a modern and rather a truculent look. The second, *Eve entering Paradise*, is a group of three figures, full of intense action. Adam, a powerful man, is struggling with an old angel who brandishes a sword. Adam is pushing the woman under the old man's arm. There is no doubt Lawrence used his wife and himself as models for these figures; but adroitly, perhaps even unconsciously, for the resemblance is so contrived as not to break the force and unity of the work. The third picture [*Boccaccio Story*] is that of a workman who has taken off his clothes in a field. He lies sprawled in the flowers and grass. A procession of shy

149

nuns veers by, startled at the sight. It was all strong coloring, big draw-ing. But I remember, in contrast to the broad heavy strokes, how deli-cately the wild flowers were done in this last picture.

I asked him if these were his first paintings. "Oh no, I used to do it years ago," he said. He deprecated them, but he had had a great time. He asked whether we thought a New York exhibition possible.

Lawrence made me think at one moment of a stripling, at the next of a patriarch. His ideas drove him to utterance—I thought, often against his will. At times his speech was as low pitched and rhythmical as a purr. At the end of a speech there was a little whinny . . . , a smiling peering up under the thick red eyebrows. At other times he spoke with abrupt-ness, with authority.

I had not been told he was a formidable host, but somehow I ex-pected it. I found him gracious, attentive, considerate. He was con-cerned about his wife's old tea things, about the bread, the jam, the flies, the temperature of the water.

Lawrence loved the Italian, spoke it with a slow relish. His tribute to Italy are his translations of Giovanni Verga, one of her greatest nat-uralistic writers.

Finally, he reached the subject of the Etruscan people. He had made visits to Volterra and Chiusi to see the tombs and pottery. The seated, smiling figures on Etruscan tombs especially had aroused his psycho-logical penetration. The man on the tomb is usually holding a cup with a small sphere in its center. This sphere, Lawrence said, was the life principle of the universe. He talked about Taos too, and his Indian friends. "We both worked too hard there," said Frieda. "We did all the heavy chores. But Lawrence would like to go back." They were indignant at the governmental stupidity which packed him out of America at the end of six months. It was that which kept him from returning to his own property in New Mexico. He had told us when we left that he was be-ginning a new book. His publisher would never print it. When I re-turned, eight months later, to the Villa at Scandicci, this book was fin-ished. It was *Lady Chatterley's Lover*. This was his first announcement, together with the information that publishers would have no hand in it. He was going to publish the book himself, through Orioli, who kept the little book-shop on the Arno, looking out on the Ponte Santa Trinità[.] Norman Douglas was privately printing a new novel, *In the Beginning*, at Orioli's. It seemed a good scheme to Lawrence. The volume would be subscribed for at two guineas. He was disgusted with the book busi-ness in England and America. He had done what he wanted to do in this book, full measure and running over. The public could make of it what it would.

At that second visit, Lawrence had looked like a very sick man. His long body was emaciated. Before and after that August [July] of 1927, if I remember rightly, he had rushed off to Switzerland as a result of severe hemorrhages.[216] In Florence the year afterward, and in Capri the spring of 1929, I heard still more ominous reports from his friends. He could not repose. There was little hope of his life.

He lived to achieve the novel he was contemplating, but it brought upon him the full venom of the moral guardians of two continents—and the consequent avarice of pirates.

I remember as far back as 1910 [*sic*] we had admired Lawrence's *Sons and Lovers*. Zoë Akins [217] had written to him and was the proud owner of a reply—a letter that expressed the naïve, modest hopes of an ambitious young author, just married and pleased over a first success. I had found his writings on Italy indispensable to the traveller, especially *Sea and Sardinia*, in which the bitter acid of his observation ate through the deceptive plumage of romance in the Italian character. His descriptions —of Etna, for example, or Italian wild flowers—were incomparable. There was no doubt that Lawrence had translated and crystallized much of the young thought of a decade. But a great deal of Lawrence's work I had not liked at all. Lawrence the psychologist, especially of women and sex, or the mystic of plumed serpents and Indians, left me cold— which may be a confession of incompleteness. His short stories seemed to me perfect—objective and relentless studies of contemporary character. I had been particularly interested in the political implications of *Kangaroo*, which reveals how closely Lawrence came to being involved in an Australian fascist movement. He was allured certainly by the theory, but his flinty individualism tore him away violently from the grip of "movements."

All of these reflections suggested questions I wanted to put to Lawrence, but I had to refrain from doing so. I had been warned by friends that the state of his health made him irascible, and it was dangerous to himself to involve him in anything like a controversy. So in reality he talked little during either of my two visits. Frieda wrote to Mabel Dodge Luhan that I had been a refreshing novelty to them, "a modest American." [218] I do remember one thing: a subtly malicious, thoroughgoing satire by Lawrence on the subject of an English novelist just then becoming popular in America. I had met the novelist, and found him stuffy to the point of tears, and I enjoyed the attack.[219]

25? July 1927   Villa Mirenda, Scandicci, Florence, Italy

❪ I am better—getting up again, and going about the house—but feeling feeble. I went downstairs and out of doors a few yards yesterday—but it's too hot to go out till sundown. However, this day week [1 August 1927] —or tomorrow week—I hope we can leave for Villach. I shall feel better a little higher. It's lovely weather here, sunny, and not too hot at all if one keeps quiet. But it's much too hot to walk in the sun. If I was well, I should enjoy it. Frieda for the first time really likes the heat. But now I feel I should like to see the world green, and hear the waters running: and to taste good northern food.[220]

31 July 1927   Villa Mirenda, Scandicci, Florence, Italy

❪ I am up and creeping around—feeling limp—but better. I had the best doctor in Florence—Prof. Giglioli—head of the Medical Profession for Tuscany. It's chronic bronchial congestion—and it brought on a series of bronchial hemorrhages this time. I've had little ones before. It would be serious if they didn't stop, he says: but they do stop: so it's nothing to worry about—only one must lie in bed when they come on—and always be a bit careful—not take sea-baths, as I did at Forte. I think he's about right. He says we're to go to the mountains so we're leaving for Austria —D.V.—Thursday night [4 August 1927]. I can get into a sleeper in Florence, and stay in till Villach, so I should be all right. . . . These hemorrhages are rather shattering—but perhaps they take some bad blood out of the system. The doctor says no good going in a sanatorium, if I will only lie down when I don't feel well—and not work. Which I shall really try to do.—I don't really feel bad.[221]

AUSTRIA AND GERMANY

8 August 1927   Hotel Fischer, Villach, Kärnten, Austria

❪ It's so nice to be out of that hot Italy, and in the mountains where the air is cool. I can imagine nothing better than a really cool bed after one that burned when you lay in it, and really fresh mountain water after that tepid Italian stuff. Of course it was a specially hot summer, even for

Tuscany—and quite exceptionally dry, no rain for three months. I wouldn't have minded if I'd been well, but being seedy, how I hated it.

I feel much better already here, and can take little walks into the country. This is a small old-fashioned town, with a nice full swift river, the Drave, and trees along the river, and seats where one can sit and watch the people and the swallows, and feel like an old veteran. There are lots of summer visitors passing all the time to the lakes and mountains —practically all Viennese. They wear any kind of clothes—the men the short Tyrolese leather trousers and bare legs. They are big strapping people —rather vague now—gone indifferent to all the woes. The country itself is dirt-poor—the shops are pathetic—all the rubbishy stuff nobody else will buy. Nearly all the banks closed for good—and the ordinary people having very little money. But they don't seem to care. They aren't very honest, they don't give you your change—that kind of thing: but even that they do so vaguely, they don't really care. There is no sense of control at all—most queer, after the bossiness of Fascist Italy. And the whole thing drifts along with no trouble, everybody really very nice, very good-mannered—pleasant. It's a great rest after Italy, and I hope I shall soon feel fit for long walks. I can only go small ways yet—. We shall stay on in this inn in town, I think, it is so amusing, and one can go excursions.[222]

11 August 1927   Hotel Fischer, Villach, Kärnten, Austria

([Frieda's junger sister [Nusch] is here with her husband,[223] staying on the Ossiachersee about six miles away. F. has just gone there swimming —it's her birthday—I shall go out to lunch. I can't swim, or bathe—or even walk very far. Makes me so cross. But it is pleasant here, in this big Gasthaus in the little town—all the Tyroler mountain people going through —and the food is really good. Also I like Villach—little old German place—and the nice full river—the Drav—that goes so quick and silent.

I think we shall stay till the 24th—then move north—we're supposed to spend September in Bavaria.[224]

17 August 1927   Hotel Fischer, Villach, Kärnten, Austria

([We stayed on here in the little town, instead of going out—about 6 miles—to the lake, because the hotel there is so hotelly. But F's sister [Nusch] and husband insist we ought to join them there. It's very nice,

153

a clear little green lake with steep pine-covered sides and little pleasant clearings—everything very green and fresh, still forget-me-nots and hare-bells—and blueberries. I find it very refreshing to come north, after a year in Italy. And the Austrians are amusing, so big and healthy and happy-go-lucky—they lie about with very small bathing-drawers, by the lake, and it's perfectly amazing, what huge great limbs they've got. They're like sea-lions, so inert and prostrate. Nobody has much money, and the poor people want to make a revolution every five minutes—but I can't see what there is to revolute against. It's all somehow beside the point—and like being asleep. . . .

I am better, but not bouncing, and the cough is a nuisance, and I wish I could get a new breathing apparatus. But it's no good grumbling.[225]

25 August 1927   Hotel Fischer, Villach, Kärnten, Austria

⟦ We've been here three weeks—me convalescing, and not very pleased with myself. . . . We're going next week to a house of my sister-in-laws [Else's] in Bavaria, to stay a month, as arranged . . . .

I think still with hankering of the ranch in the early spring—If I can, we shall come. A change of continent would do me good. Except that the altitude, for bronchials, is what the doctor calls a bleeding altitude. But who knows—I was so well again there that last summer.[226]

4 September 1927   Villa Jaffe, Irschenhausen, Bavaria, Germany

⟦ We came here on Wed. evening [31 August 1927]—met Else in Munich —it is just the same, the little wooden house in a corner of the forest, so still and pleasant.[227] I like it here, and really feel much better. . . . Autumn here, but lovely.[228]

7 September 1927   Villa Jaffe, Irschenhausen, Bavaria, Germany

⟦ I've been here a week now—it's awfully nice, the little wooden house and the forest behind, the big open country in front with the mountains. The weather is lovely, sunny all day, and the moon at night. I feel it suits me here. I drink goat's milk, and we walk through the woods—all beech and fir trees. There are lots of deer in winter and spring, but at this season

*they draw away to the more remote places. We've got a good servant:
the one we knew in the past. . . .*

*Germany is much more cheerful than Austria—much more flourishing.
In fact it seems tremendously alive and busy. Austria was too poor—too
helpless, one couldn't stand it long. . . . There's a new law that takes
20 per cent. tax on all royalties of persons living abroad—it came into
force in July last—so there's a slice off one's not very grand earnings. But
we're lucky to have got off taxes so long.*[229]

17 September 1927   Villa Jaffe, Irschenhausen, Bavaria, Germany

⟨[*The "Jugend" man [Franz Schoenberner] came—a nice little soul after
all—but they'll do him in—he'll never stand the modern mill. . . .
A rainy morning and a cold wind.*

.   .   .   .

*The "Jugend" man wants only a short-short story—four Schreibmaschine-
seiten: that's about two thousand words. No stories are as short as that
—usually five thousand. I must try and hunt something up.*[230]

Franz Schoenberner

[Among] my collaborators [on the staff of *Jugend,* the Munich literary-
artistic magazine of which I was editor for a time, were many] who
never fell for the Nazi myth, but stayed in Germany all the same. They
hoped to weather the storm, or perhaps even to establish some sort of
intellectual opposition, if only in the form of passive resistance. Some of
them were hampered by personal circumstances or even by the feeling
that their physical and moral forces were simply not sufficient for the
jump-in-the-dark of exile which most likely would mean starvation. And
it was indeed more difficult for writers than for designers or painters,
whose medium of expression is not bound to the limits of language. . . .

[What], for example, would my old friend August Wisbeck have done
in exile? He was some years older than I, a former cavalry officer who
during the war had become a major in the Turkish Army. After some
excursions in the picturesque world of the early movies, he had settled
down in Munich with his much-too-small pension in order to follow his
real vocation, that of becoming a *Schwabinger,* a bohemian of the most

155

delightful type. He had a marvelous sense of grotesque humor and was a wonderful story-teller, especially over a bottle of wine, of which he consumed more than was good for his state of health, physical and economic. Only when driven by a bitter need for money could he bring himself to writing down his stories, which were in general promptly printed by *Jugend* or some other magazine.

.   .   .   .

Our collaboration was carried over from *Jugend* to *Simplicissimus*, and provided for him finally a sort of regular income which he badly needed. Without being actively interested in politics, he heartily detested the Nazis and all their works. I don't know how he managed to live in the atmosphere of the Third Reich. But his marvelous vitality, overtaxed for so many decades, had already begun to decline. Not long before I left [1933], he had suffered a nervous breakdown from which he recovered slowly. He had not the slightest chance of making a living in a foreign country, and there was a son whom he dearly loved; a young boy of twenty living with his mother, who for understandable reasons had divorced after two years of marriage the too attractive August Wisbeck—but had remained on good and friendly terms with him. He did not see any other way out but to stay on, keeping aloof from the whole Nazi business. But it was too much for him. Some years later, in France, I received the news of his death. Only recently I learned how he had died. It seems that he developed a bad case of persecution complex—which perhaps was not only a mania but justified by real facts. For to the Nazis even the opposition of silence was a crime, and I doubt whether he could always keep silent. He finally had to be transferred to an asylum, the ultimate refuge of a reasonable and decent man in a world of madness. But he chose a refuge even more secure; he committed suicide.

It is strange to remember and to report that the perhaps somewhat flippant, but never too spicy jokes of my poor old friend Wisbeck happened to shock and even to frighten one of the most daring and most original authors of modern literature, the same D. H. Lawrence whom English prudishness stupidly enough branded as a pornographer.

Years before making his personal acquaintance I had become deeply interested in his novel, *The Rainbow*, which first introduced to Germany his later completely translated work. The person who gave me the book and told me some interesting details about the author was his sister-in-law, married to the socialist economist Professor Jaffé, who during the revolution was for some time Minister of Finance.

Mrs. Jaffé as well as her sister Frieda Lawrence must have been somewhat of a headache for their father, the old Baron von Richthofen; he was still a commanding general in the old Imperial Army when Frieda, married to an English university professor, one day simply left her respectable home and her five [three] beloved children in order to go away with a sort of literary tramp, the son of a Lancashire [Nottinghamshire] miner, some years younger than she and without a penny of regular income. In comparison even a socialist Minister must have appeared as a sort of minor evil. But evidently the two daughters had transformed the traditional military virtues of their old soldiers' family into the higher form of moral and civic courage. While Frieda Lawrence traveled around the world with her husband, who slowly began to reach fame and even to earn some money, Mrs. Jaffé lived in the liberal and intellectual circles of Munich. She had done some translating from the English for me when I was editor of *Auslandspost*. I had written some reviews about Lawrence, and so it was quite natural that she arranged a personal meeting when in the fall of 1927 he came to spend some weeks in her little country house in Irschenhausen in the Isar valley near Munich.

Even now after seventeen years my first impression of his strange and fascinating personality is still as fresh and lively as if it had been yesterday that we had tea together. It was the first time I had shared the afternoon of a faun, a sick faun who out of sheer friendliness had left his mysterious woods, adapting himself for some hours in manner and appearance to the usual human pattern; but one felt him likely to disappear at any moment with a light caper over the tea table and through the window, to return to the company of other goat-footed half gods waiting for him behind the next bushes.

No doubt he was gravely ill. Tuberculosis, the miner's illness, had emaciated his tall bony body and his stooped shoulders. It looked as if his suit was much too large for him. But the pale triangular face with the large front and the little reddish goatee was illuminated by a spiritual vitality which triumphantly denied all physical decay. The look of his eyes from deep sockets under bushy brows had the strange intensity with which an animal or some deity of nature might gaze at the curious world of human beings—half astonished and half amused, but at any rate entirely detached, separated by an unbridgeable distance, safe from any human entanglement which could endanger his unlimited inner freedom.

Only a few people whom I have met have given me this feeling of their living in a sphere of pure essentiality where everything and everyone assumes a new and higher substance. No conventional word or thought can thrive in such an atmosphere. There will be an immediate personal contact, or no approach to each other at all; a simple and direct human exchange, or a retreat into taciturnity. It was as if I had known him for many years—and I had indeed, in a certain sense, since I knew his books. But he too seemed to know me at first sight and to feel that I was not a stranger but rather a member of the great literary family to which we both belonged.

His soft, high voice carefully and a bit hesitatingly formed the German language which he had learned and sometimes used with members of his wife's family. He knew that I had some reading knowledge of English, but could not speak or understand it. He succeeded amazingly well in expressing himself in German in a very personal and even picturesque way. The German letters to his mother-in-law, for example, posthumously published by Frieda Lawrence, have a special charm. I am glad to have among his letters to me also some samples of this special Lawrence German.

We discussed extensively books and authors, but in contrast to most writers he did not speak about the circulation figures of his books or about the contracts with his publishers. He hardly seemed to know what royalties he received, and this sovereign disregard for money encouraged me to ask him if he would give me a short story for *Jugend;* though, of course, I could not compete with the big royalties which, for example, the Ullstein papers were able to offer.[231] In general I could not afford "great names," not even German great names, who were very anxious not to sell themselves under price. But Lawrence immediately promised to look for a story which—that was the only difficulty—would be short enough for my limited space.

When I sent him some copies of *Jugend,* he answered with a letter which seems to me a real contribution to the better understanding of his art and his person. This is what he wrote:

> Many thanks for the *Jugends,* which came safely yesterday. I've looked at them all the evening—but I haven't read the stories yet, only the jokes. Some of them are very good—and the whole thing is alive—but the curious sexual cynicism is a bit alarming, because it's just how the world is. But whatever will be the end of it, if there is nothing to counterbalance it? I tell you, when I've looked through ten *Jugends,* I feel thoroughly frightened.

The rest of the letter only refers to the date of our next meeting when I wanted him to see Hans Carossa, not only the poet but also the doctor.[232] Carossa was indeed one of the best specialists in the treatment of tuberculosis, and I had the same feeling which Lawrence expressed by writing "If a poet who is a doctor can't tell me what to do with myself, then who can?"

I was not in the least astonished by Lawrence's reaction to the harmless jokes of my friend Wisbeck, to which nobody else ever objected, not even the U.S. Postmaster General who strongly disapproves of Vargas girls. But I understood perfectly that Lawrence was in fact a puritan in reverse. What was called his "sexual obsession" was a kind of religious obsession. Sex for him was the sacred symbol of life, and any sort of humorous treatment of this topic seemed to him really blasphemous. He could celebrate the cult of Priapus with all the solemnity of a high priest. And deeply provoked by Anglo-Saxon hypocrisy in matters of sex, he could become a fanatical zealot in preaching his new gospel of sex, which was for him the gospel of salvation.

He was so terribly serious about it that sometimes, as for example in *Lady Chatterley,* his holy earnestness produces the opposite effect—of involuntary comicality. But he was as intransigent as the stoutest puritan in respect to naughty jokes, not because sex was impure and an invention of the devil, but on the contrary because it was the pure and holy and divine essence of life. It was nothing to joke at or to smile at. What he wrote to me in another letter is typical; he wrote this time in German:

Ich lese die *Jugend*—es amüsiert mich, und ich finde es ein bischen 'shocking.' Die Hauptsache ist, dass es lebt. Ich bin selber etwas altmodisch, und kann nie Bubiköfe liebhaben. Meine Erziehung hat sicher noch ein paar Schritten zu machen.

(I am reading *Jugend*—it amuses me and I find it a bit 'shocking.' The main thing is, it is alive. I am myself a bit old-fashioned and never can like bobbed heads. My education certainly has yet to advance some steps.)

Amusingly enough, he used the same word "shocking," although in the ironical and almost accusatory sense, when later, in April, 1928, he wrote me from Florence about his "last novel," *Lady Chatterley:*

Es ist zu shocking—shocking für die Englische Verleger; also gebe ich es selber aus. Es wird jetzt gedruckt, in einer kleinen Buchdruckerei in Florenz wo kein Mensch versteht ein Wort Englisch. Das ist sehr gut, niemand kann shocked verden.

(It is too shocking—shocking for the English publishers; so I publish it myself. It is now being printed in a small printing house in Florence where nobody understands one word of English. That is very well, nobody can be shocked.)

I saw Lawrence two or three times more in the fall of 1927, and I remember especially the day when Hans Carossa went with me to Irschenhausen in order to examine Lawrence's lungs. I suppose deep in himself Lawrence knew that he was lost, but his miraculous inner vitality could never accept this idea of death. He eagerly listened to Carossa's suggestions of further treatment, but I felt that the tone of quiet confidence in Carossa's voice was somehow forced. Lawrence himself seemed rather encouraged. Without the slightest trace of weariness he continued to tell us about his farm in New Mexico, about the Indians, the horses and all sorts of animals which he seemed to know by the mysterious instinct of some inner rapport. No zoologist, I suppose, has ever known as much about animals as the poet who wrote stories like "The Fox" or *St. Mawr.*

When we left finally, I asked Carossa, while walking to the station, what he really had found. He hesitated a moment before he said, "An average man with those lungs would have died long ago. But with a real artist no normal prognosis is ever sure. There are other forces involved. Maybe Lawrence can live two or even three years more. But no medical treatment can really save him."

"The poet who was a doctor" proved to be cruelly right. Lawrence died in March of 1930, only 45 years old. I shall always bitterly regret that I missed the opportunity to see Lawrence more often. He had offered me his house, the Villa Scandicci [Villa Mirenda] in Florence, whenever I wanted to come; but I was tied up with my editorial work. The next year he did not return, as he had planned, to the little house in Irschenhausen, but he sometimes wrote me a few lines, asking my technical advice for reproductions of his paintings or telling me that he had finally found a story short enough for *Jugend,* the lovely little story about the dog Rixi.[233]

D. H. Lawrence was one of the most extraordinary and fascinating personalities I have ever met, entirely free from social conventions, but also free from the personal pretensions and vanities which often disfigure the character of minor or even major artists. Writing and occasionally painting were for him not less natural expressions of himself than building an aqueduct or a stove, fencing a cattle range, milking a cow or whatever life might require. All these were only different expressions of his deep veneration for life.

He, too, belonged to the anti-rationalists, and I was deeply aware that his basic ideas were diametrically opposed to my world of thought. His

D. H. Lawrence, Florence, 1 9 2 8.

From a photograph taken by Robert H. Davis.
Reproduced by courtesy of the Davart Company, New York.

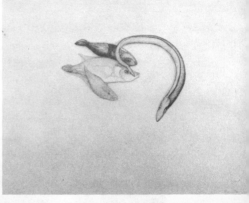

Mediterranean Fishes, by Brewster Ghiselin. See his poem "The Nets." Photographed from the original in the possession of Mr. Ghiselin.

Brewster Ghiselin, Autumn, 1928. Fro photograph in the possession of Mr. Ghiselin.

Rolf Gardiner, May, 1928. From a painting on wood by Maxwell Armfield, now in the possession of Sir Alan and Lady Gardiner of Court Place, Iffley, Oxford.

last books, especially the strange and profound novel *The Plumed Serpent*, came dangerously near to that kind of "myth" which in a much cheaper edition was so eagerly exploited by the Nazi prophets. But in contrast to [Knut] Hamsun [234] and his like, Lawrence was not a nihilist and defeatist, a bitter, disappointed detractor of life and mankind. He had faith and flame, an immeasurable spiritual passion, an ardent belief in life and man and all the great forces of nature, of which he felt himself a part.[235]

Like his father and his forebears, working underground in the coal mines of Lancashire, he had learned as an artist to drive his pits deep in the dark region of the subconscious.[236] He easily handled the psychological instruments provided by Freud's revolutionary findings. But he did not mind using dynamite in order to remove too solid a mass of petrified prejudice and moral cant. In the literary world of London, not yet used to the Blitz or to rocket bombs, these detonations and literary eruptions first evoked, quite comprehensibly, the feelings of a minor earthquake. But perhaps the time is not so far away when D. H. Lawrence's works, like those of the once so terribly scandalous Byron, will be included in the regular curriculum of English public schools; which would be good. Because, aside from his artistic values and his somewhat dubious philosophy, D. H. Lawrence always will remain an outstanding example of the highest moral courage, of the purest sincerity and of untrammeled inner freedom.

Gravely ill, fighting for many years a gallant but losing battle against death, he kept his work and his life free from morbidity, from any sort of unhealthy resentment. He never accepted defeat. He proved to be *fort comme la mort*, strong as death—or even strong as life. He lived and he died as a real man. I shall always be grateful to the fate which brought me to know him, and proud and happy that he was among the writers of *Jugend*.[237]

17 September 1927   Villa Jaffe, Irschenhausen, Bavaria, Germany

❴ Myself, I am glad to be here, in this little wooden house with the forest round the back, and in front the wide open valley going to the blue mountains. I like the dark fir-trees, and the clearings where we see the red deer. I like the deep, matted wet grass where the harebells are now so dark blue, and the chicory heavenly. I love above all the stillness of innumerable trees that are none the less silently growing, and pressing themselves on the air so softly yet so indomitably. I am glad not to be in Italy for a while. I don't mind if it rains some days, and is dark. I like it. I don't mind that it is rather cold, I like it. I find Italy has almost withered me. Here something softens out again.

I don't do much except take walks in the forest, and translate Verga's Cavalleria Rusticana and play patience. I am glad when I don't work—I have worked too much.

Tonight Frieda's daughter Barbara is coming, but only for a few days. We shall stay here, I think at least till 1st Oct., perhaps longer, if it doesn't turn too cold. Then we must go to Baden-Baden for two weeks, so we shan't be home at the earliest till middle October, probably later.[238]

Barbara Weekley Barr

The following summer (1927) I went to stay in Cologne with the old German professor who had first introduced my father to Frieda. He had a collection of photographs of her as a young woman.

At that time, Frieda and Lawrence were staying at my aunt Else's house at Irschenhausen, in Bavaria. In September I went to pay them a three-day visit.

The delightful wooden house they were staying at was a Grimm's fairy tale place. When one walked in the forest, roebuck leapt across the path.

Frieda's younger sister, Nusch, stayed with them that summer. She was the only woman whom I ever heard Lawrence describe as "desirable."

She had then just married for the second time. Her choice was a bank manager. Quite a nice man, but Lawrence was afraid she had made a mistake in becoming respectable.

"She is a bit sad inside, poor Nusch," he said. "She belongs really to the demi-monde, and should have stayed there. She has that gift for making a man feel he counts, and *is* a man. She is a good sport, ready to fall in with people's plans, and enjoy herself." She flirted with Lawrence, and he thought her fun.

When I read *Women in Love,* I thought that she was rather like Gudrun.

As a young woman, Nusch had visited England, where she had been disappointed to find that good manners prevented people staring at her remarkable good looks. "When I come into the restaurant nobody *looks* at me!" she had exclaimed, mortified. "I might just as well be the waiter!"

When his three daughters grew up, my German grandfather expressed

162

the hope that none of them would marry a Jew, an Englishman, or a gambler. (He had been a gambler himself.) To his disgust, these were just what they did marry.

Else, the eldest Richthofen daughter, was a very gifted woman—one of the very few people who could meet Lawrence on his own intellectual level. She translated some of his work into German.[239]

She married Edgar Jaffe, who was finance minister for Bavaria under the Stresemann Government. The strain brought on a breakdown, and he went into a nursing home.

Frieda went to see him there a little while before he died. From a neat, elegant man he had become a dishevelled wreck.

"You should not have come to see me, Frieda," he said. "Do you know I have not washed for three weeks?"

"Oh, Edgar, you have washed so much!" cried Frieda.

Just before I went to Germany that summer, a friend of ours had been killed in a reckless accident. Lawrence and Frieda had met the young man and some of his family in London. Frieda had really loved him.

"Poor chap," Lawrence had written to me. "It was what he really wanted, I suppose. That's the worst of it . . . life ought to be good enough. But he had that kind of life and sweetness the world doesn't want any more."

"If Barby had cared about him it might have been different," he said to Frieda.

He wrote a sympathetic letter to the mother.[240]

25? September 1927   *Villa Jaffe, Irschenhausen, Bavaria, Germany*

⟨ *This is the horridest day of all, after tea and still pouring with rain: and I would like to go out! If only I had strong boots and a rain-proof. I would of course if we were staying. —Yesterday was lovely and sunny till teatime.*

This weekend we are alone . . . . I've promised to go to Schoenberner's, and to meet Hans Carossa there. I heard from England that a man who writes plays and thinks I am the greatest living novelist (quote) and who lives in Tegernsee, may come and see me: Max Mohr . . . .

.   .   .   .

I suppose we shall stay here till Monday week [3 October 1927] . . . . I don't feel a bit anxious to return to Italy—but I think Frieda does. I don't mind, for the time being, if it rains and is dark. . . . We have gathered the apples—so bright and red—and the last two hazel-nuts. I'm afraid either squirrels or children had fetched the others. The woods are simply populated with mushrooms, all sorts, in weird camps everywhere —really like strange inhabitants come in. We eat the little yellow ones, and keep picking Steinpilze and throwing them away again. The cows come every afternoon on to our grass, with a terrific tintinnabulation, like a host of tinkling Sundays. There is a Jersey who is pining to come to tea in the porch—and a white calf that suddenly goes round the moon. Frieda reads Goethe, and I play patience—today I have finished my "Cavalleria Rusticana" translation: now I've only to do the introduction . . . .

It's nightfall—I think I shall go out, spite of rain, for a few minutes.[241]

28? September 1927   Villa Jaffe, Irschenhausen, Bavaria, Germany

〖 It has turned much colder tonight—we've both had colds. Sunday was a horror of darkness and rain but we went out and got wet. But we are better. . . . Barby is already in London. I can hardly believe she has been here. . . .

The beeches begin to turn yellow and today we gathered some violets under the balcony—they smell sweet like spring and the flowers are still wonderful. . . . Max Mohr, the dramatist, is to come from Tegernsee.[242]

7 October 1927   Hotel Eden, Baden-Baden, Germany

〖 Yes, we saw Hans Carossa, a nice man, mild like mashed potatoes. He listened to my lung passages, he could not hear my lungs, thinks they must be healed, only the bronchi, and doctors are not interested in bronchi. But he says not to take more inhalations with hot air: it might bring the haemorrhage back. The journey [from Irschenhausen, 4 October 1927] was vile, many people, much dust, and I had a cold. But it is better. We are very grand here, two rooms, a bath, and the food very good.

Yesterday it was goose, Michaelmas goose; I can eat better but they bring so much, wagonloads of potatoes, and cutlets big as carpets, and how the people feed! It takes my shy appetite away a bit.

.   .   .   .

Max Mohr came in a car from Tegernsee, where he has a pleasant house —with wife and child—a man thirty-six years old or so.

He wants to be a child of nature but we were disappointed in the nature. But he is good and interesting, but a last man who has arrived at the last end of the road, who can no longer go ahead in the wilderness nor take a step into the unknown. So he is very unhappy, is a doctor, prisoner of war in England . . . .

. . . We stay till the seventeenth. We are very fortunate here, but the world seems dark to me again. That scares me and I want to go south.[243]

10 October 1927   Hotel Eden, Baden-Baden, Germany

❨ Here my manhood . . . patiently listens to Konzerten im Kurgarten, goes to tea in the Waldkaffee with the beloved women, and in the morning sits in a white coat and hood, in a vaporous room with other figures vaguely seen through the mists in more white mantles and hoods . . . . It is my one desire, to get well as soon as possible—but really well. I am sick of books and all things literary . . . .

Really, in Baden one ought to be at least 75 years old, and at least an Excellenz, at the very least a Generalchen. This place is such a back number, such a chapter in faded history, one hardly dares exist at all. I efface every possible bit of my manhood, and go around as much as possible like a paper silhouette of myself.

The chief monument at the moment is a white Hindenburg bust, marvellous, standing among all the Wurst and Ripple in the sausage shop . . . .

We hope to leave next Monday, 17th, for Italy. The address there is Villa Mirenda, Scandicci, Florenz.[244]

SCANDICCI, FLORENCE, ITALY

20? October 1927   Villa Mirenda, Scandicci, Florence, Italy

❨ We had a good journey, few people, no difficulties, and I was not very tired. I never saw Switzerland so lovely: a still grey autumn day, grass so strangely green, nearly like fire; and then the fruit trees, all delicate flames, the cherry trees absolutely red like cherries, apple trees and pear trees yellow red scarlet and still as flowers: really like a fairyland. It has rained in Italy. But today there is gentle sun and clouds, warm air and a great stillness. The neighbours were at the station with the car, all so friendly. And here the peasants all ranged on the "aia"—Giulia radiant, she is getting quite pretty; she had the fires ready and hot water and we are here. But the house seemed foreign to me, naked and empty, and a bit uncanny, as if I had never known it, but Frieda is happy.

I don't know what it is with me, I don't feel at home in Italy, this time. . . . My pictures please me—and I listen, listen to the stillness.[245]

21 October 1927   Villa Mirenda, Scandicci, Florence, Italy

⟨ I don't feel a bit like work: yet shall have to tackle a few things. Secker wants to do my collected poems: that means typing them out and arranging and doing: then he's bringing out a vol. of short stories in January:[246] and then I ought to finish the Etruscan Essays, of which I've done just half. But I feel terribly indifferent to it all, whether it's done or not. . . . Then that resurrection story The Escaped Cock, suggested by a toy at Volterra at Easter—that the American Forum had bought—a weird place for such a story. I don't know which month they'll do it.[247] They did my Nightingale sketch in Sept. [1927] [248] and seem to have got off with it very well. As for the novel, Lady Chatterley's Lover, I'm keeping it under lock and key: I won't publish it, at least now.

I might begin a painting of Adam and Eve pelting the old Lord-God with apples, and driving him out of paradise—but I've got no canvas, and shall never go to Florence—and I don't care either.

So there's David sitting on his thumbs.[249]

6 November 1927   Villa Mirenda, Scandicci, Florence, Italy

⟨ This is already another Sunday, and the third that we are here. The weather is always like summer, so warm and clear, the windows are open all day and we don't dream of having a fire: the evenings also are quite warm. The roses are in bloom, but there are few flowers, all is still too dry, little water even in the wells. . . .

. . . Frieda has a piano again, now she wants to play Handel, the "Messiah," but she hasn't arrived at the Alleluia! I am painting a picture, not very big, of a tiger who springs on a man: such a grinning tiger.[250]

8 November 1927   Villa Mirenda, Scandicci, Florence, Italy

⟨ We've got this flat till next May, but I'm sure I doubt if we'll stay half that time in it. I am somehow bored by Italy, and when a place goes *against my grain I'm never well in it. I do really think one is heaps better off in New Mexico—sometimes I pine for it. . . .*

.   .   .   .

I did a little picture of a jaguar jumping on a man—but am not happy for working. It was a long strip of canvas left over, and cut on the skew. Now I can't afford to cut it down, to get it squared. Could I stick or sew a bit on the top edge? Otherwise I'll have to cut my jaguar's ears off.[251]

14 November 1927   Villa Mirenda, Scandicci, Florence, Italy

⟪ *It has rained a bit here, but is sunny again—we're just going out for a walk—the country is full of colour, vines yellow, olives blue, pines very green. It is Monday, so the fusillade of cacciatori shooting little birds is quieter—it makes me so mad—I am really quite a lot better—cough much less, especially in the morning—but haven't yet been to Firenze—think we'll go Thursday. There's a queer sort of unease in the air—as if the wrong sort of spirits were flying abroad in the unseen ether—but it may be my imagination. Frieda strums away on her piano, and I have to listen for when she hits a wrong note. —I am dabbing at poems, getting them ready for the "Collected Poems."* [252]

14? November 1927   Villa Mirenda, Scandicci, Florence, Italy

⟪ *We sit here rather vaguely, and I still haven't been to Florence. It's colder, and we warm up in the evening. Frieda, inspired by Maria [Huxley], has launched into puddings: boiled batter and jam. I do bits of things —darn my underclothes and try to type out poems—old ones. Reggie [Turner]* [253] *and Orioli and Scott-Moncrieff* [254] *and a young Acton came en quatre—I poured tea, they poured the rest.*[255]

Harold Acton

I only knew Lawrence slightly—usually surrounded by other friends, Norman Douglas, Reggie Turner, Orioli and Scott-Moncrieff. He was always most gentle, polite, almost lady-like, to me; and watched me with a twinkle in his bright eyes, as he showed me the collection of pictures of which he was so proud at the Villa Mirenda. I never had any "memorable conversations" with him. He was rather reserved with his Florentine cronies, listening and observing, flaring up now and then to disagree about, say, the merits of Henry James, whom he attacked. Reggie Turner and I were devout Jacobites, whereas Norman Douglas for once agreed with Lawrence about the lion of Rye, whom he had called "a feline and gelatinous New Englander." [256]

18 November 1927   Villa Mirenda, Scandicci, Florence, Italy

([. . . *I wrote a novel [Lady Chatterley's Lover] last winter that the world would call improper and all that. But it is a tender and sensitive work, and, I think, proper and necessary, and I have it, so to speak, in my arms. It is (a) no use thinking of publishing it publicly—as it stands: and I won't cut it. I thought of letting it lie by indefinitely. But friends in Florence urge me to print it privately, here in Florence, (b) as Norman Douglas does his books—700 copies at 2 guineas each—that is what he does. Production is cheap, and myself and a friend could easily do all the work ourselves. And I should make—with the gods—a few hundred pounds—even seven or eight—which would be a windfall for me. And no 20 o/o tax.*

It is not cheap, being ill and doing cures. And in January I am supposed to go up to the snow. . . .

So if this is a simple and decent way of putting the book into the world —and mind, one day I intend to put it into the world, as it stands—and also, of earning money to go on with, then I don't see why I shouldn't do it. Later, I could perhaps cut out parts. . . . But I doubt if I should. Why should I? I'm sick of cutting myself down to fit the world's shoddy cloth.[257]

Curtis Brown

D. H. Lawrence and May Sinclair [258] had the "burning glass" kind of mind. Whatever caught their eye would cause a concentration of rays. It might be quite the wrong thing; but it began to crisp and burn as soon as those intense rays were focused on it, whether it were a sex episode, or a quarrel with a publisher—or an agent. How amazed I would be when either of them suddenly fixed on some minor point in a transaction—a point that had been taken for granted as a matter of routine—and had caused a conflagration. It occurred to me that this high-power focus might be a prime quality of genius. If by luck the magic eye lit on what readers voted to be the right place, then we had a success. If it happened to hit on a subject not to be discussed happily, then we had more or less of a scandal, until public taste moved on to another view-point.

Lawrence was not, I am convinced, an erotomaniac. In various delightful talks with him on all sorts of subjects, *that* subject never once presented itself. But it is likely that his tuberculosis, with its well-known bearing on sex impulses, may have led his eye unusually often to that subject; and once focused on it, we had a *Lady Chatterley's Lover*.

.   .   .   .

Lawrence was a gaunt man who seemed smaller than he really was, with a shock of red hair; pointed red beard; pale, hollow-cheeked face; gentle hands and a gentle voice. There was a twinkle in his brown eyes, and his conversation was full of unexpected view-points. He seemed able to illuminate any topic that presented itself.[259]

18 November 1927   Villa Mirenda, Scandicci, Florence, Italy

❨ *I was in Florence for the first time yesterday. Curious, something has gone out of me—towns mean nothing to me, only noise and nuisance. I'm not interested in them. . . .*

I met Michael Arlen,[260] *too, by chance—you know, The Green Hat. He too has been sick, and was looking diminished, in spite of all the money he has made: quite a sad dog, trying to be rakish.*

The weather has gone suddenly cold and grey—very sudden. Gets my chest a bit. . . . I am busy getting my poems in order, to go into one vol.—all the poems. My word, what ghosts come rising up! But I just tidy their clothes for them and refuse to be drawn.—I think I shall publish my last winter's novel "Lady Chatterley's Lover" here in Florence, privately, myself—and take in the badly-needed shekels and avoid all publicity. I must avoid publicity with it—it is so tender and so daring. . . .

I haven't heard from the Brewsters, whether they'll come with us in March or April to New York and then New Mexico. I think he would come—but Achsah in her long white robes and floating veils—oh, I'd love to see her in a side-saddle on an ambling pad—not Poppy—wafting between the plum-bushes towards the pueblo! How I'd love it! We might have a joint, slam-bang exhibition of pictures in N.Y.—Achsah's acres of Jesus and the blue Virgin, Earl's charming landscapes and stiff white horse—my incorrigible nudes—and Brett's Trinidad. I think we'd baffle everybody—and certainly not sell a rag.[261]

12 December 1927   Villa Mirenda, Scandicci, Florence, Italy

❲ Very grey and misty and unsatisfactory here. I am in bed, as the best place out of it all. But I'm all right—cough a nuisance still, but nothing extra. I'd get up if the sun would shine. Anyhow I'll get up this afternoon.

I'm writing my "Lady Chatterley" novel over again. It's very "shocking" —the Schwiegermutter must never see it. —I think I shall publish it privately here in Florence.

We are staying here for Christmas and making a tree for the peasants. This year there'll be at least thirty of them. Dreadful thought. But Frieda wants it.[262]

18 December 1927   Villa Mirenda, Scandicci, Florence, Italy

❲ Here it has been foggy and unpleasant, and I have, naturally, coughed. But these last two days it is bitter cold, an ice wind, though the sun is warm. . . .

I have been very busy writing out my new novel [Lady Chatterley's Lover] for the third time.[263] I have done half of it now. It is so "shocking," the most improper novel in the world! that is for the conventional smuthounds, Schmutzhunde. As a matter of fact, it is a very pure and tender novel.

A la bonne heure! . . . I can never publish it in the ordinary way, so I think I shall bring it out myself, here in Florence, privately, at 2 guineas a copy: M. 42.00. Then I too shall have some money to go spreeing off with. And if we don't like New Mexico for long, we can sail from San Francisco the other way round the world. The sister of a friend of ours [The Hon. Dorothy Brett] married the Rajah of Sarawak in Borneo: an Englishman. We might even go to Sarawak. I feel like moving: am sick of Italy, especially Florence.[264]

23 December 1927   Villa Mirenda, Scandicci, Florence, Italy

⟨ *The weather here is atrocious, first cold as hell, now all warm clammy steam. Naturally I cough, but not so bad. Our friends [the Huxleys] want us to go to Diablerets, above Montreux somewhere. But I feel like a pig in a garden: I don't know which gate to go out of, and I am not going to be driven out. So I will sit here till I make up my mind.*

It is Christmas. The peasants have stolen us a handsome pine-tree. It stands there in the corner of this Salotta, with all the twinkle-things and candles on it, and looks very nice: Pietro and Giulia get so thrilled, dressing it up, that I get thrilled too. On Saturday evening we shall have all the peasants in, and they love it. But it's a bear-garden, I tell you.[265]

25 December 1927   Villa Mirenda, Scandicci, Florence, Italy

⟨ *Christmas is here again. I say, the poor chap has been born nearly two thousand times, it is enough. He might really have peace now, and leave us in peace, without Christmas and stomach-aches. But we sit still and only make the tree for the peasant children and they think it is a miracle, that it really grows in the salon, and has silver apples and golden birds: for them it is only a fairytale, nothing Christian. You've heard how Frieda wanted to act Sancta Sanctissima, she's really St. Frieda, butter doesn't melt in her mouth: because, of course, she has taken a Bandelli child to the hospital.*[266] *But, thank the Lord, the child makes trouble and Saint Frieda begins to be bored and is becoming all-too-human again.*

The Wilkinsons, our neighbours, have just been here, he with a flute and an overcoat. Tomorrow they go to Rome for a fortnight. Thank goodness I'm not going: there is an ice-cold wind these last two days and Rome is an ice-cold town.

I sit here in the corner by the stove that sings quite amiably and the world can go to blazes as far as I am concerned.[267]

Aldous Huxley

My second meeting with Lawrence took place some years later,[268] during one of his brief revisitings of that after-war England, which he had come so much to dread and to dislike. Then in 1925, while in India, I received a letter from Spotorno. He had read some essays I had written on Italian travel; said he liked them; suggested a meeting.[269] The next year we were in Florence and so was he. From that time, till his death, we were often together—at Florence, at Forte dei Marmi, for a whole winter at Diablerets, at Bandol, in Paris, at Chexbres, at Forte again, and finally at Vence where he died.

In a spasmodically kept diary I find this entry under the date of December 27th, 1927:

Lunched and spent the p.m. with the Lawrences. D. H. L. in admirable form, talking wonderfully. He is one of the few people I feel real respect and admiration for. Of most other eminent people I have met I feel that at any rate I belong to the same species as they do. But this man has something different and superior in kind, not degree.

"Different and superior in kind." I think almost everyone who knew him well must have felt that Lawrence was this. A being, somehow, of another order, more sensitive, more highly conscious, more capable of feeling than even the most gifted of common men. He had, of course, his weaknesses and defects; he had his intellectual limitations—limitations which he seemed to have deliberately imposed upon himself. But these weaknesses and defects and limitations did not affect the fact of his superior otherness. They diminished him quantitively, so to speak; whereas the otherness was qualitative. Spill half your glass of wine and what remains is still wine. Water, however full the glass may be, is always tasteless and without colour.

To be with Lawrence was a kind of adventure, a voyage of discovery into newness and otherness. For, being himself of a different order, he inhabited a different universe from that of common men—a brighter and intenser world, of which, while he spoke, he would make you free. He looked at things with the eyes, so it seemed, of a man who had been at the brink of death and to whom, as he emerges from the darkness, the world reveals itself as unfathomably beautiful and mysterious. For Lawrence, existence was one continuous convalescence; it was as though he were newly reborn from a mortal illness every day of his life. What these convalescent eyes saw, his most casual speech would reveal. A walk with him in the country was a walk through that marvellously rich and significant landscape which is at once the background and principal personage of all his novels. He seemed to know, by personal experience, what it was like to be a tree or a daisy or a breaking wave or even the mysterious moon itself. He could get inside the skin of an animal and tell you in the most convincing detail how it felt and how, dimly, inhumanly, it thought. Of Black-Eyed Susan, for example, the cow at his New Mexican ranch, he was never tired of speaking, nor was I ever tired of listening to his account of her character and her bovine philosophy.

"He sees," Vernon Lee [270] once said to me, "more than a human being ought to see. Perhaps," she added, "that's why he hates humanity so much." Why also he loved it so much. And not only humanity: nature too, and even the supernatural. For wherever he looked, he saw more than a human being ought to see; saw more and therefore loved and hated more. To be with him was to find oneself transported to one of the frontiers of human consciousness. For an inhabitant of the safe metropolis of thought and feeling it was a most exciting experience.

One of the great charms of Lawrence as a companion was that he could never be bored and so could never be boring. He was able to absorb himself completely in what he was doing at the moment; and he regarded no task as too humble for him to undertake, nor so trivial that it was not worth his while to do it well. He could cook, he could sew, he could darn a stocking and milk a cow, he was an efficient wood-cutter and a good hand at embroidery, fires always burned when he laid them, and a floor, after Lawrence had scrubbed it, was thoroughly clean. Moreover, he possessed what is, for a highly strung and highly intelligent man, an even more remarkable accomplishment: he knew how to do nothing. He could just sit and be perfectly content. And his contentment, while one remained in his company, was infectious.

As infectious as Lawrence's contented placidity were his high spirits and his laughter. Even in the last years of his life, when his illness had got the upper hand and was killing him inchmeal, Lawrence could still laugh, on occasion, with something of the old and exuberant gaiety. Often, alas, towards the end, the laughter was bitter, and the high spirits almost terrifyingly savage. I have heard him sometimes speak of men and their ways with a kind of demoniac mockery, to which it was painful, for all the extraordinary brilliance and profundity of what he said, to listen. The secret consciousness of his dissolution filled the last years of his life with an overpowering sadness. (How tragically the splendid curve of the letters droops, at the end, towards the darkness!) It was, however, in terms of anger that he chose to express this sadness. Emotional indecency always shocked him profoundly, and, since anger seemed to him less indecent as an emotion than a resigned or complaining melancholy, he preferred to be angry. He took his revenge on the fate that had made him sad by fiercely deriding everything. And because the sadness of the slowly dying man was so unspeakably deep, his

173

mockery was frighteningly savage. The laughter of the earlier Lawrence and, on occasion, as I have said, even the later Lawrence was without bitterness and wholly delightful.

Vitality has the attractiveness of beauty, and in Lawrence there was a continuously springing fountain of vitality. It went on welling up in him, leaping, now and then, into a great explosion of bright foam and iridescence, long after the time when, by all the rules of medicine, he should have been dead. For the last two years he was like a flame burning on in miraculous disregard of the fact that there was no more fuel to justify its existence. One grew, in spite of constantly renewed alarms, so well accustomed to seeing the flame blazing away, self-fed, in its broken and empty lamp that one almost came to believe that the miracle would be prolonged, indefinitely. But it could not be. When, after several months of separation, I saw him again at Vence in the early spring of 1930, the miracle was at an end, the flame guttering to extinction. A few days later it was quenched.[271]

28 December 1927   Villa Mirenda, Scandicci, Florence, Italy

⟨ *Lo, everything is nearly normal again. The tree is still standing—we want to relight it when the Wilkes return from Rome, perhaps Monday. And we have the remains of the plum pudding from yesterday. Otherwise, as I say, we are nearly normal. Frieda has forgotten her holiness for the moment. The boy [Dino Bandelli] flew away from the hospital, his padrone took him back again and promised him a bicycle. So, the operation is done, Frieda is going to visit him tomorrow. But now she is no longer the one and only saint. The padrone promised Dino a bicycle and Dante, the older brother, says: "If somebody promises me a bicycle I'll also go and be operated on." But, poor boy, he has no rupture.*

The weather is abominable—rain and little sun—evening is the best time, with fire and lamp and peace. Frieda is making herself an apron all covered with roses and birds.[272]

6 January 1928   Villa Mirenda, Scandicci, Florence, Italy

⟨ *There's not much change here. Christmas came and went without much disturbance. . . . On Christmas Day, Maria and Aldous [Huxley] motored us into Florence to a friend's villa. They have gone now to Switzerland to the snow, and they want us to join them. I'm waiting to hear from* them, what it's really like and how dear it is. We may try it for a month.

Anyhow, it is fully decided to leave this place for good in March or April. I don't want to keep it on. If my broncs will stand it, I really want to come to the ranch in April. But Frieda doesn't want to come. Still, we'll see! My cough is still a nuisance, and the weather is the devil: icy wind, then snow, then slush, then warmish fog, then feeble rain, then damp warmish days with weak wet sun, a bore. I just stay in bed a good deal. I feel that somewhere I'm really better and stronger. But my cough goes raking on. It is . . . probably a change of life one has to undergo.

I've been re-writing my novel, for the third time. It's done, all but the last chapter. I think I shall re-christen it Tenderness. . . . If only the fates and the gods will be with us this year, instead of all the time against, as they were last year. If only one were tough, as some people are tough! [273]

11 January 1928   Villa Mirenda, Scandicci, Florence, Italy

⟨ It was damp and horrid so long, we decided to join the Huxleys up in the snow in Switzerland at Diablerets, over Lake Geneva. I suppose we leave here Monday [16 January 1928]. I dread it a bit—but everyone says it is so good for me. And I would like to get myself solider this year.

I don't know quite what we'll do afterwards—but I shall give up this house in April—finally—and leave Italy—perhaps go to the ranch; if my bronchials will stand it: otherwise stay a time in Germany and England, and see.

I would really rather have come south—but everybody says the mountains, the mountains. So we'll try—4000 feet. [274]

16 January 1928   Villa Mirenda, Scandicci, Florence, Italy

⟨ Of course I got a cold which prevents our leaving for Switzerland today. But I hope we shall get off on Wed. or Thursday [18 or 19 January 1928] —be in Diablerets anyhow on Saturday. [275]

LES DIABLERETS, VAUD, SWITZERLAND

? January 1928   Châlet Beau Site, Les Diablerets, Vaud, Switzerland

⟨ Here we are, really in the snow—had quite a good journey from Florence —came tinkling along here in a sledge. There are about 100 people in the hotel—winter sporting—we have a flat in this chalet; like a ship, all wood and low ceilings. It isn't really cold, because there's no wind, and the snow is dry. I think it'll suit me, really.[276]

Witter Bynner

January 19, 1928

Dear Lorenzo:

Not wishing to dictate what I had to say about *The Plumed Serpent*, I waited. And now's a chance on this leisurely motor trip to California.

You must know, without my saying so, that I think the first half of it a consummate piece of noticing and writing. You are much better about Mexico there than you are in *Mornings*. But, after that, I'm ready to quarrel with you.

It's a fundamental quarrel. You are forever hunting out in mankind some superior being (sometimes yourself) and attributing to him mystical or semi-mystical qualities of godly leadership. In this way you try to justify man's way to God, or to yourself. There is always a physical tinge in it— an animal admiration—and often, arising out of that, a blur of spiritual admiration. You carry over, from Egypt or from England, a need of *religion:* or of authority. Touching on it, you become vague and feminine. Fair enough.

Distrusting your gesture toward religion, I see well how you must detest mine. For years, I have innerly believed that no man, not even the authoritative or prophetic leader, has any importance at all except as he foresees and furthers the ultimate amalgamation of all life into one total, completed consciousness which will somehow fulfill these imperfect and vain fragments of the totality, these individualities which we jealously restrict, when for right and happy growth we should be enlarging them toward that final merged realization of the only self.

Your way of thought for us seems to me to make man not more but less; and I don't doubt that my religious groping has the same effect on you.

Apart from this fundamental difference between us (a difference of similarity) I resented, with perhaps too personal or perhaps sufficiently reasonable irritation, the intrusion into your book of an outside influence —a presence of weakness, after your own presence had been strong. It almost seemed as though you had dropped the pen, and left behind that miraculous half-book of real observation and authoritative writing, and let Mabel take it up and proceed to impose upon your pages her idiotic bunk about Tony's spiritual qualities and to infuse into your magnificent vision her queasy female notions generally.

You emerged and shone your clear self in the narratives about destroying the Roman images and that unforgettable fight at the hacienda; but the rest of your finish sounded like Mabel. I could feel her suave presence impressing Orage,[277] or something of the sort, on the gullible. It wasn't you. She missed your person, old boy; but she caught your book—or part of it.

Now flay me.

Ever and ever,
Witter Bynner [278]

3 *February 1928*   *Châlet Beau Site, Les Diablerets, Vaud, Switzerland*

Here we sit, in the snow. Sometimes it's sunny and warm, sometimes it snows all day like yesterday—sometimes it's very cold but dazzling sunny, like this morning. I'm not up to winter-sports—sometimes F. and I drag ourselves up the hill for forty minutes with a little tobaggan, to slither down again in four minutes! Sport davvero! I trudge slowly up the snowy road, and gasp. Snow scratches my bronchials. But, on the other hand, it is a sort of tonic, and builds up resistance. So I really feel better, even when my bronchials are more scratched. But I really hate snow, it's very ungenial sort of stuff.

I've been busy getting my poems together for a collected edition—rather a sweat—but now it's done, and the MS. is ready to go off. Something else behind me.

We've got a four-roomed flat in this chalet, all wood, and low ceilings, just like a ship. Only sadly we can't sail on. But we can keep quite warm, with wood crackling in the stoves. . . .

I think we'll stay till the end of this month, then back to the Mirenda for March and April—and then whither!—to the ranch if I'm really tough enough to face that long journey. But Frieda isn't very keen on the ranch. I am.[279]

6 February 1928   Châlet Beau Site, Les Diablerets, Vaud, Switzerland

❲ I think this place is really doing me good, I do feel stronger. I don't love snow, exactly—it's so beastly white, and makes one's feet so cold. But sometimes it's beautiful. Yesterday we drove in a sledge to the top of the pass, and picnicked there, with Aldous and Maria [Huxley] and Rose, and Julian Huxley,[280] Aldous' brother, and his wife Juliette. It was brilliantly sunny, and everything sparkling bright. I really liked it. It does put life into one.

I am just getting the typescript of my novel [Lady Chatterley's Lover] in from London: [281] and Maria is typing the second half. So in a fortnight I think I shall have it all ready . . . . I am going to make expurgated copies for Secker and Alfred Knopf, then we can go ahead with our Florence edition, for I am determined to do it.[282]

Rolf Gardiner

Early in February [January] 1928 the Lawrences went up to a small skiing resort above Aigle in the Canton Vaud. It was supposed to be good for Lawrence's chest, though he hated the snow. They rented a small châlet Beau Site. Aldous and Maria Huxley stayed at another not far away, and Max Mohr and I were visitors.

On the way down through Germany I halted at Heidelberg, among other places, to talk to groups of the Deutsche Freischar, and at Lawrence's suggestion met Else Jaffé, Frieda's sister.[283] She was the widow of a Jewish socialist who became minister in one of the post-war Munich governments. Else was a fine, aristocratic-looking lady, with a good brain and vivacious interest in the things of the mind. Not florid nor queen-beeish like Frieda. I liked her very much. But I only saw her briefly as she wished to hustle to a University lecture by Max Weber's brother Alfred.[284] This was an impassioned wordy affair, dealing with Greek history. But Alfred Weber was one of the chief luminaries of academic Heidelberg, and many friends and acquaintances attended his lectures as being of importance. Else Jaffé spoke of Lawrence with affection and with admiration for his writing. She was troubled about her son, in whom the mixed blood-streams seemed to be causing some nullity of spirit.

Two days later I was in Switzerland travelling by Lake Leman to Aigle. From there I took an electric tram or funicular which grinds past the fine chateau guarding the narrow ravine from the heights. Then it goes up and up, curling upwards to Sepey in the snow, and so to Les Diablerets, lost in the snow-world, caged up in the hills between mist-capped mountains.

At the station stood Lawrence very pale and shrivelled-looking, re-treated behind his beard and a brown suit. Hovering nearby were Aldous Huxley, tall and rather distant in skiing-kit, and Maria his wife elegant with rouged lips.

A peasant woman loaded my bags on to a sledge, and Lawrence and I followed to a house where he and Frieda had booked for me a nice warm room. Lawrence sat in a chair while I washed after the journey, criticis-ing me for soaping my face: "One should never use soap on the face," he said, and I wondered how the colliers had managed in Nottinghamshire. But I felt his friendliness and glinting interest, and when we had walked along together to join Frieda at Châlet Beau Site, he insisted on my put-ting on his own warm felt house-shoes. Frieda welcomed me expansively, looking fresh and Red Indian-ish with her hair cut in a fringe.

So we had tea together and talked of Germany and the changes in Germany and England, of the young people in both countries and of the German youth Buende with whom I was deeply involved. Frieda had been impressed by the young people. Lawrence was shrewd about the political passions infecting them. (Letters written about this time re-vealed his prophetic insight.)

At supper and afterwards Lawrence asked about my Gore Farm, which I had only recently acquired and the future of which lay wrapped in the heavy mists of the Dorset downs. His concern was immediate and intense and of an almost fatherly solicitude. All the practical knowledge of his working-class youth, and the days at Haggs' farm, came to the surface in a realistic approach to the land and its economy. He said that he really longed to come and help me start up the place, to join in the work,—for Gore was the first nucleus of our Springhead estate and centre,[285] and our plans for it were fundamental and visionary. Lawrence had written in December, 1926:

I'm sure you are doing the right thing, with hikes and dances and songs. But somehow it needs a central clue, or it will fizzle away again. There needs a centre of silence, and a heart of darkness—to borrow from Rider Haggard. We'll

179

have to establish some spot on earth, that will be the fissure into the underworld, like the oracle at Delphos, where one can always come to. I will try to do it myself. I will try to come to England and make a place—some quiet house in the country—where one can begin—and from which the hikes, maybe, can branch out. Some place with a big barn and a bit of land, if one has enough money. Don't you think that is what it needs? And then one must set out and learn a deep discipline—and learn dances from all the world, and take whatsoever we can make into our own. And learn music the same; mass music, and canons, and wordless music like the Indians have. And try—keep on trying. It's a thing one has to feel one's way into. And perhaps work a small farm at the same time, to make the living cheap. It's what I want to do. Only I shrink from beginning. It is most difficult to begin. Yet I feel in my inside, one ought to do it. You are doing the right things, in a skirmishing sort of way. But unless there is a headquarters there will be no continuing. You yourself will tire. If I did come to England to try such a thing, I should depend on you as the organiser of the activities, and the director of the activities. About the dances and folk music, you know it all, I know practically nothing. We need only be even two people, to start. I don't believe either in numbers, or haste. But one has to drive one's peg down to the centre of the earth: or one's root: it's the same thing. And there must also be work connected—I mean earning a living—at least earning one's bread.[286]

Here were understanding and encouragement of my most cherished ideals and aims. And coming from the man whose vision I most revered I felt powerfully supported in my loneliness and immaturity. But I could not see Lawrence actually joining me in Wessex or Yorkshire. Already his life was fated and dated. His health could never again withstand the rigours of raw England. In the year that had elapsed since Lawrence's writing of that splendid letter I had come down to earth in accepting Gore Farm from my uncle Balfour Gardiner. The crucial words of acceptance had been written dramatically at 4 a.m., sitting in the mayor's and judge's seat of the Mayor's Parlour at Richmond, Yorkshire, in the middle of the Northumbrian expedition which I had organized for the Buende in September, 1927. The detachment, with which I had come over the soaking hills from Alston in Cumberland, lay asleep on the floor, while I dealt with the mail which had accumulated during our foray on the Roman Wall.

It was with a fearful heart that I had accepted Balfour's ultimatum over Gore Farm. I was still travelling on my missions to the youth groups of Northern Europe, and heavily involved with the starting of the Musikheim at Frankfurt on the Oder, with the Meihof at Oosterbeck in Holland, and with a dozen other interlinked projects of which I was the initiator or intermediary. To take on the major task of my English life now, frightened me. But I knew that there was no escape. Lawrence's sympathy propelled me too. As he wrote finally: "I think there's some sort of destiny in Gore Farm. We'll have to abide by it, whatever it is." [287]

Now Gore was actually mine, with seventy-five acres of land of which fifty we were planting immediately to timber. But the outgoing tenant, either from carelessness or from malicious intent, had set fire to all the out-buildings, and except for the farmhouse itself the place was a gaping shell. I had received £500 from the insurance people after the fire and this was my sole capital. Lawrence was especially concerned that I should hang on to that. And with less than the total sum I built, that coming summer, with our own labour and flints from the fields, the big Barn of which Lawrence had written, and in which we made a magnificent fireplace for festive occasions; also stables and dormitories and implement sheds, which today would cost at least £5,000 if not nearly twice that figure to build.

But in February, 1928 at Les Diablerets much uncertainty still hovered over this project. Balfour was impatient to see what I was going to do. My collaborators Ralph Coward, who a year later took over the farming side of Gore, and Thurstan Holland-Martin, who from description Lawrence considered only a possible supervisor, were quite uncommitted. So the long talks which we had around the stove of Châlet Beau Site were of considerable value to me. Lawrence's practical interest touched me deeply. I felt how he longed to come and help me run the place. But I had to tell him that it could never happen. He had worked himself too hard, straining his nervous centres. And he accepted apparently. I rather think Frieda did not comment.

That first evening I left the Lawrences about 10.30 p.m. and trudged down through the snow to my châlet above the village Boucherie. Before going to sleep I read again a few pages from *Sons and Lovers* where Paul Morel goes to work for the first time, and I felt again the old wrench from home, the courage and pain of Lawrence's life-adventure.

The next day was furled in snow. Lawrence said it was like the end of the world. I found him painting. Maria Huxley came down with a letter from Brett all about Taos and the ranch, the horses, the servants, herself. Lawrence said he wanted to go back to Taos; but Frieda was against it.

After lunch Frieda lent me her heavy boots and I stumped up the highway to the top of the pass through the snow. The Huxleys passed on skis as I went on, up into the stillness. A gleam of apricot sunlight broke through the snow-mist, and the finches in the protruding bushes began

181

singing, singing as if it were spring. It was peaceful and secluded, and I believe the place did Lawrence some good, soothing his nerves.

When I came down Lawrence was resting on the bed, and Frieda was dressed in russetty-red velvet with some soft white chiffon scarfing her throat. After I had changed I went with them slowly up to the Huxleys' châlet.

In the bright, scrubbed room, the table was set for tea with Maria sitting at the head, chic, Aldous in a pale olive corduroy suit, large and spectacled, and Mrs. Julian Huxley in skiing costume, and two Belgian girls. Lawrence was cheerful and full of boyish glee. He enjoyed stirring up Huxley, whom he affectionately called "Aldoose." The conversation ranged over the world. A lot of time was taken up in disputing the alternative merits of my travelling to Graz via Milan or the Arlberg. Lawrence had been given a boiled egg, but refused it with gay indignation and passed it on to me. After tea we sat in a circle, Lawrence with Mrs. Julian Huxley on the sofa, Frieda and Maria close together sharing a rug, and Aldous next me. Lawrence began describing outlandish events in Mexico, trying to frighten Aldous off his four-square rationalist perch. He spoke astonishingly, his blue eyes darting gleams of amusement and mimicry. Aldous found it all incredible, but he listened fascinated. Then there was some shift in the talk to history, and Napoleon became the theme. He had had to come, they said, to break the ennui of European development, to break up the dynastic pattern perhaps.

After this happy party Lawrence, Frieda and I went home through the deep soft snow and cooked some supper at the Beau Site and were very happy and at home together. I sat between them by the stove and we talked in the dark, warming ourselves. It was the happiest and closest time I had with them, recalling their lives, and places such as Garda, Nottingham and parts of England and Europe where I had also wandered in their trail before knowing them. Such parts became vivid and near in recollection as we sat there in the dark room of the châlet with the glow of the stove patterning the ceiling. I told them more of my own life. I was 25, and Lawrence exclaimed how much had happened to me for that age. His concern was so brotherly and fortifying. To me his career, the pathos of the loneliness and the fight with Frieda in an unsympathetic world, were infinitely touching. I could not help feeling a great tenderness for them both.

There was a thaw next morning, and I was due to leave. Lawrence was busy with the proofs of *The Woman Who Rode Away* and the copyright of *Lady Chatterley's Lover*. How at the mercy of these devils, the publishers, one was. As Frieda said: a writer is more married to his publisher than to his wife.

Lawrence seemed chirpy that day, however. He grinned as he stood at the door receiving the local paper from some peasant distributor: "There's nothing in it," he said in French, knowingly to the old man who came.

A rap on the door an hour later brought a masked figure into the room. Frieda was highly amused. And Lawrence exclaimed "Max Mohr!" A youngish, stout man with a boyish face and glasses was revealed. This was the Bavarian doctor-author who became Lawrence's admirer and friend. I had been to the première of his play *Improvisationen im Juni* at the Munich Residenztheater six years before, and later enjoyed his novel *Die Freundschaft von Ladiz* in which the hero is modelled on D. H. L. So I was sorry to miss the chance of any conversation with Mohr, who met a lonely death in Shanghai during the Nazi epoch.

Lawrence insisted on accompanying me to the station. It was a dripping, messy, wet world of decaying snow that day. I felt so much more at ease with him now. But sadness filled me looking at him, so brave and cheerful, but with only two more years to live.

Strangely, I never saw him again. And after the end of 1928 our correspondence petered out. It was my fault; I was hopelessly enmeshed in my own activities and tasks. *Pansies* arrived in July, 1929, and I read them aloud in the cornfields by the River Oder, and in a keeper's cottage at Abbotsbury. I cannot think why I no longer wrote.

Then in March, 1930 in the middle of the great work camp for students, peasants and workers at the Boberhaus in Lower Silesia, Eugen Rosenstock showed me a paragraph in the *Vossische Zeitung*. Lawrence had died at Vence. The blow came heavily in that bitter winter world. It seemed to presage mounting crisis in Europe. The candle of Lawrence's courage had been snuffed out. And it was very grey on the earth.[288]

27 February 1928   Châlet Beau Site, Les Diablerets, Vaud, Switzerland

⟦ We are still here—at least I am, for Frieda departed to-day for Baden-Baden, to spend a week with her mother: and I remain alone in this little house—but I take the midday meal with the Huxleys. I expect to leave here March 6th, and meet Frieda the same day in Milan: so we ought to be back in the Villa Mirenda by March 7th. I hear the spring is very early in Tuscany, all the flowers out already.

Here too it is hot sunny weather and a great deal of snow is gone from the south slope. But the north slope, and the Diablerets are still deep and white, and the sledges still tinkle down the valley. But I doubt it won't last much longer—the snow. The days are very brilliant, and I'm sure it is quite as hot as Italy. But the nights are cold. I really rather like it: so out of the world, as if the world didn't exist. That just suits my mood at present—when I don't want to work or think much about anything. But if I stayed, I think I should want to begin to paint. . . .

Well, our plans are very vague. The Mirenda is finished on May 6th—and I'm glad to be rid of it. What then I don't know.[289]

3 March 1928   Châlet Beau Site, Les Diablerets, Vaud, Switzerland

⟦ At last I have got the complete typescript of my novel [Lady Chatterley's Lover] . . . . All is ready! We can begin.[290]

5 March 1928   Châlet Beau Site, Les Diablerets, Vaud, Switzerland

⟦ I posted off the MS. of the novel to [Laurence] Pollinger [291] to-day—changed the title to: John Thomas and Lady Jane. . . .

Then the expurgations—I did a fair amount of blanking out and changing, then I sort of got colour-blind, and didn't know any more what was supposed to be proper and what not. . . .

I leave in the morning for Milan, where I meet Frieda. I do hope I shan't get any cold or anything going down, for I'm a good bit better now. This evening it's trying to rain—warm spring rain on sudden snow. Just as well to descend for a bit.[292]

SCANDICCI, FLORENCE, ITALY

8 March 1928   Villa Mirenda, Scandicci, Florence, Italy

⟦ I had a very pleasant journey—so peaceful in Switzerland—but in Domodossola a lot of nervy Italians got in. Frieda's train arrived in Milan just as mine did, and we met on the platform. Got home all right last *night*—all the peasants out to meet us, with primroses and violets and scarlet and purple anemones. Something touching about them. But I don't really like Italy: It's all in a wrong mood, nervous and depressed. And today it rains, rather dree, and is colder than Diablerets. Impossible really to warm these great stone barns. So I've been painting a water-colour: torch dance by firelight! [293]

9 March 1928   Villa Mirenda, Scandicci, Florence, Italy

❬ Today I lunched with Orioli, and we took the MS. of the novel [Lady Chatterley's Lover] to the printer: great moment. . . . Remains to be seen if Secker and Knopf will stand it. . . . However, tomorrow night I shall have a specimen page from the printer—and by Monday I may hear what Curtis Brown and Secker think of their expurgated (sic) MS. I'm prepared for anything—but shall go ahead here. —Saw [Norman] Douglas today—but nothing new about him, still thinking of Jerusalem and pre-ferring Chianti.[294]

Giusèppe ("Pino") Orioli

D. H. Lawrence was no stranger to me; I had met him years ago in Cornwall. Now he arrived in these parts and I had ample opportunities of meeting him; I ended in knowing him as well as any of his friends can have known him. Much as I like some of his work, I never had any deep feeling for him as a man. One had always to be on one's guard with Lawrence—his querulousness and chronic distrust of everybody made a real intimacy impossible. Sometimes his behaviour led me to wonder whether he was not suffering from persecution mania.

Like Scott Moncrieff,[295] he thought his merits were not sufficiently appreciated; like him, too, he had a pretty good opinion of his own talents. I have just been re-reading his Letters and have marked one or two passages bearing on this matter. To a friend he writes: "I *know* I can write bigger stuff than any man in England." [296] To his literary agent: "it [*The Rainbow*] is a beautiful piece of work, really," [297] and again, speaking of one of his short stories, he calls it a *chef d'oeuvre*.[298] Another friend is informed that his book *The Rainbow* is "one of the most important novels in the language." [299] It may be true; I am not a literary critic. But it strikes me that he might have left it to other people to say things of this kind.

A good deal—in fact, too much—has been written about Lawrence. I shall note down only a few memories that occur to me.

He lived in a pension in Florence and afterwards at the Villa Mirenda, a distant and dilapidated place among the hills with no water supply and only one small fireplace.[300] Well I knew the Villa Mirenda in summer and winter, well I remember that endless tram-ride and then the walk up! There was a peasant family near at hand and on one occasion he gave them a Christmas-tree, with carol-singing on his part, and presents for the two or three little children costing forty-eight centimes apiece.[301] These people were not very happy with Lawrence, because they expected to make a little money out of him with washing and so forth, and never did.[302] Lawrence managed his own washing and scrubbing and mending and needle-work and cooking and marketing—and very successfully too. So far as such domestic arts were concerned he might have been a woman. He took more pride and pleasure in them than many women do; much more than his wife did.

Here, at the Villa Mirenda, he wrote *Lady Chatterley,* sitting on the grass under a tree, with his knees up and a thick exercise-book resting on them and nearly touching his beard. He used to implore me to come up from Florence, which cost me a whole afternoon, and when I arrived he would say:

"Frieda has gone for her usual walk into the woods. And now I'll make some tea." Tea-making was a religion with him.

I could fill several chapters recording my experiences in various places with Lawrence, but so much has been written about him that I will only mention that up to the 10th July 1929 his profits from *Lady Chatterley* amounted to £1615:18:3, and mine were ten per cent of that.[303] It is generally the author of a book who receives the ten per cent, while the publisher—I was not officially the publisher, though I had all the publishing work to do, and a most trying job it was—while the publisher, I say, gets the remainder. In this case it was the other way round. Ten per cent of the profits and not a penny more: that was what I got. I record these figures because some people seem to imagine that I made a big sum over this work; the figures themselves I take from an account-book in Lawrence's own handwriting which lies before me at this moment, together with nearly two hundred letters from him which have never been published and which deal for the most part with *Lady Chatterley.*[304]

On the cover of this book he was anxious to have his phoenix design engraved. I had it done, though I do not care about this undignified fowl. It suggests a pigeon having a bath in a slop-basin.[305]

Looking back at my long relationship with Lawrence I come to the conclusion that it was on the whole unsatisfactory. One had golden moments with him: no doubt of that. One had also the reverse. I am not speaking of the occasions when he lay at my flat so sick that it was a question whether he would ever rise from his bed again, or when I was with him at the Mirenda during those awful haemorrhages. In matters of business he was more troublesome than any one I have ever dealt with, and as a friend so incalculable and often so disappointing, so disheartening, that now and then I wonder how many of those who knew him well were really sorry when he died.[306]

Incurably distrustful of your motives, and of everybody else's! Full of reservations! When least you expected it, he contrived to do or to say something which chilled your affection to the marrow. The friendship, I used to feel, would have to start all over again from the beginning. Or am I over-sensitive on this point? I think not, for the same trait of character has been noticed by others and was present already in youth, as can be seen by anybody who cared to read that revealing book *D. H. Lawrence: A Personal Record* by E. T. [Jessie Chambers Wood], especially the last chapter. Lawrence was a homosexual gone wrong; repressed in childhood by a puritan environment. That is the key to his life and his writings.[307]

---

15 March 1928   *Villa Mirenda, Scandicci, Florence, Italy*

❨ *My novel, Lady Chatterley's Lover, or John Thomas and Lady Jane, is at the printer's in Florence: such a nice little printing shop all working away by hand—cosy and bit by bit, real Florentine manner—and the printer doesn't know a word of English—nobody on the place knows a word—where ignorance is bliss! Where the serpent is invisible! They will print on a nice hand-made Italian paper—should be an attractive book. I do hope I'll sell my 1000 copies—or most of 'em—or I'll be broke. I want to post them direct to purchasers. . . . I shan't send the book unless the people send the two quid, else I'm left.[308]*

16? March 1928   *Villa Mirenda, Scandicci, Florence, Italy*

❨ *Frieda's daughter Barbara suddenly arrived from Alassio this morning —for a fortnight or so.[309]*

Barbara Weekley Barr

I went from Alassio to stay at Scandicci the following spring, 1928, for two weeks.

Frieda told me that Lawrence had just finished a novel which would shock people very much. Pino Orioli was discussing the publication of it at that time, and he did produce the first edition in Florence of the novel which was *Lady Chatterley's Lover*.

After Lawrence's death, a Swiss film producer in Paris, Mr. Siebenhaar,[310] planned to make a film of the novel and bought the rights from Frieda. Unfortunately he was later obliged to abandon the project through lack of funds. It was in 1933 that he sent over a couple of Swiss film directors to take a look at the "Lawrence country" and asked me to accompany them. We motored around the Midlands, and came across a country house, "Renishaw," standing above a colliery, which we were told belonged to the Sitwell family. I remembered that Lawrence had once mentioned a visit to a house belonging to Sir George Sitwell where he had seen a collection of antique beds. It was in fact the Sitwells' castle Montegufoni, some fifteen miles away in the country outside Florence, which he had visited,[311] but I jumped to the conclusion that it was this one, Renishaw, and thought he might possibly have used it as a model for the Chatterley home.

I sent a telegram therefore to Osbert Sitwell, who was in London: "Discobole, Paris, propose filming Lawrence novel. May we inspect Renishaw Hall?" To this he replied, "If you refer banned book Lady Chatterley's Lover your request gross as it is libellous." [312]

I was considerably taken aback; so were the Swiss directors. After holding a mystified council, we turned our attention to one of the other stately homes of England in the neighbourhood, timidly peeping at it from the garden with the butler's consent.[313]

That spring in Scandicci, I could not, unfortunately, do any successful paintings. But I was never bored: with Lawrence life was always absorbing, even when he was out of humour. He was brilliantly penetrating, and in assessing human relationships had an absolutely uncanny gift.

"He will leave her," he said of a young married pair. "Some other woman will want him, especially if she sees he has a wife and child." This proved true. He thought that in most people the psyche was "double," loving on one side and betraying on the other. It was our modern malady, according to him.

When my sister Elsa was going to be married, Lawrence wrote to me, "Don't let her marry a man unless she feels his physical presence warm to her."

"I don't need Lawrence's advice," Elsa told me.

In this letter he also said, I think, "Passion has dignity; affection can be a very valuable thing, and one can make a life relationship with it."

Unfortunately these letters were all lost.

"As for Barby," he said one evening as we sat at supper by the lamplight, "she will never finish anything, any relationship. If she marries, she won't finish her marriage either. I tell you, Frieda," he said, in a sharp, devastating voice, "she won't *finish* it!"

He went on: "I don't know what will become of her, simply I don't. If her father goes on giving her three pounds a week, she is very lucky. No one ever gave me that."

All this was very discouraging. But Frieda stuck up for me determinedly.

After I had gone back to London, and was drifting unhappily in the way that was becoming a habit with me, Lawrence wrote quite charitably, ending, "Don't throw yourself away; you might want yourself later on."

One day at the Mirenda we looked through an old Italian opera brochure. There was a photograph of a woman with rich dark hair piled on top. "I wish women looked like that now," Lawrence remarked. Another portrait was of a full-looking man with a big moustache. "I should like to be that man. Yes, I really would like to be just like him," he said wistfully.

In their life together, Frieda must sometimes have suffered, and felt lonely. At first, many people had been hostile to her. Lawrence was inclined to be jealous, and would often sneer at the few friends she did have. The strain on her remarkable good humour must have been colossal. She believed in him, though. He needed her belief, and was unhappy without her.

At this time she wanted a holiday by herself. I was going back to Alassio. She came too, and then went off alone.

Lawrence said to Maria Huxley, "Frieda has changed since she went away with Barby."

He did not reproach my mother. One evening at the Mirenda he said to her, "Every heart has a right to its own secrets." [314]

16? March 1928   *Villa Mirenda, Scandicci, Florence, Italy*

⟨ *No, I never said anything to Dorothy Warren about an exhibition—
only Barbey talked to her of it. I might do it—but I shan't sell the pictures
—not till I'm strong. I've done three more water-colours: not bad, but
I'd rather do oils: one can use one's elbow, and in water it's all dib-dab.*[315]

Philip Trotter

So . . . I sat on the floor with the canvas propped against a chair—and with
my house-paint brushes and colours in little casseroles, I disappeared into that
canvas. It is to me the most exciting moment—when you have a blank canvas
and a big brush full of wet colour, and you plunge. . . . The knowing eye
watches sharp as a needle; but the picture comes clean out of instinct, intuition
and sheer physical action. Once the instinct and intuition gets into the brush-tip,
the picture *happens,* if it is to be a picture at all.

At least, so my first picture happened—the one I have called "A Holy
Family." In a couple of hours there it all was, man, woman, child, blue shirt,
red shawl, pale room—all in the rough, but, as far as I am concerned, a
picture.[316]

Twice in the varied field of his essay-writing Lawrence made painting
his subject. "Making Pictures," from which the above passage is taken,
appeared twice during the month in which the events now to be related
reached their peak.[317] By an unaccountable mischance (at least in
London) the essay slipped the attention of a world focused on D. H.
Lawrence, and had to wait till after its author's death to announce its
message as at once the strangest and most convincing apologia ever written by a genuine but wholly unorthodox artist. His second venture,
"Introduction to These Paintings," [318] was a ten-thousand-word flight into
art criticism and art-critic criticism, with no mention of his having
ever handled a brush himself. Brilliant and entertaining as it is it was
an added embarrassment to the custodians of an exhibition already under
heavy Philistine fire; for it poured scorn successively on every section of
the community to whom they looked for support. If these two essays could
have changed places and roles, the "Introduction" have suffered temporary
eclipse under another name and "Making Pictures" have prefaced the
book of reproductions of the exhibits, Philistine tongues would not have
been silenced, but their pens must have been softened, for, throughout
the exhibition, column-writers pored over the "Introduction," extract-

ing the essences from which they distilled their poison. How might they have responded to the temper of sheer delight in "Making Pictures," the creative artist's delight in "the image as it lives in the consciousness, alive like a vision, but unknown." [319]

For this is the interest in Lawrence's paintings: the sick and exhausted slave of a tireless pen finds a consoling boon companion in his brush, and sitting on the floor of the Mirenda, "his is the Kingdom of Heaven," [320] so many hours of sanctuary from the struggle against his approaching dissolution. In this memoir, passages from "Making Pictures" will stand detached from the text to head sections that they seem to illumine, and "Introduction to These Paintings" will figure frequently and disastrously in the text itself.

It is rewarding to study Lawrence's pictorial inventions against a background of images and symbols in his greater medium, which the pictures sometimes echo, sometimes mock, and, in at least one case, foreshadow. One critic, among the few who braved the tumult, saw clearly the vision as it worked its way through the poet's eye to the painter's brush.

I am much indebted to the few of Lawrence's many biographers and commentators who have taken stock of this late flowering of his genius, presenting each a different aspect of it, and collectively endorsing it as the source of his happiest solitudes. Frieda's brief, ingenuous sketch of the plunge, setting the tone and temper of the whole ardent and sustained creative impulse, might have disconcerted the Philistine and muted the outcry, if it could have synchronised with the exhibition and prefaced the catalogue; [321] Mr. Earl Brewster, in his *D. H. Lawrence: Reminiscences and Correspondence,* is variously helpful: in the adventitious light his account of the Volterra visit throws on the transit of ideas between brush and pen; later, as a brother-artist, in his appreciation of the first few pictures; and throughout as the occasional recipient of Lawrence's most intimate painting experiences.[322] Mr. Richard Aldington's most valuable note in *D. H. Lawrence: Portrait of a Genius But . . .* shows the only boisterously exuberant fantasy emerging from a period of acute stress and sickness; [323] the late Mrs. Carswell, in her *Savage Pilgrimage,* recalls a "shy and eager note in every mention by Lawrence of his pictures." [324]

This slight but important body of documentation is here stressed in advance as outside witness to a part of their message that the pictures could not convey in the atmosphere generated by a section of the press and a tiny minority of the public. Competent critics attested their complete artistic integrity; but the communication of the artist's delight in their creation was held in suspense against vapours that blew in daily from the press-clippers—breath that had grown stale against *The Rainbow* and was now diverted from *Lady Chatterley's Lover* to compass the destruction of the pictures. That breath, no longer lethal but still potent to foul the freshness of the vision, pervades this history; hence the need for protective background, lacking in 1929.

So much for Lawrence's *prima facie* claim to be an artist in paint. On the effective artistic merits of the pictures the reader is referred to the very divergent views of competent critics, with the assurance that no comment from any authoritative source, written or spoken, favourable or adverse, has been withheld. The 1929 roles are here reversed—the pictures figuring collectively as the hero, their assailants as the villain. And it is the latter that have held the field up to the present time; the red herring is the Philistine's consecrated weapon against "any art of which he becomes aware" [325] and it has been drawn against every reference to the Lawrence exhibition *as an artistic event* for twenty-eight years.

Grievous it is, then, that the assignment to set the values of the drama in their right relation and perspective should have been wrested by death from the only hand fitted by endowment and circumstance to discharge it. But here the reader may measure his own loss from the correspondence presently to be submitted between exhibitor and gallery-owner, and as I briefly sketch the history and character of the unique enterprise that was destined to confront the most formidable Philistine operation of our time.

Art lovers on both sides of the Atlantic who were familiar with London in the later twenties may recall the welcome given to the new Warren Gallery in the Spring of 1927. It "opens like a May morning," wrote Mr. Charles Marriott of *The Times;* [326] if the five-word blessing seems faint and laconic beside the more voluminous and factual praise of *The Times'* contemporaries, to Mr. Marriott's accustomed readers it must have read as the promise of a new Heaven descending on artistic London, so rarely did extraneous observations intrude into his compact and luminous notices.

What critics and enlightened observers were acclaiming was the manifestation of a single intelligence. Dorothy Warren, the sole originator, in its broad conception, in every detail of its equipment, and in its objectives, of the enterprise that bore her name, inherited her extraordinary sense of form, balance and colour from both sides of her family, her collector's eye and critical judgment perhaps more from her mother's, her creative vision and rare ingenuity direct from her father, the distinguished architect, Edward Prioleau Warren. Had she been asked "What is your highest ambition in the creative field?" she might have answered, "To create in a house of a congenial period the perfect dwelling, aesthetically and practically." In such a dwelling a picture is an integral part of the room that contains it; hence, she conceived, pictures can properly be exhibited only in the setting of a congenial and livable room. Her previous employers, the Brook Street Art Gallery, deferred to her taste and judgment to the limits of conventional art-gallery procedure; among the successes that rewarded their confidence was a copious exhibition of original work, mainly etchings, by Queen Victoria.[327] This was a surprise and revelation to many, and to none more than Lytton Strachey, who, as the great Queen's most recent and colourful biographer, had failed, like so many of D. H. Lawrence's, to note that his subject made pictures.

But all this gave only a whetting foretaste of a full-scale Warren Gallery, should such materialise. It did so when, at a stone's throw from Brook Street, the second and third floors of the fine XVIII Century corner house of Maddox Street and George Street came into the market. Dorothy Warren acquired the lease, and addressed herself to carrying her comprehensive ideas on galleryship into effect.

The far-reaching stir that the news occasioned attests her versatility. Since 1924 the cameramen of *Vogue,* the art journals, and even the general press had followed her flittings from one London address to another: each house as she occupied and transformed it passed into those ephemeral records of taste which were a popular news item in the general reaction against the ugliness of war. To continental reporters, on the other hand, her name recalled the Longhi film, *The Man Without Desire,* of which she had been art director in the Berlin studios, afterwards playing a leading part in the action at Venice.

From this copious polyglot press that watched the new gallery come to completion a few sentences from an enthusiastic but rather pedestrian account are here of interest for the sinister implications they were to assume two years later. After describing the second-floor public rooms, their concealed lighting, the silver-grey velvet covering the walls of one room, the braided webbing by which the pictures hung, the writer proceeds: "Upstairs . . . will be a special gallery, where pictures . . . will be brought out one by one and placed on an easel before special curtains of pinky-grey in order that connoisseurs may appreciate them in silence and at length." [328] Surely an innocent reference to a serviceable device; but Miss Warren's activities were later to be assessed under tests unconcerned with truth or taste.

Elsewhere the stir may have had its disquietudes. It was the heyday of Bloomsbury as a compact fraternity, which at times denied its own existence as a "group," [329] yet acknowledged a common aesthetic, the product of great erudition and vision, the source of much brilliant writing. In a sense Dorothy Warren's relation with Bloomsbury dominates this history. There were, naturally, ties of friendship and mutual regard between the parties. But Bloomsbury's current *dogma*—all values are here considered subjectively—was the supremacy of French contemporary art. To this dogma Dorothy Warren made an early gesture in "One of the most representative exhibitions of Modern French painting that have been held in London recently . . . ." [330] But a gesture is not a submission; and, having made it, she resumed her essential mission of bringing the ungotten riches of native talent before a cautiously responsive public. Here, then, was a new art centre of growing stature, where Bloomsbury's writ did not run. If Dorothy Warren's fearless and independent judgment should bring her enterprise into conflict with a fiercely Philistine world, individual "Bloomsberries" would weep for a rare and delightful boon companion in trouble: but would the group leave the gallery-owner in a brilliant but perilous isolation? Events give an hesitant answer.

Within the first twelve exhibitions (D. H. Lawrence's was No. 12) it was through three members of the pit world that the Fates operated their wayward plans for the Warren Gallery. On its first miner's son, Welsh Evan Walters, [331] they showered blessings without reserve. His first week's list of connoisseur purchasers includes Mlle. Lalot, the distinguished French collector, two English and several Welsh galleries. Admiration for his young Welsh compatriot evoked Augustus John's first plunge into art criticism, a by-product of his active mind which he has never abandoned. But the inspiration was Dorothy Warren's; for the admirable illustrated article was published in *Vogue,* a pulpit which only she could have chosen for that preacher. [332] A very few, mainly continental, critics discerned the magic hand behind the framing, hanging, lighting, and general setting of the glamorous exhibition.

Yet Dorothy Warren would wish her gallery remembered—if at all— by the leaner days of her second miner's son, the young Yorkshire sculptor Henry Moore. [333] Of his massive carvings and stark but brilliant studio drawings *The Times* wrote, in a notice of impressive praise: "It is necessary to remain with them some little time"; [334] indeed the allotted three weeks proved insufficient for experienced connoisseurs to appraise the merit that Dorothy Warren's eye had so quickly and surely discerned. Accordingly, with dwindling resources she held the exhibition open . . . a fourth bleak week . . . a perilous fifth . . . and in the sixth Henry Moore awoke to find himself famous.

It is at this point, with her funds almost exhausted and her reputation at its peak, that the third miner's son signalled from Italy, foreshadowing a call for courage of a different sort, though the issue is yet far ahead. How the most impatient of men was constrained to abide Dorothy Warren's elusiveness and await her pleasure through fifteen months of being wooed by some of the leading galleries of London, is part of the function of the foregoing notes to suggest. Little need then be added to the vivid exchange of letters that brings us from the siege of Henry Moore to the battle of D. H. Lawrence.

The foregoing introduction may close fittingly with a few words taken from a letter of recent date. Dorothy Warren (Mrs. Philip Trotter since November, 1928) died on the 9th February 1954. Among tributes to her radiant personality, sparkling vitality and genius, beauty of form, voice and movement, and varied achievement, one writer recalls the stirring event just related:

> I most vividly remember the enthusiasm we shared for the early work of Henry Moore and the splendid way she encouraged it in Germany as well as in this country.
> But no one who knew her in those days can ever forget that brilliant, generous, unconquerable nature or think of that period without recalling her.[335]

I have tried to present Dorothy Warren only in the phase of her varied career that she least enjoyed. A life lived in so many fields finds no biographer: now riding a territory to design and cast a film, now planning a library, then a surgeon's theatre; now campaigning and underpinning a cause; finally enriching the exile of a forlorn minority of the country's war guests: each phase a facet of a personality too varied and vivid to be recaptured.

Dorothy Warren first met Lawrence in 1915 staying with her aunt, Lady Ottoline Morrell,[336] at Garsington Manor. Walking on the downs together they had fiery arguments, in one of which Lawrence lost his temper and slapped her in the face, but without injury to the good companionship. Later, as the Lawrences' guest at Byron Villas she formed a warm affection for Frieda and made friends with Catherine Carswell.

The latter was a frequent visitor to the exhibition; and we saw the Carswells often between then and the second war, which scattered us all.[337]

Villa Mirenda/Scandicci/Florence/27 March 1928

❨ Dear Dorothy Warren

Barbara Weekley is here, and said you might like to exhibit my pictures. There are seven biggish oils, 1 yard x 1½ yds and so on—also three littlish ones—and six water-colours. We're giving up this house 1st May, so I've got to pack my pictures and do something with them. So I might exhibit them—though really I'm not keen, and I don't want to sell them —unless one or two of the smaller things, and perhaps the waters. So what do you think? The oils are framed in plain wooden frames which I painted to fit the picture—buffish or greyish. I'd rather the pictures were left in their frames as they are. Only the waters need framing. But I can't afford a heavy expense. Just let me know what you think.

I enclose a few order-forms for my nice new phallic novel. If you know anybody who'd like it, possibly, do give them a form, if you'll be so good.

How are you after a fair number of years? Chirpy still, I hope—though people say, disillusioned. Well, that sounds romantic. And when you're through with it, you can just start being illusioned again, which is very nice.

We may be in England about August—when I shall come to your gallery, if it is open. Perhaps it shuts through the dog days, and you depart far off.

Meanwhile I hope things are going fairly gaily with you.

Sincerely

D. H. Lawrence [338]

27 March 1928   Villa Mirenda, Scandicci, Florence, Italy

❨ We had one sunny day, but grey and windy again now—no fun—F.'s daughter [Barbara] here, but leaves tomorrow. The Wilks mere wraiths, having packed up every old rag, pot, pan and whisker with the sanctity of pure idealists cherishing their goods.

Had a cable from Brett asking me to send my pictures to New York for exhibition on May 1st. Too short a notice.[339]

1 April 1928   *Villa Mirenda, Scandicci, Florence, Italy*

❲ An American [Harry Crosby] [340] asks me for [the manuscript of Sun] [341] *particularly, and offers $100. So there's a windfall, if it exists. If it doesn't, povero me! for I haven't got it, the MS. . . . I'm afraid I've burnt most of those* [manuscripts] *left on my hands . . . .*[342]

Caresse Crosby

It was that January '28 on our trip to Egypt with Harry's mother, that we discovered Lawrence and *The Plumed Serpent*. Harry found the copy of the first edition in a Cairo book shop and he read it as we churned up the Nile from Luxor to Wadi Halfa. As he sat hour after hour cross-legged on the upper deck, his nose between the pages, a native tribesman sat cross-legged on the lower deck brushing his teeth with a wooden stick hour after hour and his eyes never left his navel as he brushed. Was this a penance or a ritual? Harry's eyes never left the printed page. . . .

.   .   .   .

While floating down the Nile, Harry had sent off by overland-camel an enthusiastic letter to D. H. Lawrence, care of the London publishers.

He wrote the author of *The Plumed Serpent* about his own belief in the Sun God, described the impact of the Egyptian sun and asked Lawrence if he had any Sun story that we might bring out in a Black Sun Press [343] limited edition. Harry offered, as bribe, to pay in twenty-dollar gold pieces, the eagle and the sun.[344]

On our arrival in Paris in March our first visit had been to the rue Cardinale. There Lescaret [345] handed us a big envelope postmarked Florence. It was from Lawrence and the MSS. of *Sun* was enclosed [346] —that very afternoon the type was chorusing up the forms, the Holland van Gelder paper samples being pored over for texture. It was a Caslon job with margins as wide as a *faire-part,* the title in sunburnt red.[347]

To obtain the gold pieces was more difficult. The State Street Trust [348] couldn't send them, Steve [349] wouldn't send them and so Harry wrote to Ted Weeks. Ted, who had been in the Ambulance Corps with Harry, was our first B[lack]. S[un]. P[ress]. representative in America. Already he had sold out *The Fall of the House of Usher,* illustrations by Alastair, and was excited at the prospect of a Lawrence item. His tastes were literary, his instinct right. That is undoubtedly why he is now editor-in-chief of the *Atlantic Monthly*.[350] He promised to get those golden eagles to us somehow but it might take time. Lawrence said he didn't mind waiting, but we almost despaired and decided we'd have to smuggle them over on our next trip to Boston. Then, we had a surprise one autumn evening in '28.[351]

We had come home from the Bois in the Powels' [352] steaming Citroen, and piled out, dogs and men and girls into the echoing cobbled court-yard of 19 rue de Lille. We jostled up three flights of stairs, with nipped fingers and red noses to spread our hands before the blaze of the fire-place in Harry's library on the top floor—Narcisse Noir and Zulu yapping and excited—Peter and Gretchen bundled in polo coats, reminiscent of Harvard football days at home, Frans and Mai like story-book people, bargees as they were, and Armand, Parisien, full of suave mischief as ever.[353]

We had been running the dogs at "le Polo," a smart French club near Longchamps that had recently gone in for whippet racing. It was late afternoon in November and we were ready for hot tea and strong drink. The spacious library lined, piled and glowing with the Berry books,[354] with chintz curtains at the fourteen-foot windows and lioness and tigress skins on the polished floor, *à l'américaine,* was as pleasant and impregnable a spot that autumn afternoon as could be imagined. Conversation waxed very gay and slightly ribald. The cinnamon toast was luscious, the Cutty Sark had twang. We were enjoying hilarious fun when Ida came up the final stair to announce above the melée, "Monsieur Sex to see you, Madame."

"Who, Caresse, is Monsieur Sex," they all cried, but I had no idea. Harry had no idea.

"Ida," I said, "that can't be his name. Please go down and very politely ask again."

In a moment she returned. "Oui, Madame, Monsieur Sex. He says he is from Boston from friends of Monsieur."

"Mr. Sex must come up," they all insisted, so Ida was once more dis-patched to usher him into the arena. We waited.

"Le Monsieur," she announced shrilly from the hall below, for he had outstripped her. A dark, curly head appeared above the stairwell attached to one of the most delightful young men I've ever seen. He was about twenty. He looked shy, but advanced with authority into our midst. It was a strange entrance.

"I am Bill Sykes," he announced, "and this is my introduction." With that he pulled off one of his low tan shoes and dramatically turned it upside down over the lioness on the hearth. A shower of gold glittered in the firelight. Off came the other shoe and more gold pieces shone and clanged and rolled and spread across the floor under the desk, behind the sofa, down the stairs. The dogs barked. Ida threw up her arms like semaphores, we all exclaimed and scrambled to retrieve the precious loot.

"Ted sent you? Fine. Fine," said Harry shaking Bill's hand nearly off and turning to us, "This is the gold I promised D. H. Lawrence for his story *Sun*. Caresse and I are publishing it in the Editions Narcisee. Twenty twenty-dollar gold pieces—The Eagle and the Sun—let's find them before they roll away 'because they're round.'" Everyone set to. I pressed a glass of Cutty Sark into Sykes' hand. Soon the brilliant heap on the rug in the flamelight totaled up, and I made Bill sit down on the sofa between Gretchen and Mai and tell us all about it: how he had decided to become a painter when his father died and left him a little money; how he had to wait until he was twenty-one; how he now was twenty-one and had, like us, "escaped," from Boston to Paris; how he had promised Ted Weeks, our Press's representative, to deliver the forbidden bullion; how he had eluded the customs officers; how he had walked from the hotel to us on secret linings.

Harry, with his usual precipitousness, started to hunt for a box to send off the treasure. Lawrence was in Italy, it was nearing Christmas.[355] Harry wanted to get the gold to him as quickly as possible, but no one we knew was going to Italy. In his desk he found a small square Cartier box that had held rue de Lille notepaper, and he was busy wrapping each disk in cotton.

"The Rome Express leaves tonight at eight," he said, "what time is it now?" (He had no clock there to watch over him.) It was nearing seven. "I'll take the package to the train myself and ask some passenger to mail it in Florence"—the free circulation of gold was forbidden then as now.

"But it might fall into the hands of a crook," Armand protested. "It's too dangerous."

"If I can't tell an honest man when I see one then I deserve a crook." Harry crossed himself and went on preparing the package. He rang and ordered the car for 7:30.

Bill Sykes went off with him and he told us later that he and Harry arrived at the Gare de l'Est a few minutes before train time, Harry in his oversized mink-lined greatcoat that had been Cousin Walter's, the undeviating dark blue suit and gray spats, bareheaded as always. He hurried along the station beside the *wagons lits* through the confusion of a trans-continental *départ*, searching for his "honest man," but he hadn't found him when the guard called *en voiture*. At the final moment a distinguished Englishman with a schoolboy of about twelve at his side pulled down the windows of one of the compartments on the Florence sleeper, and leaned out. Immediately Harry spotted him and called up through the din, "Would you help me out, sir, by mailing this in Florence when you arrive?"

"Glad to—not a bomb, I trust," as he reached down a friendly hand.

"No, it's gold," shouted back Harry as the train began to move.

"Then we'd better introduce ourselves. My name's Argyll," called back the man.

"Crosby," shouted Harry, "it's gold for a poet." They both waved a salute.

In a day or two Lawrence wrote us that the gold had been delivered in person by the Duke of Argyll. Harry had not mistaken his honest man.[356]

2 April 1928   Villa Mirenda, Scandicci, Florence, Italy

❲ *I've corrected 41 pages of proofs [of Lady Chatterley's Lover], and it was almost [Maria Huxley's] typing all over again. Dear Maria, all those little mistakes you made, and I followed like Wenceslas's page so patiently in your footsteps: now it's a Florentine printer. He writes dind't, did'nt, dnid't, dind't, din'dt, didn't like a Bach fugue. The word is his blind spot.*

.   .   .   .

It's the most awful weather—pours and pours with rain. F.'s sister [Else] comes back to Florence from Capri today—it's rained all the while she was there—now she'll stay a bit with us, and it'll go on raining. My cough is as ever: but I'm no worse: really rather well, I think. Does me good to feel furious about the novel.[357]

Dorothy Warren Trotter

[The Warren Gallery, 39a Maddox Street, London, W. 1,] 9 April 1928

Dear Mr. Lawrence

I am delighted to have had news of you. I thank you very much indeed for your letter and for the notice of your book. I have ordered several copies, and I have distributed the notices in quarters that seemed suitable. I run a book department in this gallery in coöperation with a friend, Prince Leopold Loewenstein,[358] who is publishing German books in English, and buying English books for translation and publication in Germany. He would very much like to have the German rights of *Lady Chatterley's Lover,* if you have not already disposed of them. He has tried to obtain other books by you but he found that you were committed to the Insel Verlag. He was very much disappointed. In my opinion he is much more intelligent in his choice of books than are other German literary agents, who so far have boosted Galsworthy as *"der grosse Dichter"*—a term which seems quite peculiarly inapplicable and also Michael Arlen, overlooking everybody else. In a country carefully educated to approach all kinds of writing, drama, music and all the other arts, without mentioning the sciences, from a superhumanly unprejudiced and objective stand-point, the limitation is surely both lamentable and unnecessary!

Loewenstein has adopted a much wider policy, and he is placing the books he acquires very successfully.

I should really be delighted to make an exhibition of your pictures here, if you don't dislike the idea too much. When Barbara showed me the photographs I felt that I should like the paintings immensely and I wanted very much to see them. Please send them to me here as soon as it suits you to do so and I will keep them for you as long as you like.

I do all my own framing. I keep my own workman for that purpose, which enables me to frame really cheaply, as prices in London go. I never expect artists who show with me to pay for frames until they have sold pictures, and I very often take pictures for myself in exchange for frames, so please do not worry about the expense of framing the six water-colours. Have them on me, won't you?

I wonder whether I am disillusioned. No one has raised the point to me before you did. I cannot remember having been conscious ever, either of possessing or of losing illusions, so how can I judge? However I suspect that I have been regarded as fostering *idées fixes,* with which I had better be left to stew in my own juice.

In retrospect, certain obsessions, certain strugglings and stormings appear to have been exaggerated, over-coloured, over-toned—strident in fact, and certain gratifications rather anaemic.

I am convinced that I now know very clearly and inevitably what are my own tastes and distastes. So inevitable is this knowledge that I court every windfall chance of a side-track, and all tracks lead me back to the same stable!

When I used to see you at Ottoline's, in Hampstead, and the cinema parties (I wonder if you remember them, I enjoyed them so much) I was eighteen, and so full of ponderous reflections that I must have been very muddled or very glib—probably both. Now I am monotonously articulate. I am thirty-two.

I should love to see you when you come to London in August. I hope you will come before the 15th or so. On or about that date I take the only chance of getting out of London for more than a few days that I have during the whole year, except for business reasons which take me to Berlin or Paris—both of which are worse—and I rush to the Salzkammergut. My gallery is always open, day and night and Saturday afternoons. I live over it . . . .

Except for Mark Gertler,[359] now and then, I never see any of the people that we both used to know. Only through Barbara, whom I find most delightful, and through William Gerhardi, whom I like immensely, have I heard of you at all.

The latter part of April I shall be in Berlin arranging an exhibition there, but all letters will be forwarded.

Please remember me very warmly to Frieda. She was always so kind to me.

Yours,
Dorothy [360]

13 April 1928   Villa Mirenda, Scandicci, Florence, Italy

《 . . . *I am alone for a day or two, Frieda having gone off with her sister [Else] to Alassio, to see her daughter Barbara. But F. will be back Sunday night. Then we start packing up like the devil, and clear out of this house and this climate. There's no mistake, it's a poor climate; what with wind, rain, mist, scirocco and heaviness, it's a pearl. But at the end of this month we quit for good.*

And I feel I ought to go to Switzerland. It did me a lot of good—and I'd better look after these bronchials of mine, they play the deuce with me. . . . So some time in May we'll go up to the mountains, and stop a couple of months. Then perhaps to England—and in the autumn I'd like to set out towards the ranch. If I can sell my novel and have some money, I'd like to go round the world again. . . . If I have enough money, I'd like very much to do that. Otherwise we might go straight to the ranch. But it would be so nice, just for a bit, to be drifting out of reach of mail and malice, no letters, no literature, no publishers or agents or anything—what a paradise! I'm awfully tired of all that side of the world.

I painted a bit since I'm back—a few water-colours and a little Rape of the Sabine women—and I'm doing my Ravello Fauns up. It's quite amusing to paint—if only one didn't have the feeling of other people looking on. That spoils it again. People keep coming—and they want to see one's pictures—and they don't like them, they don't really want to take the trouble of really looking at them, or at anything; they stand there half alive and make the whole thing seem like lukewarm fish soup. I'm fed up with people—absolutely. That's why I'd like to move on a bit.[361]

Margaret Gardiner

The letter said:

Your brother writes that you will be in Florence. Do come and see us. You must take tram No. 16 in Via dei Pecori, just near the cathedral. Come to the very terminus—then walk on straight ahead uphill and don't turn till you see two cypresses, close together as two fingers. Take the road to the left there— dip down in the little hollow—our house is the big square box on the crown of the hill. But let us know and we'll come at least part of the way to meet you, or, if you prefer, send the peasant with the little trap, the barrocino. He'll rattle you up in no time.

She had read it many times and now, sitting in the tram, she read it again. She was solemn and excited; the whole of her life jostled in her throat to leap into expression. She was going to meet Lawrence, really going to meet him. She felt full and important. Lawrence! A person to whom one could talk, who knew and understood everything. The tram stopped with a jerk and she got out, screwing up her eyes in the glaring light, smoothing out her fresh cotton frock, already a little crum-pled and sticky from the heat. And there he was, immediately recognizable, but smaller than she had imagined, somehow a little shrunken, frail.

"Miss Wickham?"

"Yes."

He shook her hand. "I'm so glad you've come. My wife has had to go away for a few days on a visit to her sister, but she asked me to send you her greetings and say how sorry she was to miss you."

Judith was glad. It was turning out just as she wished and she would have him to herself. But she said:

"I'm sorry. I'd so much have liked to meet her."

Now they were walking slowly up the dusty road, the girl silent and breathless, the man talking easily and gaily, asking for news of her brother, questioning her about her journey and where she was staying.

"Let's look a minute," he said.

He stopped and sat wearily on a rock by the roadside, coughing. As she turned to the quivering Tuscan landscape below, Judith had a sudden realization of how ill he was and how much his quick vitality cost him.

"It's lovely."

"Yes, lovely," said Lawrence. "The world *is* lovely." And then, with surprising bitterness, "But people, how I hate them. They spoil it all."

"Oh, no," protested Judith. "Not people, just like that. Some people, perhaps. But not people, just like that."

"All modern people are rotten to the core," he said vindictively, "destroying themselves and everything else with their little beastlinesses. Well, let 'em."

Judith was shocked. He surely couldn't mean it? How ridiculous. But she was checked by his intensity and for the moment her own world darkened and was peopled by monsters.

They started up the hill again, and again Lawrence was easy and friendly and everything sparkled and looked gay in the sunlight. The climb was a painful one, with many pauses for Lawrence to rest, so that they were glad to reach the house at last and grateful for its cool darkness. But it wasn't really dark; brightly coloured pictures hung on the chalk white walls, there were striped Mexican rugs on the tiled floor and crisp muslin curtains in the windows. The furniture was painted and everything was tremendously neat and clean, enchantingly gay.

"I'm painting now," said Lawrence. "I do nothing but paint. I love it."

Judith got up and looked at the pictures on the wall. There was a holy family, a group of nuns and several portraits of peasants, all strongly, rather crudely painted in flat, bright colours. Everything he did must be wonderful, and yet she didn't really like the pictures. She gazed at them without a word, hoping, hypocritically, that her silence would be taken for admiration.

"I've cooked the dinner myself," said Lawrence. "Are you hungry? I do hope you'll like it."

He went to the kitchen and returned with a delicious smelling stew pot. They sat down.

"Oh, the potatoes. I've forgotten the potatoes," he cried.

"Shall I fetch them?" said Judith, jumping up. He looked so frail and worn.

"Yes, do. They're on the stove. Just bring them in as they are, in the pan."

The kitchen was as neat and fresh as the rest of the house. Judith loved it all. She took the pan and, walking happily back, put it down on the red and white check table cloth.

"Come on," said Lawrence, and they ate hungrily, enjoying the good food and the rough red wine. When they had finished their figs and grapes and were starting to clear the table, Lawrence looked at the girl severely.

"You need a lot of training about the house." Judith blushed guiltily as she saw the black ring on the table cloth where she had put the pan, but Lawrence laughed and said: "You should have seen my wife when I first married her! She didn't know a thing about housework, I can tell you. And even now, she doesn't know much. As for shopping! I don't believe she'll ever get these Italian weights and measures right." He himself was so quick and deft, washing the plates, putting the kitchen to rights. But his wife, it seemed, was a real lady, incompetent. He was immensely proud of her.

They sat in the wicker armchairs and talked.

"I do so love your books," Judith was longing to say. "They mean so much to me. They are more real to me than the real world." But she couldn't say that or any of the other things. All the heavy intensity that she had brought to this meeting was dissolved by his gaiety, his preoccupation with detail and his disconcerting outbursts of irritation. And yet, somehow, she felt shallow and frivolous in face of his amazing authenticity. He was a very sick man.

So he told her about Mexico and she told him about Egypt.

"I hated it," she said. "It was all so dead and old and finished. And the people, just living on the surface of it, quite disconnected. They seemed to have nothing to do with the country at all—didn't belong to it somehow. They were just living there, but they didn't belong."

Lawrence nodded.

"But Palestine," the girl went on. "That was different. I loved Palestine. It was green and growing up." She began to tell him how she had ridden up Mount Carmel with a friend and had spent the day in a Jebel Druse village. Their ponies had bolted and her friend, who had never ridden before, had fallen off. The Arabs were highly amused. And in the evening they had sat with the Chief in his big white room, lit by a single oil lamp, and all the men of the village, in their black robes and white turbans, had come silently in and sat shadowy on the floor, close to the walls. Then someone had called for music and after much chatter a man had started to play on a reedy pipe; a monotonous tune, over and over again. Suddenly a boy jumped up and began to dance, his arms and body motionless, but with delicate, subtle movements of his feet. In the growing excitement a man sprang up and then another, following the boy with a quick counter rhythm, till there were four of them dancing in single file, and the whole place was wildly alive. It was too much for the player—with a shout he flung his pipe across the room. Someone caught it and took up the scrawny tune—the black mass of men swayed and clapped till the excitement overwhelmed them and they all staggered out, drunken and laughing, into the cold, moonlit night.

Judith stopped, out of breath, a little drunk again at the memory. Lawrence was pleased.

"You're all right," he said. "You understand things a little."

Judith was delighted, triumphant. He had said she was all right! Of course—but all the same she felt troubled, a little ashamed. It had been true, about the sterility of Egypt, about Palestine and about the strange excitement of the dancing. But in a way it hadn't been her own experience at all, for it had been lived and seen with the eyes lent her by his books. And Lawrence, Lawrence who understood everything, simply hadn't seen through her; he was pleased with her for what was essentially his, not hers.

"Two friends of ours are coming up later on," he was saying, "to look at my pictures. Two ladies, sisters. They live in Florence and do a little sketching. We call them the Virgins. They're nice."

He was coughing again, looking drawn and tired. "Forgive me," he said, "I ought to rest a little now. It's quite silly, but I'm supposed to rest."

"But of course," said Judith. He did so hate admitting he was ill.

"Would you like to read one of my stories that has been published in America?" [362] he asked. "It's a good story—very good. True and tender. But that didn't prevent its readers from being shocked and from writing to the Editor to say his magazine wasn't fit for their wives and daughters to read. Not fit to read! My lovely story! Oh, their dirty, mean, poky little minds! There was quite an uproar and the Editor was frightened. He knew my story was good, but he wouldn't stand by me because he was frightened for his wretched magazine." Lawrence spoke with intense bitterness, and this time Judith shared his indignation.

"How disgusting," she cried.

She curled up in the chair and read the story. She was lost again in the magic of his writing, his delicate perception and flamelike vitality.

And again she longed to tell him how wonderful she thought his work was, how much it meant to her and how she really understood. She wanted him to know that she too was alive and aware. She wanted to tell him about herself and all that she had been through, to show him that she knew about love and suffering and death. All the time she had meant to tell him that; she had been so sure. But now doubt crept in, and again she felt curiously ashamed. Why? Lawrence, happier, lighter than she had expected, with his rather absurd grudges, his spite and his bitter outbursts. Yet, in the man himself, even more than in his books, there was a quality of sincerity that she had never met before, a clear integrity that, by contrast, made all her meanings half meant. She felt raw and untried.

Lawrence came back, refreshed and smiling, and hummed as he went into the kitchen to make tea.

"Here they come," he called.

The Misses Smith, like as two peas, came into the room. In spite of the hot Italian sun, both were dressed in trim grey flannel suits buttoned tightly over their thin chests, both wore grey felt hats and carried, rather incongruously, bright parasols. Their kindly, faded faces lit with pleasure at the sight of Lawrence and he, a charming host, chatted and teased as he handed them tea and pastries and warmed them with his attentiveness. Judith was puzzled. For all his alleged hatred of humanity, Lawrence seemed to like them so much, these rather dull, prim and elderly Virgins. And they, though they spoke to him severely, as if he were some reprehensible small boy, were clearly delighted by him, blossomed and grew animated in his presence.

With instinctive cruelty the girl stretched in her chair, flaunting her fresh roundness, her uncreased youth. But the Virgins didn't notice; they were concentrated on Lawrence.

"Now look at the pictures," he said.

Obediently they rose and stood in front of the holy family. A young Joseph, dark faced, grinning slightly, dominated the picture, standing tall and rather coarse, with his arm possessively round Mary. And she leaned placidly against him, looking up, utterly careless of the child that was perched upon her knee. Like Judith, the Misses Smith were silent and it was clear that they, like her, didn't care for the picture. But Judith now veered passionately in defence of Lawrence's work. "Silly old things," she thought, and she said:

"Lovely, isn't it?"

The Virgins didn't answer.

When they came to the bevy of nuns, however, it seemed to please them better.

"But why did you put *him* in?" asked the older Miss Smith, pointing to the figure of a peasant who peered derisively at the group from behind a corner of the convent. "He spoils it."

"Why, he's the whole point of the picture," said Lawrence, laughing.

He went to a cupboard, brought out a sheaf of water colours and started to show them.

"That's good," said one Miss Smith, and the other agreed. Here was something they understood and, looking through the pile, they spoke as fellow artists, discussing, criticizing.

"Here's one I particularly like," said Lawrence. He grinned maliciously. "It's called *Le Pisseur.*"

They all looked. "But why?" thought Judith. "Why? I don't see it."

The younger Miss Smith was the first to speak. She flushed.

"Really, Lawrence," she said, "You go too far."

Lawrence was furious.

"What do you mean?" he cried. "I go too far? What's wrong with the picture? Look at it. Look at that lovely curve. It's a lovely, natural thing."

But it was too much for the Virgins. They were really shocked and hurt.

"No, no, Lawrence," said the elder. "You shouldn't do these things. You really shouldn't."

After they had gone, Lawrence was still angry.[363]

"The impudence," he said, "the incredible impudence. To speak like that to me. I'm a real artist and they take it on themselves to say things like that to me!"

"Oh, well," said Judith, secure in being all right, in understanding things a little, in her wholehearted allegiance to him. "Oh, well—the Virgins."

Lawrence paused. He looked at her, mocking, amused.

"You're the real virgin, you know," he said.[364]

---

25 April 1928   *Villa Mirenda, Scandicci, Florence, Italy*

❪ *I hang on, waiting for proofs—have only done half, yet: wish the printer would hurry up. Orders come in pretty well—not in a rush—but all right. I can go as soon as proofs are done and binding is settled—Orioli will do the rest.*

. . . .

I feel I don't much care where I go. The outside world doesn't matter quite so much as it did—it matters less and less—so long as one can sit peacefully and be left pretty much alone. One hardly wants any more to step out of the shadow of one's bo-tree.[365]

4 May 1928   Villa Mirenda, Scandicci, Florence, Italy

❰ *You may have heard by now that we are keeping on the Mirenda. I took down the pictures and we began to pack: but Frieda became so gloomy that I hung the pictures up again and paid six months' rent. Not worth while getting into a state about. So here we are, just the same. And probably we shall stay till the end of the month, as the proofs of the novel are still only half done. I wish the printer would hurry up.*[366]

Robert H. Davis

John Ruskin in one of his pamphlets on Italian art wrote that a wayfarer rambling along the Lungarno Corsini in Florence need not be surprised should he come face to face with a genius; a suggestion that sufficed to send me along the river where Cellini walked arm-in-arm with Lorenzo the Magnificent, where Michelangelo took the air, where Dante first saw the vision of the divine Beatrice; and what not.

The month of May under Italian skies: *Multa granda.* Pausing before No. 6, I peer into a small rectangle stuffed with books, engravings, holographic letters, in frames; parchment bindings, empty but beautiful; fragments of Gregorian music. "Pino Orioli" in gold letters adorns the lower panel in the glass door. I will ask for the gentleman.

Signor Orioli is charmed and charming. "You are from the States? Be at home here," and bows me in. What a delightful litter of literature; what an intoxicating aroma of ancient books. A small folder lies on the centre of the table. What's this? "*Lady Chatterley's Lover.* By D. H. Lawrence. In preparation. By Subscription only."

I thought of *The White Peacock, Sons and Lovers, The Plumed Serpent.*

"Do you know Lawrence?" I asked with a wise lift of the eyebrows; a gesture intended to be Masonic.

"My dear sir," responded the Orioli, flashing a fraternal glance, "I have the honor to be his publisher. . . . I am expecting him to arrive at any moment. . . . I will be most happy to present you. . . . How interesting."

Ruskin was right: "Face to face with genius." Lest I be laid under suspicion, the small camera—equipped with a precious portrait lens which always accompanies me in foreign lands, was placed on a side table where it reposed harmlessly enough wrapped in a square yard of black silk.

What next? I had seen portraits of Lawrence at home; could identify him anywhere; a strapping fellow with a fierce beard; a rough rider who wore spurs in Chihuahua and lugged a heavy quirt on his wrist. Bring on D. H. I would talk Spanish with him. After establishing the entente cordiale I would pose him artistically and make his portrait.

Signor Orioli offered a chair. For strategic reasons I sat down as far as possible from my camera. No reason to feature the instrument until I had coiled the victim in the lariat of friendship. One must be diplomatic with genius.

"Lawrence has not been well," said his publisher. "His wife has been quite disturbed about him."

"What seems to be the trouble? Italian wines, perhaps!"

"He does not drink."

"Well, the Tuscan cigars and the State tobacco?"

"Nor smoke. Mrs. Lawrence prepares all his food. A very delicate stomach . . . ."

A smallish person, dressed in a loose-fitting brown tweed, appeared in the doorway, paused a moment, smiled, said "Good morning, Pino," and began to study the book shelves.

A moment of silence. "D. H.," said Orioli softly as one speaks in a sick-room, "an American admirer wishes to meet the author of *Lady Chatterley.*" The man in the tweed suit turned toward me. "Mr. Davis, Mr. Lawrence."

I took the extended hand, which was physically frail, though the clasp was cordial. The beard, tending to Van Dyke, was soft and silken. His hair was ample and glossy, falling around a splendid forehead. Whatever suggestion of sturdiness has been imparted by the portraits I had previously seen vanished when I came into his presence. The eyes were clear as crystal with a touch of brilliancy, the more so when he talked. A continuous smile, wan at intervals, played around his mouth. The voice was low, the speech modulated in accordance with his mood. What at the outset of our conversation I mistook for bashfulness proved to be commendable reserve. His whole demeanor was that of one who was unaccustomed to praise. When I spoke of his books and referred to his popularity and fame, he appeared actually to be uncomfortable. It was difficult to understand how this man—weighing not more than 140 pounds—frail as Robert Louis Stevenson, could have summoned the energy to perform the tasks that took him over the barriers of public indifference and placed him on the very pinnacle. Even so, he cannot master his delightful embarrassment. During the conversation, which consumed half an hour, he edged over to the side table and sat himself down on my small, silken-wrapped camera.

Might I take his picture? Yes, sometime before I left Florence, "but not today. Moreover, I don't make a good picture. Nor have I the time to go with you."

"Five minutes will suffice," I said. "Here and now."

"Where is your camera? Must you fetch it?"

"You're sitting on it, *hombre*," I replied, with the conviction that he who spoke Italian, French, German and Spanish would be bowled over by the last word of my sentence.

Instantly he popped off the table and surveyed the instrument. "Can you take a picture with that?" he asked. "I mean a portrait?"

"I can if you will compose yourself for seven seconds."

"Shall we go outside in the sunlight?"

"I would prefer this interior, with book shelves for a background. More intimate, don't you think?"

"Just as you wish. You're going to be disappointed in any event. Now what do you wish me to do?"

"Take a seat, opposite me, at the centre table. Look into the camera for seven seconds. Then look out across the Arno for—well, six seconds, after which you are free. With luck we shall get a front and a side view. Rogues' gallery, in a manner of speaking."

I piled up two volumes of Machiavelli in full morocco, a thick biography by Cavour and one ponderous tome dealing with the love affairs of Catherine de Medici; topping the column with my camera. One minute under the black silk for focal range. "O. K.! Steady!" Seven seconds. "Now for the side view. That's it. You looked bored."

Lawrence smiled and wet his lips. "How does one avoid that?"

"By fixing your gaze on some object outside. Select a spot on the opposite bank of the river and show some concern in it. Project your mind and the eye will record interest. Anyhow, that's my theory about portrait photography."

"I've got it," replied Lawrence, his face lighting up. "A bit of rare architecture. Beautiful lines.

Illuminated by the Spring sunshine, the little book shop, glowing with an old ivory tone reflected from the ancient parchment bindings, became an ideal studio. Six seconds were enough. The shutter clicked loudly. "That will do. Copies tomorrow. Thanks for two wonderful films. America shall see you as you are."

"Do you really think you succeeded?" asked my sitter, anxiously.

"I don't dare think otherwise. *Muchas gracias, Señor.*" And that would have to hold him.

I hustled away from the book shop, leaving Orioli and Lawrence in the clutches of baffling uncertainty, and sought out a professional photographer to whom I conveyed the information that the fates had selected him to develop nothing less than a pair of old masters languishing to be born in a bath of chemicals. He assured me that the late Andrea del Sarto was no more painstaking than himself.

True to his promise, the next morning he delivered two beautiful unretouched prints of the Lawrence portraits. With artistic hysteria I dashed out, and, as I live, ran into my sitter who, with his wife, was coming along the street. Mrs. Lawrence gazed long and earnestly at the reproductions. Suddenly an expression of infinite satisfaction came over her face. Turning to her spouse and addressing him by a pet name, which I muffed, she exclaimed: "These are you. They are wonderful. Nothing could be more natural. Just you as you are, without artifice." Eureka!

Despite this unqualified approval of the woman who knows Lawrence best, I modestly withdrew in good order and the following week left Florence for New York, fully intending to set the pictures before the American public. Upon reaching Manhattan I was plunged into the depth of despair by the discovery that both films had vanished. Men had gone gray over night for less than this.

Later I found the D. H. Lawrence films in a side pocket of my Gladstone bag. Destiny has decreed that they shall be handed down to posterity.[367]

24 May 1928   Villa Mirenda, Scandicci, Florence, Italy

❨ *You ask me, do I feel things very much?—and I do. And that's why I too am ill. The hurts, and the bitterness sink in, however much one may reject them with one's spirit. They sink in, and there they lie, inside one, wasting one. What is the matter with us is primarily chagrin. Then the microbes pounce. One ought to be tough and selfish: and one is never tough enough,* and never selfish in the proper self-preserving way. Then one is laid low. I've been in bed again this last week, but not bad, a touch of 'flu. And it's no good going to Switzerland to be bitter cold. It's even cold here.

.   .   .   .

I'm doing the last proofs of my novel now, so in about a week I expect we shall leave. I hope the book won't shock you—but I'm sure it won't. You will understand what I'm trying to do: the full natural rapprochement of a man and a woman; and the re-entry into life of a bit of the old phallic awareness and the old phallic insouciance.[368]

Bennett Cerf

As I read the inadequate four-line obituary notice [of Norman Douglas] in the Los Angeles paper, my mind carried me back twenty-three years to my one and only meeting with Norman Douglas—and D. H. Lawrence —in Florence, Italy, in the spring of 1928 (6 June).[369]

Douglas's *South Wind* and Lawrence's *Sons and Lovers* were at that time two of the best sellers in our Modern Library Series (they are still important titles on the list today, although their popularity has dimmed considerably over the years) and when I announced my impending visit in notes from Rome, both authors wrote they would be pleased to see me. Accordingly, on the tour up through the Hill Towns, while my companions were looking forward to seeing the Pitti Palace, and the Ponte Vecchio, and the famous doors of the Baptistry in Florence, I was dreaming principally of meeting two of my great heroes in modern literature. Douglas, as a matter of fact, was waiting in the hotel lobby to greet me. Silver-haired, aristocratic, and handsome in the manner of Charles Brackett, the Saratoga producer and bon vivant, Douglas was, moreover, extremely affable and anxious to please, and when he carried me off for dinner and a look at the town, I literally was in seventh heaven.

It soon developed that Norman Douglas was nursing several grievances. One was against the world at large for what he called "its imbecile attitude" toward homosexuality. Another was against rich American tourists who threw their money away on "fake antiques" but no longer seemed willing to pay fantastic premiums for the limited, autographed editions of inconsequential, slap-dash Norman Douglas trivia that his friend Orioli, among others, was publishing in ever greater profusion. "You've flooded the market," I pointed out. "Collectors of your books are

213

beginning to feel that you're making suckers out of them." "But look at the fortunes they're making overnight in the stock market," pouted Douglas. "What difference does it make to them what they pay for anything?" (What difference, indeed, I reflected some five [seventeen] months later, when the market collapsed, and more than one collector of expensive first editions took a last look at his treasures in a Park Avenue penthouse before leaping over the parapet into eternity.)

But Mr. Douglas's bitterest vituperation was reserved for the author I was bent upon meeting the next day—D. H. Lawrence. The two men had been firm friends until Lawrence wrote a long preface to a little book called *Memoirs of the Foreign Legion,* by "M. M.," published in London by Martin Secker in 1924.[370] Douglas took umbrage at some of Lawrence's remarks, and the resultant quarrel had been so bitter that the two men had cut each other completely ever since. "At lunch tomorrow I'll draw you a map showing you how to drive out to Lawrence's villa," said Douglas reluctantly, "but you're wasting your time going to see him. He's a hollow shell of the man he once was." Before we parted, Douglas proposed, "Now what sort of a companion shall I provide for you tonight?"

I explained uncomfortably that I had promised to play bridge that evening with some friends from New York. "I could scarcely imagine a more ridiculous way to spend one's first night in Florence," scoffed Douglas—and probably was right.

The next day he failed to produce the map. "It's fifteen miles over vile country roads to Lawrence's villa," he explained, "and none of the taxi drivers in Florence could get you there. I'll have to take you myself." "But I thought you loathed Lawrence?" I remonstrated. "I do," said Douglas, "but after all, he's dying [Lawrence did die, as a matter of fact, less than two years later] and this is probably the last time I'll ever see him." It soon became obvious that Douglas was looking forward to the meeting very much indeed, though throughout our entire ride up through the hills to the Lawrence villa, he expounded on the spectacular misbehavior of Lawrence and his wife, Frieda.

One last turn brought us in sight of our goal. It was a squat, two-story, stucco affair, with a balcony directly above the door in the center. Standing on the balcony was a pale, emaciated little man with a flowing red beard—unmistakably D. H. Lawrence in person. At sight of us he waved his arms excitedly, shrilled "Norman Douglas!," and disappeared within the house. A moment later the two authors were embracing warmly, babbling incoherent assurances of affection, and paying no

214

attention whatever to me. Then Frieda—the same Frieda who had been castigated by Douglas five minutes earlier—appeared, and the general rejoicing reached an even higher pitch. It was only when Frieda carried her visitor off for a tour of the grounds that Lawrence addressed his first remark to me. "Mr. Cerf," he said severely, "how dared you bring that man into my house?"

For the next twenty minutes Lawrence recited a list of Douglas's shortcomings that made the latter's own grievances sound petty by comparison. Yet the moment Douglas and Frieda Lawrence re-entered the room, the gurgles of joy and the delighted reminiscing began all over again. Those reminiscences! They embraced people and places all over Europe, and in concentrated malice and pettiness sounded, for all the world, like three old gossips cackling together on the verandah of a summer hotel.

As I sit writing this piece in the California sunshine, I can still recall every detail of that slovenly room in which we sat. I particularly remember an almost-empty milk bottle lying on its side in the middle of the stone floor, ignored by everybody—and a tray of half-eaten food gathering flies on a corner table. Bear in mind that this was the home of an invalid in the last throes of tuberculosis! And I remember, too, my sense of shock at the calibre of conversation between two of the greatest and most famous authors of their time. It amply supported the admonition made many years later by Sinclair Lewis (himself fated to die, like Lawrence and Douglas, in Italy): "Authors shouldn't gad about too much, talking and making exhibitions of themselves. That's not their business. The results are usually disastrous. An author's business is to plant himself at his desk—alone—and *write*." [371]

7 June 1928   *Villa Mirenda, Scandicci, Florence, Italy*

⟨ Here are all the sheets [for Lady Chatterley's Lover] *signed and numbered, up to 1,000: then ten extra ones signed but not numbered, in case anything goes wrong . . . and ten blank ones. So glad that's all over.*[372]

7? June 1928   *Villa Mirenda, Scandicci, Florence, Italy*

⟨ *We think to leave here on Sunday [10 June 1928], for the French Alps near Grenoble. The Brewsters are in Florence and will go with us. Very*

215

muggy thundery weather here—it will be nice to get a bit higher up. We
shall look round for a place about 3000 ft. . . .[373]

SWITZERLAND

Achsah Barlow Brewster

A year had passed without our seeing the Lawrences. It was May of
1928: they had offered us their Florentine villa, the Mirenda, for the
summer, and we had gone there to see them before they left for the
French Alps. As usual at that season the poppies were in full glory. The
little hills gambolled together as for a Bennozzo Gozzoli picture. When we
saw Lawrence we suddenly realized that he was very ill, and knew that
we must not postpone to the future our time with him, but seize each
passing day. He was fastidiously dressed in white flannels with a flax-
blue coat. (It became customary with him to wear such a coat.)

He led us from room to room showing us the walls adorned with his
paintings. Their sensitive colour and tactile qualities, their ease of
technique and their spontaneity and their expressiveness pleased me. In
the living-room hung at one end the *Holy Family;* in the dining-room was
the *Scene from Boccaccio* [*Boccaccio Story*], in Frieda's room was his
Pieta [*Resurrection*], and in Lawrence's room was a painting of nude
figures with beasts snarling around; I do not remember what he called
it [*Fight with an Amazon*], but to me it was the hounds of heaven! I
enjoyed the picture [*Red Willow Trees*] of early spring with glowing willow trees and nude figures.

The next day while we were there a group of three men arrived, among
them Norman Douglas.[374] (I believe it was their first meeting since their
disagreement over the publication of *Memoirs of the Foreign Legion.*)
Lawrence was a dignified host. The jovial Douglas talked voluble German
with Frieda. Lawrence looked pale and wan beside them.

It was decided that we should go to the Alps with Frieda and Lawrence,
instead of remaining at the villa. The trip began to have a lure.

Our farewell luncheon was gay. The train journey [10 June 1928] was
an adventure. As we sped along, the passengers descended one after
another, until by night we had our compartment to ourselves with the
adjoining ones empty. Then we began to sing hymns. Lawrence knew all
the Moody and Sankey revival songs, the Salvation Army tunes, every
word of all the verses. One followed another in growing dramatic effect,

until the climax was reached in *Throw out the life-line*. He stood up and threw out an imaginary lasso to the drowning souls, hauling them in strenuously. But the exhilaration from singing did not keep Lawrence from being tired when we reached Turin, where we decided to spend the night. The next morning [11 June 1928] a glorious magnolia blossom was placed on our luncheon table in the sun. It opened out full even as we watched it—a thrilling spectacle of a flower's response to the sun.

There was no definite notion of where we were going, only the pleasure of exploring. We thought the Savoy Alps with the sight of Mount Blanc might be what we wanted.

Our next stop was Chambéry. Early in the morning Frieda and Lawrence were up and had returned from a tour of the town, having investigated the shops, bringing back an orange cravat for Earl, before the rest of us were out. Lawrence was in a holiday mood.

How happy we felt in Aix-les-Bains. The hotel verandahs filled with gay groups dining in the open enchanted us as did the long menus. He read the list with gusto, electing fresh brook trout and grilled chicken. While he scrunched the bones of these viands he made derogatory remarks about our soufflé and salads. Two waiters vied with each other to serve us. There was bickering between them throughout the meal. When coffee was served the dark waiter gave a resounding smack full in the face of his colleague, whose cheek turned from rose to scarlet. Frieda decided it was misled patriotism, but Lawrence was grievously disturbed and felt it was a profound cosmic discord!

It was Lawrence who found the first lilies-of-the-valley; to be sure he only found them in the flower-market, but they were wild ones. We were on our way to the lake, which seemed an interminable distance, and when we arrived there we sank down in a daze of weariness, trying to refresh ourselves with tea served with eight varieties of jam, while we watched a swan careen on the lake with two of her young tucked under her wings.

From Grenoble we motored up the heights to a sunny plateau, swung out over the valley, with a view of the snow-covered mountains. The mountain flowers were in their splendour; deep purple columbine, blue gentians, pansies, forget-me-nots, lilies-of-the-valley, alpine roses. A rustic inn was found in the floweriest spot of all, christened St. Nizier-de-Pariset, and there we arranged to make a sojourn. On the following day we returned in high spirits to settle in.

Early in the morning, after our first night there, the proprietor knocked at Earl's door, announcing that monsieur had been ill in the night.

"Oh, no," said Earl, "I was not ill."

"But not you, the other one—he coughed all night."

He added that he was sorry not to be able to keep Lawrence, but there was no choice, since the law on that plateau prohibited his having guests with affected lungs. Monsieur would have to go.

Ill as Lawrence was he had never admitted to us the seriousness of his malady. He had continued to refer to it as an "annoying" irritation of his bronchials. Never before had the doors of a hotel been closed to him because of it.

Shocked and dismayed, we had to break this news to Frieda, whom it upset still more. It was decided not to tell Lawrence what had happened. Although the evening before we had all agreed enthusiastically that the place was *"perfect," "entirely to our taste," "a rare find,"* the inn-keeper *"remarkably fine"*—we now decided to tell Lawrence that we no longer liked it, and wanted to go away. *What* would he say to such a sudden change? To such fickleness of taste? We greatly wondered.

Lawrence seemed not in the least surprised, and replied quite calmly —that strangely enough he couldn't bear the place either, that he had awakened in the morning not wanting to stay. "There was something *mingy* about that inn-keeper. I felt it from the first."

Did he suspect what had happened? We never knew. But all day he kept repeating: "Curious how I hated that place!" [375]

21 June 1928   Grand Hotel, Chexbres-sur-Vevey, Vaud, Switzerland

❨ *We are in this biggish hotel, with the Brewsters—well looked after, 9 francs a day including tea—and about 2000 ft. above Lac Leman. . . . It's above Vevey, quite near Lausanne. —That St. Nizier place was very rough—and the insolent French people actually asked us to go away because I coughed. They said they didn't have anybody who coughed. I felt very mad. But it's much better here—dull, but comfortable. And it's no good shivering with cold and being uncomfortable. The Brewsters are here—Frieda has gone to Baden Baden for a week. Aldous [Huxley] has telegraphed that he and Maria will join us next Tuesday or Wednesday [26 or 27 June 1928]—from Paris. So we are not likely to be lonesome, as the Brewsters say.—They are very nice, the Brewsters, look after me so well: I ought to get quickly fat . . . . I'm so anxious to know what milady [Lady Chatterley's Lover] is doing . . . . People pelting me with letters now, to know when they'll get her. —Somehow I feel it will be safe to post*

to England, day by day: start about a week after the American copies have
gone off.[376]

Achsah Barlow Brewster

Shaken by this experience [at St. Nizier-de-Pariset] and wearied with
travel we went at once to a familiar hotel in Chexbres-sur-Vevey and
settled down there to a quiet routine [17 June 1928]. Every day Lawrence grew better, so much so that Frieda could go for a visit to her
mother in Baden-Baden.

Lawrence was in a gentle mood, and would drink down ovaltine or
mint tea like a docile child. We would take rugs and cushions out on the
green meadows over the Lake of Geneva in view of the Dents du Midi.
Sometimes we sang, often we were silent, more often Lawrence burst
forth into deeply interesting discourses.

He veered upon money one afternoon, and the more he talked the
more vehement he grew. One must fight for his just share, never mind if
peace of heart were dearer than the just share! He was furious.

"It's your duty to be rich. It's a sin for you to sneak off with your peace
of heart while other people sneak off with what belongs to you. Fight!"

Having glanced over some Indian experiences that I had been writing,
he exclaimed.

"You would not try to paint a picture without any shadows. You can't.
Without the dark side there is no brightness. Why don't you describe how
your liver felt, how terrified of the riots you were, the disgust you felt
in your solar plexus?"

On the day for Frieda's return from Baden-Baden Lawrence consulted
the time-table and decided she would arrive by ten in the morning. As
no Frieda appeared he met the twelve o'clock express, with the same
result. He ate his lunch hurriedly and rushed back for the two-twenty
local, but returned shortly looking disconsolate. "She's probably lost
her passport and been held up, or her purse."

I know not how many other trains he met, certainly the ten o'clock
train, which held no Frieda.

We tried to cheer him up, but in vain. He always looked forward so
eagerly to her return.

In the morning there was Frieda, who had missed connections and
motored from Vevey at midnight.[377]

Earl H. Brewster

Instead of accepting Lawrence's hospitable offer of his place at Scandicci, we yielded to the temptation of accompanying him and Frieda to the Alps. We were with them much of the time between May and October of 1928.

A year had passed since our "walking trip," as we always called our Etruscan journies. Now I found Lawrence much weaker. He had never allowed me to see how serious his illness was—perhaps he did not admit it to himself. He spoke of his bronchials as "very annoying" and denied that his lungs were otherwise affected. "All that the doctors can do for me," he said, "is to say—You might *try* this or that climate—they don't know—it's just a matter of experiment." He hated seeing a doctor.

For some weeks we all remained in a hotel over the Lake of Geneva. Generally he would write for an hour or so after his breakfast; then we might take a short walk in the morning sunshine and lie on a rug out-of-doors until luncheon, walking again at tea time. During this period he wrote several of the essays which have been published under the title of *Assorted Articles*. "Insouciance" describes an incident at this hotel.[378]

I ventured to remark to Lawrence that it is the unexpected which happens: every day, every hour, is different from what we would have been able to prophesy. "No, no," objected Lawrence, "the years may be different but the days and weeks are not. I will bet you two pounds that nothing unexpected will happen within three weeks." So frequently I made my point that Lawrence asked, if that could be called unexpected which one awaited so confidently?

Lady Chatterley's Lover had been published since our last meeting[379] —"I shall give you a copy. Of course I want you to read it—but it is not your type of a book. I will give you a copy to take with you when we separate"—he would say. The reception which many of his friends had given it hurt him very much. "L—— read the book, she would come to the table green with rage, she would hardly speak to me," he related. "The idea! J—— treated it as improper and returned it without reading it through." He defended the book. He declared that the animosity which it and others of his works had aroused was partly the cause of his illness. It was months before he sent me the book—obviously he dreaded our reading it.

According to Lawrence the curse of our age is machinery. The substitute of the machine for life means death. He talked much of this: he

220

hated the automobiles, so many of which rushed past us over the Swiss roads. "I would like to remove that little bridge there and let them all go tumbling down into that valley." "Oh the world is going insane, I really believe it. There is such a thing as mass insanity; that is what the world is suffering from now. But things will change—forty years from now there will not be an automobile on these roads." [380]

Grand Hotel/Chexbres-sur-Vevey/Switzerland/Saturday/24 [23] June 1928

([*Dear Dorothy Warren*

I have just heard from Barbara Weekley that you are back and expecting my pictures. But the Claridge Gallery wrote for them, and I replied almost promising to send to them, at once, as they want to show from July 12th to 28th; their July show having fallen through. I'd rather really send them to you; but let me know at once when you would show them, as I have promised to send them to New York in autumn. If you don't let me know immediately—for you seem to leave long lapses between your answers—I shall send the things to Claridges. I am not pledged to them, though.

The water-colours and the three smaller oils ought to be in London.[381] I don't know if Barbara has seen them—she doesn't mention them. But she could get them and show them to you. The big pictures are packed in Florence, waiting to be forwarded immediately I send an address.

My friends E. H. Brewster and his wife Achsah Brewster, well-known painters really, have got some things in London: about twenty canvases I think, ranging around 30 x 35 inches. If you have room I should like you to show some, at the same time as mine. You could see the canvases and decide. Let me know.

> *Sincerely*
> *D. H. Lawrence* [382]

Dorothy Warren Trotter

[The Warren Gallery, 39a Maddox Street, London, W. 1] 26 June 1928

Dear Mr. Lawrence,

By now I hope you will have received my telegram. I understood from our last correspondence that you agreed to my exhibiting your pictures in my gallery, and that you would dispatch them from Italy on or about May 1st. I only returned from Berlin, where I was holding an exhibition of young English painters (Barbara amongst them) [383] at the end of May, and found your work had not arrived. I had intended to show it now, but of course I had to carry on without it.

I know nothing about your arrangements with the Claridge Gallery, except what you have written and what Mrs. Mathias [384] said when she rang me up yesterday. Please be advised by me. Do not show from the 18th of July until the 28th. Ten days is certainly not long enough to give any show a chance, and it is much too late in the season. The only daily papers which are important as regards art criticism would hardly have time to bring out their notices, especially as one can never be sure that the critic will come to the private view, and the weeklies would have no time at all to publish anything about the show until it was over. I always do three-weekly shows and sometimes I extend them even beyond that period, and yet people come in when it is all over and another show in full swing asking to see the former show. In such cases, if I have any of the work left I always produce it, often with excellent results, and I make a point of having permanently on view here pictures by artists who have been associated with this gallery. In your case, presuming that you actually do show in London at the end of July, there would be very little chance of late-comers seeing the work as London is empty in August from the art-gallery point of view except for a few American dealers hunting up antiques. The very best month of the whole year for picture-shows is November oddly enough, in spite of the almost complete absence of day-light. October is also good, when people return from holidays and are anxious to see what is going on. Although I should like to arrange your exhibition for November, as I feel it will be an important event and should be treated accordingly, I could do it in early October, so that the pictures could be in America by early November. I need hardly tell you that I am longing to have your show. I really have been looking forward to it tremendously, and I should do everything in my power to make it a success. Do you remember the little picture you painted of the flight into Egypt [385] which used to hang over the mantelpiece in Byron Villas? I always loved it and I remember it quite vividly. I am longing to see what you have been doing since.

While I was in Germany I was badly let-down. Letters were neither answered nor forwarded to me. I left instructions for 10 guineas to be sent to Florence for 5 copies of your book, and I have only just discovered by going through my pass-book that this was not done, so I have sent the cheque myself. A stringent and sweeping reform has taken place, and everything is running so smoothly it is almost too good to be true! Business has been excellent on the whole, despite a very persistent movement to down me carried on in a very ugly manner. I seem to be in luck though, because the downing has produced defence and support, without my having to work for it, in extremely useful quarters, where my efforts had been regarded formerly merely with amiable but not particularly active approval. I feel smug! In the teeth of all kinds of difficulties, I have exhibited an extremely fine German sculptor,[386] here, and although sculpture is notoriously hard to sell, frightfully expensive to transport, and the general feeling about German work is not favourable, the show has been a financial as well as an artistic success.

I have been absolutely frank with you, by telling you all this. I really appreciate your saying that you would like to show with me, and I want to feel quite sure that you really mean it. I am collecting some work of yours from an address that Barbara has just given to me on the telephone.[387]

With regard to the Brewsters, where can their work be seen? I have often heard of them from Lucile Beckett (now Lucile Frost).[388] Until I see your pictures it is difficult to judge exactly how much I could hang with them. I can show between 40 and 50 smallish pictures, but yours are mainly large and I hate the sort of thickly hung show that one always sees in London galleries, which makes one feel that almost anything can be crowded in somehow with a lot of good will and no taste. I tend to show fewer pictures on my walls than is usual in other galleries. However I will do what I can about the Brewsters if they will get in touch with me. Please let me know how you feel about an early October date? One could open on the 2nd, which would be a Tuesday. I try to open on Tuesdays always because it is a good day. I should like to have at least three weeks clear for you, but if you want the pictures to go to America, I could close on Saturday October 20th, which would be two days short of three weeks, if that would suit you.

Yours,
Dorothy [389]

28 *June 1928*   *Grand Hotel, Chexbres-sur-Vevey, Vaud, Switzerland*

❨ *Lady Chatterley came this morning, to our great excitement, and everybody thinks she looks beautiful, outwardly. [It is] a handsome and dignified volume—a fine shape and proportion, and I like the terra cotta very much,* and I think my phoenix is just the right bird for the cover. Now let us hope she will find her way safely and quickly to all her destinations.[390]

Grand Hotel/Chexbres-sur-Vevey/Switzerland/4 July 1928

⟨ Dear Dorothy Warren

Well I have ordered the pictures to be sent on to you—so they'll arrive in due time. They are seven—and four of them in simple wooden, painted frames. I prefer them in those frames painted to merge out the atmosphere of the picture—much better than gold or black frames. So will you let your man do the others about the same. But the water-colours, I don't mind how they are framed. When you have the pictures, let me know how you like them. Probably you will like them better as you get used to them. They are quite simple, with no tricks: but I consider they are, what very few pictures are, organically alive and whole. All the modern smartness only succeeds in putting pictures together, it practically never makes a picture live as a whole thing.

I was sorry to break with the Claridge people—especially as they were going ahead. But October is really a better time. And then I felt they were just commercial. After all, I know you, and the thing is more personal. But you are an unstable person—you disappear and leave no trace, you don't answer letters when you say you will, everybody says you are going bust, and altogether it's like riding to the moon on a soap-bubble. But do be wise for a little while longer. I didn't put any price on the pictures—must think about it. What would you suggest? I'm not anxious at all to sell the big ones. I have only those seven—but the little ones I care less about.

The Brewsters have about twenty pictures in Lucille Beckett's—Lucille Frost's charge, at Marble Arch. I wish you would look at them and show them when there is a chance. I'm sure they are better than most people's pictures.

Well, please let me know when the pictures come—I am having carriage paid in advance—and how you like them. Don't lapse into the void, or I shall have to come over to London and rescue the things.

All good wishes
D. H. Lawrence [391]

Achsah Barlow Brewster

As [Lawrence] grew stronger he wanted a house of his own. We motored to Le Pont, isolated in the hills above Lausanne, thinking we might find such a place there. It was a beautiful day and we were as full of adventure as ever. The little villages with their neat gardens were left behind, and long stretches of bleak pine forest surrounded us. We were back in winter with only a promise of spring. A black, cold lake shivered beneath the hotel, thawed after the winter sports but not warmed for summer! A village huddled on one side of the lake against the blast of the wind. The hotel would open next week. A terrible dreariness came over Lawrence and the rest of us. Switzerland seemed a prison.

Frieda and Lawrence determined none the less to find a house, somewhere at once, in a higher altitude; so a few days after the drive to Le Pont they departed for Gsteig-bei-Gstaad. They found a small châlet there on a steep hill above the little village, with pine woods at the back and surrounded by green meadows. The month at Chexbres had brought about an improvement in Lawrence's health; he believed this higher altitude would continue the improvement.[392]

8 *July 1928*   Hotel National, Gstaad, Bern, Switzerland

❲ *We have decided to go out to the chalet [Kesselmatte] tomorrow, Monday evening, at six o'clock—it saves another day in this dull hotel. We went to Gsteig this morning and fixed it up. The chalet must be about a mile from Gsteig village, and climbing up all the way, alas—I panted, but it wasn't so bad—a most lovely morning.*[393]

Châlet Kesselmatte, Gsteig-bei-Gstaad, Bern, Switzerland

❲ *We are here in a small but very nice peasant châlet on the mountain just over the German side of the Pillon pass from Diablerets. It's very nice— we have two nice big rooms downstairs, all old broad planks of pale wood, scrubbed and soft-coloured, about 200 years old: then a pleasant kitchen, and another good room upstairs—then the balconies—and the steep meadows, and spring, and barn—all for 100 francs a month. It's quite cheap and very easy—they leave chopped wood, and we pay for it at the end of the month as we consume it—and they let us have butter and eggs and milk and honey. We are about a mile from Gsteig village, towards the Pillon— and about 400 ft up. . . . Our peasants are just across the valley on the north side, with their cows, and in their other house. But they send the girl to wash up and clean for us. It is really very nice,—and if I could tramp the hills, it would be perfect. But it is steep. . . .*

Our friends the Brewsters are staying in the village in the Viktoria. They come up to tea.[394]

Achsah Barlow Brewster

. . . Soon we joined [the Lawrences], putting up at a nearby hotel.

When we arrived at Gsteig Lawrence was in bed suffering from a slight haemorrhage, but was up in another day and working. He made light of it, saying he had caught a little cold in his bronchials, which had brought on asthma.

The hill was a difficult climb, especially at an altitude of four thousand feet. We puffed up daily, never failing to be there for tea. He would be sitting on his bench under the pear tree in front of the châlet, waving from afar:

"Hello, I couldn't tell whether that was you or a white goat!"

Frieda's head would pop out over a pot of blossoming geraniums in the dormer window.

One afternoon he sat holding a child's copy-book saying that he was going to read us an unfinished novel he had started on the way back from Mexico when he was very ill, and written down by Frieda from his dictation. It was called *The Flying Fish* [395] with the old haunting symbolism of *pisces*.

As he read, it seemed to reach an ever higher more serene beauty. Suddenly he stopped, saying:

"The last part will be regenerate man, a real life in this Garden of Eden."

We asked: "What shall you make him do? What will he be like, the regenerate man, fulfilling life on earth?"

"I don't just know."

The enduring beauty of *The Flying Fish* made us ask at various times if he had not finished it, to which he would reply, that we must not urge him to finish it. "I've an intuition I shall not finish that novel. It was written so near the borderline of death, that I never have been able to carry it through, in the cold light of day."

Lawrence was writing articles during those days for newspapers, which have since been collected under the title of *Assorted Articles*. Almost every day there would be a new one to read to us.

A Hindu friend, Boshi Sen, visiting us, gave Lawrence massage, with skilful fingers running lightly up and down Lawrence's spine, thumping, patting, slapping, moving the head about, rubbing the mop of hair, twisting his neck.

"Why, you must be a Y.M.C.A. man!" Earl exclaimed to Lawrence. "For I've a theory that all of them have prominent Adam's apples like yours."

While this proceeded Lawrence would open eyes and mouth and make up droll faces as he was rubbed about.

After one of these diverting performances he read his last article, "Cock-Sure Women and Hen-Sure Men," which particularly pleased Boshi Sen, who maintained every woman in India ought to read it. Lawrence shook his head—"But they won't publish it even though they have asked for it!"—which incredible as it seems, proved to be true.[396]

At that time he was painting small water-colours, among them *An Explosion in the Mine* [*Accident in a Mine*]—a group of naked men carrying the body of a wounded miner. As he showed it to us, he said: "You know the miners work in some mines naked."

One afternoon we were singing *The Two Magicians*—

> Oh, she looked out of the window,
> As white as any milk.
> But he looked into the window
> As black as any silk.

That seemed to please Lawrence very much. "I believe I'll paint that milk-white lady with the black man gazing in through the windows at her." Next time we climbed the hill he had painted her.

We sang much that summer—sitting out on the grass. How he objected to that version of *High Germany* that said:

> Besides, my dearest Harry, though man and wife we be,
> How am I fit for cruel war in High Germany?

Instead he insisted on:

> I'll buy you a horse, my love, and on it you shall ride,
> And all my heart's delight shall be riding by your side;
> We'll call at every ale-house and drink when we are dry,
> So quickly on the road, my Love, we'll marry by-and-by.

We sang *Goddesses Three.* Out on the green hill we acted it: Frieda as Venus, the child [Harwood] as Minerva, and I as Juno, Earl was Paris handing out a stone to the victorious lady, as we had no apple handy. Lawrence was stage-manager, and prompter, and a severe critic as well.

Only rarely did Lawrence come down from that hill. Once was the day before the child's birthday to buy gifts for that occasion. We started out in the hotel motor and had arrived as far as two green fields full of mauve crocuses when the motor refused to budge. There were Lawrence and Frieda, the child, Boshi Sen, Earl and I, firmly settled in the roadway. It began to pour. We were in hilarious mood, cooped up there with the rain beating merrily at the windows for an hour or more. When we arrived at Gstaad we made mad spurts between rain-drops into cafés and shops, Lawrence full of whimsical drolleries.

Another time he came down from the châlet to celebrate Frieda's birthday [11 August] with ourselves and some friends. He made the occasion a gay festival.

One fine day we made an outing to Les Diablerets by motor, but generally he stayed perched on his mountain—that terrible green hill up which even the cart horses heaved and panted.

Once we found him there as usual on his seat by the pear tree, holding in his hands a long and hectic letter from an admirer. He said emphatically how much he hated what he called literary letters, and maintained that only an egoist could write more than one sheet—but then Lawrence could say more on one sheet than any other mortal!

We were sitting among the harebells when Lawrence opened his copy-book with green emerald corners (given by the child, inscribed on the fly-leaf: "Merry Christmas to Uncle David"),[397] and began reading his story, "The Blue Moccasins," [398] which he had just finished. Before the ending he stopped and asked us how we would end it. We all agreed to the same dénouement. He replied that he also at first had closed the tale in like manner, but on further consideration he had felt forced to change it, whereupon he read the version as it stood. I have never seen the printed tale, and now although the story is vivid in my mind I cannot recall the debated point.[399]

A rustic work-bench and a table had been made in the pine-grove for Lawrence, where he sat and wrote in view of the mountains, and near him the fragrant pines murmuring in the wind. The autumn crocuses swept over the hills. Yet for all that, as the days grew shorter he longed to go down into the world. The bleak green hills with their black trees patrolling them chilled the heart.

We departed before the Lawrences, after a four months' sojourn at Gsteig. Our last night there was a grand finale. Lawrence's sister [Emily], whom he called "Pamela, or Virtue Rewarded," had come with her daughter [Margaret] [400] for a visit. It was a farewell banquet for Boshi Sen (the scientist friend) and us. Lawrence loved to offer hospitality, a slice of bread-and-butter cut by him had a special delicacy, so exactly was it cut, so smoothly spread. His exquisite perceptions met any emergency and forestalled every wish.

His Wesleyan sister may have considered Boshi Sen a benighted Hindu, and perhaps to her horror heard Lawrence saying: "Have you ever been baptized, Boshi?" "No," answered Boshi, "but I shouldn't mind. The more gods we Hindus have, the better we like it." Then Lawrence ceremoniously baptized him with wine, after which Boshi chanted a Sanskrit hymn.

Lawrence then sang *Kismul's Galley*—fit symbol of himself, a brave ship on a stormy sea. He followed with Mexican love ditties, ending with the war-whoops of the Navajo Indians, sung with such fervour that it is a wonder he did not burst a blood-vessel in his throat.

Torrents of rain were falling, and we had to plough our way down the hill through the tall grass with the cataracts of water flowing off every knoll and rock. Lawrence stood at his doorway holding a flickering light, anxiously watching until we reached the far distant roadway. The following day he wrote "Hymns in a Man's Life." [401]

Earl H. Brewster

At Gsteig bei Gstaad the Lawrences had rented a chalet [Kessel-matte] . . . .

.   .   .   .

My family and I went to live in the hotel of the village below Lawrence's chalet. He was walking less and less.

Not far from his house the forest began. I sat there painting the distant mountains, in the foreground a few trees and a house. Lawrence sat by my side telling me how he felt the motive should be painted. "Look at that tree, you have made it too solid—it isn't that way—notice you can see *through* it in nearly every part of the tree: and that distant green mountain side—see how the grass grows, notice the *form* to the hill, why it goes back there and comes out so. . . ." He seemed fully aware of "significant form"!

We spoke of Gandhi's *ashram* and his enthusiasm for hand spinning and weaving, of which Lawrence said: "He is right. We might start such a place with a few people: only I ought to do it in my own country:

229

southern England perhaps." The hand-crafts as opposed to machinery appealed strongly to him. Lawrence once wrote to me:

All we possess is life—weaving, carving, building—this is the flow of life, life flows into the object—and life *flows out again* to the beholder. So that whoever makes anything with real interest, puts life into it, and makes it a little fountain of life for the next comer. Therefore a Gandhi weaver is transmitting life to others—and that is the great charity.

I am sure Lawrence always had the hope that some time there might be gathered about him a small group of people with similar attitude and feeling toward life, who would find a new and better way to live, solving some of the problems of life. We know how profoundly Lawrence valued certain relationships—the "rainbow"—which might come to be between one human being and another. It appealed to him to create something corresponding to a Gandhi *ashram*. These two men—Gandhi and Lawrence—so far apart in some respects—yet possessed far more in common than those who did not know Lawrence personally would imagine.

Lawrence returned my copy of Coomaraswamy's *The Dance of Shiva*,[402] saying: "I enjoyed all the quotations from ancient scriptures. They always seem true to me." Of J. C. Chatterji's *Kashmir Shaivism*,[403] he remarked: "That seems to me the true psychology, how shallow and groping it makes western psychology seem."

One day I took my friend Dhan Gopal Mukerji [404] to call on Lawrence. The following remarks of Lawrence's on that occasion are especially interesting to me because . . . later he completely changed his attitude: "You don't really believe in God. You can't in this age. No, no, it is a conception mankind has exhausted: the word no longer has meaning." [405]

Kesselmatte/Gsteig b. Gstaad/(Bern)/Switzerland/20 July 1928

⟨ Dear Dorothy [Warren]

Have you got my pictures yet from Florence? They were forwarded to you some time ago. Be sure and let me know as soon as they arrive. You have the little ones, Mrs. Hilton told me you sent and fetched them. Let me know what you think of them, will you? And tell me your ideas of framing and the prices to put on them. I asked you this before, but you didn't answer. Please answer now, as it annoys me when you do not so much as trouble to reply.

It may be I should like the small pictures taken over to show to some American friends who will not be in London. If so, I should ask Mrs. Hilton to call and take charge of them for the time. So if she should arrive with a note from me, will you please deliver all the small pictures over to her: or if you are away, have them delivered?

I am doing one or two more small ones here, which I will send along later, all being well. I might even finish another biggish one, quite different. We are due to stay here till towards end of September, for my health: then I intend coming to London.

I hear that Alfred Stieglitz [406] is doing the show in New York: he is a very good man. I wrote and asked them to arrange for November. I don't really mind if I don't have a London show, since Stieglitz is arranging this in New York. So you needn't bother if you don't want to.

But let me hear from you, and do answer my questions. Hope everything is going nicely with you.

> Yours
> D. H. Lawrence [407]

Philippe Soupault

Kra, Editeur/6, Rue Blanche/Paris, Le 30 Juin, 1928
[To] Mademoiselle Scialtiel/2, Square Tocqueville,/Paris

Mademoiselle,

Melle. Claurouin me transmet à l'instant trois lignes de notice biographique sur Mr. D. H. Lawrence.

Permettez-moi de vous dire que ces quelques lignes sont vraiment trop insuffisantes; j'insiste tout spécialement auprès de vous,—et je suis sûr que vous comprendrez mon désir,—pour obtenir une biographie beaucoup plus importante. Je m'étonne qu'après nos demandes réitérées vous me transmettiez si peu de renseignements.

Je compte donc sur vous, et avec mes remerciements anticipés, je vous prie de croire, Mademoiselle, à mes sentiments les meilleurs.

> Philippe Soupault

Mr. Philippe SOUPAULT, —4, Av. Erlanger, PARIS.[408]

Jean Watson

Curtis Brown Ltd./6, Henrietta Street,/Covent Garden,/London, W.C. 2./16th July, 1928.
[To] D. H. Lawrence, Esq.,/Kesselmasse [sic],/Gsteig b. Gstaad,/Switzerland.

Dear Mr. Lawrence,

I am so sorry to worry you again about the introductory notes for the French publisher Kra, but as you will see from this letter they are very anxious indeed to have some sort of preface, either written by yourself, or by anyone else that you can suggest. Our Paris representative points out that Kra makes a great feature of his introductions, and that a good one would be extremely valuable publicity for your work in France.

I have collected all the information I can from "WHO'S WHO" and various other reference books, but apparently they want something more detailed and personal. Neither Secker nor Miss Pearn [409] have nothing which meets the case.

Yours sincerely,

Jean Watson

MANAGER/FOREIGN DEPARTMENT.

Enclosure.[410]

Autobiography

David Herbert Lawrence—born 11 Sept. 1885 in Eastwood, Nottingham, a small mining town in the Midlands—father a coal-miner, scarcely able to read or write—Mother from the bourgeoisie, the cultural element in the house (let them [struck out] read Sons & Lovers, the first part is all auto-biography—you might send them a copy [struck out]). —Fourth of five children—two brothers oldest—then a sister, then D. H.—then another sister—always delicate health but strong constitution—went to elementary school & was just like anybody else of the miners' children—at age of twelve won a scholarship for Nottingham High School, considered best day school in England—purely bourgeois school—quite happy there, but the scholar-ship boys were a class apart—D. H. made a couple of bourgeois friendships, but they were odd fish,—he instinctively recoiled away from the bourgeoi-sie, regular sort—left school at 16—had a severe illness—made the ac-quaintance of Miriam & her family, who lived on a farm, and who really roused him to critical & creative consciousness (see Sons & Lovers). Taught in a rough & fierce elementary school of mining boys: salary, first year, £5.—second year £10—third year £15—(from age of 17 to 21)—Next two years in Nottingham University, at first quite happy, then utterly bored. —Again the same feeling of boredom with the middle-classes, & recoil away from them instead of moving towards them & rising in the world. Took B.A. course, but dropped it; used to write bits of poems & patches of The White Peacock during lectures. These he wrote for Miriam, the girl on the farm, who was herself becoming a school-teacher. She thought it all wonderful—else, probably, he would never have written— His own family strictly "natural" looked on such performance as writing as "affectation." Therefore wrote in secret at home. Mother came upon a chapter of White Peacock—read it quizzically, & was amused. "But my boy, how do you know it was like that? You don't know—" She thought one ought to know—and she hoped her son, who was "clever," might one day be a professor or a clergyman or perhaps even a little Mr. Gladstone. That would have been rising in the world—on the ladder. Flights of genius were nonsense—you had to be clever & rise in the world, step by step. —D. H. however recoiled away from the world, hated its ladder, & refused to rise. He had proper bourgeois aunts with "library" & "drawing-room" to their houses—but didn't like that either—preferred the powerful life in a miners kitchen—& still more, the clatter of nailed boots in the little kitchen of Miriams farm. Miriam was even poorer than he—but she loved poetry and consciousness and flights of fancy above all. So he wrote for her—still without any idea of becoming a literary man at all—looked on himself as just a school-teacher—& mostly hated school-teaching. Wrote The White Peacock in bits and snatches, between age of 19 and 24. Most of it written six or seven times.

At the age of twenty-three, left Nottingham college & went for the first time to London, to be a teacher in a boys school in Croydon, £90. a year. Already the intense physical dissatisfaction with Miriam. Miriam read all his writings—she alone. His mother, whom he loved best on earth, he never spoke to, about his writing. It would have been a kind of "showing-off," or affectation. —It was Miriam who sent his poems to Ford Madox Hueffer, who had just taken over The English Review. This was when D. H. was 24. Hueffer accepted, wrote to Lawrence, and was most kind and most friendly. Got Heinemann to accept the MS., a ragged & bulky mass, of The White Peacock—invited the school-teacher to lunch—introduced him to Edward Garnett—and Garnett became a generous and genuine friend. Hueffer & Garnett launched D. H. into the literary world. Garnett got Duckworth to accept the first book of poems: Love Poems and Others. When Lawrence was 25, The White Peacock appeared. But before the day of publication, his mother died—she just looked once at the advance copy, held it in her hand—

The death of his mother wiped out everything else—books published, or stories in magazines. It was the great crash, and the end of his youth. He went back to Croydon to the hated teaching—the £50 for The White Peacock paid the doctor etc for his mother.

Then a weary & bitter year—broke with Miriam—and again fell dangerously ill with pneumonia. Got slowly better. Was making a little money with stories, Austin Harrison, who had taken over The English Review, being a staunch supporter, and Garnett and Hueffer staunch backers. In May, 1912, went away suddenly with his present wife, of German birth, daughter of Baron Friedrich von Richthofen. They went to Metz, then Bavaria, then Italy—and the new phase had begun. He was 26—his youth was over—there came a great gap between him and it.

Was in Italy and Germany the greater part of the time between 1912 & 1914. In England during the period of the war—pretty well isolated. In 1915 The Rainbow was suppressed for immorality—and the sense of detachment from the bourgeois world, the world which controls press, publication and all, became almost complete. He had no interest in it, no desire to be at one with it. Anyhow the suppression of The Rainbow had proved it impossible. Henceforth he put away any idea of "success," of succeeding with the British bourgeois public, and stayed apart.

Left England in 1919, for Italy—had a house for two years in Taormina, Sicily. In 1920 was published in America Women in Love—which every publisher for four years had refused to accept, because of The Rainbow scandal. In Taormina wrote The Lost Girl, Sea and Sardinia, and most of Aaron's Rod. In 1922 sailed from Naples to Ceylon, and lived in Kandy for a while—then on to Australia for a time—in each case taking a house and settling down. Then sailed from Sydney to San Francisco, and went to Taos, in New Mexico, where he settled down again with his wife, near the Pueblo of the Indians. Next year he acquired a small ranch high up on the Rocky Mountains, looking west to Arizona. Here, and in Old Mexico, where he travelled and lived for about a year, he stayed till 1926, writing St. Mawr in New Mexico, and the final version of The Plumed Serpent down in Oaxaca in Old Mexico.

Came to England 1926—but cannot stand the climate. For the last two years has lived in a villa near Florence, where Lady Chatterley's Lover was written [411]

31 July 1928   Châlet Kesselmatte, Gsteig-bei-Gstaad, Bern, Switzerland

⟨ I . . . have been under the altitude—felt perfectly wretched, and made design for my tombstone in Gsteig churchyard, with suitable inscription: "Departed this life, etc., etc. —He was fed up!" However, last Friday—or Thursday afternoon, I forget which—I decided to live a little longer—and today walked down to the village, and what is much worse, up again. It's like climbing to the Diablerets glacier. However, here I am, with a crick in my neck I admit, and Achsah et famille will be drippingly arriving to tea just now. The sun is sharply hot, the wind quite cool. But the sun sort of dissolves one's corpuscles. I daren't try another sun-bath, not for a minute. . . . I would willingly dangle myself before a shark if I could swim in the deep sea and sit in the southern sun naked and undiminished. In fact, if I don't actually sit on a muck-heap and scrape myself with a tin lid, it's because I haven't the energy.

I suppose all the ordered copies of Lady Jane [Lady Chatterley's Lover] are in England: so the booksellers have hastily written to say we must take back their copies at once, they couldn't handle the Lady, and I must cancel their orders, and will we remove the offence at once. That is in all 114 copies we have to fetch back. Of course, these children of God haven't paid. —Then there are rumours that the police are going to raid the shops: I suppose people hope they will. At the same time, the first batch has arrived safely at its various destinations in America.

I believe I have lost most of my friends in the escapade, but that is a small loss, alas! I never had any. Richard Aldington writes he gets a great kick out of it, and it's a feather in the cap of the XX century. It's a fool's cap anyhow, why should I put a feather in it. An American young man writes: But oh, your friends, Lorenzo! By their reactions shall you know them! —I shan't, because they'll keep them severely dark. . . .

I see the white flutter of our spotless friends away down on the high-road—poor dears, such a climb! Heaven is not reached in a single bound! [412]

9 August 1928   Châlet Kesselmatte, Gsteig-bei-Gstaad, Bern, Switzerland

⟨ I'm anxious about the other copies [of Lady Chatterley's Lover] sent— about 200 in all—to America, as several people sent cables saying "don't send." It went into England all right, though there was a great scare in London—police were reported to have a warrant to search for it. However nothing has happened so far: and perhaps it won't, if nobody raises a dust. But most people seem to hate the book: some dealers have returned their copies—and altogether there is a lot of fuss and nuisance. Makes one hate hypocrisy and prudery more than ever and people as a bulk.

We sit here in this little chalet near the top of the mountains—been here nearly five weeks—and until this week I felt no better. But this week I really begin to feel a difference and can begin taking short sun-baths— they only made me worse before. If only I can get a real start, to shake off this accursed cough, I ought to come along all right. But this last year I don't seem to have been able to get back to myself. Now let's hope I can.

Anyhow it's useless thinking of coming to New Mexico or anywhere far till I get this cough down.

The Brewsters are in the hotel in the village at present with four American spinster friends—quite nice women, but oh God! the meaninglessness that simply stares at one out of these women of fifty. . . .

We are due to stay here till end Sept.—and shall, I suppose, if it really does me good,—pray God it may! I'm supposed to go to London to see my pictures exhibited first two weeks in October—and I may, or may not. Here I just dibble at tiny pictures, and potter about among the trees.—A bad few years for everybody. But let's hope we'll all get steady on our legs and manage with a bit of real equilibrium, afterwards. Poveri noi! Anyhow the weather is superb.

Now I'll go and hunt my spectacles, which I lost this morning.[413]

15 August 1928   *Châlet Kesselmatte, Gsteig-bei-Gstaad, Bern, Switzerland*

❨ Nothing particularly new here. —Last week I was better, and sun-bathed —this week I've got a cold and feel all hot inside. It's a beastly climate really, hot and cold at once. I'm getting sick of it, hope we can leave in first half of September. But my sister [Emily] is coming with her daughter [Margaret] for a fortnight end of this month. Then when she goes we can go—presumably to Baden-Baden for a bit—and possibly England. I have it in my mind I want to go back to the ranch—but absolutely—in November. . . . I am still unaware of the fate of Lady Jane [Lady Chatterley's Lover] in America—some copies arrived—then we had cables saying "wait." So we are waiting. Not that there is any hurry any more; all the English copies having arrived safely. It has been good fun, really, and worth it. Though the money hasn't all come in, by any means. But I feel I've had another whack at 'em—a good satisfactory whack . . . .[414]

15 August 1928   *Châlet Kesselmatte, Gsteig-bei-Gstaad, Bern, Switzerland*

❨ Don't be alarmed about the pictures—they're quite good. Anyhow, they contain something—which is more than you can say of most moderns, which are all excellent rind of the fruit, but no fruit. And because a picture has subject-matter it is not therefore less a picture. Besides, what's a deformed guitar and a shred of newspaper but subject-matter? There's the greatest lot of bunk talked about modern painting ever. If a picture is to *hit deep into the senses, which is its business, it must hit down to the soul and up into the mind—that is, it has to mean something to the co-ordinating soul and the co-ordinating spirit which are central in man's consciousness: and the meaning has to come through direct sense impression. I know what I'm about. As for their space composition and their mass-reaction and their arabesques, if that isn't all literary and idea-concept, what is? Such a lot of canary cages, and never a bird in one of 'em!* [415]

16 August 1928   *Châlet Kesselmatte, Gsteig-bei-Gstaad, Bern, Switzerland*

❨ *Today it feels like autumn and the turning of the year. The peasants bring us bilberries, and soon it will be cranberries. . . .*

I'm pretty well in myself, but my cough is a nuisance, as ever, and I simply cannot climb these slopes. I suppose I shall just have to put up with it and leave them unclimbed. Anyhow I don't care so much any more about walking and going to see places.[416]

Kesselmatte/Gsteig b. Gstaad/(Bern)/Switzerland/25 August 1928

❨ Dear Dorothy [Warren]
   Now you must write by return and tell me:
      1. If you have the big pictures safely from Florence.
      2. How you like them—also the small ones.
      3. What are your plans concerning them.
For my part, I don't care whether you make an exhibition of them or not. So many people seem mortally offended by Lady Chatterley that perhaps a picture show might only carry the offence further. Not that I care about offending them. But you may. Personally, I think such skunks should be offended to the last inch. However, you are in business, and must have your own opinions. —Which reminds me, you never ordered any copies of the novel, as you so plainly said you would. Not that it matters, except one wonders if you ever do what you say you will.
   Alfred Stieglitz says he wants to make an exhibition of my things in New York in November. But I expect I shall be in England in September, so I can ship them off myself. If I hadn't heard from a woman that she'd seen you, and seen some of my pictures at your gallery, I should doubt whether you really existed.
   The man of the Leicester Galleries wanted to see my pictures, with a

view to showing them. Lucille Frost wrote about it—but I said there was
nothing to be done at the moment.

However, I must hear from you now.

I've got a very nice panel of Italian peasants which I did here.

Sincerely

D. H. Lawrence [417]

27 August 1928   *Châlet Kesselmatte, Gsteig-bei-Gstaad, Bern, Switzerland*

⟨ *It seems the U.S. mail is holding up some, at least, of the copies [of Lady
Chatterley's Lover] I sent—so I can send no more and those held up will
be lost. I am determined to stand by Lady C. and to send her out into the
world as far as possible. . . . I stand by her: and am perfectly content she
should do me harm with such people as take offence at her. I am out against
such people. Fly, little boat! . . .*

*I finished the second half of The Escaped Cock, about 10,000 words—
rather lovely—but I feel tender about giving it out for publication—as I
felt tender about Lady C.*[418]

Dorothy Warren Trotter

[The Warren Gallery, 39a Maddox Street, London, W. 1] 29 August 1928

Dear Lawrence,

Thank you so much for your letters. I have been so exhausted, ill and
over-worked that I had to rest a while and that is why I haven't written
before. I am so sorry! On top of all this my secretary has also been away
ill.

All your pictures arrived safely and I like them immensely. The water
colours are already framed; I enclose samples of the papers which we
have used for the mounts. The mounts are perfectly simple, just plainly
cut out and I think they look lovely. The frames are plain Hazel pine
moulding. I am now framing the oils, I quite agree with you that they
should have extremely simple mouldings so that I am doing them in 3″
flat plain wood showing 1/2″ flat plain slip. If, when you see them, you
do not like the slip it is an easy matter to remove them. I find the slip
important, because, without looking fussy, it gives a very slight recession,
but not enough to make a shadow on the canvas.

It would be a mistake to hang anything else with your pictures, they need extremely careful and wide spacing but there will be room for anything else you like to bring or send in September. I should love to see the panel of Italian peasants.

With regard to the opening day, I should suggest Friday, October 5th. to Friday October 26th., which is exactly three weeks, as the earliest possible date. That would mean that your pictures could be put back into their cases and started off for America by the end of October so that you could reckon for their arrival in New York certainly by the middle of November. If it were not for the American show I should prefer to open on Tuesday, October the 9th. as there are more people back in London in the second week than in the first.

Of course I anticipate prudish objections and attacks on myself and my Gallery. All that will have to be faced and it won't be a very new experience, although it is one to which I am not absolutely hardened! But I think your pictures fine and free and individual so that I want to show them.

It is extremely difficult to fix selling prices, as I expect you will understand one must be either prohibitive and regard them as of "Bibliophile" value or else one must present them as a first exhibition of a painter new to the public at reasonable prices. There is no middle course. In taking the latter course, both painter and dealer have to consider the fact that the painter intends to make his career by painting and work his prices up proportionately to his selling fame. Esthetic and commercial values have less and less in common these days which makes the task of pricing difficult. I should think the water colours ought to average between 12 gns. and 15 gns. apiece. About the oils I really don't quite know, you must let me hear what you think.

From a commercial point of view it might not be a bad idea to put a prohibitive price on those you do not want to sell, although that means, of course, that if the prices are given, one is bound to sell, but then if this occurs, the prices of other works go up automatically.

I am very sorry about the muddle with regard to *Lady Chatterley*. I do want three copies for which I enclose 6 gns., but please will you have them addressed to:

Prince Löwenstein/The Warren Gallery/39a Maddox Street/London, W. 1

as a great many books come here for him from abroad and I think it would be better.

The Assistant I had here while I was in Germany made such a muddle of everything that it has taken me all my strength, time and energy to straighten things out and ascertain what orders of mine were, or were not, carried out.

I hope to get away for a fortnight during the last half of September, but I shall be in or near London until then in case you should come here.

Yours,
Dorothy [419]

Frieda Lawrence Ravagli

Kesselmate/Gsteig bei Gstaad/Bern, Switzerland/31 August 1928

Dear Dorothy Warren,

We are both sorry you are not feeling well. Barby said how hard you work; but she is so much impressed with your gallery and says what an air it has. It was fun to hear of you through her. I am glad you like Lorenzo's pictures. I want to keep the *Resurrection, Boccacio,* and the *Kiss.* I was very sad to let the pictures depart. I had watched them being born and they were part of one's life. If they aren't sold I shall be glad, except for your sake. I hope we shall see you before long. England sounds the greyest *hell* to me, not even a good red hell.

Yours and may you soon be better.

Frieda Lawrence [420]

Kesselmatte/Gsteig b. Gstaad/(Bern)/Switzerland/1 September 1928

⟮ Dear Dorothy [Warren]

I was very glad to hear from you, and to know at least you are in the land of the living—and keeping up the fight. Don't for heaven's sake get into the way of being ill! That's what I've done—and heaven, I'd give anything to be well.

I've asked Mrs. Hilton to bring round the three copies of Lady Chatterley for Prince Loewenstein—she had a few in store for me, these are the last. Do show her the pictures when she comes.

We'll put a high and prohibitive price on all the big pictures, for I really don't want to sell them. Something like five hundred pounds. And then the small pictures and the water-colours you can price as you think best. Only the small picture Close-Up [Kiss]—Frieda wants to keep it, so we'll either have to mark it sold, or price it high. If, as you say, anyone offers the prohibitive price for a big picture, we shall have to let it go. But somehow I can't associate my pictures with money.

I will ask Alfred Stieglitz to let you know his date, so that if you want to open Oct. 9th instead of 5th, you could do so if his date allows.[421]

I certainly don't intend to make my living painting—far from it. I intend to paint simply and solely for the fun of it, and damn the consequences.

I shall send you my small panel of Contadini—and some others, directly. I am pining to see the pictures in their frames—pining. But my health is a nuisance—my cough a curse—God knows if I ought to come to England.

Anyhow I hope you are well and chirpy. Don't get downhearted, that's the worst. And it's good for you to have a fight for your gallery—as it's good for me to fight for my things, as I have to. Yet one does mind being insulted, bitterly.

Sincerely,
D. H. Lawrence [422]

2? September 1928

Châlet Kesselmatte, Gsteig-bei-Gstaad, Bern, Switzerland

⟨[[We] think to stay here till the 17th of this month—then to Baden for about a fortnight—then, but that I'm fed up to the nose with Englishness just now, I'd go to England. Dorothy Warren is showing my pictures from Oct. 5th to 26th—she says they are framed and look lovely. I'm pining to see them framed and hung. But whether I shall have the strength to put my nose into that stink-pot of an island, I don't know. I very much doubt it.

Richard Aldington says he is offered by Paulhan, editor of the Nouvelle Revue Française, his house, an ancient fortress, a Vigie, on the isle of Port-Cros, about ten miles off Hyères on the Riviera—and Richard wants us to go there. Frieda is pining for sea in winter. We may go then about Oct. 1st and look at the place. . . .

But one might be happy there. I like Richard Aldington and Arabella—they are in Vallombrosa at the moment. We'll see, anyhow. I don't feel quite at the point when I can go to the ranch. I'm pretty well in myself, but cursed with the same cough. . . .

Here it's turning to autumn. We had three awful deluge days—then a bright morning, brilliant new snow, brilliant new world—and slopes all bubbled over with pink autumn crocuses—very lovely. This evening it's sulking and trying to thunder: cow-bells ting-ting-ting—very still in all the world, and somehow far. Even our visitors have subsided in comparative stillness.

Am reading again Chartreuse de Parme—so good historically, socially and all that—but emotionally rather empty and trashy. Had of course to rescue F.—who is painting autumn crocuses in water, and naturally rubbed her paper with milk roll instead of stale bread, to thin off her pencil marks. Of course milk roll is so much better class! nice and greasy.

Night falling—mist on the mountains—stewed rabbit and onions in the kitchen . . . .[423]

Kesselmatte/Gsteig b. Gstaad/Switzerland/10 September 1928

⟨ Dear Dorothy [Warren]

I sent you two more panels to London [424]—nice ones I think.

There is such a fracas and an alarm in America over my novel [Lady Chatterley's Lover], such a panic, that I must postpone any thought of showing my pictures there. I'm sure the Customs in New York would destroy them! So that's off. I wouldn't risk sending the pictures across the Atlantic this year, not for anything.[425]

This leaves you free to do as you like in England, as regards the time of your show. Some of my "friends" write that this is the very wrong moment to show pictures of mine in London, it will provide an opportunity for all my enemies, that it will do me a lot of damage, and do your gallery a lot of damage etc. etc. I don't give much for such Job's Comforters myself. Nor do I tremble at the thought of my "enemies," dear Lord! But you think it over and do as you really think best. Barkis is willin', as far as I'm concerned, to agree with any decision you make. But I don't feel like being "frightened," either. Haven't my enemies been doing their damnedest for twenty years! Keep 'em running.

I hear you are in Austria, but I hope this will be sent to you from London. After the 17th my address will be:

> % Frau Baronin von Richthofen,
> Ludwig-Wilhelmstift
> Baden Baden

> > Avanti, arditi!
> > D. H. Lawrence [426]

10 September 1928
                    Châlet Kesselmatte, Gsteig-bei-Gstaad, Bern, Switzerland

❨ We leave on the 17th for Baden Baden. I don't think I shall come to
England. The thought of it depresses me. Frieda will come to England for
ten days or a fortnight. I want her to see my picture show. Dorothy Warren
opens it either on the 5th or the 9th of Oct. The first two days will be by
invitation only. . . . But the show will be open to the public till the end
of October. . . . The cows have now all come down from the high Alps—
summer is over—time to go.⁴²⁷

GERMANY

22 September 1928   *Hôtel Löwen, Lichtenthal bei Baden-Baden, Germany*

❨ We are here since Tuesday [18 September 1928]—and good weather.
F.'s mother here in hotel with us, and the Brewsters! We all drove in two
grand 2-horse landaus yesterday to the altes Schloss and through the forest
for three hours—everybody in bliss. It's rather cold—and Germany is queer
—prosperous and alive—different from other people—makes me feel a bit
queer inside. We go to the Kurhaus and drink hot waters and listen to
music and—eat, of course.

I never know quite where I am, in Germany. We leave 1st October—
Frieda for England, I for South of France, where I shall stay a bit with F.'s
sister Else, and join the Aldingtons to look at the island—Port-Cros.⁴²⁸

Achsah Barlow Brewster

[September] found us all with Frieda's mother settled in a quiet old
inn on the outskirts of Baden-Baden. Our rooms opened on to an inviting garden of stately trees, where little golden hearts were fluttering
down from the aspens. When the fickle sun allowed we sat for hours at
little tables there. Evenings we spent in the Weinstube of the inn; a
choral society of workmen met in an adjoining hall, where they practised
their songs. We would linger to listen. Lawrence liked to be a part of the
village life. One night a grocer who belonged to the choral group was
married. Down the street to the new home marched the chorus, bearing
coloured lanterns, then pouring out their heart-felt wishes in song. We

stood shivering in the road, grateful. Lawrence, although blue with cold, waited for the last note.

He would play Patience with Frieda's mother, taking as much pleasure in the game as she did. Their favourite variety was "Napoleon," in which they almost invariably had to cheat themselves to win.

In the mornings we would start out, drinking-glasses in hand, and walk the length of the Lichtenthal Allee, which still looked like a page from a Turgenev novel. We turned up the street to the stork-fountain, sending forth clouds of steam on the chill air, and we drank our potions. Lawrence prudently limited himself to one glass. Then we went to the Kursaal for the concerts. He knew all the arias and overtures without consulting the programme. Their familiarity was an added pleasure. He would sit, his head slightly drooped forward, a pensive look on his face as if he were gathering up old memories evoked by the music.

Going the round of the medicinal springs and baths, loitering in the lounges or gardens, for a time we were amused onlookers, but finally Lawrence announced that he could not bear the crowd any longer; their faces were blasted, their souls damned. He could not sit in their midst even to hear an outdoor concert.

We were walking home along the bridle-path when a servant-girl carrying a basket of groceries passed near. On seeing Lawrence she burst into a storm of sobs, shrieking that she had lost her purse and her mistress would beat her. He stood silent before the storm. Not one of us opened a purse. Lawrence shook his head seriously. He wished to be scrupulously just in the matter. "She's overdone the part. It's too dramatic."

The girl saw we were stony-hearted and, espying a gentleman in front, flew off to engage his sympathies. As she came near him she again burst into weeping, but the man stopped and raised a threatening hand. Lawrence's beard bristled and he turned to Frieda:

"You run on and tell that scullion if she does this again you will report her to the police." He felt aggrieved personally. It was a shock to his faith in humanity. Such trivial incidents moved him deeply.

Maple-leaves lay on the paths like jewels. Lawrence took a double handful and hurried on while the rest loitered. When we arrived for luncheon the table was adorned with the leaves, roses lay at Earl's place, and a mound of presents for his birthday. After this we set forth on a drive, but a real drive in baronial landaus, with spans of great horses. For hours we wound through wooded roads among great pine-boles and hemlock pillars with the light sifting transparent green and gold through the beeches on the edge of the Black Forest. Deep mystery where fairies,

gnomes and devils might be lurking. With Lawrence as master of cere-
monies we climbed through the old *schloss* to the central hall of red
sandstone where Lawrence insisted we see the aerial harp and climb "the
bastions an' turrets an' a'."

Lawrence was silent for long on the drive back through the cool green-
ness of the forest which soothed eyes and nerves. A sense of peace lay
over us; the happiness of the day, its generous giving, its glad receiving,
its communion.

Finally Lawrence began recounting that his father and X. [Norman
Douglas] [429] were the only people he had known who always followed
joy. Nothing else but the joy of life had concerned them. X. could not
admit suffering, disease, poverty, or ugliness. For X. the war did not
exist. He turned his back upon it. When Frieda and Lawrence were
desperately poor, he simply did not notice it or them! It was true, that
everyone was a hedonist of sorts. Perhaps they were right, certainly they
were consistent. As the old sundial said: "Face the sun and the shadows
fall behind." They were sun-flowers sure enough! They had their brightness too. Nothing else really existed for either of them, nothing but
themselves. One episode after another came and went; some painful and
those were deliberately forgotten, expunged; some full of pleasure and
self-aggrandizement; all real and moving at the moment, but mere paren-
theses, closed, finished. X. loved his wife and grieved over his loss when
she died, but she had gone while he was still enjoying himself. X.'s
children had passed through various vicissitudes. He was sorry, but had
kept on invincible, still finding life good in spots and choosing the good
spots. Call it courage—how much better it had been than broken-spirited
dragging on. Blithe spirits, true to themselves, they were right in a way.
They had kept themselves unbroken, while the rest of us have cared too
much and let ourselves be shattered by the depths of our affections. We
must let things go, one after another, finally even love—only keeping
oneself true to oneself, just that integrity. Nothing else matters in life
or death.

Lawrence fell into silent reverie. He felt no need of speech, and his
silences were as much a communion as his spoken word.

Before leaving Baden-Baden we wanted to see the highest place in that
region—Mercury Hill, because of the beautiful allegory Lawrence has
written about it.[430] One morning he led us through the dense shade of the
Black Forest, dappled with the early light, to the entrance of the funicular, and seating himself on a nearby bench said he might wait if it did
not turn too cold.

After being veered up over the sea of tall treetops at a terrific pitch, we arrived at the commanding height where man has felt the presence of gods known and unknown during the centuries—testifying to this are the Christian shrine, and the altar to Mercury above, another perhaps to Thor the thunderer, as Lawrence has chosen in his profound allegory. The Rhine gleamed in the distance, the Black Forest bristled up and down the round hills. The clanking chains of the funicular had brought us by a miracle of machinery to the top, high above the machine world, in the realm of the gods. As we rattled and clattered back to the lower earth, Lawrence sat on the bench near the funicular entrance just as we had left him, still as a lizard in the sun out of the green shadows of the deep woods. We walked silently home.

Lawrence's courage never failed, even though his health did. He wished to join in all our excursions and walks. One of these took us to a series of trout ponds where the fish were raised for the market. Lawrence was exhausted before we arrived, for we could never remember how limited his strength was. Even then, wearied out, his interest in the six-year-old fish-pond and the three-year-old and the spawn was keen as ever.

We sallied forth to find an old inn which had disappeared, Lawrence dragging along.

Frieda announced that she had met a famous physician who had promised to make a friendly call upon Lawrence the next day.

"I shall not be in. He'll not see me!" There the matter rested.

Nearby was a convent where we talked with the sisters, hearing of their famous eau-de-cologne, and their still more famous nun, who had the power of healing with the touch of her hands. When Frieda begged Lawrence to visit her, saying perhaps she might heal him, he shook his head, and answered that all he needed was the south and the sun.[431]

Earl H. Brewster

In September we were with the Lawrences at a rambling hotel on the outskirts of Baden-Baden.

I told Lawrence of a recent experience, when leaving the mechanization of a great modern city I had entered a museum filled with the arts and crafts of the East. The contrast had moved me so much that I was attempting to write about it in an article which I called "The Hand of Man." One day divining that I was writing he came to my room and said: —"Let me see what you have done on that article." Much gratified by his attention I showed him what I had written. He said: "Oh, that is not the way to do it; your beginning is stilted, antiquated in form. Let me have the pen and some paper, I would begin more like this . . . and then you could follow it up with topical paragraphs—thus . . . ." Of course I was most grateful to Lawrence. To me it is interesting that although I did not question his judgment, it was simply impossible for me to do the work the way he suggested!

During these last years of Lawrence's life I do not recall his once being enraged with me, as had happened in the first years of our friendship. Perhaps he felt it futile to attempt my reform! Our hours together were peaceful but with a poignancy because of his failing health. The conversations were about people we knew in common, reminiscences of Lawrence's past, the never-ending mystery of the differences between men and women, the lack of life in people—especially the youth of today . . . . He agreed that the very structure of the modern western house is not conducive to the right relationship between men and women; the oriental house where the women have their distinctive quarters is better—or as Plato pictured it in his Republic.

My fiftieth birthday occurred in Baden-Baden. Lawrence engaged for our party two carriages each drawn by a fine span of horses; we drove for miles through the forest. Such a drive in a landau behind horses was a unique experience for "the child" [Harwood] and probably the last drive of its kind for all of us.

Soon the Lawrences went to the Ile de Port Cros and I with my family returned to Italy.[432]

25 September 1928   Hôtel Löwen, Lichtenthal bei Baden-Baden, Germany

⟨ *Our plans . . . are a bit changed. The Mirenda people are sending away our peasants, Giulia, Pietro and family—and there's sure to be a great emotional stew. And I really feel the Mirenda is bad for my health. So Frieda intends to come direct to Florence, leave here next Tuesday, 2nd, arrive Florence 3rd, and finish the bit of packing—it's nearly all done —and give up the house for good. It ought only to take a few days. . . . I, coward, am staying out of it. —I shall go on Tuesday to S. of France. That Island Port-Cros is 19 kms. off Hyères, and may be a nice place to winter, no people, no villas, one small hotel, 13 families fishermen and the Vigie—fortress. It may be nice. Also F.'s sister Else is down just there till 8th Oct. So I'll try it—and Frieda can join me somewhere there. The exhibition of pictures is put off till Nov.—and F. will go to London to see it, I shan't. . . . It was so cold here, but not much rain—now is a bit warmer. Only six more days here—so much food! We are now going to the Fischkultur for tea. Hope they won't give us ants' eggs.*[433]

Achsah Barlow Brewster

Thus Lawrence started out to find the sun, going south with us by way of the French Riviera, while Frieda went to Florence to close the Villa Mirenda. Though it was cold when, on our journey, we arrived at Strasbourg, we set forth to explore the cathedral. Lawrence thought it had the beauty of both the French and German Gothic; he liked its exterior best of all Gothic cathedrals. The clock performed, purple and crimson shadows deepened down the solemn aisles.

The twilight outside was bitter cold; Lawrence decided to keep warm with *Ben Hur* at the cinema until train time. Half an hour we watched doves fluttering around baby-faced blonde dolls, brutal Romans accursed with hearts of stone, galleys of inhuman slaves, galloping horses whizzing perilous chariots. There was no human touch, nothing resembling a reality of any phase of life we knew or could imagine. Lawrence gasped out that he was going; if we did not take him out immediately he would be violently sick; such falsity nauseated him; he could not bear to see other people there open-mouthed, swallowing it, believing it to be true.

How white and weary he looked the next morning, after a night in the train. He left us in Southern France for Port Cros, while we continued our way to Nice and on to Italy.[434]

CHAPTER THREE

1928–1930: France, Majorca, Italy, Germany

Only those that die in belief die happy.
                    —Studies in Classic American Literature

? October 1928   Le Lavandou, near Hyères, Var, France

⟨ Nice down here by the sea not far from Toulon. The others have all left—Else and the Huxleys—but am expecting Arabella and Richard Aldington—and Frieda next week. We may go over to the Island of Port Cros . . . . Am feeling very well.[1]

? October 1928   Le Lavandou, near Hyères, Var, France

⟨ [I] am quite alone for the moment. But it is very pleasant lounging on the sands and seeing the men play boccie. It feels very pleasant and easy. No sign of the Aldingtons [2]—so plans rather vague still.[3]

? October 1928   Le Lavandou, near Hyères, Var, France

⟨ This is a nice quiet little place. We went out in a fisher-boat—with motor—to the island Port-Cros. It is rather lovely, all tangled forest like Corsica but the hotel is "chic"—quite a lot of high-browish people there —and the whole place a bit artificial. The Vigie—fortress—is an hour's stony walk uphill—and no way except to walk. To-morrow the Aldingtons

251

come and I decide if we shall stay at the Vigie for two months—not more —or whether we stay on this coast, which is really very pleasant.[4]

? October 1928   Le Lavandou, near Hyères, Var, France

❨ Yes, the weather, the sun, the light are lovely. Man is everywhere vile. They are just beginning to mess this coast up—but the messing seems to proceed rapidly, once it starts. Little villas "tout confort"—yes, my word. Very comforting to the eye! I think we shall go over to the island end of this week—if F. comes and sea is still. I hope she'll turn up soon, I'm getting a bit bored—have churlishly refused to talk to anybody—I'm sick of people—there are about ten in the hotel. We'll try the island—perhaps we might find a corner in it—though I saw high-brow visitors striding on every path—too precious for words, that Perle of an island.[5]

20 October 1928   La Vigie, Île de Port-Cros, Var, France

❨ Frieda arrived [at Le Lavandou on 12 October 1928] with a raging Italian cold—and of course passed it on to me, so I've felt very cheap this week. But it's much better. The Vigie isn't a castle but a top of a hill with a moat and low fort wall enclosing a bare space, about 2 acres, where the wild lavender and the heather grow. The rooms are sort of cabins under the walls—windows facing the inner space, loop-holes looking out to sea —a nice large sitting-room—a bedroom each—then across, a great room where we throw the logs, and a kitchen, pantry and little dining-room. It's very nice, rather rough, but not really uncomfortable—and plenty of wood to burn in the open fireplaces. The Italian Giuseppe, a strong fellow of 28, fetches all provisions on a donkey, once a day. We get practically everything—except milk—and plenty. But all has to be ordered from the main-land. Giuseppe does all housework except cooking—which the women take in turns. Richard and Arabella are very nice, and so is Bridget Pat- more, we get on very well, and it's quite fun, but I've felt so limp with my cold—real influenza cold . . . . I think we shall stay here till towards Christmas. The island is all green pine-tops, seen from above—then blue sea and other islands. It's nice because one is quite alone—but of course I don't want to live here. There are no other houses—only the hotel and the few fishermen at the bay—and it took me a long hour to get up from *there, so I doubt I'm perched, as at Kesselmatte. Anyhow I don't care. I don't think I shall do much work here—but it's better for me. . . .*

All feels very vague—I don't know where we shall ultimately go—and I get scared when this influenza begins biting again.[6]

Richard Aldington

[What] had happened to the Lawrences? Frieda, it appeared, was in Italy closing down their establishment at Scandicci; a complicated process, since it involved a journey to Trieste. Lawrence was at Lavandou, waiting for her, watching the fishermen play *boules* and finding out local gossip—a plenteous field. Eventually they turned up. It sounds ungracious to say so, but we had a better and more harmonious time [at Port-Cros] before they arrived. The fact is that Lorenzo's T.B. was active and he was far too ill to take any part in our expeditions or indeed to rough it in so remote and exposed a place. I used to listen to his dreadful hollow cough at night, and wonder what on earth I should do if he got worse—how I could get him carried down a mile and a half of steep rocky path, transported across twelve miles of sea in an open boat, and thence to a sanatorium. Luckily his marvellous vitality made yet another recovery, but naturally he was not in the best of spirits and apt to be bad-tempered. His talk was too often on a lower level than his best, too personal and satirical, sharp with the reckless hatred of those about to die.

We did our best to make him comfortable, but as somebody had always to stay with him, our long bathing expeditions were rather spoiled. Moreover, just at this moment when he needed quiet and gentleness, his publishers elected to send him an enormous wodge of English press cuttings about *Lady Chatterley*. We read them one evening sitting in front of a pine-log fire. I have never seen such an exhibition of vulgarity, spite, filth, and hatred as was contained in those innumerable diatribes. Every editor and peddling reviewer had eagerly seized the opportunity to vilify and if possible crush into ignominy and poverty a man who had done—what? Publish a book whose obvious intention was to rescue sex from prudery and nastiness. Now, we writers may be fools, but we are not such utter fools as to be taken in by such stuff. I had lived with men, I knew what their talk and lives were, I knew the cynicism and depravity of journalists, I knew some of the men who had written this malevolent twaddle; and I knew they were not worthy to black Lawrence's boots.

So far as I was concerned that was the last turn of the screw. I thought it vile that, without one protest, the whole press should unite in pouring out insults, innuendoes, and abuse on a man of Lawrence's integrity and gifts, one of the very few original English writers of his time. I wanted to dissociate myself sharply from such people.

It seems to me one up to Lawrence that he went tranquilly on with his writing although he was so ill, and was angry and bitter about the attacks on him in England. Every morning he sat up in bed, wearing an old hat as protection against an imaginary draught, and produced a short story or one of the little essays of *Assorted Articles*. I remember his writing an article on a book of Mr. Morris Ernst in the blank leaves of the copy which Mr. Ernst sent him.[7] He must also have been working secretly on *Pansies*, for two of them were inspired by books he read on the island. One was Aldous Huxley's *Point Counter Point* and the other a book on Attila from the pile of new French books I had with me.[8] He enjoyed the Attila book very much, as it jumped with a temporary mood of destructiveness in him.

.   .   .   .

It was interesting to see the reaction of the others to [the first draft of *Death of a Hero*]. Lawrence was entirely against it, gave me the now familiar warning that if I published it I should lose what little reputation I had, and added the original threat that I was evidently on the way to an insane asylum. One never knows; but that was twelve years ago, and I have managed to keep at large so far. As a matter of fact I took this for what it was—the querulousness of a very sick man. The women, on the other hand, were for the book, especially Frieda. I shall always feel grateful to her for this encouragement and indeed inspiration she gave me at that critical time. An author is wise to knock off about ninety-five per cent of all commendations made to his face, but it was impossible to doubt Frieda's momentary sincerity and enthusiasm.[9]

Brigit Patmore

Our last meeting place was in one of the loveliest settings in Europe: the fort on the highest point of Port Cros. The editor of *La Nouvelle Revue Française*, Jean Paulhan, had turned it into a comfortable, simple residence and let it to Richard Aldington for the autumn months.

The hill was so perfect with arbutus and pines, so clear and high that the blue space of water dancing towards the mainland of Provence, with the coast's background of heaven and snow mountains seemed to give us light with its colours, and above the sun burnished leaves and rocks.

Because of all this beauty we awaited the Lawrences' coming with eagerness. He was across the water at Lavandou waiting for Frieda to return from a visit to her mother.

The small motor-boat from Hyères came only twice a week and not at all in bad weather, so that kept us waiting also.

They arrived on a morning to match paradise, but we were saddened at once by the unexpected, dreadful weakness of Lorenzo. The long walk up from the tiny harbour had certainly been too much for him, but there was no way of avoiding this over-exertion, for no cars were allowed on the island, and not even a horse-drawn vehicle could pass over the huge stones encumbering the path at certain corners.

But Lawrence never complained: he seemed to approve the place, its loveliness and quiet, and being with friends with whom he could say what he liked and do as he pleased.

The Paulhans had left an Italian boy, Giuseppe, to do all the work except cooking. He had a donkey called Moses: the two of them went down into the valley to draw fresh water and then fetch provisions from the one shop down by the harbour. This reminded Lorenzo of his beloved Italy: it amused him to see the little donkey browsing and tiny chickens pecking around his four feet.

Frieda and Arabella shared the more serious cooking of luncheon and dinner and I looked after breakfast—"Because you don't mind getting up early, do you?"—but I think they mistrusted my power to do anything less simple.

Lorenzo had his breakfast in bed. So, about quarter to seven on those shining autumn mornings, when light itself was a flower perfumed like a god's wine, I used to carry a tray across the courtyard to his room. I'd knock and cry "Can I come in?" then plunged right in so as to save him calling out through the heavy door.

"Hello, darling. Hope you want your *lovely* breakfast!"

He was always awake and his eyes smiled, but he seemed terribly exhausted, and while putting a coat round his shoulders I could feel his pyjamas soaked with perspiration. However it was against the rules to suggest that anything was wrong.

"What do you bet I've forgotten this morning?"

"Nothing. Giuseppe's got a good memory."

"Him! You should have seen the tray he laid. Looked like a stone-mason's dinner pail. Don't know how he managed it with all Madame Paulhan's pretty Galeries Lafayette do-das."

"What's this!"

It was a triumph to have roused his interest.

"Oh just a little bit of bacon. Real old Irish, I believe. This flower to match your coat grows down the cliff under your window."

It had taken a week's plotting and correspondence to get that bacon. He seemed rather wistful for English food and this wrung our hearts. One was expected on the island to live on spaghetti, and strange minia-ture monsters from the sea, and wine: as Lawrence never drank wine, which is necessary to make a diet of *pasta* endurable, something had to be done about it.

"Here's your notebook and pencil—or do you want your fountain pen? Here's the bell. Ring like mad if you want more hot water, although I'm coming over again in a minute and you can think out your orders."

But he never had any orders. No man ever wanted less waiting on. Whenever I heard a faint shout of "Brigit" and ran to his window over-looking the courtyard, he would say something like—"Do ask Richard if one can use the word 'Catasto' in Italian for 'tithe' or is it more exactly 'tax.'"

For amusement Lawrence was translating an early Italian story called *Dr. Manente* [10] and this led to lively discussions between him and Rich-ard on technical points. The typing of the manuscript was given to me and I had to do the last page four or five times. Lorenzo inexplicably became fussy about the shape of the lines, the last word had to shrink into an inverted peak right in the middle of the page.[11] For a few morn-ing hours he would sit up in bed and write in a clear sloping script which was blissfully easy to read. The Viking Press had asked him for a short essay on the censorship of books and in less than an hour he wrote his lucid exposition on the inner cover of a book.[12] It needed no corrections. His mastery always roused my amazement; it was the same with subtler thoughts. After his death, when I was in Florence, Orioli asked me to correct the proofs of *The Apocalypse*. There were three versions in note-books to be gone through but the alterations were slight, just the rejec-tion of words which seemed superfluous.[13]

A more unique trait was that he never minded being interrupted while writing—no glare of hatred from frenzied rolling eye met the intruder. Knowing this I often told him what was happening outside the fort. He could go out so seldom and was amused to hear of the stray creatures that might wander up to our pinnacle.

One day I rushed up to his window: "Darling, there's never been anything so lovely! There are *three* rainbows in the valley! Three!"

He had a hat on, a rakish Homburg at a cavalier angle, for the draughts from the tiny window at the bed's head sometimes whisked around fiercely. He simply looked up, smiling dreamily and said: "There, there," and went on writing.

Laughing, I went back to the ramparts wondering if perhaps he hadn't yearned to curse me.

. . .

Without being too obvious we arranged that someone should always be at hand in case he was not well, for the fact that there was no doctor on the island worried us.

One sun-filled afternoon we were all sitting in the courtyard sheltered from any wind by thick, yellow cystus bushes. Lorenzo had his feet up on a chair, his knees covered with a sheepskin coat. Like most red-haired people his colour was intensified, yet more transparent, in the sunshine.

He was very gay, giving us through his imitations a gallery of portraits: it was a brilliant entertainment. Then the other three went off to bathe. It was mournful to see the expression in Lawrence's eyes: they watched Frieda until she disappeared through the door leading to the drawbridge. Richard's and Frieda's laughter came back to us. Lorenzo's eyes widened; I almost wished that Richard could have hidden his gaiety, and said: "Richard hasn't been so carefree for years. It always goes to the head a bit."

"That may be." Then snappily, as if we were in a kindergarten. "He can't live on his charm for ever." Later he added: "I don't know how it is I have no real men friends."

"But several men I know are devoted to you. But you trample on their feelings." He looked astonished.

"Well, I can't help it," he said grimly, "if these men who go to public schools can't face the truth. They're not in leading-strings even, they're in strait-waistcoats, and they tie up their tongues and develop their biceps. You can't think or feel much with a bicep. Besides, they're not such sportsmen, they hit you when you're down, my lass, and don't you forget it!"

"Heavens! your pen has much more bite in it than their swords or fists —or whatever they use."

"But you want to feel at one with your fellow-creatures . . . sometimes."

"I don't know anyone who is more so than you."

"No. Not with them. And they can go to their own inferior blazes. Even their voices are emasculate. No wonder women are restless and hard. 'A woman wailing for her demon lover' indeed! There's something for you to write about." Then suddenly, "Are you going to marry that boy back in England?"

"Of course not. I'm old enough to be his mother."

"*That* doesn't matter. Young men now seem to want to marry their grandmothers."

I was silent, so he went on:

"You know you're rather like the woman in *Rawdon's Roof*.[14] I thought that as I was reading it last night. What do you think she did?"

"I don't know. But don't *you*?" He shook his head. "It doesn't matter anyway. How witty that story is, so light the touch. Lorenzo, how wonderful it would be if you wrote a play now, turning to that side of you. Bits of *David* made me realize how easily you could. Rawdon with his 'No woman shall sleep under *my* roof.' It's unbitter, cool, soothing laughter."

He was quiet for a few moments, and then:

"Yes, I know it's time for me to write something different, but I just don't feel interested."

"Oh, why?"

He hesitated: "When you think you have something in your life which makes up for everything, and then find you haven't got it . . . . Two years ago I found this out."

It was so final, the way he said this: he was away in a loneliness where nothing but what he desired could be of use to him. And what words would help? After some moments I said:

"When I was ill a few years back and had to begin living all over again and I dreaded the effort. But from you I learnt . . . . I would say to trees 'oh tree give me your strength,' to water and flowers 'give me your soft brilliance.' Your words taught me that and they helped."

"Yes. Once I could do that. I can't any more."

Giuseppe passed us with Moses and I went to get letters for the post. When I came back Lorenzo had disappeared. I wandered round a little grass-covered hill and stood on the western ramparts, looking gloomily down into the arbutus grove and hoped our talk hadn't upset Lorenzo. Then round the pine-trees he came, as cheerful as could be.

"Here's your coat. You'd left it on a rosemary bush and the dew will soon be heavy. I've put on a kettle for tea. The others will need it after their bathe."

That evening at dinner he was happier.

"Think of it. I've made eight hundred pounds out of *Lady Chatterley*. I've never had so much money before all at once. What shall we do? I think we'll take a villa in Taormina. Yes, we'll take a villa and live like gentlemen and have a butler. Do you remember, Frieda, when the B's parlourmaid slipped and fell down the stairs to that huge dining-room and the plates crashed like a thunderstorm?"

"Yes, and Ada [Achsah?] pretended it hadn't happened. So calm. She never even looked round but just went on talking."

"That was awful," Lorenzo said, giving the table a bang, "it wasn't human. There we were, simply shattered, and that poor girl might have been badly hurt, but no, she must be a Buddha and sit there, far removed from mundane things—under a Bo-tree indeed!"

"Then do you remember how frightened they were in Ceylon? How the natives didn't like them being so holy?"

"What was that hymn Robert [Earl] was always singing?" Throwing back his head Lorenzo chanted in a horrible falsetto:

> Oh to be nothing, nothing
> Oh to be nothing, *nothing*

and put diabolic yearning into it, repeating it again.

"Stop, please stop!" Richard almost shouted. Lorenzo gravely and politely stopped, the rapt theosophist to the end.

"There was an amah who tried to frighten them about snakes."

"It was spiders, Frieda. Yes. The nights were black, oh black. The jungle was just outside the bungalow and it seemed to step closer and bend over us when the darkness came. Sounds boomed, and some animal shot a cry at you. Oooooooouh or crrcquck—like that. And this woman used to slip behind Ada [Achsah] and whisper 'Lady sleep here, *this* room tonight. *Spider* in lady's bed and if spider bite *lady*, lady die.'"

He drew out the dying into a long sigh. It would be dreadful if this gave the impression of vulgar, unkind mockery. No, apart from his intolerance of poses, Lawrence liked to present each actor to us so that we realised them. It pleased him to give us laughter, to hold us amused and wanting no other entertainment.

After coffee, when we were in the sitting-room, his mood changed. Press cuttings of *Lady Chatterley's Lover* had come and most of them were disgraceful. The critics had become so heated over imagined dirt that the odour of their sanctity was tainted. We were amused by these notices, forgetting that the author of the book was being hurt.

"My God!" one of us gave a shout. "Here, in this one, Lorenzo, one of them calls you a cesspool!"

He made a grimace which might have been a smile or slight nausea.

"Really? One's fellow creatures are too generous. It's *quite* worth while giving of one's best, isn't it?" Then as if speaking to himself, "Nobody *likes* being called a cesspool."

Beside the fire there was a heap of light branches, rosemary, thorn and myrtle. They were used to kindle dying embers, but a devil suddenly came into Lawrence and he threw a branch on the flames. It crackled beautifully and he threw another and another. Fire filled the whole hearth-place, licking over the edges.

"What are you *doing*," cried Frieda.

He didn't answer but two more branches went into the flames.

"Look out! It'd be a cold night in the open if you burnt us out."

No answer, but quicker, more branches, more thorns. Painful smoke and lovely perfume began to fill the room. But each protest only made him add more fuel in a sort of rhythmical rage. His fury died out with the swiftly burnt herbs, and having served up his enemies symbolically as a burnt sacrifice, he never bothered about them again.

.   .   .

Lawrence found it hard to endure disharmony between his friends. A discord had developed on the island, and one day he said to me:

"Let's get out of this. I don't like it. You come with Frieda and me."

"But look, darling. We're all leaving in a week's time. Can't you stand it for a few more days? Richard is one of my oldest friends. I simply don't trust those others not to do some mischief if we're not all here."

He nodded silently in agreement, saying after a moment: "A woman who uses her sex to hate with!—Awful!" Then he asked:

"What are you going to do when you get back to London?"

"Oh, I don't know. Anyway I've finished this novel and earned some of my advance. Wish I had time to rewrite it."

"Yes. I'd like to write that book for you. I know just how it should be done."

I was working in my room that afternoon when someone knocked on my door. Calling out "Come in!" I was surprised to see him walk in. He came up to the writing table holding a little paper in his hand.

"I want you to take this."

I looked. It was a cheque for ten pounds.

"*Dear* Lorenzo, I *can't.*"

"Yes you can. It would please me. Things are hard for you just now."

"But really I'll be able to get some work. I know I shall."

"Well then, give one of your parties in the studio. That would amuse me. I'd like to think of it."

And he went out quickly.

Often Lawrence was homesick for the ranch in Taos.

"You must all come out there. Look, the Brett has sent us some turkey feathers from the ranch. Would you like one? Like soft fire, aren't they? You think this place is beautiful . . . it's nothing to those Mexican mountains. The light and clarity kill you, but it's worth it. Other things seem so small after you've lived on that plateau. Yes, we'll all go back there."

Frieda said to me: "Won't you come to us and help me look after him?" 15

8 November 1928   La Vigie, Île de Port-Cros, Var, France

❲ [The] cold Frieda brought from Florence developed into the regular Italian Influenza, and I was in bed feeling low. However, I'm better and moderately well. We've had great storms and torrents of rain, and the boat doesn't come and then there's no food—so we are leaving the island, God with us, next Tuesday [13 November 1928]. I think we shall only just go over to Bandol, on the coast between Toulon and Marseilles, for a little while, just to gather our wits and decide where to go. If I were a bit tougher I'd go to Spain. We might go to that coast near Biarritz—we might go to the Garda—God knows. I don't mind very much. . . .

There's no news. . . . [There] was a great attack on Lady C. in two . . . papers in England—John Bull and Sunday Chronicle. The foulest and most obscene book in the English language. . . . In this place I tried to paint a bit—no good—I merely wrote three little articles. I don't care for islands, especially very small ones. I want to get on the mainland again.[16]

John Bull *on* Lady Chatterley's Lover
(20 October 1928)

FAMOUS NOVELIST'S SHAMEFUL BOOK

A LANDMARK IN EVIL

There has been brought to our notice within the last few weeks a book which we have no hesitation in describing as the most evil outpouring that has ever besmirched the literature of our country.

The sewers of French pornography would be dragged in vain to find a parallel in beastliness. The creations of muddy-minded perverts, peddled in the back-street bookstalls of Paris[,] are prudish by comparison.

The book is by one of the best known of modern English novelists, Mr. D. H. Lawrence. It is entitled *Lady Chatterley's Lover.*

Mr. Lawrence is a man of genius. As a psychologist he is in the front rank of living writers; as a stylist he stands supreme.

FATAL OBSESSION

Unfortunately for literature as for himself, Mr. Lawrence has a diseased mind. He is obsessed by sex. We are not aware that he has written any book during his career that has not over-emphasised this side of life.

Now, since he has failed to conquer his obsession, the obsession has conquered him. He can write about nothing else, apparently.

That his works have hitherto contained little that could fairly be called offensive to a broad-minded public is obviously due to certain police powers which enforce a standard of decency on publishers and booksellers.

Mr. Lawrence has surmounted that difficulty by having his latest novel printed and published abroad.

There is no law to prevent a man shutting himself up in an English study and creating a literary cesspool with an English pen on English paper.

WILLING HELPER

Therefore, we do not suggest that Mr. Lawrence slunk out of the country with his shameful inspiration for the more congenial air of, say, Port Said.

He may have written *Lady Chatterley's Lover* in Chelsea. The policeman on his beat would have been powerless to stop him, even had he known what this bearded satyr was up to.

That is by the way. Some months ago Mr. Lawrence found a kindred soul in Florence—the home of Dante—one L. Franceschini, master of a printing shop called the "Tipografia Giuntina."

What Lawrence had written Franceschini was prepared to print, Dante or no Dante.

The edition was limited to a thousand copies, and priced in English at two guineas. It was then broadcast to the capitals of the Continent, where it has been snapped up eagerly by degenerate booksellers.

We are informed that the thousand copies of *Lady Chatterley's Lover* have sold like hot cakes, particularly in Paris, and that they are now changing hands at from five to twenty guineas among British decadents.

UNDERHAND BUSINESS

We would not mind that. If Lawrence-lovers choose to steep their evil minds in the fetid masterpiece of this sex-sodden genius we are indifferent—so long as they don't come near us.

But some of them have seen an opportunity of making a handsome profit out of the obscenity and have succeeded in smuggling considerable numbers over to London.

These are not openly on sale, but may be had at a price, and in secret, from certain booksellers.

One Oxford Street shop which was approached last week denied with a show of indignation that it stocked the novel, but when the customer was leaving he was approached by a salesman who whispered to him that he could get a copy privately and purely as a personal favour if twelve guineas were paid on the spot and no receipt was asked for!

It is not our custom to publish an attack on a man without detailing, more or less explicitly, the offence to which we, as a public newspaper, take exception. This course is impossible in the present instance.

Lady Chatterley's Lover defies reproduction in any manner whatever that would convey to our readers the abysm of filth into which Mr. D. H. Lawrence has descended.

We have said that it is the foulest book in English literature. Though our knowledge of excursions in the lascivious by Oriental writers is limited, we do not hesitate to say that if a search were made through all the literatures of all the ages, as foul a book might be found, but certainly not a fouler.

Mr. Lawrence is a great artist. It is because of this that his book excels in filth. A merely nasty-minded novelist of limited talent could not have written it.

It was created, and created only, out of the turgid vigour of a poisoned genius. We leave it at that.

The circulation in this country of *Lady Chatterley's Lover* must be stopped.

As for Mr. D. H. Lawrence, we have no doubt that he will be ostracised by all except the most degenerate coteries in the literary world.

That there is no law at present under which he may be ostracised more completely and for a good stiff spell, we much regret.[17]

The Sunday Chronicle *on* Lady Chatterley's Lover
(14 October 1928)

LEWD BOOK/BANNED./UNDER NAME OF/NOTED AUTHOR.
PRINTED OUT/OF ENGLAND

A SENSATION has been caused in the literary world by the dramatic action which has been taken by the British Customs Authorities against an astounding book, *Lady Chatterley's Lover*, signed by "D. H. Lawrence."

The *Sunday Chronicle* learns that copies of this book have been seized by the Customs with the object of preventing its circulation in this country.

Admirers of Mr. D. H. Lawrence, the famous novelist and poet, are questioning whether he can possibly be the author of a book which the *Sunday Chronicle* has no hesitation in describing as one of the most filthy and abominable ever written, and an outrage on decency.

"FOR SUBSCRIBERS ONLY."

Privately-printed in Italy "for subscribers only," the book is limited to a thousand copies, each of which is signed "D. H. Lawrence."

Some copies reached this country before the ban came into operation, and one is now in the possession of the *Sunday Chronicle*.

It seems incredible that the D. H. Lawrence of literary fame should have written such a book.

REEKING WITH OBSCENITY.

The book literally baffles description. It reeks with obscenity and lewdness about sex. Words are used which it is impossible to print in a newspaper and which, if spoken in the street would most probably result in a charge in a police court.

No publisher in this country would dare to handle such a work, and there is little doubt that if any attempt had been made to market it in the ordinary way there would have been a clear case for serious consideration by the authorities.

Messrs. Curtis Brown, Ltd., Mr. Lawrence's regular agents in this country, told the *Sunday Chronicle* yesterday that they had no knowledge of the book except that slips announcing its publication were put into circulation from Italy, giving the price of the book as £2 2s. and stating that the edition would be strictly limited to subscribers.

PARALYSED HUSBAND.

Lady Chatterley's Lover will not only revolt decent minded people on account of its theme, but also because of the filthy words that are used.

The story deals with shocking frankness with indiscretions of Lady Chatterley, whose husband comes home from the war "with the lower half of his body, from the hips down, paralysed for ever." She takes a lover—a rough, dialect-speaking gamekeeper—and visits him in his hut.

Not only are acts between Lady Chatterley and her lover minutely described on these occasions but in one chapter the two are made to talk in the most depraved way imaginable. Such words are used between them that it is impossible even to hint at their nature.

Mr. Frank Henderson, the London bookseller, told the *Sunday Chronicle* last night that he had read a copy of the book.

"It is the sort of thing that collectors of smutty books would go after," he said. "Serious minded people would merely shrug their shoulders and lock it up somewhere out of sight. Nevertheless, despite its nature, it achieves the level of greatness in some parts." [18]

La Vigie/Ile de Port-Cros/Var./14 Nov. 1928

⟨ Dear [William] Gerhardi,

I was amused by the Beaverbrook blurb.[19] But you mustn't grumble at his inconsistencies. The heart doesn't know what the liver thinketh, and the stomach speaketh unsooth to the mind. That comes of creating a newspaper with all your anatomy. The little toe, as you remark, has a small say all on its own. One could do an amusing skit on that. I wish we created a "Monthly Express," out of our various anatomies, to laugh at it all. Just a little magazine to laugh a few things to death. "The Big Toe Points out the Point or Points in Point Counter Point."—and so on. Let's make a little magazine, where even the liver can laugh.

No, I refuse to be Rampioned. I am not responsible. Aldous' admiration is only skin-deep, and out of the Mary Mary quite contrary impulse.

We leave this isle tomorrow. —I don't like little islands. I suppose we shall stay a while on the coast here. We have given up the Florence house, and I am absolutely at a loss, where to get another. Where does one want to live? Have you any bright idea on the subject? Did you get a house west of Marseille, as you said? How is it there?

Send a line c/o Curtis Brown, if ever you want to. My wife sends her greetings, & *tante belle cose.*

D. H. Lawrence [20]

Richard Aldington

In November the weather deteriorated. We had mistrals; and then a wet southern wind from the sea which smothered us in cloud so much that Lawrence said it was *"sciroccissimo";* and indeed it was. For my part, I liked Port Cros so much and was in such excellent health that I should have been glad to stay the whole winter there—never before had I known the experience of living in natural surroundings of almost perfect beauty without the intrusion of any unwanted humans. The only people who bothered us were some French staff officers who came to investigate the suspicious alien character, Lawrence, and weren't allowed by me to see him. But they only came once, and evidently regarded the matter as absurd. It was a wrench for me to leave, but I saw Lawrence couldn't stand the exposure any longer and must be taken to the mainland, doctors, and central heating at once.

I said good-bye to Lawrence in the ugly little salon of the Select Hotel just opposite the station at Toulon. I never saw him again, for our paths went in different directions, and within sixteen months he was dead. Yet in the hundreds of times I have since passed the windows of that room I have never failed to think of Lawrence—a remarkable man, the most interesting human being I have known.[21]

Brigit Patmore

The day of departure came. It was sad, walking down the long winding path through the scented air, sad to leave the island so full of charm, but sad because a heavier parting weighed on me. To distract him I made Lawrence talk of his early life.

"What did your family call you? Had you a pet name?"

"No, they just called me 'our Bert.' "

When we reached the harbour the stretch of water outside it looked choppy: the usual afternoon wind was rising. Most people have their own cure for seasickness: mine was to keep "in the open." Lorenzo's was, to distract the mind.

On the motor-boat, which jumped and shuddered in an inhuman way, the others went into the cabin, but I chose the well outside it. Lorenzo came and sat beside me and talked all through the slapping wind and wild leaps of the boat. For the first and only time I could not listen or make sense when I tried to. A few sickly smiles of gratitude was all I could manage.

The next night Frieda, Lawrence and I dined in a restaurant in the gay Place de l'Amirauté. Toulon residents love it and carry chairs out to sit in the middle of the square under palm-trees and listen to the music coming from the café and restaurants.

Although it was a parting feast we were gay too. Lawrence spoke of Mexico, of their horses and how magnificent Frieda looked in her silver-studded saddle. A little dog came running around and looked at us with beseeching eyes. Lorenzo stroked the smooth head and said:

"So you want something of me too? There was a dog in Taos who *would* try to fight or play with the porcupines and of course got prickles all over himself. Then he'd come to me and beg for them to be taken out. After I'd done this several times, I said to him 'Don't come to me any more. I won't pull them out. You must learn not to be so stupid!' But the very next day back he came looking like a pincushion."

"And you took them out?"

Lorenzo smiled rather guiltily. "Well, you come and see for yourself."

As my train for Paris left early in the morning we went back to our hotel about half-past ten. Too soon for me, but Lawrence seemed tired. Then in their pleasant large room we said good-night—and good-bye.

Not for one second have I ever been able to think of D. H. Lawrence as dead: surely that is the greatest gift one mortal can give another— his immortality.[22]

BANDOL, VAR, FRANCE

18 November 1928   *Hôtel Beau Rivage, Bandol, Var, France*

❲ [We] *got here yesterday, quite nice, beastly crossing from that island. I think we shall stay here about two weeks—then perhaps come to Italy* to finish my Etruscans—or perhaps go to Spain. Quite hot and sunny here . . . .[23]

21? November 1928   Hôtel Beau Rivage, Bandol, Var, France

⟨ It is incredibly lovely weather, and the place very lovely, swimming with milky gold light at sunset, and white boats half melted on the white twilight sea, and palm trees frizzing their tops in the rosy west, and their thick dark columns down in the dark where we are, with shadowy boys running and calling, and tiny orange lamps under the foliage, and in the under dusk. Then we come in and have tea in my room looking south where the moon is, and get sticky with jammy cake.

. . . Orioli writes he is not well—liver. He wants to publish a series of Italian Renaissance stories . . . . I am doing Lasca—quite amusing.[24]

24 November 1928   Hôtel Beau Rivage, Bandol, Var, France

⟨ We are here on the coast near Toulon—very pleasant and warm and quiet. But I think I shall have to go back to Italy in December to finish those Etruscan essays—they nag at me for them—publishers always want "a book." They want a novel, but I'm not going to give them one. What's the good of writing books? In England the government now takes 20 per cent of all royalties of persons living abroad—and Curtis Brown 10 per cent, so they take £30 on every £100. And their royalties damn little. What's the good! It pays me far, far better to write little newspaper articles, and the papers want them now. Imagine me appearing regularly —irregularly, as a matter of fact—in the Evening News, Sunday Dispatch, Daily Express! [25] But the Sunday Dispatch gives me £25, for a 2,000 article, written in an hour and a half—and nobody would even publish a story like None of That.[26]

7 December 1928   Hôtel Beau Rivage, Bandol, Var, France

⟨ It is really blank indecision keeps us here—though really Bandol is quite nice now there are no people. Anyhow the hotel is really pleasant and the food really good—40 frs.—so it's not worth while changing. Frieda gets fidgety wanting a place of her own to spread out in. But where? Where does one really want to live? . . . Even Frieda doesn't really know—she oscillates between Lago di Garda and Taormina, and isn't sure of either. I say the best thing would be to go to Spain and try it, anyhow before settling anything. But she has left the trunks in Florence—and Orioli has gone very vague. I ought to go there. And one of us ought to come to London to see Dorothy Warren. And in this state of complex indecision we just sit here and do nothing. But anyhow it has been sunny all the time, till today, which is grey—really lovely weather. I feel I am pretty well off . . . the sun is worth a lot, so why fret.[27]

15 December 1928   Hôtel Beau Rivage, Bandol, Var, France

❲ It has been quite cold, but the sun rose brilliant, all bright and crystal, and is shining on me as I sit in bed writing. It makes me not want to come north—ever. My feeling now is, I would like to go real south, to get a house: either Sicily again or south Spain: and I'd like to look at the South of Spain first. But my instinct is to go south, not to come north. . . .

I have been doing a book of Pensées, which I call pansies, a sort of loose little poem form; Frieda says with joy: real doggerel—But meant for Pensées, not poetry, especially not lyrical poetry.[28]

Philip Trotter

The opening had been duly fixed for the 5th October 1928. Her account of herself as "exhausted, ill, and over-worked" [29] was the understatement of Dorothy Warren's condition when, on the 10th September, she set out with me for a fortnight's rest at my partner's castle in the heights of the Burgenland. But it was an unpremeditated event that occasioned yet another postponement of the Lawrence exhibition. On the second evening of a two-days' pause in Würzburg, looking down from the citadel on the baroque city in the moonlight, we plighted our troth. From the castle, replying by telegram to the good wishes of her staff, Dorothy added: "Keep everyone quiet and happy till we return." Whatever was done at the Gallery to give effect to these instructions appears to have stopped short of D. H. Lawrence.[30]

Hotel Beau Rivage/Bandol, Var./France/19 December 1928

❲ Dear Dorothy Warren,
     I think you've been a bit cool, keeping my pictures there all the time and merely doing nothing. However, now the men of the Fanfrolico Press,

Jack Lindsay and P. R. Stephensen,[31] say they want to do a book of reproductions of my paintings as early as possible in the New Year. So they want
to have the pictures photographed at once. So will you please see that the
photographer has access to them as soon as he is ready. If you are hesitating
at all about the exhibition, don't have it, as I have someone else who
would like to exhibit them. But if you still want to show them, perhaps
you could arrange with Mr. Lindsay to have the show at about the same
time as their book is ready: perhaps in February. They are doing the book
very de luxe, probably at ten guineas.

Let me know about this—and if I shall send to have the pictures removed from your gallery.

I hear you are married, and hope you are feeling jolly, and my best
wishes. But I'm annoyed at not having heard a single word from you.

Sincerely

D. H. Lawrence [32]

19 December 1928 Hôtel Beau Rivage, Bandol, Var, France

❬ We have a friend here, a young writer, quite nice and faithful. First
Frieda did not like him because he's not beautiful—but now she thinks
him quite good-looking and she likes him. We also had a young Australian
[P. R. Stephensen] here for two days, this afternoon he left for Nice. He
makes those beautiful expensive books that people collect nowadays—he
says he will make a book next year of my paintings—of all my paintings,
with a foreword by me, to be sold at ten guineas each. It seems madness
to me, but it's his money and he will pay me well—if he does it. But how
mad people are—there is quite a large vogue in editions de luxe that
cost two or five or even twenty-five pounds. I hate it.

Rhys Davies, the friend who is here, is Welsh and his grandfather was
also a miner.[33]

Rhys Davies

The winter of 1928 I was living in the South of France. A letter arrived one morning: ". . . would you care to come and be my guest in
this small and inexpensive hotel for a few days? My wife and I would
both be pleased if you came—D. H. Lawrence." [34] Some friends of his
in London had sent him my first novel [35] and told him I was in Nice.

I had always imagined him as a remote inaccessible person, brooding and alone in his later esoteric rages and fumings, impatient of the ordinary European world, flying from it to places like Mexico and Australia. Inaccessible even while in Europe. In London I had learned very little about him as a person; the younger set in which I moved had never seen him; he was becoming a legendary figure, mystic, and with more than a touch of the hieratic about him. But I had always wanted to meet him. So I was surprised and thrilled when out of Bandol, along the coast, came the note. How nice of him, I thought in excitement and a little fear, to invite me, a stranger, to stay with him.

I went in trepidation. The visit was important to me. Just as his books had meant as much to me as all my own experiences of life, becoming mixed with those experiences, I thought this meeting would intensify what he had already given me. For the younger generation of writers in England then, in that strange confused directionless decade after the war, he alone seemed to be carrying a torch. True, a smoky, wild torch. But nevertheless a light, though exactly on what path it was shedding illumination was often a matter for dispute, quarrel and even derision. I think we admired him because he was not sitting down inertly during those slack years. He was crying aloud, if sometimes incoherently, of the deceit, falseness and dangers of those apparently victorious after-war years. Not that he was political, or even social, minded. His message was directed into the heart, the loins and what he would call "the bowels of mankind." Meaning instinct as opposed to the mechanization of the individual. His work was a fresh announcement of life. Furthermore, he used language as no one had used it before.

In the train I asked myself what I thought he'd be like as a person— he had written to say he would meet me at the station, and I had seen only one photograph of him, a youthful one. I found I thought of him as a big sombre man with a vehement beard, traces of his mining *milieu* in him, rugged, savage and a little rude. Yet though he was not big, sombre or unkempt, as I descended from the train I instantly recognized him in the crowd on the platform—and he me—and there he was smiling, even gay, his high voice rippling and easy as he asked me about the journey. Standing on a rock at the gateway of the station, Mrs. Lawrence, aloft, handsome and bright-plumaged, was searching over the heads of the people for us. She, too, was gay and cheerful. It seemed something happy, even a joke, that I had come safely the short distance from Nice. In the car we chattered like magpies. My nervous excitement and twinges of fear fled. I was very glad I had come. Lawrence looked at me keenly with his bright, perhaps too bright, eyes and smiled; Frieda laughed, and I felt livelier than I had done for a long time. Just then I did not feel I had approached the wilderness habitation of one who, feeding on locusts and wild honey, was lifting his terrible voice against the world.

This first note of frivolous gaiety, alas, was not always to be maintained. I, like everybody who came into contact with him, got my share of St. John the Baptist denunciation. But for that first hour or two all was charm and ease. We entered the drowsy, placidly-run hotel purring at each other: it was the hotel to which Katherine Mansfield used to bring her nervous exhaustion and her lady-Hamlet diary. There was an air of tranquil indolence. The milky blue sea was lazy under the hotel windows.

Lawrence was a small thin man with a most fascinating head. Finely shaped, his head had both delicacy and rude strength. His beard and hair, of a ruddy brown, shone richly and, with his dark eyes, were keen with vitality. His hands were sensitively fine, and beautiful in movement. These features suggested a delicacy that at last had been finely tempered from ages of male and plebeian strength: a flower had arrived from good coarse earth. His thinness was neat, lively, and vibrant with awareness of others. To be with him was to feel a different and swifter beat within oneself. The stupid little behaviour of ordinary life, the little falsehoods, the little attitudes, rituals and poses, dropped away and one sat with him clear and truthful.

That first evening I spoke, when alone with Mrs. Lawrence, of the admiration and respect of the *young* people in London, how eagerly we looked to Lawrence, how mocking we were of the officious pomposities of the enthroned gods. "You must tell him that," she said quickly, "it will please him so much. Because he feels they *all* hate him." I told Lawrence, as sincerely as I could. But he was doubtful. I insisted. He shook his head unbelievingly. I became perplexed: didn't the man *want* admiration and disciples, I asked myself a little angrily and unable to see, just then, that he had been so wounded by English attacks that his old cry of anguish, "They are all against me," had become at last a blindly violent mania.

Thereupon Lawrence broke into such abuse of the young that I was discomfited. Ah, why didn't they stand up, he fumed, and fight to make the world theirs, why didn't they smash, smash, smash? Why did they tolerate the impositions of the old world, the old taboos and the mongrel trashy contacts of the civilization they were forced into? The men did not know even how to handle a woman: they wanted to be treated as women themselves: and the women were lost, senseless, vicious—but because their men had failed them.

Yet his arraignment of the young was not so wholehearted as his fierce raging hatred of the generation that sat in tight yet flabby ruling of the world, the moneyed and the governing classes particularly. It was they who were rotting the world, it was they who closed themselves to the voice of the spirit and lived only in the vulgar transaction of being worldlily successful, of attaining at all costs the power to grind down someone else. The young he blamed for allowing them to do it without protest.

"Kick," he said, "kick all the time, make them feel you know what they are. Because you *do* know, you're intelligent enough. The young know, they *know*, and yet they let be. Oh dear, it drives me to despair when I see them holding back, letting be. Because your chance is now; the world is all wobbling and wants a new direction."

And his voice, become shrill as he was roused—and how easily he was roused to an extreme pitch of intensity!—would finish in a heave of sighing despair. Later he spoke of the way those elders had tried to curb him, how, indeed, they *had* curbed him. "I know I'm in a cage," he rapped out, "I know I'm like a monkey in a cage. But if anyone puts a finger in my cage, I bite—and bite hard."

Uneasy though such tirades as these made me, I saw then that he was certainly caged. He was caged by censorship and persecution chiefly, but there was also his consumption and the exile this meant; and he was caged by the contempt, the laughter, the cheap sneers and the suggestive and cunning propaganda of his enemies who spoke and wrote of him at that time (*Lady Chatterley's Lover* had not long been published) as a frustrated sexual maniac, pornographic and indecent. Caged, which was the same thing as a retreat to the desert, he had arrived at that prophetic stage (and these were the last two years of his life) when the civilized human race appears one day as effete idiots, another as a pack of hyenas and wolves. But, though he writhed away, he could not turn his back on people, he could not rid himself of his vehement awareness of people: this was the motive power of his tremendous nervous vitality—and this it was that was treacherously exhausting his body. His condition at this period might have been called tragic. Yet, because of that passionate awareness still burning in him, one could not think of him as anything but a great dynamo of life, still generating with a wealthy fertility the magic of existence. Those pungent, energetic and fecund recent books of his!

At this time in Bandol he was writing the satirical poems to be called

Pansies and also painting one or two pictures. He told me he would write no more novels; *Lady Chatterley's Lover* was to be his last long work of fiction, the last large attempt to tell men and women how to live. For all his fury and rages, he got immense fun out of writing *Pansies.* He would write them in bed in the mornings, cheerful and chirpy, the meek sea air blowing in from the enchanting little bay outside his window. He sat up in bed, a little African straw cap on the back of his head—"It keeps my brain warm," he said, afterwards presenting me with another of these little native caps.[36] There was something perky and bird-like about him thus, and he was intensely happy and proud of the *Pansies;* he would read out the newest ones with delight, accentuating the wicked sharp little pecks in them. He little thought of the ridiculous heavy-handed official interference these vivid little lizards of poems were about to endure. Yet in the end they emerged triumphant, with their tails gaily up.

But it was out of his painting he seemed to get the most joy, turning to it with relief and a sense of escape that perhaps in words was denied him—for in all Lawrence's later books, luxuriant though they are with vivid life, there is an unhappy sense of recoil, as if the full blaze of his soul could not be got entirely on the pages and the writer had retired baffled into himself again, to brood and gather strength for another terrific outrush. But on a canvas he could paint those rich sensuous shades he loved so much, paint them in their own colours, not in black words; he could give a goat or a swan actual shape, a tree, a flower, a nude, in their own colours. Yet, being Lawrence and not a novelist playing about with paint, it was not enough to give them pictorial representation; there must be that exuberant surge of passion, so that every line and every shade of those nudes, flowers and animals must blaze with it. At their London exhibition (which was raided by the police) the pictures embarrassed people, the Lawrence vehemence was too naked on canvas, it confronted one too suddenly. A book is more secretive, its appeal slower: particularly the Lawrence books have to be read several times before they yield their full meaning. It was said the paintings were faulty in drawing and construction, bad *pictures*—as undoubtedly they were. But because of that Lawrence intensity in them the technical errors seemed not to matter; almost because of the errors they achieved a barbaric aliveness. And to their painter they gave intense joy, they were so .actual before his eyes, giving visual representation to a sensuousness he tried to get into words. He was almost pathetic in his absorption in these paintings; he said that words bored him now.

> . . . my soul is burning
> as it feels the slimy taint
> of all those nasty police-eyes like snail-tracks smearing
> the gentle souls that figure in the paint . . . .[37]

he wrote after the police-raid in London. The opinion, sometimes expressed even now, that Lawrence sought deliberately to incur official censorship, is completely false. I was with him often during the police and newspaper activities over *Lady Chatterley* and *Pansies*. Their effect on him was either like a spiritual vomiting or a fury that made his very appearance that of a demon. And he had not the kind of calculation to scheme all this out. Of the many accusations made against him nothing could be more fantastically untrue than that he was a humbug.

Once he rapped out at me: "All you young writers have me to thank for what freedom you enjoy, even as things are, for being able to say much that you couldn't even hint at before I appeared. It was I who set about smashing down the barriers."

The afternoons and evenings were given over to idleness. Walking tired him, so he would dawdle at the edge of the sea in the sun. These afternoons in the sun with him seemed to have a living peace that was strangely refreshing; he seemed to spread around him, his rages quietened for a while, a conciliatory atmosphere of awareness, so that the lazy roll of the sea, that ancient and ever-young blue sea, and the voices of the naked boys at play on the plage (it was his picture of these boys that was the chief cause of the London raid),[38] became a harmony that gave, to me at least, a fresh and satisfying ease. He would ask me about my childhood in Wales, my home life, my reactions to the constrictions and religious bigotry of a nonconformist period. He said:

"What the Celts have to learn and cherish in themselves is that sense of mysterious magic that is born with them, the sense of mystery, the dark magic that comes with the night especially, when the moon is due, so that they start and quiver, seeing her rise over their hills, and get her magic into their blood. They want to keep that sense of the magic mystery of the world, a moony magic. That will shove all their nonconformity out of them."

Another time he broke into a lamentation for the old pre-war England, shaking his bearded head, his voice becoming hollow with the realization that that England was dead: "Ah, you young don't know what England could mean. It's all been broken up for you, disrupted. I'm glad

I was born at my time. It's the sense of adventure that's gone, and there wasn't all this ashy taste in the mouth. The fun is gone. That's what you haven't got."

And though he would speak with contempt and anger of the economic poverty of his childhood and the horrible dreariness that trails behind mining-village life, his days in those districts of his youth seemed, as he talked, to have given him intense glee and satisfaction. He would tell of some of the characters of Derbyshire, so that bits of old England stood out before me with Shakespearean gusto.

"But nowadays," he lamented, "all pleasure takes place in people's heads. They don't *do* and *live* funny things any more, they've become much too mental and smart. The old England is gone and you've let her slip away." Again and again he harped on the inertia of the young in not springing to save the real, beautiful England. And, because of his tuberculosis, one couldn't taunt him with his own long exile from the damp soggy land. Besides, was he not protesting enough in his books?

An interesting admission he made to me was that he had come to respect his father much more than when he wrote *Sons and Lovers*. He grieved having painted him in such a bitterly hostile way in that book. He could see now that his father had possessed a great deal of the old gay male spirit of England, pre-puritan, he was natural and unruined deep in himself. And Lawrence, by implication, criticized his mother who had so savagely absorbed him, the son. Frieda told me, in answer to my opinion that *Sons and Lovers* was Lawrence's finest book, "No, it's an evil book, because of that woman in it, his mother." I was, of course, judging the book as a literary creation.

Lawrence was exceedingly puritan himself in many things, and very chapel-English. He was even an old-maidish prude. One evening I repeated a coarsely funny story that was going the rounds of the Riviera just then. It was received in blank silence. No, not blank; a silence full of freezing reproach. Stories that pulled a face at sex and teased it he abhorred. On the other hand, one was allowed to use in ordinary conversation all the "indecent" words, all those expressive words used by sailors, navvies and undergraduates which can so neatly abridge and clarify one's sentences. Which was a kind of concession.

Crotchety though he was at times, he seldom irritated me. He was so entirely without reserve, he was so aware of one, his personality came forth with such a full glow, sometimes in a martial march, true, but most often in a bright recognition that had a sturdy, ardent eagerness. To argue with him was difficult. In spite of one's frequent mental doubt, elsewhere in one's being there was the feeling that, in some burning world beyond logic, he was supremely right. If one could cut away all the weeds of principles and behaviour that had got into one since self-consciousness began, one felt that there, in the natural, instinctive self, was the truth that lived in him so undiminished. He wrote in one of his studies: "The soul has many motions, many gods come and go. Try and find your deepest issue, in every confusion, and abide by that. Obey the man in whom you recognize the Holy Ghost; command when your honour comes to command." [39] And I remember his saying to me: "When you have come to a decision, whatever your mental calculations tell you, go by what you feel here"—and with his quick intent gesture he placed his hands over and around his belly—"go by that, what you feel deep in you, not by what your head tells you."

He was obsessed by the mischief done by "mentality" when it usurped the emotions or feeling or, perhaps, that Holy Ghost of which he wrote, the uncontaminated texture in a man which must be preserved if he is to live truly. Modern literature suffered from mentality almost completely, he complained. Cerebral poems, creations of witch-novelists, with characters "like those wooden figures in a child's Noah's Ark." Cerebral fornications made modern novels indecent. And he would give a broadly amusing burlesque of some of his very famous literary contemporaries, all "gorping and puffing away importantly for success."

He had a magical talent for burlesque, and his performance of a certain novelist as a pompous whale churning the literary seas and spouting up water was so realistic that both the great industrious novelist and the stupid mass of whale were present in the room, but miraculously united. In the same way he could evoke flowers, animals and reptiles out of the air with a wonderful cunning. Once he described the lively adventures of his Italian terrier with such marvellous absorption into the canine world that D. H. Lawrence disappeared and I, too, felt myself turning into a dog: I remember especially his acting of the dog's writhing agony after it had been run over, its will to live, its pleased sniffing at life as it recovered, and its sudden bouncing forward into a fresh world of smells. He was that dog. This power of entering the soul of non-human things is the characteristic I remember most clearly. In the same way, it is for his vital descriptions of landscape and "spirit of place," and of flowers, beasts and trees, that his books yield one most *pleasure* now.

At the hotel was a young negro waiter. Lawrence took, in his usual energetic way, a deep dislike to the youth. The dislike was so intense and its object so innocently unaware of it that I was vastly amused. To see Lawrence's eyes gleam with watchful revulsion as the waiter laid a dish on the table seemed utterly grotesque to me: why be so stirred over the young man? It was his hands Lawrence watched: thin dusky nervous hands laying very, very carefully a plate of *vol-au-vent* on the table. I watched too, as I had been bade.

"You saw his hands, how uncertain they were, no feeling in them! No feeling. It's quite sickening, he can't even place a plate down properly, he fumbles, hesitates, it's like a dead hand moving, every moment I expect to see the dish go to the floor." And the denunciation came, as I expected. "All his movements are so *mental*, he doesn't trust to his blood, he's afraid. Look at him walking down the room now, look at his legs, look how they hang together and cower, pushed forward only by his mind. Ugh!" And he ended with a sharp hiss of absolute revulsion. It was true, as I looked carefully at the young man's legs, that they were rather soft and dejected-looking, clinging together as though for company as he took his short, gliding kind of step down the room. Yes, his gait was vaguely unpleasant, I decided, that hesitating glide, as though practised, and the legs with their subjected look. There was little that was spontaneous, certainly, about the youth. But this fierce antipathy!

Of course, out of such vehemence and such antipathy came *Lady Chatterley's Lover* and *Women in Love,* and the others.

Then there was the English maiden lady in the hotel, one of those respectable spinsters who were scattered all over the South of France and Italy. This lady, he swore, would have liked to kill him. Her social advances had been ignored. And one evening he wouldn't deliver up to her the hotel *Daily Mail* as she hovered and twittered about for it; he had whisked round to her demanding: "Do you *want* this paper? I'm reading it." The lady had shrunk back, mumbling that, no, she did not want the paper. But he had seen murder in her. In a shrill way he declared to me: "She would have had me taken out and killed then and there." The following morning—her bedroom was next to his—he insisted that through the dividing wall waves of hate and murder had been arriving from her. I think he saw her as some sort of witch. However, I was glad to see, on my next visit to Bandol, that he had made his peace with the lady. They now met on the common ground of painting. She made little water-colours of local scenes; Lawrence did his strident nudes. They almost flirted together with their brandished paint-brushes. Frieda was malicious. "One of Lorenzo's old maids," she said, telling me he had a weakness for these English spinsters.

Observing him strolling about in the sunshine of the plage below the hotel terrace, I mused over his extraordinary attraction as a person. In a faded old blue jacket, wispy trousers and a black flapping hat, he moved about with a springy awareness. There was something of both a bird and a lizard about him, light and winging, no flesh. Perky, bird or lizard like. Yet the thundering torrents, black hatreds and teeming awareness in that frail figure! Just then I felt, rather than was mentally aware of, the struggle against death-processes that was taking place in him. (I remembered he had just written a poem about a November sun—"my sun" sinking "wintry but dauntless" into the west: was it prophetic?).[40] The curiously fiery little figure winging about the plage was somehow electrically dangerous; it bore a high voltage of life. No, it could not die, with that bright eagerness in its wings.

His irascibility and irritation had the sharp, crackling, devouring temper of a fire. There was nothing small and fussy in his outbursts. They came in an avalanche, a torrent, a flood. Even over such a trivial incident as being half-an-hour late for the hotel lunch. I had met Frieda on the plage and we dawdled in a café over our apéritifs—time fled; it was enchanting to sit before that unspoilt (as it was then) native little plage of Bandol in the morning sun, while the villagers flopped about lazily in their carpet slippers. Unconscious that we were late we ambled back to the hotel. Suddenly I saw, watching our strolling approach from the top of the flight of steps leading to the hotel terrace, a dark sinister figure poised as if to swoop down on us, a malign vulture.

As we mounted the steps he was literally dancing with rage. What he said actually I don't remember, but as he hopped about, gesticulating in his Italian way, he poured out a flood of words that seemed to reduce the universe to nothing. He was the serpent come out of the heart of chaos to hiss forth death and desolation. I was interested, objectively, but decided that before such passion a polite apology for being late would be fatuous. And quite soon the tornado subsided into a vexed silence out of which came, presently, a charming offer. In the dining-room was a tray of newly-caught lobsters. These were a supplement on the table d'hôte price. Lawrence, the host, pointed them out and, coaxingly, was sure that I would like a lobster. I shook my head. He insisted. Then *I* became cantankerous. I refused to be wooed with lobsters. Frieda was not so silly. She enjoyed the fish with an unruffled air of "however extraordinary my husband, one does not have lobsters every day."

There were times when I could not bear to have him near me, and I would leave the hotel and go for long walks. It was the only way to keep one's will intact in this over-potent intimacy. He was too much of a magician, too much of an enchanter. There were times, indeed, when in everything he was too much. This, of course, was because I was still in a world which he had long ago left in disgust. I was even glad when it was time for me to leave Bandol, though for the next few months I returned again and again, glad to go to him, as I was glad to leave him. But such a dominant force as his was not for continual companionship. I do not wonder that his old cherished scheme for founding a community of fellow spirits came to nothing. For all his charm, aliveness and interest, men, unless they were completely negative, could never live for long in peace with Lawrence. And he had no use for negative people.

His marriage seemed to me a prosperous one. Frieda had a lioness quality that could meet his outbursts with a fine swing and dash: when really stung, she would shake her mane and grunt and growl; sometimes she charged. Their life together was an opulent one; her spirit was direct and generous, and his was laughing, malicious and subtle. Their notorious brawls were grand. She would lash out, and, gathering his forces with confident ease, he met her like a warrior. He would attack her for smoking too many cigarettes, having her hair cropped, taking a wrong line of thought, eating too many cakes in a café at Toulon, or for trying to be intellectual or aristocratic. He kept her simmering, subtly; for a natural inclination to a stout German placidity threatened to swamp her fine lioness quality.

On one occasion I remember her suffering a little from one of those odd bouts that visit women now and again—sometimes governing their lives—when they become the dupe of some shoddy mystical crank who hypnotizes them into rapt ecstatic states in which they imagine themselves angels, spirits or astral beings—anything that has no vulgar *body*. A German book on Rasputin had been sent her [41] and she read it with fascinated avidity. This incensed Lawrence to a vituperation that again, to me, seemed out of all proportion unjustified by the offence. He drew a mocking picture of women prostrate and fawning round the Russian monk, their faces gaping up for sensual religious sustenance. In Frieda's case the rapt interest in the mystic monk was only tentative. But even the gleam of interest was enough for Lawrence, who had detected it at once, and until he had swept the contamination away, his voice like a vigorously-handled broom, he could not rest. He bridled to me: "When she came down to dinner full of that Rasputin, I could have smacked her face across the soup."

To see, after their disputes, the puling, pattering little escapades of some marriages! This one had abandon. And Frieda did not impose on her husband, ill though he was, that female bossiness, that stealthy over-powering need to subjugate, which women, crying to themselves that they are doing a man good, can wind round him in oppressive folds. She could leave him alone and was cheerfully alive in her own sunny activity, or she would deftly touch him, flashing out some vain feminine illogicality that stirred him to comic denunciation. They had not *settled down* into what is known as peace but is really something else.[42]

25 December 1928 Hôtel Beau Rivage, Bandol, Var, France

⟨ *I wrote what I think is quite a beautiful article on New Mexico ["New Mexico"]* [43] *. . . . Writing it gave me a real longing to be back—and I should like to come in spring even if only to stay the six months allowed by the passport. Brett suggests creeping in unnoticed, but if I feel I have to do that I shall be spitting in everybody's eye. I'm not given to creeping in, and USA isn't paradise anyhow.—My picture show is held off—I think I'm going to have them all reproduced and appear in a book with an essay on painting, to sell at 10 guineas a copy—which is fifty dollars. That's what the Mandrake Press say they want to do—seems to me a fancy price, anyhow. And the exhibition and the book appear simultaneously. —I've done such an amusing book of rag poems—pensées—which I call my pansies—make them all cross again. But I'm holding it awhile.*[44]

28 December 1928 Hôtel Beau Rivage, Bandol, Var, France

⟨ *I am at my wits' end as all sorts of pirated editions [of Lady Chatterley's Lover] seem to be coming out in America and selling at prices varying from $6 to $20 or even $30. I am trying to get out quickly a Paris edition at about 100 frs. to put on the market and nip them if I can. But it's so difficult finding anyone to take charge, and I can't sit in Paris to do it.*[45]

30 December 1928 Hôtel Beau Rivage, Bandol, Var, France

⟨ *. . . Frieda's daughter Barby arrives on 2nd to stay a week or so . . . . I don't really want to go back to Italy. I am so much better this winter than I was last, I can feel that this place is so much better for me than Italy—something bleeds me a bit, emotionally, in Italy. I really want to* go to Spain—I feel I should be well there, too. I think it's a man's country. But Frieda hangs back. She terribly wants a house—doesn't know where —feels Spain is far. But it isn't. It's no further than Florence. . . .

Anyhow, that's how it all stands at present. It's been a lovely warm day, like spring. I lie in bed and look at the dawn, and the sort of mountains opposite across the gulf go quite translucent red like hot iron—very lovely dawns—almost like Taormina, where we had it the same. Now it is tea-time and just a bit pinky and primrosy and touches of frail grey cloud. This place is nothing much in itself—but I seem to be happy here, sitting on the tiny port and watching the "life"—chiefly dogs—or wandering out on the jetty. I find I can be very happy quite by myself just wandering or sitting on a stone—if the sun shines. Yes, one needs the sun. If anything, one needs to go further south than here, rather than further north. But it's wonderful how sunny it is here—really one can thank heaven for so shining. . . .

Ottoline [Morrell] wrote very sweetly—very sweetly—but still coughing a little over Lady C.

I have done my Pansies, nice and peppery.[46]

6 January 1929   Hôtel Beau Rivage, Bandol, Var, France

⟨ F.'s daughter, Barbara, is here, probably till next Saturday—12th . . . . It actually snowed, and is beastly cold, but I think it's calming down. . . .

Barby got herself into a very depressed state in London. Really, the young make me feel really low in spirits. I sort of want to go away to the farthest corner of the earth and never say another word. A young man appeared from California—to admire me—and you know what a depressing effect admirers have on me—I want to die. But yet he is really nice and is staying at the other hotel—and is leaving in a day or two.[47]

Barbara Weekley Barr

In the winter 1928–1929, Lawrence and Frieda were staying at the Hôtel Beau Rivage, at Bandol on the French Riviera. I spent a fortnight there just after Christmas when I was in a miserable, nervous state. Lawrence was very ill himself. It was an agonizing time.

Frieda had been in tears on Christmas day, Lawrence told me, because she did not have a single present.

"There she was, howling like an infant," he said contemptuously. To cheer herself up, she had put a photograph of Monty on a shelf, but Lawrence took it away, saying that to have photographs about was vulgar. A little while later he had burst out, "Why don't your children send you presents?"

After he went to his bedroom, which led off Frieda's, we would hear his continual cough. During the day he looked exhausted and ill.

He had just finished his *Pansies* poems, and before sending them off to his London publisher, he read them to us as we sat on Frieda's bed. These bitter poems had the effect of clearing my suffocated mind.

When Lawrence had gone to bed, I said to Frieda, "He promised to make a new heaven and earth for your children when you went away together. Well, it's true; he has." Frieda told me later that she had repeated this to Lawrence, and he had been pleased.

A young American from California, who was at Oxford, met us in the street at Bandol.

"Are you D. H. Lawrence?" he asked. He explained that he was looking for the Ultimate Reality.

Lawrence invited him to come back to the hotel with us where, sitting in Frieda's bedroom, they threshed it out. Alas! the discussion was over my head.

"There *is* no Ultimate Reality," said Lawrence, firmly, after a time.[48] I doubted if this satisfied the young man. Soon after, the American took me out to tea, and told me I was bad for Lawrence's genius and had better go away.

"He is mad, madder even than you are, Barby," said Lawrence. "He hates Oxford even more than you do your set-up. But you are both in a state of hate, and have got yourselves on the brain. . . . It's a common form of hysteria. You used to have a rather amusing temper that popped up now and then like a little devil, or Jack-in-the-box. Now it's got hold of you completely. You are cynical as well. That's dreadful."

After a few days the news came that the *Pansies* had been seized by the police in the post. This upset Lawrence painfully. The feeling of tension increased, and there seemed a malaise in the hotel.

We had arranged to meet a friend of mine, Cynthia Kent, in Cannes, but in our distraction we went on the wrong day. As Cynthia failed to appear, Lawrence, suspecting some fresh insult, became frantically annoyed.

Lawrence was relieved when a cheerful colonial he knew wrote that he was coming to pay him a visit. "Now don't say anything, but I think

Barby might like him," he said to Frieda. I think this was Lawrence's only attempt at matchmaking for me.

The young man, who was called Stephensen, proved a jolly, go-ahead sort of person. Something he had seen in a night club had given him an idea for a short story. He sat down almost as soon as he arrived and "got it off his chest." It was about an older woman leading a beautiful young woman astray. He read it to us as we all sat, as usual, in Frieda's bedroom.

When he had finished, Lawrence demolished it for him at once.

"It's false," he told him. "It wouldn't convince anybody. The emotions and situations are quite unreal. You'll have to rewrite it."

"He is *not* an artist; he is a business man," he told Frieda afterwards. "Why does everyone try to write? I don't see there's so much fun in it."

Lawrence worried about me; my depression affected him. He was rather tired now by my endless dilemmas.

"I had a dreadful dream," he told us one morning. "I was rescuing Barby from some disaster. She was in a fearful fix as usual."

When I was returning to England, Frieda said, "If you can't stand it, you can come out to us at Majorca." That was to be their next resting place. I believe it was from Majorca that Lawrence wrote to me:

I think that your headaches may be due to a deep change in the psyche, and you will just have to lie low and bear the change. Don't make too many efforts, especially efforts with people, and don't try to paint at present. Later on you might be really worthwhile.[49]

7 January 1929   Hôtel Beau Rivage, Bandol, Var, France

⟪ Today I am sending you [Laurence E. Pollinger] a couple of MSS. of the poems: Pansies. They may displease you, so be prepared. . . .

.   .   .   .

We had snow here—and it's been bitter cold—now blowing black and horrid. What a way to start a year![50]

11 January 1929   Hôtel Beau Rivage, Bandol, Var, France

⟪ We've a young Californian friend staying here now—all a bit of a whirl; not the peaceful Bandol of before Christmas at all. We went away out on *the sea on a motor-boat this afternoon—warm sun, cold wind—such snowy mountains at the back.*[51]

Brewster Ghiselin

One afternoon early in January, 1929, while walking toward the railway station on the slopes above Bandol, I heard quick steps of approach and, looking up from the red earth of the roadside, saw a blonde woman and a red-bearded man in a faded sky-blue jacket striding rapidly towards me. The man seemed tall as he came down the slope; he was slender and slightly stooped, lithe and easy in motion. There was a country looseness in his figure and clothing. As they passed, I caught the glance of his clear blue eyes, and I thought, though the photographs had suggested dark hair and beard, This may be Lawrence.

In Paris I had written asking permission to come and see him. Miss Sylvia Beach of Shakespeare and Company [52] had said he was in Bandol, and while withholding his address had agreed to forward my letter. Expecting some days of waiting for his consent, that I never doubted would come, I had gone on at leisure to the south. His reply, already long delayed, must arrive within a day, and until then it would be better to say nothing.

A day or two later, on Friday, January 4, I concluded that one of our letters must have miscarried and that if I was to see Lawrence at all before leaving for Nice the next Monday I had better try to find him. That afternoon, at the town hall I obtained his address, the Hotel Beau-Rivage. The building stood on a wooded rise along the western sweep of the shore, overlooking the harbor. On the gravel terrace before the hotel entrance, I paused to look down on the water and the plage. There, sitting alone and motionless on a bench against a small tree, was the man I had seen on the hill. He wore an overcoat and hat, and as if cold he was huddled a little, his head slightly forward and sideways in an attitude I afterwards knew to be characteristic.

Descending the long stone stairway, I crossed toward the water's edge and stood before him and said in excitement, *"Pardon,"* from habit of speaking French, and as he glanced up I asked, "Are you Mr. D. H. Lawrence?"

He was.

"I'm the young American who wrote to you," I said.

"Yes." He seemed tired.

I explained how I had waited for his answer that had never come. "Your letter or mine must have miscarried. I wouldn't have bothered you with such intrusion, except that I've needed to talk with you."

Lawrence looked at me closely and asked me to sit down. He questioned me about what I was doing, how long I was staying, where I was going. I told him I had come to Europe mainly in the hope of seeing him, partly to find a graduate school in which the whole need of the mind would be of foremost concern, in order that my education might be an organic development of power rather than only a professional discipline. But during my first term as a graduate student at Oxford I had found much the same procedures, atmosphere, and expectations as at the universities in America. I said I was trying to find a fresh mode of life, a new way of being alive, that I had only intimations of, amid the stale ways of thought and feeling the world was content with. I said I believed he had gone far in discovering some such way of being and in developing a true understanding, that everyone else seemed to lack.

To most of this he answered briefly, or merely "Yes . . . Yes," in varying intonations of sympathy or acquiescence. After a little discussion of my experience at Oxford he said sadly, "Oxford and Cambridge died during the war. Something seemed to go out in Cambridge when Bertie Russell had to leave. You could feel it, you know."

Presently Mrs. Lawrence came down the stairs from the hotel with a handsome young woman, her daughter Barbara Weekley, and I was introduced. They sat beside us awhile to talk and to eat candy out of little brown paper bags. Soon we were strolling along the sunny quay, toward the few moored pleasure boats and, beyond them, the many fishing boats scattered over the water. When the two women went on into town, Lawrence and I sat on a bench facing the sea.

There for more than an hour, under the palms in sunshine among the passing people, we talked of many things, of the intent and fate of his latest book, *Lady Chatterley's Lover*, which I had just read, of the plight of the civilized world, of England and America, and chiefly of means of reaching and keeping a vital awareness in our civilization which was tending always to destroy it. Having read a dozen volumes of Lawrence, I was familiar with his terms of expression and with the outlines of his thought. He spoke casually and freely, with much variety of tone and feeling, often with humor, sometimes scornfully, never with solemnity. The value of his conversation lay less in the force of what was being said, for all its swift flexibility, diversity, color, good sense, and constancy to a single vision of truth, than in the interest and charm of his presence,

286

that this talk made articulate. I listened a great deal and asked a few questions.

The few words of *Lady Chatterley's Lover* which he had brought back into clean usage after their three hundred years on the dunghill had lost him many of his following, he said. The old maids, as he called them with acid amusement, faithful until then, had shut the book with a snap. It was banned in America, and every copy was being seized by the customs officials because each one brought fifty dollars. And yet those words were in good use, he declared, for fourteen hundred years; then "the dirt of the Renaissance got on them." His use of them was part of his effort to restore the confused, degenerated feelings of modern people. "Sex," he said, "must be taken out of the w.c." There was no hope of a sane society otherwise.

"The uttermost mystery" for him, Lawrence said, was how man, in the state of an animal moving in instinctive unconsciousness, in dynamic relation with his environment, "came to say 'I am I.' " Now the whole world was "under a net of ideas," and one must make holes in the net as a means of slipping through—and keep them open for others. If America should ever achieve a new way of life it could be only in the far future, for the psyche of all Americans was essentially European: "Look how they take up one idea after another, while their feeling is the same old dead one!" The beaches of Southern California, Venice and Santa Monica, had made him afraid; he had never before seen "so many perfect bodies," yet nowhere any living awareness.

Still, he might be at his ranch in New Mexico in the summer, he conceded, and if he were I must come and visit him there. Even if he were not, I should go to the ranch and live there as long as I liked: a man could live in that country for a thousand dollars a year—for less on the ranch. I should see something of the Pueblo Indians, and if possible go into Mexico, learn something of the Aztec and Mayan civilizations, from which he himself had learned much. The Americans would do well to study and know the American Indians—the real Americans, now unknown to them—instead of trying to wipe them out. As for Mary Austin,[53] she only observed superficially, as if the pueblo were some American village. *Mornings in Mexico* would give me something of his own feeling for the aboriginal civilization, Lawrence said, especially the chapter on the dance.[54]

Asked about England, he said he was always miserable there: the climate, but worst of all the hopelessness of the English. The working classes were alive when he was a boy, he said, and he would go back if he thought he could waken them; but he had not gone back; and he said he would not think or talk about it. "I want to believe they aren't quite dead," he finished. But while he spoke it was plain, from the misery of his voice and eyes, that he was sure they were.

The depression of his spirit was momentary, however. Lawrence was never doleful, he could not stand lugubriousness. In disgust, he ridiculed Keats' yearning for death and quoted with scorn, " 'Now more than ever seems it rich to die'!" He went on in sweeping and vehement condemnation of Keats' falsifying feeling for the world. "The nightingale doesn't sing of death! Its song is joyful. . . .[55] And the 'Ode on a Grecian Urn'! It wasn't even an urn, it was a wine jar, more likely! With satyrs on it. 'Thou still unravished bride of quietness'!"

By this time Mrs. Lawrence had returned to sit with us. "Do you like being here in Europe?" she asked.

I answered as best I could. Some things I had liked: at Oxford, a series of lectures on Greek vases, for instance; the somber glass in the Cathedral at Chartres in the dusk; the hills and sea at Bandol. Finally I emphasized my distaste for the feeling in the cities and towns by a gesture toward the group of buildings behind us.

Lawrence, who had been musing and as if half listening, turned suddenly full around and urgently said, "What is *wrong* with it? *What is wrong with it?*"

I answered, "It's the people, it's the way of their being." And indicating the façades along the water front, I said I supposed everything a man laid his hand to took the impress of his being and gave it forth again.

He relaxed from the attitude into which he had moved with the energy of his question, and in a voice full of weariness, but alive with a profound emotion that I can attribute only to humor, he said, "Yes, yes, it's dead. Everything they touch is dead. Even if they make a little cake! Their bread—haven't you noticed it?—tastes of death."

Here Mrs. Lawrence declared with enthusiasm that Lawrence had made real bread on the ranch, very different, good.

"Yes," he nodded, "that's true."

It was tea time, then, and they invited me to the hotel for tea, but I excused myself, suspecting they must be weary of me. Lawrence insisted that I come to lunch on the following day.

At noon next day they were waiting in the sunlight on the terrace before the hotel, and we went in immediately, to a white table at the north wall of the dining room. The soft-eyed young Negro who waited on us came from French Africa, they explained. As he stepped slowly, negligently about on his errands, Mrs. Lawrence exclaimed with pleasure, "He walks like Lorenzo!" And amid laughter Lawrence sat chuckling his appreciation and shaking his head in denial.

The talk went on in gaiety and extravagance. With humorous relish, and some irony, Lawrence described a "tea" in Hollywood, at which an appalling pint of whiskey and soda was thrust into his hand by the host, an actor wearing white riding breeches and carrying a riding crop, while the shrinking, refined wife drooped in a corner and a small son marched about dressed up exactly like father and swinging his little whip. Often Lawrence spoke vividly and unsparingly of human absurdity, but never coldly, never really uncharitably. He was without a trace of the delusions that drive so many to find their own elevation in the abasement of others. I told of some fantastic tales repeated in America about his life at the ranch, which no reasonable person could believe, and he spoke with amusement of similar stories he had heard: that he was a hopeless inebriate in a home for alcoholics; that he was a drug fiend; that his wife had been a boardinghouse keeper who had captured him, her star boarder, and run off with him. As he talked on easily, always with energy and interest, I began to feel that the reports circulating in Paris of the melancholy genius dying in Bandol were no less absurd than those stories I had heard about the half-deranged eccentric in New Mexico.

After coffee on the terrace, we went upstairs to the Lawrences' rooms, on the second floor of the hotel overlooking the bay. Lawrence read aloud some of the *Pansies* and the first "Introduction," which he had recently completed.[56] Finishing the passage on Swift's poem to Celia, he looked up in concern for whatever embarrassment his stepdaughter might be suffering. "Poor Barby! *Poor* Barby!" he said, in caressing tones of sympathy tinged with amusement, much as one might comfort a rain-soaked kitten, and went on with the reading.

That afternoon he showed me some of his paintings: *Leda,* and a watercolor of two figures in grey, terra cotta, and rose, and others. He had turned to painting, he said, as a means of defining some things better expressed in that way than in writing. But it seemed clear that he felt the shortcomings of his work, and I inferred that writing would remain his major medium and interest.

At the end of my visit, I spoke of leaving Bandol on the following Monday, to travel along the coast toward Italy, perhaps as far as Genoa, then back to Oxford to begin the new term. Lawrence said, "Oxford is squalid!" and gave his opinion that I would have done better to live here and there in Europe instead of studying at Oxford. I should stay awhile in Italy and get to know the Italian people a little. And he sketched out a plan for my spring vacation that would bring me there, by stages: to Cologne for a day, to Berlin for two or three days, then to Nuremberg, which he characterized as "the old Germany," to Munich, "the old Germany in process of change," and "up the Isarthal, where *Look! We Have Come Through!* was written," to Innsbruck, and over the pass into Italy: Verona, Venice, Padua, Florence, Assisi, Rome, Naples, and Capri. He would give me introductions to people along the way.

The following morning the sky was grey over a level sea, the mimosas drooped with moisture, and the stems of the olives on the darkened hills were black with rain. The Lawrences were coming to tea at the hotel where I was staying, some distance along the road toward Toulon, quite outside the village. Though I was distressed to think they would need to come through ugly weather to see me, for I knew what was bringing them was largely a desire to be kind, I could think of nothing appropriate to do, and at last did nothing. They arrived during a downpour, in a lumbering old taxi, but cheerful and friendly and full of reassurances that nothing was amiss. During the hour of their visit, Lawrence asked if I really wanted to travel on to Nice and other crowded places. When I admitted that I had no great interest in the journey, he suggested that I stay through my whole vacation in Bandol and that I come to the Beau-Rivage in order to be near them; he would arrange for me to have the choice of two vacant rooms across the hall from his own. As he was obviously sincere I agreed gratefully.

It was an invitation, I discovered, to become virtually a member of the Lawrence household. I was expected to share their activities through the day, to be with them in the evening, and to have a part in whatever plans were made. Breakfast, of course, in the Continental style, did not bring us together. After lunch in the dining room and coffee on the terrace, we spent the hours until tea time in talk and in walking along the shore. Every evening after dinner, we gathered in Mrs. Lawrence's bedroom, Lawrence usually sitting on the bed, Barbara Weekley or I beside him, and Mrs. Lawrence in a chair by the window. Often Lawrence read briefly from the manuscript he had written during the day, and I frequently carried some of it off later to my room. In this way I read his "Introduction" to the *Paintings* as it came from his pen and some of the Pansies.

Less often there was talk of other writers. Lawrence recommended to me *The Delight Makers* and *The Golden Man* of Adolph Bandelier [57] and *In the American Grain* by William Carlos Williams.[58] He read the shorter poems in Robinson Jeffers' *Cawdor,* a volume I had brought from Paris, and found them to be tainted with that self-consciousness, that concern with the ego, which he objected to in the work of so many Americans. When I praised the musical structure of the verse, he found fault with the figures, citing the falsity of an image of "The Bird with the Dark Plumes" said to be in the "blood" of the poet. And he objected that some of the subjects were disappointingly incommensurate with the writer's excitement, as in the poem "Fawn's Foster-Mother," which describes the suckling of a fawn by a mountain woman, an occurrence that Lawrence thought insignificant. Aldous Huxley's *Point Counter Point* came up for discussion mainly as a phenomenon of the phrenetic times. Though Lawrence again and again gave evidence of a strong affection for Huxley himself, he was not much pleased with the book and he ridiculed the purported picture in it of himself, Mark Rampion, rejecting it entirely.[59] Remarking upon Huxley's preponderance of intellect and upon what Lawrence considered his deep need for a further scope of instinctive and intuitive awareness, he concluded emphatically, leaning backward and gazing before him thoughtfully as he spoke, *"Poor* old Aldous . . . *Poor* old Aldous!"

On some of these evenings Lawrence sang folksongs he had learned as a child or some of the Hebridean songs that continued to delight him, among them the Seal Woman's Song of farewell as she returns to the water:

> Ver mi hiu—ravo no la vo—
> Ver mi hiu—ravo hovo i—
> Ver mi hiu—ravo na la vo—an catal—
> Traum—san jechar—

He sang with the passion of a creature that has known and loved the endless freedom of the elements, forgotten, and remembered again.

Lawrence worked in the mornings, sitting in bed in his narrow room, facing the window and the sea, which usually was blue and white with sunshine. When I left my room after breakfast, his door was always shut, in the long, still, shadowy hall.

Until eleven o'clock or noon I was alone on the populous plage, sometimes writing or sketching. Then the Lawrences, with Barbara Weekley during the first five days, came down from the hotel to sit in the sun, to walk about, or to visit the teeming market in the square before the church, to look on or to buy fruit.

In those days Bandol was little more than a lively village. The small casino was closed for lack of business, and there were few tourists—though enough to stir Lawrence's distaste. The townspeople and the free animals of the town crowded the public areas. Dogs foraged along the shore or haunted the market place, standing or lying in the luxury of human presence, among the booths, the racks of clothing, the live catch heaped in wet baskets or dropped on bare concrete. Women passed back and forth on their errands or in idleness, many of them wearing their fashionable bright red, purple, green, or black bedslippers. Fishermen in blue jeans sat against the railing around the war monument, talking and laughing while they mended their nets or baited their lines with small prawns and wound them into a basket like a nest, the hooks plunged in along the rims. Drying nets like a gross brown lace striped the quay. Lawrence liked the warm scene, the contentment of the men and their pleasure at their work.

One morning early in the week Lawrence came from the market to sit beside me, his pockets bagging full of yellow apples. The weather had warmed, after the snow and rain of the weekend, and the sea toward which we looked was a slick of light and the sky was a bright distance. Eating one of my large sweet tangerines, he said with musing pleasure, "It tastes like Africa." Less by his words than by the full texture of circumstance and scene, I knew his feeling and meaning. I recalled that during our first conversation he had spoken of his belief that the civilizations of the future would be in the sunny lands. It was not only for his health's sake, as some have said and continue to say, that Lawrence moved about the world. He went in search of light and to explore the various life in warm places and to enjoy it.

Bandol is in southernmost France. The winters are mild and sunny, and during most of that second week in January there was scarcely a cloud. The extraordinary frost of the winter of 1929 that killed so many trees in the town had not yet come. Along the plage the broad palms flourished unpinched, and white circlets of flowers hung among the higher leaves of eucalyptus trees. Yet Lawrence was not wholly satisfied.

One afternoon we climbed the hills above Bandol, past fields of yellow and white narcissus, and up among the olives where the stones of centuries were piled between the trees, broad walls the height of a man, and further along paths among heather, where Lawrence pointed out to me wild rue and fumitory, and still higher past the pines which had been slashed for turpentine that ran down metal flanges set in the tawny bark to drip into small clay pots. On the rocky ridge, Lawrence stood musing the ancient aspect of the land and talking of the races that had possessed it before the present. We looked down on a long inland valley, on many grey rocks, wild ridges blotched with pines, and further downslope the black cypresses, the fields, the olives and the deciduous trees about the few buildings.

"It's not far enough south," he said.

One may wonder, then, why he did not set off at once for Spain, southern Italy, or Mexico. But the fact is that his needs were not simple enough to be so easily provided for. The place must be right in the nourishment it afforded for senses and spirit, for the whole being.

Coming down from the ridge, Lawrence pondered his future. Though his publishers were eager for him to write another novel, he said, he felt he did not want to; he would not do it. "If there weren't so many lies in the world," he said, looking at me earnestly, "I wouldn't write at all." What he might do and where he would go remained uncertain. Many times, he said, he had felt it would take ever so little to make him an American, though not in the way of consciousness dominant in the United States, based on money, the universal disease of mental obsession. All the real America, he declared, moves in that "deep, terrible, tigerlike vibration of destruction"—the opposite of Europe—which the aboriginal civilizations, Mayan, Aztec, Incan, and the dying civilization of the Pueblos, realized so profoundly. Somebody should study the living remnant and "find out where the Indians' energy comes from." Even now, he felt, he might end in America, perhaps in the American way of being.

Lawrence meanwhile awaited without impatience what might define itself in him. He found satisfaction in what the place and time afforded, especially in human relationships, imperfect though these might be. He rarely preferred to be alone, and when he did, as on one evening when he put on his overcoat and went out to walk in the dark, without inviting companions, he was not long away. Everyone about him enjoyed the continual lively intervention of his interest. His quick attention accented every scene and event and heightened the import of every object it seized on.

In a bookshop kept by a Frenchman who had lived in Africa, Lawrence had bought a ceremonial cup of dark wood embossed with a few Negro faces, the work of a Congo tribe, the Bakuba. He directed me to the shop, where I bought a smaller pair, evidently belonging to the same set, one full and feminine in shape, the other slender and slightly taller. Lawrence was charmed with all three, vital forms incised with loosely structured geometrical designs. One evening he polished mine, as he had done with his, working over the brittle dry wood intently with a brush and some shoe polish out of a can. These were the "Cups" and "Bowls" of which he wrote in the volume *Pansies,* the

> soft-skinned wood
> that lives erect through long nights . . . .

Lawrence responded to everything with the organic strength of his feeling for the substance and shape of life, in himself and around him. He was never indifferent. Yet sometimes he was quiet, or even quiescent, as on the blue and yellow afternoon of January 9, when we walked out to the end of the jetty and sat on huge blocks of stone, dangling our legs over water. P. R. Stephensen the publisher, who had come to see Lawrence on business, was with us. The sun was warm, the wind light, and I wanted to swim, but my suit was far back at the hotel. Standing on cold slabs in the shadow in a deep slot between the blocks of stone, I made a loin cloth of two big colored handkerchiefs, with one of Lawrence's for a belt. When I went into the breathless water over weed-darkened boulders, Lawrence nodded down to me from the rock against the sky, reassuring me: "You're perfectly decent; you're perfectly decent," he called. After some minutes I clambered on stones by the rockwall and stood in the ripple while Stephensen read aloud a story he had recently written. I was dry before he finished. Lawrence seemed content, sitting still in the wind and light amid the activity of others, effaced but observant, constantly aware and responsible.

The self of most men is important enough to demand protection and various enhancements. For Lawrence, self seemed to have no interest. This detachment was the source of some of his freedom. It perhaps accounts for his enormous, uncalculated generosity of spirit. He never withheld himself. He was unreflectingly bounteous, in kindness and sometimes, very rarely, in anger.

His anger is famous for the fury of its open outbursts, yet in all those days I saw him angry only once, in a flare of ferocity as he turned to Mrs. Lawrence with a rebuke for her launching on a thoroughly Laurentian denunciation of some aspect of the world. "You don't know anything about it!" he cried. Startled to stillness, she stared at him, her blue eyes glinting like rinsed china and her face tense and flushed. Almost at once it was over: he relaxed and turned to me quietly, smiling a little, with a brief comment on the evil of unfounded talk. Others could not change quite so abruptly, but within a few minutes the usual easy, lively atmosphere was restored.

On Thursday afternoon we took the bus to Toulon and there walked by the harbor and drank rum and coffee at a table before a café by the water. We wandered in the dark streets, bought roasted chestnuts, and looked over racks of flowers offered for sale. Afterwards we had tea in a quiet place. Waiting for Mrs. Lawrence and Barbara Weekley, who had gone shopping, Lawrence and I talked of the disruptive and constrictive effects of the presence of so many people intent on hasty routines. When I remarked that it made me feel a physical tension, as if my head were compressed with a steel band, Lawrence agreed to a similar feeling, a sense as of being pinned with a bar through the forehead.

Perhaps as a consequence of this feeling about the city, we chose on the following day, January 11, to ride out on the sea in a motorboat instead of driving in a carriage inland to one of the hill towns, an alternative we had considered. The trip was planned for the afternoon.

Late in the sunny morning, Lawrence found me on the plage finishing a watercolor of some brilliant fingerlings I had bought in the market: one emerald; one russet-gold; one green-grey with flecks of blue and purple on belly and gills; and a purple-dark eel. He remarked on their vividness and on the full detail of the painting, for which he himself could never have found enough patience, he said. If I should do a series of such paintings, he suggested, they could probably be exhibited at Dorothy Warren's gallery in London. Yet one should work only when one wanted to, he warned me; it was wonderful how ability grew if one did that.

Most of all he was concerned about the uncolored ground of white around the figures. He felt the paper—yet in all watercolor he worked with he felt "the tyranny of the paper." The feeling for the fishes themselves was true, he said, but they were isolated in the midst of bare space in a way that deprived them of their actual relation to other things, to water, for instance. My pleasure in setting them apart like intense flames in consciousness was "a form of spiritual will desiring power," refusing to admit and to express the relatedness, the vital interchange, between them and all other things, each in their special quality and degree.

"I think the consciousness of the future will be intuitive," Lawrence said, "in its intellectual form a knowledge of relations."

He himself was trying to find some expression in paint for the relations of things, he told me, perhaps by means of the touching and mingling of colors flowing from different things: as the color of the background, for example, approached any body it would diminish and take some of the color and quality of that body. Later, in his room, he showed me a black and white drawing he had been doing of a nude man and woman in a kind of complicated electric field, a drawing now reproduced in his book of paintings.[60] In it he had tried to show the special rhythms of the different parts of the body, the head, the breast, the belly, the loins, as they subsisted in themselves and in a pattern of relations.

Asked if he did not believe the quality of the life rhythm was always changing, he agreed that he did. He spoke of some translations of stories by Bushmen that he had once read, in which the qualities of things seemed to be in continual change: now the giraffe would seem to be large, now small, now vague and far, now looming over. Cézanne, he remarked, had tried to catch all the aspects of the apple he was painting, as it changed continually in the flux of death.[61] A similar need to follow the developments in the object rendered, Lawrence said, accounted for the flowing and changing form of free verse.

Early that afternoon, in an open motorboat, we traveled out on the sea to circle some lonely islands. All but one of them, on which the lighthouse stood, were desolate stones stuck up into the mist of sun and sea. As we passed over pale green streaks in the deep channels Lawrence remarked that the color was of sunken limestone, but the boatman confirmed my belief, based on knowledge of similar waters and seaground in California, that it was the pallor of sand. Passing one of the smaller islands, a sunny slab over a cold shadow of waves, I remarked that I would like to go onto it.

"Why?" Lawrence asked sharply, as if scenting folly.

"Just to be there," I answered.

"Yes," he conceded after an interval, as if he had been considering.

Beyond the familiar hills of the shore other hills had lifted into view, the inland upland rising snowless toward the white bar of the farthest mountains. We must have been four or five miles from land when Lawrence told the boatman to turn round. The ride back was colder. When we reached the landing, I stepped out ahead in order to pay for our excursion, knowing that Lawrence would not consent to it except as an accomplished act. He protested even then, just as he had done when I arranged to supply some portion of the wine we used at table.

It was probably that same afternoon that we went downshore past the town to a little tea garden under pepper and eucalyptus trees by the sea. The sun would be down in an hour. Though the air was beginning to chill, I intended to go swimming again; I had brought a suit and towel this time. But Lawrence fiercely forbade it, because of the increasing cold, and in order not to distress him I gave up and sat still with the others, talking and drinking hot coffee.

While Mrs. Lawrence told how she had once saved Lawrence from drowning, he laughed and protested, shaking his head and assuring me, "It *isn't* true, you know; it *isn't true!*"

"Yes," she went on, "near the place where Shelley was drowned." [62]

"Then," I said, "what a shame you didn't let him drown!"

And Lawrence agreed, nodding over the lost opportunity, "*Yes—what a mistake!*" Half laughing, he spoke slowly, almost drawling, with the variety of tone and emphasis usual with him, shaping the sound into the fullest meaning.

We used to go a good deal along that eastward stretch of shore. One of our pleasures was seeing a flock of about forty goats that often grazed near the roadside, attended by a fat man. Idly watching his flock, he would sit like a slightly deflated balloon, while beside him his dwindled black dog lay breathing with closed eyes and pricked ears. The man's faintest whistle would make the goats swerve like a pool of minnows. When we whistled, the goats heard nothing. Then at a low slight blast from the goatherd, the hillside would heave. Or he would send the dog to wring the heels of the stragglers.

On my last afternoon in Bandol, Tuesday, January 15, Lawrence and I walked along the shore a mile or so eastward toward Toulon. Near the mouth of a little creek we sprawled on the gravel beside the waves to talk. "A flower is the most perfect expression of life," Lawrence said. He liked the symbol of the Lotus, "coming up out of the mud." What was wrong with all the religions was that they had always "plucked the lily," had found one or another symbol and had clung to it, refusing to relinquish it as its vitality was exhausted. Yet a symbol, he had found, lasted only about twenty minutes—he didn't know why; then it had to be replaced by another. The ultimate symbol he called "the Sun, the great central sun around which all the universes are circling." Sometimes he preferred, he said, the symbol of the great white bird beating the water with its wings and sending out waves. I asked why he did not write a book about symbols, and he answered slowly, as if reflecting, that he might, sometime.

I looked at him without speaking, feeling that though I had understood in some degree I could not wholly reach him. Coming down the shore, we had talked of the difficulty of conveying new insight, of the likelihood that even the clearest embodiment of it will be misunderstood, as so much of his work had been, and of the fact that apprehension of any new work of art requires a growth of consciousness, an expansion of the psyche, in the perceiver. I knew that insight is a living thing and that in full understanding of Lawrence's work I must comprehend in myself a vast fabric of living experience.

Knowing he would interpret my words by their context and sense their irony, I said, "Even I don't really understand you."

"No," he said soberly, "no . . . ."

Early next morning when I was ready for the train, I went to the Lawrences' rooms to say goodbye. In the clear full light before sunrise Lawrence sat in bed, propped against the headboard. We said only a few words and shook hands. His eyes were on mine while I crossed to the door at the foot of his bed and went out.[63]

Brewster Ghiselin

The Nets

That morning when I painted in Bandol
Beside the Mediterranean fiery fish
I left white paper blank about their blue,
Violet, burnt orange, and bird green,
Netted them in no meaning but their flame.

There Lawrence came (a devil's advocate)
With the blue question of his eyes to weigh
My jewels, while the palms around his head
Swayed in his honor. And his venerable
Red beard of judgment praised—but soon denied.

Spiritual will would have them so, in white
Tyrannic paper, islanded from life.
Painting as if his European need
Must be my own, I saw my need betrayed
In that white stained with common light and shade.

For now the flesh of elemental fire
Smouldered in opal folds, a borrowed light,
Quivered in colorings of the world's flame,
Not metal-bright as if those bodies rang
Belled by a hammer of the abounding forge.

"Better," the beard said. But in grief I gazed—
Though taken in a golden amplitude.
I saw the worn face turn and blue pain stare
Like mine: the buildings of that happy town
Nourished by light and by the tourist trade,

The market heaped with pride, with feasts, with trinkets,
Slippered dowdies shuffling on parade,
The fishermen beside the war monument
Mending the antique treasure of their nets,
The idiot boy entangled in his hands.[64]

11 *January* 1929   *Hôtel Beau Rivage, Bandol, Var, France*

⟨[*[Barbara] leaves tomorrow for Paris. Some time next week I expect the Huxleys will appear—Aldous and wife. Stephenson [sic] came, and stirred us all up as usual. But I thought he seemed a bit more downhearted than the first time. He is rushing back to London to work. I think they'll do my pictures all right . . . .*[65]

Philip Trotter

In mid-January 1929 the Lawrence pictures were collected by Mr. P. R. Stephensen and two colleagues for reproduction in the "sumptuous" volume that was to inaugurate the re-emergence of the Fanfrolico Press as the Mandrake. Dorothy pleaded for the return of the pictures in time to open the exhibition in April and thus avoid its running on into the London season.

A few days later an astonishing passage appeared in the *Daily News.* After citing Blake and Rossetti as the only other "outstanding examples of the painter-poet," the writer continued:

Now a friend of mine who has just returned from the Riviera has *brought back with him* twenty-four oil paintings . . . from the brush of no less a person than Mr. D. H. Lawrence.

My friend is Mr. Jack Stephensen of the Fan Frolico [*sic*] Press, and *he is arranging a special spring show* of Mr. Lawrence's work at the Warren Galleries. (My italics) [66]

For a brief moment at this time the fate of the Warren Gallery was in suspense. Dorothy received a very favourable offer for her two floors; we had just acquired a house in St. John's Wood, and for my semi-precious stone business I still had wholesale premises in Hatton Garden. Dorothy left the decision to me, pointing out that Lawrence had throughout been *menfichiste* about the exhibition, that other galleries were angling for it, and that it might well give a strident send-off to our partnership in the enterprise. What she did not tell me was that she was longing to be quit of gallery-owning for ever and to devote herself to creative work. I pondered the advantages; then looked round at the miracle of harmony she had created. "No," I said, "let's go on"; and preparations for the Lawrence exhibition went forward.[67]

Jack Lindsay

I came to London from Sydney, N.S.W., Australia in early 1926 with John Kirtley to start the Fanfrolico Press—we had hand-printed my version of the *Lysistrata* [1926] with drawings by my father, Norman Lindsay,[68] and the book had been well received in England. Kirtley wanted to found a fine press there. The Fanfrolico Press ran from 1926 to 1930. Kirtley soon decided to go back to Australia, and I took over the Press.

In October, 1928, I spent a couple of weeks in Florence with Norman Douglas at his invitation. Lawrence had already left, but Frieda came on a visit round that time. Orioli showed me a couple of water colours by Lawrence that he had, and I remarked on their interest and suggested that an exhibition should be held in London. I also suggested a book of reproductions.

On my return to London I forgot about the idea, but Orioli took it up and wrote to me about it. I presume that he was the person who persuaded D. H. L. to carry on with the exhibition. I was offered the right to publish the book of reproductions, but decided not to take it up. The reasons for my refusal were twofold:

(a) I was not much in sympathy with Lawrence at that time, and his whole outlook and aesthetic ran counter to the positions taken by the Fanfrolico Press, which were based on the ideas of Norman Lindsay (set out in his books *Creative Effort: An Essay in Affirmation* [1920] and *Madam Life's Lovers: A Human Narrative Embodying a Philosophy of the Artist in Dialogue Form* [1929]—the first published in Australia, the second by the Fanfrolico Press) which we were loudly expounding in our magazine *The London Aphrodite*.[69] The title of this periodical was meant as a polemical joke directed at *The London Mercury*—John Squire [70] and James Douglas of *The Sunday Express* [71] being particularly disliked by us. I may summarise our views as a sort of Nietzscheanism, with a pronounced aesthetic-subjective idealism plus something of the metaphysics of Yeats in *A Vision* (I do not mean derived from Yeats, but owning certain affinities with his views). My *Dionysos: Nietzsche contra Nietzsche* (1928) carries these positions to their limit. It will be understood that we were thus rather far from the positions of Lawrence, though I was beginning to come unwillingly under his spell (which I belatedly succumbed fully to in 1934–5).

(b) The feud of Lawrence and Joynson-Hicks [72] was at its height and the police were extremely keen to find any ways of taking action against Lawrence, whose *Lady Chatterley* they were watching for in the post from France. The Fanfrolico Press was also in a rather precarious position. We had received a number of anonymous letters threatening police action, and we had a good idea that these were not without basis in fact. With our magazine we were deliberately provoking the Squirearchy and the self-appointed guardians of public morals. Further, P. R. Stephensen,[73] then working as manager of the Press, with myself, had published —though not under the Fanfrolico Press imprint, a verse booklet *The Sink of Solitude* [1928] about *The Well of Loneliness* [74] uproar, in which we tried to satirise both that novel's author and its critics. I therefore felt that to publish Lawrence's paintings would be sure to bring the police down on us; and I still think this idea was correct.

However, I was keen that the book should appear. About this time my relations with Stephensen were wearing rather thin. I suggested that he should start a new press (which he ultimately called The Mandrake Press) on the basis of the undoubted profits that would come in from the Lawrence book if it was not suppressed. And I suggested that for interim capital he should draw on Edward Goldston, who had a bookshop at 25, Museum Street (near our own offices at 71, High Holborn, in Bloomsbury Square) and who had several times said that he would be ready to invest some money in the Fanfrolico Press. The three of us got together, and the new press was started off.[75]

At the same time both Orioli and Lawrence kept in touch with me about the book and the exhibition. Stephensen, still working for the Fanfrolico Press, said that he'd like to take a holiday in the South of France—killing several birds with one stone by also selling Fanfrolico Press books at the fashionable resorts and calling on Lawrence to finalise matters about the paintings. Stephensen made his journey, though he sold at most one book out of the huge trunkful he had taken. He was very much struck by Lawrence and fell strongly under his influence.

Lawrence sent me the text of his Introduction to the paintings and

301

asked me to check various points—in particular his remarks about Henry VIII and syphilis. (I assume that he had read the book *Post-Mortem* by an Australian doctor [76] while in Sydney, where this matter was dealt with.) I remember him writing something like, "Now don't say you'll do all this and then do nothing about it," remarks which showed he knew all too well the way that fellow-writers can let one down in such matters. However, I did do what he asked. He also sent some poems (which later came into *Pansies*) for *The London Aphrodite;* but I did not use them for the same reasons I did not publish the paintings.

I do not know who fixed first with Dorothy Warren for holding the show at her gallery. But Orioli and Lawrence wrote to me about it and asked me to look over things and report. I went along with one of Frieda's daughters, I forget her name, and, I think, with Stephensen.

The book of the paintings was a great success, and on the strength of it Stephensen got a flying start with The Mandrake Press. I had, however, no part in the further publishing decisions he took, some of which, such as the issue of *The Legend of Aleister Crowley* (1930), I thought injudicious. It was not long before much money was lost. The times, however, were bad just then for fine presses; they practically all ceased or suspended operations. The Fanfrolico Press itself was soon in difficulties and was wound up in 1930.

I recall in one of Lawrence's letters that he mentions getting a second copy of my *Dionysos* sent to him.[77] This makes me look rather foolish; but in fact I was not responsible for the duplication. Stephensen had given him a copy during his visit; then on his return, forgetting what he had done, he pressed me to send one. I objected as I knew that the book would be anathema to Lawrence, but at last agreed. (I think, however, the book did have some effect on Huxley, who under Lawrence's influences was weakening in his rationalism.)

There is also a story which Stephensen told that is, I think, worth repeating. Rhys Davies was visiting Lawrence at the time when Stephensen looked in. During lunch Lawrence worked up a terrific attack on the inoffensive Davies, accusing him of forgetting his working-class origin, and ending with an order-and-appeal, "Don't desert your class! don't run away from your class!" Taken in conjunction with *Lady Chatterley* and some of the *Pansies,* etc., these words seem clearly to express what Lawrence was feeling about himself.

Unfortunately I lost all my letters from Orioli, Lawrence, etc., in the difficult period after the liquidation of the Fanfrolico Press, when for some three years I was in dire poverty. One that I rather treasured ran in part something like, "Give up writing all this muck about love. Leave it to the Sashy Sitwells. You're right in what you hate. Stick to that and you'll get somewhere. Stop the love slush. Stick to your hate. That's what's real and good and creative in you." It expatiated on this theme at some length. Lawrence had been presumably reading *The London Aphrodite* and *Dionysos*. Why he dragged Sacheverell Sitwell in, I don't know, unless perhaps because in an essay on contemporary poetry I had praised him and Roy Campbell.

I recall the occasion when I lost this letter. Several people were drinking in Edgell Richword's [78] rooms. There was an argument about Lawrence, and I produced the letter and passed it around. As someone presumably pocketed it, it may yet be extant. The occasion is sharp in my memory as I also then lost in the same way a letter from Freud in which he made some interesting remarks on the early influence of Nietzsche upon him. [79]

24 January 1929   *Hôtel Beau Rivage, Bandol, Var, France*

What I am concerned about is my manuscript. There are the two copies of the poems, Pansies, sent to Pollinger on January 7th from Bandol, registered, as papiers d'affaires, No. 587. There is also the manuscript of my essay on painting, for the introduction to the book of reproductions of my paintings. This was sent to Pollinger as registered letter on January 14th, No. 718. —Now these two MSS. we must recover, whoever is interfering in their delivery. The essay on painting is my original manuscript. I have no copy. I sent it to Pollinger to be typed. It is about 10,000 words—is perfectly proper—and I can't have it lost. [80]

Rhys Davies

Pansies was finished and typed in Bandol; an incomplete set was dispatched to England from that village post-office of tolerant France. We dawdled through the mild days, sometimes taking long drives into the country in the village droshky: Lawrence disliked motor-cars. Out in the country, while the ancient nag munched the herbage and Frieda and I strolled about, he would squat on his heels collier-fashion and remain thus for an hour, unmoving, hunched up like a very old and meditating bird, his shut eyelids lifted to the sun. There was something eternal and primitive about him thus; and a delicate, untrammelled peace. Sometimes he would open one eye like an owl, keep it briefly on me and Frieda, and lapse back into his meditation.

There was nothing of the cathedral air of the great writer about him; no pomp, no boomings, no expectation of a respectful hush from apprentice hands such as myself. One warm afternoon he announced, after a hint from me, that he would read a selection of *Pansies* to me and Frieda. After a rather heavy lunch we went to my bedroom, where there was a sofa, on which I foolishly lay. And Lawrence had not a good reading voice; it was apt to become stringy and hollow. Very soon, to the sound of verses about the harsh flight of swans clonking their way over a ruined world,[81] I went off into deep slumber. When I woke he and Frieda had stolen away. But when we met at tea-time he twinkled with amusement. Only Frieda's face contained a surprised rebuke.

In a few days news came of the fussy official interference with *Pansies*, the opening and seizing of the packet of incomplete MSS. in the post by the English authorities. It afterwards appeared that anything posted from Bandol to England just then was subject to scrutiny; it was known that the author of *Lady Chatterley* was living in the village. What a surprise the authorities must have had, really, for there was nothing in even the complete *Pansies* which could be described as indecent by a normal person. A few quips and bits of plain-speaking, in good household English; that was all. Still, they kept this incomplete collection. Afterwards I despatched from Nice another incomplete set, which arrived intact, and later I took to England a complete set, which was duly printed—though privately—and sold unexpurgated.[82] Though I had no hand in the printing of this private edition, it was whispered to me one day on good authority that the flat in which I was staying had become of interest to the police: it was believed to be a distributing centre for the banned works of D. H. Lawrence. The fussiness!

Lawrence, sick in the face, crying out in his bedroom of the seizing of his darling, innocent poems, or raging on the beach as he talked of it, was depressing. He could *not* understand this new mealy-mouthed England. Ah, how the old robust England of strong guts and tongues had died! Why, why couldn't they let him have his say! The charge of indecency had an effect on him like vomiting. It was almost painful to look at him. It was in such moments as these that I felt that, more than his consumption, an evil destructive force was attacking him successfully.[83]

Hotel Beau Rivage. Bandol. Var/27 Jan 1929

⟨ Dear Bruce [Brewster Ghiselin]

I had your letter—we are still here, as you see. The Huxleys also are here—Aldous has a chill & is staying in bed a day or two—will leave when it's better. Frieda too has a chill & stayed in bed since lunch—so Maria & I went down to dinner alone. Of course the old waiter wouldn't believe that Frieda was ill, while I survived. —It's the wind, which has been bitterer than ever, I never knew such a nasty wind, worse than maestrale or tramontana, by a long chalk. It's got my bronchials too—but that's inevitable.

The only news is that the police have started seizing copies of Lady C that enter England, and they have even seized the two MS. copies of the Pansies, which I sent to my agent—they say they are obscene & indecent. I must get back at them some way about that—must, must. They even held up the only existing MS. of the Introd. to Painting, and I trembled with rage. But they've let that go! That's what it is to write for a civilized world.

Stephensen sent a proof in colour of that picture—Accident in a Mine —Not bad, but oh, it loses a lot. I've nearly done that panel of which I made the sketch the night before you left—rather nice—& part done another, of bathers. Now I'm having to type the Pansies again, to rub salt into my sore against Scotland Yard and such gentry. Attendons!

I read The American Caravan,[84] and I wonder it's not called the ambulance Van instead, they are all so sick. Why they don't all quietly take hemlock I don't know. But of course they wouldn't be able to wail any more print across any more pages. The wailers! Edward Dahlberg [85] has asked me if I'll write a foreword to his novel which Putnams are publishing, & I've said probably. Nothing like asking.

I'm really hoping we'll get away to Spain by 10th Feb.—away from the wind. Such a lot of fusses through the post to attend to. —I hope you're bearing up at Oxford & being a good little, good little boy.

Regards from both

D. H. L.[86]

5 February 1929 Hôtel Beau Rivage, Bandol, Var, France

⟨ . . . I want to go soon, now. Frieda has not been contented here in an hotel—she wanted a house. But I liked the hotel—warm and no effort.

Then lately they have been making a great fuss over Lady C. Scotland Yard holding it up—visiting my agents—sort of threatening criminal proceedings—and holding up my mail—and actually confiscating two copies, MS. copies of my poems, Pansies, which I sent to my agent Curtis Brown —saying the poems were indecent and obscene—which they're not— and putting me to a lot of trouble. I don't mind when I'm well, but one gets run down. And those dirty canaille to be calling me obscene! Really, why does one write! Or why does one write the things I write! I suppose it's destiny, but on the whole, an unkind one. Those precious young people who are supposed to admire one so much never stand up and give one a bit of backing. I believe they'd see me thrown into prison for life, and never lift a finger. What a spunkless world!

.   .   .   .

I wanted to go to Spain, but now it's upset—and Frieda doesn't want me to go. So I don't know what we shall do. I can even be arrested if I come to England—under the Post Office Laws—oh, la, la! I feel like wandering away somewhere—south—south—perhaps to Africa.[87]

7 February 1929   Hôtel Beau Rivage, Bandol, Var, France

❲ This hotel, thank goodness, is always pleasant and warm, and the place is practically always sunny, though the wind can be devilish. I don't think Frieda should have been discontented—but discontent is a state of mind. Now that I am beginning to come to the end of Bandol, and the sojourn here, she's beginning to like it, and I expect her, as soon as I'm ready to go, to refuse to leave its paradisal strand. *La donna é mobile*. But I'm grateful to the place, it's been very kind to me—and though I've had a bit of 'flu now, I've not had to stay in bed at all, and have eaten my meals and thanked the gods. I'm really a lot stronger, even with a bit of 'flu on me.

.   .   .   .

I feel rather like wandering—going to Spain—Morocco—Tunis—anywhere south. I want to go south again, to the southern Mediterranean. I wouldn't mind even going later to India for a spell, to see if I could do an Indian novel—novel with the Indian setting. It tempts me. If one could be fairly sure of not getting ill . . . .

.   .   .   .

. . . *If one is a man, one must fight, and slap back at one's enemies, because they are the enemies of life, and if one can't slap the life-enemies in the eye, one must try to kick their behinds—a sacred duty. We are passive when we are dead. Life is given us to act with.*

To-night is the Bandol philharmonic concert, so of course we've got to go—and Madame says we shall be enchanté, so let's hope so. I only hope we shan't be enrhumé into the bargain.[88]

Hotel Beau Rivage/Bandol. Var./16 Feb. 1929

⟪ Dear Bruce [Brewster Ghiselin]

I have not heard again from you—I suppose you had my letter in answer to yours. We are still here—it's been so cold that the railway stopped running, so did all the water in the hotel—now it's warmer. We both had flu, but fairly mildly—hope you haven't got it, it seems universal.

My sister [Ada] is here staying a while with us—when she leaves we shall go, I really think. I was rather surprised when she told me you had not sent that little African musical instrument [89] *to her boy—and he on tenterhooks to get it, poor lad. Would you sent [sic] it him please, if it's not too much trouble:*

Master Jack Clarke [90]/"Torestin"/Broadway/Ripley near Derby

The Huxleys were here for ten days—both rather seedy. Now they are freezing in Florence, where there are 50,000 cases of influenza, and ice over the Arno!

How are you bearing up against Oxford? —I hope it's not doing deadly things to you.

We sat out on the end of the jetty this afternoon—where you swam. It was just warm enough to sit for an hour, but colder than that time. A palish octopus kept rising & sinking in the water, pale green like a streak of slime. You wouldn't have bathed today.

Do let us know how you are, and many regards from us both

D. H. Lawrence [91]

18 February 1929   Hôtel Beau Rivage, Bandol, Var, France

⟪ *My sister [Ada] is here, arrived a week ago: and I am fond of her, but she fills me with tortures of angry depression. I feel all those Midlands behind her, with their sort of despair. I want to put my pansies in the* fire, and myself with them—oh, dear! But this afternoon Frieda and she have gone to Toulon—and it was a lovely warm day, the loveliest . . . . O the blue sea! But all the palm trees and eucalyptus trees of Bandol are dead—frozen dead. They look funny and dry and whitish, desiccated—but I can't believe they'll not put forth. But Madame says the gardeners say no, they are killed. I feel as if half the town had died. Then these wonderful blue tinkling days so still and fair!

We had a bit of 'flu—I had—but not bad. Every single body in the hotel had it—but mostly mildish.

.   .   .   .

We now think of Corsica. Frieda has read it up in Baedeker, and is thrilled! So I expect we'll go—perhaps even end of next week.[92]

Parliamentary Debates on Seizure of Pansies MSS
(28 February 1929)

MR. DAY [93] asked the Home Secretary whether any books or other publications have been seized and confiscated by the officers of his Department during the months of January or February, 1929, and will he give particulars; and is he considering, together with his legal advisers, any further action?

SIR W. JOYNSON-HICKS.[94] The officers of my Department have no power to seize and confiscate books or other publications. During the period from the 1st January, 1929, to 26th February, 1929, the Postmaster-General, acting in pursuance of warrants issued by me, has intercepted copies of six books and of 10 other publications of an indecent nature. The answer to the last part of the question is in the negative.

MR. DAY. Can the right hon. Gentleman say whether, before these books are seized, his officials have any expert literary advice as to their nature?

SIR W. JOYNSON-HICKS. No, Sir. I think the hon. Member will see that I have seized not merely books but photographs and all kinds of matter of a very unpleasant character which are forbidden to come through the post, as I shall show in an answer to another question which I have before me to-day. I would ask the hon. Member to leave his supplementary questions over until I have answered that question.

MR. MORGAN JONES.[95] Are we to infer from the answer that it is possible for the Postmaster-General to open postal communications on the chance that they are undesirable?

SIR W. JOYNSON-HICKS. I am dealing with that fully in reply to another question, and I do not think that it is right to take up the time of the House at this stage.

MR. DAY. Shall we now have the answer to the question, to which the right hon. Gentleman refers, as the hon. Member on this side who has put it down is not at present in the House?

SIR W. JOYNSON-HICKS. Someone will ask it.

SIR FRANK MEYER [96] asked the Home Secretary whether he gave instructions to the police for the seizure of copies of the novel, "The Sleeveless Errand"; [97] and on what ground such action was taken?

The following question also stood upon the Order Paper in the name of Miss WILKINSON: [98]

11. To ask the Home Secretary whether he gave instructions for a manuscript of poems sent by Mr. D. H. Lawrence to his literary agent to be seized before any question of publication arose; if he will give the names and official positions of the persons on whose advice he causes books and manuscripts to be seized and banned; what are the qualifications of such persons for literary censorship; and whether, to assist authors and publishers, he will state what are the rules and regulations the contravention of which causes a book to be seized and banned by his Department?

MR. PETHICK-LAWRENCE.[99] Can the right hon. Gentleman answer at the same time Question No. 11, which stands in the name of my hon. Friend the Member for East Middlesbrough (Miss Wilkinson), who is prevented from being present by a family bereavement?

MR. SPEAKER.[100] No. That would be creating a very bad precedent. If an hon. Member is not present, the question cannot be asked, except when time permits, and questions are gone over for the second time.

SIR W. JOYNSON-HICKS. I will explain the position fully to the House in order that they may understand that I do not in any sense exercise a literary censorship. The Obscene Publications Act [101] makes it lawful for any Metropolitan Police Magistrate, or for any two Justices of the Peace, on sworn information, to issue a search warrant to search for and seize any indecent or obscene book, picture, writing or article, and there is a Common Law duty upon the police to secure the prevention of crimes of this or of any other character. Accordingly when information was conveyed to me that the book referred to in the question was about to be published, I handed the matter over to the Director of Public Prosecutions, and under the provisions of the above-mentioned Act he applied for and obtained a search warrant at Bow Street, in the execution of which a large number of copies were seized and are now in the possession of the police, by virtue of the Magistrate's directions.

The procedure directed under the Act referred to is being followed with a view of obtaining from the Magistrate an Order of Destruction and a Summons to the publisher is now pending at Bow Street. In view of this circumstance it would be impossible for me to make any observation on the character of the book in question. The question whether it comes within the Statute is a matter for the Magistrate's decision.

SIR F. MEYER. Has the right hon. Gentleman considered whether the present position of the law in this matter is the best way of dealing with clearly obscene publications, without imposing upon the police and magistrates a duty which they should not have—a literary censorship or a moral censorship?

SIR W. JOYNSON-HICKS. I hope that the hon. Member does not want to impose that duty upon myself. At present, I have the magistrates to fall back upon, as it were, in a very difficult duty. While there are Acts of Parliament passed by this House, my only duty is to see, as far as I can, that they are carried out.

MR. PETHICK-LAWRENCE. Is not the right hon. Gentleman aware that his action, in the first instance, is taken as if it were a censorship? If we are to have a censorship, would it not be very much better that the whole matter should be discussed in this House, and a censorship formally appointed, than, in effect, bring about a censorship by this indirect means?

SIR W. JOYNSON-HICKS. When my Estimates are put down, I should be only too glad if my hon. Friend wishes, to raise a Debate on the whole question. At present, there is no censorship. It is not until a book or any other obscene document is brought to my notice that I exercise my position. A censorship would imply that every book should be read by the body of censors, which would be an impossible position.

MR. RAMSAY MACDONALD.[102] Will the right hon. Gentleman make it quite clear whose responsibility it is to put the law into operation?

SIR W. JOYNSON-HICKS. Undoubtedly, the police, but I do not want to shed any of my own responsibility for my own action. In this particular case, the book was sent direct to me by a friend. I thought that it was a proper case to send to the Director of Public Prosecutions, which I did. There my responsibility ceases.

MR. PETHICK-LAWRENCE. Does not the right hon. Gentleman see that, when he sets the law in motion, he is, in fact, exercising a censorship, whether he calls it by that name or not?

SIR W. JOYNSON-HICKS. Really, the hon. Member must see that my action or the action of the police in dealing—I am assuming for the moment that it is indecent—with an indecent publication, is exactly the same as dealing with an indecent act which may be committed to the detriment of the public weal. The law has decided that these indecent publications should not be permitted, and I have to carry out the law.

Lieut.-Commander KENWORTHY [103] *rose—*

MR. SPEAKER. Further discussion must be deferred until the Home Office Vote.

11. MR. PETHICK-LAWRENCE (for Miss WILKINSON) asked the Home Secretary whether he gave instructions for a manuscript of poems sent by Mr. D. H. Lawrence to his literary agent to be seized before any question of publication arose; if he will give the names and official positions of the persons on whose advice he causes books and manuscripts to be seized and banned; what are the qualifications of such persons for literary censorship; and whether, to assist authors and publishers, he will state what are the rules and regulations the contravention of which causes a book to be seized and banned by his Department?

SIR W. JOYNSON-HICKS. The answer to the first part of the question is in the negative. I will explain to the House exactly what has happened. Under the Post Office Act of 1908 the duty is laid upon the Postmaster-General to refuse to take part in the conveyance of any indecent matter, and the Postal Union Convention of Stockholm, 1924, also prohibits the transmission through the post of indecent matter. In this case the typescripts were sent through the open book post from abroad and were detected in the course of the examination to which a proportion of such packets are subjected for the purpose of detecting whether letters or other matter not conveyed at that rate are contained in the packet. The typescripts were sent to the Home Office and by my directions were then forwarded to the Director of Public Prosecutions. I am advised that there is no possible doubt whatever that these contain indecent matter and, as such, are liable to seizure. I have, however, given instructions that they shall be detained for two months to enable the author to establish the contrary if he desires to do so.

As regards the remaining parts of the question, I have explained in reply to the question by my hon. Friend and Member for Great Yarmouth (Sir F. Meyer) that there is nothing which can properly be described as a literary censorship in this country. It is a misdemeanour to publish any indecent or obscene book, and the Obscene Publications Act provides machinery by which the publication of an indecent or obscene book may be prevented or stopped if a competent Court so decides. I have no authority to discriminate between offences of this character and offences against any other part of the criminal law, and it is my normal practice, when information reaches me with respect to the publication or intended publication of an alleged indecent or obscene book, to refer the matter to the Director of Public Prosecutions, who takes action in the ordinary course of his duty where the facts seem to warrant it. The publication of a book cannot in any circumstances be prevented except by decision of the Courts.

MR. PETHICK-LAWRENCE. Is it not clear from the right hon. Gentleman's answer that some person or persons came to a preliminary decision that this book is of an indecent character? The question which my hon. Friend wishes to put is: Who are these persons who are entitled to give this provisional opinion, and what qualifications have they to make a literary discrimination of this kind?

SIR W. JOYNSON-HICKS. In the first place, in this case the Postmaster-General makes the first determination that this is *primâ facie* a case of indecency. He then sends it to me, and, if I agree, I send it on to the Director of Public Prosecutions. It is not a question of literary merit at all, and, if the hon. Member has any doubt, I will show him this book in question. It contains grossly indecent matter.

MR. AMMON.[104] Is it to be understood by the House that in endeavouring to discover these publications the Postmaster-General does not violate any sealed packet or anything sent by the letter post?

SIR W. JOYNSON-HICKS. I think it would be better to put a question to the Postmaster-General on that point, but it is clear that the Act of Parliament and the International Convention both direct the Postmaster-General not knowingly to carry indecent matter of any kind. That applies to other things besides letters, and, if he finds indecent matter in the post, it is his duty, by law and by International Convention, not to deliver it.

MR. AMMON. Is it not understood that under the Berne International Convention sealed letters cannot be opened unless by direct order by a Secretary of State? I am trying to elucidate that this sort of thing is not arrived at by a violation of that order, but simply by examination of open packets, which are always liable to inspection. I understand from the Postmaster-General that that is so.

SIR W. JOYNSON-HICKS. It is quite clear that nobody, no official of the State, can open a sealed packet without the direct warrant of the Secretary of State.[105]

2 March 1929   Hôtel Beau Rivage, Bandol, Var, France

〖 Have you heard the row in London about [Pansies]—seized by Scotland Yard and now questions being asked about them in Parliament? It's just March lunacy—those poor bits of Pansies. Everybody is of course quaking, at the same time they are getting the wind up against that imbecile Jix, the Home Secretary.—And the colour-printers are frightened too, and refusing to reproduce some of the pictures—perfectly harmless pictures. But the people are going ahead—and I suppose they'll get the book out about May . . . .[106]

? March 1929   Hôtel Beau Rivage, Bandol, Var, France

〖 . . . I've decided to come to Paris to see about an edit. of Lady C. —else I'll feel minchione, with all those other pirates. So expect to arrive Paris at 10.0 on Tuesday night [12 March 1929]. Frieda says she wants to go straight to Baden-Baden—by Lyon, Besançon, Strasburg—and join me in ten days or so. . . .

Rhys Davies will probably be coming up at the same time, so I'd have company.[107]

PARIS, SURESNES, ERMENONVILLE

Rhys Davies

[Lawrence] and I went together to Paris later; Frieda left for Germany to see her mother. Pirated editions of *Lady Chatterley* were appearing and Lawrence wanted to arrange for a cheap edition in Paris so that the expensive pirated editions might not command such a ready sale. In addition, he badly wanted the book to reach the masses—of England particularly. Like Tolstoy he was indifferent to any royalty there might be from such an edition. For the pirates he had utter contempt, but was angry to think of the money they were making. One of them in Paris, hearing of the contemplated cheap edition, got into communication with him and offered royalties on all the copies already sold, on condition that no cheap edition was issued. The sum due was substantial. Lawrence wrinkled his nose in disgust, and yet, as was only to be expected, was half attracted. He twittered and was unusually indecisive: finally he went off late in the afternoon to the pirate's office, and found the place shut up: it was after office hours. "I knew then," he sighed, when he arrived back at our hotel, "I didn't want to see the man. I stood there on the pavement with relief and was utterly glad the office was closed." I think he had consulted his midriff on the pavement. He refused to meet or correspond with the pirate after that.

In Paris I witnessed another of his strange rages. We took a taxi to Sylvia Beach's book-shop [108] in a little street near the Odeon; he wanted to ask Miss Beach if she would publish *Lady Chatterley;* [109] she had already dared Joyce's *Ulysses* (a book Lawrence had not much respect for: too *cerebral*).[110] The taxi-driver, a big bull-necked creature, couldn't find the little street. As we cruised for the second time round the Odeon, Lawrence began to start and writhe. The powerful, unmoving back of the driver roused him to a yell. "The fat fool!" he screeched—in English— "A taxi-driver! Fool, fool, fool," he stamped and writhed. "Or else he's doing it purposely, knowing we are foreigners." In the tiny enclosed space it was like having a shrill demented monkey beside me. After dipping into another street, again the cab cruised round the Odeon. To Lawrence's yells and bangs on the glass screen the driver's steady bull neck remained unperturbed. Ruddy beard stuck out, Lawrence's pale face was lifted in agony. The immovable neck in front was bringing on a psychic crisis.

At last the shop was discovered, and the taxi skipped up to the kerb softly as a purring cat. Lawrence's thin body exploded out of the door; I followed in readiness for a brawl on the pavement. But I was disappointed. The two men faced each other. The driver's big moony face was shining with a most childlike grin; it was all a friendly joke to him. And in heavy French he told us that he was a Russian, an exile, and had only recently begun his job as taxi-driver. He beamed with good humour; Russian-like, he accepted Lawrence's fury with benign understanding. Lawrence had started back from that broad Slav fleshy face. I could almost see the steam of his rage evaporating. His prancings became stilled. As we entered Miss Beach's shop he said to me, "*I couldn't* be angry with him, I couldn't. Did you see his face! Beautiful and human. He lives in his blood, that man, he is solidly in his blood—not like these slippery French who are all mind. I saw it at once and I respected him." Miss Beach was not interested in an edition of *Lady Chatterley.*

Though the weather was warm and sunny, and Paris at its best, he hated it, like all cities. He couldn't bear people close-packed about him, the grey slick city faces, and he would scuttle back to our hotel in Montparnasse after meals. We stayed there a month, and all the time he fumed to get away, a city darkened his spirit and humanity became almost completely hopeless. Knowledge of his presence got about, and he was offered a banquet by a literary organization: to his horror. His chest became ominously troublesome. But such was the vitality he spread about him, even in Paris, that alarm and suspicion of his physical state would vanish.

It was in Paris that he dauntlessly refused to keep an appointment, made by a friend, with a first-class specialist in bronchial diseases. Half an hour before the time fixed, and ready dressed to go to the specialist, he suddenly refused to leave the hotel. It seemed to me that he believed a submission to medical art was an act of treachery to the power within him, his gods.

But his nights became restless; often I woke to his coughing and writhing in the next room. One night, instinctively, but half asleep, I hurried through the communicating door and found him as though in mortal combat with some terrible invisible opponent who had arrived in those mysterious dead hours that follow midnight. The dark tormented face and haggard body was like some stormy El Greco figure writhing on the bed. Was this the perky bird or lizard figure of Bandol! He seemed to be violently repudiating some evil force, a wretched man nearly overcome by a sinister power of superhuman advantages. Alarmed, I suggested a doctor and went towards the telephone. But at once he flew into anger. No, he would *not* have a doctor. But if I would sit quietly by the bed for a while. . . . I think he needed the aid of some human presence. Soon he was calmer, lay back exhausted, unspeaking but triumphant. The opponent had gone.

A month passed before a publisher for *Lady Chatterley* was found.[111] Frieda returned from Germany; I left for England. My regret at leaving him was mingled with a strange willingness to go. He seemed to have given me as much as I wanted, and for me he would always be near. I have spoken to many people who did not know Lawrence personally but who read his books sympathetically, and to each of them he has been alive and of the same significance as though they sat with him and were warmed by that rich personal glow of his: and they too, like myself, when he died felt for a time as though there was no sun in the world. There must have been few men who inspired such personal—but I cannot find the word: not *affection,* not *homage, love* is too specialized a word, and I must say, almost meaninglessly—reactions, as Lawrence. Almost that emotion he inspired has been lost: to-day particularly we are consumed with distrust of the world and therefore men. Perhaps if that emotion had been garnered and understood and cherished, the life of man would have taken a more fruitful direction—for has the world ever been more sterile than it is now, except of wars? He was a Christ of an earthly estate, and those about him knew the Godhead he had found in himself, and were warmed by it. His humanity was so purely aristocratic and undefiled. Here was the complete flowering of the spirit in flesh. Let me not be misunderstood: Lawrence was a man and no Jesus in rapt love with the Heaven that is to come; but a Christ of himself as every man can become who has once found the pure centre of his being and keeps it uncontaminated. This is what he had done. He had not submitted to the contamination that seems inevitable. Civilization had not dirtied him, in himself, though enough mud was thrown at him, and some clung for a space. It was the mud that caused those rages which seemed to be so insane.

He wrote to me now and again: gay, amusing letters, gay even in his furies against certain actions and persons in London. He wanted to start a little magazine, to be called *The Squib*,[112] which was to consist of lampoons, leg-pulls and satiric pieces; he sent some verses for it and asked if I would be editor, with himself as guarantor of half the expenses. If he had lived it would have been a lively magazine, though I had a taste of how difficult it would have been to obtain suitable contributions; people jeered and lampooned amusingly enough in their conversations, but to get them to set their antipathies and violences on paper!— no, they became self-conscious and wary, the labour was impossible. The idea of *The Squib,* with Lawrence adopting the pseudonym of John Doolittle, came to nothing in the end.[113]

18 March 1929   3 rue de Bac, Suresnes, Seine, France

⟨[*I am staying with Aldous and Maria [Huxley] for a few days.*[114]

23? March 1929   3 rue de Bac, Suresnes, Seine, France

⟨[*. . . I am here—staying at the moment with the Huxleys—Frieda in Baden, joins me next Wed.—and I go in to Paris. . . . Got a cold—feel sort of feverish—don't like Paris—but think I shall manage to do an edition of Lady C. pretty cheap—to sell about 60 frs.—so that's what I came for. Otherwise no news and no wits and feel very tired of seeing people and wish I was on a desert island or in Bandol or even Capri. We'll leave next week—after Easter—D.V.—but I don't know where for . . . .*[115]

26 March 1929   Hôtel de Versailles, 60 Bvd Montparnasse, Paris 15

❨ *I came back here yesterday and Frieda arrived last night.*[116]

Secretary, The Warren Gallery

[The Warren Gallery, 39a Maddox Street, London, W. 1] 28 March 1929
D. H. Lawrence, Esq.
Dear Sir,
   Mrs. Trotter has been ill and is now away in the country but she has asked me to write to you about the forthcoming exhibition of your pictures at this Gallery.
   The pictures, at present, are away being reproduced but as soon as we get them back we will be able to make definite arrangements for the Exhibition to take place at the end of this month and during May.
   We are looking forward to it very much and hope and expect to have a great success.

Yours truly,
Secretary
The Warren Gallery [117]

?30–31 March 1929   *Le Moulin du Soleil, Ermenonville, Oise, France*

[Lawrence and Frieda spend a weekend with Caresse and Harry Crosby.] [118]

Caresse Crosby

   In spring [1929] D. H. Lawrence and Freda, his wife, came to visit us at our "Moulin du Soleil." Lawrence, fugitive, strung taut and full of wisdom—Freda, upholstered, petulant and full of pride. I loved him and disliked her. Lawrence was like a prickly pear when people wanted more. I wanted more of him because of Harry. Freda didn't want any of us. Lawrence used to sit for hours on the sun-warmed paving stones in the courtyard, his back against the ancient pillar, brought there from Chalis by Cagliostro when Cagliostro was in retreat at that nearby Abbey.
   It grew more evident every day that the Mill was builded on magic ground: Jean Jacques, Cagliostro, Lawrence and Harry, all felt the spell and from the mill stream at the foot of the tower little fishes leapt mys-

teriously twenty feet in air to land safely in the pool above, and there were tree trunks like tortured lovers in the forest. Once a flock of sheep had walked right through our thrice-barred gate. I have said we kept our tombstone on the sun tower and it was inscribed with our Harry-Caresse Cross, and with the dates of life and death. When Harry died, too soon, it leapt the high balustrade and exploded to a thousand bits below.

Varda,[119] the mystery-loving painter of Greek descent, has a theory that if one founds one's house upon ground beneath which water flows, the house will be one's touchstone with magic. This explains, he said, how spiritually arid some houses are, others how full of invisible power.

Less than a mile from the Moulin tower and seen from its heights, a sea of sand had appeared five hundred years before and this has never been explained. Suddenly the forest opened and golden sand filled those hollows, Atlantis receding beneath the waves, perhaps tossed back a handful of her shores to keep one earthbound toehold. Some day the ocean tides may seep again into the *Mer de Sable* and transfuse their qualities, mermaids in the tree tops, wild deer under waves.

It was the season of daffodils and we went searching. Lawrence and I in the donkey cart, jogging down long aisle-like paths where no flowers grew. We hunted in the most unlikely places and with a shawl tucked round his knees, collar up and his soft hat pulled over his scorching eyes, we briefed each copse and sward, talking, talking, talking all the while, and Eclipse trotted briskly along urged on by my ear-tickling willow wand. We would return to find Harry still writing and Freda still playing the gramophone. On one of these occasions, Lawrence in a fit of exasperation, broke record after record over her head.

That week end I had stemmed the usual onrush of Sunday visitors. Lawrence disliked meeting people, but Constance [Atherton] [120] was not prewarned. She appeared at noon with two swains, Merritt Swift, diplomat, and Felton Elkins, dilettante. Felton had never heard of D. H. Lawrence, but was an aspiring though uninspired playwright and insisted on telling Lawrence how to write a play. Lawrence, unfortunately, did not tell *him!* [121]

5 April 1929   Hôtel de Versailles, 60 Bvd Montparnasse, Paris 15

⟨ *I have been here a month, and at last have managed for a cheap edition of Lady C.—in English—produced here—and to sell at 60 frs.*[122] *Paris gave me grippe and I was miserable: the town is too depressing. To-morrow we leave, going south to Lyon, Avignon, Perpignon, and so to Spain.*[123]

MAJORCA

15 April 1929   Barcelona, Spain

❲ We have got so far—and tomorrow night we cross to Palma, Majorca. It is queer, Barcelona—so modern, and yet not, so full of wealth, yet so proletariat. At first one recoils—but I think I really like it. The people are self-contained and calm, they don't gibber like most moderns. The air seems good and alive and a bit tonicky, bracing—rather cold too. And the flowers in the street are marvellous, so are the vegetables and fish in the market—a certain rich splendour and abundance which I had not expected . . . . I think it may be really good for my health—a tonic. So if we like Majorca, we shall contrive to stay, find a house if possible. Unfortunately, everything is rather dear, especially hotels. But if one could have a little house, I think it would work out like Italy.[124]

18 April 1929   Hotel Royal, Palma de Mallorca, Spain

❲ This island—Majorca—is rather like Sicily, but not so beautiful, and much more asleep. But it has that southern sea quality, out of the world, in another world. I like that—and the sleep is good for me. Perhaps we shall stay a month or two—and come to Italy and find a house for the winter. Frieda will never take to Spain, and she won't even try to speak Spanish. So I expect we'll be back in Italy in autumn. But I like this sleep there is here—so still, and the people don't have any nerves at all—not nervous, anybody.[125]

24 April 1929   Hôtel Príncipe Alfonso, Palma de Mallorca, Spain

❲ [Everybody] seems to think I ought to be in ecstasies over this place, even including Frieda—Majorca is one of her oldest dreams—and I don't really care for it. True, the sea is usually a most heavenly blue, and the old town lies round the bay, pale, phantom in the strong light, all a funny heapy-heap of buff and white—and the flowers are nice—and I like this hotel. But there is a cold little wind, and some days it is all funny and grey and clammy, scirocco, and they give one far too much food to eat, quite good food here, but too much—and my bill last week was over eleven pounds, merely the hotel—and the Spanish wine, my God, it is foul, catpiss is champagne compared, this is the sulphurous urination of some aged horse—and a bottle of Julien, the cheapest claret, costs 9 pesetas—over six shillings—and worst of all, the place gets on my nerves all the time, the people are dead and staring. I can't bear their Spanishy faces, dead unpleasant masks, a bit like city English—and my malaria came back, and my teeth chattered like castanets—and that's the only truly Spanish thing I've done. We nearly took a house—and I must say, in some ways it was very nice, but thank God my malaria came on in time to save us from deciding on it. And that's about all the news—except that we ran into Robert Nichols [126] in the street the second day we came here, and saw quite a lot of him and his wife, and we liked them very much. They had been here three months, and just got fed-up, and had booked their berths, so they sailed off to Marseilles on Tuesday morning, and at that moment I wished I was sailing too. But in the morning when it is lovely and sunny and blue and fresh, I am reconciled again, for a time. We may stay another twelve days—we might stop a month—but I think, by June surely, we shall be sailing also to Marseilles, and going either to Lago di Garda or somewhere like that. I don't want to take a house here, to stay. I think, all in all, Italy is best when it comes to living, and France next. Triumphant Frieda! [127]

Hotel Principe Alfonso/Palma de Mallorca/Spain/27 April 1929

⟨ Dear Bruce [Brewster Ghiselin]

Your letter came on to Paris, but your telegram took eight days to wander here to us—and by that time I was afraid you would have left Naples: moreover Spain was too much off your map. Did you have a nice trip, I wonder, or were you only the more disillusioned after it? I think one shouldn't ask too much from the outside world, especially if one is not interested at all in the tradition, as you are not. You rather dislike the tradition, really, and any manifestation of it—so perhaps it is a mistake travelling to look at old countries.

This island is very pleasant, very quiet, very Mediterranean, and very dull. I quite like it, but don't contemplate ending my days here. Still, for the time being it is soothing and calm, so I think we shall stay till it gets too hot. The trouble is that I had a whack of malaria, and shook in my skin—I suppose that's with coming so far south—and it was a muggy clammy day. But I mistrust a place where malaria comes back.

You haven't much longer to endure Oxford and Europe. I shall be quite relieved to think of you safely returned to California, & comparatively happy there.

Frieda has gone off to a concert in Palma, but she'd send her greetings, with mine.

Yours
D. H. Lawrence [128]

27 April 1929 Hôtel Príncipe Alfonso, Palma de Mallorca, Spain

⟦ I wish, somehow, the mysterious bars would lift that keep us from coming back to the ranch—a sort of fear, a sort of instinct. Now I am in a Spanish-speaking country, I have New Mexico before my eyes every moment. After all, it's so much bigger and lovelier than this is. Europe remains a bit poky, wherever you go. Yet I feel the stars are against my crossing the Atlantic just now.[129]

9 May 1929 Hôtel Príncipe Alfonso, Palma de Mallorca, Spain

⟦ Yesterday we motored to Valdemosa, where Chopin was so happy and George Sand hated it. —It was lovely looking out from the monastery, into the dimness of the plain below, and the great loose roses of the monastery gardens so brilliant and spreading themselves out—then inside, the cloister so white and silent. We picknicked [sic] on the north coast high above the sea, mountainous, and the bluest, bluest sea I ever saw— not hard like peacocks and jewels, but soft like blue feathers of the tit— really very lovely—and no people—olives and a few goats and the big blueness shimmering to far off, north—lovely. Then we went on to Soller, and the smell of orange-blossom so strong and sweet in all the air, one felt like a bee. —Coming back over the mountains we stopped in an old Moorish garden, with round shadowy pools under palm trees, and big bright roses in the sun, and the yellow jasmine had shed so many flowers the ground was brilliant yellow—and nightingales singing powerfully, ringing in the curious stillness. There is a queer stillness where the Moors have been, like ghosts—a bit morne, yet lovely for the time—like a pause

321

in life. —It's queer, there is a certain loveliness about the island, yet a certain underneath ugliness, unalive. The people seem to me rather dead, and they are ugly, and they have those non-existent bodies like English people often have, and which I thought was impossible on the Mediterranean. But they say there is a large Jewish admixture. Dead-bodied people with rather ugly faces and a certain staleness. Curious! But it makes one have no desire to live here. The Spaniards, I believe, have refused life so long that life now refuses them, and they are rancid.[130]

Glenn Hughes

[I had a conversation with Lawrence in May, 1929.]

Big and fiery in his writing, yes; but in the flesh he was a small man, quiet and incisive. Illness gave his figure an added slenderness and his manner an unusual delicacy. His head . . . was long, and it narrowed as it descended. Dark red hair fell loosely over the forehead; a beard concluded the downward sweep of the face. The very blue eyes were sharp, alert, quizzical, and taunting. . . .

Meeting him, one found it difficult to believe him the creator of the many powerful works which bear his name. There appeared to be no physical basis for such energy. The easiest explanation of the anomaly would be one suggested by his own semi-mystical beliefs—one which would make him the sensitive medium of great hidden forces. Any non-magical theory must certainly tax the resources of the analyst.[131]

17 May 1929   Hôtel Príncipe Alfonso, Palma de Mallorca, Spain

⟨ We have been on this island for a month—very pleasant and sunny, right on the sea, and very peaceful. They call it the island of calm, and indeed it is. Yet there is a certain deadness in the human atmosphere at least, which makes it unattractive in the long run. We went across to the other side of the island. There are lovely lonely little bays with pine trees and sand and no people—and big stretches of a sort of heath-land or moor. One could be a lonely hermit here if one wanted—and the climate seems to me very good, about the best in Europe, I should say. Yet I don't want to stay—and I don't want a house here. I think in about a fortnight's time we shall take the boat to Marseilles and come to Italy and see if we can light on a suitable house. We hesitate whether to take a trip in

Spain—to Granada and Sevilla and Madrid—but the railway journeys are so long and tiring, and as I get older I care less and less about merely seeing things or places—or people.[132]

26 May 1929   Hôtel Príncipe Alfonso, Palma de Mallorca, Spain

⟦ It is really rather lovely here, warm and sunny and blue, and so remote, if one goes a bit away. Of course we know a number of residents—come-to-lunch kind of thing—but nice. Today we motored along the coast to a lonely bay with pine trees down to the sea, and the Mallorquin servants cooked Spanish rice over a fire in a huge pot, and the others bathed, and I sat under a tree like the ancient of days and drank small beer—microscopic bock—and it was really very lovely, no one in the world but us. This is a wonderful place for doing nothing—the time passes rapidly in a long stretch of nothingness—broken by someone fetching us out in a motor, or somebody else in a donkey-cart. It is very good for my health, I believe.[133]

2 June 1929   Hôtel Príncipe Alfonso, Palma de Mallorca, Spain

⟦ I have corrected proofs [of Pansies] for Martin Secker—he has omitted about a dozen poems, with my consent—no use raising a fuss—and he expects to get the book out this month. . . . But probably I shall get a small private edition issued, complete and unexpurgated, so that the poems appear just as they were written. . . . No definite news yet about the pictures—nor the book of them. I have got proofs of all except one—so I shouldn't be surprised if Stephenson [sic] issues the book this week or next. . . . [Since] the great scare of Jix and suppression, all publishers are terrified of the police—lest they come in and confiscate the whole edition. That would be a terrible loss in the case of my book of pictures, as it has cost about £2,000 to produce. But already there are orders for more than half—and the ten copies in vellum at fifty guineas each were ordered six times over. Madness! [134]

12 June 1929   Hôtel Príncipe Alfonso, Palma de Mallorca, Spain

⟦ We want to leave here next Tuesday—eighteenth—by the boat to Marseille. Frieda sprained her ankle, bathing, but I think it will be better by

then—it's not too bad.[135] *I want her to go [to London] and see after my
pictures, as the show is supposed to open this week. And the book is ready
today—I have a set of the colored plates . . . .*[136]

*If Frieda comes to England from Marseille, I shall probably go to North
Italy, the Garda, where it won't be too hot. This year I don't want to come
very far north—I feel I am better south of the Alps—really. Probably,
Frieda will come to Baden on her way back from England.*

*This island is a queer place—so dry—but at last it has rained. We might
possibly come back next winter.*[137]

ITALY

23 June 1929

Pensione Giuliani, Viale Morin, Forte dei Marmi, Lucca, Italy

❲ *We left Majorca last Tuesday [18 June 1929]—it was too hot. Frieda
has gone to England to see her children, and to see about the pictures.
The show began on June 14th, and I've heard no definite news—a long incomprehensible telegram here—saying show great success—press critique
bored or scurrilous and apparently some pictures sold, but I can't make
out quite what. The book is out—a very handsome volume . . . .*

*I am staying here in a pensione for a fortnight or so—Aldous and Maria
[Huxley] have a little house—then I shall probably go to Switzerland to
meet Frieda.*[138]

Pensione Giuliani/Viale Morin/Forte dei Marmi/(Lucca)/Italy/24 June
1929

❲ Dear Dorothy [Warren]

I received the enclosed telegram Saturday night [22 June 1929]—had it
repeated this morning—am not much further. I still don't know who wrote
it—did you? —and what I am to reply to—there is a reply paid. Anyhow
I am glad the show is a success: though whether you sold 17 paintings or
17 painting-books I still don't know. If you haven't already sold Boccaccio
Story and Red Willow Trees and A Holy Family, please don't sell them,
I very much want to keep them. Stephensen said they would buy Boccaccio
Story, but I shall tell him I want to keep it. I am sure you have worked
heroically, and are worn out: I do hope you feel it's been worth it.

I suppose by now you will have seen Frieda, and heard whatever she has to say. But send me a line of definite news.

> Ever
>
> D. H. Lawrence [139]

Pensione Giuliani/Viale Morin/Forte dei Marmi/(Lucca)/24 June 1929

[To Frieda]

❨ *Your letter from Paris today—sorry you didn't feel well—it's the change —guess you are better now. Damn Billy Nell* [140] *and all wash-outs. As for Titus,* [141] *the copies of Our Lady of Paris haven't come yet.*

I want very much to have real news of the show—have written [Dorothy Warren] *today please to keep Boccaccio, Red Willow Trees, and Holy Family, if they are not already sold. Hope you've been to see Lahr,* [142] *taken him the drawings, etc. I particularly don't want him to print mine of me unless they (in general) like it.* [143] *And Rhys Davies wrote anxiously about seeing you—and Kot.* [144] *Of course you must see Kot.*

Don't butt in heavily about my money affairs with Pollinger. I don't wish it, and it is no good.

Probably you'll see my sisters this week—find out how they are, and all.

Great stews of Brett and Mabel, Georgia O'K[eeffe]. [145] *and my manuscripts and the Taos bank!!* [146]

Buy a packet of Carter's Little Liver Pills for me. My little pensione is very nice—eat out of doors under a big plane tree—with a little cat— and a bedroom rather like my Mirenda one. Go to Il Canneto to tea —and see them [the Aldous Huxleys] *on the beach. They are very well indeed, nice to me—but a bit queer together. Maria still tangled up in a way I dislike extremely with Costanza.* [147] *Poor Peterich* [148] *lots of spots on him.*

. . . Weather a bit scirocco, but not so bad—not so hot as Palma. I expect Pino [Orioli] *down this week—he'll be my guest here. I somehow am not pining for a house here—or anywhere. We must leave it till it happens. What's the odd's! People who do have houses only leave them.*

I'm quite comfortable and quite all right, so don't bother about me —but mind your foot, and have a good time in London, and stay while you feel like it, and write to your mother, and if she wants you to go there now, perhaps best do so.

> Love to Barby, and all
>
> Lorenzo non santo [149]

Frieda Lawrence Ravagli

Kingsley Hotel [36 Hart Street, London, Late June? 1929]

Dear Dorothy [Warren],

It was so very jolly to spend the evening with you! I enclose this—I also have a *Lady C* for you, new Paris edition, if you would like it. And let's have a party, not the next few days, you are so busy too, but then you lend the rooms, the rest is "my show"! I hope you aren't too tired, you and Philip. Take it as gently as you can! I do write to Lawrence and try to tell him all I can.

So let's hope for luck right along!

Frieda

Forgive the pencil! [150]

Philip Trotter

The advice so freely offered in 1929, to look at things in perspective, is more plausible at a quarter of a century's distance from the scene of action than during the fifty-five days from the private view to the trial at Gt. Marlborough Police Court. Events then in fevered and bewildering motion have become static and remote; and in any case perspective is not a constant, but determined by the viewer's angle of vision. From early in the fifty-five days the dominant figure in the exhibition was not Lawrence, nor art, but the Obscenities Act of 1857, first its shadow, later its substance. We shall encounter it stalking the pages of this narrative, but no longer as the central theme to which Lawrence, with his pictures, has contributed a serviceable case history, but as an alien element, which has jarred and dislocated the functions of a world not its own into which it has intruded. And observe that this shift of focus derived mainly from the camp sympathetic to Lawrence and the exhibition and opposed to the self-appointed guardians of public morals and their Act. Lawrence became the hero destined to open the door to a broader approach to the scope and functions of the visual arts and to confine the Obscenities Act within its intended limits, "the suppression of the trade in obscene articles." But in this missionary vision all other aspects of Lawrence's visual art, its relation to his literary art, how and what he painted, whence his inspiration, whither his direction, passed out of sight. And in due course, compelled by the spectre of this Morality Moloch hungering for his sacrifice, we were ourselves drawn into the current, uttering our own formula of disavowal; "With the merits of Mr. Lawrence's paintings we are not for the moment concerned." [151] That bleak moment has passed; but to appraise Lawrence's artistic merits belongs now to another generation. Believing, against *prima facie* evidence, that a second Lawrence exhibition is no longer impossible, I offer this memoir in homage to those who have the courage to attempt it and the skill and integrity to carry it through. The sources, besides the biographical and autobiographical material already cited, are personal memories, crossed and recrossed by the happenings of two strenuous decades and a copious but defective documentation salvaged from the office floor of a 20th Century war ruin.

The following are the principal dates of the period: days of the week are given only when they are material to the history.

Private view	Friday	14 June 1929
Exhibition open	Saturday	15 June 1929
Adverse notice in *Observer*	Sunday	16 June 1929
Outcry, "The Much-censored Novelist . . ."		
1st phase	Monday	17 June 1929
2nd phase		26 June 1929
Evening party for Frieda at the Gallery		4 July 1929
Police raid		5 July 1929
"More Paintings by D. H. Lawrence"		28 July 1929
Hearing at Gt. Marlborough Street		8 August 1929
Warren Gallery closed for repairs		September 1929

From the first week in April the Warren Gallery waited for the Mandrake Press to return the pictures and deliver their "sumptuous" publication, *The Paintings of D. H. Lawrence.* "Oh, that Mandrake—vegetable of ill omen!" wrote Lawrence in one of his last published letters,[152] a sentiment frequently and variously expressed in the Warren Gallery during the previous spring and summer; for the opening of the exhibition in a mid-June weekend was its first misfortune. Every Warren Gallery exhibition, as the curtain went up on the private view, had that May morning freshness and peace that Mr. Marriott savoured on its first birthday, and no pictures ever responded better than Lawrence's to that peculiar magic of light and level, juxtaposition of colour and subject, and placing of furniture and flowers: crudities were hushed and Lawrence's unerring sense of overall design gave full value to a brilliant hang. But such spells have a brief total effect; flowers shift and fade, objects are displaced; during that hot Friday-to-Monday most of the Warren Gallery faithful were restoring their flagging social energies in the country; [153] and by Tuesday a more sinister magic from another world would be cast over the scene—the press saga of "The Much-Censored-Novelist-Turned-Painter." Avoiding so ungracious an introduction let us try, in the company of the few that have left unprejudiced memorials of the exhibition, to capture something of its quality, remembering its origin: that Frieda said "Let's have some pictures"; [154] and that Lawrence, thus prompted, painted on to amuse himself; remembering, too, that his most intimate and penetrating apologist assesses him as "always and unescapably an artist." [155]

The Warren Gallery catalogue is here reproduced with the following additions: an asterisk (°) denotes that the picture was seized by the police on 5th July; the dimensions of each picture are given, taken from the Mandrake Press reproductions, but always in the order, height before length; the continuous catalogue is divided into "Big Gallery" and "Velvet Room."

EXHIBITION XII

Paintings/by/D. H. LAWRENCE

OILS

Big Gallery

1. Flight Back into Paradise	39″ by 58″
2. A Holy Family	26″ by 30″
3. Resurrection	38″ by 38″
°4. Boccaccio Story	28″ by 47″
°5. Fight with an Amazon	39″ by 29″
6. Fauns and Nymphs	38″ by 32″
°7. Dance-Sketch	15″ by 17″
°8. Family on a Verandah	14″ by 19″
°9. Contadini	16″ by 13″

Velvet Room

°10. Accident in a Mine	16¼″ by 13¼″

11. Rape of the Sabine Women	12″ by 16″
°12. North Sea	16″ by 13″
°13. Spring	12″ by 9″
14. Finding of Moses	18″ by 15″
15. Red Willow Trees	26″ by 40″
16. Close-Up (Kiss)	15″ by 18″

WATER COLOURS

17. The Lizard	9″ by 12″
°18. Singing of Swans	9″ by 12″
°19. Leda	9″ by 12″
20. Renascence of Men	9″ by 12″
°21. Yawning	9″ by 12″
°22. Fire-Dance	9″ by 12″
23. Throwing Back the Apple	9″ by 12″
°24. Under the Mango-Tree	9″ by 12″
25. Under the Hay-Stack	9″ by 12″

Summer Dawn, a small water-colour, though reproduced in the book, was not considered suitable for exhibition; *Dandelions*, referred to in a letter to the Huxleys and by Catherine Carswell in *A Savage Pilgrimage*,[156] was neither exhibited nor reproduced.

One may see the divine in natural objects; I saw it to-day, in the frail, lovely little camellia flowers on long stems, here on the bushy and splendid flower-stalls of the Ramblas in Barcelona. They were different from the usual fat camellias, more like gardenias, poised delicately, and I saw them like a vision. So now, I could paint them. But if I had bought a handful, and started in to paint them "from nature," then I should have lost them.[157]

The view so often heard during the exhibition, and confirmed later by Mrs. Carswell, that this was "work that could have been done by no-body but Lawrence" [158] is impossible to deny but difficult to explain. An attempt to do so in an otherwise admirable notice in the *Scotsman* attests the difficulty: "As readers of his novels and poems might expect," wrote this critic, "his interests as a painter are concentrated entirely upon the beauty and force of the human figure." [159] They are indeed; but why should his readers expect it? Even if we exclude *Birds, Beasts and Flowers,* the compacted mystique of his communion with nature, and "Making Pictures," where this communion seems held in readiness for his new art, his prose and earlier verse are littered with evidence of the comprehensiveness of his vision. In the only two landscapes the exhibition gave us, *Red Willow Trees* (15) and *Boccaccio Story* (4), his brush followed his pen, and not such a long way off, in the two countryside features that move and stimulate him most. "If I were a painter I could paint them," he writes in *Sea and Sardinia,* first of "a cluster of naked poplars," then of "the mauve silver fig." [160] Trees are what he perceives most intimately; and, in a greatly simplified setting, *Red Willow Trees* echoes the poplars with their "grey, goldish-pale incandescence of naked limbs and myriad cold-glowing twigs, gleaming strangely" [161]—only the glow of the poplars is warm. In the *Boccaccio Story* something in the surging file of nuns recalls—though the contexts are poles apart—the peasant procession, again in *Sea and Sardinia,* seen far off as the bus swerved into the sunlight on the road to Nuoro.[162] Everything is different: the purpose of the peasants is pious, of the nuns licentious; [163] the peasants, men and women, each in their different colours, are following a hideous image to a remote church; the nuns, uniform in their huge headpieces and stiff, pale, pleated habits with white capes, are advancing on the naked sleeping gardener. All that the two scenes have in common is that the artist who painted the one must have written the other. Behind both picture and passage is the downright directness of Lawrence.

Before we pass to the nudes the two draped-figure oils claim attention. *Resurrection,* which the visitor looked straight across to as he entered the Gallery, retained its central position after the raid. It aroused little conscious interest; but its potent tragic appeal possibly gave rise to the strange error recorded in good faith by competent critics that nearly every picture contained a self-portrait. Actually the only other is in *Flight Back into Paradise*. Lawrence was working on *Resurrection* intermittently through the winter and spring of 1927. He writes Brett on 8th March: "I began a resurrection, but haven't worked at it. In the spring one slackens off." [164] Then to Brewster, 28th May: "I've finished my Resurrection picture, and like it." [165] No one who has read *The Man Who Died* and looked at *Resurrection* can fail to associate Lawrence's only tragic picture (of those exhibited) with his saddest story, whose genesis is assigned to Easter morning, 1927, at Volterra. [166] But if we are right in identifying its central figure with the self-portrait in *Resurrection*, this most poetical of Lawrence's creations was first pondered and worked on with his brush—to be transmuted to its final form and into his greater medium by the impact of an external image—a toy in a shop window.

A Holy Family, on the left of *Resurrection* and slightly recessed from it, becomes a fascinating study in the light thrown on it by Lawrence's essay, "Making Pictures." [167] It was, in fact, the "plunge," the response to Frieda's "Let's have some pictures"; and it "happened" in two hours. What emerged—the perfect poise and masterly characterization of the three figures, the complete sureness of touch and design, the rare harmony of colour—was possible only with the "brush-tip" in total possession of the "intuition." Catherine Carswell's felicitous interpretation has, I think, one flaw. She was

delighted by the true believer's touch of mockery in the rendering of the Eternal Triangle of Father, Mother and Child posed in front of their cottage crocks—that cheeky, clever little Jesus who was going to upset everybody's apple-cart, that mindless, smiling, big-breasted mother Eve, and that moustachioed Father and Husband who was so clearly the master in his own house! [168]

Her mistake was in naming the Child, for all three figures are as remote from Nazareth as they are from Montmartre, and the indefinite article in the title absolves the subject from a charge that might otherwise have gladdened Lawrence's enemies. True, each figure has its nimbus; and above the Child's a tapering shaft of light shoots upward.

I stick to what I told you [Lawrence wrote to Brewster], and put a phallus, a lingam you call it, in each one of my pictures somewhere. And I paint no picture that won't shock people's castrated social spirituality. I do this out of positive belief, that the phallus is a great sacred image: it represents a deep, deep life which has been denied in us, and still is denied. [169]

We knew nothing of the law of the "lingam in each of the pictures *somewhere*"; but, embarrassed by its position in *A Holy Family*, we supplemented the work of the police by withdrawing the picture on the morning after the raid. Whether it propounds a longing to correlate, or a need to contrast his own deeply felt convictions with the Christian mystique, *A Holy Family* provides the text of the sermon in paint that Lawrence was to preach, from his Kingdom of Heaven, in the next two years.

For a key to the remaining twenty-one pictures we must turn to Lawrence's "Introduction to These Paintings" in the Mandrake volume.[170] In fact this vehement essay concerns this memoir at least twice on different planes; for it acquired during the exhibition a shadow history of its own in the devastating use made of certain colourful passages by the servicemen of the "Much-Censored-Novelist-Turned-Painter" campaign, who had access to the book in the Gallery. It is a brilliant synthesis of Lawrence's familiar indignations and rejections woven into the texture of a review of contemporary art, largely based on Lawrence's own findings of history and science. Empirical facts do not count among his sources of power; but the force and passion of his conviction generate a pragmatic truth out of which the forms in his new medium are fashioned.

For the part of the "Introduction" that immediately concerns us I am privileged to quote from Mr. T. W. Earp's [171] review of it published in the *New Statesman* ten days after the police-court hearing. The following is a very able summary of the first seven thousand words:

The English, says Mr. Lawrence, have produced few good painters because the national spirit became atrophied with fear at the time of the Renaissance. This fear was caused by the wave of venereal disease which then swept over Europe. High and low alike were tainted—Mr. Lawrence gives a lurid account of the Tudor and Stuart dynasties—and the result was a shuddering, universal attack of sex-repression, which obliterated "Merry England" and has continued with gathered strength to the present time. It was reflected in literature by the morbidity of the Elizabethans, the emasculated intellectualism of the cavalier poets, and the coarseness of Restoration comedy. Thus a mental attitude towards life took the place of an intuitional one. By the time English painting really got started with Gainsborough and Reynolds we had lost our imagination and freedom of expression. France, because it had affected some sort of rational compromise with sexual necessity, was a little better off. But gradually everything has gone from bad to worse. This sex-repression, caused by the fear of disease, has by now robbed us of the power both of artistic creation and appreciation. "We, dear reader, you and I, we were born corpses and we are corpses." Such is Mr. Lawrence's general thesis, and such his general nonsense.

In order to make our poor dead flesh creep, he turns history into a dirt-track and rides round it on a hobby-horse.[172]

This masterly, but coldly factual condensation of a long-sustained out-pouring of Laurentian fire gives us history as Lawrence saw it, but not as he felt it. Now, having demolished English painting in general, Lawrence brings out his great exception.

Landscape, however, is different. Here the English exist and hold their own. *But, for me, personally, landscape is always waiting for something to occupy it. Landscape seems to be MEANT as a background to an intenser vision of life, so to my feeling painted landscape is background with the real subject left out.*[173] (My italics)

Actually, what we have in at least ten of the pictures is Subject with the background left out—or, to be accurate—squeezed out by the nudes. And yet? "[Let] me wander . . . across . . . the world empty of man . . . ." The words are again from *Sea and Sardinia*,[174] but surely they echo through Lawrence, a longing for background with the human subject left out. Lawrence's Daimon manifests itself variously at different times. Here, and in his pictures, it is more than a Socratic obstructionist, the recurrent "Balaam's Ass in my belly." Here, Lawrence is himself Balaam: he "cannot go beyond the commandment of the Lord." In a letter to Dr. Trigant Burrow (3 August 1927), he writes: "[We're] going to Austria tomorrow, D.V.—whoever D. may be . . . ."[175] We, too, may well wonder and—with no disparagement to the nudes on their own merits—lament that so teeming a genius should obey so fettering a deity. Of his eleven non-human creatures contained in six paintings the most engagingly Laurentian is the goat in *Dance-Sketch*, a delightful woodland fantasy that passed almost unnoticed, except by the police, who seized it.

Of great biographical interest, since they propound trans-fertilisation of images between pen and brush, are two fantasies from the Eve-Eden-apple myth, Lawrence's most copious symbolic source. *Flight Back into Paradise* was the largest painting in the collection; it hung alone on the East wall of the Big Gallery, square to *Resurrection* both before and after the raid. Not a pleasant room companion, but Lawrence at the highest pitch of exuberance. A provincial critic who described it correctly as a picture "of writhing brown and white flesh, huge strained muscles and burning white light," missed the essence of its achievement, the compacted tragedy, pathos, and satire in the poignant face, struggling form, and huddled figure of the machine-shackled Eve. At least twelve years separate this pictorial variant from its parent poem in *Look! We Have Come Through!*, where the lovers "storm the angel-guarded/Gates" in contempt for the proffered disembodied bliss of eternity.[176] The picture delighted Lawrence. "And I challenge you to a pictorial contest," he wrote describing it to Brett, and added,

I should like to do a middle picture, inside paradise, just as she bolts in. God Almighty astonished and indignant, and the new young God who is just having a chat with the serpent, pleasantly amused, then the third picture, Adam and Eve under the tree of knowledge, God Almighty disappearing in a dudgeon, and the animals skipping.[177]

In the event, Parts 2 and 3 of the projected triptych contracted into the small water-colour *Throwing Back the Apple,* and the animals, alas, have skipped right out of the conception. This little picture is foreshadowed in a letter to Brewster: "I might begin a painting of Adam and Eve pelting the old Lord-God with apples, and driving him out of paradise . . . ."[178] This was on the 21st October, 1927, shortly after a searching letter to Dr. Trigant Burrow on man's religious relation to the Universe and the antagonism between mental and physical consciousness, where he writes:

The Edens are so badly lost, anyhow. But it was the apple, not the Lord, did it. . . . How to prevent suburbia spreading over Eden (too late! it's done)— how to prevent Eden running to a great wild wilderness—there you are.[179]

In both these pictures the brush seems to echo the pen in a loose satire.

The voice of serious criticism cried rarely in the wilderness of irrelevant clamour and its few words are precious. The outstanding notice, most happily headed "The Eye of a Poet's Mind," appeared in *Everyman* over the signature of Gwen John.[180] Its note of critical admiration is the more valuable since it has to surmount the writer's evident distaste for the general character of Lawrence's art. I am privileged to quote from it, summarising at times most reluctantly, since it mutilates a fine piece of work. "Profoundly introspective," attracted by nature "because, like himself, it is colourful and egotistical," but with a "stupendous" "gift of self-expression" —these are points from Gwen John's introductory remarks. "[Lawrence] surprises by the power with which, through a new medium, he states his inner vision; rhythmically, and with tremendous assurance." Working, "apparently, red-hot," his composition is "unpremeditated, yet usually happy." In his best pictures a "balance and scheme both of line and colour are preserved, because Mr. Lawrence is an artist." Pondering Lawrence's quest for "joy" the writer proceeds: "that he should seek it, self-tormented, in the globy female . . . to him the paradise of sex, or in the provocative and slightly more vital woman who has stepped from his poem of the

'Cherry Robbers' [181] to sit under the mango tree . . . and that he should paint what one feels is a self-portrait in nearly every picture, is a mood akin to that of El Greco." Only the unprepossessing "Amazon" in No. 5, a trump-card, if not a paradise, of the trouble-makers, can be justly called "globy," from which it seems evident that Gwen John recalled the Amazon's rude canvas-mate, as well as the male figure under the mango-tree, as self-portraits—an illusion only to be explained by the overmastering impression made unawares by *Resurrection* and *Flight Back into Paradise,* neither of which figures in the *Everyman* review. Present admirers of Lawrence will read with alternating assent and dissent that he "personifies . . . a mighty mutiny; without religion [*sic*], without hope . . . in flight from an overcrowded, commercialised, vulgar . . . social machine. He believes in nothing but indulgence, and he hates all that he attains. That," she adds, "is why his pictures will shock, and, I think, rightly." Points from Gwen John's concluding paragraph are: "*The Finding of Moses, Red Willow Trees,* and, politeness apart, *Boccaccio Story,* are pictures of real beauty and great vitality." *Close-Up,* in which she saw "power and passion," proving Lawrence able to "surmount even ridicule," [182] was otherwise appraised in the Gallery. To my wife, even before *Pansies* reached us, the masterly composition of two unlovely heads contacted in an unfulfilled kiss is the pictorial rendering of Cold Passion, condemned in cruder terms by the gamekeeper in *Lady Chatterley's Lover* and delicately but cruelly in "When I went to the Film," "and caught them moaning from close-up kisses, black and white kisses that could not be felt . . . ." [183]

The late Frank Rutter's [184] *Sunday Times* art column gave a kind but rather colourless notice, but filled a gap unaccountably left by Gwen John: "Technically," he wrote, "his best exhibit is the half-length male nude entitled *Contadini,*[185] in which we feel there has been a genuine personal search for form as well as colour, and, consequently, it is superior in drawing and modelling to all the other exhibits." After praising the design and drawing of the *Rape of the Sabine Women* Rutter concludes: "The exhibition as a whole reveals a temperament that is sensually romantic rather than sternly realist." [186] The *Scotsman,* after noting Lawrence's debt to Renoir and Cézanne, observes well, "With the former he shares the love of luxuriant forms, with the latter the horror of the 'cliché,' the desire to do all he can to rid his work of commonplaces and see things entirely for himself." [187] In the *Western Mail,* a Welsh organ, Mr. Evelyn Herbert, after balancing Lawrence's amateur crudities of draughtsmanship against his striking individuality "which flames through the canvas," concludes: "As a contribution to art this exhibition is not perhaps great. As a contribution to the autobiography of Mr. D. H. Lawrence it is invaluable." [188]

Within the small compass of authentic criticism devoted to the exhibition two writers only condemned it out of hand, one on technical, the other on moral grounds. Mr. Earp, part of whose summary of the "Introduction to These Paintings" has been quoted, closed his review of it with a withering glance at the paintings. "Because he is so good a novelist," he wrote, "we are interested in his views on painting. His own pictures alas! do not give him interest as a painter."

> For painting to Mr. Lawrence is simply what his violin was to Ingres. It may be a delightful hobby, but the exhibition as a whole showed no signs of a vocation. There was imagination and there was passable draughtsmanship; but the alternate muddiness and garishness of colour, and the clumsiness with which the pigment was laid upon the canvas, revealed a basic inability in mere picture-making. [189]

There are a few more lines; but the above is enough—and interesting. To painting, as a hobby ("to amuse myself"), pictures that were "rolling with faults, Sladeily considered," [190] to "painting wet," and making considerable use of his thumb: [191] to all these solecisms of the craft Lawrence himself pleads guilty. But "alternately muddy and garish" as a description of Lawrence's colour simply won't do. But it *will* do admirably—in fact there is not much else that will—for the "colour-work" carried out for the Mandrake Press "under the supervision of William Dieper." [192] The inference seems clear: While reviewing the "Introduction to These Paintings" Mr. Earp sought to refresh his memory out of the Mandrake pictures —and blurred it. As for the lack of vocation: this record serves little purpose if it does not show Lawrence's painting as a source of refreshment, sometimes of direct inspiration to his essential genius, and as capable of stating his inner vision to the amazement of competent critics. But I recall a conversation in 1934 with an eminent authority on art—the holder of many Chairs, keeperships, and curatorships. "Lawrence paint? He should never have tried it; it wasn't his job." And he repeated, "It wasn't his job," diminishing to a whisper, with the finality of a tale that needs no further telling.

Entry No. 3 on the table of dates heading this section reads: "Adverse notice in *Observer:* Sunday, 16 June." It is the chief reason why the weekend opening was reckoned a calamity. The late Paul Konody,[193] principal art critic of the Rothermere Press, had been from its inception a keen and kind supporter of the Warren Gallery. But on the 14th June 1929, he came, he saw, and was disgusted. Opening hopefully on the note: "Opinions . . . are alleged to be broader nowadays; yet the prurient attitude to paintings of the nude figure . . . convinces one of the fallacy of any statement that the worst elements of Victorianism have lost their sting," Konody proceeds: "There are still things which are not permissible. . . . Pornography is probably the worst form of lewd expression, and when undeniable skill is present to increase its effect, a firm stand should be taken against any display of it." Coming by stages of prolixity to Lawrence, he utters what was to be quoted and requoted in scores of provincial papers: "This author-artist, weary, perhaps, of being subtly misbehaved in print, has elected to come straight to the point, and is frankly disgusting in paint." How straddling was the disturbance wrought by Lawrence's nudes in Konody's mind and eye is revealed as this frequenter of the world's picture galleries proceeds: "His choice of subjects—the Boccaccio story of the gardener and the nuns, Leda, Rape of the Sabine women, Fauns & Nymphs, and so forth [*sic*] is sufficient to reveal his bent . . . . If critics and the public regard such a display [*sic*] as an outrage upon decency, I am in hearty agreement with them." Then, in the closing paragraph, we are brought back, by a devious route, to the "sting" of Victorian prudery, with which this amazing notice opened. It must first be explained that what was then being referred to as the "other big sensation in the art world" was a very blatant Spanish exhibition in a neighbouring gallery, with which Lawrence's was constantly compared. And it is instructive to note the comparisons, first in the *Scotsman,* then in the *Observer,* each the closing paragraph of a notice on Lawrence. Here, then, is the concluding paragraph of the *Scotsman's* notice, already twice quoted in this memoir:

In contrast to this small exhibition [D. H. Lawrence's] is the huge one at the New Burlington Galleries, where after a distasteful publicity campaign, the work of the Spaniard, Beltran Masses, was opened to the public. . . . Neither his portraits nor . . . compositions have any . . . originality or power. He is mainly a painter of "daring" nudes, and has found an attractive formula for depicting vamps, "wicked mahas," and the like.[194]

And here is Konody's conclusion:

Unfortunately, in the same week as the outburst against Mr. D. H. Lawrence's defiance of propriety, there appeared various tirades . . . on the alleged flaunting immorality of Señor Beltran Masses' *Salome* . . . . The sleuth-hounds who whip out their magnifying glasses as soon as they catch sight of a painted or drawn limb would convince one more of the purity of their motives were they also to notice other features—the acceptable features—in the pictures which so shock their senses.[195]

Truly the Warren Gallery's third miner's son had come in under altered aspects. For it was the week-end opening (necessitated by extraneous delays) that gave weight and priority to Konody's Sunday assault. It condemned the pictures virtually before they were seen, and gave the authoritative lead of a great paper and a competent critic to the flood of opportunist column-writing that was to follow. At the time, too, we held it responsible for a keenly regretted silence: for the first and last time in the Warren Gallery's history, no notice of its current exhibition was printed in *The Times*, although its critic had called, and lingered, within a few hours of Konody's visit. I am privileged to give his impressions of Lawrence's work, as recalled after a quarter of a century. Mr. Charles Marriott [196] remembers Lawrence as "a genuine artist, imaginative and vigorous in expression," but with "an imperfect sense of the fundamental difference between the mediums of writing and painting: that what can be suggested in words has to be stated flatly in paint." Lawrence might have replied by claiming pioneer licence for introducing "phallic beauty" into his pictures,[197] as for doing violence to the conventional structure of a novel. But Konody's prompt and querulous outburst demands investigation; for we cannot suspect an experienced critic of condemning pictures on the analogy and merits of a banned novel: something in the paintings put his critical acumen out of focus, and his chaotic reaction was not an isolated case. Balancing Mr. Marriott's weighty aesthetic objection was the less respectable but widespread recoil from anything new and unaccustomed in art. Lawrence's most strident innovation falls to be discussed at a later stage of this memoir. But one comment, refreshingly *à rebours* against the background of the exhibition's history, is here pertinent. "You know," observed a genial dilettante a few days after visiting the exhibition, "I don't care for those pictures. *They are so oppressively proper.*" He had lingered, apparently, in front of *Family on a Verandah,* and here, once again, the appeal of a single Lawrence painting seems to have echoed in the viewer's memory. I now interpret this incongruous invention as an impish caricature of some mid-nineteenth century conversation piece, the caricature consisting in presenting the exact scene, only with the intensely bourgeois family of father, mother, and two children stark naked.[198] The mother (centre) reclines full length, with nothing concealed, in a hammock, the foolish-looking father squats, profile perdue, near her feet. It left one with the impression that, had Lawrence been attracted, instead of repelled, by city scenes, we should have had naked solicitors and stockbrokers bowing naked clients into office chairs.

Neighbouring this absurdity on either side were the two paintings best fitted to correct the malaise induced by its amateur treatment of the nude:

Contadini on its right, drawn from life, had, as its centre figure, a finely drawn and modelled male head and torso; the head looks rightwards, and its shadow on the nude shoulder is delicately painted. *Dance-Sketch* on the left, with its rhythmic beauty and lyrical sense of ecstasy, could take anatomical liberties unwarranted in the plump conventionality of the verandah scene.

Monday, 17th June, was the exhibition's second open day. The rooms filled rapidly with a crowd of visitors new to any picture gallery, mostly carrying the current issue of the *Daily Express*. Here is what had brought them to the second floor of 39a Maddox Street:

D. H. LAWRENCE/AS PAINTER
CENSORED NOVELIST'S PICTURES
INTIMATE NUDES

Another sensation in the art world has been provided during the weekend, writes a special correspondent of the "Daily Express," by the opening of an amazing exhibition of paintings by Mr. D. H. Lawrence, the much censored novelist.

Twenty-five paintings, signed Lorenzo, in oils and water colours are on view, and in nearly all of them the human frame is shown in its most intimate details.

The ugly composition, colouring, and drawing of these works makes them repellent enough, but the subjects of some of them will compel most spectators to recoil with horror.

"Spring," a study of six nude boys, is revolting.[199] "Fight with an Amazon," representing a hideous bearded man holding a fair-haired woman in his lascivious grip, while wolves with dripping jaws look on expectantly, is frankly indecent.[200] "Boccaccio Story," another of these works of art, is better not described.

Mr. Lawrence holds revolutionary views on art. "Hogarth, Reynolds, Gainsborough," he writes, in an introduction to his pictures, "they all are already bourgeoisie. The coat is really more important than the man."

"CRYING FOR ESCAPE"

"The northern races," he adds later, "are so innerly afraid of their own bodily existence, which they believe fantastically to be an evil thing . . . that all they cry for is an escape. And especially, art must provide that escape."

According to Mr. Lawrence, English artists excel in landscapes—"which do not call up the more powerful responses of the human imagination, the sensual, passional responses"—because they form that escape.

The glorification of the spirit, the mental consciousness which distinguishes us from beasts mean nothing to Mr. Lawrence. Indeed, he describes the history of our era as the nauseating and repulsive history of the crucifixion of the procreative body. And the gross and the earthly are the main features of his pictorial art.[201]

Variations on the above theme were countless. Konody's antithesis of the "subtly misbehaved in print" and "the frankly disgusting in paint" echoed round the provinces, in the formal "One distinguished London critic writes: . . . ." There were two other elements in the first phase of the campaign: the facetious, and the pityingly-patronizing. Examples of the former were: that a better title for *Fight with an Amazon* would be *Before the Obesity Cure,* that the poor Contadino had such a squint that he couldn't even see that he was naked; and that *Boccaccio Story* depicts "a troop of nuns fleeing past a nude sleeping gardener—and no wonder!" [202] The motif of patronizing pity sums up in the formula: "Unfortunately the poor man just can't paint."

What seemed to justify dividing this unlovely chapter of the exhibition's history into a first and second phase is the appearance of a new leitmotif at the end of the second week: the call for action on the part of "the authorities"—whoever they might be—and the duty resting on the press to protect the public against corrupting influences. Remembering the stir created two years previously by the appearance of the Warren Gallery, and the crescendo of interest as one exhibition succeeded another, readers will learn with surprise that the following—not from the hand of an art critic—is the first cutting from the *Daily Telegraph* in the Gallery's press album: dated 27th June 1929:

A DISGRACEFUL EXHIBITION

PROBABLY NO greater insult has ever been offered to the London public than the exhibition at the Warren Galleries in Maddox street of twenty-five paintings by Mr. D. H. Lawrence, whose name is better known to the public as a writer than as an artist.

So long as the exhibition remains open it must be a standing source of amazement that the authorities permit the public display of paintings of so gross and obscene a character.

To encounter a friend, particularly a friend of the opposite sex, in the Warren Galleries is, to say the least of it, highly embarrassing, and one can detect that attitude of mind in the furtive entrance of those who climb the narrow staircase.

To pretend that such subjects can be justified on any artistic grounds is sheer nonsense. Mr. Lawrence's qualifications as a painter appear, to the normal mind at least, negligible, and his subjects, lacking all sort of restraint, are of a character such as has never been seen in London before.[203]

The above sentiments had been anticipated, though in more temperate language, in a general news column of the *Morning Post,*[204] whose accredited art critic had hitherto reviewed all Warren Gallery events. The immediate effect of the entry of the "Heavies" into the crusade was a burst, among the "Populars," of interviews with "spokesmen" of the Home Office, House of Commons, and Police, on what could be done, should be done, and how difficult it was to do. Even the President of the Royal Academy was lured into speculative but non-committal utterances on possible currents of obscenity in the art world, none of which had come under his personal notice—hence his inability to express an opinion. The 1857 *Obscenities Act* became a best seller in Fleet Street; every columnist had the definition at his fingertips. What none of the pundits had grasped— none, at least, foreshadowed—was the simple but repulsive machinery provided by the law, and the willingness of a certain type of individual to manipulate it. Here we must return to the Gallery.

By the end of the first week the rooms were filled to capacity, apparently, during most of the day, though the sale of catalogues—the condition of entrance—showed a fairly steady increase right up to the 5th July.[205] Throughout the growing congestion three schools were clearly distinguishable: those who condemned the pictures as obscene, but split wide on the question of repressive action; those who defended the pictures as not obscene, and/or asked what, in any case, was meant by *obscene*, and what its legal definition. The third group, welcome only for its non-use of the hideous word *obscene*, had come in search of dirty pictures and, in varying degrees of forcefulness, expressed disgust at finding none. Probably because our contacts were mainly with the second group, we remembered it as the most numerous. But, in fact, their relative strengths were not assessable; the odious word *obscene,* with its phonetic quality of a furtive but penetrating whisper, was an auditory presence in the Gallery, dominating and constant. The daily litter of cast-away catalogues on the stairs and landings was interpreted as a manifestation of outraged modesty; but disappointed prurience was at least an equal contributor.

Prominent and frequent among the denouncers of obscenity from the last days of June was a short, thick, hook-nosed, sallow-faced, bespectacled man whom the Gallery came to know and dislike under the name of "Jaundice." Calling late in the morning he buttonholed small groups and harangued them in corners in a strangled voice. At last, interrupting one of these séances, I asked him why, since he appeared to dislike Lawrence's pictures, and the Gallery was in nobody's way, I had had the honour of seeing him four or five times, generally accompanied by a different lady. His answer was incoherent, but, if he had not already been to the police, he must have gone there hot-foot; for this was on the 4th of

July, and it has always seemed fair to assume that Jaundice was the Common Informer—the unknown warrior—whom the Law has enlisted, and whose anonymity it protects, in its zeal for the detection of crime.[206]

Under normal Warren Gallery procedure the exhibition was due to close on the 6th July, three weeks from its opening on the 15th June. But all three miners' sons were exceptions: the first because his sales were still booming; the second because his sales had not begun; the third?—his pictures must hang until the rabble made way for those able and willing to view them on their merits, and/or "the authorities" either moved against them or let it be known that no action would be taken. They elected to move on the 5th.[207]

2 *July 1929*
Pensione Giuliani, Viale Morin, Forte dei Marmi, Lucca, Italy

❨ *It is rather hot here, I am going to Florence on Saturday* [6 *July 1929*], *just for a day or so. The address c/o G. Orioli, 6 Lungarno Corsini, Florence. Then on the 10th I shall go to Milan, probably to meet my wife there, and we may stay a week or two on Lago di Como. I don't think it will be too hot. Later we shall come to Germany* . . . .[208]

7 *July 1929*   c/o G. Orioli, 6 Lungarno Corsini, Florence, Italy

❨ *Maria* [Huxley] *drove me to Pisa yesterday afternoon—very sirocco and overcast, but not hot, not at all uncomfortable. Unfortunately my inside is upset—either I must have eaten something or it came from drinking ice-water very cold on Thursday when it was very hot. Anyhow my lower man hurts and it makes my chest sore—which is a pity, because I was so well. Now I'm rather limp. But I've kept still all day in Pino's flat, and he looks after me well—so I hope by tomorrow or Tuesday it will be all right.* . . . *Pino's flat gets a bit hot just at evening, but in the night and the most part of the day it is pleasant and cool—it's not really a hot year.* . . . *Pino and I will have a cup of tea now, then perhaps take a carriage-drive for an hour.*[209]

8 *July 1929*   c/o G. Orioli, 6 Lungarno Corsini, Florence, Italy

❨ *The pains were a chill—have been in bed all day today—damn! Pino very nice, but oh the noise of traffic. I'm a lot better. I want to get up* tomorrow, and leave if possible on Wednesday night [10 July 1929] for Milan. I might arrive Baden on Thursday night—otherwise Friday—all being well. Hot internal cold I've got, real Italian. I hate this country like poison, sure it would kill me.

I should rather like an apartment for six weeks or so—Ebersteinburg, Baden—anywhere—where I can lie in bed all day if I want to—and where I needn't see people. . . .

Rained a bit today—quite cool.[210]

c/o G. Orioli/6 Lungarno Corsini/Florence/9 July 1929

⟨ Dear Dorothy [Warren]

Well there's a go!—even the Boccaccio Story and Eve [211] shut up in prison now, with only Mr. Mead to look at them. Hope he'll get his meed. But send me news. If only one could shoot a few of the old fungoids!

I've written to Frieda to the Kingsley—is she still there? I hear nothing from her. . . .

D. H. Lawrence [212]

Philip Trotter

Appropriately for the eve of battle the Warren Gallery had been *en fête* the previous night (4 July) in a reception given for Frieda. Catherine Carswell has recalled her resplendent appearance: "She wore a gay shawl, red shoes and a sheaf of lilies—the last to symbolize Lawrence's purity!" [213] For those few hours the pictures came into their own. There was, of course, earnest discussion of the fate now probably awaiting them. But unprejudiced eyes enjoyed them as works of art; to Frieda's profound relief Mrs. Ada Lawrence Clarke, who had travelled south for the occasion, found them agreeable and not shocking; *Finding of Moses,* lovely and luminous and praised even by Mr. Earp, had many admirers, but had been sold that morning to a Cambridge undergraduate for 50 guineas. *Boccaccio Story* and *Leda* were purchased during the reception, the former to a high officer of the Crown, the latter to a Scottish collector. Both pictures were seized next day and both purchases cancelled within the week. My memories of the reception include an argument with Frieda on how to prepare a German *Erdbeerbowle,* for which *fraises des bois* had been flown from France. She insisted on adding soda-water to

342

the white wine and champagne; to me, having come of age in the Black Forest, this was an unwarrantable adulteration.

A letter written by the late Geoffrey Scott [214] to Arnold Bennett (then abroad) twelve days after the raid gives a vivid eye-witness impression by a brilliant and sympathetic observer. But the letter as a whole belongs to different stages of this history, and was written with the express purpose of enlisting support, Bennett having been foremost among Dorothy's personal friends in advocating the Lawrence exhibition.[215] Here I wish to record the exact facts of the 5th July in order to detach the story from the "apocrypha" in which it quickly became embedded, which has grown with the years, and from which nearly every biography of Lawrence that I have had access to has absorbed something. Even Catherine Carswell writes: "The police raid on the Warren Gallery, with the *confiscation of all the pictures*" (None were confiscated, and only thirteen out of twenty-five seized) ". . . came very *soon after* Frieda's return." [216] (She did not leave London till several days *after* the raid.) Nearly every biographer I have read states that the exhibition was *closed by the police*. It ran three weeks longer than Henry Moore's, finally closing seven weeks after the police raid and nearly three after the trial at Gt. Marlborough Street. Most of the newspapers reported that the raid was carried out after close of business. The police may well have wished it had been; but here are the facts:

As we were finishing lunch on 5 July, two plain-clothes detectives, Detective-Inspector Gordon Hester [217] and Detective-Inspector Humphreys were announced. I received them in the office, while Dorothy went upstairs for a moment.

"Are you responsible for this exhibition?" asked Mr. Hester.

"It is my wife's gallery, and we are jointly responsible for the businesses carried on here."

"Am I right in understanding that you live above these premises?"

"Yes, that is so."

An oration followed in which "the authorities," "a member of the public," and "the reputable press" seemed to have got inextricably tangled. But the conclusion was clear:

"I have therefore to call upon you to close this exhibition *herewith, forthwith and now,* failing which proceedings will be taken against you."

As a number of the pictures could not be condemned on any conceivable criteria I was protesting that this was an unreasonable demand when Dorothy came in and the speech was repeated word for word.

"You have no right to ask us to close the exhibition," she replied, "and we deny that any of the pictures are obscene; but, if you can specify which of them have been the subject of *bona fide* objections, we shall withdraw them from view, and undertake not to show them again."

The tense atmosphere relaxed.

"That is a reasonable proposal," said the Inspector, abandoning the browbeating tone, "but I have no authority to accept it."

"Perhaps," I suggested, "you could go back and put it before the learned magistrate."

"That is what I propose to do; but," he added, "I think the law will have to take its course."

"Would you care to take a turn round the pictures with me before you go?" I asked.

"Well, now," said Mr. Hester, calling up as many words as the context could be made to contain, "as a matter of fact I rather think I would."

During our tour, which was punctuated by ejaculations of "Very crude, very crude," Dorothy took the unorthodox step of briefing her own counsel on the telephone. St. John Hutchinson [218] had been at the reception the previous night. He now approved all we had said; but feared the raid was inevitable if, as seemed probable, the Common Informer had been at work. The Inspector and I parted amicably; but he had stood rapt in front of *Leda,* and I realised that a policeman who had not yet raided a major picture gallery must interpret the venerable legend as a plunge by Lawrence into unrestrained bestiality.

In less than an hour a commotion among the upward stream of visitors gave warning of fresh happenings, and the crowd within was forthwith convulsed with news of a cordon of constables forming round the corner-house and a police van standing at the door. The purpose of the latter was obvious; that of the cordon can only be guessed. Two uniformed constables entered with our previous visitors, whose bearing was now conciliatory.

"You will like to close your gallery while we are busy," said Mr. Hester.

"No," we answered, "we close at 6."

And they addressed themselves to their task with fresh crowds pressing in from the stairs. They started counter-cataloguewise; so *Contadini* came down first and was turned face to the wall. They had deposed *Dance-Sketch* and were exempting *Fauns and Nymphs,* when there was a halt.

A tall figure had entered carrying a glittering silk hat and jewelled cane. "Aga Khan," [219] muttered the four executants, and stood, not quite to attention, but very much not at ease. His Highness, who had broken away from the Royal Garden Party at Buckingham Palace, the other outstanding event of the 5th, paid his compliments, expressed his sympathy, and turned to the pictures in catalogue order. But since the well-draped biblicals (Nos. 2 and 3) were presumably immune, I begged to cut a passage through for him to *Boccaccio Story*, whose turn was now imminent and whose fate was inevitable; and there he and Hester met, and bowed, to the latter's embarrassment. On the Aga's heels came a shabby little man from Nottingham, to see his famous co-citizen's pictorial work. I expressed regret that he was too late for *Contadini*. He sidled towards it and began furtively revolving the frame as on an axis. Hester, glad to relinquish *Boccaccio Story* to the Aga Khan, muscled back to *Contadini*.

"Stand aside, please," he said sternly. "That picture is no longer on view."

The little man slunk away.

But the Aga Khan had followed Hester. Pointing his splendid cane at the stretchers of *Contadini*:

"Will you turn that picture round, please? I should like to see it."

Dorothy's formula, as she related the story of the raid, hit the spirit of the scene that followed, though her facts were heightened. "The police," she used to say, "made easels of themselves. 'Light all right, your Highness?'"

Then the Aga Khan signed the man from Nottingham to his side, and they enjoyed *Contadini* together. This gracious incident, besides contributing one of the few moments of comic relief to an essentially tragic chapter in our social history, has historical significance. It will be recalled that the Aga Khan was among Lawrence's last visitors at Vence, that he had plans for a further exhibition of the pictures in Paris, and was believed anxious to acquire some if the Lawrences were willing to part with them.[220]

The seizure of four copies of the Mandrake Press book of reproductions of Lawrence's paintings (including one of the ten printed on vellum and priced at 50 guineas) was a foregone conclusion, since we had failed to hide them. But this is a faint memory in the counterchange of hopes and despairs that the raid evokes. The news that Blake's *Pencil Drawings* had been impounded, with the prospect of showing cause why it should not be destroyed, had brought half-an-hour's elation. The public claimed to know that the Police had opened the book on *Adam and Eve*, where the sexes are indeed realistically distinguished. But the two stand side by side and hand in hand, embodying the total innocence of the newly-created. Their seizure as "obscene" is a beautiful irony. The raid was over and Mr. Hester was writing out his receipt when a visitor apprised him of the literary, artistic and religious significance of Blake. "I find I shan't want this after all," he said, as he handed the book back to its bitterly disappointed owners. But it had lain impounded for upwards of an hour, and owed its release to the jibes of the public. As such it was to figure large and often in the coming weeks. A pictorial affinity of Lawrence with Blake was occasionally canvassed before and after the raid. I cannot discern it in temperament, style, or execution. But their approach to the art, or the art's to them, makes their seizure at the same time and place extraordinarily apposite. Compare the following passages from Sir Geoffrey Keynes' [221] Introduction to the impounded book of Blake drawings with the appropriate passages in "Making Pictures":

He never tired [writes Sir Geoffrey] of decrying realism in art and of exalting the imaginative faculty above all others. In this he was quite consistent. Making studies from models or painting portraits he called "copying nature" and complained that such pursuits "smelt of mortality." [222]

And again, where he quotes Blake's words:

He believed . . . that he had been suddenly "again enlightened with the light I enjoyed in my youth, and which has for exactly twenty years been closed from me as by a door and by window-shutters. . . . For I am really drunk with intellectual vision whenever I take a pencil or graver in my hand, even as I used to be in my youth." [223]

Suppress *intellectual,* and substitute a "brush full of paint" for "a pencil or graver," and it is Lawrence's apologia. That way, it seems, lies the house of detention.

Two further books remain to be mentioned. Hester and his assistant had been intent on a book that their persons concealed until the former came forward with a large, flat, red volume with a sampler design on the cover.

"I have to ask you what this is, Mrs. Trotter," he said gravely.

"It is a literal translation into French of *The Hunting of the Snark.*" [224]

"But what is *The Hunting of the Snark?* I never heard of it."

"Possibly not; it was written for children by an English clergyman."

"No need to be rude, Madam," replied the Inspector, for once giving vent to his discomfort. But he put Lewis Carroll back where he had found him.

The other book was more serious, and the only extraneous volume to reach Gt. Marlborough Street. The *Ecce Homo* portfolio by George Grosz [225] belonged upstairs, had been brought down by a guest during the reception, and placed next day by a member of the staff on a shelf in the Gallery marked "not for sale." Grosz's brilliant drawings were a frightful and passionately sincere commentary on post-war, *schieber* Berlin. But no policeman could be expected to approve the visions that his indignation evoked.

Our own sense of time was suspended throughout that afternoon; but the most trustworthy reports put the preliminary visit at 4 o'clock (Our lunch was a movable feast throughout the exhibition), and a police document in my possession states that the officers "withdrew" at about 5.30. Thus the whole operation, with the "exercising of a sound discretion" (as we were to hear later), and certainly of a fine forbearance with the public, and with a private view to the Aga Khan of the three pictures then in eclipse, had occupied less than an hour. A few visitors lingered to express sympathy and indignation. Their impressions agreed with ours as to the lines along which the sound discretion had operated, and the opening speech for the Prosecution a month later seems to confirm them: any picture showing pubic hair was automatically proscribed. Hence the taking of *Contadini*, a finely modelled study of head, trunk and arms, which would have been saved by a half-inch slip along the bottom of the canvas. Hence, too, the taking of *Family on a Verandah* (where the reclining lady was generously endowed in that respect), and the leaving of *Flight Back into Paradise*, where Eve's belly is hidden. *Leda* and *Spring* were presumably Mr. Hester's own selection, since neither contains the offending feature.

As for the books: a paragraph in next day's *Daily Chronicle*, and echoed throughout the provincial press, said: "With Inspector Hester, who carried out the raid, was Detective Inspector Humphreys, of Scotland Yard, *who has figured in all cases in recent years concerning the seizure of books* and postcards." [226] (My italics) So there was an expert in our midst after all. Whatever his qualifications and training when he came to Maddox Street, did he, on the next occasion of *"Marlborough s'en va t'en guerre,"* go forth better equipped for his adventures with William Blake and Lewis Carroll? The 1954 "obscenities" bag in the courts shows little evidence of any lasting change.

The shadowy bogeys moving behind the raid were further illumined by a late-lingering visitor that evening whose profession associated him with the police, and who joined the group of friends, art-lovers and Lawrence-readers, whom we had made a practice of entertaining after business hours throughout the exhibition.

He said: "Did they ask whether you live above these premises?"

"Yes," I said, "it was Hester's second question: 'Was he right in understanding so?'"

"You see," he continued, "the picture in the raiders' minds was of an upstairs premises, where salacious pictures are shown to the unwary, who are then lured one floor higher for more intimate rites. These illusions are part of the price we pay for operating the law through a Common Informer."

He turned later to the press album to study the "Much-Censored-Novelist" campaign, and there became interested in the early notices of the new Warren Gallery.

"My word," he said, "here's something for them."

He read out from the *Westminster Gazette* column quoted above: "Upstairs . . . a special gallery, where pictures will lie on shelves, and will be brought out one by one and placed on an easel . . . ."[227] Whatever the value of this startling assertion there were undoubtedly sinister visions behind the vehemence of Mr. Hester's initial address; and his rapid and total change of orientation attests the "exercise of a sound discretion" though in a context not envisaged by Prosecuting Counsel on the 8th August. Our cordial relations with the principal raiders were happily maintained, not only throughout subsequent proceedings, but until, in 1934, the Warren Gallery closed serenely with its thirty-third exhibition, "Pictures by Angna Enters," the American dance-mime.[228]

That "The Authorities," so frequently and glibly invoked during the press campaign, were contained in the person of the Common Informer seems established by the following, dated 6th July: "The Home Secretary [Mr. J. R. Clynes] informed the *Daily Dispatch* last night that he had no knowledge of the raid."[229]

The end of that eventful day saw the birth of a curious item in the "apocrypha" of the Lawrence case. The last visitor to the Gallery was Frieda. Coming from her hotel she can have looked neither right nor left at the news-posters at every street corner, for, like the Home Secretary, she "had no knowledge of the raid." Nor had she believed it possible. To her the daily crowds had been witness to the long-delayed triumph of Lorenzo. She loved the pictures, and it was right that people should come in thousands to see them. We found her standing in the doorway, staring aghast at the eloquent gaps on the walls. We gave her an account of the raid, consoling ourselves with the remnants of the previous night's *Erdbeerbowle*. A sympathetic American woman was present, who was to render valiant service with her camera in the coming weeks. But there was an atmosphere of suspended animation until Dorothy said: "Let's all go to the Russian Ballet just as we are"; and off we went. We arrived late. Whispered references to the "seized pictures" were audible as we pressed to our seats.

On that first evening the impressions of the day were vivid but disconnected, and the mechanism of plan-making was in suspense. But one thing was certain: Every answer we gave to the questions that would bombard us in the interval between the first and second ballet must lead back to William Blake and the seizure of his drawings. And so, in the pause between the second and third ballets, came from all sides the facetious suggestion: "Mr. Mead [230] will by now be busy preparing a warrant for the arrest of William Blake."

That facile joke has had an interesting career. It echoed round the clubs for a week; then went to sleep (or I suppose it did) for a quarter of a century. In May, 1954, while I was collecting the bomb-scattered records of the Lawrence exhibition, it awoke in a new role as historical fact from the pen of a barrister, writing against the law of Obscene Libel in a serious journal devoted to literature and the arts, and with the Lawrence case as his point of departure.[231] The hackneyed error of the closing of the exhibition by Mr. Mead was brought out from the existing legend; but the barrister's major surprise was his recollection of a club lunch with "the late Mr. Mead," who told him that "a man named Lawrence was holding an exhibition of obscene pictures . . . near Bond Street"; that "the police had applied for two summonses, against Lawrence and a fellow called Blake; but, as Blake could not be found, Mr. Mead had issued a warrant for his arrest. Blake's reproduced drawings," concluded the barrister, "had shocked the police, and *Mr. Mead, too.*" (My italics) The four-column article contains useful information and comment; but readers of the foregoing authentic account of the raid, ending with the sheepish return of the Blake book, will accept the "Barrister's Dream" with an appropriate pinch of salt.[232]

Our earliest visitors next morning (6 July 1929) were two young reporters desiring to be put in touch with Mr. William Blake, whose name had figured in the previous night's report of the raid. Since William Blake was now the only feature of the raid that was not *sub judice,* and a section of the press to whom his name was unknown had discovered the Warren Gallery, Dorothy drafted the following statement, with which reporters had for the moment to be content:

We are going to have immediately another show called "D. H. Lawrence and his Masters." We shall show, besides paintings by Mr. Lawrence, photographs of famous pictures that may have . . . inspired him in producing the paintings that have been taken away. They will be of pictures . . . on view in the public galleries of England.

Variants of this announcement, which I have taken from the *Notts Evening News*,[233] appeared in a great number of London and provincial papers. The newspapers were, however, to receive fresh material for reports and comments in the coming week, and it will be convenient to review the press of the no-man's-period between raid (5 July) and trial (8 August) at a later stage.

The march of the twelve thousand had ended with the raid. Attendance at the Gallery reverted to normal, reinforced by newcomers whose attempts to view the full exhibition had been frustrated by the mob. Two other callers were Inspector Hester and his lieutenant, bearing the summonses; these were "returnable" on the 12th, but an adjournment could of course be granted. Meanwhile the bearers begged to know of any way they could be of service to us between now and the hearing. An opportunity offered on the 9th.

Colin Agnew, head of the famous Bond Street firm and a connoisseur of international reputation, had returned from abroad in the weekend, and on Monday, having read the events of the 5th on his journey, came round to see the remnant exhibition. He was unexpectedly pleased with it and agreed to my invoking the good offices of the police for a private view of the eclipsed thirteen. This was fixed for next morning, when we were received by Inspector Hester, his accustomed shadow, and, I think, two uniformed constables. A popular tradition has located the pictures in a cellar; I remember only a long slow march along a corridor, to the accompaniment of great keys jangling, which recalled the entry of Hunding in the first act of *Walküre*. The condemned cell was small but light; the pictures were stacked face to the wall, for their own protection or that of susceptible constables. A constable assumed the office of showman; the rest stood round holding their chins. Some five or six pictures were seen and approved; but at *Boccaccio Story* there was a long pause. It will be recalled that a troop of nuns is advancing to the foreground, where the gardener is lying on his back, fast asleep, his shirt blown back by the

wind. I ventured a series of observations on the serenity of the landscape
. . . on the rhythmic surge of the nuns . . . on their charming headgear
. . . on the cloud of blue-grey, feathery willows in the background; but
the pause continued. The escort grew restless; the showman's hand hovered over the frame. At last:

"Yes," said Agnew. "Those are charming features. But I think you have
missed what I find so interesting in this picture. All the different elements
in the scene have subtly converging lines, which is what gives the composition its harmony; and the point of convergence is this dark mark *here*"
—and he put his forefinger on the part of the gardener that had caused
the picture to be seized.

If policemen ever dropped their keys—even so infrequently as soldiers
their rifles—the condemned cell would have resounded to the impact of
steel on concrete. All I remember is that it was Inspector Hester who now
reverently replaced, in its position face to the wall, the picture which, a
few nights before, he had waited the pleasure of the Aga Khan to impound. The rest of this memorable séance has escaped my memory if
it ever entered it. But, while hesitating to describe it as a sequel, I append
here a letter from the Warren Gallery's solicitors to those acting for the
Commissioner of Police:

Messrs. Richardson Sowerby, Holden & Co.[234]/5, John
Street,/Bedford Row, W.C. 1/13th Aug. 1929

[To Messrs. Wontner & Sons] [235]
Dear Sirs,

Police – v – Trotter.

We are sorry to have to report that apparently the Police have damaged one
of the pictures returned to our Clients. The picture in question is known under
the title of "A Bacaccio [*sic*] Story" and a hole has been made in the canvas
and it has been most inexpertly repaired from behind by having a piece of
canvas stuck on to it and we understand that an attempt has been made to put
paint over the front part of the picture where the injury took place.

This picture was in perfect order when it was examined at the Police Court
by Mr. Colin Agnew and our Clients, and the reason why the injury has not
been discovered sooner is that when the pictures were handed back by Inspector
Hester, he particularly desired that they should not be kept at the Gallery or
in any place where they could be seen and our Clients put them in a locked
room at their private house until they could fully carry out the undertaking that
they have given to the Court and on taking the pictures out of this room the
other day, their head workman immediately noticed the damage and called
our Clients' attention to it.

We desire to write in a quiet manner about what has happened but, of
course, we must hold the Police responsible for the damage to this picture,
which we are informed is of very considerable value.

Perhaps, in the first place, you would like to take your own instructions and let us know what the Authorities are prepared to do.

There seems to be no doubt whatever about what has happened. The repair work is obviously the repair work of someone who has no knowledge of pictures at all.

Yours faithfully
RICHARDSON SOWERBY, HOLDEN & CO.[236]

Why, out of the thirteen pictures, was *Boccaccio Story* damaged? Did an enquiring officer of the law return to the condemned cell and try, with the help of a sharp instrument, to trace the lines that Agnew discerned? [237]

10 July 1929   c/o G. Orioli, 6 Lungarno Corsini, Florence, Italy

❲ *Well, now the police have raided my picture show in London, and carried off 13 pictures, and have them locked up and want to burn them! Autodafé! My wife is staying on in London, I don't know how long.*

I think I should like to come to the Tegernsee. If my wife does not make some other plan, I think I shall take the train on Sunday or Monday to Munchen from here, and then come to Rottach.[238]

Frieda Lawrence Ravagli

Meanwhile Lawrence was ill in Florence. What with the abuse of *Lady Chatterley* and the disapproval of the pictures, he had become ill. Orioli telegraphed in distress. So off I set on my journey to Florence, my ankle still wabbly and aching and with constant worry in my mind of how I would find Lawrence. Orioli told me that after receiving my telegram saying I was coming, he had said: "What will Frieda say when she arrives?" And Lawrence had answered: "Do you see those peaches in the bowl? She will say, 'What lovely peaches,' and she will devour them." So it was. After my first look at Lawrence, when his eyes had signalled to me their relief, "She is here with me," I felt my thirst from the long journey and ate the peaches.

He always got better when I was there. But Orioli told me how scared he had been when he had seen Lawrence, his head and arms hanging over the side of the bed, like one dead.[239]

Philip Trotter

Within a week of the raid Lawrence, having struggled back from Mallorca to Forte dei Marmi and thence to Florence, had collapsed at Orioli's flat, and the latter had telegraphed recalling Frieda from London. The fatigues of that ill-advised journey were cause enough for a serious attack, and only Richard Aldington [240] and, in a casual phrase, Frieda [241] have noted the effect on his failing health of the fall of his "Kingdom of Heaven" before a Philistine assault. But the reaction, as his next two letters to Dorothy Warren Trotter (13 and 14 July 1929) reveal, was more complex. Out of the Lawrence who had lain several days "with head and arms hanging limply over the side of the bed, looking . . . like an old picture of the Descent from the Cross" [242] springs a flame of energy, burning on a strange compound of défaitism and defiance, dictating the procedure of defence to those on whom had fallen its whole burden, responsibility and expense. It is the Lawrence to whom his own values are universal, all others of no account, the Lawrence who had once resented Frieda's solicitude for her own children. The rally was as brief as it was spectacular. Two months later—again according to Richard Aldington—Lawrence comes back to the Mediterranean, visibly to himself and everyone a dying man.[243] But here is the background to what now follows.

Frieda, before her rush to Florence, had attended our first conference in Counsel's chambers on the 9th July, and applauded a proposal put forward by one of the lawyers for avoiding a dangerous clash on the character of the pictures. The Magistrate might, it was suggested, agree to release them and adjourn the hearing *sine die* if the Warren Gallery would undertake not to exhibit them again. It was an unexceptional proposal and merely the application to pictures in prison of the offer we had made to Hester when the police first visited the Gallery. But in the context of this jittery meeting it started an unhealthy round of mutual misinterpretations. They were of short duration and would have no place in this history if they were not reflected in nearly all the letters now to follow. Some account of them is therefore necessary.

Olympian lawyers, whose battlefield, if any, is the High Court, are generally at a loss when called upon to operate on the mortal level of magistrates. It will be recalled that Dorothy had adopted the unheard of procedure of briefing her own counsel, St. John Hutchinson, while I was showing Mr. Hester round the pictures; she had then instructed her devoted solicitor, the late Ralph A. Holden, to consult with Hutchinson.

353

It was, I think, their first association. Since, under the Obscenities Act, the author or painter of the offending work is no party to the case, their first step was to obtain the consent of Lawrence's solicitors to co-opt a Mr. Percy Robinson to watch his interests. Mr. Robinson was an able solicitor of Gt. Marlborough Street, whom constant practice in the police courts had endowed with the skills essential to the safe handling of their occupants. Before the conference began this triumvirate had reviewed the situation with some misgiving due less to the contents of the Act or the character of the pictures than to the personalities of the prosecution, to the vision of the solicitor Herbert G. Muskett pleading before the Stipendiary Magistrate Frederick Mead. Thirteen years earlier Mr. Muskett's eloquence had sent a thousand copies of *The Rainbow* to the stake. But *The Rainbow* had risen from its ashes and Mr. Muskett might be indulging the pleasurable reflection that a painted picture has not the phoenix properties of a printed book. Mr. Mead was eighty-two; Magistrates tend, in the course of long service, to focus their fury on a particular breach of the law; Mr. Mead's preferred victims were the elderly and often distinguished perpetrators of nocturnal park incidents.[244] Gt. Marlborough Street was therefore reckoned an unlucky tribunal for Lawrence's pictures.

Dorothy and I were not blind to the menace of the Muskett–Mead axis, but were inclined to offset it by certain salutary features in the case. First among these was Dorothy's offer above referred to; next, almost all the seized paintings would be shipped back to Italy, for whose morals the metropolitan police are not responsible. Lastly, a belated study of the Act had revealed that, for its incendiary powers to operate, Obscenity is not enough: the object must be exhibited *for purposes of sale and gain.* Six of the seized paintings were not so exhibited; for Lawrence had reserved them for himself or his friends; and two of these, *Boccaccio Story* and *Fight with an Amazon,* may fairly be assumed to have precipitated the crisis. Lawrence's vetoes had been a disability in the exhibition; they might be an asset in the police court.[245]

Our concern, second only to the release of the pictures, was their vindication before the press and public. That the Magistrate would reject artistic evidence was tolerably certain; but in disallowing it he would merely publicize its existence so long as Hutchinson was in a position to cite authoritative names before (or until) he was silenced; accordingly he had assigned us the task of furnishing him with names that the *Daily Telegraph* and *Daily Express* could not ignore. Frieda, with an anxiety at either end of her forthcoming journey, was concerned only that no word or gesture before or during the trial should delay for one moment the release of the pictures or the Magistrate's decision to grant it. These were the dispositions of the parties that met in Hutchinson's chambers.

The redundant undertaking came from Mr. Robinson preambled by a rather unctuous invocation to the agony of the artist threatened with the destruction of his cherished creations and epilogued by a hope that it might be so handled as to obviate any dangerous discussion of the pictures on their merits. We had decided to leave all talking to our legal betters, and waited for them to put Mr. Robinson's mind at rest since the desired undertaking was already in existence. Instead they acclaimed it as Mr. Robinson's compromise. Nor did they seem to boggle at his conception of it as the one perfect and sufficient plea for the release of the pictures. Here, on the evidence of the letters before me, we broke our silence in terms that caused unnecessary dismay. But I have no recollection of what we said, or of having spoken at all.

Now came farewell to Frieda, which was both a mourning and an anxious moment. For the past fortnight her gusty visits to the Gallery had been as draughts of champagne. Now there were common anxieties, and apprehensions on both sides concerning the intentions of the other. She asked wistfully but not hopefully if we were satisfied with the conference in general and Mr. Robinson in particular. We must have answered unequivocally in whatever terms were current before Munich laid its overtones on *Appeasement*.

Two opposing theories issued from the conference: ours, that our lawyers had sold the pass to the *Daily Express* and *Daily Telegraph*, theirs (deducible from the following letters) that Dorothy and I were resolved to fight to Lawrence's last seized picture. Whatever either of us may have said I recall that Mr. Robinson's compromise seemed to be acquiring a viability of its own independent of the purpose it was to fulfil, which might bedevil our quest for artistic support.

Richardson Sowerby, Holden & Co./5, John Street/
Bedford Row/London, W.C. 1/10 July 1929

Dear Trotter,

I have been thinking over what you said last night, and I have never in my life arrived at such a definite conclusion on any subject before.

Here are some of my reasons why I think it would be a fatal mistake if you refuse to compromise:

1. I am absolutely convinced that whatever defence you put up the ultimate result will be the destruction of these works of art.

2. Apart altogether from your position as a Gallery you have the very definite legal obligation to protect

(a) the painter himself, whose property the pictures are, and

(b) those people who have purchased examples of his work.

If the pictures are destroyed the rights of both (a) and (b) have gone.

3. If you accept the compromise and give an undertaking not to exhibit the pictures again your Counsel will have an opportunity of stating in open Court the reasons which have influenced you, and we shall make abundantly clear that you have not agreed to the compromise through any fear of having the pictures destroyed so far as their character is concerned, but that you have been legally advised that this is the only possible step for you to take in order to avoid the risk of destruction and to protect the interests of the absent painter and your own customers, and that in fact you are being forced to take this step by the very circumstances of the case.

4. You mentioned to me that the painter himself were he consulted might disagree with his wife as to the wisdom of accepting the compromise. I think that is a very strong point, but I now present you with a complete answer to it.

   If, after this business is over, and you have given the undertaking (and you must remember that that undertaking will be given by the Warren Gallery, and not by the painter who is no party to these proceedings) and then the painter objects to the course which has been taken, he can himself exhibit or threaten to exhibit here such pictures as are not sold, and can in that manner directly challenge the authorities, and if the matter is taken up by the Court he himself runs the risk of their destruction.

5. You will not misunderstand me when I say that art of this description is not the popular conception of art, and while I entirely agree with your policy in making the Warren Gallery a means of showing what you yourself consider to be best modern art, yet I am quite convinced as an ordinary man of the world that if you fight this thing and lose it, and an order for destruction is made it will not be a good thing for the Gallery.

It is frightfully easy in a matter which so closely concerns yourself as this affair does to become what I would call obsessed with it. I do not mean thereby to merely magnify the importance of it to yourself, but I mean that you get so obsessed with your own views on the thing that you do not get a very clear view of the cold facts.

You see, the Act of Parliament does not really admit of any proper discussion or evidence about these matters. It places you entirely at the mercy not of any artist of some rival school but of a very commonplace practical person, and even if you appeal you go before people of the same type, and in reality you never get a fair trial at all from your point of view. Now, if the painter wants to take the risk himself he can do so subsequently, and while you would have to keep out of any actual exhibition yourself there would be no reason why you should not help him in fighting the case.

The decision, of course, must be yours, and I am always open to be convinced, but I never felt so certain of anything in all my life, and I think if we do accept this compromise you will be able to get before the public in one way or another all the views you desire to express.

You pointed out to me that if the matter was compromised certain sections of the press would in due course make comments upon it. I hope they do. They will present us with a wonderful opportunity of answering these comments, and while I am sure you will do it better, I myself, if the compromise were effective could write a wonderful article upon this business. The absence of the painter has presented us, in my view, with a golden opportunity, and if you think there is anything in my argument to-day it may be a question whether it would not be wiser that the painter should not be represented at all at the Court.

Yours sincerely,
Ralph A. Holden [246]

Holden's point that our undertaking could bind none but the Warren Gallery was as unconsoling as it was obvious. We, the Gallery, did not exhibit Lawrence's pictures to 12,000 prurients and a common informer. So far were we from wishing to woo an unstable public that we had even cut down private view invitations to a selected list of seasoned viewers. The march of the 10,000 was the work of one or two newspapers for purposes of sale and gain.

Dorothy now hand-wrote a long and bracing letter to Lawrence, lest Frieda should infect him with the submissive overtones of Mr. Robinson's compromise; for this might mean the ignominious return of the pictures as undesirable objects not worth a bonfire, in complete vindication of the filthy campaign. The letter was taken by Victor Cunard to be posted from Rome, where he was special Correspondent of *The Times*. He was to telephone Lawrence on his arrival.[247] This letter crossed with the following: [248]

[*Hotel Porta Rossa?*] *Florence/Sat. night* [*13 July 1929*]

❨ *Dear Dorothy* [*Warren*]

Frieda came all right—but wrenched her foot again, and limps—otherwise is blooming, and all sorts of fine feathers making her a fine bird. She says she had a coruscating fortnight. I had a nasty chill in my inside —special Italian sort, Forte beach, Forte water etc. etc. —but it's passing. No need for poor F. to rush here.

Your telegram come—but you don't say if you've got the pictures out of prison—and I'm so anxious about that. The letter has not come—Victor Cunard wired about it. I will answer at once when it does. You know Almari's have a shop in London, near Brit. Museum—but I'll hunt here on Monday.

I'm sure you are worn out. But do get me all my pictures back safely—

I am so anxious about that. And don't sell any more of them at those prices—I'd rather keep them: why sell them at all?

Very many thanks for the lovely jade box—but I had to drop a tear in it when I thought of my Boccaccio in gaol.

Waiting your letter—and thank you both for being so nice to Frieda. She'll write too—but now her limp is an occupation!

D.H.L. [249]

Philip Trotter

It would have been difficult to get the pictures out of prison before we had shown cause why they should not be destroyed; and "why sell them at all?" was an inopportune question to a gallery owner who has paid all expenses of the exhibition even to the framing of the water-colours and is now facing a legal action in respect of the pictures. But here is Lawrence's reply to Dorothy's letter. With its mounting tempo and rally of symbols, new, or echoing *Apocalypse* of nearby date it marks a single momentary return of the vitality so long missing from his letters. [250]

Hotel Porta Rossa/Florence/14 July 1929

〘 Dear Dorothy [Warren]

Your long and very interesting letter this morning. [251] Lord, what a go! But I think it's a mistake to want to go to High Court. [252] What to do? prove that the pictures are not obscene? but they are not, so how prove it? And if they go against you there, then more is lost than will be got back in years. No no, I want you to accept the compromise. I do not want my pictures to be burned, under any circumstances or for any cause. The law, of course, must be altered—it is blatantly obvious. Why burn my pictures to prove it? There is something sacred to me about my pictures, and I will not have them burnt, for all the liberty of England. I am an Englishman, and I do my bit for the liberty of England. But I am most of all a man, and my first creed is that my manhood and my sincere utterance shall be inviolate and beyond nationality or any other limitation. To admit that my pictures should be burned, in order to change an English law, would be to admit that sacrifice of life to circumstance which I most strongly disbelieve in. No, at all costs or any cost, I don't want my pictures burnt. No more crucifixions, no more martyrdoms, no more autos da fé, as long as time lasts, if I can prevent it. Every crucifixion starts a most deadly chain of karma, every martyr is a Laocoön snake to tangle up the human family. Away with such things.

I want you to get my pictures back. If you have to promise never to show them again in England, I do not care. England can change its mind later if it wants to—it can never call back a burnt picture. If the things are burnt, I shall not break my heart. But I shall certainly have much less hope of England, and much less interest in it.

If you want to arrange a show in Germany, and can, I don't mind, but I am not keen that you should do it. I should like you soon to wind up the show altogether—sell the pictures at much better prices, if there are purchasers. If there are no purchasers, I am just as well content, I have no need and no desire to sell. You can have Contadini for £20, if that is the one you want—it is a favorite of mine. I want you to give North Sea (of course, if you recover them) to St. John H[utchinson]. for Maria Huxley, according to long promise. Orioli wants to buy Dandelions for £20. About the disposal of the others I will write you in detail when you are ready to close the show. But we want to take a house in France or Italy this autumn, and I shall have most of the pictures back to hang in the rooms, as at the Mirenda. I am most grateful for all you and Philip Trotter have done, but now it is about enough, and anything else will be in the nature of an anti-climax.

Tante belle cose!

D. H. Lawrence

We leave here Tuesday [16 July 1929] for Baden Baden
c/o Frau von Richthofen/Ludwig-Wilhelmstift [253]

Frieda Lawrence Ravagli

[Hotel] Porta Rossa [Florence]/Sunday [14 July 1929]

Dear Dorothy [Warren],

Your long letter to Lawrence only came this morning. So you got an adjournment we guess. There is a lot to be said for your fight to the finish plan. But Lawrence and I who have been up against it so often, know what can be done at one go. If you overdo our side the Soloman's baby i.e. pictures will be burnt. That would be a feather in *their* cap. You have won so far with showing the pictures at all, and it's all been a great advertisement for us all round. One has got the thin end of the wedge in, a new way of looking at things started. Let's go slow and sure and with a *far* vision. Keep some of your fighting spirit for future occasions, keep some in reserve. I have so enjoyed these London days and you and Philip. I am glad to be with Lawrence, we are so *sure* of ourselves in the long run. Don't take it too seriously!

Love

F.[254]

Philip Trotter

An adjournment of the hearing from the 12th to 18th July, negotiated by Mr. Robinson, was the only concrete result of the conference of 9 July; but this was almost immediately extended by the police to the 8th August to accord with Mr. Hester's summer holiday. We thus had virtually a month for the tasks Hutchinson had assigned to us. We were to seek testimony from authorities in every field of art that Lawrence was a true artist of the brush as well as of the pen, and from the walls of the great public collections that his subjects and treatment were in an accepted tradition; we were also to draft and issue a protest for signature by a much wider section of the public, against the application to irreplaceable pictures of an act framed for the suppression of pornographic books and postcards. Work among the living fell naturally to Geoffrey Scott on his long round of farewell visits and parties among precisely the people whose support we craved.[255]

Geoffrey Scott

17 July 1929

My dear Arnold [Bennett],

I do not know if you have seen in the papers anything of the action taken by the Police in regard to the Lawrence pictures, but I feel sure that if you were in the country your artistic spirit would have been shocked by what took place, and that you would have felt moved to lend your moral support in defense of common sense and decency. I am sorry you did not manage to see the pictures before you left, for they are exceedingly interesting. . . . Augustus John,[256] Colin Agnew, and other first-rate painters and critics, were greatly impressed by Lawrence's work. There [are] some smaller fry who would not allow that literary men should take to painting. The charge of obscenity was ridiculous. The force of the pictures was naturally disturbing to common minds; the nudes un-figleaved—and that is all there is to it. In no sense can they be regarded as the pictorial equivalent of *Lady Chatterley;* Lawrence is clearly exceedingly serious in his pictures, and there is a certain great lack of [latent?] [257] force of imagination in some of them.

One or two papers elected to "stunt" the Exhibition as a challenge to propriety. This brought a host of undesirable Philistine gazers to the Gallery. The Authorities visited the Gallery privately, and decided that no action was called for; but almost at the end of the show, when it had been running over three weeks, some fanatics forced the Police to take action. As a result, four burly policemen arrived at the Gallery. I happened to be present at the moment of the raid, which was indescribably farcical. The raiders had a warrant to impound books as well as pictures, and after close examination and prolonged confabulation, they seized the Nonesuch Edition of the drawings of William Blake. This will give you an idea of the competence of Scotland Yard to deal in such matters. The Blake was subsequently released, because it was pointed out to the Police that his centenary was recently [celebrated] with Divine Service in several churches. Thirteen of Lawrence's pictures were removed to the Police Court. Dorothy was summoned to "show cause why they should not be burnt." The Law, it appears, precludes the Gallery from calling witnesses to give their opinion on the point of issue; the destruction or survival of the Lawrence pictures lies entirely at the discretion of Mr. Justice Mead. Quite apart from any particular question as to the merit of Lawrence as an artist, this obviously raises a point of principle of the first importance. The lawyers say that the action is entirely without precedent. The methods employed are those devised for the exculpation of the indecent postcard trade, and no such raid has previously been executed on the work of a serious man shown at a serious gallery. ([Other galleries] were exceedingly anxious to procure this exhibition for themselves.) Ignorant and ill-qualified censorship is bad enough as applied to books, but where it threatens the existence of unique and irreplaceable objects it becomes a menace indeed. The sole criterion adopted by the Police was the presence or otherwise of pubic hair in the nudes (hence the impounding of William Blake).[258] As it has obviously come to splitting pubic hairs, the National Gallery will have many gaps on its walls.[259]

Meanwhile, the pictures are in jeopardy, and Lawrence, who is gravely ill, is in great distress about them; while Dorothy, whose Gallery has been a singularly serious and disinterested enterprise, is subjected to the treatment devised for pornographic street vendors. It is difficult to take effective action owing to the strictness of the law debarring the discussion in print of a matter which is "sub judice." An adjournment of the Police proceedings to the 29th July has been secured. Her Counsel is St. John Hutchinson.

It seems wise to distinguish between two aspects of the case, the general, and the particular. Even those who have not seen Lawrence's pictures, or who do not admire them, or even think them objectionable, may feel very strongly against the principle of summary destruction of works of art at the discretion of four policemen and a Police Magistrate. On this account, signatures will be invited to a protest based simply and explicitly on this one point. Whichever way the case turns, those who admire the pictures as works of art, or respect the sincerity of Lawrence as an artist, can give most valuable assistance by notifying Hutchinson of their willingness to have their opinions cited should opportunity offer, and the Law permit it. I feel very sure that the whole situation is one which would have engaged your sympathy had you been here, and there is no one whose support would have been more effective. I am hoping that even at a distance you will identify yourself with those who think the matter calls for defense action. Will you consent to add your name to the signatories of the enclosed statement? (It has only just been drafted, and I think can hardly fail to obtain powerful backing.) If so, you will be doing both Lawrence and Dorothy the greatest kindness by wiring your consent. Anything further, or stronger, that you may feel prompted to do would, of course, be invaluable, and, I need not say, would be most deeply appreciated by Dorothy as an act of friendship, though it is on the wider grounds of liberty and good sense that I am writing to you.

Unfortunately, I have to return to America in a few days. It was great luck that I had a chance to see you in my tantalisingly brief visit.

My homage to Dorothy and yourself,

Yours ever
Geoffrey Scott [260]

Philip Trotter

We ourselves set round the London galleries. The eye trained rapidly to the technique of sweeping a great wall, skipping huge masterpieces to alight on a square half foot of defence detail. In a few days we amassed a collection of photographs which, by comparison, threw an almost conventional propriety over the forlorn thirteen in the condemned cell.

Most of our impressive haul of reproductions is now dispersed; but I have before me photographs of two representations of Leda and the swan: the superb Michel Angelo painting in the National Gallery,[261] which was to figure in the trial; and, from the Wallace Collection, an inkstand of Italian majolica, surmounted by a group representing Leda and the swan,[262] made probably at Urbino in the late 16th century, perhaps the most realistic treatment ever applied to this venerable legend. The latter, Frieda said, would have shocked Lawrence deeply. What would have happened if the Michel Angelo had been in the Warren Gallery on the 5th July is one of the might-have-beens that defy speculation; for in it the lady is up and doing, complete master of the situation. I must pay quick but grateful tribute to the initiative of our American friend of the raid-and-ballet evening round the open-air statuary of London. I find a "Kodak Ltd." envelope containing twelve shots, close-up and otherwise, of Peter Pan in Kensington Gardens; our friend thought the anatomical dawnings allowed by the too short tunic more unsettling to the immature than Lawrence's forthright nudes. The collection delighted Hutchinson; but was voted unlikely to impress the Magistrate.

But with Musketts ahead there was one big gap in our defences. In his letter to Arnold Bennett, Geoffrey Scott had written:

The sole criterion adopted by the Police was the presence or otherwise of pubic hair in the nudes (hence the impounding of William Blake).[263] As it has obviously come to splitting pubic hairs, the National Gallery will have many gaps on its walls.[264]

This begged a question to which our search was to give an unequivocal NO. From our tour of all the great London repositories we went on to explore the galleries of the world as contained in the files of the splendid Witt Library of reproductions, whose founder, the late Sir Robert Witt, had charged the Custodian to give us all assistance. We found much that we should have shrunk from exhibiting ourselves; but neither on the walls of London nor in the files of the library was there a single occurrence of the feature that had formed Mr. Hester's terms of reference. This was Lawrence's innovation: if the police had visited us as custodians of a rigidly maintained aesthetic convention, their case would have been unassailable. All new forms of art shock or repel by their newness, and I think Lawrence's uncompromising realism created a certain malaise in most of us [265] and since Mr. Muskett will distil the last drop of prejudice from the venerable ban it is pertinent to quote a famous scientific authority on its merits:

The omission of the pudendal hair [writes Havelock Ellis], in representations of the nude (in classic art) was, for instance, quite natural, for the people of countries still under Oriental influence are accustomed to remove the hair from the body. If, however, under quite different conditions, we perpetuate that artistic convention to-day, we put ourselves in a perverse relation to nature. There is ample evidence of this. "There is one convention so ancient, so necessary, so universal," writes Mr. Frederick Harrison (*Nineteenth Century and After*, August 1907), "that its deliberate defiance to-day may arouse the bile of the least squeamish of men and should make women withdraw at once." If boys and girls were brought up at their mother's knees in familiarity with pictures of beautiful and natural nakedness, it would be impossible for anyone to write such wicked and shameful words as these.[266]

Meanwhile our quest for eminent artistic testimony had opened auspiciously with the assent of a Big Four, later augmented to Five, handpicked it might seem not only for their stature, but for the diversity of their roles in the complex of art. But three of them would have been appealed to in any crisis affecting the judgment of the Warren Gallery. These were Augustus John, who telephoned his assent from his Hampshire home, Colin Agnew, of the genuineness of whose judgment the police were witness, and later, on his return from a professional tour, Dr. Tancred Borenius.[267] The remaining two were Glyn Philpot[268] and Sir William Orpen.[269] The former was secured to our purposes by Geoffrey Scott, and it was fitting that Glyn Philpot should give his name in defence of D. H. Lawrence; for he too had a Daimon that once or twice compelled him away from the fleshpots of fashionable portrait painting to renew the springs of his self-expression. On the need for Orpen the world was unanimous and Hutchinson insistent. For Orpen was twice a rarity: a genuine artist who enjoyed the favour of the State (first rarity) and used it without detriment to his artistic integrity (second rarity). For this rich prize it was felt a little wooing might be necessary; an interview in Orpen's studio was arranged by his brother-in-law, the late Sir William Rothenstein,[270] Principal of the Royal College of Art. We went through portfolios of enchanting drawings, rough sketches from the battlefields and impish private intimacies from Versailles; boon-companionship was his famous secondary art. But sundry teddy-bears and other nursery trappings littered among the gems from his brush and pencil betrayed an infantilist streak; it soon became clear that Orpen liked to be told by an attractive woman that he was really just a big baby. This was too high a price for Dorothy to pay for any favour, and the observation finally came from the great man himself; but he said "child." I think he had all along intended to support the defence; and we came home grateful and triumphant.

But in that hot July five swallows did not make a summer, for Dorothy had sensed a winter wind from Bloomsbury in the dudgeon of Lytton Strachey [271] and the silence of Roger Fry.[272] To Geoffrey Scott, after what he described as an enchanting half hour, Strachey had lapsed into sulks on the mere mention of the Lawrence exhibition. He thought it a mistake and the pictures poor, and with that he tried to dismiss it. But at the end of the visit he praised it with faint damns in the context of the impending trial. "At least you think the pictures respectable?" asked Geoffrey. "Much too respectable," he snapped in his high falsetto. The reaction was symptomatic rather than intrinsically tragic; for Strachey was neither artist nor art critic. But he was a hierarch of Bloomsbury, as eminent in letters as Roger Fry in art. Mr. David Garnett has recorded how he boiled with rage over the suppression of *The Rainbow*; [273] but Dorothy may not have known this.

From Roger Fry we had expected unsolicited support. A few years earlier, in his essay "London Sculptors and Sculptures" [274] Fry had seemed to engage himself as the lifelong champion of exactly such a cause as we were now fighting. The erection of Epstein's [275] *Rima* memorial to W. H. Hudson in the unfrequented corner of Hyde Park where pet dogs have their last resting-place had been the occasion of a militant uprising of the Philistines, who smeared the figure with green paint and clamoured for its removal. In a section of his essay devoted to Epstein, Fry wrote:

We [Fry and Epstein] can settle our quarrels elsewhere and at another time; for the moment all who care for art of whatever shade must face the common foe and stop once for all his arrogant attempt to lay down the law out of the abundance of his ignorance and insensibility. I say once for all, but . . . his voice will never be completely silent; only, from time to time, the Philistine can be made to see that as he has always made a fool of himself in the past, the probabilities are that he always will.[276]

Actually Lawrence's claim on Fry was stronger than Epstein's; for, since *Rima* was not posted over the canine dead for purposes of sale and gain, the custodians of Hyde Park could not be called upon to show cause why the work should not be destroyed. Moreover, the Warren Gallery had earned Roger Fry's gratitude on the 5th July. In a prominent alcove of the Velvet Room an exquisite alabaster male statuette from Fry's collection was displayed for purposes of sale and gain. We might have been excused if, in the breathless pause between the two police visits, we had forgotten to hide it. And what then? for the little figure's phallus was a tiny shaft of alabaster loosely held in a socket; Lawrence's flat two-dimensional "obscenities" might have been almost forgotten in the convulsions that must have followed its discovery. But, as the blind van drew up at the street door, we rushed the Gaudier to the top floor and buried it under the mass of tow and tissue that lurks behind a wedding.

Dorothy pondered: were the sins of the Warren Gallery so inexpiable as to stifle Fry's knight-errantry? We turned to Lawrence's "Introduction to These Paintings." All Bloomsbury is there lampooned, not by name, but round Mr. Clive Bell's [277] famous phrase *Significant Form*. This is placed, as the slogan of the "New Primitive Methodists of Art Criticism," side by side with the Lamb of God, that symbol which Lawrence, though aware of a Balaam's Ass in his own belly, could tolerate in no one's church window; and its votaries are mocked with his two bugbears, Goethe and Plato. To be lampooned in such high company is tolerable; but Roger Fry, Bloomsbury's tribune of the plastic arts, is named and taken to task. One of Fry's few unguarded phrases, in his brilliant study of Cézanne, gives Lawrence his chance. "With all his [Cézanne's] rare endowments," wrote Fry, "he happened to lack the . . . gift of illustration, the gift that any draughtsman for the illustrated newspapers learns in a school of commercial art . . . ." [278] "[This] sentence," flashes Lawrence, "gives away at once the hollowness of modern criticism. [Can] one learn a gift in a school of commercial art . . . ?" [279] and he launches into a defence of Cézanne's draughtsmanship, which Fry has nowhere assailed. It is a question, which is the more incongruous picture: the amateur artist belabouring the Olympian critic in an essay introducing his pictures at their first exhibition, or D. H. Lawrence defending Cézanne against Roger Fry, who looked back to Cézanne as the "tribal deity" and "totem" of his circle in their formative years. [280]

The Cézanne section of the "Introduction to These Paintings"—some fifteen pages in all—is autobiographically fascinating and invites a digression in this history, since it contains the essence of Lawrence's artistic experience, and stands, far more than the earlier sections, as introduction, not only to the paintings, but to the police raid and court action. Its mood of truculent exuberance is the measure of what painting could do for his spirit when the flesh was failing him. But that is only its manner, and even Mr. Earp finds "his eulogy of the Master of Aix noble and moving." [281] Yet most of Cézanne is swept aside, the portraits and genre paintings as banal, the landscapes as "acts of rebellion against the mental concept of landscape." [282] There remain the still-lifes with their apples; and Cézanne's apple, as symbolic to Lawrence as Eve's, evokes his most inspired and sustained exaltation of intuitive over mental consciousness, his most vehement and colourful assault on the cliché. It is the story of a dual conflict, Cézanne against "the tyranny of mind, the white, worn-out arrogance of the spirit," whose domination, says Lawrence, tortured him, and Cézanne against "the hydra-headed cliché, whose last head he could never lop off." So Cézanne is the hero of a struggle in which he is ultimately worsted. "After a fight tooth-and-nail for forty years, he did succeed in knowing an apple, fully . . . . That was all he achieved." "So," he concludes, "the conflict, as usual, was not between the artist and his medium, but between the artist's *mind* and the artist's *intuition* and *instinct*." [283] It is Lawrence's own conflict projected on to a brilliantly observed Cézanne.

Hostility notwithstanding, Lawrence's tribute to Cézanne is indebted to Fry's masterly study, though the latter issues in a grand panorama of achievement, sees the conflict as between the artist and his medium, and traces Cézanne's development in plane sequences, volumes, colour harmonies, and all the current coin of criticism of which Fry was the master minter, and which Lawrence satirizes so boisterously in the closing paragraphs of his essay. The panorama is eclipsed to Lawrence by the shadow of the cliché, his life-long dread, which here covers a multitude of merits as well as failings. But throughout the essay the shadow lifts and falls; and once, after a rather fatuous digression from art to science, which is dismissed as "just occult," an exquisitely observed passage shows Cézanne surmounting the cliché and bidding defiance to its static view of the inanimate world in "landscapes" where "we are fascinated by the mysterious *shiftiness* of the scene," which "has its own weird anima . . . and changes like a living animal under our gaze." [284]

Interesting, too, is the attack on Roger Fry; for it was inevitable without the adventitious pretext of a logical slip. Mr. Bell has written that Fry "had a genius for holding his aesthetic emotion in suspense, analysing its object, and expressing the result in admirably lucid equivalents." [285] Could Lawrence ever have come to terms with a process of vision so alien to his own?

Both heartening and sobering reflections arose out of our two quests. From eminent living authorities we had magnificent support; but the dedicated slayer of Philistines was sulking in his tent. Old masters had furnished a rich bag of obscenities; but Lawrence had transgressed an ancient rule which, though remote from any possible moral issue, had revealed the police as upholders of artistic as well as civil law. This chequerboard forms the background of our third and last quest, the issuing of a circular letter and protest form.

For this we had distinguished drafters. Geoffrey Scott, after preparing and rejecting several attempts, took his choice of them to Desmond Mac-Carthy; [286] and, during part of a visit that was to figure exactly one month later in MacCarthy's obituary tribute to Geoffrey Scott,[287] they worked on it together. MacCarthy did little more than approve; but this was a happy break in the dark cloud hanging over our relations with Bloomsbury. All Geoffrey's drafts contained the fruits of his conviction, obstinately held, that the convergence of D. H. Lawrence and the Warren Gallery was a value to be exploited in any appeal to cultivated people. But Dorothy was not converted; her sole message to her readers was the peril to serious art from the Common Informer with his secret oath, and the consequent seizing of Blake's drawings by arbiters appointed under the Obscenities Act. The letter, as it went out over the last weekend in July, is almost entirely Geoffrey, with the background embellishments left out:

The Warren Gallery/39a Maddox Street, W. 1
Dear

We have recourse to you in defence of a public principle raising an issue of serious moment to all cultivated English people. The matter arises out of the pending police proceedings against the pictures of Mr. D. H. Lawrence, but goes far beyond the controversial question as to the merit of any individual artist's work.

The principle which we ask you to support is embodied in the following formula:

"Since many pictures admittedly of great artistic value contain details which might be condemned as 'harmful to the morals of those who are unstable in mind or immature,' we protest in principle against the destruction of pictures on that ground. The burning of a book does not necessarily destroy it, and condemned books have sometimes taken their places among the classics, but the burning of a picture is irreparable."

Although Mr. Lawrence's pictures have been admired by several distinguished painters, critics and connoisseurs, we are not here inviting your judgment on his ability in the field of painting, or indeed on any other question specifically relating to his case.

This is the point at issue.

The law as it stands allows that an anonymous "common informer" instigated by the sensationalist section of the press, may put in action machinery by which a serious artist's work is placed in peril of total destruction.

It is not difficult to recall instances in the past where work of the highest

Dance-Sketch

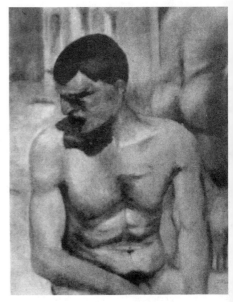

Contadini

Oil paintings by Lawrence exhibited in the Warren Gallery in 1929.

Rape of the Sabine Women

A room of the Warren Gallery, 39a Maddox Street, London, W. 1, with some of the early paintings replacing seized pictures. At left, *Fauns and Nymphs.* In center, *Finding of Moses.* At upper right, *Rape of the Sabine Women.* From a photograph, taken after the raid of 5 July 1929, now in the possession of Mr. Philip Trotter.

The Warren Gallery, photographed after the raid.

The Warren Gallery, photographed after the raid. Over the mantel, *Resurrection*. Above the sofa, *Flight Back into Paradise*. Over the bookcase, *Red Willow Trees*. From a photograph in the possession of Mr. Philip Trotter.

Dorothy Warren Trotter and Philip Trotter, photographed in the Velvet Room of the Warren Gallery after the trial of 8 August 1929. Mr. Trotter is holding the copy of *Pencil Drawings of William Blake*. From a photograph in the possession of Mr. Trotter.

Throwing Back the Apple

Renascence of Men

Water colors by Lawrence
exhibited in the Warren
Gallery in 1929.

The Lizard

value has aroused a prejudice, when first seen, which has afterwards given place to acknowledged and general acceptance. It is noteworthy that, during the raid on Mr. Lawrence's exhibition a volume of William Blake's pencil drawings after careful examination was selected for seizure. It was subsequently released on attention being drawn to the fact that Blake's centenary was recently celebrated with services in various churches.

To protect contemporary art from the grave menace implied in the terms of the summons issued in regard to Mr. Lawrence's work is the sole object of our present appeal. On the merits of a case which is sub judice we are debarred from entering. We only ask your support for the broad principle stated in the above formula. If, as we feel confident, you are in agreement with its terms, will you please give us your signature? The names of signatories may be quoted by our counsel Mr. St. John Hutchinson, at his discretion, as endorsing the precise statement here set forth.

We enclose a form for signature and an envelope stamped and addressed.

Form for Signature
On the principle set forth, I protest against the destruction of D. H. Lawrence's pictures.
Signed:
Enclosed: Envelope addressed to: Secretary, the Warren Gallery,/39a Maddox Street,/London, W. 1

I find no record of the number sent out, or the total of signatures received. Large numbers of these little slips are undoubtedly lost; but from approximately seventy still extant I make the following selection.

Lytton Strachey	Sir William Orpen
Roger Fry	Jacob Epstein
Leonard Woolf	Frank Rutter [288]
Virginia Woolf	Albert Rutherston [289]
Clive Bell	Allenby [290]
Vanessa Bell	Sefton Brancker [291]
Duncan Grant	C. P. Scott [292]
Desmond MacCarthy	Mansfield Forbes [293]
Maynard Keynes	Nancy Mitford [294]
Augustus John	V. Sackville-West [295]
Colin Agnew	The Rt. Hon. Harold Baker [296]
Dr. Tancred Borenius	Gladwyn & Cynthia Jebb [297]
Glyn Philpot	Numerous members of Parliament

Gwen John,[298] for whose luminous notice see p. 333, sent the following:
Aug. 1 1929
To the Directors of the Warren Gallery
I could not sign the formula embodied in your letter to me of July 31 on a detached and inadequate form where the words "set forth above" have no

application. But I object strongly to the destruction of any serious and sincerely created work, even though in my opinion such work may not be suited to public exhibition. Such action seems to me to be cruel and indefensible, because without sincerity we can have no art. Therefore I object to the destruction of D. H. Lawrence's pictures.

Gwen John

Miss John did indeed put her finger on an oversight on our part. Her other reservation adds weight to her tribute to the artistic value of Lawrence's painting.

It is doubtful whether the names of those who took the trouble to specify their reasons for not signing are public property like those of the signatories. But the following was never intended to be private and was a cherished exhibit until the 8th August:

Beefsteak Club/9 Green St./Leicester Square W.C. 2/ 2 August, 1929
My dear Philip
I never sign protests, and even if I wished to, I haven't seen the pictures: but as the police are the only people in England who take any interest in art or literature, I think it is only fair that their opinion should carry a preponderating weight.

Yours,
MB [Maurice Baring] [299]

And the following is fair game:

The Manse/Eastwood/Notts
Rev. E. C. Shave, MA   August 7 1929
Dear Madam,
Even though I live in Mr. Lawrence's home-town I fear that I must refuse my signature even though I agree with the actual principle involved.

I don't seem to remember Mrs. Hilton who recommended you to write to me, but that may be my faulty memory!

Yours truly
Eric C. Shave

All my life I have from time to time gone back to paint, because it gave me a form of delight that words can never give. Perhaps the joy in words goes deeper and is for that reason more unconscious. The *conscious* delight is certainly stronger in paint. I have gone back to paint for real pleasure—and by paint I mean copying, copying either in oils or waters. I think the greatest pleasure I ever got came from copying Fra Angelico's "Flight into Egypt" and Lorenzetti's big picture of the Thebaid, in each case working from photographs and putting in my own colour . . . . Then I *really* learned what life, what powerful life has been put into every curve, every motion of a great picture. Purity of spirit, sensitive awareness, intense eagerness to portray an inward vision, how it all comes.[300]

Before returning to the Lawrence country after the raid, Mrs. Clarke had promised to collect a few specimens of Lawrence's early work to fill the gaps on the gallery's walls. This took her over a fortnight; but on the 28th July we were able to announce "More Paintings by D. H. Lawrence" in *The Times*. With our gleanings from the public galleries accessible on the table, this was as near as we got to our post-raid project of "another show called 'D. H. Lawrence and his Masters.'"

In an earlier section of "Making Pictures" than that quoted above, Lawrence, after describing how, when he tried to paint from nature or plaster-casts, "the 'object,' be what it might, was always slightly repulsive to me once I sat down in front of it . . . ," continues:

I learnt to paint from copying other pictures—usually reproductions; sometimes even photographs. When I was a boy, how I concentrated over it! Copying some perfectly worthless scene reproduction in some magazine. I worked with almost dry water-colour, stroke by stroke, covering half a square-inch at a time, each square-inch perfect and completed, proceeding in a kind of mosaic advance, with no idea at all of laying on a broad wash. Hours and hours of intense concentration, inch by inch progress, in a method entirely wrong—and yet those copies of mine managed, when they were finished, to have a certain something that delighted me: a certain glow of life, which was beauty to me. A picture lives with the life you put into it. . . . Even if you only copy . . . an old bridge, some sort of keen, delighted awareness of the old bridge or of its atmosphere, or the image it has kindled inside you, can go over on to the paper and give a certain touch of life to a banal conception.[301]

Here is the catalogue of this strangely-wrought collection:

OILS

Flower-piece

WATER COLOURS

After Fra Angelico [Flight into Egypt]	Elm Trees
	The Orange Market
Study of a Tiger	The Road
The Stick Gatherer	Still Life (Apples)
Autumn Trees	Boy Paddling [302]

The season was over; art critics and their readers were scattered; but the annual August invasion from the provinces brought us visitors from the Lawrence country, among them Mr. Arthur Statham, Producer of the Newstead House Players of Nottingham; and this is what he contributed to the (London) *Evening News* (It will be observed that, though not published till a week after the trial, it was written while the pictures were still in custody, also that Mr. Statham had visited the original exhibition):

The gaps left upon the walls of the Warren Gallery, London, after the recent seizure by the police of a number of paintings by Mr. D. H. Lawrence, the well-known Nottingham novelist and poet, have been attractively filled by a further selection from the same artist's works. . . .

In some respects the reconstituted exhibition is even more interesting than the original arrangement, since the newly-added paintings belong to an earlier period than many of those so dramatically seized, and by reason of their more conventional subjects and treatment serve to dispel very effectively the charge put forward in some quarters that Mr. Lawrence, apart altogether from any moral issues raised, could neither draw nor paint with sufficient merit to justify the exhibition of his paintings.

AN ABSURD ALLEGATION.

The allegation was absurd to any but the most casual critic. People who disliked, or shrank from the frank honesty of the paintings, sometimes preferred to fall back upon reference to "ugly composition, colouring and drawing."

The newly-shown pictures are a most complete answer to these critics, for we have here a dozen paintings in oil and water colour which, while comparatively unimportant productions when measured against the strength and intellectual force shown in the paintings comprising the original exhibition, are yet notable for qualities of composition, harmony of colour, and delicacy of touch such as would do credit to the most graceful of artists.

There is "The Stick Gatherer"—recalling some early Corot's; there's a study of two green apples, and a little sea-piece called "Boy Paddling"; these are wholly delightful.

FORCE OF EXPRESSION.

Avoiding a discussion of any of the dozen or so pictures at present under lock and key, the case being still sub judice, there remain on public view paintings forming part of the original exhibition with which to compare the earlier and simpler paintings now added.

The difference is one affecting subject, size and treatment. In the earlier examples of his brushwork he has a good deal less to express; in the later work the importance of what he has to say overshadows all the time mere manner and technique. Force of expression rather than draughtsmanship is pulling at the artist here.

Mention may be made of "Flight back into Paradise." This picture, one may suppose, is one of those embodying the points summarized by the superficial critics as "ugly composition, colouring and drawing." Yet what a forceful expression of the idea underlying it!

Contend as you may about the qualities of composition, drawing and colour, this picture remains a fitting, forceful expression of what the artist desired to say.[303]

Mr. Statham's evident appraisal of the new pictures as original compositions is perhaps a tribute to Lawrence's ability to assimilate these rather banal little photographs to his own vision; but it is strange that he should have missed, or failed to record, the one gem in the collection. His water-colour copy of a great master, Fra Angelico's *Flight into Egypt,* which Dorothy recalled from Byron Villas in her letter to Lawrence of 26 June 1928, and which she and Catherine Carswell hailed with delight in Mrs. Clarke's consignment, was a miracle of skill in draughtsmanship and of taste in the selection of colour.

"Making Pictures" was not the only product of Lawrence's pen to appear between the raid and trial. I have taken the following from the *Notts Evening Post;* it was published rather more fully in the *Daily Express* of the same date (11 July 1929) under the sub-title "Censored Painter on Shocking Pictures."

SEIZED PICTURES

MR. LAWRENCE REPLIES TO/HOME SECRETARY

NOTTS. PAINTER ON MOB/LAW IN ART

BEAUTY OF SEX APPEAL

Mr. D. H. Lawrence, the Notts. novelist and painter, who has recently had some of his pictures seized by the police in London, is publishing at the end of this month in a Paris periodical named "This Quarter" what he terms a reply to the British Home Secretary.[304]

The London "Express," by the courtesy of Mr. E. W. Titus, publisher of "This Quarter," gives some extracts from Mr. Lawrence's remarkable essay in his own defence. He opens with some pungent remarks:

"If a play shocks ten people in an audience, and does not shock the remaining five hundred, then it is obscene," he says, "to ten and innocuous to five hundred; the play is not obscene by a majority. 'Hamlet' shocked all the Cromwellian puritans and shocks nobody to-day, and some of Aristophanes shocks everybody to-day and did not galvanise the Greeks at all.

"Man is a changeable beast, and words change their meaning with him and things are not what they seemed and what's what becomes what isn't and if we think we know where we are, it's only because we are so rapidly being translated to somewhere else. We have to leave everything to the majority, everything to the mob, the mob, the mob.

"They know what is obscene and what isn't—they do. If the lower ten million doesn't know better than the upper ten men, then there is something wrong with mathematics. Have a vote on it! Show hands, and prove it by counting it!

"You cannot tamper with the great public, British or American. 'Vox populi, vox dei,' don't you know! At the same time, this vox dei shouts with praise for moving pictures and books and newspaper accounts that seem to a sinful nature like mine completely disgusting and obscene. Like a real prude and puritan I have to look the other way.

"When the vox populi, vox dei is hoarse with sentimental indecency, then I have to steer away like a Pharisee afraid of being contaminated. There is a certain kind of pitch that I refuse to touch.

"YOU ACCEPT THE MOB"

"So, again, it comes down to this: you accept the majority, the mob, and its decisions, or you don't. You bow down before the vox populi, vox dei, or you plug your ears not to see [? hear] its obscene howl.

"You perform your antics to please the vast public, deus ex machina, or you refuse to perform for the public at all unless now and then you pull its elephantine and ignominious leg. When it comes to the meaning of anything, even the simplest word, then you must pause, because there are two great categories of meaning forever separate. There is mob meaning and there is individual meaning.

"Even quite advanced art critics would try to make us believe that any picture or book which had a sex appeal was, ipso facto, a bad book or picture. This is just canting hypocrisy.

"Half the great poems, pictures, music, stories of the whole world are great by virtue of the beauty of their sex appeal. Titian or Renoir, the Song of Solomon or Jane Eyre, Mozart or Annie Laurie—the loveliness is all interwoven with sex appeal, sex stimulus, call it what you will.

"Perhaps it may be argued that a mild degree of sex appeal is not pornographic, whereas a high degree is. But this is a fallacy. Boccaccio at his hottest seems to me less pornographic than Pamela or Clarissa Harlowe or even Jane Eyre, or a host of modern books or volumes which pass uncensored.

"Then what is pornography after all this? It isn't sex appeal or sex stimulus in art. It isn't even a deliberate intention on the part of the artist to arouse or excite sexual feelings.

"There is nothing wrong with sexual feelings in themselves so long as they are straightforward and not sneaking or sly. The right sort of sex stimulus is valuable to human daily life. Without it the world grows grey.

"I would give everybody the gay Renaissance stories to read. They would help to shake off a lot of grey self-importance which is our modern civilised disease." [305]

Otherwise the press of the period is not edifying. A particularly offensive paragraph by F. G. Stone in the *New Leader,* "D. H. Lawrence and Art," [306] drew a dignified protest in the paper from S. Hilton; [307] *John Bull,* in "Art for Dirt's Sake," published a burlesque trial of this exponent of "the higher pornography" before Mr. Justice Bull, who directed that "any further filth from Florence shall be immediately consigned to the nearest public incinerator." [308] *Bazaar,* in a full column, "Censoring Art," congratulated the police on their "wise & salutary step," only regretting that 8,000 had been allowed to visit the exhibition.[309] It rejoiced in "another instance . . . of the banning of nudes" when a book of drawings by Epstein was seized by the American Customs. Welcome relief came from the *Glasgow Bulletin* in "Artist of Ideas," "from our own Correspondent": "[From] the 'expurgated' exhibition that remains it is plain that [Lawrence] is an artist of ideas not merely in . . . subject but in the artistically more important points of arrangement and rhythm which one expects from a poet, and he has a real sense of colour." [310] The writer closes with special praise for *Red Willow Trees* and *Finding of Moses*.[311]

16 July 1929   Hotel Porta Rossa, Florence, Italy

❨ We are off just now [for Baden-Baden].[312]

Norman Douglas

I once asked [Lawrence] whom he was aiming at with *Lady Chatterley*, which was just then appearing. He said:

"The young writers. I want them to come out of their shells and be more frank. I want to encourage them—give them some 'kick.' As for the old ones—I don't care a pin whether they read *Lady C*. or not. There's nothing to be done with them; they are past human aid. Let them stew in their grease."

At that meeting I induced Lawrence to pay several whiskies-and-sodas for Orioli and myself; the surest way to win his regard was to make him suffer small losses of this kind. There must have been something wrong, however, with my masochistic theory, for not long afterwards he played a much better trick on us.

He was leaving for Germany with his wife and had invited Orioli for a farewell luncheon, his train being due to start early in the afternoon. Then it occurred to him that he would like to have me too, and he sent round word to that effect. I had another engagement but threw it over: "Lorenzo" was no ordinary person and, besides that, so ill that who could say whether I was ever going to see the poor devil alive again? We sat down at midday in a certain restaurant, Orioli and myself ordering the simplest dishes in view of Lorenzo's relative impecuniosity. He himself could not make up his mind what to eat. He was not feeling particularly hungry that day, and Frieda waited for him to decide. At last he thought he could manage some fish. They brought for his inspection the usual platter of raw fish, red mullets and the rest of them. He waved it aside; these small sea-beasts with their ten thousand bones were troublesome to deal with. Then the manager himself appeared, bearing an enormous tray in his arms. On it lay a sole, a single sole, a monster, one of the largest I ever saw in Italy; it would have done credit to Bond Street. He set it down ceremoniously and observed:

"This, gentlemen, is no fish. It is a museum-piece. It is a wonder. Lucky the client who gets it."

Lorenzo fell in love with the museum-piece. Frieda and he would have that wonder for luncheon, or nothing at all. I thought: that's going to cost him fifty or sixty francs. Well, it was no affair of mine; this was Lorenzo's luncheon; let him do as he pleases! The sole was long in cooking. Frieda had patience, but Lorenzo fumed and grew more and more concerned about the possibility of missing his train. He continually looked at his watch: was that wretched fish never coming? At last it arrived, and the two of them devoured what they could with irreverential haste. Lorenzo glanced at his watch—

"Good God! We're just in the nick of time. Hurry up! I can't pay now, because I've got only a few coppers and a five-hundred franc note which they'll never be able to change; we must settle up later. Now let's rush! You, Douglas, take Frieda to the station in a taxi. I'll go with Orioli in another, because I must fetch my bags at his place."

Arrived at the station Frieda, of course, had no money for the fare, because Lorenzo always kept the cash; I paid it. Orioli paid for the other taxi and porters, because Lorenzo had only a few coppers and a five-hundred franc note which they'll never be able to change. On our way home we also settled up the combined luncheon-bill; it amounted to a little less than a hundred francs, for which we have not yet been reimbursed. Meanwhile Lorenzo made himself comfortable in a corner seat, with his tweed overcoat thrown about him. No reference was made to the museum-piece either then or thereafter, and as the train moved out I thought to detect —it may have been imagination on my part—the phantom of a smile creeping over his wan face.[313]

GERMANY

20 July 1929   Hôtel Löwen, Lichtenthal bei Baden-Baden, Germany

❲ *Well, here we are, all right—it was hot yesterday, we just did nothing, but last night a long and lurid thunderstorm poured out endless white electricity and set us free—now it's delicious and cool and fresh.*

.   .   .   .

This is a nice old Gasthaus, quiet rooms on the garden, 9 marks a day pension. Lichtenthal is about 1½ miles from Baden, but it joins on now and is incorporated—and there is a tram. Even I can remember when it was a separate village. . . . Baden itself is incurably 1850, with the romance and the pathos and the bathos of Turgenev rather than Dostoievsky. Just now the trees are very green, the roses very pink and very numerous, the fountains very white, the visitors not many, and the music also a little pathetic. . . . But my wife and her mother want us to go on Wednesday [24 July 1929] up to the Plättig—about 3,000 feet up—only an hour or so drive from here. Everybody is crazy for altitude—except me, and I don't like it very much.[314]

Frieda Lawrence Ravagli

Hotel Plättig/bei Baden-Baden/23 July 1929

Dear Dorothy [Warren],

You are having such a bad, long strain on your nerves and Philip's. It's horrid! but I know you won't give in. I only wish Lawrence were strong enough to really fight, but he is not very well. I am glad we had the show, I am glad there's been a rumpus, future generations may want to pay vast sums for those pictures. Let the mud come to the surface, it's there right enough. I think of you with real affection, of your relation with Philip, do let's try and agree on details, because fundamentally we do! Lawrence just can't conceive the ordinary point of view! He is depressed about his health! He is so, so frail! But in a little while we'll all meet and have a good time! I am just ordering more canvasses for L. If I possibly can I'll come on the 8th [August 1929]. So I can do nothing, except my moral support!

It's hot, but lovely and fresh in these mountains.

Love
Frieda [315]

25 July 1929   Kurhaus Plättig, bei Bühl, Baden-Baden, Germany

⟨ Quite cool up here—had a huge storm—it's the usual Kurhaus with 150 people—and I am rather unhappy, and wish I was back in the south, and could see the olive trees and the Mediterranean. I hate these great

black pine forests—and this heavy, though good food. I should pine away
quite soon if I had to stay—fortunately I haven't.[316]

Frieda Lawrence Ravagli

Kurhaus Plättig/bei Baden-Baden/Tuesday [?30 July 1929]

Dear Dorothy [Warren],

Lawrence says, write to Dorothy. We had your long letter. Lawrence
has come up again and is writing. He just read me a bit:

> All stare at the spot
> Where a figleaf might be
> And was not— [317]

He is better, thank goodness. So, think you both of the good, quiet time
you'll both have soon and come and see us, but don't forget that Lawrence is as frail as one of those blue bird's eggs—but you know. I can't
really worry, it seemed all so very *interesting*, I mean worry about the pictures but I hate that they are in a cellar. Keep them till we want ours,
please, you have room in your Maida Vale house, haven't you. In the
long run we win, that I know in my bones. And I hope you are all right.
You have lots of friends, real ones, your brother and Monty and the others
let them go. It's cold here and I wish we were further south. Victor Cunard
wrote a nice letter. Agnew might be helpful. I wrote to Aldous, he ought
to do something. Do people still come to the Gallery? The ring of
Lawrence's influence seems to widen almost frighteningly—it seems too
much for his frail person. Philip and you must see him, I feel. I feel he is
so *alone*, people are so small and merely personal with him, when bigger
things are at issue. It seems to me only with genuine, frank human relationships can we win—some joy in each other and other living things. The
Mexicans (Aztecs) had a goddess of dirt, who was a filth eater, she must
have come to Europe for a change! and is swamping it. I don't know
why I write all this stuff. I fear you have all the actual brunt to bear,
but you enjoy it too, if you aren't tired! I would love to come on the 8th,
have you seen Mr. Meade's face? but Lawrence isn't well enough. I hope
we get news from you soon. You'll send a wire on the 8th. —Sometimes I
feel bodily in your gallery—and greet Mrs. Grover and Miss Young,[318]
and don't work too hard. We use the jade, Lawrence and I. When the
Italian, who printed Lady C (he didn't know one word of English) was

warned that it was obscene, he asked how? And when he was told just "lovemaking," he said: "Well, we do that every day," in great astonishment. Really I am indignant that you and Philip should have to fight the low canaille—you are *too* good for it!

Love and luck to us all!

Would you have lots of duty to pay if I sent you some Kirschwasser? I am sorry this is so dirty, my cast.

F.[319]

2 August 1929   Kurhaus Plättig, bei Bühl, Baden-Baden, Germany

⟨ *It has rained and been bitter cold all the time we have been up here on this beastly mountain, and I have hated it, and only stayed because my mother-in-law got into a frenzy at the thought of going down, because she says it does her so much good here and gives her so much strength —es gibt mir Kraft, Kraft! —She is 78, and is in a mad terror for fear she might die; and she would see me or anyone else die ten times over, to give her a bit more strength to drag on a few more meaningless years. It is so ugly and so awful, I nearly faint. I have never felt so down, so depressed and ill, as I have here, these ten days: awful! What with that terrible old woman, the icy wind, the beastly black forest, and all the depressing and fat guests—really, one wonders that anyone should be so keen to live, under such circumstances. I know I'm not.*

But tomorrow we are going down, and it will be better. We shall stay a week or so in the

Hotel Löwen, Lichtenthal bei Baden Baden

It is better there—I can sit in the Gaststube where the men come in from the village to drink their beer and smoke their pipes, and I can escape a bit this awful atmosphere of old women who devour the life of everything around them. Truly old and elderly women are ghastly, ghastly, eating up all life with hoggish greed, to keep themselves alive. They don't mind who else dies. I know my mother-in-law would secretly gloat, if I died at 43 and she lived on at 78. She would feel an ugly triumph. It is this kind of thing which does kill one.[320]

I think we shall stay in the Löwen about a week, then come south again to Lake Como. I feel I can't stand much more Germany. It's given me a bad blow this time. . . .

. . . At present I can do nothing: except write a few stinging Pansies which this time are Nettles. I shall call them nettles.[321]

Order. Obscene Prints.

In the Metropolitan Police District.

BEFORE the Court of Summary Jurisdiction sitting at the Marlborough Street Police Court.

The 8th day of August One Thousand Nine Hundred and Twenty nine

Gordon Hester, Detective Inspector, "C" Division

having made a Complaint that Philip Trotter and Dorothy Trotter (hereinafter called the Defendants) on the 5th day of July One Thousand Nine Hundred and twenty nine were the occupiers of certain premises at Maddox Street, in the District aforesaid, in which were seized by virtue of a certain Search Warrant bearing date the 6th day of July One Thousand Nine Hundred and twenty nine diverse obscene oil paintings, water colours and books

that the same were kept there for the purpose of sale and gain, and were of such a character and description that the publication of them would be a misdemeanor, and proper to be prosecuted as such, on hearing the said complaint it is ordered that four books seized on the said occasion be destroyed

at the expiration of the time allowed by law for lodging an appeal herein, unless notice of appeal be duly given, and that in the meantime such articles are impounded.

F. Mead.

One of the Magistrates of the Police Courts of the Metropolis.

K. 5/Order./Obscene Prints [322]

Philip Trotter

As for the Robinson-Wontner target of quick disposal of the proceedings, which had so distressed us at the conference on the 9th July, we were to find an unexpected ally in the Magistrate, though for reasons other than our own. It became clear as the case proceeded that Mr. Mead was taking his chance of getting level with his senior colleague, Chief Magistrate Sir Chartres Biron of Bow Street, whose handling of *The Well of Loneliness* in 1928 had raised the stature of that Court a cubit or two.

D. H. Lawrence was finer game than Miss Radclyffe Hall, and better than all the titled dotards in Hyde Park at night.

[Richardson Sowerby, Holden & Co. 5, John Street
Bedford Row London, W.C. 1] 8th August [1929]

Dear Trotter,

Mr. Hutchinson has just spoken to me and asks . . . that he shall be definitely instructed by me, as the solicitor concerned, with regard to the use of the various names mentioned at the conference last night, particularly such as that of Lord Allenby.

You told us that you had sent out a letter to various people asking for an authority to use their names. Now can you send me back by bearer (or . . . have without fail, at the Court at 2.15)

(1) A copy of the letter you sent out.
(2) All original letters you have received back again from people.
(3) In other cases where this does not apply, some definite instructions from you in writing stating that Mr. Hutchinson is entitled to say in Court that persons comprised upon his list have authorized the use of their names.

Yours sincerely
Ralph A. Holden [323]

On 8 August 1929, we drove to the judgment hall with Philip and Ottoline Morrell. Our reception by Inspector Hester and his subordinates suggested that accorded to a minor royalty arriving to dedicate a building to some such chastening purpose as an approved school for fallen girls. Within the Court we were separated: Philip and Ottoline were ushered to the back, Dorothy and I were led forward and bowed into two armchairs placed immediately in front of the dock. Hester's whole bearing indicated that, if the latter convenience were occupied, it would not be by ourselves or by Lawrence, but by Massetto di Lamporechio [324] and his fellow-nudes. The Court filled rapidly; but press intelligence on the character of the public is conflicting: "Many well-dressed men and women," [325] "Many young people from London's Bohemia"; [326] the recent congested routine at the Warren Gallery accounts for the fact that "Mr. Trotter, *although* conventionally dressed, wears his hair long." (My italics) [327] Actually Mr. Hester, true to his promise when serving the summonses, had done his best to reserve his limited public space for our friends and Lawrence's admirers. Among the latter were the Carswells, Eders, Lows, and Hiltons. I do not recall Kotelianski. A good many lawyers were present and the law press gave prominence to the case.[328]

Mr. Muskett,[329] having first apprised the Magistrate of his duty to decide whether the pictures were obscene and, in that event, to order them to be destroyed, gave, as background of the raid, the "outcry in the reputable press" and the number of complaints received by the Home Secretary and the Commissioner of Police, all pointing to the need to look into the matter "in the interests of public morality."

Describing the raid he said that Inspector Hester, after a preliminary visit, returned to the premises with a search warrant. "This officer," he continued, "exercising a sound discretion, selected from the twenty-five pictures thirteen which he thought of such a character that they should be submitted to you for adjudication whether they were obscene or not." In addition he found four books of colour reproductions of all the pictures. This book also contained "30 or more pages of printed matter for which it would appear the author Lawrence was responsible." Mr. Muskett might "call attention to one or two matters in the text if necessary."

The Magistrate, continued Mr. Muskett, was the only person who had to form an opinion whether these works, if they might be called such, came within the definition "Obscene." "These paintings, I submit to you, are gross, coarse, hideous, and unlovely from any aesthetic or artistic point of view, and are in their nature obscene."

Mr. Muskett went on: "For generations past now—I can speak with an experience of over forty years in this class of case—it was always, in my young days, and has been ever since, the test of obscenity in this class of case, whether there was a gross and unnecessary exposure of the private parts of the male and female, and if the pubic hair was represented in any pictures, or paintings, or engravings, or the like. That was an almost invariable test that they were to be regarded as obscene, and I do not suppose, although my ideas on these matters may be very mid-Victorian, there is very much difference that could be applied to-day in this class of filthy production, as I call it." [330]

Hutchinson now read a letter from our solicitors, elaborating "Mr. Robinson's Compromise," urging that the destruction of original works of art was irreparable, and that in this case legal problems arising out of contractual rights might flow from it.

Mr. Mead said that that was a suggestion he could not yield to. Assuming the pictures were obscene, "It is just as bad to exhibit them in private houses as in public places; it is rather worse, because in a public place they could be discovered and put a stop to, but a man could collect obscene pictures or books in order to corrupt people who visited him."

Mr. Hutchinson: Such a man could be prosecuted. It is advancing the censorship to apply it to works of art in private houses.

Mr. Mead: It is utterly immaterial whether they are works of art. That is a collateral question which I have not to decide. The most splendidly painted picture in the Universe might be obscene.

Mr. Mead's sibilants possessed a train-whistle quality that heightened the sinister values of *obscene*. The fatuous invocation of the "Universe"

Hitherto unpublished cartoon by Boswell: "The Day's Good Turn or Marlborough Street Triumphant." From the original cartoon in the possession of Mr. Philip Trotter.

as an art centre suggests its opportunist use as a scream-bomb. It was at this point that the Magistrate began to fidget in his chair, as if wishing to leave the room. "Can nobody find that lady at the back a seat?" he asked testily. We heard a shuffle of chairs behind us, and muffled voices: "Please sit here, Lady Ottoline." But Ottoline had her own seat and had risen;

standing her statuesque height, with a long forefinger pointing at the Magistrate, she was gently intoning an incantation:

"He ought to be burned, he ought to be burned."

Before examining Inspector Hester, Mr. Muskett handed the Mandrake Press book of reproductions to the Magistrate, drawing his attention to a particular page.

Mr. Mead: Some vulgar words I think I saw.

Mr. Muskett said the printed matter was signed "D. H. Lawrence."

In reply to Muskett, Hester said: "When I told Mrs. Trotter that the pictures were objected to as being obscene she said she was aware of press criticism both adverse and otherwise, and she felt [*sic*] that they were not prepared to close the exhibition down."

Mr. Muskett: Did she make any suggestion?

Inspector Hester: Mr. [*sic*] Trotter said he was prepared to remove any offending picture.

(Throughout the evidence Dorothy's words were attributed to me.)

Mr. Hutchinson asked if, when Witness told Mr. Trotter that if he closed the Gallery the authorities would not take steps, he made that offer on instructions.

Inspector Hester: I was asked to tell him and report what I was told.

Mr. Hutchinson suggested that if the Gallery had been closed the pictures could have been sent anywhere.

Inspector Hester: I take it so.

Mr. Hutchinson: Mr. [*sic*] Trotter offered to remove any of the offending pictures if you wished and not to exhibit them further?

Inspector Hester: We did not get quite so far as that.

(Mrs. Trotter interrupted with an emphatic "Oh, yes, excuse me.") [331]

Mr. Hutchinson: You would have been prepared to accept the word of a lady like Mrs. Trotter?

Inspector Hester: I was merely there to report on what I was told.

Mr. Hutchinson produced another large volume, and suggested that Inspector Hester had wanted to seize that also.

Mr. Mead: Did you seize it?

Inspector Hester: I did not. I had decided to seize it and then changed my mind.

Mr. Hutchinson: You put it on one side and it was pointed out to you that this book had drawings by William Blake, who was possibly one of the finest draughtsmen that the British School has ever produced. Was that pointed out to you?

Inspector Hester: I think it was.

Mr. Hutchinson: Perhaps you felt your instructions did not go so far as seizing William Blake's books?

Mr. Muskett: Possibly it did not convey anything to him.

Mr. Mead: Have you ever heard of William Blake?

Inspector Hester: No.[332]

Mr. Mead intervened, remarking to Mr. Hutchinson: You are pursuing a hare. That is not before me. It is absolutely irrelevant.

Mr. Hutchinson: It is part and parcel of what you have to decide whether these are works of art or not. I am laying the foundation for the suggestion that, unless you decide on this ground, people like Blake and Hogarth can be seized. I am asking this officer if he was prepared to seize William Blake's productions until it was pointed out to him that he was an Old Master.

Mr. Mead: Did anyone speak of the Old Master?

Inspector Hester: No.

Mr. Hutchinson: Was it pointed out to you that there is a room at the Tate Gallery entirely for his pictures?

Inspector Hester: No.

Mr. Mead: I cannot allow this to go on any longer. . . . This has nothing to do with that gentleman's work. It complicates it unnecessarily.[333]

Mr. Hutchinson suggested that the chief leader in the crusade against the exhibition was the *Daily Express.*

Mr. Mead (interrupting): I do not think we need go into that.

Mr. Hutchinson said he wanted to ask the officer this question, and if he also knew that there were eulogistic comments.

Mr. Mead: No, you cannot go into that. I cannot regard either press eulogy or press comment.

Mr. Hutchinson: Were the proceedings started by a private individual or the authorities?

Mr. Mead (to Inspector Hester): You need not answer that.

Mr. Hutchinson questioned the Magistrate's ruling.

Mr. Mead: It is before *me;* it does not matter who started it.[334]

Mr. Hutchinson, addressing the Magistrate, said the case was one of great seriousness both to the defendants and to British art. He paid tribute to the objectives and achievements of the Warren Gallery and the integrity of its owners.

Mr. Hutchinson: Mr. Lawrence is an Englishman, and a very English Englishman. The case seeks to establish quite a new form of censorship.

He could find no precedent for it.

Mr. Hutchinson: We have had to wait until 1929 with a so-called advanced government in power before that new form of censorship seems to have been set up in this country.

These pictures were the work of a serious artist painting serious pictures, he went on. If they were found obscene, where would proceedings stop? Were they going to have police officers going to the Wallace Collection and saying that Bouchers were obscene?

To show that they were serious works of art, he proposed to call Sir William Orpen, Mr. Glyn Philpot, Mr. Augustus John, and a number of art professors.[335] Mr. Hutchinson referred to a panel of Venus in the Dulwich art gallery.

Mr. Mead: I have been there, and my feelings were not offended with that.

Mr. Hutchinson: I am very glad to hear it, Sir.[336]

It was open to the Magistrate to decide that these were not works of art, Mr. Hutchinson continued, but was it not essential that he should be allowed to call experts to show that they were? He dealt with prudish attacks on occasional indecencies in great masters of art and literature, for which protective authorities existed.

Mr. Hutchinson: There cannot be one rule for Lawrence and one rule for Dryden simply because Dryden lived a long time ago.

Mr. Hutchinson said he hoped the Magistrate would deal with each picture separately. There was the picture of Leda and the Swan which, he suggested, could not be said to be obscene, and, compared with a Michel Angelo in the National Gallery, had not a touch of indecency. No one would dream of bringing a Michel Angelo here "for you to decide whether it was obscene or not, and if they did you would dismiss the summons on the grounds that the picture was a great work of art." Referring again to the letter received by Mr. Muskett, it would, he said, completely carry out what obviously the police wanted. The Trotters were honourable people and would give their pledge. He recapitulated the terms of the compromise.

And now the anticlimax came full circle. Mr. Mead, says the *Daily Telegraph,* asked Mr. Muskett what his view was. Mr. Muskett, who had admonished the Magistrate on his duty to destroy the pictures if he found them obscene, who had then instructed the Magistrate that the pictures were "from their nature" obscene, now addressed the Magistrate. The letter received by him was submitted to the Commissioner of Police, he said, and he knew it went to the Secretary of State or Permanent Head of the Department.

Mr. Muskett: I have authority, if you consider it proper, and it must be within the strict limitation of your view, to accept such an undertaking as Mr. Hutchinson is prepared to give.

But Mr. Mead had not quite finished. He had had, I think, two digressions into *The Well of Loneliness* at Bow Street, though neither of them is reported, and he meant to provoke one more.

Mr. Mead: You have never considered the question of what volume of evidence you could call of eminent persons who might hold contrary opinions to those called by Mr. Hutchinson?

Mr. Muskett (reacting as required): I should never attempt to do it. I submit it is quite irrelevant and could not be heard. The Chief Magistrate considered that point very carefully in the case of Radclyffe Hall's *Well of Loneliness,* when he was threatened with the same kind of evidence. He decided after consideration that he could not hear it on the grounds that it was irrelevant.

Mr. Mead: Independently of Sir Chartres I should have given the same opinion. I do not at all regret that the case has been heard at length.

Mr. Muskett submitted the draft terms of an undertaking; and Mr. Mead and Mr. Hutchinson agreed to them: The case to be adjourned *sine die,* the pictures released and restored to their owners, and the four books of reproductions destroyed. In consideration of this latter clause, Mr. Mead awarded £5.5.0 costs against the Warren Gallery. To close the proceedings he observed, but only *The Times* reported: "Mr. St. John Hutchinson has put forward powerful arguments, but they have not convinced me." [337]

Back at the Gallery our first acts, after getting rid of reporters and photographers, were to send a telegram to the Lawrences and a long night letter cable to Geoffrey Scott, news of whose illness had not yet reached England. He received it on the 10th, four days before he died, and we do not know whether he read it. Insofar as there was a viewable exhibition of Lawrence's pictures, Geoffrey's contribution was outstanding, apart from his splendid assistance in preparing the defence and rallying support. During the full exhibition, pictures could be effectively looked at only after closing time; and then, while the cigarette ends, paper bags, and apple-cores were being swept from the gallery floors, little parties were entertained round the office table. Here Geoffrey was in his element. "He was happiest talking and listening," wrote Desmond Mac-Carthy, "the charm of his company was that he was so responsive to other minds and the feelings of others." To these private views he brought valuable supporters in the coming crisis, including Glyn Philpot, and many were drawn there in the hope of finding him.

Scott and Lawrence were at opposite poles of life and letters. But chance threw him heart and soul into the defence in Lawrence's most seering battle as the final episode in his short life, and it is fitting to draw a little from Desmond MacCarthy's portrait of him, which recalls the fruitful farewell visit already recorded. After relating his early triumph as Newdigate prize-winner at New College, Oxford, his first post as secretary to the famous art collector Bernard Berenson, for whose villa at Florence he designed the new library, "one of the most beautiful and suitable of modern rooms," where, too, he wrote *The Architecture of Humanism* (1914), MacCarthy proceeds:

His death is a grave loss to English letters and to his friends. . . . I even believe myself, though this I only expect a few others to believe, that his Life of Boswell, which he would have written when his task of editing the *Boswell Papers* [338] was finished, would have been one of the most remarkable biographies in the English language. . . . When he was asked by Col. Isham to edit Boswell he knew that the chance of making a lasting name in literature had come his way. He was far from being a confident man, but he knew the subject was made to his hand and too interesting ever to be forgotten. The last time we met before he sailed for New York we smiled together over his luck. "You will win your niche in literature," I exclaimed enviously. He nodded with just the degree of ironic assent appropriate, for he was far too good a student of literary fame not to know that it is not only works of genius that are lastingly remembered but the result of happy combination between author and subject. Alas! He will not have that niche now. It would have been a happy combination. He would have understood perfectly Boswell's hypochondria, his eager sociability, his craving for distraction, his diffidence. . . . He would have seen all the tragedy of Boswell's life. WE HAVE LOST A VERY FINE BOOK.

Geoffrey Scott had a strong streak of melancholy in him. He was looking forward immensely to returning to his editorial work with Col. Isham. He was happy in America. When I said I was afraid of going there myself because I should never be allowed to mope in that country he replied, and it was true, "But I am the king of mopers, the curious thing is, one does not want to mope there." . . . I have written as though Geoffrey Scott's achievement was before him rather than after him when he died at 46. This is true, but *The Architecture of Humanism* is a task which has made its mark. Its effect was damped down by the war for a time, but it has been deep. The book marks the first turning point in contemporary taste away from the Gothic toward the Baroque. His *Story of Zelide* is a charming book. It made him well known, but he took its measure as the slight thing decently done. . . . He ever was critical of himself and generously appreciative of others.[339]

More, I think, than "the few" whom MacCarthy counted, felt that here the enchanting companion (much of which is here omitted) was stressed at the expense of the writer of rare distinction and genius. But it is a happy picture of an exact contemporary of Lawrence whose last weeks are woven into the texture of this history.[340]

12 August 1929   *Hôtel Löwen, Lichtenthal bei Baden-Baden, Germany*

⟮ *We are much better down here—an old inn, with old garden with such nice trees, and I have a room with a balcony among the leaves, might be a sparrow. The weather has been very nice again, sunny and warm with a touch of autumn. I like it, really—but the atmosphere of Germany itself somehow makes one irritable. Frieda is really very irritable—but then she always is, in her native land. She never feels free, yet seems to hug the thing she isn't free of, and altogether I just leave her alone. She has massage for her foot, and all sorts of baths at the Kuranstalt, and takes it out that way. Yesterday, evening, we celebrated her 50th birthday— we were nine people, five of whom were over seventy, and we drank Pfirsich Bowle with 2 Flaschen Sekt in it, and ate trout and ducks—very nice. It was quite nice—but the Germans themselves are very depressed, and they leave me hollow. There are lovely roses on the table, and I dread the effect on Frieda of four large boxes of chocolates.*

I have been going to the old Medizinabrat who examined me two years ago. He says the place on the lung very much healed, the bronchial condition better but not very much better, and the asthma no better. I needn't bother about the lung—but must look after the broncs and asthma —must not go to high altitudes, not even 3,000 feet—and am best living near the sea—and otherwise there's not much to be done, except avoid damp, sudden changes, and dust: keep as even temperature as possible, and not try to walk or climb much, as I should never exert the asthma to make me pant. —I knew it all. Meanwhile another Medizinabrat gives me a little treatment for my ear, and life is a jest and all things show it, and my name's Mr. Gay.[341]

Hotel Löwen/Lichtenthal/Baden Baden/14 August 1929

⟮ *Dear Dorothy [Warren]*

We haven't received any letter from you, after the telegram when the case was settled. Today only Percy Robinson's letter arrived, written on

389

the ninth. Why it should have been five days on the way, when ordinary letters take two days, I don't know.

He, however, insists that the pictures which are to be returned to me should be packed up at once and sent to me, out of England. Of course there are those that are sold—and then North Sea to go to Maria Huxley, either via Hutchinson or direct to Paris: then there is one promised to Enid Hilton, and the Dance Sketch was promised to Frieda's daughter Elsa, and Renascence of Men to Monty: and you were having one— Contadini—and Mary Hutchinson one. It won't leave many to be sent back. But I don't know if you are free to dispose even of these. Anyhow I will send you a definite Florence address in a day or two, that you can forward those returning ones to me as soon as they are packed up.

Then I wish you would close the show altogether. My sister Mrs. Clarke will take care of all the big pictures you still have hanging in the gallery, and I will write you about the disposal of the smaller ones. I must think out carefully, which they are.

Well Dorothy, there is the end of my first, and probably my last picture-show in England. I must say it leaves me feeling depressed and nauseated —so many insults, such silly extravagance of insults, and a meek or gloating public. Heaven helps him who helps himself, and really, the English seem as if they can't help themselves. A lily-livered lot: that's where all their purity lies. Alas, that they should be a nation of poltroons, in the face of life! But that's what they are: bossed by the witless canaille and off-sweepings of a dead 19th century.

Well, I'm sure you feel a bit weary and depressed and bitter also. The sooner we wind the whole thing up, the better. Take the Contadini then for love, for money is a weariness too. Mañana es otro dia! We'll come back in triumph one day—you see. But at the moment, I'm sick.

My regards to Philip.

D. H. Lawrence [342]

21 August 1929   Hôtel Löwen, Lichtenthal bei Baden-Baden, Germany

⟨ Frieda says she wants to stay till Sunday, to have her bath and her masseuse once more. She is still troubled about the foot though it is much better. —So I suppose we shall arrive in München on Sunday evening [25 August 1929]. —Max Mohr says he will meet us at Rottach station with a Wagon—and he knows of a nice little house for us. So it sounds quite good, if only it will not rain.[343]

Interview with Ada Lawrence Clarke

(28 August 1929)

D. H. LAWRENCE AND HIS ART/"No motive excepting Sincerity"/BANNED PICTURES/Spirited Defence by Sister at Ripley

The recent condemnation by the law of D. H. Lawrence's pictures and books has aroused particular interest in local circles as Mr. Lawrence is a native of Eastwood, Notts.

The famous painter and novelist's attitude towards art and his native place were described by his sister, who lives at Ripley [Derby.], in an interview with a [*Nottingham*] *Journal* representative.

EASTWOOD MEMORIES

Story of Early Struggle for Self-Expression

"And what does your brother really think of Eastwood?"

"He hates it. It makes him ill whenever he sees it."

Some time ago a local writer indignantly announced to his fellow townsmen that D. H. Lawrence, the perpetrator of "obscene" pictures and books, had sullied the fair name of his birthplace.

The offended gentleman and his friends will be glad to learn from the above quoted conversation which took place between Mr. Lawrence's sister and myself, that they are not likely to be disturbed by the "criminal's" presence since Eastwood makes him ill, and he prefers to stay away and consider his health. The hatred is extended only to depressing buildings and people who seem to delight in talking a great deal and in very loud voices about things of which they know nothing. They learn that some of his work has been declared obscene by a magistrate, and read sensational journalism which relies upon scandal, and especially sex scandal to attract its public. It never occurs to them that they have insulted Mr. Lawrence, and that they have dragged his name in the mud.

BEAUTIFUL DRAWING

Yesterday I met Mrs. W. E. Clarke at her home in Ripley. Before her marriage she was Ada Lawrence and perhaps she understood her brother more than anyone. She visits him every year on the Continent. She possesses all his books and many of his pictures. To her the recent police raid on his paintings and books, which were being exhibited at a London gallery, is simply incomprehensible. There are many people who probably imagine that for financial reasons Lawrence welcomed the publicity which was given to that raid and subsequent police court proceedings. Perhaps they have forgotten that he made no protest and did not defend himself. In other words he doesn't stoop to that kind of fame.

There are some who have said that he paints pictures which don't conform to any rules, because he can't really draw according to accepted standards. Once more they are wrong. In Mrs. Clarke's home there is a lovely copy of M. Greiffenhagen's *An Idyll*. Lawrence painted it at Eastwood when he was a lad.

ENEMY OF UGLINESS

"They all think my brother has a motive—to be indecent for the sake of frankness or some such nonsense," said his sister. "He has no motives excepting sincerity. He says and writes exactly what he thinks. He has never written or painted a single thing just because he thought he could sell it. When I was on the Continent with him a few weeks ago he received scores of letters from editors of sensational newspapers imploring him to write articles for them. He could have made a great deal of money, but he said No to all of them. He has always stood alone. He will never live in England again. The sensation hounds would never leave him alone. He doesn't seek publicity. He hates crowds. He hates Eastwood. He cannot bear the sight of poverty-stricken homes and the squalor of mining areas. He had a great struggle to gain financial independence, and he had a surfeit of poverty when he was young.

ADMIRATION FOR THE MINERS

"Our father, Arthur Lawrence, was a butty at Brinsley Colliery. Our mother came from Kent. She was a refined woman who fought all her life to give her children opportunities of becoming something more than miners and factory hands. Had it not been for her my brother would have gone down the pit with father. He likes the miners. We have fine men round about Ripley. I know many of them. But he couldn't stand the idea of living most of his life in darkness and poverty.

"When we were children we spent most of our holidays walking in the country—to Clifton Grove and Matlock and the Hemlock Stone and Bert began to paint. He worked in the office of a Nottingham surgical goods manufacturer. He didn't like it, but he wanted to help mother. Then he went to Nottingham University College and taught for a short while at Eastwood elementary school. Later he taught in London.

HIS FIRST NOVEL

"When our mother was dying of cancer he sat with her in her bedroom every evening and painted. That was when he copied *An Idyll*. Before she died he had written his first novel *The White Peacock*. In those early days he was a shy boy with an intense love of beautiful things. Ugliness made him feel physically ill. I suppose all geniuses suffer a great deal and he has certainly suffered much because he is honest with himself and everyone else.

"Cheap, suggestive revues are regarded as jolly entertainment. No-one worries about cheap suggestive novelettes, but a serious and sincere artist is pilloried by every so-called moralist who thinks he has a divine right to express an opinion on literature and art."

Mrs. Clarke thinks that *Sons and Lovers* is her brother's greatest novel. Much of this is autobiographical and contains beautifully written descriptions of Clifton and the river, and Eastwood and the surrounding countryside.

A RAID JOKE

Some of the pictures which were exhibited in London were sent from his sister's Ripley home. They were painted when he was young. She has many of his original manuscripts including that of *Sons and Lovers*. She also possesses two University College notebooks in which are written some of his unpublished poems.[344]

I have seen reproductions of all the pictures which were seized by the authorities.

If the nude human body is obscene then the critics are right, and we should all feel thoroughly ashamed of ourselves for possessing one.

And surely this is the joke of the century. I understand that when the police raided the galleries where Lawrence's pictures were exhibited they pounced on some work and were about to take it away when they were informed that it happened to be by a man whose centenary had just been celebrated—William Blake!

Lawrence's sister Emily and brother George are now living in Nottingham. Ernest, who was the eldest, died in London when he was 23.[345]

William Edward Hopkin

(29 August 1929)

THE LAWRENCE PICTURES/Notts. Artist Defended by An Old Friend

That the [*Nottingham*] *Journal* should take up a defence of that brilliant Notts. genius Mr. D. H. Lawrence is a sign of his fairmindedness and the sanity of his outlook.

A great deal of silly and disgusting stuff has been written about the Lawrence pictures and *Pansies,* his latest book of poems.

The latter I can understand, but the former not at all.

I saw the pictures prior to the very stupid raid by the police, in fact I was at the Warren Galleries the morning the police paid their first visit.

I was also present at the Marlborough-street court during the farcical trial and heard the very early Victorian remarks made by Mr. Muskett, as well as the unnecessary declaration by Mr. Mead (over 80) that he "had seen the 'Venus' in Dulwich Art Gallery, and it had not excited his feelings."

"Scasely," as Uncle Remus would say. From the Warren Galleries I went to that temporary abode of mediocre art the Royal Academy, and there to my surprise and amusement I found that No. 75 displayed the figures of a man and a woman nude and in detail.

Curiously enough the artist was also named Lawrence, but as his picture was in the Academy the pornographic Puritans who instituted the raid on D. H. Lawrence's pictures said and did nothing.

If the human figure is obscene somebody really ought to haul the maker of the original before Mr. Mead for so lavishly scattering copies about the earth.

I have the honour to be one of D. H. Lawrence's oldest friends, and I know him more intimately perhaps than anybody outside his immediate family circle, and I have been both pained and disgusted by the attacks made upon him in certain circles—attacks by men void of understanding or filled with silly jealousy.

The last thing to charge D. H. L. with is pornography. He is first, last and all the time an artist, no matter whether his medium is painting, poetry or prose writing. Some of his prose is fine poetry.

Every one, or nearly every one, of the pictures represents an idea and that the pornographists failed to see. Anatomical perfection was not in the least necessary to convey the meaning intended.

His critics are so used to the conventional photographic art of the art schools that anything transgressing their accepted canons is either lewd art or bad art to them.

Augustus John and Sir William Orpen praised the Lawrence pictures unreservedly and it was left to police sergeants who owned to possessing no knowledge of art, and back numbers like Messrs. Muskett and Mead to damn them.

Taking their cue from such men and from a certain daily the pseudo-Puritans up and down the land conspired to denounce what they had never seen and would not have understood had they seen.

Between their idea and imagination are the twin impulses of the art of Mr. D. H. Lawrence. To sit down before Wingfield Manor, or at the head of Dovedale and reproduce the scene on canvas is mere copying.

It may be good painting but it is certainly not creative art.

The fact is that we are afraid of our natural impulses.

As D. H. L. said the other day: "One would think that the Almighty created us down to the waist and the devil finished us off," judging from the fear the average person displays of his own and other people's natural actions.

Sex is the strongest of all urges outside the instinct of self-preservation, and is merely the instinct of nature for prolonging the life of the species.

But for a century or more what should be a splendid part of life and experience has been made a taboo and the subject of nods, winks and whispering. There is nothing more beautiful than the human figure, but thanks to the way it has been spoken of and vilified by us it has become something to be hidden and ashamed of.

The body is clean and sex is clean, but the mind with both conjures up filthy associations, and so the noblest work of God is degraded by a depraved mental outlook.

Nine-tenths of our immorality is mentally inspired and a perversion of our natural animal instincts.

Not the human body nor pictures of the human body are obscene, and if we had clean minds we should realise the truth of it.

In twenty years time there will be no need to defend D. H. Lawrence, for he will have justified himself to a more enlightened and charitable world.[346]

30 *August 1929*
Kaffee Angermaier, Rottach-am-Tegernsee, Oberbayern, Bavaria, Germany

❨ We are here among the mountains—rather a lovely place—and very peaceful, a little inn smelling terrifically of cows—but we eat out of doors under the trees, and live in a little house to ourselves. It is much more the old Germany here. I simply can't stand the new Germany—it's awful, so empty and depressing and in a hurry to get nowhere.

I think in about a fortnight's time we shall go down to Italy again. Give me the south, the Mediterranean.[347]

5 *September 1929*
Kaffee Angermaier, Rottach-am-Tegernsee, Oberbayern, Bavaria, Germany

❨ . . . I've had such a nasty sort of cold, laid me out, and am as weak as a rat and no happier—rats never look happy. I'm but a stranger here. Heaven is my home?

.   .   .   .

Frieda is glad because she had a bone-setter from a neighbouring village —a farmer—and he set her foot in one minute. The bone was off the centre and resting on the side of the socket—and in another month or two the socket would have filled in and it would have been too late. And I paid 12 guineas to a Park Lane specialist, and the long-bearded Medizinalrat in Baden-Baden is still to pay. Doctors should all be put at once in prison.[348]

6 *September 1929*
Kaffee Angermaier, Rottach-am-Tegernsee, Oberbayern, Bavaria, Germany

❨ I've been so seedy this week—and in bed most of the time—but now a new doctor has descended on me—in fact, three doctors—and they say I can soon be well, with proper régime and diet: that the animal man is in a state of change, and needs a whole corresponding change of food and rhythm. I feel this is true, and shall start in. They also say eliminate salt as much as possible, as there is excess of chlorine in the body—and substitute some other salt in place of NaCl: the common salt. I feel that *may be true. They say I can get well in quite a short time. I hope it's true—it may be, really.*[349]

Max Mohr

. . . I would rather tell you of one of the last days I spent with Lorenzo at the time he lived in the mountains with his wife Frieda near to my place in Bavaria . . . .

A little peasant-boy comes with a message from Frieda. I must go down to their house. She is standing on a wonderful blue autumn-day before the little farm-house, five minutes away from ours. She thinks that Lorenzo is going to die. She had been in his room and thought him dead already. Often before she has had this experience: again and again she had gone to his bed to see whether he was still alive or not.

Now I go into his bedroom with her. He is alive. One can see it, as his breath passes over his red beard. He opens his ice-blue eyes and smiles. He knows what we have been thinking. He gets up and we breakfast together. He laughs heartily over a story I tell him: during the preceding night I had assisted at a poor peasant-woman's delivery, and the father of the child, who was drunk, did not come back from the village-inn, in spite of the repeated urgent messages I had sent him. Lorenzo laughs heartily. And that evening he shows me a little poem he had written on this husband:

Good husbands make unhappy wives:
so do bad husbands, just as often;
but the unhappiness of a wife with a good husband is much more devastating
than the unhappiness of a wife with a bad husband.[350]

And I see him on this same evening. He comes to my house hand in hand with my three-year-old daughter, Eve. Frieda and my wife are sitting with me in front of the house, waiting for him. The little child trips beside him, shy, and yet under a spell. She looks up at the tall man, whose blue jacket hangs loose around his thin body. She stops and picks a small blue flower for him. . . . Frieda feels perhaps that my wife is a little afraid of the contagion for the child, if she plays constantly with Lorenzo; and she asks me, if I do not think it dangerous. But I deny it as so often before. For nobody can believe that any harm can come from Lorenzo.

And so it was. No harm could ever come from him, from his person, from his work, from his sickness, from his troubles, from his sharp criticism of our times. Behind everything there stood and stands forever the power and saving magic of his life.[351]

Frieda Lawrence Ravagli

[?Kaffee Angermaier, Rottach-am-Tegernsee, Oberbayern, Bavaria, Germany] Monday [?9 September 1929]

Dear Dorothy [Warren]

Is it really true that Geoffrey Scott is *dead?* Really dead? He is so vivid to me standing at the gallery sofa, with rather grim dimples laughing at things; what a *loss* for you, my dear. Philip was fond of him too. Really life does such bitter, bitter things to one, it's hard not to become a fiend with bitterness. Did he die *alone?* how—what of? So big and strong; I am glad I knew him and even so short a time, I'll keep him a warm corner in my memory; no, but he *shouldn't* have died. Really, Dorothy, you do get your whack of misfortunes. But about the show I don't feel depressed, a fight's a fight and it was our victory I consider. Jack Hutchinson was evidently splendid. And for us it is a comfort to leave the pictures in yours and Philip's hands. You know really much better than Lawrence or I how to deal with people. And there's no hurry about anything. It's been a great advertisement, people are also coming round to *Lady C.* In 5 years time she will be as "salonfaehig" as *Jane Eyre.* So the pictures. I am glad people are still coming, but really don't collapse—it isn't worth it. I wish poor Lorenzo was better. You must see us, after the first. Where would we meet? This is a little damp for Lawrence, we want to go south soon. The French Riviera suits him. We'll take a house in Cassis or thereabouts, I think. But I am sure it will be hard for you to get over this unexpected blow of Geoffrey Scott's death. There is *much* bitterness because one feels so much in him never blossomed to its full, the beastliness of modern life for anything a little splendid. So one must fight! You have got Philip and I think of you both with so much love and belief in your genuine beings, and I do so want you to be *fulfilled.* I am so looking forward that we meet. It will do us all good. So don't worry any more. Robinson is only clumsy, I think. And look, we all made our definite stand against this antiquated dirt. Now people can follow and profit by it!

So think of your getting away and forgetting all the bother. Glad to get your letter. I haven't heard from Barby for some time. I hope she is well.

So much love to you both.

F.[352]

13 September 1929
Kaffee Angermaier, Rottach-am-Tegernsee, Oberbayern, Bavaria, Germany

⟨ *I have been doing my cure—first taking arsenic and phosphorous twice a day. This made me feel I was really being poisoned, so I gave it up. Now I am only doing the diet—no salt, and much raw fruit and vegetables, and porridge in place of bread. I must say I don't feel much better—in fact I have been rather worse these last two weeks. . . .*

And I am still waiting to hear from the Trotters about meeting them in Venice. They are perfect demons to have anything to do with: never answer, never come to the point. The picture-show is still going on. I feel it is all bewitched.—They wanted us to meet them in Venice . . . .[353]

Philip Trotter

Lawrence's approaching death was to frustrate any shipping of the pictures to Italy or France. As asked in Frieda's undated [?30 July 1929] letter from Plättig, we stacked the whole collection in our empty house, and it was probably fortunate for her that we later ignored Lawrence's instructions to send them on to his sister Ada in the Lawrence country; for though Mrs. Clarke remained neutral in the sordid proceedings now to follow, her benevolence was towards her family; and their rapacity extended even to the pictures, pictures which Frieda had called into existence. I find a letter from Percy Robinson dated 11 June 1930, applying for the pictures "on behalf of Mrs. Frieda Lawrence and Mr. George [Lawrence], administrators of the estate." [354]

Lawrence meanwhile had entered that phase of petulance which is best reflected in letters to Orioli published in *The Intelligent Heart;* and from this series of outbursts Dorothy and I are not exempted. We were repeating our last year's autumn programme of a business-cum-pleasure visit to my partner's castle in the Burgenland, breaking the journey at Würzburg, where, exactly a year previously, we had plighted our troth.

There had been tentative suggestions for a meeting with the Lawrences. But fresh trouble was brewing for the warrior gallery.

While the informer and police were performing on the stage, a fresh villain unbeknown to us was waiting in the wings. The London County Council was serving a dangerous-structure notice on the landlords of 39A Maddox Street, which was to cause dislocation of our future business. Dorothy at once filed a petition for trespass; the landlords countered with an injunction restraining her from displaying posters; this was quashed under the terms of her covenant; then Junior Counsel for the Defence propounded a plea that our loss of business was due, not to the landlords' interference, but through our becoming "vendors of obscene objects." The case did not come on till 1931; but it delayed our plans.

Early in September came a letter from Lawrence, now missing from the records. The first paragraph almost recalled the relation-severing letter to Bertrand Russell,[355] and the "spit in the face" to Katherine Mansfield.[356] Then the rage evaporated, and we were admonished to remember that "the love was just the same." We bundled exhausted from London at the first possible moment, and telegraphed Lawrence from Würzburg. He wrote Orioli from Rottach, September 11 [1929]:

> There was a telegram from the Trotters last night—they are in Würzburg, about five hours from here, and are on their way to that place in Hungary [*sic*] where they buy [*sic*] that beastly jade—and they say they are writing and sending a cheque. Which means of course that they don't want to see me, because they don't want to answer my questions. So they are slipping past.[357]

I find no trace and have no recollections of any questions. It was a disappointment to both of us: I was as anxious to make Lawrence's acquaintance as Dorothy to renew it. But we were many days late at Bernstein, and she was suffering from strain. So we hurried on.[358]

14 September 1929
Kaffee Angermaier, Rottach-am-Tegernsee, Oberbayern, Bavaria, Germany

⟨ *We are leaving here on Tuesday [17 September 1929], to go to the South of France. I was so well and so cheerful in Bandol last winter— such a sunny winter—that, all things considered, it is perhaps madness to go to Italy. We ought to be in Marseille by Friday at latest. . . . We want to look round first at Cassis, to see if we can't find a nice small house there, that we can keep permanently. . . . If Cassis is unpromising, we shall come on to Bandol, which I know I like. It has its ugly side—the French* made their places ugly—but somehow the little port is so friendly and nice—I was happy there.[359]

27 September 1929   Hôtel Beau Rivage, Bandol, Var, France

(We arrived Monday evening [23 September 1929]—three days ago. It seemed very lovely—so full of light and a certain newness. I am already much better. In Germany I felt I should certainly die—awful. It was psychic depression. The Germans are in an awful state, inwardly—but horrible. I feel that nothing will ever again take me north of Lyon. I dread and hate the north, it is full of death, and the most grisly disappointment. I feel already nearly myself again here—the sun and sea, the great light, and the natural people. I can breathe. In the north, I can't breathe.

We have taken a house for six months—Villa Beau Soleil. . . . It is on the sea—rather lovely—a smallish bungalow, six rooms, terrace—bath, central-heating—some neglected garden. . . . It is ordinary—but not poky —and wonderfully in the air and light. . . .

.   .   .   .

From here, one feels Africa. It is queer—but the direct vibration seems to be from Africa. Next winter we'll go.[360]

4 October 1929   Villa Beau Soleil, Bandol, Var, France

(Here we are already in a house of our own, a nice little bungalow villa right on the sea—and with bathroom and all conveniences—and a nice woman to cook and clean. It is very easy and I like it. I still love the Mediterranean, it still seems young as Odysseus, in the morning. And Frieda is happy. The only trouble is my health, which is not very good. For some reason, which I don't understand, I lost a lot of strength in Germany. I believe Germany would kill me, if I had to stay in it. . . .

It is very lovely, the wind, the clouds, the running sea that bursts up like blossom on the island opposite. If only I was well, and had my strength back!

But I am so weak. And something inside me weeps black tears. I wish it would go away.

Max Mohr is quite near in the Goelands Hotel—always very nice and willing to do everything he can to help.[361]

23 October 1929   Villa Beau Soleil, Bandol, Var, France

⟨ The Brewsters arrived suddenly from Naples, and are also looking round for a house. . . .

. . . .

No news here—Max Mohr has gone back to Germany, but says he'll return here with wife and child in January. The little house—this—which Achsah finds truly terrible because it is so lacking in "Beauty," is quite pleasant, for the time being, and I believe will be cosy enough. It was the "love-nest" (Frieda's word) of a femme-tenue, hence the sunk-in marble bath and rather expensive plumbing, including the central heating. But it is, none the less, a rather hard square box. . . .

We've got a cat—a young yellow "marmalade" cat with a white breast, who simply forced himself on us. He is very nice, but I never knew a French cat before—sang-froid, will of his own, aimable, but wasting no emotion. I like him very much, but I don't love him—which is perhaps as it should be. He simply abandoned his French home, and howled like a lion on the terrace till I let him live here—he's about eight months, I suppose.

. . . .

Brewsters having a bad time with their vegetables in the Beau Rivage.[362]

Achsah Barlow Brewster

[In] the autumn [1929], we came to Bandol to be near the Lawrences. They were living in a little villa (Beau Soleil) by the sea, which with its heliotrope-tinted walls and gold-framed mirrors, must have been designed for some lady-love, and was drolly incongruous for the Spartan Lawrence who denied himself most comforts. Frieda put up bits of embroidery that she and Lawrence had made, some sketches by him, a few of their own household gods to modify the effect. Here they offered hospitality to a stream of visitors. Lawrence could view from his large room a vast expanse of sea stretching to the eastern sky.

402

He was in bed seriously ill, having recently arrived from Germany. He announced that the psyche of Germany had been killing him, and that we never ought to go north of the Alps into the spirit of unbelief—man could not live without faith. "Now, I believe, in the centre of my being," he said solemnly, as if it were his confession of faith.

Whatever remedy was suggested he would try hopefully. Shortly he was up, resting on the couch, walking out to his verandah. Max Mohr—a physician as well as playwright—was with him for a short time. We all tried to aid Frieda in finding ways for his improvement. Every day would find us sometime at Villa Beau Soleil. Earl massaged him with cocoanut oil until Lawrence's blue fingers began to take on a hue of life.

By the end of November Lawrence was walking to the pine grove skirting the sea, where we would find him absorbed in contemplation, sometimes sitting in the wind, on cold stones, without an overcoat, in his reckless way. He was refreshed by short motor trips, and began planning a longer excursion to the Magdalen's cave at St. Baume, which dwindled to a morning's drive to the hill-towns of La Cadière and Castelet.

This drive was after the heavy rains, and the vines were a final burst of colour, the sun glistening through every leaf. We have never seen the foliage so wonderful in colour as on that day: it ranged from purest yellow through golds to deep russet, from vermilion to purples—against silver olives and dark pines, with the emerald of wild turnip springing from the brown earth. Beyond all were the blue sea and sky.

Lawrence grew tired: we were conscious of his aching weariness. Our attention was caught in the windows of a village house by some coarse lace curtains with a design of a triple fountain from which two doves were drinking; I declared that I should like to have them. Lawrence exclaimed in exasperation: "Would you go and rip them down from the woman's window? It would be quite as base as Y——, who would take the only blanket off an Indian's back!" This outburst seemed to relieve the pressure; it had offered a tangible object outside his own aching body.

During those days he was reading the Bible in Moffatt's translation, also Dean Inge's essays on *Plotinus* [363] and Gilbert Murray's *Five Stages of Greek Religion*.[364] He was annoyed with Murray for teaching that civilization keeps evolving into something better. The old gods were as important to Lawrence as the new, different but not inferior.

On the bed beside Lawrence was a yellow and white kitten, "Mickie Mussolini." It was startling to see the two side by side, both so still, both red-gold and white. Mickie would put his paw on Lawrence's hand as he wrote; or he lay curled under the down coverlet, peering out, while

Lawrence said: "Yes, you're a cave-man." The kitten had adopted him, refusing to depart, and paying little attention to others. Lawrence had an awareness of the cat's real nature and did not treat it as his "pet" and property, but as a creature with a life of its own to be respected: he insisted that it sleep outside the house at night lest it become "bourgeois and comfortable"!

He watched the little creature play with the chains of a hanging clock. Madame [Douillet] of the hotel [Beau Rivage] had brought to Lawrence two gold fishes in a globe; they sailed around, magnified by the water into large golden lumps which Mickie watched fascinated. The fish were banished to the bathroom, where Mickie was forbidden entrance. Of course the expected happened: Mickie burst in and caught the fishes. Frieda was so upset that for days she would not speak to the cat! Lawrence lectured him. ("He understands every word I speak to him.") And Lawrence spoke long and earnestly to the unrepentant Mickie. "You knew perfectly well that I wished those fish left alone and therefore you should have respected my wishes." Again: "Who ate the butter? You are a thief."

Lawrence took great interest in our search to find a house where we might be neighbours, and in the old farmhouse [Château Brun, St. Cyr-sur-mer, Var] we finally unearthed. He would lie awake at nights worrying—supposing it was too isolated, supposing the neighbours were hostile. He wanted to help paint the doors. He planned every detail—we must have fire-screens, our beds must be comfortable. He asked exactly how much each article cost. He was pleased that we had a refectory table of teakwood made by the village carpenter, for he held that the life should be kept beating in living artisans instead of seeking out antiquities. This table was a gift from Lawrence, and he was to carve his initials under the bevel. Whenever he came to the house he would examine the surface to see how it was taking the wax.

He would sit contentedly by our hearth warming his feet, and insisting that it was the first time during the winter that they had been warm. He declared that if he had the actual presence of a fire before him in his house, instead of *chauffrage centrale,* he would gain new strength: for man lived by the elements and he should not deny fire. It was at this time that he wrote a poem to fire.[365]

29 October 1929   *Villa Beau Soleil, Bandol, Var, France*

❲ *The doctors seem to think the lung is not troubling—it is never very much—but the bronchials and asthma are awful, and affecting my heart* a bit . . . . I say, as the ancient said, there is an evil world-soul which sometimes overpowers one, and with which one has to struggle most of the time, to keep oneself clear. I feel so strongly as if my illness weren't really me—I feel perfectly well and all right, in myself. Yet there is this beastly torturing chest superimposed on me, and it's as if there was a demon lived there, triumphing, and extraneous to me. I do feel it extraneous to me. I feel perfectly well, even perfectly healthy—till the devil starts scratching and squeezing, and I feel perfectly awful. So what's to be done! Doctors frankly say they don't know.

.   .   .   .

As I grow older, money bores me, and one smells it in people like a bad smell. Which is not because I'm hard up at all, because I'm not. I put myself on my feet by pushing Lady C. for myself.[366]

Earl H. Brewster

I had hoped the Lawrences would go with us to Africa for the winter of 1930; but Lawrence was anxious to find a place for permanent residence in the country east of Marseille. He rented a villa at Bandol, intending to search in the country between there and Marseille for such a place as he desired. During that autumn and winter I saw him almost daily. He continued to grow weaker, generally passing his mornings in bed writing or reading. Our walks were short: the few drives tired him.

The Lawrence villa was close to the sea, and on a pleasant road bordered by pine-trees where we took brief strolls or sat on the rocks. Something in the lay of the land there reminded us both of the African country Lawrence had pictured in *The Escaped Cock*. As always, he and Frieda made us feel welcome. . . .

.   .   .   .

Lawrence's conversations during his last months interested me more than ever; in one of the first he said to me: "I intend to find God: I wish to realize my relation with Him. I do not any longer object to the word God. My attitude regarding this has changed. I must establish a conscious relation with God." These remarks surprised me, remembering how previously he had declared to my Brahmin friend [Dhan Gopal Mukerji] that "God is an exhausted concept." [367]

He spoke often of his illness, assigning different causes for it: "The hatred which my books have aroused comes back at me and gets me here"

—(tapping his chest). "It seems to me there is an evil spirit in my body; if I get the better of it in one place it goes to another." He strongly believed that psychic conditions are the cause of bodily ills. During this time he gained a greater tranquillity. But his illness depressed him; often he expressed his yearning to be well. Never did he give me the impression that he thought his recovery doubtful. He was willing to try many remedies.

Lawrence's humour was quiet and rather ironical. Sometimes he showed me the strange contents of his post, on which his remarks were highly interesting. Once a long letter came from a woman chronicling her career, and offering to give him the fullest details if Lawrence would use them for a book, and share the proceeds with her. His comment was: "I feel like replying—it doesn't matter what the events are, if the person, to whom they befall, is without character." Again a letter arrived from a reverend gentleman—the head of a large religious group in America— saying that his congregation were divided in the interpretation of *Lady Chatterley's Lover*, would he please tell him what he meant by the book. Lawrence sent him his pamphlet *Pornography and Obscenity*. His rule was never to answer letters from people unknown to him, and to disregard all requests for autographs.

He often expressed himself as ashamed that he had any money saved in banks or stocks. Lawrence so intensely resented the power of money over life, that when the financial crisis fell upon the New York markets, that winter, he furiously objected to being informed, or to Frieda's even looking to see, if it had affected their investments. Yet he worried about my financial affairs, sternly warning against improvidence.

He was speaking of good and evil: "Both exist. There is good and there is evil. There is no higher plane where evil is justified. You can *never never* justify murder." He had no sympathy with my remarks that by means of experience, through suffering and error, we arrive at wisdom which justifies all. He said: "I don't care for wisdom." At other times he reiterated this.

Again I was holding forth that my surest conviction is that everyone is acting as well as he is able to do, therefore utmost compassion is the most logical attitude toward people. Lawrence sat up in bed, his eyes blazed—but not in anger—and with tremendous force and emphasis he said: "*Don't you think* that I KNOW YOU?" What he meant to imply I do not know. Then he declared that he had more compassion than I. I was taken back by his personal remark, for I had been speaking impersonally. It might seem from this account that Lawrence resented my talking of what he felt I held in theory rather than in practice. On the contrary, I am sure his words contained no such resentment: he was simply stating the truth as he deeply felt it—that he *knew* me, that compassion was stronger in him. He was aware of his suffering which his compassion had entailed. But the incident still haunts me, as though I had missed some of its meaning: it was more of an affirmation than a question. Was it the declaration of his insight into our spiritual being, and the ties which unite us; the brotherhood which exists between us?

I reflect now from that incident how differently compassion manifests. Lawrence's compassion was of his *feelings* and ravaged him; in this respect he was Christian. It was actively manifest in many ways. He felt keenly the suffering of individuals and promptly sought to aid them: constantly, gifts of money and thoughtfully chosen things were being made by him to people of all sorts in various lands. He tried to help young writers. Injustice done to others he felt as much as most of us do when it is meted out to ourselves. It angered and wore on him. But does not compassion include more? Is that not also compassion which is of the mind, not suffering yet *understanding* and *forgiving*? Probably Lawrence cared less for this, and would not have agreed with the saying that "to know all is to forgive all."

Lawrence believed himself to have been more deeply aware of the ancient and prehistoric culture than our modern historians. One afternoon when we were alone together I listened thrilled by his description of ancient Egyptian life. Occasionally he would hesitate, stop, and then say: "No, I shall not tell that—no, no, why should I? You have only to look at Egyptian and Babylonian sculpture to see how different their culture was from what historians have described. Look at the seated Egyptian gods. The ancients had an ideal of splendour and power of which the man of to-day has no comprehension." I wonder if the modern reader is not unprepared for Plato's emphasis on splendour as a personal ideal. Lawrence often spoke in a way which implied that he was in possession of occult knowledge.

Lawrence was enjoying the Moffatt translation of the Bible; he remarked: "A great book should be retranslated every ten years." He used to say Jesus should not have allowed Judas to betray him: and that it was not enough to have said to Satan "Get thee behind me." He felt that men of spiritual insight should not renounce power, that for the sake of the world it was their duty to exercise power. Lawrence remarked: "I am almost certain that Jesus never expected to be crucified." Once Lawrence asked: "What would Jesus have done if when he told the rich young man to go and sell all that he had and give it to the poor, the young man had offered his wealth to Jesus?" [368]

Villa Beau Soleil./Bandol. Var. France/3 November 1929

❲ Dear [Brewster] Ghiselin

We had your letter yesterday, and you see where it finds us. We were in Germany the summer, very bad for my health, I was ill as could be, and am still rather wretched. However, I am thankful to be back in Bandol, where the sun shines and the sea sparkles. We have got this very ordinary little house right on the sea—on the Marseille side of the village, near the pine-grove. It is unpretentious but comfortable enough, my wife likes it, hangs up curtains and buys chairs—and I lie in bed and look at the islands out to sea, and think of the Greeks, and cough, and wish either that I was different or the world was different. No, but I really do wish my health was better—and I hope yours is perfectly good.

The Brewsters are here, also looking round for a house. They have left Capri for good (for the moment) and Mrs. Brewster wants to find a house she can buy and live in for ever and ever. As for Earl, I think he feels, as I do: "heaven is my home." We were talking about you just before your letter came, wondering about you as a married man, wondering if you hated Europe as much at a distance as you did at close quarters, wondering if you minded teaching, if you were more content, and what you were doing besides teach. Your letter answers a little of the wonderings, but not all.

I'm doing nothing at the moment. What with my health, and the stupidity over my pictures & the Pansies, I feel sort of fed up. —I suppose by the way, you've seen Knopf's Pansies. I see they are out, but haven't received a copy yet. I suppose there'll be another stupid press. How boring it all is!

I was once in Salt Lake City for a few hours. Such a clean, respectable place with a glorified chapel! But the country round was weird—seemed to me a bit macabre. One day you must run down to Taos, you are not far off. Mabel Luhan is there, & Miss Brett, and they'd be nice to you.

Do you remember the little fishes you painted here? Madame at the Beau Rivage recalled them and said what bijoux they were. And do you remember the drawing I was doing when you left? It became the painting "Spring," which I liked very much. Perhaps you'll see the reproduction one day—the original is sold.

Souvenirs:

D. H. Lawrence [369]

9 November 1929   Villa Beau Soleil, Bandol, Var, France

⟨ Rather changesome weather here—yesterday lovely, today raining. We've motored a bit with Brewsters, looking at houses. The country is lovely—yesterday, the lovely wide valley full of brilliant vines, beautiful, beautiful! I think they will take a little stone house, just like a smaller Mirenda on a hill-top, Château Brun—about 5 miles from here—quite lovely situation, lovely—but lonely, and no light nor bath nor water-closet—and water from wells—but very nice—and unfurnished, only two thousand five hundred francs a year—a pleasant old place. But hunting, one could find all sorts of things—and fascinating country. But I don't want to be so isolated. We shall get a bit bigger house in the spring—perhaps here—perhaps at St. Cyr-s.-mer or Les Lecques—about 7 miles nearer Marseilles from here. But it's easy and pleasant living here, suits me.

.   .   .   .

I'm feeling a good bit better—Frieda pretty well. From the outside world, little or no news.[370]

14 November 1929   Villa Beau Soleil, Bandol, Var, France

⟨ . . . Frieda is happy. She is now singing Schubert at the piano: but the gramophone [371]—"kiss your hand, Madame"—I only allow in the kitchen, with the doors shut. I do mortally hate it. Then we have pictures on the walls, covers on the "divan" etc. etc. —and Frieda is proud of her little house, though I call it a little railway station, and Achsah despises it terribly, calls it a vulgar box. She, however, is only too happy to come to it. The Huxleys are in Madrid, shivering, but admiring El Greco. . . .

There is no news in the world—our world. I was better and taking my little walks, but mostly through the pine trees towards the English-woman's house. Now I have got a chill—a touch of grippe—so am staying indoors a day or two. The country looks very lovely, the vines all red and yellow—we have been motoring several times with the B[rewster].'s—we had a very special octopus for supper on Saturday evening, and it was quite good, but still I had to shut my eyes.[372]

21 November 1929   Villa Beau Soleil, Bandol, Var, France

⟨ Yesterday Madame Douillet and her daughter—from the Beau Rivage —came to tea, and she talked of Earl and Achsah [Brewster], in all respect,

409

but it was rather funny. Pourquoi, Monsieur, pourquoi mangent-ils comme ça? pourquoi? C'est manger sans vouloir manger, n'est-çe pas? —It was a serious problem to her. And when I said: Voyez-vous, ils sont Bouddhistes, les devotes du dieu Bouddha, de l'Inde—she was all the more astonished and mystified. Can't get it at all. She brought us a pretty little palm tree in a pot, saying: J'ai pense à Monsieur—and she is going to send us some little gold-fish—and alive and swimming: also for Monsieur, I suppose. I am afraid Monsieur Mickie Beau Soleil, le chat jaune, les trouvera fort à son gout.

. . . .

I have been better lately, taking my little walks. We have had three lovely brilliant days, very blue, with a yellow sun sinking down in the sea at four o'clock. The wind is rather blowy, but from the east, and warm. We light the chauffrage centrale at tea-time, but all the day is warm. On Monday we baked bread, five loaves only, and white bread, because one cannot buy Vollkorn Mehl. But Mme. Douillet is getting us some—she calls it farine de saigle, which is Roggenmehl, but I hope it won't be, because that is so difficult to bake. Madame Martime, our femme de menage, was very jealous when we baked the bread, and bounced about the kitchen, and burnt Frieda's Apfelkuchen black. But I sat in the kitchen like a lion and watched my bread bake safely. It is very good, but nearly all eaten.[373]

21 November 1929   Villa Beau Soleil, Bandol, Var, France

❰ Here all goes very quietly. [Frederick Carter] is here, staying in the Beau Rivage. It is six years since I have seen him . . . .[374] He is not really interested in Apocalypse or Astrology any more—but of course he would like to get published this work he has already done. So I must see if I can manage it.[375]

Frederick Carter

At intervals in the autumn of 1929 I sent portions [of the *Dragon of Revelation*] along to [Lawrence] and near the year's end, as I had some affairs to look to in Paris, he suggested that I should go south and stay in Bandol for a little while to discuss the prospective book with him.[376]

410

In Bandol he was fixed, it seemed. He had decided in the summer that they would take a house in Florence, but it had been impossible; something milder and more equable was necessary. During his stay in Paris and whilst the disturbance in London over his paintings was going on, the illness of which he complained seemed to have caught a firmer grip on him. The wrangle about his pictures had distressed him. Police Court proceedings about their destruction conjoined with the strain of a piratical raid or two on his novel, *Lady Chatterley's Lover,* had been disastrous in their effect on his unstable throat and lungs. The dry and dusty air of Paris had helped the mental irritation. Later, in Germany, as I heard, he had collapsed desperately.

So there he was in the South of France held down by it. And he took a villa, "Beau Soleil," for six months' rest and to recover. They knew the place and liked it, for it had agreed with him when they had been there before. And the little house named after the beautiful sun that he adored, praised and glorified. It sounded pleasant.

When I left Paris that November night it was foggy and as chilly as is London of that season. But the next morning, at Marseilles, was full of sunshine, light and warmth. How ridiculous my heavy overcoat seemed. And all along the coast that morning beside the railway was the fabulous blue of the Mediterranean, either that or sun-browned earth, palm trees and cactus plants. What a land; ancient, stony, tumbled amongst rocky little hills, but warm. Yet it could change quickly enough to mist and rain and hard-blowing wind as I found before I left, for I was caught for a wetting in the walk from Beau Soleil villa back to the hotel the day I left.

Bandol itself is a small place, a little town yet abuilding with a few score yards of sand at the centre of a rock-bound bay, just enough stretch of it to make a *plage*. This is its asset as a summer pleasure resort, the bay with its patch of sand guarded by a jetty and a dozen cafés looking out on it. Rocks on the seacoast there are plenty, which are used as foundations for hotels that house visitors in the season. But in the winter these are empty in the main. The town is occupied by its own folk then, except for a few foreigners, the wandering invalids from the north and those few other strangers who live all the year round in the villas.

These villas are still being built every day, a little more and a little more they creep up, one and another. Splashed about here and there, of every size and shape, they gleam with all those sharp colours customary in Neapolitan ices. Sunshine makes them glow cheerfully along the slopes of the grey-brown countryside, but on a dull winter's day with a dash of

411

rain and mist they look sadly ephemeral against the hard landscape. They seem as sugary as sweetstuff, and as soluble and frail.

All the slopes up beyond the town here and there, even among the fungus-like villas, the ground is divided up into cultivated strips tilled by peasant folk. There they work all the time bent over close to the earth day in day out, loosening the soil with their very hands, watering it actually with their sweat, holding it together with stone terraces on the steeper places. Their way with it is strange—affecting even—to Northern eyes. How close they hug it, intent, concentrated, man and woman turning it over with short-handled, large-bladed hoes, both of them at work in a slow, easy way, but none the less unremitting, urgent, pressing and scratching it into more life and productivity. Flowers and vegetables they grow amongst those stones; indeed, anything profitable they drag out with the sun—the friendly sun—to aid.

There alongside Lawrence's villa in late November bloomed a whole field full of narcissus flowers. Brilliant against the dark pine copse beyond, they stood, day by day coming to fuller profusion and glory. Even on the dullest of days and in the rain, that field shone and flashed. And sitting on the veranda of the villa on sunny days it radiated its pure clarity of colour through the whole air, reflecting back the sun's cool winter light.

How Mrs. Lawrence gazed with round eyes and round mouth in ecstatic longing—longing just to creep through the wire fence and come back again with an armful. They could be begged from the grower, of course, but that would be no fun. The way to enjoy them was to gain them by skill, cunning, adroitness, coming back in warm laughing triumph from the expedition with face splashed with dew from the mass of blooms in one's arms. But after all they could be bought cheaply enough of a morning on the *plage;* she consoled herself with the thought, and the field of bloom remained unravished until they were cut for market.

At the extreme point of the cape that guarded the little bay of Bandol lay the villa they had taken. It was protected from direct sea-winds by the little pine wood that grew on the very verge of the rocky shore. Walking out from the town towards it the road took one behind the hotels and villas built into the rocks at the edge of the bay and then, coming out beside the water a little way from Villa Beau Soleil, became a lane—a path—by the water's edge. At one's feet as one walked the sea—the Mediterranean—ran amongst the rocks, slapping sharply at the hard edge of the land. One forgot the enormous advertisement at the lane's corner directing to the Splendide Hotel, except that it marked the proper turning in a tangle of similar side roads.

When I got off the train at Bandol station Earl Brewster met me. Lawrence, he explained, was not well enough to come along. He took me to the hotel, where he too was staying, and after lunch we strolled along to the villa. A very different Lawrence from the one I remembered sat on the *terrasse* awaiting us in the warm afternoon sunshine. He rose from his seat as we came up the steps; he rose slowly and turned towards us. The tall, sharp-shouldered figure was exaggerated now to the extreme of fragility. Before, he was slight but very brisk and alert, now he was frail and tired. Fatigue and weariness lay on him.

Live and direct were his eyes even yet, and firm in gaze. And the ruggedness of brow and head with hair tumbled across above the eyes was still the same. But the heavy head overweighted those thin shoulders in the wrinkled blue flannel jacket. Colour, too, had gone out of his beard, its redness had darkened, the vividness, length, the aggressiveness had gone.

A few days before, as Brewster had explained, Lawrence had been desperately ill and they had been truly alarmed at the condition he had fallen to. He was worn down beyond all seeming. Every day Brewster went along to massage him with oil and he told with distress how emaciated and martyrized was his body. It had become terrifying in its meagreness, just like, as he described it, one of the haggard, mediaeval, carved figures of the crucified Jesus.

And even when I looked at him the frailty of his limbs beneath his clothes made me afraid. The knee-bones of him showed tiny in his grey flannel trousers and his little flannel coat seemed corrugated by the shoulder bones beneath.

His voice, too, was tired, though it still had the same fluting note in it. For the moment he was worn down and subdued. But a few days later his spirit had risen again and once more he delivered his long monologues on people and things, broken with sharp questions, teasing, sudden, embarrassing interrogations. About acquaintances and friends of ours, people we knew, their ways of life, their interests, thoughts, prejudices and familiar interests he told, with all the queer humour and acrid penetrative analysis that was so characteristic of his conversation.

Spiteful, as Frieda Lawrence called it sometimes, and particularly when the names of certain familiar targets came up. When [H. G.] Wells was mentioned one day, for example, she called out to him: "Now don't be spiteful, Lorenzo," as he began an anecdote. It was one of Huxley's stories he recounted, I believe. But, of course, he went on only the longer for the interpellation and only the more sinister was the curious high whinny

413

of a laugh that he gave when he had achieved the droll revelatory traits of character in his tale. A feminine-sounding laugh it was too, near to a cackle and old-maidish. Uncontrolled, something of sharp disappointment burst out in it, and of malice; ungenial it was, as if something baffled and sterile cried out in him.

But for all that, one had to admit real hard sense behind these mannerisms. However acrid his expression in judgment, there was penetration, accuracy and often remarkable exactness in his final summing up. A certain satirical turn, but with that a deep significance lay in his gossiping and jesting. He was a real tale-teller. His malice gave the piquancy and sauce to his tale, touching it with a gleam of that deliberate exaggeration in fact, which makes revelatory the penetration of true caricature.

Actually, and perhaps obviously, he had a remarkable feeling for the natural grotesque which exists in character and makes that variant from the norm lying in everybody. It gave gusto to the description of people in his conversation. As it existed in his books it was less obvious, less hard and direct, being interspersed with so much that existed peculiarly in his writing giving a quite feminine warmth and intimacy. Yes, he was more masculine in his talk than he was in his writing. Perhaps it would be better said that in his actions he was more positive and male, but in thoughts more feminine.

As he retold stories of which one had already seen a version in print— some from *England, My England,* as an example—giving the true names of people and places, the queer closeness with which the published story followed the original facts made one gasp. What hard penetration had been in the eyes he had cast upon the personal affairs of his friends. No wonder they had been perturbed when the stories had appeared.

How he had loved to pillory a father god in the household: papa dominant, affable, prosperous, alert, full of warmth and affection towards his daughters—and jealous, too, being a possessive god of the house and god of the garden. It had a bitter sense—this sort of fatherhood—not to his taste. Maybe had he possessed children of his own begetting he would have less resented the lordly dominance of paterfamilias.

A jealous god he seemed to be to Lawrence, Eden's Lord. And he was suspicious of Jehovah. How Lawrence stood up for Eve—lived for her emotionally and strove to her justification so soon as he sat down to write. But not nearly so much was he of that disposition of mind when he talked. More obvious in his satire, perhaps more ready to jeer laughingly at both parties, but rather more on the side of his own sex, too—and even, it may be, more just and fair in the main issues between man and woman.

Tales like this he told for the company sitting after tea. His wife was German, his visitors were American, but there in the stucco villa on the Mediterranean tea there was about four every afternoon, English fashion. It was homely, too, even there, for the winter sun set early and there came a warmth of atmosphere to the cold evening light as we sat around the tea-table.

So when the Brewsters, his American friends, came he introduced them by means of his tales to far-off English circles and presented patriarchs and adoring daughters to them. Less frequently he told of riotous sons. Figures of old time they seemed, bearing all the characteristics of the age now just gone when families strove to breed masterful men and biddable women.

But with that, too, were gossiping stories about his own family and his youth where he clearly lived again, very often, in memory. The dominant figure of his mother, the striving devoted woman of the north country, informed it; all her voice spoke through him, and her estimates of the circle of relations gave the ultimate standard of their values.

Some days, at Achsah Brewster's instigation, he would be induced to sing his favourite old English songs. Whilst Frieda Lawrence played on the small upright piano in the corner of the room we others joined in a chorus or sang out the words of any tune that came up as the songbook's pages were turned over. Lawrence was particularly fond of one or two quaint country songs, one especially esteemed, *Turnip Hoeing*, which he gave with a strong Derbyshire accent. Pleasant was the winter evening as the light died over the southern sea to the sound of the broad-spoken country words as he sang.

He was not too short for breath for that, indeed, but very often it showed as he talked, that weakness in his lungs and throat. He became breathless and his remarks died away in a kind of sighing aspiration. Lacking resonance his voice fell flat and without ring in it. It beat at one like the sound of a knock on a board.

Most difficult of all to pass over without alarm and even horror was his incessant spitting, that in itself gave an atmosphere of fear and threat. He didn't cough loudly, but simply and carefully spat into an envelope. Once one's presence became familiar and he sensed himself secure from comment, he gave the slightest coughs, an apologetic throat sound, and took out an envelope. These he had about everywhere from his ample correspondence, and they were kept to expectorate into. In his jacket pocket he kept them, and they were folded up when used and neatly returned into his pocket again. He would discuss his illness as if it were due to throat trouble from a bronchial cold—a weakness of the bronchial tubes that was difficult to overcome—and to get rid of; and it was tiresomely liable to recur. Only that, nothing more.

Mornings he usually lay abed and wrote in his room. One entered through a large glazed double door from the *terrasse*. But ordinarily it was not till the afternoon that I went, taking tea, and after a talk left at seven for my dinner at the hotel.

At this time the Brewsters were taking over a house called Chateau Brun, a few miles off. A pleasant, Provençal farmhouse, standing high up on a hillside. The man who farmed the land, working it right up to its very doors, lived a couple of hundred yards away. I saw him stolidly at work behind the house apparently ploughing the top of a low stone wall. It was a little containing wall holding together a strip of soil on the hillside, but from where I stood he, his horse and plough moved along the level of the wall top, diligent and preoccupied. He never even looked up towards me.

One morning we all went by automobile to look at the new place, taking Lawrence with us. He pottered about and watched the painting and finally squatted on his heels by the fireplace, making a fire with twigs to dry the new colour-washed walls. He sat there feeding the fire with the bits of stick I carried in. Looking like a collier, he stayed all morning perched on his toes, elbows on knees. Frieda called out: "Look at Lorenzo sitting on his heels. He always does it—just like a miner." She seemed almost vain of his accomplishment.

While I was staying there, of course, a certain amount of time was spent discussing the project of the book on Revelation and its symbols, for that was the main reason for my visit. He wanted opinions and urged for anything suggestive that could be used to define the place of the author, who and what he was in the new world religion. Perhaps it would be better defined to say that to displace the accepted author was what he wanted.

Still he held to the same point that had been in his mind when we had discussed the thesis of Revelation and its symbols years before. The matter held in suspension in the book fascinated him and the glimpse it gave of a great and splendid world order. But not the author St. John the Divine. No, no, he hated him. How he snarled at John's Christianity and refused him even the credit of having assembled together an old inheritance of stellar myths in the interest of the new-found faith. No, it was a work written long before Christianity, taken over and mauled about and plastered up with pious Jewy texts.

This was one notion he put forward. There were others, for he busily devised scheme upon scheme to eliminate the Johnisms—the sentiments and morals of the new religion.

Of all the writers dealing with the origins of this Apocalypse he preferred Dupuis' version in the *Religion Universelle*.[377] Not that Lawrence had read Dupuis, but I had, and gave him a synopsis of the argument. This was to the effect that in it existed the only document that had come down to us of all the secret cults, the sole survivor giving a full description of the Mithraic initiation with its symbols and figures. He liked this notion of an exposition derived from the one cult and preserved as canonical and inspired by its foe. But his critical sense made him doubtful of it.

Well, after all, that to him was the grand idea, a pagan document uncovering all the secrets of the cosmos and revealing the mysteries of the heavens as they are imprinted upon the mind of man within him. Yes, in the end, did it matter much who told the story of the stars and the skies and the way through them to the mansions of new life in the many coloured city above.

.　.　.　.　.　.　.　.　.　.　.　.

. . . Against the feeling of striving back to heaven, of climbing painfully there amid protestations of sin and repentance for it, [Lawrence] reacted violently. As he said with grim humour in reply to a reassuring comment when he left Bandol and was taken from "Beau Soleil" to the sanatorium under doctor's orders fearing—declaring—that it meant the end: "Our next good times together will be in heaven, I'm afraid—and I've never believed that I should like it."

.　.　.　.　.　.　.　.　.　.　.　.

These things of course came up again and again whilst we talked in the little villa's sitting-room or in the bedroom with its brass bedstead where he lay a-mornings. But he said little of what he was doing, stopping his writing and putting aside the exercise book in which he did his work without remark, as one arrived. In fact, he usually was secretive about his work in progress, whatever it might be.

However, before I left to return to London in order to prepare the last chapters of the book—the *Dragon of Revelation* as it was to be called —our joint book, he let me know that he had already written nearly twenty thousand words of introduction. But news from New York was bad and he could not decide to which publisher to offer the book. His confidence on the acceptance by an American publisher had been sadly

417

broken by the stock market collapse there. Could I find one in London? What form should the book take? All was in flux again.

When, after my work was finished, I suggested that it was time to decide, he had changed his opinion again. He wrote that in his view the long introduction would not be suitable, and that he had done another, much shorter one, which he believed to be more suitable. Better for my purpose. One that I should prefer.[378]

Plans again had to be changed. But before this new scheme had been more than agreed upon the last dolorous succession of collapses had begun. He wrote a note to announce the abandonment, unfinished, of his longer essay on Revelation, the probability of going into a sanatorium: "No luck," he wrote [4 February 1930], on a postcard, which on its reverse bore the picture of a grinning tiger's head in colour—all teeth and tongue and snarl. A strange premonition seemed to hang about that deadly grin—it gave a shiver in its conjunction with his message.[379]

But strange, and more strange, coming after this last endeavour to expound the book of the last things—the Revelation—after all the talk of the way of the seeking spirit-books discussed, planispheres examined and manipulated to discern the path through the heavens and the way of the little creature man back to the Father of stars—after this Apocalyptic strife to discern the course of the last Judgement and the ultimate secrets of the seven heavens—after writing to the last permitted instant until the work was ended by a specialist and a sanatorium. What then? Why, that of all things, the name of the place—the sanatorium—in Vence to which he was carried off should have been Ad Astra. Yes! from the house with the name of the divinity he loved and applauded, the house of the Beautiful Sun—Beau Soleil—he went to a house of Stars to face the end.[380]

10 December 1929   Villa Beau Soleil, Bandol, Var, France

❨ *My health is rather a nuisance—doesn't recover very well from the setback in the summer. But I hope the turn of the year will improve it. Walking is the worst—I hardly go a stride—much worse than last year. Yet in myself I don't think I'm worse. But what a weariness it is! We've had a few lovely sunny days, but really rather too warm. The yellow narcissus are in full flower—and the fresh young radishes and new potatoes are very good—grown since the rain. That Obscenity pamphlet [381] has already sold over 6,000—quite a stir.[382]*

15 *December 1929*   Villa Beau Soleil, Bandol, Var, France

❲ *I have roughly finished my introduction* [to the Dragon of Revelation], *and am going over it, working it a bit into shape. I'm hoping I can get Brewster's daughter to type it—she comes this week. —God knows what anybody will think of it. . . .*

We've had the most beautiful weather lately—brilliant sunny days, and warm. This morning is another calm and lovely morning. —The Brewsters are still in the hotel—had no money to go to their house with—not a sou even to pay the hotel: but thank goodness, some has come at last—or almost come—so are a little nearer. Today the grand piano is being sent up from Toulon, and they are going to welcome it. It will be the first piece of furniture in the chateau!—all alone. —We are quite a party—Mr. and Mrs. di Chiara,[383] from Capri, are in the hotel—also Mrs. Eastman,[384] from New Mexico. They all troop along to tea, so the Beau Soleil resounds with voices, and the cat goes away in disgust.[385]

19 *December 1929*   Villa Beau Soleil, Bandol, Var, France

❲ We are still a colony here, the Brewsters still in the hotel . . . . The daughter [Harwood] comes to-day from England: and on Saturday Ida Rauh's [386] son comes from Geneva: the di Chiaras are still in the hotel: so we have parties. I went to lunch at the hotel on Tuesday, but had a headache after, drinking Chablis, I suppose, so I shan't go again. My sister sent plum-pudding and cake and mincemeat, so I expect we shall have a little Christmas party.

Did you read of Henry Crosby—the American in Paris who printed "Escaped Cock"? He shot himself in New York, and shot a young woman along with him. Horrible! The wife is bringing his ashes back to Paris.[387]

.   .   .   .

The world is certainly mad: and worse than ever.

The pamphlet on Obscenity which I wrote at Rottach, at the Angermeier, has made the old ones hate me still more in England, but it has sold very well, and had a very good effect, I think. Toujours la guerre.[388]

19 December 1929   Villa Beau Soleil, Bandol, Var, France

⟨[It was very warm, lovely, and sunny here till Tuesday! When it went
cold. Today is sunny and clear, but cold, the sun has no strength. I keep
mostly indoors. It's a bit too sharp for me.

.   .   .   .

The cat made an attack on the goldfish today, and a few small brilliant
gold scales are floating loose. I spanked him, and he looked like a Chinese
demon. Now he's trying to make up to me, but I'm cold.

The sun is just going down: coldly, from a milk-blue sea.

There come the friends.[389]

23 December 1929   Villa Beau Soleil, Bandol, Var, France

⟨[[My] health is enough to depress the Archangel Michael himself. My
bronchials are really awful. It's not the lungs.

I shall be pleased to see Dr. Morland, if he really wants to take the
trouble to stop off here. But I don't like the thought of troubling him.[390]

Achsah Barlow Brewster

Lawrence began a preface to Frederick Carter's essays on the Apocalypse. He would say that the final proof of insanity was to have a theory
about the Apocalypse! That preface grew beyond bounds and became a
book. When the Christmas holidays arrived Harwood typed it off for him,
his last book.[391]

She had returned from school in England bringing hampers from
Lawrence's two sisters. He served out their contents at a Christmas Eve
party, supervising every detail, even helping to make lemon tarts. With
his unfailing generosity he had carefully selected gifts for everyone. He
had painted a clock putting a sun-burst design around the face that—"the
sun might never set" for us!

During the school term Harwood had been given the subject for an
essay, the sketch of some great man. When she wrote that she was un-
decided whether to choose the Buddha or her Uncle David (as she called
Lawrence), Lawrence chuckled and when he saw Harwood asked: "Well,
who has won out, Lord Buddha or My Uncle David?" He took satisfaction in being the chosen one.

Ida Raugh [*sic*] arrived from Taos telling him the latest news, among other items a tale of the murdering of a young man who was picnicking with his bride on a mountain, when an Indian joined them and shared their luncheon. Afterwards they were walking on in single file when the Indian suddenly shot the young man dead. Some of us decided it was sheer mountain madness such as seizes a lonely shepherd. Lawrence emphatically disagreed. He asserted that it was because the man had his back turned to the Indian, and that deep in the heart of every primitive being is the impulse to creep out and kill anything that had its back turned. "You've no right to walk on ahead of a primitive creature. He'll shoot you, or stick a knife into you, if you do. It's his nature."

News of the suicide of Harry Crosby reached Lawrence, a terrible blow, for he was a man whom Lawrence had loved and admired. Lawrence sat in bed, his eyes showing large in his pale face, swathed in a scarf of Frieda's to protect his ears, which were troubling him. Some of the flame of his beard seemed to die out. He looked utterly miserable and sorrowfully reiterated: "That's all he could do with life, throw it away. How could he betray the great privilege of life?"

Lawrence attended a New Year's luncheon given by the Di Chiaras which he enjoyed with his usual zest, but he lingered overlong, and walked to the village to sit down in a cutting wind. From that time he steadily lost flesh.

He still came out to our place bringing friends with him. It was a pastime with him to watch the repairs we were trying to make to an old house and garden. He would look over the olives telling us that they must be pruned, sniffing the wild thyme crushed into fragrance by his feet.

One afternoon we were with him and Frieda at Villa Beau Soleil, he began selecting some of his "Nettles" for a small volume. There were to be others called "Dead Nettles," because they were to have no sting in them. He turned the pages of his notebook, adding that he had been writing some verses about death and would read them; then, shaking his head wistfully, he closed the book, saying: "I can't read them now."

Lawrence's friends in England sent Dr. Morland, who proved so sympathetic that Lawrence followed his advice and lay still on a couch screened off in a sheltered corner of the garden. He lay there meditating, with a great calm over his face.

Before this he had been reading methods of mental healing. He exclaimed critically that you must not lie to yourself, a lie flies back and hits you twice as hard in the end. When you go on saying to yourself that you are good and sweet, but feel ugly all the time, you'll just grow into horrid, hideous old things. It was suggested that you can turn your thoughts from your own imperfections and meditate on perfection. He grew more and more to look as though this were what he was doing.[392]

6 January 1930   Villa Beau Soleil, Bandol, Var, France

❨ *I'm rather better but don't get on much. Still, I think I'm better—warily. Frieda's got a cold for a change.*

Already the year is changing round. Ida Rauh being here, we talk, of course, of Taos and the ranch, and plan to go back in the spring. It might pick me up again: who knows?

Pino and Douglas were very sweet, but rather on the holiday razzle, so rather depressing. I find that people who are on the razzle, enjoying themselves, are so inwardly miserable and agacé, they are a real trial.[393]

Norman Douglas

The last time I saw Lawrence was at Bandol on the 4 January 1930. They were living in one of those dreadful little bungalows built of gaudy cardboard—there may have been one or two bricks in it as well—which grow up overnight, like a disfiguring eruption, along that coast. Lawrence was a sick man; sick to death. His voice was weak, and he moved about with difficulty. He produced a bottle of French cognac: wouldn't I have a glass? He spoke of the flowers in their garden, of the clamour of the waves on stormy days. Not much later, in the beginning of March, I strewed a few red carnations on his grave at Vence—an inoffensive gesture.[394]

6 January 1930   Villa Beau Soleil, Bandol, Var, France

❨ *We talk and make plans: plans of coming back to the ranch . . . and perhaps having a sort of old school, like the Greek philosophers, talks in a garden—that is, under the pine-trees. I feel I might perhaps get going with a few young people, building up a new unit of life out there, making a new concept of life. Who knows! We have always talked of it. My being ill so long has made me realise perhaps I had better talk to the young and try to make a bit of a new thing with them, and not bother much more* about my own personal life. Perhaps now I should submit, and be a teacher. I have fought so against it.

For my own part, though I am perhaps more irascible, being more easily irritable, not being well, still, I think I am more inwardly tolerant and companionable. Who knows! Anyhow, people's little oddities don't frighten me any more: even their badnesses. . . . Frieda is suspicious, but I think even she is weary of the old watchful and hostile attitude, and doesn't care very much when people affront her a bit. So many of our feelings are illusion. We don't really have them. . . .

I wish we could start afresh with this year.[395]

21 January 1930   Villa Beau Soleil, Bandol, Var, France

⟨ The doctor from England [Dr. Andrew Morland] came on Monday [20 January 1930]—says the bronchitis is acute, and aggravated by the lung. I must lie still for two months.—Talks of my going into a sanatorium near Nice, but I don't know if it's suitable. And I don't know if I shall go. He says with absolute care for two months, absolute rest from everything, I ought to be well enough to come to New Mexico and there get quite strong.—I believe I should get strong if I could get back: but I'm not well enough to travel yet. I must see. As soon as I can come I want to come. The thing to do is to take one's hands entirely off the body, and let it live of itself, have its own will. It is by the body we live and we have forced it too much. Now it refuses to live.[396]

Dr. Andrew Morland

My acquaintance with D. H. Lawrence was only of a few days duration and began within two months of his death in March, 1930. Mutual friends in England [397] had become increasingly anxious about his health and I readily agreed to the request that I should see and advise him during a visit my wife and I were paying to the South of France early in January; I had been warned that he did not like doctors and might well refuse to be examined and moreover that any advice given must be simple and precise as he was in the habit of twisting round doctors' prescriptions, accepting the small part that suited his mood at the time and forgetting the rest.

We began with a social visit—afternoon tea—walking from Bandol to the Lawrences' villa on the sea coast just outside the little town. He was waiting for us when we arrived, a colourful figure with bright blue coat, red hair and beard and lively blue eyes; he lost no time in making us warmly welcome. While his wife prepared tea he made the toast himself treating the operation as though it were a serious matter and at the same time great fun. After tea we talked for a while by the fireside, Lawrence being altogether charming and gently witty, but it was not long before it was obvious that, although enjoying himself, he was tiring rapidly. We therefore hastened to say goodbye and I arranged to come again in the morning on a professional visit.

The next morning I found that although Lawrence had obviously been suffering from pulmonary tuberculosis for a very long time—probably 10 or 15 years [398]—he had either never been properly advised about treatment or, much more likely, he had chosen to ignore most of the advice given while remembering a few unimportant details. I found him extremely emaciated, obviously very ill and needing bed rest of many months if he were to have a chance to arrest the disease. All he seemed to know about the treatment of tuberculosis was what he had learned from his friend Mark Gertler who had fully regained his health after some months in a sanatorium; the only lesson he could remember was that he should walk three or four miles every morning and that he should drink a lot of milk. Lawrence had tried with pathetic determination to do these walks but recently they had been quite beyond his strength and he had taken to driving instead. He admitted to getting tired very quickly particularly when visited by admiring strangers from across the Atlantic.

Although the severity of his illness was clear I did not feel altogether hopeless as he had never given proper treatment a chance and his resistance to the disease must have been remarkable to have enabled him to survive so long while doing all the wrong things. My difficulty was how to arrange for him to have the medical supervision and surroundings he needed. His own idea was to get back to New Mexico but, quite apart from the immigration difficulties, he was so ill that I did not think he would survive the journey. He was strongly averse to treatment in either Switzerland or England and the only possibility seemed to lie in finding some reasonably suitable place not too far away. The Mediterranean Coast itself has a bad reputation for this type of case and the exposed situation of Bandol aggravated his bronchitis. I therefore recommended that he should move to a small sanatorium at Vence which is a well-situated resort about 1000 feet above sea level and some miles inland.

Lawrence would never have tolerated a strict sanatorium but this one was more like a private hotel but with medical and nursing facilities available.

The Lawrences moved up to Vence about a fortnight later and the X-ray which was sent to me confirmed my impression of a remarkable resistance. There was a very extensive scarring but only one tiny cavity. At first the change seemed to do a little good, in any case Lawrence wrote to me that he found the air better and that Frieda, his wife, was relieved at having him under proper care. Unfortunately within a few weeks an attack of pleurisy precipitated a relapse which his emaciated frame could not withstand. Characteristically he turned against the sanatorium and insisted, within a few days of his death, on being moved to a villa in the village.

This sad story illustrates the incompatibility between a certain type of genius and the ordered way of life necessary for recovery from tuberculosis.[399] Those very qualities which gave Lawrence such keen perception and such passionate feeling made it quite impossible for him to submit for any length of time to a restricted sanatorium existence; the ingredients for tragedy were therefore present from the start and its course, although slow, was inexorable.[400]

21 January 1930   *Villa Beau Soleil, Bandol, Var, France*

❨ *All very quiet here . . . doctor says perhaps I must go into a sanatorium for a couple of months. Perhaps I will, I am tired of being always defeated by bad health. It has been rather bitter to me, this not being able to get better, for such a long time. But the body has a strange will of its own, and nurses its own chagrin.*

Frieda's sister [Else] is staying with us—and her daughter Barbara comes next week—so we are not lonely. The weather has been quite lovely— a grey day today, but I don't mind it. It is nice here, but there is something curiously flat and uninteresting about the French—though they are very nice to us here.[401]

Dr. Else Jaffe-Richthofen

After the years of separation caused by the war, Lawrence, Frieda, and I met many times at my mother's in Baden-Baden. I was with them

425

at the Villa Mirenda, and in the autumn of 1928 Prof. Weber,[402] my daughter and I met the Lawrences at Le Lavandou after I had spent a few days with them in the cold and unfriendly town of Gsteig-bei-Gstaad in Switzerland. We went on a trip to Port-Cros to the Vigie, the fort on the romantic island, which, with its damp walls, was singularly unsuited for an invalid such as Lawrence. But he and my sister had come to a rational way of dealing with his illness—everyone must live and die according to his own precept. So one can scarcely excuse Dr. Mohr for enticing Lawrence, when the latter was in Germany once more in the late summer of 1929, and already then a very sick man, to stay with him in a shady valley by Tegernsee. We visited Lawrence there—he was lying in a bare room in the mean village inn. Beside him stood a great bush of pale blue autumn gentians as the only furnishing.[403] When in the winter of 1930 the news became progressively worse, I spent a fortnight in January of that year with Lawrence and my sister at Beau Soleil, Bandol. Even now, Lawrence was working. Often he would endeavour to spend a few hours in the garden, lying in the sun, with a view over the rocky coast, against which the blue waves broke. He was still full of plans for travelling, but how sadly he said, "Else, I would do anything, to get well."

In these long years of close relationship, I experienced only happy and harmonious hours with Lawrence—perhaps our relationships, for all their warmth of feeling, were not sufficiently intimate for him to direct his "outbreaks" at me. (Even the fact that there was a mistake in his name in my translation of *The Boy in the Bush* and he was called "H. D. L." instead of D. H. L. did not make him angry. He only laughed at me.) But I have him to thank for a wealth of intellectual stimulation, and to be with him was a privilege. Among my books are many volumes of Thomas Hardy which he gave me and of which he was very fond, especially *Far from the Madding Crowd*,[404] and Samuel Butler's *The Way of All Flesh*. He did not appreciate Galsworthy at all.[405]

When *Sons and Lovers* appeared he asked me if I would translate it— more perhaps because he had the gift of stirring and stimulating people "to do something" than for the sake of his book. That he should entrust it to me was an honor. You see, I still remember it today. At that time I had other things to do. Later I translated *The Boy in the Bush* (*Jack im Bushland*), published in Deutsche Verlag-Ansbach, 1925; "The Fox," in the Insel Verlag; and "The Woman Who Rode Away," also in the Insel Verlag. I am especially fond of "The Woman Who Rode Away." The Insel Verlag have not published a cheap translation of *The Plumed Serpent*, and had Herbert E. Herlitschka revise it.[406]

30 *January 1930*   *Villa Beau Soleil, Bandol, Var, France*

⟨ *Here all has gone rather badly . . . . The doctor came from England, and said I must lie in bed for two months, and do no work, and see no people, only rest. So I do that. On sunny days I lie out of doors in the garden on a leigestuhl—otherwise I am in bed. And I get weary in my soul. My cough also is a great nuisance. So this year Bandol has not been much help.*

Frieda's sister Else, Frau Jaffe, was here last week: and now F's daughter Barbara is with us: I don't know for how long. In February my two sisters are coming together. The Huxleys are in London, because Point Counter Point is being made into a play, a drama—the first night is to-night. . . .[407]

. . . If I can get well, I want to go to America, to the ranch, because I believe I should get better there. I wish it were possible to sail at the end of March.

.   .   .   .

The weather is sunny, the almond trees are all in blossom, beautiful, but I am not allowed any more to go out and see them.[408]

Barbara Weekley Barr

In the winter of 1929–1930, I had a letter from Frieda from a villa they had taken at Bandol called the "Beau Soleil." Lawrence was now extremely ill and spent a good deal of time in bed. People were trying to persuade him to go into a sanatorium. "They say he must have a nurse. He says, 'Can't I have Barby?'" she wrote. This pleased me, and I went out to Bandol, arriving there one winter evening.

The Beau Soleil was a little box of a villa near the sea.

Lawrence was sitting up in bed, wearing a blue cloth jacket. A ginger cat was sleeping on his bed, making him look quite homely.

After supper we sorted out some papers together. "Don't yawn, Barby, it's boring!" he said, engrossed.

"The nights are so awful," he told me. "At two in the morning, if I had a pistol I would shoot myself."

Sometimes Lawrence walked feebly into the garden, and lay on a chaise longue. He felt Frieda could not help him any more, and this made him resentful. Covered with rugs, and lying in the garden with a grey, drawn expression on his face, he said, "Your mother is repelled by the death in me."

Some Americans came to see him. Lawrence said the wife was going mad because she had tried to insist on the ideal of goodness and beauty. The proprietress of the hotel came and chatted with him in her bright French way, but she, too, got on his nerves.

The person who seemed to tire him least was the cook's cracked old husband, who would come and stand at the foot of his bed, waving his peaked cap, talking inconsequently, and laughing like a noodle.

A young doctor from an English sanatorium came to see him with his consumptive wife. Lawrence liked her. "She is like all people with chest trouble . . . gives too much life away," he remarked.

I cooked some of Lawrence's meals, especially his breakfast, because he liked porridge. Frieda found me a little "managing," I think—a little like Ada.

We all three decided to go to the ranch in New Mexico for which Lawrence longed, believing he could recover there. Frieda thought that I could go out first, and stay with Mabel Luhan.

Lawrence was amazed at this suggestion. "What on earth do you think that Mabel would want with Frieda's daughter?" he demanded. "You might just as well throw Barby into the sea!"

"But if you and your mother really could love each other," he said to me later, "you might make a life together." [409]

30 January 1930   Villa Beau Soleil, Bandol, Var, France

⟨ *Here all is the same—I lay out today in the mouth of the garage, because the mistral is blowing—a sunny, brilliant day with blue sea and sharp white foam.*

Barby helps Frieda to look after me, and all goes very well. Yesterday the bronchitis was much better, but today it is tiresome again—probably the wind.

The doctor sent word about the nursing home at Vence—it is not much of a place—like a little hotel or convalescent home. If I make good progress here, I shall not go to Vence—but if I don't get better, I will. But truly, I am already much stronger for this rest.[410]

Villa Beau Soleil/Bandol/Var. France/30 January 1930

❲ Dear Dorothy [Warren]

I am thinking you won't want to be bothered holding my pictures much longer, and as I never want to show any of them again, and care nothing about selling them, I think the best thing to do would be to turn them all over to my sister Mrs. Clarke, and let her store them in her attic, where she has lots of room. So would you give Maria Huxley her North Sea—and you take Contadini—and then perhaps the others could go in their cases and be sent off to Ripley (Derby.). You have the address: Mrs. W. E. Clarke, Broadway. Anyhow let me know. I haven't written my sister yet, about it, but I'll do so.

My health is rotten this winter. Now I'm ordered to stay in bed for two months, and not budge. Am very tired of it.

I hope you and Philip are well and flourishing—and I hope you think of us affectionately, as we do of you.

Send a line

D. H. Lawrence [411]

3 *February 1930*   Villa Beau Soleil, Bandol, Var, France

❲ I have decided to go to the Sanatorium that Dr. Morland recommended —Ad Astra, Vence A.M. . . . . It is above Nice. I've arranged to go on Thursday [6 February 1930] . . . they say it's nice there. . . . Of course I hate going—but perhaps it won't be so bad.[412]

Achsah Barlow Brewster

The morning before they left, Mickie sat disconsolately outside the shut door of Lawrence's room. When this was opened it disclosed Lawrence propped up in bed, galley sheets piled thick about him, correcting proofs of his *Nettles*. He raised his eyes from the pages, saying that he would be coming back soon to stay in our pine grove. I believed him. In his last letter to me, as in one of his first,[413] he asserts that he shall pitch his tent near us, a hope to which we all had remained constant through the years.[414]

Earl H. Brewster

Remembering how often people with affected lungs live for many years in that condition, we could not believe those were Lawrence's last days. We thought with proper care he would recover. Perhaps he intentionally hid from us the seriousness of his conditions; but he always spoke cheerfully of future plans. I cannot believe he thought his death was near. My wife and I had taken an old farmhouse a few miles distance from Bandol. Lawrence motored over to see us several times and talked of coming to stay with us in the spring; we planned to have a tent for him under a great pine-tree near our house.

Yet the time came (in early February) when after much debating he decided to try a sanatorium at Vence—which is on the hills behind Nice and Cannes—about five hours journey from Bandol. I drove with him and Frieda to Toulon, where we took the train for Antibes. The train was so crowded that Frieda engaged a private compartment. It was a day of bright moving clouds and intermittent sunshine. All three of us were depressed by the thought of a sanatorium: now it seems that the seriousness of our mood had been like a dim intuition. But we enjoyed the beauty of the country and marvelled at the blossoming almond trees. Like the fleeting sunshine of the day itself the conversation at times became gay and amusing. At Antibes Lawrence was met by friends who motored us to Vence: he talked and seemed very much himself.[415]

VENCE, ALPES MARITIMES, FRANCE

7 February 1930   Ad Astra Sanatorium, Vence, Alpes Maritimes, France

⟨ *I have submitted and come here to a sanatorium—sort of sanatorium—and Frieda is in the hotel—I came yesterday. It doesn't seem very different from an ordinary hotel—but the doctors are there to look after one. . . . It's quite a nice place here—the air is good, and one is aloft.*[416]

Earl H. Brewster

At the sanatorium Lawrence was assigned a room with walls of a deep overpowering blue, but it had a large terrace overlooking a vast expanse of mountains and sea. He at once gave me the impossible task of finding him something readable from the library of the sanatorium, which was largely composed of French translations of Walter Scott. It seemed remarkable to me that Lawrence had brought no books with him. He was grateful when I brought masses of orange-coloured flowers to his room, counteracting those awful blue walls and making them recede somewhat.

There were days when he liked the place, and was glad that he had come; again he was in pain and it was all wrong. . . .

. . . .

The doctors had encouraging reports, but Lawrence's weight was shockingly little. He said that he would try the sanatorium for a month, then he would see, perhaps he might learn how to care for himself better by being there. Yes, in the spring he might come to us for a bit, and if he were strong enough—oh, he would like to go back to New Mexico. I referred to the hard railway journey that would entail in America, but he was strongly of the opinion that our great trains are more comfortable than the European ones.

There seemed the possibility of my making a brief visit to India—returning in May: Lawrence declared that surely I must go. It seemed the vaguest possibility, and when I said good-bye to Lawrence, after a couple of weeks, our thought was rather that I would soon return to Vence with my painting materials to work in that neighbourhood.[417]

12? February 1930   Ad Astra Sanatorium, Vence, Alpes Maritimes, France

(*It isn't a sanatorium, really—an hotel where a nurse takes your temperature and two doctors look at you once a week—for the rest, just an hotel. They examined me with X-rays and all that. It is as I say—the lung has moved very little since Mexico, in five years. But the broncs are awful, and they have inflamed my lower man, the ventre and the liver. I suppose that's why I've gone so thin . . . . Of course they can do nothing for me—food, the food is good, but it's hotel food—they say milk is bad for my liver, and it's true. They don't say rest all the time—I go down to lunch, down two flights of steep stairs, alas—and I'm going to practice walking again. I think they are right and the English doctor wrong. A certain amount of movement is better. I've got a good balcony and lovely view—and the air is much better than Bandol. . . . Frieda is in the*

Nouvel Hôtel in Vence—she goes back to the Beau Soleil Saturday—her daughter Barbara is there. They will pack up and go to a little house in Cagnes, which the di Chiaras are giving up. Then they'll come on the bus, about 20 minutes, to see me. —It's dull here—only French people convalescing and nothing in my line. But I'm feeling more chirpy, and shall try to get on my legs. . . . I wish we could have been somewhere to have a good time like Diablerets. Or I wish I could sail away to somewhere really thrilling—perhaps we shall go to the ranch. What I want is to be thoroughly cheered up somehow—not this rest-cure business.

Well, it all sounds very egoistic—that's the worst of being sick. The mimosa is all out, in clouds—like Australia, and the almond blossom very lovely, especially around Bandol. Today was a marvellous day—I sat in the garden.[418]

Frieda Lawrence Ravagli

"Ad Astra"/Vence A.M. [? February 1930]

Dear Mr [H. G.] Wells,

I think it pleased Lawrence to hear from you. He is here in a sanatorium, hoping it will do him good. It is not very far from Grasse, is it? If you'd like to come to tea with me at the sanatorium, I will tell you all about him & you may see him, if he hasn't had a bad day! Lawrence told me how Ford Hueffer took him to see you years ago. Yes, I met your wife several times.[419] I see her very plainly in a grey & blue pale garment like a cloud. I am worried about Lorenzo & the only thing I can think of for him is a journey on a big yacht. It's so *dull* for him! Do come about 4 o'clock, you might wire.

Sincerely,
Frieda Lawrence [420]

27 February 1930   Ad Astra Sanatorium, Vence, Alpes Maritimes, France

⟪ I'm about the same—I think no worse—but we are moving into a house here in Vence on Saturday [1 March 1930], and I'm having an English nurse [421] from Nice. I shall be better looked after.

H. G. Wells came to see me Monday [24 February 1930]. . . . To-day the Aga Khan came with his wife—I liked him—a bit of real religion. . . .

He wants to take my pictures to Paris—perhaps buy some—we'll see.[422]
The Huxleys are in Cannes—came Tuesday, and coming again tomorrow. . . .

. . . .

Ida [Rauh Eastman] and Barby are both very good. . . .
It's beastly weather.

. . . .

Jo Davidson came and made a clay head of me—made me tired.[423]

Jo Davidson

. . . I was lunching with H. G. [Wells] and he said:
"Jo, you ought to do D. H. Lawrence while you are here." It turned out that Wells had just been to see Lawrence in Vence and had told him what great fun it had been sitting for me and that he should do likewise. Lawrence, very ill at the time, agreed to do it. And Wells told me:
"If I were you I shouldn't go back to Paris without having a shot at it. I am not doing this for you but for him. You will surely do him good. I am sure he is not as ill as they think he is. You can cheer him up."
The following morning, instead of heading for Paris, Yvonne [424] and I went to Vence. We went directly to the Hotel Ad Astra, where the Lawrences were staying. Mrs. Lawrence received us as if she were expecting us. I told her of my talk with H. G. She told us that they had been talking about me and she knew her husband would be very happy to see me. I was glad I came.
It was a beautiful sunny day and Lawrence was having his lunch on a terrace. I had brought my clay and paraphernalia along with me, and I had it sent up to Lawrence's room. After lunch I started to work, while we talked of mutual friends. I knew Lawrence had painted, and I asked him if he had ever done any modeling. He had—once, in plasteline. But he hated the material, its feel and odor, and never touched it again. I gave him a piece of my clay. He liked the feel of it—because it was clean and cool. I promised to send him the very clay I was using as soon as the bust was completed. He thought he would like to do some little animals in clay.
After I worked for about an hour or so, Lawrence suggested that I had better go down and have some lunch, while he had a nap.

A little later a servant came down and said that Mr. Lawrence was awake and had asked for me. When I went up, I found him in bed. He asked me if I could work if he sat up in bed. I told him it did not matter. If he would rather, I would come back tomorrow or any other time. He stayed in bed and I worked for another hour.

When I told Lawrence I had been experimenting in polychrome sculpture, he asked me to do him in color, and not to forget the blue of his dressing gown, of which he was very fond.[425]

The bust was finally completed [426] and we got back to Paris. About a week later, Mrs. Harry Payne Whitney [427] came to lunch. I told her how ill Lawrence was. She was distressed, and said, "Can't you call up Mrs. Lawrence or someone and tell them not to spare any expense?"—she would look after that. When I called H. G. at Grasse, he told me that Lawrence had died that morning.[428]

Barbara Weekley Barr

In early February, 1930, Lawrence had left Bandol for the Ad Astra sanatorium at Vence in the Maritime Alps. Frieda went with him; I stayed on at the Villa Beau Soleil.

A friend of mine met them at Nice, and motored them to the sanatorium.

"Blair [Hughes-Stanton] [429] has been as kind as an angel to me," wrote Lawrence from there, adding, "Here is £10 for housekeeping." To this Frieda put a postscript. "Be careful with the money." This admonition impressed me so much, that when Blair and his wife came to see me, I gave them only a few rags of boiled meat from the soup for lunch, and offended them.

A little later I joined Frieda in Vence where she was staying at the Hotel Nouvel. When I went to see Lawrence at the sanatorium, I found him worse. In his balcony room, painted a dreary blue, he seemed wretchedly ill and wasted. For the first few days he had gone downstairs for lunch, but the other patients depressed him.

The superintendent was a cheerless person. "Monsieur Lawrence is a lamp that is slowly failing," he said to me unctuously.

Lawrence wanted to leave and go into a villa somewhere near. We had difficulty in finding this, because the French, often so reckless, seemed terrified of invalids. Many whom I approached refused to let their villas on that account. At last we found the Villa Robermond [430] on the hill just above Vence. It was a comfortable house, with a little cottage where an Italian peasant lived with his wife, who acted as concierge.

Lawrence still thought that if he could rest, and regain a little strength, he might be able to travel to New Mexico. To go there had also become my dream. In Nice I made enquiries about our passports.

Before Lawrence left the sanatorium several people visited him there. H. G. Wells, whom he did not like, came one afternoon, and told him his illness was mainly hysteria. The Aga Khan and his wife also came, when the Aga cheered Lawrence by saying he admired his paintings.

Lawrence complained to him of the way his work had been treated, and said: "The English kill all their poets off by the time they are forty."

Before taking Lawrence from the sanatorium, we engaged an English nurse.[431] We also found another doctor—a Corsican—who was recommended by an American friend.

On March 1st, Lawrence drove up to the Villa Robermond with Frieda in a taxi. I saw him, in hat and overcoat, stagger up the few steps of the verandah, supported by the chauffeur. He was saying, "I am very ill."

After he was put to bed, the new doctor examined him. When he came out of Lawrence's room, he said, "It is very grave. There is not much hope. Do not let him see that you know." To our American friend Ida Eastman, he said, "He is simply living on his spirit."

The next morning Lawrence got up, washed, and brushed his teeth. He did not care much for the ministrations of the nurse, though she was unobtrusive enough, poor thing.

"She is so insipid," he whispered. She was very unhappy, and sulked a good deal.

Lawrence said he thought he should rewrite the will he had once made but lost, in which he left everything to Frieda; but she feared it would tire him too much.

I cooked Lawrence's lunch, and took it in to find him sitting up in the blue jacket, tranquilly reading a book about Columbus' voyage to America.

The Huxleys came in the afternoon, and the nurse voiced her woes to Maria. Towards evening Lawrence suddenly became worse. His head began to distress him. Sitting up in agony, holding his head, Lawrence cried, "I must have morphia."

I put my arm round him for a few moments. I could not understand why the doctor had not come, and decided to go for him. When I left, Lawrence said to my mother, "Put your arm round me like Barby did; it made me feel better."

As I was leaving to go to Vence, Aldous and Maria came again from their hotel. Maria went and soothed Lawrence, holding his head in her hands. He had said she had his mother's hands.

He sat up in bed with startled brilliant eyes, looking across the room, crying, "I see my body over there on the table!"

When I reached the Corsican doctor's house, I found that he had gone to Nice, so I hurried with a friend to the Hotel Nouvel. There the proprietor telephoned to the superintendent of the sanatorium, asking him to come and give Lawrence morphia. This was a lengthy talk, as the doctor at first refused. At last the proprietor won him round, so we called for him in a car and took him up to the villa. He complained all the way.

When we arrived there, however, his professional manner asserted itself. He greeted Lawrence kindly, and his greeting was returned. He gave him morphia, and left.

Aldous Huxley thought we had better go to Vence and try again to find the Corsican doctor, in case the effect of the injection wore off. We went to his house, but he was still away. It was about eleven at night when we walked up the hill to the villa again, talking of Lawrence and his illness. We found Frieda and Maria in the kitchen, with the peasant of the conciergerie standing by.

"We could not get the doctor," I told them agitatedly.

"It doesn't matter," said Frieda, gently.[432]

Frieda Lawrence Ravagli

Now I am nearing the end . . . . I think of Bandol and our little villa "Beau Soleil" on the sea, the big balcony windows looking toward the sea, another window at the side overlooking a field of yellow narcissus called "soleil" and pine-trees beyond and again the sea. I remember sunny days when the waves came flying along with white manes, they looked as if they might come flying right up the terrace into his room. There were plants in his room and they flowered so well and I said to him: "Why, oh why, can't you flourish like those?" I remember what a beautiful and strange time it was. One day a cat, a big handsome yellow-and-white cat came in; Lawrence chased it away. "We don't want it. If we go away it'll be miserable. We don't want to take the responsibility for it"; but the cat stayed, it insisted on it. Its name was "Micky" and it grew more and more beautiful and never a cat played more intelligently than Micky . . . he played hide-and-go-seek with me, and Lawrence played mouse with him . . . . Lawrence was such a convincing mouse

. . . and then he insisted: "You must put this cat out at night or it will become a bourgeois, unbeautiful cat." So very sadly, at nightfall, in spite of Micky's remonstrances I put him out into the garden. To Mme. Martens, the cook, Lawrence said: "*Vous lui donnez à manger, il dort avec moi, et Madame l'amuse.*"

But in the morning at dawn Micky and I appeared in Lawrence's room . . . . Micky took a flying leap on to Lawrence's bed and began playing with his toes, and I looked at Lawrence to see how he was . . . his worst time was before dawn when he coughed so much, and I knew what he had been through . . . . But then at dawn I believe he felt grateful that another day had been given him. "Come when the sun rises," he said, and when I came he was glad, so very glad, as if he would say: "See, another day is given me."

The sun rose magnificently opposite his bed in red and gold across the bay and the fishermen standing up in their boats looked like eternal mythological figures dark and alive against the lit-up splendour of the sea and sky, and when I asked him: "What kind of a night did you have?" to comfort me, he would answer: "Not so bad . . ." but it was bad enough to break one's heart. . . . And his courage and unflinching spirit, doing their level best to live as long as he possibly could in this world he loved so much, gave me courage too. Never, in all illness and suffering, did he let the days sink to a dreary or dull or sordid level . . . those last months had the glamour of a rosy sunset . . . . I can only think with awe of those last days of his, as of the rays of the setting sun . . . and the setting sun obliterates all the sordid details of a landscape. So the dreary passages in our lives were wiped out and he said to me: "Why, oh why did we quarrel so much?" and I could see how it grieved him . . . our terrible quarrels . . . but I answered: "Such as we were, violent creatures, how could we help it?"

One day the charming old mother of Mme. Douillet who was at the Hôtel Beau Rivage brought us two gold-fish in a bowl; "*Pour amuser Monsieur,*" but, alas, Micky thought it was "*pour amuser Monsieur le chat.*" With that fixed, incomprehensible cat-stare he watched those red lines moving in the bowl . . . then my life became an anxious one . . . the gold-fish had to go in the bathroom on a little table in the sun. Every morning their water was renewed and I had to let it run for half an hour into the bowl. That was all they got, the gold-fish, no food. And they flourished. . . . "Everything flourishes," I said to Lawrence imploringly, "plants and cats and gold-fish, why can't you?" And he said: "I want to, I want to, I wish I could."

437

His friend Earl Brewster came and massaged him every day with coco-nut oil . . . and it grieved me to see Lawrence's strong, straight, quick legs gone so thin, so thin . . . and one day he said to me: "I could always trust your instinct to know the right thing for me, but now you don't seem to know any more . . . ." I didn't . . . I didn't know any more. . . .

And one night he asked me: "Sleep with me," and I did . . . all night I was aware of his aching inflexible chest, and all night he must have been so sadly aware of my healthy body beside him . . . always before, when I slept by the side of him, I could comfort and ease him . . . now no more . . . . He was falling away from life and me, and with all my strength I was helpless. . . .

Micky had his eyes on the gold-fish. One sad evening at tea-time the bathroom door was left open. . . . I came and found both gold-fish on the floor, Micky had fished them out of the bowl. I put them in quickly, one revived, a little sadder and less golden for his experience, but the other was dead. Lawrence was furious with Micky. "He knew we wanted him to leave those gold-fish alone, he knew it. We feed him, we take care of him, he had no right to do it."

When I argued that it was the nature of cats and they must follow their instincts he turned on me and said: "It's your fault, you spoil him, if he wanted to eat *me* you would let him." And he wouldn't let Micky come near him for several days.

I felt: "Now I can do no more for Lawrence, only the sun and the sea and the stars and the moon at night, that's his portion now. . . ." He never would have the shutters shut or the curtains drawn, so that at night he could see the sky. In those days he wrote his *Apocalypse;* he read it to me, and how strong his voice was still, and I said: "But this is splendid."

I was reading the New Testament and told Lawrence: "I get such a kick out of it, just the same as when Azul gallops like the wind across the desert with me."

As he read it to me he got angry with all those mixed-up symbols and impossible pictures.

He said: "In this book I want to go back to old days, pre-Bible days, and pick up for us there what men felt like and lived by then."

The pure artist in him revolted! His sense of the fitness of things never left him in the lurch! He stuck to his sense of measure and I am often amused at the criticism people bring against him . . . criticisms only reveal the criticizers and their limitations. . . . If the criticizer is an in-teresting person his criticism will be interesting, if he isn't then it's a waste of time to listen to him. If he voices a general opinion he is uninteresting too, because we all know the general opinion ad nauseam. "My flesh grows weary on my bones" was one of Lawrence's expressions when somebody held forth to him, as if one didn't know beforehand what most people will say!

One day Lawrence said to himself: "I shan't die . . . a rich man now . . . perhaps it's just as well, it might have done something to me." But I doubt whether even a million or two would have changed him!

One day he said: "I can't die, I can't die, I hate them too much! I have given too much and what did I get in return?"

It sounded so comical the way he said it, and I ignored the depth of sadness and bitterness of the words and said: "No, Lawrence, you don't hate them as much as all that." It seemed to comfort him.

And now I wonder and am grateful for the superhuman strength that was given us both in those days. Deep down I knew "something is going to happen, we are steering towards some end" but every nerve was strained and every thought and every feeling. . . . Life had to be kept going gaily at any price.

Since Doctor Max Mohr had gone, we had no doctor, only Mme. Martens, the cook. She was very good at all kinds of tisanes and inhalations and mustard plasters, and she was a very good cook.

My only grief was that we had no open fireplaces, only central heating and, thank goodness, the sun all day. Lawrence made such wonderful efforts of will to go for walks and the strain of it made him irritable. If I went with him it was pure agony walking to the corner of the little road by the sea, only a few yards! How gallantly he tried to get better and live! He was so very clever with his frail failing body. Again one could learn from him how to handle this complicated body of ours, he knew so well what was good for him, what he needed, by an unfailing instinct, or he would have died many years ago . . . and I wanted to keep him alive at any cost. I had to see him day by day getting nearer to the end, his spirit so alive and powerful that the end and death seemed unthinkable and always will be, for me.

And then Gertler sent a doctor friend to us, and when he saw Lawrence he said the only salvation was a sanatorium higher up. . . .

For the last years I had found that for a time mountain air, and then a change by the sea, seemed to suit Lawrence best. Lawrence had always thought with horror of a sanatorium, we both thought with loathing of it. Freedom that he cherished so much! He never felt like an invalid, I saw to that! Never should he feel a poor sick thing as long as I was there and his spirit! Now we had to give in . . . we were beaten. With a set face

439

Lawrence made me bring all his papers on to his bed and he tore most of them up and made everything tidy and neat and helped to pack his own trunks, and I never cried. . . . His self-discipline kept me up, and my admiration for his unfailing courage. And the day came that the motor stood at the door of our little house, Beau Soleil. . . . Micky the cat had

Originally printed in *The Evening Standard* (London), 6 October 1937, with the following caption: "From D. H. Lawrence's Death-Bed. This doodle was made by D. H. Lawrence, the novelist, while lying in what turned out to be his death-bed in the South of France. It is sent by Evelyn Thorogood, of 12, Lloyd's-square, W.C. 1. She found it one morning on his breakfast tray."

been taken by Achsah Brewster. She came before we started with arm-fuls of almond blossoms, and Earl Brewster travelled with us. . . . And patiently, with a desperate silence, Lawrence set out on his last journey. At Toulon station he had to walk down and up stairs, wasting strength he could ill afford to waste, and the shaking train and then the long drive from Antibes to the "Ad Astra" at Vence. . . . And again he had to climb stairs. There he lay in a blue room with yellow curtains and great open windows and a balcony looking over the sea. When the doctors examined him and asked him questions about himself he told them: "I have had bronchitis since I was a fortnight old."

In spite of his thinness and his illness he never lost his dignity, he fought on and he never lost hope. Friends brought flowers, pink and red cyclamen and hyacinths and fruit . . . but he suffered much and when I bade him "good night" he said: "Now I shall have to fight several battles of Waterloo before morning." I dared not understand to the full the meaning of his words. One day he said to my daughter:

"Your mother does not care for me any more, the death in me is repellent to her."

But it was the sadness of his suffering . . . and he would not eat and he had much pain . . . and we tried so hard to think of different foods for him. His friends tried to help him, the Di Chiaras and the Brewsters and Aldous and Maria Huxley and Ida Rauh.

Wells came to see him, and the Aga Khan with his charming wife. Jo Davidson did a bust of him.

One night I saw he did not want me to go away, so I came again after dinner and I said: "I'll sleep in your room tonight." His eyes were so grateful and bright, but he turned to my daughter and said: "It isn't often I want your mother, but I do want her tonight to stay." I slept on the long chair in his room, and I looked out at the dark night and I wanted one single star to shine and comfort me, but there wasn't one; it was a dark big sky, and no moon and no stars. I knew how Lawrence suffered and yet I could not help him. So the days went by in agony and the nights too; my legs would hardly carry me, I could not stay away from him, and always the dread, "How shall I find him?" One night I thought of the occasion long ago when I knew I loved him, when a tenderness for him rose in me that I had not known before. He had taken my two little girls and me for a walk in Sherwood Forest, through some fields we walked, and the children ran all over the place, and we came to a brook . . . it ran rather fast under a small stone bridge. The children were thrilled, the brook ran so fast. Lawrence quite forgot me but picked daisies and put them face upwards on one side of the bridge in the water and then said: "Now look, look if they come out on the other side."

He also made them paper boats and put burning matches into them; "this is the Spanish Armada, and you don't know what that was." "Yes, we do," the older girl said promptly. I can see him now, crouching down, so intent on the game, so young and quick, and the small girls in their pink and white striped Viyella frocks, long-legged like colts, in wild excitement over such a play-fellow. But that was long ago . . . and I thought: "This is the man whom they call sex-obsessed."

I slept on his cane chair several nights. I heard coughing from many rooms, old coughing and young coughing. Next to his room was a young girl with her mother, and I heard her call out: "*Mama, Mama, je souffre tant!*" I was glad Lawrence was a little deaf and could not hear it all. One day he tried to console me and said: "You must not feel so sympathetic for people. When people are ill or have lost their eyesight there is always a compensation. The state they are in is different. You needn't think it's the same as when you are well."

After one night when he had suffered so much, I told myself: "It is enough, it is enough; nobody should have to stand this."

He was very irritable and said: "Your sleeping here does me no good." I ran away and wept. When I came back he said so tenderly: "Don't mind, you know I want nothing but you, but sometimes something is stronger in me."

We prepared to take him out of the nursing home and rented a villa where we took him. . . . It was the only time he allowed me to put on his shoes, everything else he always did for himself. He went in the shaking taxi and was taken into the house and lay down on the bed on which he was to die, exhausted. I slept on the couch where he could see me. He still ate. The next day was a Sunday. "Don't leave me," he said, "don't go away." So I sat by his bed and read. He was reading the life of Columbus. After lunch he began to suffer very much and about tea-time he said: "I must have a temperature, I am delirious. Give me the thermometer." This is the only time, seeing his tortured face, that I cried, and he said: "Don't cry," in a quick, compelling voice. So I ceased to cry any more. He called Aldous and Maria Huxley who were there, and for the first time he cried out to them in his agony. "I ought to have some morphine now," he told me and my daughter, so Aldous went off to find a doctor to give him some. . . . Then he said: "Hold me, hold me, I don't know where I am, I don't know where my hands are . . . where am I?"

Then the doctor came and gave him a morphine injection. After a little while he said: "I am better now, if I could only sweat I would be better. . ." and then again: "I am better now." The minutes went by, Maria Huxley was in the room with me. I held his left ankle from time to time, it felt so full of life, all my days I shall hold his ankle in my hand.

He was breathing more peacefully, and then suddenly there were gaps in the breathing. The moment came when the thread of life tore in his heaving chest, his face changed, his cheeks and jaw sank, and death had taken hold of him. . . . Death was there, Lawrence was dead. So simple, so small a change, yet so final, so staggering. Death!

I walked up and down beside his room, by the balcony, and everything looked different, there was a new thing, death, where there had been life, such intense life. The olive trees outside looked so black and close, and the sky so near: I looked into the room, there were his slippers with the shape of his feet standing neatly under the bed, and under the sheet he lay, cold and remote, he whose ankle I had held alive only an hour or so ago. . . . I looked at his face. So proud, manly and splendid he looked, a new face there was. All suffering had been wiped from it, it was as if I had never seen him or known him in all the completeness of his being. I wanted to touch him but dared not, he was no longer in life with me. There had been the change, he belonged somewhere else now, to all the elements; he was the earth and sky, but no longer a living man. Lawrence, my Lorenzo who had loved me and I him . . . he was dead. . . .

Then we buried him, very simply, like a bird we put him away, a few of us who loved him. We put flowers into his grave and all I said was: "Goodbye, Lorenzo," as his friends and I put lots and lots of mimosa on his coffin. Then he was covered over with earth while the sun came out on to his small grave in the little cemetery of Vence which looks over the Mediterranean that he cared for so much.[433]

443

CHAPTER FOUR

The Man Who Died

Where do I pay homage, whereunto do I yield myself? To the unknown, only to the unknown, the Holy Ghost. I wait for the beginning, when the great and all creative unknown shall take notice of me, shall turn to me and inform me. This is my joy and my delight. And again, I turn to the unknown of the end, the darkness which is final, which will gather me into finality.
—"Life," in Phoenix, p. 698

3 March 1930: *Nice.* Mr. D. H. Lawrence, the novelist and poet, died at Vence, near Nice, at nine o'clock last night after a short illness. He had been suffering from tuberculosis. News of his death was kept secret until this afternoon by his literary friends, who were at his death-bed.
—British United Press

3 March 1930

Star (London): D. H. LAWRENCE/DIES ON RIVIERA./MINER'S SON: STORMY PETREL/OF LITERATURE./NEWS KEPT SECRET./NOVELS AND POEMS BANNED/ AND PICTURES "RAIDED."

Birmingham Mail: MR. D. H. LAWRENCE./DEATH OF A REMARKABLE/WRITER./ CONFLICTS WITH CENSOR.

Nottingham Evening Post: MR. D. H. LAWRENCE./EASTWOOD NOVELIST WHO/ ACHIEVED NOTORIETY./PICTURES SEIZED BY POLICE.

Nottingham Evening News: MR. D. H. LAWRENCE/DEAD./NEWS HELD BACK BY HIS LITERARY FRIENDS./A MASTER NOVELIST/EASTWOOD MINER'S SON WHO/ WROTE ABOUT NOTTS. LIFE.

Sheffield Mail: FAMOUS AUTHOR'S DEATH/RECALLS CENSORSHIP BATTLES./ D. H. LAWRENCE DIES AT NICE./MINER'S SON WHO/HATED UGLINESS./EX- PONENT OF MANY/FORMS OF ART./OVERNIGHT SECRECY.

Glasgow Evening Times: DEATH OF MR. D. H./LAWRENCE/UNTIMELY END OF GREAT/NOVELIST/NEWS KEPT SECRET/UNTIL TO-DAY.

Oxford Mail: DEATH OF MR. D. H. LAWRENCE/AMONG ITALY'S MOUNTAINS./ NOVELIST, ARTIST AND POET, WHOSE CANDOUR BROUGHT/HIM UNDER THE CENSOR'S BAN.

Evening Standard (London): LAWRENCE/NOVELIST WHOSE/BOOKS ENGLISH/ CENSOR BANNED.

Manchester Evening Chronicle: D. H. LAWRENCE/DEAD./DEATHBED SECRET
KEPT/BY FRIENDS.

Daily Telegraph (London): PAINTER AND/AUTHOR./D. H. LAWRENCE'S LIFE/
AND DEATH./A MINER'S SON./LAUNCHED ON LITERARY LIFE/BY A GIRL.

Liverpool Echo: FAMOUS NOVELIST'S/DEATH./MINER'S SON BECAME/LIT-
ERARY LION./ENEMY OF CENSORSHIPS./MR. D. H. LAWRENCE AND HIS/
STORMY CAREER.

Edinburgh Evening Dispatch: MR. D. H. LAWRENCE/DEAD./POET AND NOVEL-
IST WHOSE WORKS/WERE BANNED./POLICE RAID RECALLED.

Liverpool Evening Express: D. H. LAWRENCE/DEAD./AUTHOR OF BOOKS THAT
/WERE BANNED./SEIZURE OF/PICTURES/RECALLED.

Evening News (London): DEATH OF D. H. LAWRENCE,/AUTHOR OF BANNED
NOVELS./PAINTER AND/AUTHOR./D. H. LAWRENCE'S LIFE/AND DEATH./A
MINER'S SON./LAUNCHED ON LITERARY LIFE/BY A GIRL.

Bradford Telegraph: NOTED NOVELIST/DEAD./NEWS KEPT SECRET/BY FRIENDS.
/MR. D. H. LAWRENCE./OUTSPOKEN WRITER ON/SEX PROBLEMS.

Yorkshire Evening Post: MR. D. H. LAWRENCE/DEAD./AUTHOR OF MANY
BANNED/WORKS.

Barbara Weekley Barr

Three days later [4 March 1930], a light hearse carrying Lawrence's
coffin was drawn to Vence cemetery by a small black horse, which picked
its way intelligently down the rough hillside. Two wild-looking men accompanied it.

Robert Nichols, Achsah Brewster, the Huxleys, Frieda and I went to
the grave. The English chaplain at Vence had sent a message, saying if
he could be allowed to come and say one or two prayers, he would waive
the usual burial service. This offer was refused. There was no religious
rite.[1]

The head of Lawrence's grave was against a sunny wall. One could see
the Mediterranean far away below, and nearer, the dignified cypresses.

Two young Italians were commissioned to make a mosaic phoenix for
the headstone. They worked it in pebbles of rose, white, and gray. Sometimes we watched these two—Dominique and Nicola—at work.[2]

One day a tall dark woman came into the cemetery, but, seeing us,
went away. This was the "Louie"[3] of Lawrence's early days. They had
been engaged for a short time, but he broke it off, telling her, "You see,

I don't think we could make a life together." A fortnight later he met Frieda.

Speaking once of her he said, "She was dark, good-looking. I liked her and she attracted me very much physically. But I didn't live with her, because she would have given too much—it wouldn't have been fair. I would like to do something for Louie one day."

After we had left the cemetery, she came back and left some flowers there. On her return to the Midlands she wrote to Ada: "I went to Vence and saw the poor lad's grave." [4]

Achsah Barlow Brewster

A telegram came saying: "Lawrence died ten o'clock night of March second, funeral four o'clock March fourth."

At the funeral there were ten of us gathered together—each with his own memories, very separate, yet held together by the depths of sincere affection for Lawrence. The plain oak casket placed at the foot of his bed was covered with spring flowers—freesias, violets, mimosa, primroses and garden posies. There were no words spoken, no services read. We followed to the cemetery on its ledge over the valley where the afternoon sun shone. We laid the spring flowers over the fresh earth. That was all—simple friendliness and sincerity.

In June, when we visited the grave, little yellow and white pansies from his sister's gardens were nodding at the foot. A mosaic design from Lawrence's drawing of the phoenix made with black, white and red pebbles picked up on the Bandol beach, marked the place. The song of the nightingale echoed across the valley, swallows darted in high circles against the mountains. The Mediterranean shimmered in the distance. [5]

Capt. Angelo Ravagli

After my last visit [to the Villa Mirenda in 1927] I lost track of the Lawrences and time went by. It was 1930. Suddenly one night on the train going home to Savona for a month's furlough, during a long stop in the railway station, at Voghera, near Genova, I left my compartment to buy the newspaper *Il Corriere dela Sera* and what I read was "D. H. Lawrence dies, March 2, 1930, in Vence, Alpes Maritimes, France." It was a great shock to me, it took me by surprise. The next day, from home,

I sent a telegram of sympathy to Frieda, inviting her to stay with me and my family in Savona as soon as she felt she would like to do so. Before my month of furlough expired, she really came, and spent a week with us. That was the time we made plans to go together to America and I was to help her on the Kiowa Ranch in New Mexico, as Lawrence had predicted several years before. It was a strange coincidence, but it really happened.[6]

Douglas Goldring

On the day of Lawrence's death I happened to enter an Anglo-American bar in Nice which was frequented by the Riviera correspondents of English and American newspapers. One of these—not perhaps the noblest of God's children—had a much-thumbed copy of *Lady Chatterley's Lover*, extracts from which he was reading aloud to his friends in the shocked tones of a Sunday school teacher. When I came in he buttonholed me, supposing (rightly) that I might have known Lawrence but not realising that I had no wish to discuss him. For I was overcome with the sense of loss. Why hadn't I had those few hundred francs which would have enabled me to see, for the last time, the man who had meant so much more to me than any other contemporary writer: Lawrence *dead* screamed itself at me while this brother of the pen said: "Look 'ere, damn it all, this is wot 'e writes. Sheer muck." I lost my temper and told him that if he and his colleagues sent obituary messages describing Lawrence as a pornographer they would disgrace their profession and the papers which employed them. I think his story was watered down a bit as the result of my outburst, but he adopted an attitude of outraged virtue and he did not forgive me.

I was not given a chance of attending Lawrence's funeral at Vence and a day or two later I left for London. Some days after my return to England I was staggered to see in the London *Star* and in several provincial newspapers the following paragraph, supplied by a news agency:

SCULPTOR ATTACKED.

Sequel to Taking of Study of D. H. Lawrence

Nice, *Tuesday* [11 March 1930]
Strong criticism of the action of the American sculptor, Mr. Joe [*sic*] Davidson, in making a bust of the late D. H. Lawrence, the English novelist, is made by the British author, Mr. Douglas Goldring. Mr. Lawrence died a few days ago and Mr. Goldring alleges that Mr. Davidson had only a slight

acquaintance with him, and that "he broke into the sickroom" to make a study of Mr. Lawrence, when the patient was much too ill, as events proved, to be disturbed.

Mr. Goldring has left for London, where he intends to make the matter public.[7]

This story was printed in the Paris editions of two American newspapers, and probably in the Continental *Daily Mail*. It was, I need hardly say, an entire fabrication from beginning to end. The only explanation of it I can give is that a Jewish-American novelist, who disapproved of Joe [*sic*] Davidson, had said something of the kind and that his story, to pay me out for having defended Lawrence's memory on the day of his death, had been fathered on me by one of the Riviera correspondents. I denied it promptly but, to my surprise, I was unable to get *The Star* to print my contradiction until it was too late to do any good. (Not that it is ever possible in England, where to be accused and acquitted is just as damaging as to be condemned, to catch up with a lie of this kind.) The provincial papers behaved better. *The Sheffield Independent*, under the caption "Dying Author's Bust. Author Repudiates Alleged Criticism," promptly quoted my brief denial.

> Mr. Goldring has written repudiating the paragraph. He says: "I do not know Mr. Davidson and have never made any sort of allegation against him. I left Nice on 6th March, nearly a week before the alleged criticism was made." We tender our apologies to Mr. Goldring for any annoyance the news agency paragraph may have caused.[8]

Unfortunately few people ever see protests or denials. A few days later H. G. Wells wrote to me: "My dear Goldring, go slow on this Lawrence story, etc." This was decent of Wells, as it enabled me to send my repudiation to an influential quarter. The whole business worried me out of all proportion to its importance.[9]

William Gerhardi

I heard of Lawrence's death, one morning, as I happened to look in at the office of a New York publisher. "Is that true?" I asked, and I was thinking that at last he had severed the tortuous cord of his own thoughts, which now went on, coiling and winding on their own; while the publisher, note-book and pencil in hand, addressed in insistent whispers the deceased author's agent: "Is there anything? A completed book? No? Any unfinished manuscript that could be issued as a novel?" [10]

451

Jessie Chambers Wood

43, Breck Hill Road,/Woodthorpe,/Nottingham./March 10th. 1930
[To May Chambers Holbrook, Cuffley, Sask., Canada]

My dear May,

I hope this letter will not be a shock to you; perhaps you have seen of Bert's death in your papers. I can only enclose cuttings, and cannot tell you any details because I never resumed correspondence with him. I had no idea he was ill, so it was a great shock to learn that he was dead.

I should very much like to be able to talk to you about things. Did you ever write to him from Canada, and did you ever hear from him? I think he has had a very strange and stormy life; to my mind he has made no development. I think he has been afraid to face the real problems of his own personality, but I am sure he has suffered terribly, and endured awful loneliness.

I feel terribly grieved when I think of what he has suffered, but I do not feel that I could have helped him. During all these years I have never regretted returning that letter to him—you remember it? It was the first after a year of silence; I showed it to you, and you said: "Send it him back, send it him back." Which I did because I felt it necessary to make a clean break. Yet, when I remember how he used to tell me, almost in despair, that, as an artist, he could not do without me, my heart aches, and I wonder if I did wrong. It can make no difference now, of course, but I never really felt hard-hearted towards him, and it was hard, indeed, to be parted from him. You understood best of any one in those days, and I want to thank you for all your unspoken kindness that helped me so much during that first terrible winter.

These last months I have felt such a desire to write to him, particularly when there was all the trouble about his pictures. Did you read of it? I felt he was Ishmael, with his hand against every man, and every man's hand against him, and I just wanted to tell him that I thought of him still with the old affection. But I did not write, partly because my operation came on just about that time. I feel sure, in my own heart, that all the fuss with the authorities over his pictures & his poems, has killed him. No doubt he was deeply mistaken about life, poor chap. Now I learn that David wrote to him a year ago, and have seen his reply,[11] and how much his old self that was, but such yearning. If I had known of that, I could not have kept from writing. But they never told me until now.

I am going to ask you, my dear May, if you will send me back two books I once sent you. Never mind what condition they may be in; it doesn't matter, I should just like to have them for old times sake. They are (1) The Golden Treasury of Songs & Lyrics, in a *green* binding, and full of pencil marks. Bert gave me that little book for my birthday when I was nineteen; he dropped it into my hands when we [were] in the wood all among the anemones. I sent it to you at a time when I felt I must part with everything that could remind me of him, and indeed I have nothing left. So if you will let me have it back I shall be glad. The second one is a little collection of Browning's poems I sent to you. A little red book, I think. That we had read together many times, and I have never been able to find that particular edition in the shops. Do you know the two books I mean? If they are still in existence, do let me have them. To send you that Golden Treasury was like sending you my own heart, but it had to be done.

Now in return, please tell me some book you would like to have, and I will get it for you.

Don't let this grieve you; it is all so long ago—but some things last while life lasts. I cannot understand why feeling should be so deep and so constant, can you?

I shall trust you not to let any one see this, not even Will, because it just reveals a little of what never has been revealed. But Death is a great and august event, and feeling, for once, may be forgiven. I think he had reached a terrible "impasse" in life, where he could go neither forward nor back; I was so afraid he might lose his reason, which would have been so much worse than death. Let us hope he has found the peace he never found on earth.

With love to you,

J.

I never saw him after that Sunday father & I drove over to your cottage & he returned with us as far as Watnall.[12]

Rhys Davies

After brief wanderings in Spain and Germany [Lawrence had] settled in Bandol again, and again I was eager to see him. A melancholy note had crept into his letters: "—there was a great storm yesterday—huge seas—to-day is quiet, but grey and chill and forlorn: imagine me the same." [13]

But he was moved from Bandol to the sanatorium at Vence. I did not believe he was dying: it could not be. Notes arrived from him; he was making arrangements for the publication in England of one of his very finest stories, *The Man who had Died* [*sic*]; a story of Christ's escape from death, a story rich with newly discovered splendours on earth. The newspapers published their contradictory reports; he was dying and he was very much better. They had announced his approaching death often before. And still one persisted in believing him very much alive. To read one day in the cold print of the afternoon London papers that he was dead was a strange experience. One's soul stood still and denied that death. Curious how it could not be accepted, as it had been accepted so often before in others. He who had been working in the full fructifying shine of the sun, while others produced from tombs.

But of course he was dead; at forty-five; and if we desired further proof, rude and raw proof, what more could we want than the obituary notices? Nearly all of them. But one could only read them in astonishment and horror, and avert one's head in shame as from an indecency.

Most of them did not lack length, it was true; surely this was an important writer, to demand such space! Double columns. But filled with such repetitions of revilings that one had the impression of a pack of evilly surly convicts released at last. The bad-tempered squealing, the patronising superiority, the wearisome insistence on his faults—especially this last, as though by continued repetition these particular critics were trying to convince themselves that this meanness in obituary notices was just and proper.

There were two exceptions to this deluge of hostility in England: the notices in *The Times Literary Supplement* and *The Manchester Guardian* [14] were warm and truthful in their tributes to Lawrence both as a writer and a person. From the others one gathered that he was nothing but a frustrated maniac with small occasional flashes of talent. One is not entirely at a loss to explain this insensibility to him. There are people who hate to admit the insufficiency of the existence we are forced to live. Lawrence cried this insufficiency aloud, brought out all the stale old corruptions from our being and told us what they were and what they were doing to us, particularly the corruptions of sexual life. Far better to shut them up, let them be, and go on living the pretty little make-up-a-tale of modern life. But he went into the root of life in its pristine strength. He believed that the instinctive purity and the original fertile innocence in man could still be found; he refused to accept the cynical distortions of a mechanized life, he refused to have the holiness of life blasphemed, he saw only too clearly that man was in danger of becoming barrenly closed in on himself and that soon the imprisoned spirit, lacking the radiance of true primal exchange, would turn into dark ways of destruction. His was a hateful creed, unscientific ("All scientists are liars!" cried this lover of the magic of night, when the instincts reign over their empire), illogical and retrogressive: it was maddening to be reminded of it. And of one's interior barrenness and fear.

As the days went on I began to think that his physical martyrdom and its so brutally celebrated end was inevitable. And it did not really matter now. There was the victorious magnificence of his work and of his example. But there was, too, the personal loss, the loss of a friend who had inspired that strange (alas that it should be strange!), living emotion of which I have spoken. I had written to Frieda Lawrence before he died, asking for the truth, since the papers were so contradictory; I had written that it must not be that he was very ill, that he must greet the Spring triumphantly as before. She replied:

. . . No, you won't make him a chaplet of anemones any more, but anemones crown his grave now. His death was so simple and somehow great, his courage in facing death and fighting inch by inch and then at the end asking for morphia. He looked so proud, so beyond all these silly ugly dogs barking, so unconquered when he was dead. —I know you grieve too.

Yes, his death did not matter. Still he was unconquered, standing richly in life, the warmth of the sun in his hands.[15]

Richard Aldington
(13 March 1930)

D. H. Lawrence was a great example of the English Heretic. In England, contumely, persecution, exile, fierce solitariness show the man of genius. Think of Shakespeare, throwing up a social career in London, leaving his plays unpublished and going contemptuously home to Stratford to breed bullocks. Think of Swift exiled to Dublin and shaking the Government with his pamphlets, Pope at Twitnam ("Men who do not fear God, fear me"), Shelley a public scandal, Byron the world's exile, Blake playing Adam and Eve with Mrs. Blake in the greenhouse, Tennyson hiding behind the juniper bush. Not *la gloire*, not the triumph of a doctrine or a party, but the vindication, the assertion of a man's own soul in the man's own way—that is the English heresy. And if you want a tradition for Lawrence, there it is. Let the heavens fall, let Rome in

Tiber melt, but the Lawrenceness of Lawrence must be asserted. "You tell me I am wrong," wrote Lawrence indignantly, "I am not wrong." [16] Of course he was not wrong; he was Lawrence. It is not a question of being right or wrong (*i.e.*, by reference to some outside standard, some body of doctrine, some Absolute), but of being oneself, a person, a man.

Lawrence despised Socialism, it was too conservative and organized. He was a true Anarchist (this Lawrence denied, but it was true), living outside human society, rejecting all its values, fiercely concentrated on his own values. Those who thought him a danger to social order would be right if there were the slightest chance of any considerable number of people being made to think by a set of unpopular novels and free verse poems. Lawrence was the champion of the individual in his age-long struggle against collective tyrannies. He was rude, cantankerous, vain, presumptuous, pig-headed, satirical, but he was a man, a savage defender of his own liberty; and I loved him for it. Put the old test to him: "If every man lived as Lawrence lived, if every man did as he taught, what would happen to the world?" Well, society would collapse. And a good thing too, he would have said. I confess I am more cynical; if this society collapsed, we should only get a worse one, for in times of confusion the scum always rises to the top. But the main trend of our social life is for a vast mediocre majority, with mean aims and paltry ideas, with limited capacities and inane ideals, to impose its views on every human activity and to crush the individual. Lawrence was a living protest against this flopping tyranny.

Among all the writers I have met (and some of them are very paltry fellows) Lawrence possessed the most vivid and uncompromising personality. He had a wounding capacity for not adapting himself to others. His psychological insight enabled him to flatter women into bubbling sympathy and to irritate men into sharp hostility. Like most geniuses, he preferred women because they have been trained not to contradict and would not puncture his assertions with argument and fact. Few things enraged him more than to be convicted of an error in fact. Need I add that his assertions were sometimes more daring than true, more picturesque than accurate? But a great personality is not at the mercy of an encyclopaedia. Not that Lawrence was ignorant; he picked up several modern languages which he talked with fluency and grammatical incorrectness, and he read omnivorously, though he pretended not to, and sedulously avoided possessing books. But the amount of formal or general knowledge possessed by a poet (a "creator") is comparatively unimportant; it is only a means of illustrating his perceptions and intuitions.

The strength, the profundity, the range, the acuity of Lawrence's perceptions and intuitions made him so interesting. One went to him, I repeat, not for a doctrine but a personality.

Lawrence's face was moulded by his personality, just as his prose was made to carry the very tones of his voice. When I first saw him (in 1914) I was rather disappointed. It was at an inane dinner—in a private suite at the Berkeley Hotel, of all places! At that time he was successful and the debacle of *The Rainbow* and the War had not driven him into the wilderness so unpleasantly necessary to the Heretic. He was clean-shaved except for a small ginger moustache and he came into the room looking rather like a competent private soldier in evening dress. But you were immediately impressed by his fiery blue eye and the pleasing malice of his talk. Latterly his face had grown harder and finer, all vulgarity was purged away in Heaven knows what agonized communings; the head looked moulded of some queer-coloured stone, the beard gave the right touch of Mohammedan "touch-me-not-ye-unclean," and the blue eyes were more assertive than ever and seemed to exist independently of their owner. And his voice—such a pleasant devil's voice, with its shrill little titters and sharp mockeries and even more insulting flatteries. At any moment one expected to see him sprout horns and a tail and cloven hoofs and to run trotting about poking his dull or resentful guests with a neat little pitchfork. He adored playing the game of smashing people's values. If he suspected you of any social snobbery he would plunge into stories of his childhood as a miner's son and drop into Derbyshire dialect. He invited worshippers at the Great Man's Shrine to assist him with the washing-up. He loathed a scholar, and tittered and tee-heed and too-hooed at all the monuments of literary research. He was more restless than a legion of devils, and yet he could live perfectly happily in remote places, so long as the weather was fine, the prospect beautiful, the peasants or Indians or other aborigines docile, and the callers infrequent. He had his vanities, little and big, but never was there a man who more hated humbug, pedantry and all the apparatus of the "literary."

Where Lawrence was, there talk—his talk—abounded. I think I have never heard better, nor have I read of any in the past more alert and interesting and amusing. But suffer him not to inveigh upon mysticism, metaphysics or politics—there he could be, and often was, a crashing bore. He needed space and no competitors for his talk, though he could be witty enough in ordinary chatter. At his best, he talked novels—almost better than he wrote—and needed only an attentive and moderately intelligent audience, murmuring interjections at the right moments. Were you lucky enough to get him after a meal and start him on his proper line—character, human relations and the penetration of the human personality by savage life and strange countries, the magical effect of landscapes on the mind, his mind—you would not say that talking is a lost art. It was a great spectacle to see Lawrence building up a "situation," starting from the merest silly gossip and rising, like a sharp-tongued hawk, in sweep after sweep of words to a literary display of the first order.

Of course, this wandering in distant places of the world, these prolonged spells of comparative solitude, this absence from the intellectual centres, inevitably resulted in a slight provincialism. In some respects Lawrence never got beyond 1912, and at odd times startled one by some echo of London life in those distant days. His objection to any form of serious literary culture dated from that period, when it was fashionable and perhaps necessary as a revolt against a tediously erudite Romanticism. But that is the price the Heretic pays; in trying to be for all time he is inevitably and always a little behind the times.

As I proceed to paint the portrait of this respectable man, the memories of his virtues crowd thickly upon me. Might it not be well to recast these haphazard notes into a formal éloge? Or into a funeral oration beginning: *Mes frères, Dieu seul est grand?* Yet I must praise him because he possessed a negative virtue dear to me. He had no social, moral or intellectual affectations. He was neither Oxford nor Chelsea, neither Cambridge nor Bloomsbury ("My dear fellow, they're *quite too* marvellous"), neither red nor primrose, innocent alike of simple faith and Norman blood, spitting with equal contempt on kind hearts and coronets. Never have I known a man so free from every kind of snobbery. He had not even the inverted snobbery of the drawing-room revolutionary. He was even free from the snobbery of the working-man who is too proud to speak to a gentleman. As for intellectual snobbery, there I welcomed his "tee-hees" and "too-hoos," which puffed away a deal of silly cant and affectation.

Again he won my approval by his total indifference to sports of all sorts. Since he lived intensely, since his mind was perpetually active and his senses acutely employed, he had no need to kill time by killing animals or birds or by propelling balls in competitive feats or by glowering over indoor games. Superior even to the great Gibbon, he never felt it necessary to relax over a game of cards. Is life so long, is the mind so dull, is there so little to see and do and feel and know, that we must waste the unique (if diabolical) gift of consciousness in silly games? If anyone presented Lawrence with a golf-club or a cricket-bat he would have cracked him over the head with it.

This character of Lawrence which I discover (or invent) has found expression in a series of novels and poems, travel books and stories, which have appeared with startling rapidity in the past fifteen years. There were people who deprecated Lawrence's fertility. I think they were wrong. An intense fertility is one of the signs of genius. Nearly all great writers are fertile, and the notion of a small highly-wrought output—one or two volumes—representing the lifework of a great artist is the apology of sterile pedants. One of the elementary requisites of a great writer is a ceaseless industry. Lawrence, I admit, worked too carelessly and his lack of form was sometimes an exasperation. But unpremeditated and spontaneous creation is the very essence of the Romantic and the Heretic. All this regrettable splurging was a condition of Lawrence's genius. It must be accepted and the reader must bump over the rough and arid and silly spots as best he can. And this fundamental principle of criticism must never be forgotten when judging Lawrence: That a writer is to be judged by his positive and not by his negative qualities. Any laborious fool can be correct, any plodding pedant can avoid many of Lawrence's faults, but only a man of genius could equal his positive achievements.

These are the qualities I think I discern in Lawrence's books: A remarkable intuitive insight into character, a subtle sense of complicated human relations, an exquisite sense of beauty, a sense of the mystery of things, a power of using countries and landscapes and animals to interpret the human mind and its moods and tragedies, a great gift of description and evocation, and lastly the "gift of interest" which is very hard to analyse but which one feels almost unconsciously—I mean that Lawrence could make you interested in almost anything he wrote, whereas other authors with all kinds of negative virtues are merely boring. His personality, at once so forcibly interesting and so annoying, was faithfully mirrored in his books. Another virtue in Lawrence's books is that the good portions are unforgettable. For instance, in *The Lost Girl* there is a lot of balderdash about people playing at Red Indians, puerile stuff; yet who can forget the characters of Alvina and the Italian, and the magnificent description of the journey into the lonely Italian mountain village in winter?

It is not possible to illustrate the major gifts of a novelist by quotation. The slow building up of character, the development of "situations," the play and relations of minds and bodies, the dramatic intensity, cannot be scooped out in selected passages. I shall not pretend to do more than turn over some of his books and to tear out some passages I like. Almost at once I find something very characteristic, his love of flowers and subtle ability to make them interpretative of human emotion:

> After a spell of hot, intensely dry weather she felt she would die in this valley, wither and go to powder as some exposed April roses withered and dried into dust against a hot wall. Then the cool wind came in a storm, the next day there was grey sky and soft air. The rose-coloured wild gladioli among the young green corn were a dream of beauty, the morning of the world. The lovely, pristine morning of the world, before our epoch began. Rose-red gladioli among corn, in among the rocks, and small irises, black-purple and yellow blotched with brown, like a wasp, standing low in little desert places, that would seem forlorn but for this weird, dark-lustrous magnificence. Then there were the tiny irises, only one finger tall, growing in dirty places, frail as crocuses, and much tinier, and blue, blue as the eye of the morning heaven, which was a morning earlier, more pristine than ours. The lovely translucent pale irises, tiny and morning-blue, they lasted only a few hours. But nothing could be more exquisite, like gods on earth. It was the flowers that brought back to Alvina the passionate nostalgia for the place. The human influence was a bit horrible to her. But the flowers that came out and uttered the earth in magical expression, they cast a spell on her, bewitched her and stole her own soul away from her.[17]

I am not sure of many things, hardly of anything really, but I am sure that this is the work of a great artist. And there are scores and scores of such perfect pages in Lawrence's books.[18] People are so strangely unwilling to admit the genius of a living artist. They feel so meanly of themselves that they cannot believe that one of the gods is moving among *them,* that genius lives in *their* time. They are insulted by superiority and try to ignore it or to crush it. They are afraid they might have to do something about it, pay some money or get up a vote of thanks. They are only interested in authors when there is a chance of getting some reflected glory, as when their friend Bilge issues his original imitation of an imitation of an imitation. But Lawrence gives you direct contact with his own mind and with the earth and with human life; and so—to our eternal shame—we called in the police-spies and the military and the lawyers and saw to it that he was exasperated and hounded into exile and bitter rage.

I think England owes Lawrence an apology.[19]

John Middleton Murry
(13 March 1930)

I should like to put down in haste a few of the most enduring personal impressions which a close friendship with D. H. Lawrence, lasting (alas!

with catastrophic interruptions) over sixteen or seventeen years, have left upon me. I regret that I must put them down in haste; but I desire (if I can) to correct the impression, which is widespread, that D. H. Lawrence was a madman of genius, savagely bent on violating sanctuaries, and bruising the finer conscience of his fellow-men.

To defend Lawrence's passionate convictions is no part of my hasty undertaking. These do not need to be defended, only to be understood, and understood in the light of an experience extraordinary in its depth and comprehensiveness. And again I am not invoking the beauty of his personality to excuse his work. It is right that I should make it clear that I do not consider his work needs any excuse. If it was wrong, it was passionately wrong; and to be passionately wrong is far better than to be coldly right. What I have to say concerning Lawrence the man could easily be corroborated from his work, if it is read by sympathetic and discerning eyes. But who knows how long sympathy and discernment may be in coming?

Lawrence was the most remarkable and most lovable man I have ever known. Contact with him was immediate, intimate, and rich. A radiance of warm life streamed from him. When he was gay, and he was often gay—my dominant memory of him is of a blithe and joyful man—he seemed to spread a sensuous enchantment about him. By a natural magic he unsealed the eyes of those in his company: birds, beasts, and flowers became new-minted as in Paradise; they stood revealed as what they were, and not the poor objects of our dull and common seeing. The most ordinary domestic act—the roasting of a joint of meat, the washing-up of crockery, the painting of a cottage room—in his doing became a gay sacrament. He surrendered himself completely to whatever he had in hand; he was utterly engrossed by it. And the things he took in hand were innumerable. In bare record they may seem fantastic, as when for weeks together he decorated little wooden boxes, or, years later when, during his last Christmas in England, he fashioned a marvellous little Adam and Eve beneath the tree in Eden, made of modelling clay and painted; but those who shared in these makings will remember them for some of the most simple, happy hours in their lives.

As his happiness was radiant, so his gloom was a massive darkness in which his intimates were engulfed. I see him sitting crouched and collapsed on a wooden chair when the long horror of the war had begun to gnaw his vitals—forlorn, silent, dead. One could not speak against the numbness of that sheer desolation. But sometimes, in those bitter days —out of which sprang his lifelong passion of rebellion against the European consciousness, and his unresting search for a land and a way of life to which he could surrender himself—sometimes, in those days he would rise to the surface with a flickering smile and begin to sing:

> Sometimes, I feel like an eagle in the sky . . . .
> Sometimes, I feel like a moaning dove . . . .[20]

With the first line he soared; with the second he sank, down, down, down.

He was completely generous. At a moment when there were not ten pounds between him and destitution he thrust five of them upon a friend and, because the friend refused them, flew into a transport of high-pitched rage. Friendship was to him a blood-brotherhood, an absolute and inviolable loyalty, but not to a person, but to the impersonal godhead beneath. I do not believe that he ever found the friendship after which he hungered; and perhaps this was the tragedy of his life. The men he knew were incapable of giving that which he demanded. It was not their fault, though in his heart of hearts he believed it was.

He had an infinite capacity for making warm human contacts. In whatever part of the world he found himself in his quest for newness of life, he left his mark and memory among the common people. Whatever may be our intellectual judgment of the theories he built upon his immediate experience, no one who knew him well has any doubt whatever that he had a mysterious gift of "sensing" the hidden and unconscious reality of his fellow human beings. He did not sentimentalise about them, but he did *know* them, in ways more direct and ultimate than any of which ordinary men have experience. What is vague and dimly apprehended instinct with most of us was in him an exquisitely ramified sensibility, responsive to realities which elude our blunter organisations and for which our common language has no appropriate expression. Hence the seeming violence which Lawrence, a native master of the delicate and creative word, did to the conventions of style and morality. His sacrifice of "art" was quite conscious, and quite deliberate; he was not concerned with it any more. "Fiction," he said in a letter, "is about *persons;* and I am not interested in persons." [21]

Perhaps he never clearly understood how extraordinary were these gifts of his for making contact with the life that is prior to personality. No doubt for a man of genius such as his to admit that he is in some sense radically unlike his fellows—a queer creature, an animal of a different species—is almost impossible. Such absolute isolation is not to be endured. Because Lawrence found his friends and mankind at large lacking in faculties which were native to him, he inclined to believe that they had deliberately buried in the earth a talent which was never theirs. So he was often, in his later years, induced to think men perverse and wicked when they were merely dull; and he grew exasperated with them.[22]

Catherine Carswell
(14 March 1930)

The picture of D. H. Lawrence suggested by the obituary notices of "competent critics" is of a man morose, frustrated, tortured, even a sinister failure. Perhaps this is because any other view would make his critics look rather silly. Anyhow to those who knew him (and I knew him since 1914 as friend, hostess and guest in varying circumstances, often of the most trying kind, at home and abroad) that picture would be comic if it were not in the circumstances disgraceful.

Lawrence was as little morose as any open clematis flower, as little tortured or sinister or hysterical as a humming-bird. Gay, skilful, clever at everything, furious when he felt like it but never grieved or upset, intensely amusing, without sentimentality or affectation, almost always right in his touch for the *content* of things or persons, he was at once the most harmonious and the most vital person I ever saw.

As to frustration, consider his achievement. In the face of formidable initial disadvantages and lifelong delicacy, poverty that lasted for three-quarters of his life and hostility that survives his death, he did nothing that he did not really want to do, and all that he most wanted to do he did. He went all over the world, he owned a ranch, he lived in the most beautiful corners of Europe, and met whom he wanted to meet and told them that they were wrong and that he was right. He painted and made things, and sang and rode. He wrote something like three dozen books, of which even the worst page dances with life that could be mistaken for no other man's, while the best are admitted, even by those who hate him, to be unsurpassed. Without vices, with most human virtues, the husband of one wife, scrupulously honest, this estimable citizen yet managed to keep free from the shackles of civilization and the cant of literary cliques. He would have laughed lightly and cursed venomously in passing at the solemn owls—each one secretly chained by the leg—who now conduct his inquest. To do his work and lead his life in spite of them took some doing, but he did it, and long after they are forgotten, sensitive and innocent people—if any are left—will turn Lawrence's pages and will know from them what sort of a rare man Lawrence was.[23]

Mabel Dodge Luhan
(19 March 1930)

When D. H. Lawrence died in France on March third, a soul passed out of this world that was unique and inviolate. He was protected all his life by something that preserved his spirit in him whole and undissipated.

Where others squander the little bit of gold in them, tossing it out here and there in ha'pennies, this one contained it intact within himself; for he formed new friendships and he had no love affairs, save the long, intense relationship with his wife, with its splendor and its misery, a relationship that took perpetual readjustment and endless understanding. She was, in a sense, the guardian of the treasure within, and her role was allotted to her, perhaps by the gods who watch over unusual men.

To those who knew him only slightly, Lawrence appeared to be a puritan. He was very conventional in many ways and had inherited a certain uprightness and directness from his mother, but he had evolved, individual opinions that he had worked out early in his own life. He held that women got their consciousness from men and men their power from women. Or, rather, he thought a man gets his power from *a* woman. Monogamy seemed to him to be important because only through it can a man experience sex. That is to say, love, power, creation. Where many people look for one in the many, Lawrence knew he could find the many in the one. All his knowledge, imagination and development were the fruits of his simple passion. He passed up the difficult, darkened stairs and through the doorless corridors, rising painfully year by year, forever faithful, no matter what disillusionment he met, eternally true to his belief.

"Fidelity is worth more than love," he told me once.

For Edwin Arlington Robinson, love is "a stair-case leading to the sea, down which the blind are driven"; [24] for Lawrence it was a stair-case to the stars that a man may choose to climb, and climbing find it the Path the initiates tell about.

Now Lawrence, in his own person a reservoir of unspent ecstasy, Lawrence, frail and irascible, had an extraordinarily potent effect upon people.

Involuntarily, possibly quite unconsciously, he awoke new rhythms in people, latent sleeping energies and untried potentialities. He changed people. One could not be quite the same person after knowing Lawrence that one was before. He had a magical presence. He had creative vision.

That is to say, when he saw the possibilities in people, they became actualities. This worked two ways! When he had a negative intention about a person, seeing the dark chance, it was quite likely to manifest itself. The man was essentially creative but he was also destructive, and so he was one of the most dangerous as well as one of the most highly developed people that has ever lived.

There is something to be learned here; for, kept "centered" as he called it, by his woman, sheer power emanated from him. This, then, is perhaps the lost meaning of continence, lost in these days of outlets, canalizations, and self-expression.

The man who has written the most continuously, exhaustively and freely about sex, of anyone, was one whose own life was self-contained and restrained, not inhibited, not repressed, but "centered" by one woman.

This, possibly, gives a meaning to the instinctive jealousy that guarded him, since behind it may be inferred the gods' intention that the sacred fire be saved for more ultimate ends and diviner satisfactions than other men know.

Compared with Lawrence's life, other people seem lost in intricate futilities. Complicated social customs, extravagant motivations such as govern politics and most social patterns, were nothing but chimeras in his eyes, and when one was with him, many things that had appeared real before fell away into ashes and revealed themselves for what they were.

He could make an unreal feeling or opinion fade away out of one, and he made the small, usual, unconsidered acts and automatisms of life come into reality, and, assuming a new life, grow significant once more.

He liked to do things. Natural things. He liked to do the chores around the ranch in Taos. He liked to bake bread in the outdoor adobe oven, and to feed the animals and milk the cow.

When Lawrence went down to milk the cow, the meadow awoke to one who went along because he himself saw it so living, the wild flowers in the grass glowing and glistening, the lupin, the aster and "the little scarlet rain," as he called that red flower growing small bells along a slender stem. They all appeared more vivid and more lovely after he showed them to one.

He knew the immediate and continuous life about him, and nothing bored him except "the inessentials," too much furniture, automobiles, or "modern conveniences"! These seemed deadly to him, who knew how to savor a piece of crusty bread on the side of a hill.

Coster says in *The Living and the Lifeless* [25] that the most important achievement in this century will be *the return to the ordinary life*. When

465

one has known Lawrence well, these words seem deeply true, for he gave back the magic to ordinary life. He had a perpetual sense of wonder. For him there was no dullness in the ordinary life. He had escaped the commonness in most of the small, daily, insignificant activities that most people suffer under and from which they long to escape to larger, more glamorous scenes. He had a constant awareness of the life in everything, an exquisite perception of the aspects and flavors of all passing moments. It was the difference between complete wakefulness and a dingy sleep to be with him after others. He gave one realization.

If that is what Coster means by the *return* to the ordinary life, the new awareness, in little, usual things, of a beauty never seen before even in glamorous scenes and large horizons, then Lawrence was the forerunner —one who found the way and embarked upon it.[26]

Barbara Weekley Barr

A few weeks after Lawrence's death Frieda went to London to see to her affairs. I stayed on alone at the villa. At night the peasant's dog slept on the floor by my bed for company. I never shut the door of Lawrence's room across the salon, thinking that if there should be an after life, his spirit might like to go in and out of it.

When Frieda returned, we went to visit my German grandmother. I found that Lawrence's description of her hearty appetite was correct, and together we devoured apple cake and cream. When she said to me, though, "You ought to speak German; your mother is German," I was annoyed, and answered, "My mother left me."

It rained all the time in Germany, and I caught bronchitis. By the time we were back in Vence I was seriously ill. This lasted many months and caused Frieda more strain and worry.

Some of the memories of that time are mixed up with queer fantasies. One clear picture I have at the onset of the malady is of the tall, grey-bearded Vence doctor bending over me with a benevolent look. Near him stood Madame Lilli, our staunch, queenly cook. On a chair Frieda was huddled in helpless misery.

When I was getting better, I lay in bed one bright autumn morning and Frieda came in, bringing Lawrence's early letters to her for me to read. I picked one up and began, but halfway through, feeling listless, wretched and confused, put it down again. At that moment I clearly saw Lawrence's image bending over me. It was made up of little shimmering particles. His form was filled out, glowing, and he looked at me with a very benign expression. I blinked—startled by the vision: it vanished and, to my regret, never appeared again.

When I could travel, I returned to England, and stayed at my uncle's vicarage at Maplestead in Essex, a place I loved.[27]

Frieda Lawrence Ravagli

Villa Robermond/Quartier Chabert/*Vence* AM/France [Postmarked: London, 31 March 1930]

Dear Brewster [Ghiselin],

I must just tell you how Lawrence died, so splendidly that I am filled with admiration— You do understand, he gave me most of my *life* and now he gave me death—that great other that I knew nothing about— now I know— When he was dead he looked so proud and unconquered and fulfilled, another Lawrence I didn't know and I only want for the rest of my life, that he should never have to be ashamed of me— I want to bring him to the ranch, with a red Indian funeral and make it a lovely place for him— Yes, he wanted me to write to you and said you must see the ranch— Barby and I will come— And I know that you were one of the few so far who *got* him—

Yours with many sad greetings
Frieda L——[28]

Interview with Jessie Chambers Wood
(9 April 1930)

A TALK WITH LAWRENCE'S "PRINCESS."/GIRL WHO BROUGHT FAME TO/BOY OF GENIUS./BUSY HOUSEWIFE TELLS HOW SHE "LAUNCHED"/D. H. LAWRENCE: NAME STILL SECRET./VILLAGE MEMORIES—AND REGRETS.

It was while I was at Croydon that the girl who had been the chief friend of my youth, and who was herself a school teacher in a mining village at home, copied out some of my poems, and, without telling me, sent them to the *English Review*, which had just had a glorious rebirth under Ford Maddox Hueffer. Hueffer printed the poems, and asked me to come and see him. The girl had launched me, so easily, on my literary career, like a princess cutting a thread, launching a ship.[29]

Who was "the chief friend" of his youth, to whom D. H. Lawrence thus paid a tribute in *Collected Articles* [*sic*],[30] the book now published only a week or two after his death? He corrected the proofs on his deathbed, but to the end he kept silent about this autobiographical chapter which might explain much that is confusing in his literary development.

His publisher did not know. Mr. Michael Joseph, of Curtis Brown, his literary agents, one of the few men in London who knew Lawrence, told me that he had never heard the novelist-poet mention her. At the offices of the *English Review* all trace of any correspondence has been lost.

SPRING-CLEANING.

To-day I have talked with this "Princess" who launched that youth of genius twenty years ago. She is now a woman entering the middle years, happily married and utterly aloof in spirit from the world of affairs.

The interview interrupted the spring-cleaning of her distant suburban home. Also, every now and then, despite her intense interest in her recollections, she had fears for the bread that she was baking.

But as she lingered to talk of her dead friend she did not attempt to disguise her grief.

"I did not even know that he was ill," she said. "Our last meeting was eighteen years ago. I saw the announcement of his death in the *Daily News*. It has been a great shock to me."

THE SECRET.

It was only on condition that I would not divulge her name during her lifetime that she consented to tell me the story of her friendship with the youthful Lawrence.

"We were children together," she said. "Our families were close friends, and we grew up together in the same village. He began to write quite early, and he showed me everything he wrote. He used to send me poems in his letters, and when he began to write *The White Peacock,* he read it over to me as he worked on it. I was twenty and he was nineteen."

In the pause that followed, it was only too clear that the past had become suddenly very vivid. Lawrence's "Princess" looked into the fire and seemed to have forgotten her visitor.

"But the story?" I asked.

"There is no story," she said quietly. "I simply said to him, 'Why don't you send some of your poems to *The English Review?*'

"He replied: 'I can't bother.' So I copied them out and sent them. That is all the story, as you call it."

WHAT MIGHT HAVE BEEN.

For a few minutes we discussed Lawrence's books. I commented on the strange way in which in the last years his mind had seemed to turn in upon itself, in a crescendo of self-torture. I amended some lines from Meredith—"his sense was with his senses all mixed in."

"I think his life was a tragedy," she said then. "I have the greatest reverence for his memory, and I only speak from a literary point of view, but I know what he might have been.

"His last writings and those terrible paintings ought never to have been given to the world. His friends might have saved him from that."

"Why don't you write the full story of your friendship?" I suggested.

She shook her head. "It is not for me to write. Besides, I haven't the time."

NOT HISTORY YET.

"It must be written one day."

"Yes."

"It is literary history."

The dark eyes flashed. "It is not history yet. Lawrence is just dead. Let him rest.

"In fifty years' time it will be history. In fifty years the story may be told. When I am dead, it will not matter."

"You used to write?" I suggested.

She smiled at this. "No; I hadn't the time. I was too busy preparing for my career."

"EVERYTHING GONE."

During that school career, finished now, she met her husband, a man who, though alert and well read, is content to do his obscure work, and is also a trifle contemptuous of the hurly-burly where people fight fiercely for a place in the limelight.

I spoke of those early letters and poems which Lawrence had sent her. "You kept them?"

Her answer was decided. "Everything I had of Lawrence's has gone."

"They would be valuable now?"

"Valuable, yes," was the half-ironic answer. And then: "I have not kept any of them. I have not seen or heard anything of Lawrence since 1912. I have kept nothing."

Although their lives have been entirely apart, she has followed his books closely. I quoted his tribute to her. Again she was silent, looking away. Then: "It was fine of him to write that," she said slowly.

THE NEW BOOK.

She asked eagerly about the new book—what was it like, when would it appear, its title?

We talked of the many letters Lawrence is said to have left, letters written in his early years. The past came up again vividly in that quiet room.

"I had a fear when I first knew of his death that somebody would hunt me out," she said.

"But I am afraid I have not the interest in publicity that so many people seem to have nowadays. I want to be left alone."

Her dark eyes flashed again. "During the whole of my life I never want my name mentioned in connection with D. H. Lawrence."

IF ONLY—

There was nothing more to be said. Spring cleaning was delayed, a husband was coming home to his midday meal, and bread was baking. I just paused by the bookcase to note a pocket set of Hardy.

"If only he had written books like those," she said quietly.

In the moment of parting I looked finally at this woman who had brought fame to the boy she had known 20 years ago.

Jet-black hair above a fine brow, features sensitive and clear cut, most of all the eyes, by turns dominant and appealing; a woman Hardy might have painted.

Her fine lips had curved ironically when she spoke of the public's interest in Lawrence. They softened when they framed his name.

THE FAREWELL.

Most certainly, one would have said, a woman destined to mould genius.

Instead, she stood in the doorway of this small house remote from affairs, completely uninterested in the ways of the world.

She has lived for years among quiet people who have never dreamed of her friendship with the stormy, frustrated genius who died in exile.

Outside, the cold rain of reluctant spring fell upon the daffodils and the opening lilac bushes in the little front garden.

"Please forgive me . . . my bread is baking," said D. H. Lawrence's "Princess." [31]

The Times (*London*)
(12 June 1930)

Mr. DAVID HERBERT LAWRENCE, of the Villa Robermond, Vence, near Nice, novelist and poet, died intestate on March 2, aged 44, leaving £2,438, so far as can at present be ascertained.[32]

Jessie Chambers Wood

43 Breck Hill Road,/Woodthorpe/Nottingham./July 6th. 1930
[To May Chambers Holbrook, Cuffley, Sask., Canada]

Dear May,

I'm rather late in answering your letter. I found it waiting at the end of the Whitsuntide holiday, when we returned from a few days in London. I couldn't reply quickly because I was busy doing some writing which I will tell you about some day. Just yet I cannot say much, but when I can tell the whole tale, you shall hear it. You will be interested.

I am very glad you are sure now that I am truly alive. It is so indeed. When you went away, the time was still young; I have fought many a hard fight since then, but I have kept really alive with no veneer. Of course, one must have a face, 'to face the world with,' but that also is a true part of me, and I was always an excellent hand at keeping my own counsel.

Thank you for the enclosure. I shall keep it on account of the passages you have underlined. How very revealing they are! Poor chap—he must often have cursed himself for a "flat," as he used to say. It was precisely because he was naturally good that it all happened. But he has paid the price, to the uttermost farthing, and for that I honour him; it tells me that I was not mistaken when I looked at him and felt that he was a living manifestation of God. What I saw in him I can never tell to any human being, and you are one of the very few to whom I would try. But I *was* right, he was as great as I thought; I shall prove it to you later on. The trouble with him has been, that as a youth, the ideal of goodness that was rammed down his throat was a thoroughly rotten one. He submitted to it, knowing no better, and after he found out his mistake, he spent the whole of his strength in tearing it to pieces, like a tiger rending his prey. This has hardly been discernible yet, but it will be seen, and

471

then he will take his place among the great—perhaps not the great artists, but among the great benefactors to mankind.

I remember well, when I put the anemones on the grave, you said, "It isn't finished; it's only just started." You were the best friend to me; you were always sympathetic, and you asked no questions,—how great a boon that was, you can never know. If you had tried tiresomely to 'understand,' it would have been fatal. So once more I thank you for your help and *real* 'understanding.'

I like the article you sent; it is in the book of "Assorted Articles." In a while I'll send this book for you to read; and then perhaps you will post it back to me—it costs 6/- which is more than it is worth (of our money).

I must disagree with you when you say that inspiration is off its pedestal. It is rather the other way about. The greatest scientists of today admit that science can only go so far, and that the kind of truth that true inspiration teaches is beyond the reach of science. That is true of Einstein and all the great figures in the scientific world of today.

Speaking on my own little account I must tell you in all seriousness and sincerity that, but for divine help, I could not have come through unmaimed. For I was really stricken unto death, and I had to fight for my life, but in very truth help came to me that I can only call divine. I am sure that it is so—it must have been so with the saints of old, those who died and suffered for a faith. And you know, no faith is *the true* faith, because faith itself enlarges according to our vision, and thus changes from age to age.

What do you think of 'The New Adelphi'? [33] You like the Portrait, don't you? Of all the articles I think Bert's own is far and away the best. How well he remembered the old places! In my opinion, had he but had the physical strength to live, we might have witnessed something in the nature of a miracle. But we are all too unbelieving for such things to happen, and it is hard to see aright.

How are things going with you? Here it is a perfect, fresh Sunday morning. I did the cooking yesterday, so am free to write today. What are your crops looking like? How I wish you could get a bumper year, and sport a holiday.

Did you get a dress length recently? Did you care for it?

We are hoping to go abroad this year, to Slovenia—Ljubljana is the town we are making for, if it comes off. Will tell you more later.

With love to you and Will,

(By the way, does Will need more powder?)

Jessie.[34]

Frieda Lawrence Ravagli

Kingsley [Hotel, 36 Hart Street, London] 4 February 1932

Dear Dorothy [Warren],

No luck! I was sorry to miss you just as I had ventured out rather feebly. Your flowers are like a gay and gallant red and yellow flag and challenge in my room, like you and Philip, they seem. That you never give *into* the low ones is such a joy, and that you have a real tenderness and gentleness for each other is so rare and good. It's *everything*, it frightens me, the absolute *toughness* and hate, envy and spite and misery I feel in most people. Barby came and said yours are the only parties she likes. I am so sorry I couldn't come, awfully so. I would have liked to see Mrs. Eames.[35] I want to. I also want to show you a picture of Lorenzo's that I have with me. I called it my *Garde du Corps,* it hung over my bed. I'll go to Margate and look at and smell the sea. Then I want to see you next week. I like to be with Philip and you *alone* also.

Much love and so many thanks.

Did the Elizabeth Arden materialise?

F.[36]

Rolf Gardiner

3rd July, 1932   Wallington,/Cambo,/Morpeth [Northumb., Eng.]

Dear Mrs. Carswell,

Your vindication of Lawrence is a benison. I got the book [*The Savage Pilgrimage*] at Elliot's in Edinburgh and was able to race greedily through its pages in the train to Jedburgh before walking back here across the Border. I meant to write to you when your first articles came out in the *Adelphi;*[37] now I must indeed thank you. It's something to be thankful for, a straightforward just account to which people can turn amid all these frightful personal outpourings over poor Lawrence: Murry's venomous self-justification which made me feel so physically sick that I could not finish it, and Mabel Dodge Luhan's book writhing with her awful will and personality. You seem to be one of the very few normal, human beings among the circle of Lawrence's literary friends. I always thought it pitiable that Lawrence had to find companionship among the neurotics, intellectuals, people to whom books and book-talk were more real than the kind of action for which Lawrence himself was looking. As a young man growing up under the spell of his writing, I ever hoped that some-day we should be able to claim him as the leader (which posthumously he has become) of a younger generation engaged in doing rather than recording. But when I first met him in the flesh in July [August] 1926, I realised that it was too late and that the great onset of illness which struck him at Oaxaca during the winter of 1924–25, had left him too frail and that he would never be able to join in with us. (Perhaps Aldous Huxley showed you copies of the letters which he wrote to me between 1924–1928?) [38]

Nevertheless I firmly believe that by desire Lawrence was a man of action and a leader of action and, that given robust health and other friends than writers and artists, he would have been a great pioneer in forms of living. It is typical that none of his literary friends and critics, least of all Murry, have begun to realise his interest in practical leader-ship. *The Plumed Serpent* is surely a religio-political book. Lawrence would have lived the action of the book, had he been able.[39]

As it was, he led us *through* his books. Think how marvellous it was for a boy to grow to manhood with the companionship of Lawrence's writ-ing! His books were an imaginative projection and biography which de-veloped as he advanced further on his great journey. As Lawrence wrote one travelled with him or followed him: his books were never escape or distraction, they were always intensely relevant to the here and now; they deepened and intensified and made powerful and significant the present. And growing up with these records of immediate living, warm and flushed with intense experience, one learnt to see and feel in his way: one's facul-ties and perceptions went to school in his books. Lawrence educated one in the literal sense of the word.

But it was the greater Lawrence of his imaginative experience that led one, more than the Lawrence who later wrote letters and for whom one felt gratitude and respect, and more than the Lawrence whom still later on one met in the flesh, and for whom one felt tender veneration and affec-tion. It was this greater Lawrence who mattered to us, who was and is our leader. Therefore all books about his personal life are bound to affect bathos: they try and save the personal Lawrence from the work which he created! We have verily got to "save the tale from the artist who cre-ated it"; [40] we have got to cling to the greater, richer, more powerful Law-rence, the *voice* of his books and not to his suffering personality, however much we may have loved and venerated the latter.

474

For "a man is more than a man," and the power in Lawrence's books was vaster and richer than in Lawrence's personality. Which is not dishonouring him but accepting the circumstances of his life that he a man, who might have been a great practical leader, was compelled to lead through the imagination in writing. He would, I feel sure, have us *live* the example of his books, become potent and alive as he saw life through his writing, and tap the sources of power through obedience as he bade us through his characters.

It always seemed to me that country spoke through Lawrence. It was indeed the dark, fecund forces of Nottinghamshire which threshed through his earlier books filling them with the quality of imminence and dark presage, the secret hidden power of Nottinghamshire. Lawrence became the vehicle for the dark gods of country to speak to us and claim us: so the Midlands again and again, Northern Italy in the most harmonious of all his books *Twilight in Italy*, Tuscany, Australia, Mexico. The spirit of the place, this dominated him and fed him with power. All his books throb with this dark exciting spirit of place, subduing our picture-postcard imaginations, teaching us to sense and experience afresh the intense power of the gods in the earth. I feel that this aspect of Lawrence's writing has never been appreciated by the critics: probably because they are too numb and mental to experience country vividly in the flesh. But it seems to me one of the great clues to Lawrence's teaching. He knew that we could draw power from the earth and only live significantly if we worked in communion with the authorities of the past in the earth, in particular landscapes, as well as with the authorities of the cosmos, with the sun and the rhythmic order of the stellar universe.

I think this is important because what Lawrence experienced and showed through his books has been experienced by many of the younger generation, by the Jugendbewegung in Germany and to a lesser extent in Britain. Such as these will accept the greater Lawrence as their prophet and leader and will live and do his work. He has torn the veil of the old vision across and allowed us to see through; he has given us the clues to a new heaven and earth.

I have felt for a long time that some vindication of Lawrence's teaching, of his *vision* must be made, and not by literary critics, but by people trying to live his vision. You, Mrs. Carswell, have vindicated Lawrence the man whom you knew and loved, and have thereby rebuked the slanderers and self-justifiers with pure factual truth. It still remains to vindicate his vision: to vindicate the greater Lawrence who led us and leads us through his imaginative projection of his own experience in his books.

This can only be done by younger people, probably. When I was at Cambridge in 1921–24 I often thought of doing it. But none of my contemporaries had begun to understand Lawrence: I was utterly alone and my vehement proclamations merely bewildered my friends and drew mockery from my opponents.

Now however in the course of time there are many who feel similarly to myself: who recognise Lawrence as their chief. With such one should, I feel, build some small monument of veneration in a book *vindicating his vision* and acknowledging his leadership of those who are attempting to live it after him. A friend of mine, Christopher Scaife,[41] wrote the "introduction to Lawrence" which I think is a clear and useful guide to the uninitiated to the meaning of his books, and which I am taking the liberty of sending you with this letter. I think it might well serve as the introduction to a book of essays by Lawrence's younger friends and followers such as I suggest.

I would be grateful for your opinion on this matter. Perhaps you could also suggest people who might be asked to contribute to such a book. In addition to Scaife and myself, I thought that possibly(?) Adrian Stokes [42] and W. H. Auden might take part in such a book. Do you know of any other young men who knew Lawrence personally and could write of him and his work, or who did not know him personally but might write of the effect of his work on themselves and their contemporaries? We should only need half a dozen contributors at the outside. I should like to undertake this book in the autumn when all the summer activities are over. Scaife's essay could, I think, stand; I would like to write on Lawrence as a religious-political leader as I experienced him through his books and later through letters and as a person. I have hesitated for a long while, partly because I have been too absorbed with practical work, partly because I felt that all literary and personal gossip and discussion over Lawrence's grave would have to subside a little first.

I should be very grateful if you could be so very kind and let me know what you think about all this. Perhaps later on sometime we might meet and discuss things together. I'd be grateful, having read your book. But until the autumn it will have to wait since I shall be busy with activities in the Baltic till then. Curiously enough these undertakings have all developed from a meeting at Rendsburg in Holstein in October 1926 to which Lawrence hoped to come himself. But of course he didn't.

With gratitude for your book,

I am, yours very sincerely,

Rolf Gardiner.

P.S. My permanent address is: 9, Landsdowne Road, London, W. 11.

2. Who was the doctor from Frankfurt/Oder whom you met in the Harz? [43] The Musikheim at Frankfurt/Oder is our headquarters. Lawrence was to have come there too! [44]

The Times (*London*)
(4 November 1932)

A settlement was announced [3 November 1932] of this probate action which concerned the testamentary affairs of the late Mr. David Herbert Lawrence, the novelist, who died at Vence, France, on March 2, 1930.

The plaintiff, Mrs. Frieda Emma Johanna Maria Lawrence, the widow, residing at the Kingsley Hotel, Bloomsbury, propounded a will of November 9, 1914, under which she was sole beneficiary, and asked that letters of administration granted on June 5, 1930, to herself and Mr. George Arthur Lawrence, a brother of Mr. D. H. Lawrence, be revoked.

The defendants were Mr. G. A. Lawrence, of Laurel Street, Nottingham, and Mrs. Lettice Ada Clarke, of Broadway, Ripley, Derbyshire, and Mrs. Emily Una King, of Norwell Lane, North Markham, Newark, Nottinghamshire (sisters of Mr. D. H. Lawrence).

Mr. T. Bucknill appeared for the plaintiff; Mr. Walter Frampton for the defendants Mr. G. A. Lawrence and Mrs. King; and Mr. Noel Middleton for the defendant Mrs. Clarke.

Mr. BUCKNILL said that Mr. D. H. Lawrence had made a will on November 9, 1914, which could not be found. There was no question of its contents and date, because there was an identical will of the same date in existence made by his friend, Mr. Middleton Murry, the author. Mr. Lawrence's will remained in his possession for years, and it was still in existence in 1925, when Mrs. Lawrence saw it. Three days before he died he asked where the will was.

He and his wife were a couple most devoted to each other all their married life.[45] During the latter years they might be described as *citoyens du monde*, travelling from place to place all over the world. Mr. Lawrence carried his papers about with him and some had been recovered in various places, but not the will.

Mrs. Lawrence, the widow, in evidence, said that her maiden name was von Richtofen [*sic*] and that she was born in Germany. The marriage took place in July, 1914. On November 9, 1914, they were living at Cholesbury, Buckinghamshire. A discussion arose between Mr. Lawrence and Mr. Middleton Murry on their financial position and how little money they had. It was War time, and they were discussing the possibility of being called up. Mr. Lawrence remarked something like: "We shall be great men some day and we must make our wills." Each wrote out a will for the other.

Mr. Lawrence's will, leaving all he possessed to her (the witness), was witnessed by Mr. Middleton Murry and Miss Katherine Mansfield.

The last time that she (the witness) saw the will was when they were on her ranch at Taos, New Mexico, in 1925, when they were packing up to return to Europe. Her husband put it among some papers. He was arranging some papers at that time to be sent to New York. She had not seen it since. He was reading a book a few days before his death and an incident in the book about a Chinese making a will caused him to ask about his own will. He was very ill, and she told him not to worry about it. He said that in any case she would have everything.

Mr. J. Middleton Murry, of the Old Rectory, Larling, near Norwich, gave evidence of the execution of Mr. Lawrence's will.

The PRESIDENT said that the evidence was quite clear. He suspected that the will was in the papers intended to go to New York and was lost. The letters of administration already granted would be revoked, and he would pronounce for the will. The terms of settlement, which were generous terms, would be made a rule of Court.

Solicitors. —Messrs. Field, Roscoe and Co.; Messrs. Percy Robinson and Co.; Messrs. Neve, Beck, and Crane.[46]

Jessie Chambers Wood

[43 Breck Hill Road, Woodthorpe, Nottingham] ? 1933

[To Helen Corke]

I'm sorry to be rather late in returning the book,[47] but the spring-cleaning was fairly long and exhausting, and gave time neither for reading nor writing. Now it is over, and I am rejoicing in a clean house and a little leisure.

Well, your book [48] will rank along with the other Laurentian literature; it is a document; and if it bears witness rather to the author than to the subject of the work, it is not the less interesting and significant. I can't wax enthusiastic about it, because it is concerned with that aspect of D. H. L. that I have always found least interesting. As an artist, when he is dealing with the immediate and concrete, he is superb, but when he assays to be a thinker, I find him superficial and unconvincing, and quite soon boring. The Revelation of John of Patmos, and Apocalypse of D. H. L., can never have any but a secondary interest for me. I have never been able to read the biblical Revelations—when I have tried, I have soon felt that here was the basis for all the Old Moore's Almanacs that ever existed, and the guesses and speculations and the monstrous beasts are only weari-some. As a fragmentary and mutilated account of mankind's early attempts to understand his place in the universe, it *is* interesting, but that was not really D. H. L.'s concern with Revelations. His concern was to find some means of escape from that narrow prison of his own ego, and to do so he was prepared to assault the cosmos. So, whenever I read his almost de-lirious denunciations of what he pretended to regard as Christianity I only see the caged panther lashing himself into a fury to find some way out of his strait prison.

D. H. L. was a man in bondage and all his theorisings and philosophis-ings only bear witness to his agony. The more I ponder upon his life and his death, the more significant becomes to me the fact of his suffering—of course I don't mean his physical suffering, *that* was the direct outcome of his spiritual anguish at his own frustration. Well, why was he frus-trated, and why was he in bondage? Some of his own words come to my mind. The day before his mother's funeral we went a walk together, and during that walk I reproached him for having become engaged to X. Y. I said: "You ought not to have involved X. in the tangle of our relation-ship." . . . D. H. L.'s reply took my breath away; he said . . . "With *should* and *ought* I have nothing to do." If you will think out the implica-tions of that statement you will see what was the nature of D. H. L.'s bondage; he was the measure of his own universe; his own god—and also his own hell. He deliberately (or perhaps he couldn't help it)—anyhow, he regarded himself as exempt from the laws that hold mankind together (I am not referring to conventional morality) and when a human being does that, he is of necessity cut off from contact with his fellows. It seemed to me that D. H. L.'s great powers—far from exempting him from responsibility, conferred upon him a much greater and higher order of responsibility. I could only think that time would prove. At the end of that same walk, as we stood within a stone's throw of the house where his mother lay dead, he said to me:

"You know J, I've always loved mother."

"I know you have," I replied.

"I don't mean that," he answered. "I've loved her—like a lover—that's why I could never love you."

Then he handed me the three poems he had written since she had died.[49] I think this partly explains why he had placed himself beyond ordinary human sanctions. He was, as it were, driven out of the land of the living into a fearful wilderness of egoism. It explains, too, why, as you remark in your book, he looked in woman only for the animal—female—qualities.[50] It made his dilemma a cruel one, because it compelled him to deny what was best in himself. Consequently his prison was also a terrible battleground where his two selves were constantly fighting each other.

I'll tell you one other incident. On the day when he first met Mrs. Weekley at lunch, he came to tea at the Farm here; and after tea, in the parlour, he said to me in accents of despair:

"When we are not together, since we have been parted, I'm not the same man. I don't think the same, feel the same; *I* can't write poetry." There was his dilemma; one D. H. L. saw one thing with intense clarity; the other went the way of a doomed man. As he said so often; he couldn't help it. But what a price he paid.

I don't propose to write a book about him, and yet I know an aspect of his life that no one else has ever known or can possibly know. So I hope to leave a simple historical record of all I know about him, so that if at some future time some biographer with no pre-conceived theories about him, but a genuine desire to find out what manner of man he was, and what forces went to his making, should arise, my record will exist as one of the "sources." That, I feel, I owe to D. H. L. and to what he stood for. But I loathe exhibitionism, so that only a later generation will read my record, if indeed it is ever read.

Strangely enough, the record will extend just beyond his death, and perhaps you will be interested to hear that part. As I have said, the fact of D. H. L.'s suffering is the dominant fact in his life for me, and it was only after the publication of *The Plumed Serpent* that I realized he was a tortured spirit. As you know, I returned his last letter in 1913, and since then no word ever passed between us, and I never heard news of him; his name was never mentioned to me. I did not know he was ill; the letter he sent to David [51] was never shown to me until weeks after his death, so that whatever knowledge I had of him came through other channels than those of ordinary communication. For some eighteen months or so before his death I felt acutely drawn to him at times, and wondered intensely how some kind of communication that seemed so urgently needed, was to be established. It seemed to be not just a matter of writing a letter—something else, something different was needed. The feeling that some

Frieda Lawrence Ravagli, June, 1956. From a photograph taken at the Upper Ranch, Taos, New Mexico, by A. Alvarez.

Painting of Lawrence (1938) by the Hon. Dorothy Brett.

drawing together was imminent scarcely ever left me. Once quite suddenly, as though he had spoken, the words came into my mind—"We are still on the same planet." There were other things too of a like nature. Please remember I had no idea D. H. L. was ill. On the morning of the day he died, he suddenly said to me, as distinctly as if he had been here in the room with me: "Can you remember only the pain and none of the joy?" And his voice was so full of reproach that I made haste to assure him that I *did* remember the joy. Then later on in a strange confused way he said—"What has it all been about?"

The next morning I was busy with my housework when suddenly the room was filled with his presence and for a moment I saw him just as I had known him in early days, with the little cap on the back of his head. That momentary presence was so full of joy that I simply concluded it was an earnest [52] of a real meeting in the near future. I remember saying to myself, "Now I *know* we're going to meet."

The following day his death was announced in the paper, and was a terrible shock to me. I give you this for what it is worth . . . smile it away, if you will, it doesn't matter; the experience was just as real as the fact that I am now holding a pen. I don't think it was self-suggestion, because I didn't know he was ill; I was full of anxiety on his behalf, but I judged his trouble to be of the soul.

I am sure that he broke through his prison before the end, and died a free spirit, though he had lived in bondage. I think his last poems show that he found the way to freedom and wholeness, so that he achieved a triumph, but not the kind that he used to write about so much. It had been my conviction all along that he would find out what the trouble really was, and I had almost dared to believe that having achieved the inner unity, without which he spent himself in vain, he would be strong enough to reshape his life on positive values; but it was not to be. By the time he understood his malady he had spent his vital force. I was expecting too much from one earthly span; the suffering of self-division of the utmost limit was a life-time's work, maybe. The story of the unification lies in the future.

So you see this is how D. H. L. appears to me, and his long arguments about aristocrats and democrats and the rest are only the dusty miles he covered in his pilgrimage. The only interest they have for me is the internal evidence they bear as to the state of his soul. Apart from that they are utterly unreal. There is no such thing as a division of people into aristocrats and democrats; it is the same with human beings as with the wheat among which the enemy had sown tares. "Let both grow together till harvest." The only definition of democracy that appeals to me is this: "Democracy is that arrangement of society in which every individual has an opportunity of becoming an aristocrat." . . . "By their fruits ye shall know them." [53]

Again, is that Golden Age of which D. H. L. dreamed in some remote past any further back than his own boyhood and youth? It is a great error to suppose that his early life was unhappy. In our home his name was a synonym for joy—radiant joy in simply being alive. He communicated that joy to all of us, and made us even happy with one another while he was there; no small achievement in a family like ours! No, D. H. L.'s Golden Age was the time up to nineteen or so, before that fatal self-division began to manifest itself. What was it Keats said about a great man's life being an allegory, and his works the comments upon it? Something of that applies to D. H. L. You see that in essentials my feeling for him has not changed in spite of other deep affection. What he said about the indestructibility of love is quite true, on a particular plane.

I hope this long letter will not bore you. I haven't said much about your book, but I think you will understand my attitude.

You may like to read Carter's book.[54] I prize it for the little biographical touches . . . D. H. L. sitting on his heels feeding the fire with sticks —how clearly I see him, and his sombre face. Keep it as long as you like, but sometime I'd like to see it again. My very best wishes for the success of your book.

[Jessie Chambers Wood] [55]

Jessie Chambers Wood

43 Breck Hill Road,/Woodthorpe/Nottingham/June 21st. 1935
[To May Chambers Holbrook, Cuffley, Sask., Canada]

My dear May,

I was very glad to get your letter of a week or two ago. It seemed such a long time since I had heard from you. Now you are in the midst of the busy season, and I hope that things are promising well. By the way, it was not *your* parcel that I thought was "a bit of a fluke," but the one we sent to Will, containing old socks & tobacco.

.   .   .   .

Now to leave Keyworth news and come to some of my own. I told you some time ago that a young Frenchman, Emile Delavenay,[56] had applied to me for information about Bert, on whom he is writing a most exhaustive thesis. I supplied him with notes as to our reading and so on. Later on Professor Lavrin [57] happened to see these notes, and begged me to let him publish them in a magazine he was bringing out called "The European Quarterly." [58] Then Jack suggested I should make a book of my notes etc. He pointed out that I was giving away this information to others who were making use of it, and that I might just as well publish it myself. So the long and short of it is that I have written a short book on our old friend, which has been published by Jonathan Cape. I am sending you a copy in a day or so. Perhaps you won't have time to read it in this busy season, but never mind, it will be there for when you have time. I think you will be interested in it, and I shall be delighted and anxious to know what you and Will think of it, and please tell me just what you *do* think. Remember there is no hurry; bide your time, and talk about it in a letter when you feel inclined. *You,* more than anyone, know what those years were to me, and you may guess what the writing of this book has meant, in joy and in sorrow. But I am very glad it is done. It is a great relief to mind and spirit. I felt, too, that I had a duty to discharge. I knew a chapter of Bert's inner history that no one else did or could know, and it happened to be a vital chapter, lacking a knowledge of which his critics and commentators went sadly astray.

I want you to realise that I can never forget your sympathy of those times, which was the more precious because it was nearly always unspoken. Nevertheless, I knew it was there, and it made all the difference. Your cottage was a haven in a world that had become almost wholly a desert. I don't think I need say any more. It goes deeper almost than words can go, but I have never once forgotten what it meant to me. So, as you shared in the joys and sorrows of those days, I want you to share a little of the fruits of them. Cape's have paid me £25. on account of royalties on the book. Whether there will be any more depends upon the sales, and I believe the book is doing pretty well. So in the course of a few days I shall send you an order for £10. and I hope you will enjoy it in the way that appeals to you most. But *do* enjoy it, buy yourself something you've always been wanting.

Now I want to make a request. Do you mind not mentioning anything about the book to mother, or even perhaps to Hubert & Bernard. I have not spoken of it to any of our people except David. There is no reason why father & mother should not know, but I think it would only waken old, unhappy memories, and I simply don't want to talk about it with them. That's all. You'll understand, I'm sure. I must hurry now to catch the post, and will send on the book and money order within the next few days.

Jack joins me in sending love to you both. I hope you are both well, and enjoying the summer.

Yours with love,
Jessie [59]

Witter Bynner

Though funds had been pledged to bring [Lawrence's] body from the temporary grave in Vence to his hill in New Mexico, Frieda now resolved, with the suit ended in her favor, that she would bear expenses and that cremation would be more feasible and fitting. Ashes were truer to the phoenix symbol than a coffined body would have been. So, returning from Europe herself, she arranged to have their Italian friend, Captain Ravagli, attend to details and follow with the urn.

The sequel may be, in part, another legend. Sometimes legends, though not quite accurate, are truer than the truth. Being in Chapala at the time, I was told the tale by letter. When Frieda and some companions met the train at Lamy [Spring, 1935], the junction which connects with Santa Fe by bus, they were so cordial in greeting the Captain and he—speaking only Italian—was so confused, that not till they had almost reached town nineteen miles away were they aware of having left on the station platform the urn containing Lawrence's ashes! Back they went, recovered it and took it safely to Del Monte, where a tiny chapel was built for it under tall pines on a rise behind the ranch house.[60]

Louis Untermeyer

Six years after Lawrence's death I saw Frieda Lawrence again. It was during the Christmas holidays in Boston at one of Merrill Moore's [61] cosmopolitan week ends. Frieda was round and exuberant, handsome, lustier than ever. We spoke of Lawrence's happy days, when he baked the bread and Frieda served it, of the many women who tried to mother him and the quarrelsome biographers who claimed him—Frieda's own *Not I, but the Wind* still seems to me the most unaffected and revealing of the portraits— of the intense and comic rivalry betwen Frieda and Mabel Dodge Luhan; of our meeting in London and Frieda's subsequent experiences in Taos' "Mabeltown."

Then Frieda told us an incredible story. Someone who wanted Lawrence—and Frieda named the possessive admirer—wanted him in death as well as in life. Frieda's house was invaded and Lawrence's ashes were stolen.

"You can believe," said Frieda, "I had a hard time getting them back. But I recovered them. And I made up my mind that nothing of this sort should happen again. So I fixed it."

"How?" we asked. "What did you do?"

"I had the ashes mixed with a lot of sand and concrete. Now they are in a huge concrete slab. It weighs over a ton." She laughed heartily. "A dozen men could not lift it." [62]

Barbara Weekley Barr

Frieda went back to Kiowa ranch and made it her home.

In 1935 she had Lawrence's body disinterred and cremated, afterwards taking his ashes to the ranch, where she had built a little chapel for them on the hill above.

I had married a year before, and was with my husband in America. We went to stay with Frieda for the ceremony of placing the ashes in the chapel.

Captain Ravagli (whom Frieda has since married) met us at Cimarron and motored us seventy miles to Kiowa. It is nine thousand feet up—a wild, beautiful place. The altitude makes one breathe faster, and gives all the flowers an intense brilliance. Beside a newer, large cabin was the small one where Frieda and Lawrence used to live. Near it their horses, Azul and Aaron, cropped the grass with two young piebald horses—"Pintos."

The ceremony was to be at sundown. Frieda invited some of the Taos Americans, and asked the Indians from the pueblo to come and do their ritual dance.

A local judge she knew was to give the oration. Unfortunately some Taos busybody "tampered" with him. The judge failed to appear, so my husband took his place.

When the casket of ashes had been put in the chapel, the sun set and the skies grew dark. A big fire was lighted on the level below, and the Indians, in feather dress, did their ceremonial dance. Trinidad, a young Indian whom Lawrence had known, led the dancers.

Afterwards a storm broke out. The horses neighed in fright. Lightning and thunder circled the ranch and the mountain.[63]

T. M. Pearce

The great bend in the highway was as lovely as ever as it swept away from sky and sunlight into shadow and then came out on the Taos plain. There the mountains loomed beyond the village and the pueblo. D. H. Lawrence had called it "the most dramatic landscape I have ever experienced," [64] and today none of the power of space and clarity had diminished. We weren't hurrying; our date was not until 3 o'clock. We had time to stop at an art gallery or two, perhaps to visit with a friend. At Ranchos de Taos (the village with the wonderful old Spanish colonial church) we sought out the gallery called The Ruins, named appropriately enough. It was behind an adobe wall with exterior and interior a bit crumbling, but the walls whitewashed clean for the framed colors so brightly spotted against them. Some other visitors followed us, and we heard a babble of voices. Then we overheard the attendant say, "Oh, yes! The funeral is this afternoon. It is very shocking. The ground is trembling under our feet!" Her tone was not ironic—just the dramatization one anticipates in an art colony. The moments of life—and death—are always heightened. One of the visitors remarked, "She was so sweet. Everyone loved her." "Yes," said the gallery woman. "It ends an era. It was an era. My husband had just installed a banister at the house, so she could go down the steps. She tested it three days before the stroke. She was so pleased with it. She had been very ill."

Later we talked with the attendant, who said that Frieda had been well enough to go to the Taos Fiesta. But then she went back to bed. She had never really recovered from the spell in the Santa Fe Hospital last winter when influenza had joined the chronic asthmatic condition to cause a crisis in her health. In addition, Frieda had been a diabetic for many years. On Wednesday, August 8th, 1956, at 9 P.M., she suffered a stroke. It completely paralyzed her body. On Friday, she seemed a little better. She was able to make her wishes known, and one of them was to tell her husband, Angelino Ravagli, to send a small volume of Lawrence's poems (from an edition consisting of only 200 copies) as a birthday present to her friend, the poet, Witter Bynner in Santa Fe.[65] This Friday was Bynner's birthday. Saturday was Frieda's own. They were to have celebrated their days together in Santa Fe on Saturday. It was at 7.30 A.M. on Saturday, 11 August 1956, that Frieda died.[66]

I remembered the birthday party at Kiowa Ranch when Frieda was sixty and Hal Bynner was fifty-eight. The big log chalet had just been finished, built in front of the low adobe where the Lawrences had lived in 1922 and 1923. There were luminarios outside, tallow candles that burned in brown paper sacks half-filled with sand, and their dim glow was a yellow necklace around the white flood from the Coleman lamps hanging in the house. There was dancing in two big rooms and *vino*, beer, and cider as refreshments. The dancing was nothing Arthur Murray would have imitated, but it was turbulent and gay. The *Beer Barrel Polka* was popular then and the couples skipped and whirled while Frieda talked to groups of her friends, both inside the house and outside where the night was gentle with shadows on the slopes of Mt. Lobo and luminous above with stars. Between the dances, Bynner amused with dramatic monologues about himself, his acquaintances, and a famous Aunt Harriet, whose idiosyncracies became a scenario in his gifted dialogue. Frieda had a genius for friendship, as Lawrence did not: she held the friends they had, for both of them, and now, in her life since Lawrence's death, the community of her friends in Taos, Santa Fe, and Albuquerque were with her for shared fellowship on a memorable occasion. Somehow this occasion at 3 o'clock didn't seem real though Frieda had again drawn her friends to Taos on a day that was to have been a party and a birthday.

The grey coffin rested before red velvet curtains with a gold panel in the center. Tall silver candelabra held burning tapers and electric reflectors threw light to the ceiling. Frieda wore a grey silk dress with a pattern in pink, and in her right hand she held a summer hat with a ribbon around the crown of the same grey-pink silk. In her left hand was a spray of delicate blue flowers. She looked unmarked by illness, her face serene, her hair like spun gold. On her feet were soft soled shoes that looked like beaded moccasins. Gladiolas—yellow, white, pink—were among the massed flowers. Red roses, carnations, asters, purple gentians were there. A cross of white carnations stood at the foot of the coffin. There was no funeral service there at the mortuary. People simply sat, some with bowed heads, while the candles burned, smoking in the currents of air-conditioning fans which hummed in the stillness. People sat and no words were spoken, other than whispered remarks. But what is there to say, really? The age old words of Scripture? Yes! They were to be read later, at the ranch. Here there was nothing expressed. But wasn't everything said by the presence of the many who knew Frieda and loved her?

The pallbearers were in the front row of chairs, and after a half hour or longer we stood while younger men came to bear the casket to the carriage.[67] The engines of the cars outside started to sound, and the procession gradually formed to drive through Taos and out the north road to San Cristobal and off to the east, up the sinuous mountain road to the ranch. How well I knew that trail, though today I was not to take it. Once I slept in my car on a slick stretch of that road after the rain had fallen. I made it into the ranch the next morning, where Frieda had breakfast waiting and where Angelino protested he would have come down to help me if he had known I was stuck in the mud. I knew every turn the cortege took—where the fenders scraped the branches of scrub oaks and fir, where the tires grated on rocky stretches or kicked up gravel. I knew where the hearse would stop, at the foot of the slope north of the house where the Lawrence chapel was, that tiny building with its altar of concrete in which the urn holding the ashes of the English poet-novelist became one with the massive thrust of Mount Lobo. How many times I had walked up this incline, through the turnstile and the carved wooden candelabra and past the avenue of evergreens until I came to the white little cinder block building and unlocked the gilded wooden door and stood before the carved red fox which was the altar piece. Above the altar was a painting on glass of a brilliant red flower. A registry book lay on a shelf near the entrance; the signatures of visitors from Europe as well as from America filled its pages. An old hat and a jacket Lawrence had worn lay there, too, at one time. The birds flew in the unglassed "rose window," which consisted of a gilded cogwheel, ornate enough however humble its origin. On the peak of the roof was the carved figure of the golden hawk of Horus, or the Phoenix symbol, which Lawrence had made his own. Whatever the logic of Lawrence's mind and thought, this symbol of creativity was forever his. In the struggle for achievement in his art as well as in the struggle for success in his marriage and in his personal relationships, new life rose from every disappointment or failure. Whenever I visited the chapel, I felt that Lawrence was there where, in his last illness, he said he wanted to be. He wrote from Mallorca less than a year before he died, "Now I am in a Spanish-speaking country, I have New Mexico before my eyes every moment." [68] And nine months later, "I want so much to get well enough to be able to start for New Mexico. I feel I'd get better there . . . ." [69] D. H. Lawrence died at Vence in southern France on March 2, 1930, and Frieda returned to New Mexico three years later. In 1935, she had the chapel built at Kiowa Ranch, where Lawrence's ashes were placed in that year. Now it was August 13, 1956. Both Lawrence and Frieda were again together at the ranch.

With the permission of Willard "Spud" Johnson, a friend of both the

Lawrences during all their Taos days, I quote from a letter telling of the services at the ranch.

As you will see, the ceremony there was just as stark and simple as the one at the Hanlon chapel. I'm sure Frieda would have liked it that way. Bill Goyen's few words were most touching, and even with the reading of the poem by Lorenzo and the one Psalm which followed, the "ceremony" lasted but a few moments. Carrying the coffin from the lower fence up that steep slope to the chapel was in itself impressive—and the fact that people like 80 year old Blumenschein and Mrs. Wurlitzer also managed the ascent. There was not a large crowd there, which was lucky, since, as you know, the parking facilities there at the ranch are most limited.[70]

The words of William Goyen, young American novelist and poet,[71] who was Mrs. Lawrence's neighbor and friend, were printed in the Taos newspaper, *El Crepusculo,* August 16, 1956. They were as follows:

For our beloved Frieda, a few words, a poem and a Psalm in behalf of all who loved her.

We remember her for her rare gift of life—her cooking, her sewing, her gayety, her love of all living things; and we think of her as being joyful and peaceful at home forever here on this mountain in a place she loved so deeply. Our hearts and our friendship are with dear Angie.

And Frieda, I want to read for you a poem that you loved and a little Psalm that I know you cherished.

The poem which Goyen read was Lawrence's "Song of a Man Who Has Come Through." [72] Frieda had chosen from the first line the title for her own great tribute to Lawrence, published in Santa Fe in 1934, *"Not I, But the Wind . . . ."*

Not I, not I but the wind that blows through me!
A fine wind is blowing the new direction of Time.
If only I let it bear me, carry me, if only it carry me!
If only I am sensitive, subtle, oh, delicate, a winged gift!
If only, most lovely of all, I yield myself and am borrowed
By the fine, fine wind that takes its course through the chaos of the
    world . . . .

        .   .   .

We hear the 121st Psalm of David in Frieda's strong confident voice.

I will lift up mine eyes unto the hills, from whence cometh my help.
My help cometh from the Lord, which made heaven and earth.
He will not suffer thy foot to be moved: he that keepeth thee will not slumber.

Behold, he that keepeth Israel shall neither slumber nor sleep.
The Lord is thy keeper: the Lord is thy shade upon thy right hand.
The sun shall not smite thee by day, nor the moon by night.
The Lord shall preserve thee from all evil: he shall preserve thy soul.
The Lord shall preserve thy going out and thy coming in from this time forth, and even for evermore.

Because Frieda had one word more to say to her friends, I close this tribute with the words of "Spud" Johnson's editorial in *El Crepusculo* on the date previously cited.

FRIEDA

It is hard to know what to say about a friend who has gone, when that friend's whole existence has been such an overwhelming affirmative of life.

No one who ever met Frieda Lawrence Ravagli, even casually, can ever forget the eagerness and assurance of her booming "Ja!" It always made them feel their own importance as living creatures, and certainly impressed them with her significance as a vital force and as a lasting influence for good on all who knew her.

In the final paragraph of her Last Will and Testament, is this simple message to all of us:

I further order and direct that my executors shall insert a notice in the Taos newspaper, after my death, as follows:

To My Friends: A last farewell to all my friends, thanking them for all their friendship.

Frieda Emma Johanna
Maria Lawrence Ravagli

But it was she who inspired these friendships, and she who should be thanked for what she so bountifully gave to so many of us.[73]

CHAPTER FIVE

Five Who Went Back

A. L. Rowse

It is sometimes a mistake, if one wants to write about a subject, to know too much about it: one loses something of the sharpness, the tang, the excitement and the mystery. D. H. Lawrence meant something special to the men of my generation: he was an essential part in our awakening to maturity. We saw something of life through his eyes: his mode of experience intimately affected ours. He meant, naturally, even more to me. I could never regard him externally, as one does most writers. He was a part of me: he had entered into my veins at a very vulnerable moment, of adolescence changing into maturity. He was entwined in the fibres of my mind and heart, so closely that I remember a curious experience when he died. The day the news of his death came I went to walk alone on the coast of the bay at home in Cornwall: it was evening, and the image that consciousness of his passing took was that of a ship of death passing slowly along the darkening waters of the bay from west to east. It was only later that I learned that that was the image that had haunted his mind for weeks before his death, that the subject of the poem he left unfinished.[1]

There was a very natural reason why he should speak specially to me: he was then the only writer of genius to come from my own class, the working people, and his books—especially his masterpiece, *Sons and Lovers*—were the only books that described the life of the people from the inside, with absolute fidelity and conviction, and at the same time transfused it with imagination and poetry, made a work of art of it. I was a predestined victim: my nerves vibrated in sympathy with his: the same sensitiveness, the touchiness, the irritability of the one skin too few, the confusion of emotion and intellect, the keen but easily discouraged response to life, the brittleness and toughness, the mixture of masculine and feminine: I was an unknown, unrecognised, younger brother. How much he would have disapproved of me and the way I went: politics, the way of the intellectual, pride of the intellect, historical research, learning, burying the response of the senses to life under many weary tomes, living in libraries and colleges he so much despised, progressively withdrawn from life; but reaching, if by another avenue, the same disillusionment and despair. (One could not arrive at a greater despair than his.) And yet underneath the libraries, the works of history, the layers of academicism, the buried life, something of him goes on in my veins, the seed forgotten, its life not extinguished. It is years since I read anything of his—once I had read him almost all, absorbed him whole; and I had never yet visited the place where he was born and grew up, that made him what he was —though I had always meant to.

Here, at Nottingham, was my chance. At lunch-time I did not know where I was going. My friends knew. I thought I was going to the University. They said I was going to Eastwood. After lunch we parted, they for Wollaton and Derby. Emerging into the great Market Place, I felt lonely without them. My footsteps led me to the Eastwood bus. When I returned late in the evening, transported, beside myself—

> Nor did the wisest wizard guess
> What should bechance at Lyonesse,
> When I set out for Lyonesse
> A hundred miles away— [2]

I asked them where I had been. "To Eastwood, of course," they said.

I took my place humbly, apologetically, on the bus, front row in the stalls, upstairs: excited to think that I was following the road he knew so well, had so often come into Nottingham and out along it. A kind young man took charge of me—the Midlands courtesy, the Midlands niceness, I noticed; pointed out the sights to me. Some I registered silently to myself, having already entered the dream. Here was the cemetery that must have been so familiar to the Lawrences—on the slope of the hill, the last lap into Nottingham: as on that merry walk of Lawrence's father with his pal Jerry into Nottingham, when after several drinks on the way he lay down and slept in the last field under an oak in view of the city, and came home drunk to put his wife out of doors in the last weeks before Lawrence was born. It is all wonderfully described in *Sons and Lovers:* the moonlit night, the scent of phloxes in the garden, the wife looking under the drawn blind to see her husband asleep on the kitchen table, tapping at the window to be let in.[3]

We passed through Basford with the large house where Philip Bayley, author of *Festus,* a poem famous in its day, lived and wrote too much —for it is intolerably tedious, forty thousand lines of Victorian moralising. (No less popular in America, where thirty editions of it were pirated.) Thence past Nuttall Temple, the ruined shell of which surmounted the rise on the left. It was built in the mid-eighteenth century by Sir Charles Sedley—it is said, on the winnings of one race: a magnificent domed Palladian villa, like Chiswick House or Mereworth in Kent. It is mentioned somewhere by Lawrence in a description of the countryside.[4] My companion told me that his father had helped to redecorate it in the years before the war. Now deliberately dynamited, a fragment of hollow-windowed wall on the horizon—like a Piper scene of war damage. But the Nuttall Temple petrol-filling station is all right, standing beside the dismantled entrance-gate, the forlorn pillars and the overgrown drive.

It is the end of a civilisation. Piper and Betjeman, Osbert Lancaster, Gerald Berners, Martyn Skinner, Jack Simmons—all my friends are right. In the heroic days of 1940–45 I used to put up a resistance and argue that there was a future. Now I know that they are right. There is no point in resisting any longer. It is the decay of a civilisation that I study—like Leland and Aubrey before me: the one "roving maggoty-headed" about the country, wishing that there were monasteries still for such as he to retire to; the other ending up off his head, the spectacle of dissolution and destruction too much for him. Yes: it is a vanishing culture that I pursue, the débris that I lovingly cherish.

Descending from the bus, on the pavement I fell into the arms of luck. A passing fellow didn't know the house where Lawrence was born, but he could tell me the man who did, an old man of eighty-seven who had been his great friend and would tell me all about him. No, he himself had never seen Lawrence. No, Eastwood people usedn't to think much of him —until later years when he became famous, they began to take notice. He always understood that Lawrence resented Eastwood. He had been unhappy at school—no good at games, laughed at by the other boys, who thought him eff-eff-effo—what was the word? Effeminate? Yes, that's it.

I explained that he would not have been a man of genius, able to create as he did, unless he had had a strong streak of feminine as well as masculine in him. He thought that was right. But Lawrence resented Eastwood, and the last time he visited it he said he hoped never to see it again.

The usual story, I registered, but said nothing. One knows the difficulties a neighbourhood will make over one of their own who stands out: no such trouble if it is the son of a squire or of a local bourgeois. Is it any wonder that Lawrence grew to hate it? He said again and again that he would never come home to Eastwood. Nor did he. Switzerland, Germany, Italy, France, Australia, New Mexico—but never Eastwood. His father and mother, that ill-assorted couple—the drinking coal-miner who was such a beautiful dancer and his serious little wife with a soul above her surroundings—whose union yet produced a son whose genius was ripened by their jarring tension—lie in Eastwood Cemetery: not so their son. Yet how often, under alien skies, he revisited in mind the loved familiar places: the Breach, with its country look in spite of the proximity of the pit, the house in Walker Street with the ash-tree in which the wind moaned on winter nights and its broad view down the valley, and uphill to the trees behind which lay the farm where Miriam lived; Strelley Mill and Nethermere and Beauvale, Hucknall where Byron lies buried. Perhaps, in glimpses of the moon, the wraith—not of a bearded famous man but of a grey-eyed schoolboy, eager of step, lingers about those spots.

> He hears; no more remembered
>   In fields where I was known,
> Here I lie down in London
>   And turn to rest alone.
>
> There, by the starlit fences,
>   The wanderer halts and hears
> My soul that lingers sighing
>   About the glimmering weirs.[5]

The first thing that struck me about Eastwood—and what surprised me—was that, allowing for differences of colour and accent, it might have been a china-clay village at home in Cornwall. Not at all one's usual idea of a mining town, as it might be South Wales or Yorkshire or Tyneside. For one thing, it was clean, blowy, healthy. There is still country round about, fields and holdings and trees, and distant views toward Ilkeston and Ripley, places mentioned in the novels, towards Moorgreen Reservoir— the Nethermere of *The White Peacock,* towards Hucknall and further afield, back to Nottingham. The lie of the land reminded me of the china-clay district: windy ridges like that along which Eastwood lies, in the valleys the pits. There was the same rawness and rudeness about the place—as it might be Bugle or St. Dennis—the rough-edged angularity, the sharpness, the hideousness. Everything recent and ugly and Philistine, the chapels in evidence: a working-class and petty-bourgeois community. Nothing of the grace of life: no taste, no culture, no relenting: nothing whatever to stay the mind on or comfort the elect soul. How he must have felt about it, once he had come to know something better—just as I used to feel about St. Austell and the china-clay district!

Directed to the bungalow where Lawrence's old friend now lived, I entered at once into the aura—there were photographs of the lad he was, the one with the boyish hair and moustache, wide-apart eyes and an amused, enigmatic smile at the beholder, keeping himself in reserve, the withdrawal of youth, self-conscious yet friendly; next to it the image of the famous man, the bearded Christ with the infinitely sad eyes. So this was what he had come to—the suffering servant of Isaiah. His friend was away in Nottingham for the afternoon but would return to his shop. Back through the main street, past the "Wellington" inn—no doubt patronized by the father, though the "Ram" was his usual haunt—past the little shops Lawrence would still recognise if he could come back: Hunter's Tea Stores must be the same and the Nottingham Trustee Savings Bank next door, and surely the shop with the lettering "Drapery—Millinery—Mantles" must be pre-1914, though not that of John Houghton of *The Lost Girl*, who had a passion for fine clothes and filled his windows with them, and was laughed at by the mining folk to whom he had to sell them at a loss in the end. In the window of the only bookshop there was a copy of *Forever Amber* and Daphne du Maurier's latest—but no D. H. Lawrence. How right, I reflected: it could not be more right! First to be disconsidered, and then forgotten.

At the shop the old friend's wife made out an itinerary for me to follow —again the Midlands kindness to the stranger—and all the afternoon I went over the ground alone. It was all the more poignant so. Only a step across the street was the house where Lawrence was born. Again, not exactly a miner's cottage: a small, mean house in a squalid street, with a little shop-window and gate-entrance at the side to a back-court, the row of outdoor privies against the wall at the end of the potato patches. Mrs. Lawrence in her early married years had tried to sell baby-clothes and ribbons and lace in the front room to help out, but had had no luck: off the main street, nobody came. It was from this house that she came with her baby, when the friendly shopkeeper first set eyes on him as she drew back the shawl: "I'm afraid I s'll never rear him."

This is 8A Victoria Street: the whole neighbourhood gone downhill and really squalid now. The mean street runs steep down to the valley and the pit at the bottom, the sharp February wind blowing bitterly up, with occasional skiffs of rain from which I take shelter in a doorway opposite Searston's Groceries and Provisions, across the large ugly Wesleyan Methodist chapel MDCCCLXVI. A few miners are coming uphill, black from their work. In the street behind me a loud-speaker van tours up and down: "What about the promises the Socialists made in 1945? The Conservative Party will *not* nationalise industry if they come in." An old miner's wife clops crippling up the hill to do her Saturday shopping at Searston's, trudges back wearily, hopelessly with her carrier, her old shoes worn over, her ankles swollen: Saturday afternoon and the end of life for her. My heart sinks for her—but what is the point? One can do nothing. A blowsy slut peeps out of her den, keeps me under observation the whole time I am in the street. Perhaps they take me for somebody to do with the Election. But all that is long over. They wonder at the well-dressed stranger who huddles about in doorways, sheltering from the showers, but who will not move away, is rooted to the spot—so strangely moved he does not know whether it is raindrops on his face or tears, for the thought of all that this huddled street gave birth to, the intensity, the passion, the mingled bitterness and sweetness of life. Thoughts come and go like flickering lights of an aurora, as I once saw them in a snowstorm over Hensbarrow. How can language express these intense moments when the sense of life passes through one's mind with such poignancy, when one sees it all in a flash, in all its layers and dimensions simultaneously, as they say a drowning man sees it, all the pathos and manifold insatisfaction, yet touched by joy and love and incomprehensible consolations? Hardly thinking at all, I see the little family they were, making up the street for the Congregational chapel on Sundays, down the hill to the Breach where they next lived, the growing boy, the lyrical journeys to the farm and Miriam and her brothers, the obsessive love of mother and son excluding everyone else until she died, the brave face she put on life, the tragic division she inflicted on her son, the tension and the genius she gave him.

> I kiss you goodbye, my darling,
> Our ways are different now:
> You are a seed in the night-time,

I am a man, to plough
The difficult glebe of the future
For seed to endow. . . .

Is the last word now uttered?
Is the farewell said?
Spare me the strength to leave you
Now you are dead.
I must go, but my soul lies helpless
Beside your bed.[6]

The street has now an upper room, a Kingdom hall, of Jehovah's Witnesses. Lower down there is a clothes-drying ground: young Nottinghamshire lads cross it from time to time this Saturday afternoon, as it might be Bert Lawrence. But no Bert Lawrence will appear here again—ever.

At last I tear myself away to go on with my pilgrimage.

Back in the main street I retrace my steps past the Congregational chapel: very Early English and with a sharp little spire that looks as if it might prick you. Here it was that Mrs. Lawrence met Miriam's mother and the children first became acquainted—all described in *Sons and Lovers* and in the touching Personal Record that Miriam wrote after Lawrence died. The young minister used often to come down to the collier's house in the Breach to talk books and theology with the serious-minded wife, the best tea-things would be put out and the miner would be on his worst behaviour when he came home to find the minister there. Somewhere in a story of his, I remember, Lawrence recalled years after the text that was inscribed on the walls of the chapel—I forget what.[7] And in an article he wrote shortly before he died he remembered the hymns he liked: "Awake, my soul, and with the sun." The Lawrence children used to sing in the choir:

Dare to be a Daniel, dare to stand alone,

and

Sound the battle-cry,
See the foe is nigh,
Raise the standard high
For the Lord. . . .[8]

Lawrence was certainly a Nonconformist writer, one of the greatest of them: he had no difficulty in daring to stand alone: it came naturally to him. *Ich kann nicht anders.* Impossible to over-estimate the Nonconformist element in his make-up: he was always sounding the battle-cry, raising the standard high, pedalling away at the harmonium of the Sunday school in which he taught. He thought of himself as a prophet: he was certainly a missionary, a local preacher, yes—and alas—a prophet too, a prophet of the destruction that would come on us. It fascinated me to think, as I went along ("What did Mr. Aneurin Bevan say in 1945?" The voice pursued me, an echo from my past. I'm sure I don't remember)—I wondered, my mind set on better things, what would have been the effect if the Lawrences had gone to the dead, deserted church at the other end of the town: a less harsh inflexion, a more graceful, a more tolerant culture, a greater sense of history and tradition, a kindlier, easier spirit? There was the Sunday school they had all been brought up in, now an Employment Exchange. I longed to go into the little chapel: barred and bolted, the gate chained: I don't suppose anyone goes there now: there too an end of a way of life.

I go on my way along Dovecote Lane, suddenly noticing that it is the road to Hucknall and Byron's grave. In the playing-fields by the Greasley Miners' Welfare Centre, a dead-looking place, boys are playing football, white shorts and blue jerseys, green and black and red colouring the field. There is a gleam of sun. The wind is very fresh up here. In the distance the bells of Greasley church ring sweet in the sad February air. (Suddenly, a strange experience: a man in a passing car scrutinises me: I thought I recognised the sloe-black, adder-black eyes: a false friend of former days in Cornwall.) Hereabouts, in this parish, were the meadows that Miriam's father and his sons used to mow, and the young Lawrence would help.

[We] used to pack a big basket of provisions to last all day [Miriam wrote], so that hay harvest had a picnic flavour. Father enjoyed Lawrence's company quite as much as the rest of us. . . . I heard father say to mother:

"Work goes like fun when Bert's there, it's no trouble at all to keep them going." [9]

There is a lyrical description of it all in *The White Peacock*, written when those days were but just over, the dew still upon them. It is in the chapter called "A Poem of Friendship"; a chapter in which one sees Lawrence's sense of ecstasy in the life of Nature at its quietest and best. It is dedicated to his love for Miriam's eldest brother—the real, if transposed, subject of the book: in it he came as close as he could to the subject of their coming together. Afterwards,

We went together down to the fields, he to mow the island of grass he had left standing the previous evening, I to sharpen the machine knife, to mow out the hedge-bottoms with the scythe, and to rake the swaths from the way of the machine when the unmown grass was reduced to a triangle. The cool, moist fragrance of the morning, the intentional stillness of everything, of the tall bluish trees, of the wet, frank flowers, of the trustful moths folded and unfolded in the fallen swaths, was a perfect medium of sympathy. The horses moved with a still dignity, obeying his commands. When they were harnessed, and the machine oiled, still he was loth to mar the perfect morning, but stood looking down the valley.

"I shan't mow these fields any more," he said . . . . This year the elder flowers were widespread over the corner bushes, and the pink roses fluttered high above the hedge. There were the same flowers in the grass as we had known many years; we should not know them any more.[10]

Now all about is asphalt and new roads, and bungalows and houses for the too many people who inhabit England. Having gone too far beyond the little Board School with its bell that called the young Bert to school, I returned on my track to Eastwood, going downhill to Lynncroft, where they lived last, and along Walker Street to which they moved up from the Breach. There in the bottoms was the house where their life was at its unhappiest: the four stark blocks of miners' houses Mrs. Lawrence so much hated. Yet there are still fragments of country within reach, on the doorstep: trees, a sounding stream, fields, a farm—and then the former colliery-manager's house in its grounds, I suppose "Highclose" of *The White Peacock*. House-proud, yoked to a man who would not pull with her, and whom she gradually excluded from the life of the family, the mother was proud of the house in Walker Street: a bay-window, three steps up to the front door.

We loved living here [the youngest sister wrote]. We had a wonderful view of Brinsley, Underwood, Moorgreen, and the High Park woods in the distance. Immediately in front were fields stretching to the Breach which made the best playground one could have. What fun we had round the ancient ash tree which stood just opposite the house—although the moaning wind through its branches scared us as we lay in bed in the winter.[11]

D. H. himself has described it, more vividly, in *Sons and Lovers:*

They all loved the Scargill Street house for its openness, for the great scallop of the world it had in view. On summer evenings the women would stand against the field fence, gossiping, facing the west, watching the sunsets flare quickly out, till the Derbyshire hills ridged across the crimson far away, like the black crest of a newt.[12]

But the children were terrified of the moaning of the ash-tree at night.

The west wind, sweeping from Derbyshire, caught the houses with full force, and the tree shrieked again. Morel [i.e., the father] liked it.

"It's music," he said. "It sends me to sleep."

But Paul [i.e., D. H.] and Arthur and Annie hated it. To Paul it became almost a demoniacal noise. The winter of their first year in the new house their father was very bad.[13]

The moaning of the tree became a symbol of the discord within the house, the tension that imprinted itself upon the children, that left its stigmata ineffaceably upon one of them. One of his earliest poems is about it:

> Outside the house the ash-tree hung its terrible whips,
> And at night when the wind rose, the lash of the tree
> Shrieked and slashed the wind, as a ship's
> Weird rigging in a storm shrieks hideously.
>
> Within the house two voices arose, a slender lash
> Whistling she-delirious rage, and the dreadful sound
> Of a male thong booming and bruising, until it had drowned
> The other voice in a silence of blood, neath the noise of the ash.[14]

No ash-tree now stands outside the house to disturb the peeping ghosts. All is as quiet as the grave.

It is indeed very quiet this Saturday afternoon. A couple of coal-miners are crossing the open space, their dogs rushing madly across where the children used to play. The view is much the same, the great tip that dominates the valley even large; the wide view spreads upwards to where on the horizon are the trees behind which was Miriam's farm, and where lived the people of Nethermere. Life was not all misery at Walker Street: joy was inextinguishable in young hearts, and there is a delightful description in *Sons and Lovers* of the games in the street under the one lamp-post on winter evenings when it was not too wet and the boys and girls came out to play.[15]

From Walker Street the Lawrences moved just round the corner, going up one again, to Lynncroft. D. H. showed Miriam—they were now in the phase of adolescent friendship ripening into love—over the new house

with quiet pride. It had a little entrance hall, with the stairs and the doors to the other rooms opening out from it. There was a cooking range in the scullery as well as in the living-room, a china closet in addition to the pantry, a cupboard under the side window where the school books were kept, and from the big window of the living-room was the view over the roofs of Eastwood to the square church tower standing high above. The garden was pleasant and adjoined a field. This is the house that Lawrence describes in *Aaron's Rod*, where the husband returns surreptitiously at night.[16]

It is also the house of Lawrence's martyrdom: the long-drawn-out agony of his mother's dying from cancer. Other people have experienced a like *supplice;* but few people have loved with such intensity as this mother and son, have held on to life with a more terrible will-power until she had to be torn apart from him, or have had such capacity for suffering as this son born of it. It makes the most painful, the most unforgettable scene in our modern literature: once read one can never forget that, whatever else one forgets.

That house was also the house of Miriam's defeat and frustration, the working out of her own tragedy, the condemnation of her love for D. H. to nullity, breaking against the rock of his mother's will. She early sensed the tension within which he lived.

Perhaps it was the strong emotional tension between mother and son, and in a directly contrary sense, between husband and wife, and father and son, that made the strangely vibrating atmosphere.[17]

Or there were those gatherings on Sunday evenings after chapel.

There was the rustle and scent of Sunday clothes . . . . A general talk would go on, with Lawrence giving quick conversational change all round. . . . Mrs. Lawrence, in her black dress, would sit in the low rocking-chair like a little figure of fate, coldly disapproving, while Lawrence fetched cakes and pastries out of the pantry, which he would press upon us who had a long walk home. Sometimes we went into the parlour, and A. would play the piano while we sang "The heavens are telling," "O rest in the Lord," "Yes, the Lord is mindful of His own," and the exquisite "Hymn to Music" Lawrence liked so much. It was exciting, but there was an undercurrent of hostility running strong beneath it all.[18]

How well one recognises that baleful atmosphere: it was the same in my own home, except that there weren't any friends who came in. "The father I rarely saw," says Miriam. "He was always out in the evenings." [19]

"He hates his father," the mother once told her. "I know why he hates his father. It happened before he was born. One night he put me out of the house. He's bound to hate his father." [20]

The result was this tragic division in Lawrence that made it impossible for him to respond to Miriam. Something was destroyed in him by this insatiable demand of his mother. Miriam's parents understood: "Bert belongs to his mother. She'll never give him up." [21] Even after his mother was dead, it was "Don't imagine that because mother's dead you can claim me." [22] "I began to realise that whatever approach Lawrence made to me inevitably involved him in a sense of disloyalty to his mother." [23]

Hence the distortion he made in the presentation of Miriam in his great novel, in order that the mother might triumph.

[As] I sat and looked at the subtle distortion of what had been the deepest values of my life, the one gleam of light was the realization that Lawrence had overstated his case; that some day his epic of maternal love and filial devotion would be viewed from another angle, that of his own final despair.[24]

It was Lawrence himself who taught Miriam to be a penetrating, watchful observer. "It was his power to transmute the common experiences into significance that I always felt to be Lawrence's greatest gift." [25] And then—"With all his gifts, he was somehow cut off, unable to attain that complete participation in life that he craved for." [26]

But, of course, hence the genius: it comes from the fissure. The artist, the writer of genius, is half in life and half out of it—Henry James thought: if he were not drawn in he would not feel sufficiently acutely to write about it; if he were not half outside he would not be able to see it and describe it. It is the acute discomfort, the maladjustment that creates the tension; the desire to be within, enclosed like everyone else, secure and safe, that gives the nostalgia, the poignancy, the colouring— that looking-backward which is the infallible signature of the artist, whoever he is, Shakespeare or Scott or Hardy, Flaubert or Poussin or Duparc. No wonder Orpheus has always been the image, the symbol of the artist, the fated figure.

Back over the ground I trudge, a more dogged figure than Orpheus, more substantial than Persephone, to take Lawrence's place in the chair by his friend's fireside in the sitting-room behind the shop. All the afternoon I have waited for the friend [W. E. Hopkin] to come back from Nottingham, at last with growing anxiety. The door opened and he came in: eighty-seven looking like sixty-seven, bearded, bright as a bird, untired at the end of a busy day. Extraordinary to think that here was the man whose life enclosed Lawrence's, lapped it round at either end: twenty years older than Lawrence, he is still alive twenty years after Lawrence died.

He had known Lawrence all his life, from the time he was two months old and he had asked Mrs. Lawrence across the way how the latest arrival was. But she was a foolish woman to think she could alter her husband and force him into her ways. She had never seen him dirty before her marriage: they met one Saturday night at a dance in Nottingham and fell violently in love with each other. He was a really *beautiful* dancer when young, known for miles around. (Lawrence one day to Miriam:

"Father says one ought to be able to dance on a threepenny bit."
He seldom spoke of his father and we at once exclaimed:
"Why, does your father dance?"
"He used to, when he was a young man. He ran a dancing class at one time," he replied briefly.
It seemed unbelievable; we had never thought of his father in that light.[27])

When they were married, the first day he came home from the pit and insisted on eating his dinner—as miners do, tired with the day's work—without washing *appalled* her: she never got over it.

(Ada, Lawrence's youngest sister:

I wonder if there would have been quite so much misery in our childhood if mother had been just a little more tolerant.

. . . .

As we grew older we shut him more and more out of our lives, and instinctively turned to mother, and he, realising this, became more and more distasteful in his habits. He was never really intolerable, and if, instead of wanting the impossible from him, we had tried to interest ourselves in the things for which he really cared, we should have been spared many unhappy and sordid scenes.

. . . My brother's description of him in *Sons and Lovers*, when mother was dying, seems to me to be writing too deep for tears. He shows a lost man, bewildered by the realisation that she was going from him, and that somehow he had no part in anything.[28]

How relentlessly the wife made him pay for his failure to come up to her expectations of him! The irony of it is that his part in his son's genius goes unrecognised—and yet one sees that his was the artist's temperament, not hers; that the instinctual sense of life that made the creative strain came through him, the miner living his underground life of the senses, primitive and animal, shut out from the family, excluded, forgotten. Yet his was the dance, the ecstasy, the escape into dream. Some spark from his blood carried the germ from which the artist was born. D. H. had his father's cleverness with his hands, for ever making things, his dance-like rhythms of body. The poet was his father's son, the father unrecognised; the prophet, the uncompromising, relentless spirit of the mother.)

When Bert was in his teens (I had made a mistake and said David: he was never David here, always Bert) you would have thought he and his mother were more like a courting couple than mother and son. When she was dying I thought he would have gone off his head, clean off his head! He had written his first book, *The White Peacock*, and all Mrs. Lawrence was living for was to see Bert's book. He sent message after message, telegrams to the publishers for a copy to put into her hands. At last it

came, and he rushed upstairs to place it in her hand. She was already unconscious. It was a great grief to him that he never could be sure whether
she knew what it was that she was holding.

What Lawrence wanted all his life long was a man friend. (I remembered what he once said to Miriam: "If only you'd been a man, things
might have been perfect," then added immediately, "but it wouldn't have
been any good, because then you wouldn't have cared about me." [29]
Miriam noticed his longing for the friendship of her elder brother—it is
the inspiration of *The White Peacock*. The real emotion in the book is
Cyril's love (suppressed, perhaps hardly realised) for George, the young
farmer brother: whenever George is being described there is always passion behind the writing. Cyril is the pallid girlish type as his mother would
have him. He only releases himself in disguise as Lettie—she leads George
on, rouses his love and then does not satisfy it, leaving him to go to pieces
in his own way. It is a sad piece of wishful *schadenfreude*. People understand these things better nowadays: no reason why Lawrence should have
been so hopeless: but perhaps here too he was before his time. One realises
why, in the novel, Cyril is about so much with Lettie, like a curious attendant shadow: he was not so much her brother as the same person, two
extrapolations of Lawrence.)

But Lawrence never found the friend he needed. He himself, twenty
years older, was the only man friend he had that stayed his friend all the
time. Lawrence had had a false friend—he too. Of him Lawrence said—
"He is my Judas Iscariot. And he will betray me. Not in my lifetime: he'd
be afraid of what would come to him. But after I am dead, you will see."

I said, was it not partly or even largely his own fault that he never
found the friend he needed? One could not say such passionate things,
quarrel violently and lacerate people's feelings, and then expect all to
go on as it had been before. No friendship—no human relations could
stand it. Curious that he never learned that, that he had not more self-
control. I asked: "Did he never try to tell him when he was younger?"
"Oh dear, no. I never interfere with people. I let them go their own way."
I said that lads growing up like D. H. as good as had no fathers, no-one to
tell them or help them.

The thought struck me that if one has too intense a struggle in early
days perhaps one needs unconsciously to perpetuate the struggle later
on—one creates enmities, antagonisms. H. said that Lawrence had extreme antipathies. If he were sitting there where you are sitting—when
the news went round that he was staying here, there'd be a lot of women

school-teachers who'd drop in in the hope of seeing him—if someone came in he took a dislike to, he'd sit there and not say a single word the whole evening. And yet—he was a wonderful conversationalist. (Oh, the usual story: how well one knows the symptoms.) Bert said to me one day when I was putting out chairs for them to sit down: "What are you putting out chairs for the bitches for? You know, Willie, you are making a great mistake. When you get to Heaven for your good works, rather than your faith, you'll be so busy putting out chairs for the bitches that you'll fall backward—into Hell."

Clearly, the way Lawrence went, following his intuitions and impulses absolutely, with no attempt at control, made him pay a heavy price—an extreme loneliness and friendlessness in the end. It was the penalty for his abnegation, his hatred of the rational, and the compensatory subtlety of his intuitive senses, his response to the blood and the unconscious.

The last word has been said about him by Miriam, the girl with whom he grew up here in his youth and whom he left to make her own life while he travelled so far away in space and in spirit. He always used to say that she would write his epitaph. On H.'s last walk with Lawrence, a sad one for him, he had said to him, "Why didn't you marry Miriam?" He burst out: "Mind your own bloody business!" and then, apologising, "I'm sorry. But she wasn't the one for me." He continued in German—so like this little circle: as a youth he would frequently come out with French phrases to Miriam. I think I know the psychological explanation: a sign of malaise. The upshot of it was that she would have destroyed his genius; he needed something to stimulate him. (In other words, too much of a yes-woman. Like N., I registered from long ago. No, Lawrence was right.) Miriam had married afterwards and had had children. Mrs. H.: But she always loved Bert. The last time she had been over to see them—she died two years ago—they went up to Walker Street and looked into the distance to the trees behind which was the farm where they had lived. There was a pause between the two of them. The shrewd, practical, kind Mrs. H.'s eyes glistened as she remembered: "She was very sad." He, after a pause: "Yes. She always loved him." The memory was too strong: they couldn't speak about it.

All the same, Mrs. H. realised, it was Lawrence who had made Miriam. And Miriam recognised it:

[The] realization that our long, and in many ways wonderful friendship had actually come to an end was a very deep blow, comparable to a kind of death. . . . In the passing of Lawrence I saw also the extinction of my greater self.

Life without him had a bleak aspect. I had grown up within his orbit, and now that he was definitely gone I had to make a difficult new beginning. For a long time in a quiet and deliberate way I wished I had done with life.[30]

And no woman understood Lawrence as Miriam did. "Whatever my own lot it was easier to bear than his, for at least I had the positive value of love, and I was not frustrated as he was by inner division." [31] She understood that at bottom "the whole question of sex had for him the fascination of horror, and that in the repudiation of any possibility of a sex relation between us he felt that he paid me a deep and subtle compliment." [32] I am sure that that is true. It all meant that "one could do nothing. He was like a man set apart. Only Lawrence might help himself. Anyone else was powerless." [33] (How like Swift it all is!) And yet, there was his extraordinary capacity for joy—

No task seemed dull or monotonous to him. He brought such vitality to the doing that he transformed it into something creative.

. . .

There was his sensitiveness, too, his delicacy of spirit, that, while it contributed vitally to his charm, made him more vulnerable, more susceptible to injury from the crudeness of life.[34]

Hers is the last word about him:

He was always to me a symbol of overflowing life. He seemed able to enter into other lives, and not only human lives. With wild things, flowers and birds, a rabbit in a snare, the speckled eggs in a hole in the ground, he was in primal sympathy—a living vibration passed between him and them, so that I always saw him, in the strictest sense of the word, immortal. . . . And with the clarification that time brings and its truer perspective, those of us whose youth was the richer for knowing him see again the dear familiar figure, and we remember how much of our joy came to us through the inspiration of Lawrence's gay and dauntless spirit.[35]

I asked his old friend when did he realise that the boy he knew had genius and would be a famous writer. He said that he had always known it, from the time he grew up into young manhood. Miriam says that she realised it quite early—"I had so clearly the knowledge that he must inevitably move far beyond us, and felt that he knew it himself, and was trying to devise some means of not severing himself from us all." [36] There is a certain sadness in the way such a man passes out of the ken of his early friends. And yet—they had him at his youngest and best, when there was a charm upon life and horizons were illimitable.

Turning away to say goodbye, I said to Lawrence's old friend that he had been a most fortunate man. He said simply, "I have been." I said it was astonishing the way that a life like Lawrence's could light up a whole landscape, so that the place lived in him. It was obvious how these good kind people had been touched by the intensity of the dead man's personality, so that it *made* life for them—as Shelley's life was all in all for Trelawny and nothing that happened after had any significance.

But my last impression—so strong that the dream has gone on ever since—was of Eastwood, to which he would never come home: those raw streets and miners' terraces, the wind blowing gustily along the ridges and up Victoria Street from the Breach, the harsh corners and the sharp spire of the Congregational chapel pricking the sky from the places where he lived. Not palaces nor great houses nor castles nor monuments ever moved me so much as this small mining town with the February wind blowing through—and something else that made it so poignant and alive: the spirit of the dead boy who lived and suffered and was often happy there and, leaving it, has touched every lane and corner and view with the shadow of his genius—all springing, like that first glance of Hardy's mother and father in the church at Stinsford, from the mating of that unhappy couple, the miner who was such a beautiful dancer and the wife who felt herself superior to the life she lived with him and yet gave birth to all this: both of them now sleeping together in the cemetery under the hill from Eastwood church.[37]

Witter Bynner

In 1950, a young Sicilian poet showed me, outside Taormina, Fontana Vecchia, the hillside villa where Lawrence wrote his famous snake poem and much else. "The landlord, Ciccio Cacópardo," explained the poet on our walk, "owns three houses now and rents them and is very rich." "A friend of David Lawrence is here" he called across high terraces. A sturdy middle-aged man clambered from the garden where he was working, greeted us warmly in good English, and led us up to the house, overlooking rural slopes and blue sea. "It then had only lamps and water which was carried, but now is electricity, and we have a bathroom where their little kitchen used to be." He and his wife had in the old days lived on the ground floor and the Lawrences in the two upper stories, "where now lives a Swedish girl, a painter," said the poet, bright eyed. His eyes glistened still more when she opened the door for us. We were all bound by Lawrence. "I have copied his Taormina poems into a book," she beamed, "and set my water colors round them. It is beautiful to be where he was and to hear the feet of the goats go by in the morning as he heard them, like leaves blown in the wind. I read him once when I was unhappy," she continued, "and he comforted me, and I am translating these poems into Swedish." Then Ciccio remembered "David H. Lawrence's early mistakes in Italian. It was in 1920. '*Avete del latte di capro?*' 'Have you he-goat's milk?' It has been ever since in the community a laughing memory. He used to put his head back when he spoke and close his eyes, and his face was thin with a beard." Ciccio compressed his own face between his palms. "And is Frieda still large and light-haired?" Then Emma, Ciccio's wife, put in, "There was a bench here outside my mother-in-law's room and he would sit on it and talk with her and everyone said she had a new beau!" "My mother died twelve years ago," mused Ciccio. "Frieda will remember Grazia."

Then he poked among dead leaves and petals on the ground near the front of the house and exposed a metal plaque. "Look up there where it was," he said, pointing to an oblong blotch on the wall, "but it was not accurate, I had to pull it out. See, it says 'D. K. Lawrence.' I would not have that. So I took it down." And he prodded it under leaves again with his foot. "But the other plaque is still on the wall at the rear by the lane where the goats passed." We went and looked. And it read:

D. H. LAWRENCE
English Author
1 9 1885 + 2 3 1930
Lived Here
1920–1923

"Three years!" he gloated.
At Taormina in 1922 and 1923?
Perhaps the western months recorded in [*Journey with Genius*] are a dream.[38]

Roland E. Robinson

Not long after I had "discovered" D. H. Lawrence for myself and had learned that he had visited and written about Australia, I determined to explore the country of his novel and find, if possible, the house on the low cliff overlooking the "huge rhythmic Pacific" where, with his wife Frieda, he had lived and worked.

A collection of Lawrence's letters, edited by his friend Aldous Huxley, contains a photograph of the house, which is called Wyewurk, not Coo-ee as in the novel. These letters also supplied, for me, the information that Lawrence's address had been Thirroul, on the N.S. Wales South Coast, not "Mullumbimby" as related in *Kangaroo*. This knowledge apart, the novel, which I was reading as I travelled in the train, was my only direction, but the book proved to be a true guide.

Lawrence must have sat in the train and sketched-in the scenery all along the way. You will find his description of Sydney and its suburbs. Then "the waste marshy places, and old iron and abortive corrugated-iron 'works'—all like the Last Day of Judgment, instead of a new country." [39]

Botany Bay is there, Como, "that curious sombreness of Australia, the sense of oldness, with all the forms worn down, low and blunt, squat, and the sombre bush with its pale-stemmed dull-leaved gum-trees, and the great spiky things like zuccas." [40] It is the bush that makes one of his characters say:

"Most Australians come to hate the Australian earth before they're done with it. If you call the land a bride, she's the sort of bride not many of us are willing to tackle. She drinks your sweat and your blood, and then as often as not lets you down, does you in." [41]

Leaving the train at Austinmer, I started out along the highway that goes over the hills by the sea. As I crested the first rise a sleet of rain swept over the sea and the land. Through the rain I saw the township of Thirroul. Somewhere, near the sea, was the place I had come to find. Then I realised that many things could have happened since Lawrence lived there. I stopped on the rise and read a passage in the book:

A long high jetty straddling on great tree-trunk poles out on to the sea—a spit of low yellow brown land, grassy with a stiff little group of Noah's Ark-trees and, further in, a little farm-place with two fascinating big gum-trees that stuck out their dark clots of foliage at the end of slim, upstarting branches. [42]

There, sure enough, was the scene in front of me! Not far from there would be the house, I assumed.

But when I descended into the township, the houses, shops, and, over all, the dark mountain at the back, closed in on me. It seemed that after all those years I could not hope to find the place. I turned in towards the sea, looking for a big red bungalow where the Lawrences used to get their milk. Then, ahead of me, I saw a group of coral-trees, "the trees with the bright scarlet flowers perching among the grey twigs." [43]

511

A milk-cart with a boy driving it was coming down the road. I waved to him to stop and asked him if he had a house called Wyewurk on his run. He said he had and gave me directions. I remembered that I would first see a white gate. I cut across a grassy footpath, turned the corner and looked eagerly down the road. I thought I could see the gate. As the angle lessened I was sure. "A brick house, with a roof of bright-red tiles coming down very low over dark wooden verandas—deep verandas like eyelids half-closed." [44]

I was having some difficulty with the loop on the gate, in my haste I was trying to wrench it off, when I became aware of a girl standing in the doorway watching me. I tried to explain what I was about.

"I came to see this house—you see, a writer named D. H. Lawrence lived here once. I wanted to see where he lived," I told her.

The girl seemed to think I wanted to rent or buy the house.

"Oh, wait and I'll get my father," she said, disappearing. So the father came out to see what the trouble was.

"D. H. Lawrence?" he queried. "No, I don't seem to know that name."

"Oh, yes, he lived in this house, I know. Here," I said, opening the book, "here's a description of it, the surroundings, everything. You couldn't mistake it."

The old man had been eyeing me as he talked. "Well, you had better come in and have a look around," he said.

Lawrence's bent windswept tree, bigger now and thick in leaf, was thriving in the middle of the lawn at the back of the house. I talked to the old man and the girl on the lawn above the sea, reading out of the book to them descriptions of the coastline spread out before us. Beyond, where Lawrence's little path still led down through the ragged hedge, "the great Pacific was rolling in huge white thunderous rollers not forty yards away, under the grassy platform of a garden." [45] . . . "The morning was one of the loveliest of Australian mornings, perfectly golden, all the air pure gold, and the great gold effulgence to seaward, and the pure, cold pale-blue inland, over the dark range." [46]

Afterwards, I walked alone on the wide smooth beach in the late afternoon. Where the sea ran back, leaving the sands glistening wet, the beach was littered with smooth, shining pebbles. The purple-blue, transparent little bladders, like Venetian-blown glass, which Lawrence had described so surely,[47] were left lying in solitary places. I walked under and past the jetty and stood on the smooth rocks where Lawrence had said his spirit would stand looking across the sea.[48]

The essential part of Lawrence's writing of Australia is praise, it is

May Chambers Holbrook, *ca.* 1916.
From a photograph in the possession of William
Holbrook.

Ad Astra Sanatorium, Vence, Alpes Maritimes, France. From a photograph in the possession of Harry T. Moore.

Villa Jaffe, Irschenhausen, Bavaria. From a photograph in the possession of Harry T. Moore.

Interior of Lawrence Memorial Chapel. From a photograph by Warren Roberts.

Exterior of Lawrence Memorial Chapel at Kiowa Ranch, San Cristobal, New Mexico. From a photograph by Warren Roberts.

poetry in prose. He was given the experience of an Australian spring. He and Frieda drove with a pony and sulky into the bush in spring. The wattle was out. Frieda gathered whole armfuls of wildflowers and filled the sulky with them. Lawrence kept jumping out from among the flowers to plunge into the bush for a new one. This is in the last chapter of *Kangaroo* called "Adieu Australia." This chapter was written and added in September at Taos, New Mexico. It is ecstatic, intoxicated with the sights and scents of the Australian bush in flower.

"They splashed through a clear, clear stream, and walked up a bank into the nowhere, the pony peacefully marching." They found "the little, pale sulphur wattle with a reddish stem that sends its lovely sprays so aerial out of the sand of the trail. Then beautiful heath-plants with small bells, like white heather, in tall straight tufts, and above them the gold sprays of the intensely gold bush mimosa, with here and there, on long thin stalks like hairs almost, beautiful blue flowers, with gold grains, three-petalled, like reed-flowers, and blue, blue with a touch of Australian darkness."

Then "great flowers, twelve feet high, like sticky dark lilies in bulb-buds at the top of the shaft, dark, blood-red." Then "queer gold red bushes of the bottle-brush-tree, like soft-bristly golden bottle-brushes standing stiffly up, and the queer black-boys on one black leg with dark-green spears, sending up the high stick of a seed-stalk, much taller than a man." . . . "Yet a stillness, and a manlessness, and an elation, the bush flowering at the gates of Heaven." [49]

Yet always in this writing is the ominous note that is even more truly Australia.

Sometimes from the interior came a wind that seemed to her evil. Out of the silver, paradisical freedom, untamed evil winds would come, cold, like a stone hatchet murdering you. Sometimes a heavy, reptile hostility came off the sombre land, something gruesome and infinitely repulsive. All the uncontrolled gentleness and uncontaminated freedom of Australia, was it going to turn and bite her like the ghastly bite of some unclean-mouthed reptile, an iguana, a great newt? Had it already bitten her? [50]

But the novel ends on praise and nostalgic regret at leaving, with Lawrence looking out from the ship until he could see the dark shape of the mountain, far away behind Coo-ee, and thinking of the empty house, the dark tor, the bush and the Australian spring. Then, "It was only four days to New Zealand, over a dark, inhospitable sea."

Comparing the result of this writer's three months' stay in Australia with the product and knowledge of indigenous writers, Lawrence is by no means shamed. It is no easy matter to absorb and express such a harsh and enigmatical country as Australia. Lawrence once defined genius as "the ability to absorb." [51] Enduring prosecution and then dire poverty as the results of his writing, and then enough recognition and recompense to make it possible for him to obey the dictates of his "daimon" and travel the world and pour out his novels, travel books, essays and poems, his writing reveals that he possessed chameleonic powers when it came to absorbing and expressing the widely different geographical and spiritual entities of the earth.

Each country has its own indigenous human voices, creators who, long-looking, long-loving, long-desiring, win to the inmost being of their love and speak from that authentic source. England has such voices as Clare, Cobbett, Jefferies, Hardy and Thomas who are the very earth and flowering of England. In Australia writers have been confronted with what was at first to them "a barren accurst land." In the evolutionary development of a national literature there were, as in our painting, painful adaptations, selections and survivals before we in Australia produced even the beginnings of an expression that was the unmistakable voice of this strange new world.

These observations make D. H. Lawrence's achievements all the more remarkable. An Englishman, he produced novels, stories, essays and poems that are lyrically and intensely English. No English writers have given us the vividly alive flowering, character and mythological significance of Italy as Lawrence has done. This is true of his writings in Mexico and, again, of *Kangaroo* and the poem, also of that name, which is included in so many English-speaking anthologies.

A passage from one of Lawrence's travel books, *Twilight in Italy*, reveals his sensitivity to the different "spirit of place" that is the inmost being and emanation of each country of the earth:

> Each country has its own flowers, that shine out specially there. In England it is daisies and buttercups, hawthorn and cowslips. In America it is goldenrod, stargrass, June daisies, Mayapple and asters, that we call Michaelmas daisies. In India hibiscus and datura and champa flowers, and in Australia mimosa, that they call wattle, and sharp-tonged, strange heath flowers. In Mexico it is cactus flowers, that they call roses of the desert, lovely and crystalline among thorns; and also the dangling, yard-long clusters of the cream bells of the yucca, like dropping froth.[52]

Kangaroo contains much of Lawrence's best writing. In plot and form it may not compare with the great English novels, but it is in sequence with the very essence of Lawrence: such inspired writing as *Twilight in*

Italy, Sea and Sardinia and *Etruscan Places.* Lawrence used all the forms of literature to express himself, the sensitive, personal, intensely vivid self that could enter into the very soul of man and woman, beasts, birds, flowers and landscape.

A walk into the bush at night in Western Australia, the journey by train from Sydney to Thirroul, excursions, driving into the bush around Thirroul and the stay in the cottage on the edge of the Pacific, formed the conception and background for Lawrence's novel. He had no other experience of Australia, he knew only the fringe of "Australis Incognita," yet, from this experience, he was able to produce the novel which causes Lawrence's most recent biographer, Richard Aldington,[53] to report Australians as saying that its evocations of the country are the most vivid and perceptive yet written.[54]

John C. Neff

I am not a native of New Mexico, nor do I live there. But from my home back here in Ohio I pass many hours thinking about the long weeks I've known in the Sangre de Cristos packing for four hundred miles, and the months I've spent on the flats south of Las Vegas in roundup time. There are many tales to be told, but today there stands in my mind the picture of my visit to Kiowa Ranch far above Taos where I went to visit Mrs. D. H. Lawrence.

During two previous winters, I had come to know John Middleton Murry, Lawrence's friend of the early years, now a brilliant man of letters. He would always have me tell what little I could about New Mexico and the country from which Lawrence got so much. He wanted to know about the Indians and their pueblos and the sun setting over the Jemez Range and the smell of wood coming through the air at night. But like every man who has not seen the land, he was only half impressed. He will never know what tied Lawrence there until he sees it for himself. Two years ago, when he learned that I was going to spend the summer near Santa Fe, he begged me to visit Mrs. Lawrence and bring her his best wishes.

That I did, though I wasn't sure that I had any right to go calling at a house I didn't even know. When I arrived in Taos from Santa Fe one morning I began to get cold feet. Almost, I wanted to chuck the whole business. But when I thought of the hundreds of miles I'd come for just this hour, I shoved aside all my inhibitions and walked boldly into a store to inquire the way to Kiowa Ranch. A young German woman overheard me and came to my assistance. "You go up, up, up all the way," she said, "and the road is terrible. But she'll be happy to see you, with your greeting from Murry."

This was a good start. I didn't concern myself about how terrible the road might be, but I was glad of the encouragement in the German woman's voice. Past the road to the Taos Pueblo I drove, and up and over the long winding road to Arroyo Hondo. The sky was a brilliant one, and the sun was very warm. Almost to Cristobal I went, and then turned off in the direction of the mountains, following the sign pointing to "Brett." The private road was bad. It was so miserable my car bounded from rock to rock, just missing the springy juniper branches. The twists and turns made the going hard, but in what seemed no time at all I found myself at the end of the drive.

There was the house. A long, low place with a gabled metal roof and fine colored shutters. A magnificent view of the westward-sweeping country spread before it, with the mountains rising strong behind it. Little wonder why Lawrence loved the place. Or why he loved to stand and watch the sun melt into the little gap where the road goes down toward Santa Fe. Or why he yearned to be back there during his last months in far away Europe. I had for many years been familiar with the beauties of New Mexico and had accordingly thought I understood Lawrence's love for the land. But not until I saw the view from Kiowa Ranch and the house itself did I fully realize what held him to the country and what in his last years made him say: "I think New Mexico was the greatest experience from the outside world that I have ever had." [55]

But there was no one on the porch, and the house seemed empty. I found a little bell near the portico and was about to ring when someone called out, "Come in!"

A dark short Italian stood near the door of what I presumed was the kitchen. He bowed, asking what I wanted. When I told him, he spoke to someone I couldn't see, someone beyond the door. In Italian he said, "A young stranger wants to see you." A woman's voice in guttural Italian answered him. "Have him come in." And then the man swept his arm in the direction of the wall beyond the door. Stepping inside and turning to the right, I saw sprawled out on a bed a large, reddish, smiling woman. It was Frieda Lawrence, looking much older than I had expected to find her. She was wearing a long print dress and a colored apron. She greeted me hospitably, but when I mentioned that Middleton Murry had asked me to see her, she jumped from the bed and cried: "Ach! Murry! Yes? Murry! You know him?"

The ice was broken. Mrs. Lawrence was all smiles. Her lips stretched across her face, and she hurried about the room to bring a chair for me. All the while she carried on a conversation about Murry and his visits to America. How was he? Would you describe him? What does he think of America? Suddenly she went across the room. "Ach! Will you have some of my wine! It is very good." And without waiting for an answer, she poured me a long glass and made me sit by the table with the man who was glancing through a copy of an Italian newspaper. The table was covered with a red and white checkered cloth, and there was a large bowl of fresh dark cherries and another filled with cakes and cookies. I sat there with them eating and drinking and talking as though they had known me all their lives. It had been the most comfortable entry into a strange house I'd ever made. The Italian spoke with Mrs. Lawrence in his own language. He wanted to know what Murry I was talking about. When he was told it was Middleton Murry who had brought about my visit, he was satisfied and sank back into his chair with the paper.

But Mrs. Lawrence had been ill that winter and was easily tired. She went back to her bed and stretched out again, still talking about Murry. Presently she began on Lawrence, always using his last name. She told how he loved the Indians and their dances, how he used to go down to the pueblos and sit in the sun to watch them dance. How he used to stand on the porch of the house and watch the glowing sun sink deep behind the far mountains. And then she would exclaim in German and laugh. Sometimes her words came sharp and quick, but there was always a twinkle in her eyes that made me laugh with her. She seemed the easiest person on earth to get on with.

In a little while the Italian got up and left the house. But she would not hear of my going, "after how far you've come!" We were not alone long, though, for soon her daughter and son-in-law who were visiting from England came in. Naturally, they were interested in hearing about Murry's lectures in this country and how they had been received. We talked about American colleges, contrasting them and comparing them with Cambridge and Oxford. They seemed to object to our system of education and our noticeable lack, as they put it, of worthwhile scholarships. The Americans were wonderful people, but oh so slow. The hundreds of colleges, what did they mean? Too much sameness, too similar. Their graduates were so slow in grasping the real significance of a situation, they so easily misunderstood. They were thick like oil.

This brought Mrs. Lawrence into the conversation again. She put out a cigarette and began. "You must never read Lawrence while you are young. Too many young people read him, and they do not know what he is saying. It is so difficult, then, to explain to them what he is saying. You must have had experiences and bitter tastes of life before you can read him with intelligence." And she would smile and laugh in her jolly way. "He was such a great man."

The son-in-law interrupted to ask if I'd read *Sons and Lovers*. He thought, along with the rest of England, that it was his best book. But Mrs. Lawrence broke in, saying, "No, no, you must read *The Plumed Serpent*. All of Lawrence is in that book. Two years he spent writing it, one winter in Chapala and the next winter in Oaxaca." I admitted that though I liked the earlier book immensely, I thought *The Plumed Serpent* more significant. Sometimes while we were talking, I had a chance to look about the room. It was like an old kitchen I had once seen in Munich. There were gaily colored plates on racks along the walls. Huge pots and pans hung in the corner near the stove, and lively curtains were at the small windows. The daughter came round and filled our glasses with more deep red wine and passed the brown crock of cookies. These people were hospitable to their finger tips. But I could not wear out my welcome. Through the open door that looked down toward Taos, I could see great dark clouds hanging low over the mountains. A storm would be coming up at the end of the afternoon. I thought of the miserable road back to the highway. It was time to leave.

As Mrs. Lawrence walked with me to the gate, the wind caught stray ends of her fine long hair and whipped it across her face. Her apron sailed out in front of her and her eyes grew bright in the cooling air. When I turned to bid her good-bye, her real character seemed to come to me. She was standing on a little knoll near the gate and her head was dipped toward the lowering sun. The sun glowing on her made her a radiantly handsome middle-aged woman. But it struck me that she was at once very much like a small happy child and a woman of wide wisdom. Her eyes were twinkling and her mouth laughing, swallowing and laughing in turns. She raised her arm high above her head and waved her hand vigorously. "Good-bye, hmmm, good-bye. It was good of you to come. Good-bye!" [56]

Mark Schorer

In April or May of 1926, D. H. Lawrence, who was careless about dating his letters, wrote to Dorothy Brett from a Lungarno *pensione* that "Perhaps now we shall take a little flat in the country here—outside Florence—for a couple of months, and I wander about to my Etruscans."[57] How he found Villa Mirenda, isolated in the country beyond that ugly little town of Scandicci and the mere crossroads of Vingone, I have been unable to discover, but to find it today is easy enough, since we have only to follow Lawrence's own directions.

When is your sister Margaret coming out? [This to Rolf Gardiner.] Here we are—if nothing drives us away—so tell her to come and see us when she will. If she will walk out, then tram *No.* 16 from the Duomo to *Vingone:* to the very terminus and dead end (½ hour). Then there's another 25 minutes' walk —straight ahead uphill from Vingone till you come to two cypresses, just beyond the house marked *Podere Nuovo.* Turn to the left there, and dip down into the little valley. Our house is the square big box on top of the *poggio,* near the little church of San Paolo.[58]

How the Lawrences found Villa Mirenda remains a mystery, but why they did is clear enough. Lawrence was suffering with the tubercular infection that killed him, and from that point of view, he should have been back on his ranch in Taos, but he could not bring himself to go back; England was out of the question, he found it so intolerable ("a kingdom, a tight and unsatisfactory one in which I should die outright if pinned to it");[59] he was not at work on a major effort, but he had interested himself in doing a series of essays on Etruscan art and life, and the monuments of that civilization were scattered all over to the south and west of Florence; he wanted a particular kind of isolation, separation, loneliness; finally, they needed a *pied à terre,* and they needed it cheaply: they rented Villa Mirenda (or their top half of it) for three thousand lire, which was then twenty-five pounds, or about one hundred and twenty dollars a year. They kept it for two years.

We do not take tram No. 16, but drive out through the Porta San Frediano, and then follow directions and the trolley tracks. Through the long narrow Via Scandicci, with its scaling walls off which posters peel almost as soon as they are pasted up, but on which they are nevertheless pasted in great number—out through this hazardous street we circumspectly ease the second-hand Austin. It is a poor district, and the hazards are not provided by other cars, because they are few, but by the multitude of mule-drawn carts, bicycles, Vespas and Lambrettas, and, since it is a Sunday afternoon, half the Vespas are charging out into the country carrying hunters, their thick thighs splayed widely on the broad seats, their guns strapped to their backs, off to the tidy woods and fields to shoot the small birds, the larks and nightingales, for the markets and their own tables. Twenty-five years ago, when there must have been more birds in Italy than there are now, the hunters bothered Lawrence, who wrote to Aldous Huxley from Villa Mirenda, "Under cover of the mist, the Cacciatori are banging away—it's a wonder they don't blow one another to bits—but I suppose sparrow-shot is small dust. And it's Sunday, *sacra festa*." [60]

Driving slowly, we peer into the dark one-room dwellings that open immediately upon the street and each of which houses at least one large family, many of them more than one. Here there are no great houses nor a long history to invite our speculation, but only, for block after block, the terrible evidence of the life of the European poor. Then at last the houses thin out, the solid walls of low buildings break up, we pass more rapidly through Vingone, and presently we see a square house painted orange, and under the paint we can still read the words *Podere Nuovo*. We decide to walk, park the car beyond the two cypresses, and proceed uphill. Now we are in open country, and the landscape is soft and still curiously precise, as only Tuscany can be, but the road is narrow, rutted, and covered with loose gravel, and, as bumblingly we climb, we wonder not only whether Sister Margaret ever made it, but, aware of our own clumsy progress, remember also Lawrence's lines about inveterate motor-ists: ". . . the vibration of the motor-car has bruised their insensitive bottoms into rubber-like deadness." [61] The Lawrences never had a car; they always walked, and not only on this rough road, but on every kind of road all over Europe.

The house is a great square block of whitish-gray stone that stands, like the typical farm villa of Tuscany, alone on its hill, its fields and vine-yards falling away from it in all directions, and the matchstick dwellings of the *contadini* scattered here and there among the fields. Our gravel road climbs up toward it, then drops down again, then up once more, and at last we leave the road and climb up to the house by its own circuitous dirt path that brings us to a long, low, peasant house and an iron gate. A woman is spreading bits of laundry on stones in the sun, and we ask if this is Villa Mirenda. It is. Is there a dog? None but this, she tells us, and indicates a sleeping creature near her that has hardly lifted its ears at our approach. So we push open the gate and proceed. Near the great central door of the house, standing open, is a well—again, the character-istically Tuscan well, charming in its symmetry, a round gray stone cylinder perhaps six feet across and ten feet high, simply domed, with a small lion's head looking out in each of the four directions from the base of the dome. At the well is a young girl who is staring curiously at us as we approach. Is the owner at home? She turns her head and calls sharply to the open door, "*Zia! Zia!*" and in a moment her aunt, who is Signora Mirenda, appears, wiping her hands on her white apron. Then the explanations: who we are, why we are there, what we would like. "*Il gran scrittore inglese, Signor Lawrence . . . molto tempo fa, venticinque anni fa . . . abitò qui?*" we stumble, half convinced by her stern, questioning regard that we have surely come to the wrong place in spite of those detailed instructions. But the name of Lawrence brings recognition and a smile; suddenly she understands us and bursts into a string of *si, si, si's,* and calls her husband with a shout flung over her shoulder. In a moment he appears in the doorway behind her, and now she explains to him, and we are welcomed.

Signor Mirenda appears to be a moderately successful farmer. He is wearing breeches and polished black boots to his knees, a rough jacket, and a curiously high corduroy cap. The boots are new and creak at every step, and the cap remains on his head, inside the house and out, through the entire time of our visit. He explains that the Lawrences used a different entrance, and leads us around the house so that we may enter as they did. How old is the house? "*Quattrocento,*" he replies, but that you do not take seriously, since it is the answer that nearly every Italian gives when you ask about the age of any structure, and you conclude that it is more probably eighteenth or early nineteenth century. At the front of the house are a wide green lawn and pleasant trees and, in line with the door, a straight avenue of cypresses that leads for perhaps a quarter of a mile downhill to the house of the peasants who helped the Lawrences. The double door, a handsome, arched affair painted dark green and standing at the head of five or six wide, stone steps, opens from the inside, and Signora Mirenda appears again.

We enter a large, cool, rather dark room, entirely devoid of furniture, and are startled by the walls, which are decorated with evenly spaced, quite large and very badly painted murals of allegorical subjects, and for a moment we wonder whether it is possible that Lawrence, who first took seriously to painting in this house, could have exercised his talent in these dubious studies of nymphs and clouds and winged heroes. But no; they were painted, Signor Mirenda says, by someone's mother—we cannot be sure whose. They were here in the time of Lawrence? Ah, yes. We do not ask what he thought of them, but go silently up a flight of rather narrow wooden stairs to the second floor.

Now huge keys are produced. The flat is used by Signor Mirenda's brother, but only in the summers, and it is differently furnished, but the rooms are of course the same. The narrow hall in which we are standing divides the apartment in two. Signor Mirenda unlocks one door and shows us into a living room. The floors are of dull red brick. There is a plain tile stove. The thick walls are plastered and scarcely finished off with whitewash. The deep windows are barred with iron grilles. (I have not inquired, but these grilles, which appear so frequently in old Tuscan houses even on high windows, must have been a mode of protection against the more ingenious of those bandits who thrived in such lively numbers in this part of Italy in past centuries.) The furniture is moderately comfortable and scanty. Beyond this room are two ample bedrooms, each containing a large dark bed, a chest, a chair, little else. We remember how Lawrence described the apartment in his *Letters:* "The rooms inside are big and rather bare . . . spacious, rather nice, and very still. Life doesn't cost much here. . . . I told you we'd fixed up the *salotto* nice and warm, with matting and stove going and Vallombrosa chairs." [62] The description suits, except that the stove is cold and those particular chairs do not seem to be here.

On the other side of the hall we see three more rooms. First, the kitchen, with an enormous open fireplace that still serves for cooking, the hearth raised about a foot from the floor, a black kettle hanging from a hook over a neat pile of dead ashes. Beyond the kitchen is a room for dining and intimate sitting, and beyond that, another bedroom, smaller. And that is all. Very simple, very plain, and although the rooms carry now the musty air of shut-up places, we are vividly reminded of Lawrence's preferences, of the things he loved and the things he despised, and particularly of one of these as set down in a poem written late in his life, perhaps here:

> Some women live for the idiotic furniture of their houses,
> some men live for the conceited furniture of their minds,
> some only live for their emotional furnishing—
>
> and it all amounts to the same thing, furniture,
> usually in "suites." [63]

The house speaks of him, and bears, in fact, an uncanny resemblance to another house of his that we had previously seen and where he also lived for exactly two years—at the edge of Taormina, where a vegetable garden grows just outside the kitchen door and barnyard fowl energetically peck away on the terraces.

Where did Lawrence work? In bad weather, in the *salotto*, but in all good weather, either in the tower or in the woods. From the narrow hall, we ascend by tight stairs to the tower. It is not much more than six feet square, with two deep romanesque arches open to all weather. The sun streams in, and we look out through one arch to the valley of the Arno and the whole miniature spectacle of Florence, every dome and tower as clearly limned as in an old engraving, and to the mountains beyond it, and immediately below to the vineyards and the olive groves and the small fields of grain that belong to the Mirendas, and we watch two white bullocks slowly moving up a field, and near a road, a flock of long-legged, gray and black sheep munching grass under the supervision of a placid dog and a girl asleep in a ditch. From the other arch, we look out at other villas on other hills, at clumps of cypresses like omnipresent sentinels, and at the spread of the *pinèta,* the pine woods, where Lawrence took his daily walks and worked when he could. It is spring, and everything is green and stands out with gemlike clarity, but we remember Lawrence's reference in a letter written in mistier autumn, to the yellow leaves dropping from the vines against the barbarous red of sumac.[64]

I begin to take some notes, and when the others thread down the narrow stairs, I stay behind, for it is possible here, high up and looking out and down, to feel a number of things that Lawrence felt, chiefly his desire to be out of the social world, to make something positive of his loneliness. In one quarrel after another, he, too, had lost many friends, but he had retained those he wanted (*"Tu stai con me, lo so,"* he wrote to one of them from Villa Mirenda).[65] Now, however, he did not want to see even them, and in this outlandish place he was quite safe. Few visitors came. An English couple living in a nearby villa came occasionally—the Wilkinsons, "sort of village arty people who went round with a puppet show, quite nice, and not at all intrusive."[66] The Huxleys, who lived in nearby Forte dei Marmi, the Lawrences saw in this period, but not at Villa Mirenda. A daughter of Frieda Lawrence came once for a short stay. An occasional British friend trekked out from Florence now and then, and the Lawrences went into Florence once or twice a week. But chiefly they had the peasants and themselves. One reason that they took the place was because it was "a region of *no* foreigners."[67] Lawrence knew quite well what he was facing ("Have you built your ship of death, oh, have you?")[68] and he was trying to face it. ". . . people don't mean much to me, especially casuals: them I'd rather be without," he wrote;[69] and, "the Florence society is no menace."[70] He did not want what he could have, and he could not have what he felt he needed.

I suffer badly from being so cut off. But what is one to do? One can't link up with the social unconscious. [This is a letter of August 1927 to Dr. Trigant

Burrow.] At times, one is *forced* to be essentially a hermit. I don't want to be. But anything else is either a personal tussle, or a money tussle: sickening: except, of course, just for ordinary acquaintance, which remains acquaintance. One has no real human relations—that is so devastating.[71]

Better to have no social relations at all than to have them and pretend that they are real! So he wrote disgustedly to Huxley of Beethoven, "always in love with somebody when he wasn't really, and wanting contacts when he didn't really—part of the crucifixion into isolated individuality— *poveri noi.*"[72] Every future holds but one final fact, and what Lawrence loved about Villa Mirenda was that it served to school him in that ultimate isolation.

> I never know what people mean when they complain of loneliness.
> To be alone is one of life's greatest delights, thinking one's own thoughts,
> doing one's own little jobs, seeing the world beyond
> and feeling oneself uninterrupted in the rooted connection
> with the centre of all things.[73]

In these bare quiet rooms, in this quiet country landscape, the rooted connection might be found.

> There is nothing to save, now all is lost,
> but a tiny core of stillness in the heart
> like the eye of a violet.[74]

Most of those many poems that Lawrence scribbled in his notebooks toward the end of his life have no interest as poems, but, as I flatten my palms on the crusty gray walls of his tower and look out toward his pine woods where just now the violets are blooming, I feel their charge as facts.

He was ill much of the time, of course—with an illness that could only be alleviated, not cured, and, in spite of his somewhat fantastic notions about sickness and health, about the relation of physiology to temperament, he knew this fact, and knew what he must expect. "My bronchials," is a kind of refrain in the letters of these years. "I am itchy." But it was worse than that: "I've been in bed the last eight days with bronchial haemorrhage—and Dr. Giglioli!"[75] It was this illness quite as much as his native restlessness, his spirit of *andiamo*, as he called it, that took the Lawrences away from Villa Mirenda and the Florentine climate so frequently. Five or six times in two years they left it for a month or two at a time—for Switzerland, for Germany, for Austria, for Ravello, even briefly for England—but always to return; and even when they left it for good, it was the Mirenda that they hoped to find in duplicate somewhere else. Yet their two years in Villa Mirenda were punctuated with outbursts of dislike for Italy.

I've had a spell of loathing the Italian countryside altogether [Lawrence wrote to Earl Brewster], and feeling that Italy is no place for a *man* to live in. I nearly decided to go off to Bavaria. But it all costs so much—and I think the discontent is inside me, and I'd better abide and wait a bit. But O miserere!—I've taken the house at least for six months more.[76]

In this mood, he could build up his own "paper castles," and with his own excitement.

I *am* somehow bored by Italy, and when a place goes against my grain I'm never well in it. I do really think one is heaps better off in New Mexico—sometimes I pine for it. Let's go in spring—and you help me chop down trees and irrigate pasture on the ranch. I'm sure you'd be happier—if we were all there. After all one *moves*—and this deadening kind of hopeless-helplessness one has in Europe passes off. Let's all go in March, let's go. I'm sick of Here. . . . And let's make an exhibition of pictures in New York. What fun! For Easter, an exhibition of pictures in New York, then go west. We might afterwards sail to China and India from San Francisco—there's always that door out. Let's do it! Anything, anything to shake off this stupor and have a bit of fun in life, I'd even go to Hell, en route.[77]

If illness and the image of a black ship lay under this restlessness, they also affected in a curious way Lawrence's attitude toward his work. A lethargic indifference, a weary kind of rest after all the high-strung battles, came over him.

In the real summer [he wrote his British publisher], I always lose interest in literature and publications. The *cicadas* rattle away all day in the trees, the girls sing, cutting the corn with the sickles, the sheaves of wheat lie all the afternoon like people dead asleep in the heat. *E più non si frega.* I don't work, except at an occasional scrap of an article. I don't feel much like doing a book, of any sort. Why do any more books? There are so many, and such a small demand for what there are. So why add to the burden, and waste one's vitality over it. Because it costs one a lot of blood. Here we can live very modestly, and husband our resources. It is as good as earning money, to have very small expenses. Dunque—[78]

And to his agent: "I think perhaps it's a waste to write any more novels. I could probably live by little things. I mean in magazines." [79] And yet, he did work, and under circumstances that few except Lawrence among modern writers could have found advantageous:

We have come to the lying in the garden stage, and I go off into the woods to work, where the nightingales have a very gay time singing at me. They are very inquisitive and come nearer to watch me turn a page. They seem to love to see the pages turned.[80]

The result of this kind of work was not only the articles that finally made up *Etruscan Places* (which called for a tour of cemeteries to the south and west in March and April of 1927, the essays themselves written rapidly in June when he was back at the Mirenda) but also the revision of all his poetry for the collected edition, that remarkable fable called *The Man Who Died*, a good deal of short work, and the three quite different versions of *Lady Chatterley's Lover*, all written here between February of 1927 and January of 1928. After that, Lawrence waited until June, when his queer friend Orioli, the Florentine bookseller and publisher, produced the private first edition, and then he left.

Downstairs, the others are standing in the doorway to a room off the big, shadowy hall. They are studying two plain chairs and a table, and Signora Mirenda explains that these belonged to the Lawrences, who gave them to the Mirendas when they left Scandicci. The Vallombrosa chairs! They are upright, walnut chairs with slim arms and straw seats, and this one, the signora continues, was his, and that, somewhat less comfortable with its single crosspiece in the center of the back, was hers. The room seems to be used for storage; on the floor, spread out on a large cane mat, are many lemons, and their fragrance fills the room.

The Mirendas invite us into their apartment, and we walk through rooms identical with those upstairs, through the kitchen with the same vast fireplace, and sit around the dining table with them. Signora Mirenda produces a decanter of white Chianti. Theirs? *Si, si.* ("They finished bringing in the grapes on Wednesday, so the whole place smells sourish, from the enormous vats of grapes downstairs, waiting to get a bit squashy, for the men to tread them out.") [81] Now Signor Mirenda produces a photograph album and shows us a dim snapshot of the villa taken by Lawrence for them. Did the Lawrences have servants, we ask. They had the help of the *contadini*, but Lawrence liked to do the marketing himself, walking to and back from Scandicci, and he liked much to work around his house. He cooked, the signora says with a chuckle, and he washed the floors, he washed the clothes. He was very handy with the needle, and he turned his own shirt collars. He was *molto simpatico, molto, molto.* Was Signora Lawrence happy here? They do not know, but she cried much of the time. Did they quarrel? Was he cruel to her? Again, "*Non lo so,*" and the discreet Italian shrug. But he was very kind to the poor.

"The poor" must mean the peasants, of which there were twenty-seven on the place in the Lawrences' time. Lawrence has written in his letters how on each of their two Christmases at Villa Mirenda, they gave a party for all the *contadini*, with a tree brought in from the *pinèta*, presents for all the women and children, cigars for the men. Once, when they returned from Switzerland, all the peasants were "out to meet us, with primroses and violets and scarlet and purple anemones," [82] and the peasants, say the Mirendas, enjoyed Lawrence's pictures and liked to watch him paint them. Lawrence pointed out that in this taste, they were rather different from the British magistrates who ordered the raid on the London gallery where they were shown.

Somewhere in another room a radio begins to sputter over an Italian version of *I Want To Be Happy*, perhaps to the young girl we saw by the well, and it jars the easy flow of reminiscence to a stop. We ask whether we can walk to the wood, and the Mirendas take us on a sunny terrace on the south side of the house and point out the way. From a wicker rack on the wall of the house, Signora Mirenda takes a handful of figs ("great big figs that they call *fiori*") [83] and offers them to us. We thank her and thank her husband, and they come to the door with us and wave as we go.

We take the path through the vineyard that stretches out beyond the well. A turkey puffs and swells at us, and spreads his feathers protectively between us and his unconcerned hens. Eating the figs, we pass the stream where, in warm weather, the Lawrences picnicked ("I can go about in shirt and trousers and sandals, and it's hot, and all relaxed"),[84] and then walk over the fields for about a half mile and presently we are in the woods. They are deep and cool, the umbrella pines old and tall, with straight, thick trunks, and high above, their curious spread of branches. Nearer the ground grow bushier trees with very small dark leaves that one Italian has told me are "elms" (when you solicit this kind of information, most Italians would rather misinform you than tell you nothing at all), and under them and all over the ground is that whole array of spring flowers which Lawrence so liked to catalogue and describe: crocuses and grape hyacinth, primroses and violets, enormous purple anemones, and some heavy-petaled chartreuse lilies that are strange to us. Here Lawrence once found a white orchid, but we find none; and here, in this most Italian wood, he imagined his English forest on the estate of Clifford Chatterley.

Lady Chatterley's Lover, like almost everything that Lawrence wrote, is a protest against the mechanization of human nature. At one point his heroine reflects that "civilized society is insane," and the novel opens with the assertion that "Ours is essentially a tragic age, so we refuse to take it

527

tragically." This is a strange old wood to which Lawrence came every day: he had backed almost entirely out of society in order to give us this measure of it.[85]

Then they moved again. ". . . at a certain point the business of the thistle is to roll and roll on the wind," he wrote about three months before they gave away their chairs and left for good.[86] "We've given up the Villa Mirenda, and are once more wanderers in the wide, wide world." [87] Much of what Lawrence wrote at Villa Mirenda was bitter, but the place seems to have preserved him from his final savagery of feeling. When, in his tower and in these woods, he worked over his many poems for the collected edition, he felt, he said, "like an autumn morning, a perfect maze of gossamer of rhythms and rhymes and loose lines floating in the air." [88] It was only after he left that he was impelled to write the inscription for a hypothetical tombstone in Gsteig churchyard: "Departed this life, etc. etc. —*He was fed up!*" [89]

Here in his woods the nightingales are singing like mad.[90]

CHAPTER SIX

The Chambers Papers

Dr. J. D. Chambers

R eferences have recently been made to the family background of Jessie Chambers by Harry T. Moore and Edward Nehls.[1] The authority for them is Mr. William Hopkin who, Mr. Moore tells us, went to school with her father and, of course, knew him and the family during the period when D. H. Lawrence was a frequent visitor to the Haggs. Mr. Hopkin himself was not a member of the Haggs group and as far as I know never visited us there, so that his knowledge of our family life is necessarily superficial and in so far as it bears on the character and influence of my sister, somewhat misleading. In these notes written at the request of Mr. Nehls, I have attempted to give an account as it appeared to one who, if not a very active participant in the incidents described, was at any rate on the inside and knew them at first hand.

The subject of the short story "The Bankrupt" written by my sister Jessie and here published for the first time supplies a suitable starting point. It concerns the death of our great-grandfather, a Nottingham lace manufacturer, who was caught up in one of the periodical panics of the Nottingham lace industry and took his life by drowning. The story of this tragic event was passed on by my mother to her children, and it is perhaps not without significance that this should be the choice of subject of the one exercise in creative writing which, as far as is known, my sister undertook apart from the novel which she wrote and later burnt.[2]

The story, perhaps, has another significance. The incident described had the effect of plunging our great-grandmother and her family of small children into great distress from which they were rescued by the dead man's colleagues and fellow business men who took one or more of the children into their various families and brought them up as their own. What happened to our great-grandmother I never heard; but our grandmother was taken into the family of the Morleys, a well-known and highly respected member of the business community at Nottingham, in fact one of the leading families of the town. Her portrait, taken at her marriage at the age (I believe) of twenty-five or -six, shows her to have been strikingly handsome, with flowing black hair and finely chiselled features and a look of absorption and of determination on her face that betokened great strength of character. She was always said to have been very much like my sister Jessie, and her portrait, which I very clearly remember though it must be many years since I saw it, showed a quite striking resemblance.

Her history was recited to us again and again by my mother and must have made a great impression on my sister. It was, as far as I remember, as follows. She was brought up as a member of the family of the Morleys but not without those subtle indications of a difference which a prudent mother would naturally employ in the interests of her own family which included a son of about the same age. Whether their attraction was mutual I never knew; certainly Miss Newbold (as she was then) had hopes, and she was much too proud, I should have thought, to confess this to her own daughter if she had not received encouragement. She was, of course, disappointed; the boy's mother saw to that; and she then lost no time in looking elsewhere for a husband.

We were always told that she consulted a fortuneteller about this, and she was informed that she would marry a man who did this, *i.e.*, the motions of using a plane. And sure enough her husband, David Oates, was skilled in the use of all joiner's and carpenter's tools and may have been of higher rank. At any rate, my mother used to tell me that he was employed in the carving in St. Mary's Church, Nottingham, which was being renewed at this time.

Perhaps a short digression on our grandfather, David Oates, may be permitted. He came from Yorkshire, of farming stock. His father grew teazles for use in the whipping up of the nap in the manufacture of cloth. David, however, was brought up to be a joiner and as a skilled man he would be in demand, but he chose to try his luck in the U.S.A. He went twice, first in a sailing boat, and owing to his foresight in equipping himself with a bag of oatmeal which he shared, as my mother was never tired of telling me, with another member of the ship's company, he was one of the few passengers to complete the voyage without suffering the pangs of hunger. It was, apparently, a long and perilous voyage and a mast was blown down, missing my grandfather by a margin that probably got narrower as the story went down the family tree. On the second occasion he went by steamer without recorded incident.

Instead of following his trade, he preferred to make his living by playing a maplewood flute (which accompanied him on all his wanderings and is now with my brother Bernard in Saskatchewan) on the famous steamboats which plied dangerously and uproariously on the Mississippi in the middle of the last century. He also told of being held up on one of his journeys while two duellists settled an argument by shooting at one another with revolvers from behind trees. He was a merry, musical, adventurous, lovable fellow; he loved his three children, especially his son George, who responded by developing an uncontrollable temper which resulted eventually in his dying in early middle age from a heart attack brought on in the course of one of his rages. George was dark and handsome, with flashing black eyes, the image of his mother (we were told) but lacking the iron self-control which she had acquired during her long sojourn as a ward in the house of the Morleys.

My grandmother accepted her matrimonial fate with dutiful resignation; she felt she had been destined for higher things but she had been cheated by a cruel fate. She eked out the family budget by taking in "clipping and scalloping" from a warehouse in the lace market, a task in which the whole family took part. This was made necessary by the addition to the household of two other female members of her family who had fallen on evil days. My mother, the eldest of the three children, was thus inured from childhood to the mischances of life, and the shadow of her mother's childhood seems never to have been entirely dissipated by the sunny optimism and protecting love of her father.

She always looked back on her childhood, however, as a period of almost unalloyed happiness, her only regret being the necessity of leaving school at an early age and being unable to continue her education at the newly-opened People's College in Nottingham. This was a real grief to her, but she never blamed her parents for it. She worshipped her father, admired and, I think, feared her mother, and absorbed with passionate intensity the puritan message of nineteenth century nonconformity. This was conveyed through the medium of the Congregational Chapel in Castle Gate which she attended with a terrifying earnestness. She used

533

to talk to me with rapt absorption of the doings of the minister Mr. Loosmore whom she had probably not seen for twenty years; and I remember as a young man going into the chapel and trying to recapture the reality of the image which she had impressed so indelibly on my child mind. It can be imagined, therefore, how deep and lasting must have been the impression left on the mind of my sister, more than ten years older than myself and that much nearer to the events my mother described, and far more sensitive and sympathetically disposed. Perhaps I may add that, as quite a small boy, perhaps eight or nine, I remember turning away from my mother as she recited once again some of the soul-stirring drama which she believed she had experienced and asked her not to tell me these things any more. I felt instinctively I must disentangle myself from these memories of a dead past which was being made to live again; and the fact that my sister chose to write up the central and most tragic incident of the story is perhaps a measure of her greater involvement in it.

My mother, of course, was to have her own troubles. They came with her marriage to my father. The description of a comfortable and placid pair given by Mr. William Hopkin as quoted by Mr. Moore and Mr. Nehls is only part of the truth, the visible part of the iceberg, as it were. My father may, as he says, have been a plodding, inoffensive schoolboy, though it is so far out of character as I knew him that I find it hard to believe. He certainly grew up to be a dashing, handsome, irresponsible and quick-tempered young blood, riding his penny farthing bicycle with reckless speed down hills, his feet over the handle bars, and with a capacity for falling off without getting hurt, which stood him in good stead in his various tumbles from ladders, horses and haystacks in after life. He was a man of considerable physical strength and of fearless courage, and was as quick to answer a challenge whether it came from a truculent neighbour or an angry bull.

Two early ventures in business failed and then, with the help of a gift from his mother in anticipation of his inheritance, he started farming, in a haphazard, happy-go-lucky sort of way and was moderately successful mainly as the result of the hard work of my eldest brother Alan. When he was in the mood, he could be irresistibly charming and gay; he could sing (as we all could) and had some small skill with a concertina and a flute; as a young man he tried his hand at poetry and went with a friend to conduct the service at various small chapels.[3] Apparently they both occupied the pulpit, and as each got up to do his piece the other surreptitiously leaned forward to feel if his companion's knees were trembling. It was he, not my mother, who remembered the stories of my grandfather's two trips to America; the two men apparently got on splendidly and the visits to the house for the ostensible purpose of courting my mother seem to have been more usually spent in long and no doubt rollicking discourses with her father.

This was unfortunate as she knew very little about him when they married. He was pale and thin from overwork at Burton's grocer's shop where he was the youngest of the assistants. They worked incredibly long hours: they closed the doors at 11 p. m. on Saturday night (my father used to say) and then had to serve the customers who had edged their way in, and have everything tidy and shipshape for Monday morning before leaving. He met with sympathy as well as admiration when he joined my mother's family circle on Sunday. They were anxious about his health; he might, they thought, be sickening for a serious illness, possibly consumption. And he was always vowing he would set up on his own as soon as he had the money. I think his temper was also being tried at Burton's. He was young—nineteen or twenty—and hot-tempered, and the older men teased and tried to bully him. But he was handsome, with curly brown hair framing a pale face and clear blue eyes, and was vaguely religious; he sang hymns and dabbled in poetry, and gave no sign of the rougher, tempestuous, barbaric side of his nature which his hard upbringing and frustrating grind at Burton's brought out in him. My mother thought of herself as his helpmeet; she would lift him out of all this and they would go on with the blessing of her father and the minister and make a new life together. They succeeded, but not quite in the way Willie Hopkin imagined.

There were incompatibilities which he evidently did not suspect. My mother had been brought up in a household in which the Christian injunctions of love and duty were literally rules of life, extending even to forgiving your enemies and turning the other cheek. Grievances must be silently borne, and frayed tempers must not give rise to hard words. In my father's family, on the other hand, frayed tempers and hard words were part of the currency of living. Life was a fight in which moods of anger, elation, love and hate alternated according to the swaying fortunes of the struggle. Words were counters of exchange, not symbols of eternal verities. Say what was in your mind, get it over and forget all about it: that was the rule. His mother was known to be a hard woman.[4] She had to be. She kept a shop in the Breach at Eastwood in the riproaring days of the 1870's and 1880's. Across the way was a public house where workmen from Barber and Walkers' Pit—including a notorious contingent of Irishmen—gathered because of the quality of the ale— "fighting ale," it was called. They caroused until closing time and frequently finished their arguments under my grandmother's window.

My mother knew nothing of this. She worked in the lace market at

Thomas Adams's where the day's work always began with a service in the chapel. It was a happy, above all, a respectable place, though there were stories of dashing young men in magnificent waistcoats and hints of gallantries which we would have dearly loved to explore. Her real world was at home with her stern and saintly mother, her doting and indulgent father, two aunts who paid in gratitude and love—the only currency they had—for sharing the hearth of the humble joiner, and, of course, the Congregational minister. It was from this background that my mother entered marriage. My father's background was that of an untamed mining and farming community in which gentleness and restraint were unknown and love the synonym for physical possession. Later in life my mother used to shudder when the subject of sex was mentioned.

Jessie was my mother's confidante. Alan and May, the two elder children, also shared my mother's life and lived much of it at first hand. (It is a thousand pities that they are not writing this memoir instead of me.) But they reacted differently. They did not make my mother's life their own; they asserted their independence, Alan by a silent, dogged, almost supercilious indifference; May by a flaming vitality of her own that would admit no powerful infusion of another personality into her private world. She was very much like my father, as fearless, gay and tempestuous, but with a more sustained tenderness for the people she really loved. She fought my father, defied my mother, bickered with her brothers and sisters, including Jessie whom she thought, in those days, sentimental and melodramatic,[5] and went off at the earliest opportunity to find a job and a husband. I loved her for her gaiety and the noise of the outer world she brought into the house; I can still hear her singing in a ringing soprano voice as she scurried around in preparation for some errand or expedition. She was a great favourite with her fierce old grandma at the Breach and spent a good deal of her time looking after her and the shop when she got old.[6] She knew everybody and everybody knew her; but she held herself aloof from D. H. Lawrence and his circle. It was, however, to her house, the cottage at Moorgreen, that Lawrence took Frieda. As far as I know, she is the only member of the family who ever saw her.

The burden of my mother's troubles thus fell on Jessie. She remained, it seems to me, in the orbit of my mother's mind—and of *her* mother's too, when the other children were striking out on their own. That does not mean that she was merely impressionable clay which reflected the mould of my mother's more powerful personality. Not at all. Jessie had a still stronger personality: one of the sayings credited to her, and frequently quoted against her in the family circle, was "If I can't be boss

I'll be equal." And she certainly was—equal to anybody. My brothers, Hubert and Bernard, knew that to their cost when they carried their teasing too far. They were the next in succession to her and took delight in bursting in on her rhapsodical moods and shattering her poetical day-dreams in a wild scrimmage of slaps and bangs. I remember them once waiting for her as she came along reciting *The Lay of the Last Minstrel* or "Lucy Gray" and springing out on her as she went by. Then they took to their heels, for the chase was on. In lighter moods, she would wind a scarf round each fist and challenge them both to a fight. I saw her myself, when she was a teacher in Underwood school, call out a great hulking lad nearly as big as herself, and give him two strokes of the cane. His mother—a vast woman—waited for her as she came out and told her what would happen to her if she ever dared to lay her hands on her Sam again. The children shouted after her as she went down the village street. She walked on with her head high as though she saw and heard nothing. She was about nineteen at the time, at the height of her glory.

She was, therefore, very much a personality in her own right. But she was endowed with an almost preternatural sensitivity, and my mother tended to focus it within a particular field bound by her own life's experience of man and God. Of course my sister went far beyond it; she was passionately interested in poetry and literature and the beauty of the natural world long before she met Lawrence. But it was all part of a cosmos bounded by the criteria of right and wrong, of good and bad. She knew what was right—in taste as well as in conduct; she did what was right and expected to receive what was due to her for her universal rightness. If that was refused her, she would have nothing. I always imagined her as Rebecca of York. She could have stood on the battlements of Torquilstone and hurled defiance at the Templar; and, rather than yield, she would have hurled herself down.

Perhaps her relations with Lawrence would have been the same without the special kind of influence exerted by my mother. I am inclined to think that they would. Her inflexible will would have taken some other direction, and if it had diverged from his it would not have been bent or broken. But I think it is possible that the early emotional strain to which she was subjected may have had lasting effects. It should be remembered that she entered into the whole gamut of the sorrows of two intensely self-centered women while she was still a child, and an exceptionally sensitive and gifted child at that. This premature plunge into the vortex of adult experience may have overstimulated her sensibilities while thwarting growth in other directions. The break with Lawrence was, of course, final, complete and bitter. For a time she was distraught, but there was no breakdown, and she soon regained her self-possession and apparently her peace of mind. In 1915 she made a happy marriage with Mr. J. R. Wood, schoolmaster and a farmer's son. She studied Russian under Professor Janko Lavrin [7] and had many literary friends including, in particular, Max Plowman. [8] She was a socialist and pacifist. She talked on these questions with passionate conviction, never doubting the rightness of her opinions which she arrived at as though by the guidance of an inner light. She was regarded by her husband and neighbours as a saintly woman, always engaged in good works, as a woman out of the ordinary. To her disappointment, she had no children. She died of cerebral haemorrhage in 1944. [9]

Jessie Chambers Wood

THE BANKRUPT

A little girl sat in the glow of firelight singing. She clasped her doll tightly with small brown hands and rocked herself in a low rocking chair.

On the hearth rug another girl, ten years old, knelt, cutting out paper men to amuse a fat baby boy. He was not interested in paper men and stretched out his hands trying to catch hold of his mother's skirt as she passed to and fro, laying the table for tea.

"Do keep him quiet till I've finished. He's getting so heavy to carry about." The mother spoke wearily, keeping with an effort her tone free from irritation. She unloosed the baby's fingers, while the sister rapped the steel bar of the fender with a spoon. This pleased him; he seized the spoon and aimed weak blows at the fender: the spoon flew from his fingers and Matilda had to search for it.

"Look here, our John, it isn't fair. I've minded baby all afternoon, and you've done nothing but read," she said in an aggrieved tone, to a brother a year younger than herself. A volume of *Chatterbox* lay across his knees and he bent towards the firelight, reading eagerly.

"That's what girls are for; it's your work," he muttered without looking up.

"Well it isn't very fair. That's my book—you know it is," she answered, with tears in her voice.

The baby had tired of the music of the spoon and began to cry fretfully.

"Let's show him the pictures! Shall you?" Matilda asked pleadingly. The boy assented, laying the book on the rug; the girl brightened.

"Now, baby, look! Pretty pictures, oh-h pretty!" John turned over the pages while his sister held back the baby's struggling hands. To keep him interested and to preserve the book from damage was a difficult and exciting occupation: they became flushed and noisy. The child in the rocking chair sang on imperturbably: the mother, passing between kitchen and dining room, found herself moving to the rhythm of the little one's hymn.

It gave additional fluency to the easy motion of her body. She was pleasing to see as she came towards the firelight and its glow rested upon her white skin, and thick smooth fair hair. Her mouth was firmly set, and little shadows danced about it pencilling heavily the lines which childbirth had traced there. But for these one might have discounted her thirty-three years: yet she carried a sense of latent power which lived in every ordered movement.

Each time she went down the passage to the kitchen she glanced at the door of the back parlour which faced that of the dining room. It was closed; it had not been opened since early morning.

She paused before it in returning for the last time, the filled tea pot in her hand. The noise from the dining room deterred her: she passed on. "No, I'll put them to bed before I disturb him."

She called the children to the table. The boy and girl lifted the baby upon their joined hands, and so, with his arms about their necks and his fingers clinging in their hair, carried him noisily to his high seat. The little girl laid her doll in the rocking chair and tucked it round with a tiny shawl; then stood sucking the end of her finger and looking thoughtfully at the table.

"Come and sit down, Dorcas, there's a good girl."

"Where's Dadda?" she asked, not moving.

"Oh he'll come soon. See, I've poured out your tea."

"Let me fetch him. I want to. Can I?"

"No, dear, he's busy."

"I want him. Can I fetch him? He likes me to fetch him," she persisted, slowly backing towards the door.

"Oh, he's ever so busy. He didn't hear me when I knocked a little while ago."

"I don't want my tea." The child's voice shook, she reached blindly for the door handle. "I want to fetch Dadda. Can I?"

The baby had crammed his mouth too full: he was on the point of choking. While the mother attended to him Dorcas slipped from the room. She closed the dining room door and stood an instant staring along the dark passage, then she ran to the door of the back parlour and beat upon it with the palms of her hands.

"Dadda—Dadda—let me in," she called softly.

There was no answer. She waited a moment and battered the door afresh.

"Dadda. I want to tell you something—Dadda, let me in—it's Dorcas."

She leaned her head on the door and listened eagerly, but heard nothing from within: she straightened herself and took a step backwards, glancing fearfully towards the deserted kitchen where a point of gas light like a strange little eye looked at her. Then she began again, beating and calling low, her voice growing thick with tears.

Presently a chair was pushed, as if someone moved it in rising, and she stood tense and quivering. Footsteps crossed the room and the door opened. She ran forward and hugged her father's knees. "Why didn't you let me come in, Dadda. I've been waiting ever such a long time."

He lifted her without speaking: she clung about his neck. He sat down in his chair by the table and set her on his knee, drawing her warm trembling little body close. So they sat a moment; then he began to realise the stiffness of his limbs, and rose slowly to pace about the room with her in his arms.

"Well, what did you want to tell me?"

She began running her fingers through his fine dark hair.

"Should I make you some curls, Dadda?"

"But I thought you had something to tell me," he persisted gently.

She pressed her face against his neck. "I didn't want my tea," she whispered.

"And you do now?"

"Um!"—with a nod—"if you come with me."

He sat down for a moment, still holding her tightly. His gaze wandered absently round the room. The open bureau and the table were littered with papers: more papers, which appeared to have been sorted and arranged, lay upon the seats of three leather-covered chairs.

"Well, then, must we go, Dorcas," he said wearily. She hugged him, laughing: he rose and carried her into the dining room.

"I didn't know it was tea time till Dorcas fetched me," he said apologetically to his wife as he set the child in her chair.

"I thought you didn't want to be disturbed; I had knocked once or twice."

"Yes, I've been very busy," he answered without looking at her.

The children were eating silently, gazing at him with grave curiosity. He felt he could not bear their scrutiny: it imposed upon him some demand that he might not meet. He drank a cup of tea and left the table with a muttered apology. The mother had devoted herself studiously to the baby's needs: the two had not exchanged a single glance.

After tea began the bustle of getting ready for bed. The mother sat by the fire on a low chair holding the baby; the children stood by, watching her deft untying of each little garment: ready to receive it as it was slipped off. They must play each in turn with the rosy bare limbs, kicking and waving in the firelight. While the mother spread the bath sheet and carried in the bath Matilda was in charge: she held the baby, naked but for his tiny vest, very carefully. She clasped him tightly round his soft little body, but he wriggled and squirmed to get down on the rug. The other children laughed, but Matilda was frightened, for without clothes there seemed to be no way of keeping hold of him, and the faster she hugged him the more did he struggle. At last she let him slide down before her, and knelt over him, playing with his hands and feet.

In the bath he was regal. Each child went up to be splashed, and retreated in mock terror, while the baby shouted and slapped the water till it hissed upon the hot iron of the grate.

They all undressed by the fire. When they were ready for bed Matilda led the way, carrying the candle. Dorcas crept behind and stopped at the door of her father's room. The mother missed her and turned round half way up the stairs, the baby in her arms.

An unusual anger flashed into her eyes at the sight of the child lingering by the door. "Dorcas!" she exclaimed. The child shrank at the strange harshness of tone. She followed the others upstairs and got quickly into bed.

The house was large, built at the time when the lace trade had been in its first flush of prosperity. With its decline and the need for an ever-narrowing economy the unnecessary rooms had been one by one divested of furniture till now but three bedrooms were in use. The empty rooms seemed sinister as if they harboured a spirit of loneliness that was secretly seeking to eject the inmates and claim for itself the whole. The mother hated the place, marked with so many tokens of lost things, and hated more to leave the children there: their room but a small oasis of light and warmth in a waste of desolation.

She glanced resentfully at the closed parlour door as she came downstairs. She emptied the water out of the bath and folded the bath sheet. When the children's clothes were put away she decided to lay supper.

She took the table cloth from the drawer, and stood with it a moment in her hand. She half unfolded it, then flung it down upon the table and went impetuously to the parlour, opening the door quietly and closing it with a steady hand. Within her husband sat beside the fire.

He shivered slightly as she entered and turned involuntarily from her, bending towards the grate, which was choked with the ashes of burnt papers. She knelt on the rug before him and put her hands on his shoulders.

"Why do you stay away from me? Can I do nothing but keep your house?" her voice vibrated with pain and resentment. He moved, stretching his muscles to control them.

"I'm sorry," he said. His throat felt closed: he fancied the words like air bubbles rising, unchosen. "I . . . what is it you want to know?"

"What do you think I want to know?" she retorted passionately. "There is only one thing I care about: you know it well enough. Why do you shut yourself up alone? Why can't I share your trouble? You are cruel —you are cruel and wrong!"

She leant against his knee: he could feel the long sobs she suppressed. He looked away: stared at the uncurtained window where the gas flame reflected. The soft dark blue of his eyes dilated and his forehead quivered. He sat still, one hand supporting his head, the other hanging loosely by his side. Soon she raised herself and became calm. She rose to her feet and spoke coldly.

"I'm very sorry I've troubled you. I ought to have known better, considering all things. Only I fancied that if something was hurting you I might be able to help."

She stood for a moment looking down at him. She trembled a little and could scarcely restrain herself from clasping him to her. But she set her mouth resolutely and turned to go.

He moved uncertainly, almost writhing, averting his face yet more.

"No—no—you're wrong, very wrong," he said, huskily.

She stopped and echoed him: "Wrong?"

He felt her eyes upon him: they seemed to burn him. He got up and walked across the room as if to escape. The bitterness faded out of her eyes as she watched him: he was beautifully made, all supple and winsome. Her protective instinct asserted itself suddenly: for the moment there seemed but little difference between the man and the baby, only the man was infinitely more pathetic. He faced her and her eyes hardened as he avoided a direct gaze.

"Well, perhaps I only pain you. You would rather I did not know," she said, evenly, and moved towards the door.

542

"Don't go," he said. She waited, near the door; he walked to the table and stood leaning over it, his eyes fixed upon the litter of papers.

"What is there I can tell you? I don't know myself." He moistened his lips and forced out the words.

"No?" she said, gently and encouragingly. He winced and threw himself again into his chair.

"You see I've never looked far enough ahead—" She waited, but he did not continue.

"Well, don't worry. We shall manage to get along all right," she said sympathetically. The ready and tactless optimism stung him. She started at his harsh laughter.

"There—now I can tell you. No, we've done getting along; there's no more road for us: we've done, altogether."

"What do you mean?" she asked sharply, watching him with anxiety. Her change of tone braced him; he went on more calmly.

"You know there's to be a meeting of the creditors?" He paused, watching her; she nodded.

"I've been trying to straighten things out—and they're worse—even—than I thought." He stopped and dared her eyes—she answered his gaze steadily.

"I'm a bankrupt," he said simply. She started: her eyes filled with tears.

"No, look what you've got to realise upon. There are all the machines —and the warehouses," she cried eagerly.

He shook his head a little impatiently. "The machines will fetch the price of scrap iron," he said bitterly. "No," as she began to protest, "they've been valued."

"But they're in working order," she cried breathlessly.

"You know they can't compete with the new ones," he said.

"What of the combine that was going to keep new ones out. You joined that?"

"Ay—useless—foolish. The men who have brought in the machines could buy out the combine."

"Well, if your machines are obsolete there'll be other people bankrupt too," she said.

"Ay—there's Packer and Goode. They can't be fixed much better than I am. But it's different for them—" His voice dropped, the last words were barely audible.

"Why?" She looked at him in great distress. He did not answer, and she repeated the query.

"They'll go under and come out again." The words came with difficulty.

"Well, and so will you!" Her voice rang sharply, slightly touched with scorn at his easy acceptance of defeat.

"Ay!" he said, and was silent. His long hands twitched convulsively. His eyes were dull now, and the looseness of utter weariness hung about every line of his face. The woman stood motionless: he seemed to have cast a momentary spell upon her; she felt baffled as if she were groping in fog. She had to rouse herself to throw it off. She stood up and went to the fireplace: taking up the tongs she carefully placed the half burnt pieces of coal in a little heap over the dull embers. The slight occupation brought relief: the absolute hopelessness vanished. She felt in touch once more with familiar things.

Her husband watched her deliberate building of the fire: the calmness of her movements fascinated him. Some great change had taken effect between them: he realised dimly that it had been long working unrecognised. But now he watched her as if from another state of consciousness. Presently she put down the tongs and turned to him resolutely, taking his hands and pressing them tightly in her own.

"We must be brave. We won't admit failure: we must win through in the end." She spoke rapidly, with dogmatic assertiveness. She looked at his drooping head and unstrung face—she grew strong with the instinct of motherhood, and rich in possession. "You must not think about it any more alone. There's nothing disgraceful in bankruptcy. It's misfortune, that's all. We'll begin again: we'll go slowly: we'll work together."

Her eyes were bright and defiant. A little smile touched his face. It was so curious to hear her talking on, blundering and blundering. Yet she was so self content and so very far away that it did not seem to matter. Better that she should not understand.

"We shall have to send the children away. Mother would have Matilda and John until the worst pull was over, at any rate. Baby's too little to send anywhere, and Dorcas hardly makes any difference."

She was deliberate again; he was fascinated as before, wondering at the immense essential difference between her and himself. He looked into her clear grey eyes and assented to what she said without having heard her words.

At last she noticed his abstraction.

"Well, we needn't stay here talking. I was just going to put supper on the table. You've had scarcely anything to eat all day." She waited anxiously for his reply, but none came. He passed his hand restlessly over his forehead. Her anxiety increased.

"Come, dear—come and have your supper." He rose and stretched himself and then stood upon the hearthrug with his back to the fire: his hands behind him.

"I'll go out a bit first, I think."

"But you ought to eat something." Then, as he made a movement of impatience: "Very well—perhaps you'll get an appetite if you go out awhile. But don't be long."

He went into the hall to get his coat and hat; she extinguished the lamp and returned to the dining room. As he pulled on his overcoat he heard a movement on the stairs behind him, and turning, saw Dorcas creeping down close to the baluster, holding her long nightgown above her bare feet.

"Why, Baby!" He picked her up quickly; she clung fast to him. Her feet were icy, he clasped them in one hand.

"I never said goodnight to you, Dadda—and—and I had nasty feelings beside."

"Did something hurt you, Dorcas—where?"

"No—not hurt," she shook her head vigorously. "Nasty feelings—close round me."

The mother came into the hall on hearing the child's voice. She opened her lips to chide, then paused with an intuitive alarm. Dorcas was shrinking from her, almost cowering in the father's arms. He carried her to the fire.

"Why, you ought to have been fast asleep long ago," he said soothingly.

"I wasn't sleepy." She blinked in the strong light: she stared vaguely about the room, then dropped her head again on his shoulder. The roughness of his overcoat surprised her, she sat up suddenly and looked at him. "Are you going out, Dadda?" she asked with a deep sob in her breath.

"Not far. Now let mother take you to bed."

But she clung to him more tightly than ever and began to cry softly, her shoulders heaving.

"Give her to me. I shall have her ill," the mother said, frightened. He tried to loosen her arms, but she clutched him, shaking. "I think I had a fancy, Dadda," she whispered hoarsely, imploring.

"No, no, go to mother, like a good girl," he said very gently.

"Now I'm going to be cross, Dorcas, if you don't come to me at once," the mother said firmly, adding: "Father is tired tonight." The child was cowed at the tone and turned obediently.

"Why, you're like an icicle. Yes, you'll be coughing all night now!" She drew the rocking chair nearer the fire and sat down, chafing the little one's feet.

"Don't be gone more than half an hour, Henry. It isn't good for you to wait so long between meals."

He stood an instant looking at them, pulling on his gloves the while. The child had closed her eyes and lay inert upon her mother's lap, the dark curls rumpled against her sleeve. His wife did not look up, but rocked gently and rubbed the child's limbs. When he turned and went she did not notice the soft closing of the door. She sat until Dorcas was warm and sleepy—till to all appearance sleep had come, then she rose to carry her upstairs. But Dorcas stirred, and opened eyes flooded with the unreasoning fear that comes between sleeping and waking. The mother was troubled: she watched thoughtfully, looking for symptoms of some childish sickness.

Presently she was able to lay her upon the couch: she covered her with a rug and began to set the supper.

The front door slammed: the man walked quickly down the hill, descending between the warehouses from the elevation of the Lace-Market into the river flats. When the townlights were all above him—not until then, there came to him the sound of the slamming door. It stayed with him as he walked, strangely persistent; neither repetition nor re-echo, but an unvarying continuous sense in the background of his consciousness, like the sense of moving looms to one who spends the half of a lifetime among them. At first it brought the memory of the exterior of the house, and impressed peculiarly the appearance of the cracks in the wood panelling of the door. He thought of Dorcas, hoping that the noise had not startled her. He turned his steps the while by long habit through an open meadow by the river side.

It was a breathless autumn night: the trees seemed to be listening for a sound too rare and fine for human ears: the heavy dew-soaked grass seemed weighted with an intense life of its own. The pungent scent of the rotting leaves was as arresting as a voice: these were the only things in the depths of the soft silent night that had a distinct articulation. He picked up a handful and inhaled their keen fragrance. They were the more intensely living, he thought, through the working of death. He walked slowly under the trees that bordered the path.

Gradually the sense of the slamming door lost its local significance, assuming one more intimate; becoming unified with the feeling of disintegration he had experienced earlier in the evening. It became the snapping of a bond between self and self. He felt an utter detachment from all that had grown about him since the time when between childhood and manhood he had put aside, at his father's bidding, the demands of the eternal child within him: submitting himself to the iron tradition of his house. He breathed the atmosphere of a night twenty years before, when in the same small business parlour where he had passed today, he learnt something of his fundamental weakness. He had entered the room vowing defiance to his father's will—clinging passionately to his ideal, a wider, freer life than that of the counting house and factory: a more generous aim than any permitted by the following of a business career. He had stood before his father seeing that ideal as it appeared in his father's eyes, seeing it shrink and wither and become of no account, feeling himself powerless to sustain it. He had forced himself to make the protests which had seemed so compelling, and had been abashed at their feebleness. And in the end he had yielded and bound himself to the gratification of his father's wish, and to the business fortunes of his family. Heaven and earth reeled in the revulsion that followed: in his self-abasement he could draw no relief but from the determination to make at least a success of his life upon its inevitable plane. He would put away all the visions of beauty for which he was not worthy.

He had straitly disciplined himself, striving to excel, painfully familiarizing himself with the minutiae of his trade, studying assiduously the movements of the industrial world. But always the progress of his affairs was checked by an unbalanced judgment and the actions of a spasmodic generosity. After the death of his father the prosperity of the house steadily declined.

Beyond the point where he now stood he could see nothing. He had no more faith in the virtue of his struggle: subconsciously he had realised the growing domination of the old self: it was rising, untrammelled, the stronger for its long repression. And while he was glad to feel it lifting, sweet and strong, he yet suffered an anguish of defeat, knowing that in face of the sure judgment of the world he had no intelligible plea to put forth. The bitterness of the past day had centred round this conviction.

He reached the path which followed the river, a little above its sloping green banks, and sat down upon the protruding roots of a great elm. A thin mist floated over the river; beneath the mist the water ran swiftly—a deep stream neglected of the city, for it gave nothing willingly, and brooked ill the harness of men. He listened to the whispering of innumerable eddies as they swirled softly away in the dark under the mist covering, and the quiet lapping of the water against the banks suggested to him the warm patting of a child's hands. Beyond the river the mist spread itself out over the marshes white and boundless, broken only by the shadowy forking of an isolated tree. There seemed to pass from him, as he sat, the last traces of the superficial self he had so hardly acquired— its pursuits, its standards, its interpretations; in the mist world before him was nothing more formless than they; scarcely more real appeared the surrounding of his physical existence. And though a lethargy woven of weariness and the spell of the river was upon his senses, there was yet an activity working tirelessly beneath them and by its agency he knew assuredly the dissolution of these things to be complete and final.

He rose suddenly, and moved nearer to the water: as he crossed the path the clock of St. Mary's struck nine. It was time to return home.

He stood still, trembling violently while throughout his dulled body there surged, like a cold wave seething, its dread of an essential, inevitable change. He stumbled towards the bank and leaned against a tree, faint and shuddering: gradually he slid downwards and lay in the grass. Before his brain, doors were swinging noiselessly, swinging backwards and forwards without reason or impetus.

Presently the shuddering ceased. "The door *did* slam," he said, and lay quiet.

Then through his stupor flowed the soothing of the river's voices: the current was swollen with heavy autumn rains, and the water slid past but a few inches below his head. When he opened his eyes he beheld the river: it absorbed him with its imperturbable flow, with the eternal measure of its irresistible motion. Its strength, its being, assumed gigantic proportions: it became a majestic, conscious power, filling the whole valley, lifting itself upwards and outwards to the hollowing of the night.

Supper was laid: Dorothy sat waiting her husband's return. She still felt uneasy about the child, and listened with some anxiety to her breathing. It was uneven, and the nostrils too worked rapidly. The eyelids were barely closed; between the upper and lower lids a tiny strip of the iris could be seen, and below the eyes were dark rings.

Dorothy bent down, putting her ear close to the lips, listening for the muffled sound heralding bronchitis. The child suddenly opened her eyes wide, and shivered with a terror of half waking. The mother shaded the light with her hand and stood motionless. In a little, Dorcas slept again. Dorothy glanced at the clock. The time was half past eight.

She went softly to her sewing table under a window in the corner of the

548

room, and took from a drawer the twill frock she was making for the baby. She seated herself so that her shadow fell over the couch, and began to sew rapidly, absorbed in thought. She tried to see clearly the immediate future with its limitations and possibilities. She would have to part with the two elder children for a time, but for their welfare she was not concerned: her parents would take them gladly. The two younger ones cost little as yet. Henry, she knew, would never give up Dorcas. So, having roughly arranged the matter of the children, she turned to the consideration of her husband's position. This gave her more trouble.

She was not entirely ignorant of the ordinary course of circumstances following upon a man's bankruptcy. But it was difficult to imagine Henry in such a situation. She felt baffled with regard to him: she could not plan for him. Something in him puzzled her: she had never felt so foiled before: she hated the feeling of helplessness his attitude imposed upon her. As she thought of him she grew inquiet, sewing more and more rapidly, until her hands became unsteady, and she laid the work down almost from exhaustion. The clock struck ten. She turned in astonishment: she had not noticed the striking of nine. The table, set for two, was a mute interrogation. She folded up the little frock and went to the outer door, where she stood looking up and down the street.

About a hundred yards below the house, on the opposite side of the street, rose the tall straight outlines of her husband's factory. She looked intently at the windows of his room, and her heart leaped as she fancied she saw the glimmer of a light in one of them. She ran forward to make certain, and found the glimmer to be the reflection of a street lamp. She retraced her steps slowly and stood again in the bar of light which streamed through the open doorway.

She returned to the dining room on tiptoe, afraid lest Dorcas should be roused by her entrance. She felt a repugnance to the intensity expressed in the child's eyes, and to the terror that swept visibly through her newly awakened consciousness. But Dorcas slept, breathing unevenly still, as if she had sobbed herself to sleep.

For lack of any other occupation, Dorothy took up her sewing again. Presently her ear, keenly alert, registered the more regular breathing of the child, and after a while, seeing that the eyelids were completely fallen, and the little figure in deep repose, she decided that she might safely carry her to bed. When she came downstairs, she found it impossible to rest alone: the dining room with its generations of associations became articulate. Dorothy had never taken root in the old house. Its spirit was antagonistic, and she felt on sufferance with relation to it. Its furniture was not of her choosing, dating mostly from the time of the marriage of Henry's father. She had no real heritage, and in earlier days, before the birth of the children, fancied herself regarded as an intruder. Even now, her nerves being at a tension, the sideboard seemed frowning upon her, and all the silent furniture expressing an unalterable antipathy. The portraits of Henry's father and grandfather, reflected in the mirror above the mantelpiece, looked down austerely.

At eleven o'clock, steps came along the street. She sat erect and listened, holding her breath. They passed straight on, and as the sound of them died away far down the hill she found herself trembling.

She remembered the glimmer of light on the warehouse windows, and began to persuade herself that she had been mistaken in supposing it the reflection from a lamp. Perhaps, after all, he was only lingering about the place that had been his so long. The idea, once conceived, grew rapidly: she pictured him in the deserted rooms among the useless machinery, grieving for the consequences of his mismanagement. Suddenly impatient, she rose to go and find him, reproaching herself for not having done so sooner.

She fetched an old lantern, dusted it, fixed a candle in the worn socket, and, taking the emergency key, went out quietly, leaving the door ajar. She would not look again at the illumined window, but, fumbling, fitted the key into the great lock, setting the lantern on the ground and pressing with both hands to turn it. Then she pushed the door back slowly and went in. Her light seemed devoured by the darkness of the hall.

The warehouse had once been a family residence. From the entrance a flight of shallow stairs led to the rooms where the machines stood. She mounted, holding the lantern high to light the steps before her. At the top she paused and listened, but the heavy throbbing of her blood deafened her: she could not trust her hearing. She wanted to call his name, but she had not the courage, dreading the empty echo of her own voice.

The room was very long. One end from ceiling to wainscot was glassed: this great window gleamed grey in the dusk, its crosswork of frames standing high and black. There was a gangway leading from the doorway down the centre of the room, flanked on either side by the machines, each like an animal, crouching for the spring. Dorothy made an effort to control the beating of her heart, and forced herself to take long breaths. Then she walked slowly along the gangway, turning the light from side to side, fearing almost equally what she might or might not see. She reached the window: nothing had moved but the great shadows of the machines which sped silently behind at each turn of the lantern. It suddenly occurred to her that the machines were condemned and awaited destruction. A feeling of pity gave her courage: she looked with interest and commiseration over the grim iron outlines. They had dignity and purpose; the rigidity of their form belied their subtlety. She remembered the long quiet days succeeding the birth of each one of the children, when she had lain inert in a warm calm of existence, and the humming of the machines had woven into her drowsy soul. She grieved to think that they would spin no more.

As she went downstairs she knew she had not expected to find her husband in the factory. She hurried home, trying to believe that he had entered during her absence. His overcoat was not hanging in the hall.

The fire was low in the dining room. She put on coal, and sat down in the small rocking chair, bending forward, propping her head with her hands, pressing the temples as though she would press back the invading dread. Glancing suddenly at Henry's chair opposite, she rose and went to it, trying to be still, but a great longing for him, a great overmastering physical longing strained every fibre: she drew tight breaths painfully and rocked to and fro. When the clock struck twelve she went upstairs to the children's room.

The night light burned softly upon its high shelf, leaving the beds in shadow, mellowing the yellowish paint of the old ceiling. She took it down and stepped to the side of Dorcas' cot; the child slept calmly, breathing easily. She went to each bed in turn. There was deep rest here, but she might not stay: yet she waited after replacing the light. The baby stirred slightly—she went quickly to the cradle and lifted him out: she wrapped a blanket round him and carried him swiftly downstairs.

He whimpered a little. She began to pace up and down the dining room with him. Long after he had fallen asleep again she walked, swaying her body automatically, to and fro, up and down. At last she sank into the arm chair in a half stupor, but never relaxing her grasp of the child.

The light of the lamp burned low and became thick and smoky, then flickered out, leaving the room oppressive with fumes. The fire settled, the red glow died sullenly, and white ash lay thick on the bars of the grate; there was darkness. Dorothy still slept. When the dawn came grey creeping, thinning the darkness imperceptibly, it clung about her, showing her white face and fair hair in outline against the chair back. It dwelt upon the spread table, emphasizing its neglected hospitality: it gave an added desolation to the ash-strewn hearth, and a greater rigour to the lines of the family portraits. It permeated the whole room touching into a harsh

551

significance one object after another. As it strengthened it lifted Dorothy's face from the shelter of the shadows. A strained expression grew more and more marked, the eyelids lifted slightly. When the actual sense of light penetrated to her brain she sat suddenly upright.

The brutal light struck and confused her for a few seconds. The cold and the pain of her cramped limbs brought recollection rushing back. Following upon a sense of the antagonism of the desolate room came the swift realization of her abandonment. It was absolute: there was no gainsaying her divination: the force of it swept through her overwhelmingly.

The light lay heaviest in a pale beam which crossed the couch and dropped to the floor below. It became more vivid, and she watched it from irritation, staring till it hurt her eyes. Then she moved and the baby woke.

She carried him upstairs.[10]

Dr. J. D. Chambers

May Holbrook's manuscripts were found when I visited my brother Bernard at Mervin, Sask., at Christmas 1956. My sister had left a box with him when she ceased to live at Brightsand and moved to Sidney, British Columbia about 1954 or 1955. My brother had no objection to my searching the box, and in doing so, I came across the memoirs which now appear for the first time. The fact that one was typed implies that a third person knows of their existence, as my sister did not possess a typewriter. It is not possible to say when the memoirs were written; perhaps soon after the appearance of *D. H. Lawrence: A Personal Record* by E. T., but this is pure surmise.[11]

May Chambers Holbrook

When D. H. Lawrence was a child, the Colliery Company provided a cricket field for their workmen. It lay in the valley beside the brook, on whose other bank was my grandmother's [12] orchard. By jumping and wading I had crossed the brook—a thing forbidden—and stood fascinated by the game of snobs [13] some big girls were playing on the lawn turf of the corner reserved for tennis.

Presently one big girl looked up and asked: "Is there a pig to be shaved?" Jumping up she shoved the crowd of little ones away.

A red-haired girl with thin lips said: "Let her stay," and beckoning me asked my name, age, number in family, and school I attended.

Her companion asked: "Who do you lie with?" which I didn't understand. It was explained as "Who do you sleep with?"

Their curiosity satisfied, the red-haired girl told me to sit down and learn the game, but my hand was too small to hold the five snobs or staves, and she said: "You'll have to play with our Bertie." In a shrill voice she called the name.

A tall, thin, pale boy came from the crowd of small children unwillingly, crying "What do you want, our Pem?" [14]

"You take this little girl and play with her," she ordered, and, his face clearing, we ran off together to play with the crowd of small children.

There was an empty house in the Breach where they had lived formerly —"But we don't live there now," explained his sister as we crossed the plank that bridged the brook. "We wouldn't live in the Breach for anything. We live up at Brickyard Closes in those houses with bay windows." [15]

. . .

It was some years before I got as far as the bay windows. But the Lawrence children were among those who played on the cricket field where we used to crawl under the pavilion which stood on piles about eighteen inches high, pretending we were down in the pit among the props that supported the roof. In the semi-darkness we were laughed at as "mard" if we dared not crawl the full length and back. "Them as'll ma'e good colliers crawl all o'er and dunna screet," cried the boys. But I was always glad to see the light and feel the fresh air as soon as possible.

Another jaunt was to the hut used by the man in the clay of the brick field where a leather-faced man with a wide grin used to offer us toffy he had made: we called him Mako Koko. We used to scrape off all signs of clay, because it was a forbidden adventure. Dark tales were told of Mako Koko and the toffy he made—and some of us threw it away when we got outside.

Just above these clay pits was the road, like a cliff, on which perched the row of bay-windowed houses. A rough, steep path ran under the high hawthorn hedge down to the Breach, which was a double row of blocks of houses, built by the Colliery Company for their workmen. In the bottom of the valley was the brook along which my grandmother's property lay. From here I carried a can of milk on Saturday mornings up the Brickyard Closes, and up the dark entry at the houses with the bay windows to the Lawrence home. I was greeted as a playmate and as the child of a friend, for our mothers had walked and talked on Sunday nights after Chapel.

One night, Mother was so long coming home I went in the darkness to meet her and heard them talking.

"I knew he'd come home to me," Mrs. Lawrence said in dramatic tones. "I never went to bed that night, but looked up the trains, and walked from our entry to the end of the road to meet him. Aye, I'd been many times before he did come—but he came, and I knew he would. I knew he'd come home to his mother . . . ."

She went on, and I ran home to something more interesting.

So now on my first visit to the Lawrence house, I was warmly welcomed and taken in to be shown with pride the parlour, the carpet, the suite, the vases and ornaments, the family group in a handsome frame on the wall facing the bay window.[16] We peeped through the curtains at the wide view over the valley crowning its far side. They turned again to the family group, telling me when and where taken, and I stood admiring everything when the elder sister [Emily] asked:

"Have you got a suite?"

"Mind your own business," snapped the mother. "If you ask me no questions, you get no lies, do you, child?"

She was a short, robust woman with a heavy, plodding step, her thick hair greying, shrewd grey eyes, and a kindly smile. She drooped slightly, and carried her head bent to one side a little, as if weary and discouraged. Her black dress and the apron tied around her waist bore signs of work about which she complained and was rebellious. Her expression changed swiftly from the sympathetic to the combative. In Chapel she sat at the entrance of their pew. She wore a small black bonnet with the ribbons tied very neatly, sitting with downcast eyes, her head slightly on one side. Her eldest son [George Arthur] was dark and quiet looking, his brother [William Ernest] was brilliant with flashing eyes and teeth, and unruly, tawny hair. He was popular with the night-school boys to whom he taught shorthand and with the athletes. He had an irresistible smile and seemed to find difficulty in sitting still so long, so he took down the sermon in shorthand sometimes. There were the two sisters [Emily and Ada] between whom Bert was sandwiched. Only on very rare occasions did I see the father in Chapel. He looked handsome in a rugged way: black curly hair and beard streaked slightly with silver; blue eyes smiling kindly in a rugged face, glancing over the congregation with a friendly air; well-built and strong in figure; and a genial manner. By comparison the mother appeared bitter, disillusioned, and austere. Her attire was black, as I recall it.

On Sunday morning was Sunday School followed by Chapel. In the

554

afternoon was school in the big schoolroom, boys on one side, girls on the other, in small groups, each class with its teacher. Some Sundays "pieces" were said, and the Sunday Bert was told to say his piece he stood on the raised dais speechless, till a titter ran through the room. Then he was allowed to look at a sheet of paper from his jacket pocket; just one glance, and unfalteringly he went to the end. But I don't remember seeing him on the platform ever again. I said "pieces" to my mother's intense disapproval, but at the special request of our young Scots minister,[17] whose wife provided my "pieces." Sunday evening found us again at Chapel. Sunday was the big day for both our families. We went to different day schools because we lived in different parishes, but the brook drew children to play at the sheep-bridge where we also used to watch the shearing of a few sheep in the spring.

Bert was ten when first I went to his home, and Saturday mornings found him cheerfully helping in the work, cleaning boots or knives and forks, with an apron tied under his armpits, a smudge on his face, and his thick, fine hair rumpled. Whatever he was doing, he was merry with lots to say. One morning he was waiting for me. "I must show you Mother's flowers," he said, skipping about while the milk was put away, and then led me through the scullery into the yard where a bit of space made a drying ground for the wash, its line-post between the house and the ash pit. A tiny spot like a tablecloth was protected by a few bits of board for palings, and here bloomed a handful of flowers. Bert hopped on one foot as he excitedly explained:

"Mother calls it her 'wilderness.' They're all mixed together, they're best that way. It's a wilderness because they're all mixed together. They're lovely, aren't they?"

"It's a 'wilderness' right enough, isn't it, child?" said the mother. "I just took the seeds and scattered them all together. He thinks they're pretty, but they're nothing, are they, child?"

"Oh, I think they're ever so nice, don't you?" insisted her son, hopping from one foot to the other, and said when I was dubious: "Well, anyway, they're better than none, and I think Mother's wilderness is lovely."

He always spoke rapidly and in a high voice tingling with excitement or perhaps enthusiasm.

.   .   .

"Did you find your teapot lid?" Bert asked one morning of the bent old woman with a black chenille net over her grey hair who came out of the scullery door opposite theirs, and he explained with concern that she always emptied her teapot at the back of the fire, and had forgotten to remove the lid so that it fell and must be retrieved from the ashes. His polite inquiry was full of genuine interest, and he comforted her: "It's better than if you had knocked the spout off, you know." He walked down the entry with me, explaining how very old she was or it would not have happened.

His sister scolded: "Our Bert, come on and get on with your work. She's got to go and get on with her work."

"Do you catch it if you're a long time?" he asked as he went backward up the entry.

He was never still, a quick, lively boy interested in everything, but not strong enough to play with boys, they said. He had a slight cough. Sometimes they made him sit still, and then he looked like a captive as he sat by the window, his elder sister beside him, a big rug in the making, like a barricade over their knees. He was snipping lengths of cloth while his sister pegged them into the rug.

"She's making him cut rags for her," complained the mother, "and she's no call to. There's no hurry for that rug."

Her daughter began to complain shrilly why she wanted to finish it.

"Aye, you want, right enough," said the mother tartly, "and what you want you make him help you with!"

The girl again upheld her reasons, but the boy snipped viciously at the cloth and said nothing, his lips tight shut. He gave me the flicker of a smile as I passed the window which looked onto the gloomy back yard, as if he longed to be free.

.   .   .

One midsummer morning his sister exclaimed in her shrill, scolding way:

"You must be hot in that stuff frock! Why don't you have a cotton one like me? I couldn't bear a stuff frock."

Her mother gave her a vigorous nudge. "Shut up, fool! What'll keep cold out'll keep sun out, won't it, child? She's big enough to help with the washing and ironing. That's why she can have a washing frock. I know how useful you are—your mother's told me you're wonderful for your age. Never you fear, you'll have a washing frock just as soon as you can look after it."

At the bottom of the entry her son said with a warmth in the blue of his eyes, "Never mind!"

I stared at him because it was the first time I noticed his eyelashes were white, like his hair—the same shade as parchment I had seen at my grandmother's.

"Never mind!" he said again, kindly.

And I laughed: "I don't want a washing frock. It'd be too hard to keep clean!"

Instantly Bert returned to the defense of his family: "But they're very nice and cool, and they look so nice and fresh."

I wasn't interested. His shirt collar was open, and I saw he had large, yellow freckles on his pale skin. I was tempted to remark on them, but knew it would be ill-mannered. So I went home and told my brother.

.　　.　　.

One dull, heavy morning [1898] I came upon mother and son at the end of the entry. I thought Mrs. Lawrence must have a headache. Her elbow was on the coping stone on the low wall, her head resting on her hand. In her black dress and soiled apron she impressed me as one in deep misery.

Bert came a few steps to meet me, and said in a tense voice:

"I've won that scholarship."

My eyes and mouth opened in speechless admiration, and his face suddenly shone with joy, then clouded with anxiety.

"She's wondering if she'll let me go. I hope she does. I want to go."

The mother didn't change her position, but stared out over the wide valley as she said:

"I don't know what to do, child. He's told you they both won the scholarship."

The other boy had been forgotten. I hardly knew him. I said I was glad, and asked when would High School start? She had not altered her position, and stared over our heads to far tree-clad hills.

"I don't know that I shall let him go."

Bert stood digging the toes of one foot in the dust, hanging his head, and said tensely, "You will let me go. I know you will."

"Oh, shall I?" she queried tartly.

"Yes, you will," he repeated very low and vibrant. "I know you will."

She stepped away from the wall and shook and tossed her head.

"Aye, if I can pinch it out of the pennies, he knows I'll let him go. He knows, oh, he knows right enough." Bert glanced with a face puckered with varying emotions, and she continued, appealing to me, "It takes money, doesn't it, child?"

But Bert broke in, "There is some money found, Mother."

"Aye, my lad, there's a little found, but there's a lot wants finding. Why, look at his clothes and boots and dinners and train fare and books."

"There's enough for books and train fare and a little more, I think, and I can wear my Sunday suit and boots," he arranged eagerly.

"And they won't wear out? And what will you wear for Sunday? Tell me that. Oh, I don't know!"

And she turned up to the entry with her weary step and her shoulders a little more bowed.

"Skimp, skimp, I'm tired of skimping."

The next time I went, it was all settled that somehow means should be found for Bert to attend the High School at Nottingham.

.　　　.　　　.

Somewhere about this time the Lawrences took me into their parlour to show me a photograph of the girl [18] engaged to the handsome, auburn-haired brother Ernest. He was bringing her home for the holidays, and the elder sister declared:

"We're going to tidivate everything up. This parlour's going to be done so that you'll hardly know it."

"There's a lot she says is going to be done that won't get done, varnishing and such like," declared the mother.

"Well, we shall have to—" began the daughter, but the mother broke in.

"We shall have to do just as far as the money goes and that's all! That's as much as you can do, isn't it, child?" she said to me. "Besides, what's good enough for us is good enough for them who's coming."

We turned to the photograph again.

"She's nice, isn't she!" said Bert, quivering with excitement, and I said she was handsome.

" 'Handsome is as handsome does,' we shall see!" said the mother, grimly.

The sister pointed to the family group, saying, "That's him."

"Fool!" ejaculated the mother. "She knows him, don't you, child? Aye, I wonder how he's changed," she said mournfully. "They're never the same men once they go out into the world. You lose them—you might as well never have had them." Her tone filled me with sadness as if she were crying, "Woe is me."

The only change I could see was that Ernest was more dashing and handsome. Arm-in-arm with the two sisters and Bert, he and his fiancée swung down the hill to the park where the annual Band of Hope Demonstration was in full swing with all the brass bands of the town which was *en fête*. Gaily they marched in the sunshine, all brimming over with joy of life. I suddenly felt grieved to think of the mother alone at home looking out on the gloomy back yard, apart from the fun and laughter that they made.

But the next time I saw Mrs. Lawrence, she was in a fury and began talking:

"They're gone! Aye, they're gone, and I for one am not sorry. Why, child, she lets him buy her boots!"

The tirade continued. Bert had heard it before and stood patiently waiting till he could go down the entry with me and said:

"I don't think it matters, do you?"

I didn't know. Such a torrent shrivelled me and left me dazed. I said it must matter, or his mother wouldn't be so angry.

"I don't think it does," Bert said. "They're sweethearts. If they give presents, they can just as well be useful. They were very pretty boots. He paid— Guess how much he paid for them . . . ." And he named a sum that filled us with awe. "But I don't think it matters, she's his sweetheart."

I thought his mother knew best, but Bert stuck to his own opinion.

.   .   .

Now Bert was at High School [1898–1901], the Lawrence house seemed very quiet. Their pew at Chapel had lacked the presence of the two elder sons for some time. Even the elder sister was absent for short periods. But the mother in her black bonnet sat at the entrance of the pew, and always Bert was with her. Coming down the aisle, he would be looking straight ahead in perfect behavior, but a faint blow with his fist made communication. And while our mothers talked at the entrance gates, we children exchanged remarks.

Mrs. Lawrence was often alone when I called at the house, and always she seemed weary and dejected. "Eh, child!" she would say in tones that filled me with fear of the woe and wickedness awaiting me in life—the hard work, the deception, the scratching and scraping to make ends meet, the ingratitude of children. I used to look over the wide valley with relief after the gloom of that back yard.

My mother was now able to attend Chapel only when Father could drive her in the mornings; and as Mrs. Lawrence attended only at the evening service, they had not met for some time when Mrs. Lawrence, looking bleak and nipped as if she had been in a bitter wind, said to me:

"Eh, child, tell your mother not to spoil her sons. Mine's married! [19] Aye, he's married."

Presently I went down the entry, frightened at the enormity of getting married. Her tones and expression conveyed the idea that we children were a wicked lot, and I wondered how I could avoid causing such bitterness. I wished Bert were there to give me his opinion. Perhaps I should not feel such distress. I always thought his mother was right; perhaps he thought otherwise. But he was at school.

.   .   .

One afternoon, Bert was in high glee and hopped about the doorstep, his eyes shining.

"You'd never guess. I shall have to tell you, because you'd never guess in ever so long." He paused dramatically. "Mother's writing poetry! She is, you may not believe it, but she is."

His mother came to the door, an exercise book almost hidden in the folds of her skirt as it hung from her hand.

"Well, child, how's your mother?"

But he burst out, "I've told her!"

"Aye, clatting! [20] I might have known. It's nothing, child."

But Bert cried, "It is, it is. It's poetry."

"Nonsense. I just amuse myself sometimes with making up verses."

"She's going to send it to a mag," he announced.

"He means a magazine, child," Mrs. Lawrence explained.

"She sent some once before," Bert volunteered.

"Aye, and that's all that came of it. I expect it got into the wastepaper basket. But come in. We are all by ourselves, for a wonder. Just the two of us."

Nothing more was ever said about the poetry, though that afternoon her son sketched glowing pictures of his mother becoming famous and making them rich.

.   .   .

During High School [1901] it was arranged that Mrs. Lawrence and Bert should visit our farm [the Haggs] which lay three miles away among the woods they could see from their bay window. The way lay along the valley and skirted a sheet of water seventy acres in extent. This was the [Moorgreen] Reservoir which lay at the foot of a great hill clothed with a remnant of Sherwood Forest.[21] Here they left the road for the field path which angled across to a spinney of young firs known as the "Warren" because of the many rabbits. It was the way I came from school and to me seemed a walk of matchless beauty at any season of the year. At the time of their visit the short grass was full of violets, and the birds filled the air with music.

I dawdled all the way home that afternoon, rather dreading those people from the bricks and mortar of streets of houses where bay windows and front room furniture and new clothes were so very important. They would think our old house and severely plain furnishings very countrified. They would complain of the distance and the loneliness and perhaps never see the violets, for they liked the town and we liked the country. Slowly I sauntered across the sunny yard and into the kitchen. Bert rushed from an inner room.

"Oh, I say, you *are* late. Why are you late? I began to think you were staying at your grandma's. Your mother says you are hardly ever as late as this, and you knew we were to be here!"

The entrance of the two mothers saved me from replying. His mother sympathized.

"Eh, child! you have a long walk! You must be tired out, and ready for your tea, I'll be bound. Let her get her tea in peace and save your questions till she's rested a bit. He's just full with everything, and wild over that well of yours in the wood. I'd like to see him carry all the water your family needs bucket by bucket, eh, child? Wouldn't he be crying out for a tap? He'd hate the sight of a bucket before he was many days older."

"Let's go now," Bert urged, as I finished my tea.

"Let her alone," scolded his mother. "She's tired. I don't see how she does it—school at eight o'clock, on her feet all day in front of a class, and that long walk home. I don't think you'll stand it. It may be too much for her yet," she said to my mother, who laughed:

"Oh! she'll go through a stone wall to get to school."

"Aye, they're wasteful at this age. They're bound they'll have what they want. Our two young madams would boss me, but I lay down the law to them, and to this one too. I'll make them do as I say, or I'll know the reason why." She laughed. "But it's not school they're after, they don't want learning. They haven't brains like this one, he's bookish. They're not a patch on him, but Ern was clever too, though not bookish. He was after a good position. And bold, too. He raised himself by his bootstraps, as you might say. When he said, 'Mother, I'm going to apply for that position,' I said, 'Why, my boy, you're not fitted for it—you've no business training.' But he said, 'No, but I've picked a lot up, and I've worked up pretty good in shorthand. I'm going to try for it, and if I get it I'll pick more up as I go along. I can—I'm sure I can.' And he did. He got the job, and he worked himself up and bettered himself all along the line, till now he's high up and improving himself all the time. Aye, but you lose them, though. The mother's forgotten for the young ones. But I must

say he's a good son, he's a real good lad to his mother, even if he is courting strong."

We all listened appreciatively—she was so obviously enjoying herself—
but her son held out a book he had picked up from the window ledge,
asking:

"Who's reading *Bonnie Briar Bush?*"

And the talk swung to books, and presently his mother said:

"Oh! but you should read *When a Man's Single* by that writer Barrie. I
mean to get that to keep some day, and another of his, *Margaret Ogilvy*."

There was now a good audience, and Bert twitched my sleeve and went
outside. Reluctantly I followed.

"Why don't you want to show me the wood? I'd go myself, only I'm
afraid the keepers would turn me back, or I might lose my way and be
out a long time and upset Mother."

I was loath to show him the wood because it was like showing my heart.

"Did you see the violets?" I asked.

"Am I blind? Why, we were ever so careful not to tread on any. I never
saw so many."

That was enough. "I'll show you the most secret spot in the wood for
that," I cried.

And in the rich glow of late afternoon we entered the shadows of the
great oaks, and followed a narrow path to the heart of the wood, then
in between trees, where I signalled him to be silent. I sniffed and listened,
then drew him towards a tiny clearing where stood a little pavilion of
poles with the bark still on. His eyes widened with amazement as we
stepped on the deep green grass.

"What is it?" he whispered.

"The keepers' hut," I whispered back.

"They might be around," he suggested.

"No, there's no smell of tobacco smoke."

We drew away down a path.

"They've never caught me here yet," I said, "and I've been scores of
times. It's like a fairy tale. I could make a story about it, couldn't you?"

"I don't know. Where are we going now?"

"To the spot I like best."

We were now on the broad main riding and came to the tip of the wood
and looked out across the wide valley with the stretch of water from
whose edge rose high beach-land clothed with great oaks. Straight ahead
over the placid water, a large, gentle, green slope was crowned with
trees under whose shadows stood a tall white house.

"Why, we're looking out from the wood as if we were looking from a big window," Bert cried in delight. "The land drops so suddenly from the wood you'd think we were standing in a room up lots of steps. No wonder you like this spot. Would you like to live there?" He nodded towards the house.

"Yes, very much, but I like to look at it."

"Why?" he rapped out. "Why do you like to look at it?"

And I said—because it looked so orderly and peaceful.

"But to live there!" he objected. "Don't you like where we live?"

"No," I answered bluntly, off my guard.

"Why?" he demanded.

"Well," I began in confusion at my ill manners, "I'm not used to streets, so I don't like them much, especially the back yards. Perhaps if I lived in a street, I should like it when I was used to it."

"You've always someone to play with or talk to, and you're close to town if there's anything going off. I know my mother wouldn't live here: she's sorry for your mother, I can tell by the way she talks. I expect Mother will say she'd die if she had to live here."

I replied that all my mother's people from the city pitied her for having to live in such a lonely place and said it wasn't good for us to grow up away from the world as we were doing.

"Why, you're all right," Bert declared indignantly. "I've always thought you were nice, and so does Mother."

When we reached home, I turned at once to my lessons.

"Oh, don't while we're here," Bert begged.

"I must have them ready for tomorrow morning."

"Well, then, let me help you," he offered generously. "Let me help you, now I've hindered you so long."

"You can't, it's study."

"I bet I could tell you and save you swotting—"

Mrs. Lawrence appeared on our old oak stairs and said as she stepped down into the room:

"You'll be glad when we're gone, I know."

"I have to do my lessons for tomorrow. I apologize."

"Yes, and she won't let me help her," complained her son.

"You let him help you, child. He'd be glad to. Do him good, too. He's been skipping about like a goat long enough."

"Go on, let me," Bert urged. "We'll do it in a jiffy. Then we could go out again."

His mother was a different person from the house-weary woman I knew. Her eyes snapped with enjoyment of an audience, her chin was high, she laughed often and shook her head in vigorous emphasis as she talked of how he had enjoyed everything.

"If only Bert could come on his Thursday holiday, it would give him new life. The doctor thinks he's got to get more country air. He's just wild to come."

My mother invited him to come any time he cared to, and Mrs. Lawrence declared:

"I'll take my oath he'll be no trouble. I had boys as good as a girl in the house, and quick to see when you need help. He doesn't wait to be told to do a thing. My father was exacting. He made us wait on him hand and foot, and I used to say, 'I'll never have a husband like you,' then I'd have to fly. But it taught me not to dance attention on a man and to let a boy learn to help himself."

All our family formed an audience, and in the pause Bert offered again to help me. But I refused, afraid to expose my ignorance against his high school learning, and so his mother said they had better start for home and let me work.

It was agreed he should come next Thursday.

"You don't know what you are doing for Bert," declared Mrs. Lawrence. "But I'll see to it he brings his own bread and butter. I'll not let him sponge on you. I know what it is providing for a family. Isn't it astonishing what they can put out of sight? It makes you frightened to see the food disappearing at the rate they can eat it up."

We walked with them to the spinney, Mrs. Lawrence declaring what a world of good such a weekly outing would do Bert and how much obliged she was to us.

"I don't care what you say," she said as she shook Mother's hand, "he's going to bring his bread and butter. You're doing me a favour in having him, so I'm not going to put on you any further."

And "Goodnight, Goodnight" echoed on the wood as they went down the spinney.

.   .   .

The following Thursday, as I emerged from the fields, Bert ran across the sunny farmyard, took my bag of books, and announced with shining eyes:

"Your mother's a lady."

He hovered around while I ate my tea, and I knew he was trying to keep me from settling down to my lessons.

"Mother said I wasn't to pester you to go in the wood because you're tired, but you're not, are you?" he urged. "I've been to school and walked to the station and back and up here, and I'm not tired."

"No," I returned, "because it's all new to you here and makes you excited."

"Well," he bargained, "we'll do your lessons first then."

"Yes, and they'll soon all know at school, and I shall be ordered to bring my own work, not yours."

And my father coming asked, "Haven't you got to your lessons yet!"

We went to my study table, and I showed Bert the book cupboard deep in the thick, ancient wall, and we talked about the probable age of the house and its connection with the ruined Abbey.[22] As I opened my books at last, Bert said brightly:

"I know what I'm going to do! I'm going to come on the Saturday holiday, then you won't have to study and we can have lots of fun."

But he came the next Thursday and insisted on helping me so that we could go in the wood. His hurry to get into the wood made him very impatient, and he hammered the table with his fist to drive some points home, and soon said:

"You know that. Come on, let's go."

So we went to what I laughingly told him was "Gog and Magog," barrows of ancient chiefs, but the delight he showed in the woods was spoiled by my resentment at being dragged from my lessons.

"You're mad," Bert said. "It's your lessons, I know—but you do know them."

"I do! Well, you're clever and I'm not, and I'm as tired as a dog."

"Oh, I'm sorry. Don't say anything, will you, or I shall get a wiggin'[23] from Mother."

"You said you should come on a Saturday!"

"They won't let me," Bert said swiftly. "Don't say anything, will you, about taking you off your study. I don't want them to stop me. I love to come, and your mother doesn't mind. The boys don't like me, though, but they're getting to," he finished hopefully.

"They've been told not to be rough with you because you're not strong. Besides, you seem like a girl sometimes."

"No, I don't!" he said indignantly. "It's you who don't know. There's lots of thin, lanky boys at high school. You only know the rough ones who play tethes[24] at school and dust you with their cap soon as they go down pit, and send you home crying with a black face. I bet they dusted you when you was little, and I bet you didn't like it. I suppose you like boys like that, though, not like me."

"You're with girls so much, it's silly."

"It isn't silly. I like girls. I like boys as well. Why can't you be with both? I think it's silly to stay just with boys all the time, especially when you can't play rough games like football."

His voice grew plaintive, and I was sorry.

"Well, you could go bird-nesting. The boys know a robin's nest in a tree. And you could play duck with them."

"I'll play anything so long as I can keep coming," he said earnestly.

"Mother and Father say you can come, so no one can stop you," I assured him.

"Oh, I like them ever so much," he said enthusiastically. "They let me talk to them about all sorts of things. Grownups usually put you off, but they don't."

.   .   .

Bert's genius for making friends soon won the entire family, and if he was late, someone looking in would ask: "Isn't Bert here yet?" And on the rare occasion when he didn't come, there was real disappointment, for each separate member looked for some special pleasure he could give. He was a mine of information and a fine organizer of games, and the fun ran high in the yard while I tried to study. When an extra one was necessary for a game, Bert would help me. But in the hurry to get out to play, he would beat the table and raise his voice energetically, and I would run out for a few minutes to the game to get rid of him, and then return to plod along in my own slow way.

One evening he exasperated me with his hammering the table and his storming, and I closed the book. He sat, lips apart, knuckles raised, staring at me, then called out:

"Mrs. Chambers, your May won't let me help her."

Mother came, amusement in her fine dark eyes: "I think it's very good of Bert to help you."

And I replied, truculently, "He doesn't help me, he only shouts at me!"

Bert apologized and coaxed and promised not to shout or hammer the table, but I refused his help and was secretly glad of the excuse. Already I had heard that his family had said, "Our Bert helps her," and I was determined to give them no chance to say that. I'd "do or die" alone. Remarks that my brothers were just "rough country lads" came to my ears; and, though I laughed it off, it nettled one to find that Bert was letting his family cross-examine him and answering all their questions.

So one afternoon in my holidays when Bert sat in our kitchen talking to Mother, my brothers came in from school, and I turned to them, laughing:

"Bert's been telling us how very nice lemon juice is for the hands!"

"I bet he uses it. His are white like a girl's, aren't they? Do you use lemon juice on your hands, Bert?"

"No, of course I don't," he said angrily.

"I bet you do, or how can they be so white? Look at ours—brown as a nut."

"They'd be several shades lighter if you'd wash them," he returned spitefully.

"Oh, would they? They are as clean as yours, only they do some work and you're lazy. Always with the girls. Daren't go with lads because you daren't fight."

Here Mother intervened—to my disappointment, for I badly wanted to see how Bert behaved towards boys when alone with them.

The next Thursday the minister [25] came up with his little son and a camera, and grouped us all on the grass plot. Bert sat with the boys and shows a smiling, boyish face on the faded photograph. We were all flustered at being photographed, and had scrambled into our Sunday clothes. But my eldest brother's dickey was not yet starched and ironed. We were at a loss, but Bert seized a piece of writing paper and fixed it under Alan's collar and arranged his tie.

"Now, if you hold your head still, it'll manage. It looks spiffin'," Bert declared with great satisfaction.

We all crowed with admiration of his smartness. But he laughed at our simplicity, saying:

"I've seen that done many a time. If you fasten them down to your shirt, it'll do even for Chapel."

We felt we had much to learn.

.   .   .

Since Mother refused to have Bert bring food, I was invited to tea at his home in his holidays. He had been on some errand and met me as I came from school. We looked into the confectioner's.

"What would you like?" Bert asked.

I said, "Some of everything," and he turned away with a laugh.

"Well, you won't get any, not even a tantafflin.[26] We don't have them till Sunday, so come thy ways."

This banter and laughter continued till we all sat down to the table. Bert and I sat on the sofa; and when his father took his place, I felt Bert draw himself together, humping himself up and bending his head over his plate. When the father talked to me, the son twitched my dress or nudged me. He hardly answered when his father spoke to him. His mother kept her eyes down and spoke only in monosyllables. But the father talked, and ate and handled the food as the man who paid for it all. He chatted amiably with me, and his young daughter [Ada] told of some prank that made us laugh. But his son nudged me so hard I felt I was misbehaving. There was such a hateful feeling coming from Bert that I was almost frightened. It was as if Prince Charming had changed into a toad.

The father went out when the meal was over, and Mrs. Lawrence said:

"He hates his father. That little minx will sit on his knee, but not the boy. He keeps his distance, he never goes near him if he can help it. He hates his father."

Bert's gaiety returned as his father's steps echoed in the entry; and when a couple of neighbour girls came in, he was sparkling with them. He seemed to be very happy to be the only man in a houseful of women, or rather girls, for his mother joined in the banter, enriching it like a dash of spice with iron caustic wit. After a noisy burst of hilarity, I thought how different it would be if a father wanted to sit quietly reading his newspaper, and I asked:

"Does Mr. Lawrence go out every night?"

"While his money lasts," said his wife, grimly.

"Oh, but then he goes to bed," put in one of the girls quickly, as if to assure me we need fear no intrusion of the father's presence.

Next time Bert was at our tea table, I offered him the cream.

"You know Bert doesn't take cream," remarked Mother.

But I pressed it on him till he said:

"I don't like it, I like the taste of the tea."

And I informed my family, "Those are the very words his father used when I passed him the cream jug!"

Bert reddened. "Yes, he doesn't take it."

And I followed up: "Fancy you inheriting his taste!" For I couldn't forget the waves of hate that came from him as he humped himself up.

One of us always went as far as the Warren with Bert, and I seemed to be the only one not reading when he was ready to start. So I went, and carried a couple of books with a string around them. The string was twisted around my finger as I passed them to him. He steadied my hand as he spun the books to unwind the string, then dashed away my books spitefully.

"Goodnight," he said laughingly.

"Goodnight, prince into a toad!" I returned.

But he was running and did not turn to answer me.

.   .

His auburn-haired brother [Ernest] was again to spend the holidays at home, bringing his fiancée. I was taken into the parlour and shown how it was "to be tidivated till you won't know it for the same room." The family showed me her portrait—a different girl, if I remember rightly, but handsome.[27] I didn't see the visitors, but Bert told me all about them.

"Mother's wild because they lay on the sofa all one afternoon," he said to me as we walked. "It was raining, and they couldn't go out, and they lay on the sofa and talked. Mother's furious about it, but I can't see how it matters, can you?"

No, I couldn't see, but I thought his mother knew best. Bert looked worried.

"But why should it matter? What is it that matters? What is it that's not right about it? They just lay and talked softly. Perhaps they went to sleep, I don't know. But what if they did? I think it's silly to make such a fuss, or any fuss at all. Why should there be a fuss because two people lay on the sofa to talk instead of sitting on it and talking? We were all sitting about doing something. I thought they seemed more out of the way on the sofa. Mother's carried on ever since they went about it. I wish she'd let the matter drop. You'd think it was a crime by the fuss it has raised! I can't see any need for fuss, and I don't see any harm or anything wrong, do you?"

I was as puzzled as Bert, and we walked in silence for a while. He seemed to be worrying like a puppy with a shoe. Then he said:

"There's other things I'd like to know. This 'safety in numbers'—what does she mean? Safety from what? Anything I ask brings, 'Wait till you're older.' I hate growing older to find things out. It's like getting lost before you can find the proper way. I wonder why they don't tell us what it is that's so wrong, if there is anything wrong. If there's a mystery, tell us straight out, and let us see the reason for making a fuss, instead of hiding something from us that we have to get to know. What could that be? I am a kid. I don't know. I ask why shouldn't they lie on the sofa and talk? And Mother says, 'Because they shouldn't!' But I want to know why, and that's what she won't explain!"

"I give up!" I announced.

"Yes, and you're always wondering if you're doing something you shouldn't. At least I am."

"So should I be if I went about with a lot of boys as you do with girls!"

"It doesn't matter. Oh, what do you think? Mabel says I'm a monster. Imagine, a monster! Me a monster!" he cried.

"I bet she means it, too," I said.

"She pretended to, but she doesn't really. She doesn't know what it means. I was making fun of her, and she got mad. Why should she mean it?" he asked aggressively.

"Because perhaps she thinks you don't play fair. You don't stay friends with just me but have a lot of friends because you like each one for something the others haven't got."

"Well, that's all right, isn't it?" he wanted to know. "I do like one for this, and one for that, but what's wrong with that?"

"I bet that's why she called you a monster, just the same!" I answered.

.   .   .

A few days later, I had tea again at Bert's home. The father had come from the pit and ate heartily of his dinner of meat and vegetables, ignoring the attitude of his wife and son who sat next me on the sofa, humped up and uncivil. The father talked of his work and of my grandmother, and listened indulgently to his little daughter [Ada]. I tried to find a word to fit Bert's attitude and discovered it was *vengeful*. He was totally unlike the boy who lit up the rather drab room with a dancing light like a sunbeam. He seemed to gather the gloom of the back yard into his being and crouch among the shabbiness like something sinister. The wooden chairs, the well-worn sofa, the dresser with the ill-fitting drawers showed only honest wear and tear of years of service, but Bert seemed to send out jagged waves of hate and loathing that made me shudder. The father was hungry after his day's work in the pit and ate heartily as he talked—evidently so used to the atmosphere of animosity that he did not feel it. I wanted to get away. The queer behaviour of mother and son made me tremble internally till I couldn't swallow my food. The mother poured us more tea, and her husband drank thirstily.

"I was dry," he said to me. "You like milk in your tea? You should try it wi'out. You'd soon get used to it, then you'd like it better. You get the taste of the tea. Milk just spoils the taste of the tea. You just try wi'out."

He rose from the table and bade me "Come and see us again before long," and went out immediately.

As his step echoed in the entry, his son shed his malignancy. He brought in a basket full of clothes lately off the line, and as we folded them the mother said:

"Eh, our Ern has to use handkerchiefs only mangled. She won't iron them. You'd think she would, wouldn't you? Aye, that's what you get in lodgings. He says he's so ashamed that he hates to pull it out of his pocket in company. Imagine a young man like our Ern having to be ashamed of his handkerchief! It doesn't take a minute to rub the iron over them. Well, his mother never sent him out ashamed of his things. Aye, you'll learn, all of you, when you go into lodgings. Do some of you good!"

There was a laugh, for the two neighbour sisters had come in, and Mabel said: "Especially the monster!"

.   .   .

A few days later I had an errand to do in my dinner hour. As I entered the store, Bert turned from the counter and importantly showed me his purchase, expounding on the difference of two qualities in a high voice that arrested the attention of customers and assistants. But Bert's back was turned to them, so he did not see the broadening smile on all faces, which broke into a titter as he announced, "But these are really very nice," and happily bade me goodbye.

At the counter, the young man said, "He's not right in his head!"

I was shocked, but he shook his head.

"Anybody'll tell you he's not right in his head!" he insisted. "Do you know another lad as 'ud stand and talk like a woman about groceries? Do you ever see him with a gang o' lads? Do you ever see him without two, three girls? You can't tell me he's right in his head. Anybody'll tell you the same!"

In the following years this accusation was so common that I learned to answer it with only one remark: "I wish I had his head!"

.   .   .

As the autumn drove us indoors, Bert begged permission to bring a pack of playing cards—the first to gain admittance into our house.

"Not to play cards but games," he explained to Mother.

So we sat around the big dining-table and played games till we had learned all he knew. When we grew tired of them, we asked him to teach us whist. He sat shuffling the cards in his hands below the table, and whispered:

"I'll teach *you*, but not these."

"Why?" I demanded resentfully.

"They'd be slow," he muttered. "You could teach them afterwards."

I shrank from him as I whispered, "You're a snake!"

Immediately he dealt to the three eldest of us, and proceeded to initiate us into the deep mysteries of whist. By hectoring and scolding and ridiculing, he eventually got us playing a fair game, and then scolded us for dealing clumsily, for letting him see our cards.

"If I catch a single glimpse, I know it and where it is," he assured us. But we protested, "You can't remember!"

"I can and I do, and I play accordingly."

"Well, then, don't look," we advised.

"I can't help but look if you give me the chance," he declared. "It's you who've got to keep me from seeing. You must keep them absolutely out of my sight. It's your fault for letting me see, not mine for looking."

But no matter how we dealt, he could see if he was in the mood to say so, and he suggested we all play as if we were gamblers "out for blood." Some of us told him he would be a bad man, but others of us agreed with him that he was sharper than the rest of us.

That he was clever was a fact we never disputed, but we often wondered why he came so regularly. Only when he had to help his father in the allotment (which we called "common gardens") was he absent on his holiday.

"Why do you come to our house when you don't like us?" some of us asked him.

"Of course I like you!" he protested indignantly.

"Well, you're always grumbling at us and finding fault."

"No, I'm not. I'm setting you right. That shows I like you. You don't think I should take the trouble to bother with you if I didn't like you, do you? I'm going to teach you to dance now."

First he taught us songs for dance tunes. *The Lowther Arcade* was sung by the rest while he taught me the steps.

"We'll polka first because you're as light as a feather," he decided. "Then we can both take a new one."

How hard Bert worked, till he was flushed and panting. And when we all could "get around," he declared it was time to learn the waltz, and held forth very wisely on the grace and elegance of the waltz.

"Now one, two, three," but I always broke into a polka, and next week he announced:

"I was wrong—it should be one, two, three, four."

"But who told you?" we inquired.

And, reddening, he admitted it was his father, and having broken the ice and allowed his father to have any good points, he talked a lot about Mr. Lawrence's knowledge of dancing. It was easy to see he was proud of him as an authority on dancing.

"I don't know anybody else's father who knows the science about dancing, do you? Some can dance, of course, but Father knows how to teach it, he says."

And he repeated his father's praise of the different dances as I ran down to the Warren with him on his way home.

As we slowly grew more adept, we complained that our kitchen floor was too small for us all to be up together, but Bert dismissed the notion:

"Father says you should be able to dance on a threepenny bit. Come on, now, and everybody sing."

So we sang, and danced, and laughed, and enjoyed it all.

.　　.　　.

High School was over [July, 1901], and Bert was to go out to work. Mother was very interested in his search through Nottingham, which was her native place, and they talked about the different firms with mutual interest. When eventually he became a clerk in a small concern making surgical bandages,[28] she was very disappointed that he should be going into such an old building without modern lighting and ventilation, and feared for his health.

"How awful!" I said. "Surgical bandages!"

"Why awful?" Bert asked, and I explained that the thought of all the suffering these bandages represented might harm him. He shuddered then, and said with a grimace:

"Their brass is as good as the next one's, and we've got to have money—so I've got to put up with it."

Mother had known the two old ladies—overlookers of the concern—when she was a girl, and so Bert talked of them and imitated them till we laughed to exhaustion. But he sat and rested after his walk on Saturday afternoon, and looked flushed with feverishly bright eyes. Anxiously my mother questioned him, and he shuddered.

"Oh, those old women! They smell so funny. They think I'm not strong and fuss around me, and I get the full blast of that stuffy, musty smell and the scent of the pomade they use on their hair! I'm sure I nearly faint. But they mean to be kindness itself, and so I shall have to put up with it."

And he sent us into gusts of laughter, mimicking their tones in forcing him to accept and use cough lozenges they had bought for him. But my mother saw trouble coming, for the healthy tinge under his fair skin gave place to a flush and his eyes glittered.

.　　.　　.

Then tragedy struck. Ernest, the auburn-haired brother, was so ill in London that his parents had been sent for. He had paid a flying visit home at Goose Fair, and had seemed abounding with life. I had seen his dazzling

573

smile with a touch of the audacious which added to his attraction. Now he was at death's door.

On a Saturday night in October [1901], I was at the Station to meet a friend of Mother's, standing as arranged under the one lamp. The train came in, the carriage doors flew open; but in the stream of passengers I saw only one figure, short, black, bowed, but tearless, stunned with grief but wearily attending the work of the moment. Her husband followed heavily behind as she went to attend to the coffin's transfer. Her face looked shrunken under the small bonnet; grief and pain seemed concentrated in the pitiful eyes.

My mother's friend was kissing me under the lamp, but all I could say was, "Look at poor Mrs. Lawrence, she's brought Ern home in his coffin!" The night was very black, and the city friend complained bitterly of dark, country roads. But the blackness seemed in keeping with my thoughts of Ern in his coffin and the family grieving—and now for evermore a sadness in our lives like a black band running through bright colours.

.   .   .

Bert did not visit us for a week or two, and sadness seemed to envelop the world, for he was sickening with a cold. Then there was a heavy, grey fog for several days, and he went down with pneumonia. Daily at school we talked of the tragedy of Mrs. Lawrence's life and the progress of Bert's illness. As the crisis approached, there seemed a breathlessness among people. "Eh, that Bertie Lawrence'll ne'er o'er break it," would say a woman to me on my way to school; or "It'll be t'biggest wonder in t'world if he isna laid wi' t'other lad," would say a collier on my way home. Our house was stricken. Father and Mother talked of Mrs. Lawrence's troubles, which were never out of Mother's mind, while we waited for the crisis.

"It'll break his mother's heart if Bert dies. He's all she's got, all that counts with her. He's her one consolation for all she's gone through in life."

"Well, perhaps he won't die," Father said. "The doctor says there is a spot about the size of a crown on his lungs that is clear. If that can be kept clear, he may live—that's what I heard today."

The crisis passed, the long slow climb back to health began. I went to see Bert one Sunday after tea. The night was black and foggy, and the lights of our house beckoned to me as I turned into the pasture where only darkness and emptiness surrounded and almost daunted me. Down the Warren along the bridle path, over the fence into the road that skirted the Reservoir, down Engine Lane, past the pit, past the sheep-bridge, by the Breach, up the Brickyard Closes, and I was at their bay window. Up the entry into the back yard where the only light was over the scullery. My knock brought footsteps downstairs, and Mrs. Lawrence held a light to see who was at the door.

"Why, child!" she exclaimed, "this black night! Aye, he'll be pleased to see you. I tell him his heart's more at your house than at ours."

I followed her upstairs and down a narrow, narrow passage to a tiny bare room like a big box, where Bert lay on a tumbled bed, gaunt, flushed, and bright-eyed, his cheeks sunken, the bones showing keenly, but the old smile on his face—his gaiety springing back to life. His voice wavered and cracked and went hoarse as he asked about us all and about the animals and what we had been doing and if we missed him. He was already planning his next visit eagerly.

"When can I go, Mother? When shall I be ready? How long before I can walk?"

"That's what I want to know, my lad, and it can't be too soon for me. Eh, child, I'm worn out, cooped up here night and day. Believe me—he can't get downstairs quick enough."

"I can't walk," he giggled, "but I shall soon. As soon as I can stand up, I shall squirm around somehow. I'm sick of lying here. I'm tired out with lying."

"Aye, we're both sick of it," Mrs. Lawrence said. "Look at him, child, look at the length of him. He's grown out of his clothes. He'll need a new suit before he can be dressed, and new boots, I'll wager."

Bert tossed ceaselessly on the bed, tumbling the clothes about. He seemed like a jackknife opening and shutting.

"Lie still," I said.

He shook his head violently, and in his cracked voice declared:

"I can't—I can't keep still a moment. I am twitching all over. Look, I can't control myself!" He giggled as his knees shot up and down. "You hold me. She can't!"

"Eh, child, he wants me to hold him," said Mrs. Lawrence. "He wants me to hold him on my lap like a child, but I can't. He's too big and too long. And thin as he is, he's too heavy for me now."

"Don't be a baby," I laughed at him.

"I'm not," he wheezed. "I just want somebody to hold me still. It's awful, twitching like this." He giggled again. "I think Mother should tie me down with ropes."

"Aye, poor lad," Mrs. Lawrence said, "he tosses even in his sleep."

Bert coughed and seemed exhausted, lying flushed and bright-eyed, but his knees shot up and down.

I was overcome with pity, and knew if I did not soon get out I should cry, and though they begged me to stay, I dared not and made the excuse I must go on to service.

"Why, child, it's late," said Mrs. Lawrence. "Our girls have been gone ages."

I said I must hurry away, I wanted to hear the church service.

"Church!" Mrs. Lawrence's eyes bored into me, and her thoughts seemed to shout, "She's got a young man!"

But I looked back steadily, and Bert was croaking:

"What do you want to go to church for? Stay here with me."

"Nay," I said, "I want to hear the service. I like the church service."

"She wants to hear the service, don't you, child?" Mrs. Lawrence said. "I don't blame you. I'd like to hear a service myself. Eh, won't Chapel seem grand when I get there again!"

"You've not been away any longer than I have," Bert croaked, and jerked over. "I don't know when I shall go to Chapel again. When shall I go, Mother?"

"I wish I knew, lad," she lamented.

"Well, write me a long account of you all and about what you're all doing." Bert coughed and jerked about on the tumbled bed. "Tell them all I shall soon be up, then we'll do all the things we like to do. Goodnight, fraud!"

"Fraud!" his mother repeated, as we went downstairs. "That's because you won't stay. But I know how it is, child. You want a bit of brightness for a change with that long walk in the darkness and all. I wonder when I shall get a change. Eh, even the black night smells fresh after that room all these weeks. I sometimes wonder what it's all for. A few years and his mother comes second. Well, goodnight, child. I hope you get home safe. It's an awful walk all alone. Tell your mother about him growing so. She'll know what that means in extra expense!"

My mother was aghast that I had not stayed at their request:

"You should have put your feelings in your pocket and tried to have been company for them. I'm ashamed of you! You should have shown more kindness."

.   .   .

It was a long time before Bert drove up [to the Haggs] with Father, and we all made much of him, delighted at his recovery.

"I do like spoiling a bit," he told me. "I need a little spoiling to bring out the best in me. I'm much nicer here than at home. I've been an awful expense, you know."

He sounded fearful of the debt, so I tried to comfort him by saying:

"The expense would have been as great if you had died, and they still have you."

Then he laughed ruefully.

"When I was little and folks made me mad, I always used to say, 'You'll be sorry for that when I am dead.' But now I know it doesn't make much difference."

A long holiday with an aunt who kept a boardinghouse at the seaside [29] restored him, and sent him back ready to enjoy life as he used. Many letters had passed between him and us, and now he filled in all the details of life in a seaside boardinghouse. And he was angry with me when I said that now he had described it all so vividly, I never need go.

"It ought to make you want to go," he said. "Why, I've described the bluebells to Mother, but she's got to come to get their scent, and to really see them as they are, to sort of feel them."

Mrs. Lawrence came with him, and after tea she set out, but would have my mother go too.

"Come along," said Mrs. Lawrence. "I want to talk. He's talked about these bluebells till I know all I want to know about them, but there was no pacifying him till I'd come to smell them. I did smell those he brought, but he declared the whole woodful smelled different, and made me take that long walk. Aye, if he gets a thing in his head, he never rests until he's got it into yours!"

She chuckled often as she talked good-naturedly, but her son winced and called two of my brothers [Hubert and Bernard]. They walked behind the two mothers, who sauntered deep in conversation; and when they came to the particular spot Bert thought so beautiful, he called a halt, and his mother turned her head and said, "Aye, they're lovely," and continued her conversation. My young brothers saw Bert redden and look so disappointed that they felt bound to call more of her attention, so they lay down and rolled in the deep carpet of bluebells. Bert had an unexpected outlet for his disappointment, and pounced on the two young boys and punched and thumped them. His mother laughed and cried:

"Hit him back, hit him back. Serve him right. What's a few bluebells when all the wood's just carpeted with them. Hit him hard."

My mother sent our boys home, but Mrs. Lawrence protested:

"I believe in retaliation. This 'bear and forbear' gospel is too one-sided for me! Give him some of his own medicine, I say."

.   .   .

Since Bert was recuperating, he spent much time at our farm, the walk back and forth thought to be beneficial. He roamed the fields with these two young brothers; and when they spotted the first mushrooms, his long legs carried him to them first, and he pocketed them, to the disgust of the young boys, who argued:

"They are on our land—they're ours."

"Findings' keepings," Bert retorted hotly.

"You didn't find 'em. It's just cos you've got such long legs. They're ours on our land."

"They're wild, and wild things are free for him who's sharp enough to get them."

"Well, I don't reckon to be as sharp as you, but I spread salt to make them grow, and so you're stealing them."

They brought the dispute home, and Bert was allowed to keep them.

"All that fuss," he said to me angrily, "over four or five mushrooms, a measly few like that! Be different if it was a score."

"Yes, why did you make such a fuss?" I asked.

He threw up his head defiantly.

"I found them, and they're wild, salt or no salt."

I shook my head.

"Well, if you want to know, I want them for my father's tea," he announced.

"Well!" I cried in sheer surprise, "and you hating him as you hate him! You don't hate him as you pretend you do, or you'd never make trouble with your friends to take their mushrooms for him!"

"I have to hate him for Mother's sake," he replied. "But I can take mushrooms home when I find them, and they'll be for his tea because he loves wild things you find. I hope you're satisfied, now you know!"

The next time he came, Bert brought a small gift for my brother who had spread salt, and Bert looked at us all and said frankly:

"I find I have no sense of possession. I just want to grab anything without thinking it belongs to somebody."

And we all thought him much nicer than ever for such a frank admission. He continued to roam the fields with the two young lads, and often brought home mushrooms, giving them up to Mother, who complimented him, to the great disgust of the boys who complained that they knew where to look and first spotted them. But Bert reached them first and smilingly took the credit for industry in searching for them.

This rankled, as also did the memory of his attack in the bluebells, so the younger of the two boys [Bernard] challenged him to "put on the gloves" and soon got the worst of it, because of Bert's long arms and better science, and nearly five more years of age. This tussle cemented a friendship that taught my brother to say:

"I love Bert for himself, and alone, but I hate him in a crowd."

.　　　.　　　.

We sometimes talked in the dialect. Bert was very good and gave us samples new to us.

"Hoad the faece, woman!" his father had said to his mother.

I told this to my grandmother, who drily remarked:

"His father said what he meant, 'Hoad the faece.' Thee calls it 'shut up.' That's what he meant, 'Shut your faece.' Aye, that an old 'un, 'Hoad the faece!'"

And her eyes grew wistful with memories.

.　　　.　　　.

Bert drove with Father to the hay fields and sat about in the sunshine which he loved. It could never get too hot for him, he said, to which I retorted that it would if he had to work; for when I took the lunch, Father made me work while they ate, and I found the July heat exhausting. At dusk we rode home, singing, in the wagons, passing under the lime trees that scented the evening air and felt glad to be alive in the world, declaring there could be no better life. Bert was so tall now that he could look down at me and sing:

> She looked up and I looked down,
> Handsome, sunburnt Johnnie Brown.

"True, except for the 'handsome,' isn't it?" he said.

Bert wanted to have a picnic with a fiddle, but Father objected:

"I shan't have that lot of lasses that traipse about with you. We've got to get this hay up while the weather lasts, and the lads'll never work while the lasses are around."

The lasses that "traipsed" about with Bert were neighbours and his sisters. It was rare to see him alone, but on Friday afternoons the colliers received their wages at the Company's offices. As the men were not yet home from the pits, wives and daughters went to the offices. During his convalescence I saw Bert several times on his way to fetch his father's money, for he had to pass my grandmother's where she and I watched the stream of black and white, as the black colliers passed their women folk. He was a very different Bert from the one we knew, striding along, head bent in thought, paying no attention to his surroundings. Sometimes the collier boys jostled him in passing, and the swift lift of his head and thrust of his shoulders made me feel he had lots of fight in him, if only his strength would hold out. My grandmother would remark, "Eh, that Bertie Lawrence is none long for this world, I'm thinking." The other boys laughed at him for associating with girls. Kindly folk dubbed him "Jack among the Maidens." Youths passed him up as a "tea leaf," but the majority were harsh in their judgment, the general remark being "He should see a doctor." He was well aware of all this but disdained it.

"I like girls, and I'm going about with them whatever they say. Why shouldn't I?"

"Why not boys?" I asked.

"Girls are ever so much nicer. Besides, I don't like boys' games, they're so rough. It's beyond me why they make such a fuss about it."

.   .   .

One summer evening, returning from my grandmother's, I met Bert coming out of the wild land we called the "Gullets." It bordered the Reservoir on the opposite bank from our fields, and led into the wood once part of Sherwood Forest. With permission we could enter the wood and climb the long hillside under the splendid oak and ash, elm and beech and alder, to Robin Hood's Well and Maid Marian's Dancing Green. On one side of the hill in the deep valley were the ruins of Beauvale Abbey. On our side, across the shallow valley, the windows of Felley Priory flashed in the afternoon sun at just one particular angle, betraying for a few minutes the presence of the Priory which otherwise would never be suspected, the grey stones merging into the face of the hill under whose brow it stood. How often I have run to catch that instant's flash of silver from the windows!

At this romantic spot, suddenly around the corner came Bert with a troop of girls—his sister and cousin and two others. It was midsummer holidays, so I invited Bert and his sister to come up the following afternoon and bring a friend of mine, too.

"And can we bring these, too?" begged Bert, indicating his companions. "They've never been, you know. We couldn't leave them. They would so like to come."

I couldn't say no, and I daren't invite so many. So I compromised with, "Oh, well, you'll see when you start. Perhaps they won't feel like a long walk if it's hot!"

But they all appeared, and an uproarious time we had with all our family joining in. And what a lot we ate! Every crumb of bread was devoured, and we had to bake a new batch to be ready for breakfast. For a long time afterwards I was chaffed about inviting a Sunday School tribe by various friends who declared they should have met such a tribe with the remark: "I'm at home and I wish you all were!" as if they had been my parents.

.   .   .

One day I was telling my family of my visit to a palmist, and Bert watched and listened so intently that I urged him to have his palm read.

"Oh, I daren't," he shivered. "I daren't."

Pressed for a reason, he admitted:

"I know I should believe it. Fancy knowing what the future holds! I wouldn't dare to peep, would you?"

He appealed to Mother, who said she thought it a wise provision that the future was hidden from us. Bert shook his head.

"I'm frightened to even think of the future. I've a feeling I should be terrified to know what is in store for me." He shuddered. "No, I'll never peep. 'Enough for the day is the evil thereof.'"

He was very much in earnest.

.   .   .

One Saturday afternoon we were coming from the well with water, talking of *David Copperfield*.

"I bet you like Agnes," Bert said.

Of course I liked Agnes.

"I bet you think David was a fool to marry Dora."

I thought David married Dora out of the kindness of his heart.

"Well," said Bert, "I don't think he did. I think he married her because he wanted to. He liked her best. I like her best, too."

I said she was a silly, frivolous thing, useless and babyish, a plaything.

"I know," Bert replied, "and I know Agnes is the best woman and would make the best wife. But I like Dora best, and I should want to marry her instead of Agnes. I like her because she is frivolous and useless."

"I'm certain you'd have more sense than to marry her," I said.

But he insisted sadly, "I should want her so badly because she was so nice to look at. I should marry her."

"And make a rod for your own back?" I asked incredulously.

"I should be doing that, shouldn't I?" He flushed. "But I know I should marry her because she would make me feel there was no hard, rough work, or ugliness, or hate, but only nice things."

The next heroines we fell fond of were those of *Adam Bede*. I was polishing the small windowpanes with a chamois, and Bert stood leaning against the gate nearby, and suddenly said with sadness in his voice and look:

"You don't like Hetty, do you?"

"No," I said emphatically.

"I knew you wouldn't, but I do. I can't help it, and really I'm glad I do like her best, because hardly anybody will like her. She's frivolous and pretty and wants a different life, and so you think she's wrong, but I don't."

"I think you are sorry for her because of her punishment. But I think we ought to know better than to do things and not expect to be punished."

"I know that, but still I like a girl like Hetty."

"But not to marry!" I asked.

"Why?"

"Why, because she was foolish and would always be foolish, and a foolish wife is a nuisance, and you'd always have trouble."

He shook his head sadly.

"I like Hetty all the same, though she isn't a patch on Dinah."

It was a different story when we came to *The Cloister and the Hearth.* I was praising the description of the journey across Europe, which delighted me immensely.

"But Reade's so proud of it," Bert said, superciliously.

"Why shouldn't he be?" I asked.

"It's just research," he declared. "Anybody could do it."

"Well, you are funny! A man who does some hard work shouldn't be proud of it, but a girl who apes the fine lady, and a girl who is empty-headed you like. Why *do* you like girls to be vain and silly?"

"You're quite disgusted, aren't you?" he mocked.

"Yes, and it isn't sour grapes, though I know you'd like to say it is."

Among new books we read Barrie's *Tommy and Grizel,* and I remember a few years later Bert coming across the yard laboring with the great heat and a packet of books that seemed very heavy, and gasping out as we met him:

"Barrie's wife's left him for a writer he had helped ever so much. Don't let's ever read any of his books."

We stood in the sunshine, stunned, asking questions which he answered briefly, insisting over and over that we "VOW never to read any of his books. Let's make a pact!" [30]

. . .

When sufficiently recovered, Bert became a pupil-teacher [1902]. He was in the boys' department of the school connected with the Chapel we all attended.[31] He was to take lessons from the headmaster [George Holderness] for an hour before school commenced, then teach a class. I had lessons from the headmaster from eight till nine in the girls' department. Bert begged me to look out for him and "give him a smile to cheer," for he was frightened to death. The sort of boy he was not strong enough to play with he was now to try to teach. All the boys' classes were in the one big room used for Sunday School, and there was one classroom besides. On the mornings he took his class of boys for a lesson in the classroom, I sent in my watch to be set correctly, and he generally sent a scribbled note back. It was always signed "D. H. L.," and it was by his initials he preferred to be called. He looked a little anxious with his forty-odd boys passing in to their seats.

"What sort of question do you get?" he asked one day. "This morning my question was: 'Why do we teach boys poetry?' What do I know about teaching boys poetry?"

"What did you say?" I asked.

"What could I say, except that it is to train memory and teach good expression?"

He was much encouraged to find that the headmaster marked him "Correct," and that he was hailed as far above average at doing his own thinking. We clustered about him, admiring his cleverness of which he seemed far less conscious than we were. "He knows everything," we pupil-teachers, both boys and girls, declared. "He's never been stuck with a question yet." And his doubt of himself and his modesty only added to our sincere esteem of him.

But out on the street people would say, as he raised his cap in passing: "He's not right in his head."

And one of us would answer viciously:

"He's a sight more in his head than you have!"

Bert's little band of followers was enlarged, and his home of an evening was lively with several girls and a boy or two come for help from D. H. L., who sat at the table hammering something into one or another, or studying while they and his family larked. His concentration was a marvel to us. Suddenly he would look up and take part in the general conversation of which his mother was the centre.

"The women say I shall never get old mixing like this with the young ones," Mrs. Lawrence beamed.

And Bert observed indulgently:

"The little woman fancies herself among the lads and lasses. It is rather flattering, isn't it, Lyddy?" (Her name was Lydia.)

There were derisive cries of "Oh, Dickie!" for Bert would not acknowledge his third name Richard from us. His mother vigorously applauded.

How different a mother and son from when the father was present! She liked the attention of the little group, and he liked playing host. Her caustic wit and positive advice drew the young people who delighted in their young host instead of an elderly father who might have scowled on their intrusion. The mother was a different woman from the complaining housewife of the mornings. The banter of the young folk stimulated her, and their inexperience of life brought out her most emphatic statements and her opinion of people, so that to them she sounded very wise and absolutely sure of herself. And at the back of all was pity that she had a husband who spent his evenings in public houses. We spoke with bated breath of the story she told some of us of being put out one night before one of her children was born.

"He put me out and locked the door," she said in bitter remembrance of the night she spent in an outhouse. "Aye, there's a reason for hate and nasty temper. It was in them before they were born."

Some of the group were so impressed that it seemed a duty to stand up for Mrs. Lawrence against the divided sympathy found among the older generation.

.   .   .

Occasionally the girls discussed him:
"Isn't Bert nice!"
"Isn't he gentlemanly!"
"He never spoons."
"There's never any soft mushy talk where Bert is. You should have heard him rave over a note I showed him from a fellow. It started, 'My own sweetheart.' I thought it was spiffin', but Bert said it was 'drivil and piffle and utter rot.'"

.   .   .

We used to laugh at Bert as examinations approached and he feared he might fail. We didn't think he could ever fail on any subject, but he would look desperate and say: "What if I fail?" We would say he was too modest, that if we knew half he knew we should go down on our knees and give heart-felt thanks. But he refused to be assured and would look tragic and say, "Wouldn't it be awful if I did fail!" When results came out, his name would top the list or come second. But not before he had made himself look quite ill with worry and doubt.

To prepare for my final exams, I lodged near school. One evening, alone in the house, I was surprised on answering a knock to find Bert at the door. He came in saying he had come to see my digs. Blinking in the light, he looked tired, having just come from an oral test.

"It's nothing, you know," I assured him.

"No, but you feel a goat just the same."

As we stood talking, the family returned and made a great fuss of him having been at school where the oral tests were made.

"He's as clever as they make 'em," said the man, when Bert had gone.

"He's more than that," said his wife. "He can draw the girls like flies around sugar."

"He did the best of all of them tonight," the man said. "He's far and away above average. Strikes me he'll make his way in the world. Keep your eye on him. He's got something about him. You just wait and see!"

.   .   .

My mother wanted an errand done in the neighbouring town of Ilkeston, and I was expected to walk from my lodgings after school. But I had heard so many evil tales of a long, lonely lane to be travelled—all the girls assuring me "It isn't safe, I dare not go alone to save my life"—that I determined to ask Bert to go with me. So after tea I went to the Lawrence house. He was studying at the table, his mother in her place between the fireplace and the window, doing some mending. They looked up in mild surprise at my entrance, and I spoke at once.

"Mrs. Lawrence, you know we always come here when we want a kindness done. May Bert go to Ilkeston with me?"

She gave him a nod of command as she said:

"Why, yes, child!"

I told her why I dare not go alone. She agreed heartily.

"It isn't fit to go alone, and there's no occasion with our Bert here."

He had pitched his books into the dresser, gathered up his papers, and was pulling on his cap.

"Come on," he said, "the shops will be closed. We'll have to sprint."

Down the entry, across the [public house?] yard, where he said: "You'd find Father in there!" Up Hill Top, then a sharp turn down a narrow footpath, where ash pits spilled over on one side, and on the other the land dropped abruptly to the valley, green and quiet before us.

"It always seems to me I've been here before in a former existence," I said, as we ran down the steep, rough path, and came into the still valley lying in shadow with an odd cottage or two and a tiny chapel with knarled old trees whose roots ran over the narrow path.

Bert struck a tree with a bare patch of earth all around it.

"This has been played around for generations."

"It should have a name like a lane or corner," I said as we hurried on. "It's just as much a landmark. Can't you feel the generations of people that have trod this path?"

For the still, summer evening seemed communicative of the life that had travelled the ancient paths since time was. Across the flat, green water-meadows we went, and at last into the lane of evil repute ending at the tram lines.

"Did you notice we never met a single soul from the Brockhills' to here?" Bert observed as we waited for a tram.

We reached the shops and did my errand, and returned as we had come. But the glow of color had deepened in the sky, and the water-meadows reflected the pink in shallow pools in the vivid green grass. The little wild flowers took on a saintliness in the shadowed valley where sound only came like an echo in the still air.

"Even the air seems violet," I remarked, "and the valley seems full of what has gone before, doesn't it?"

That set Bert talking about fairy tales. As we gained the high land, the flaming sunset met us in startling grandeur, and a faint breeze wafted away the magic spell of the valley.

"I believe people who write fairy stories feel as I felt in the valley," I said, "but I'm sure that sense of all that has been means much more than fairy tales."

"To you it does, but what about these?" Bert asked, indicating the mean street and playing children. "Fairy tales may teach them to look for what's behind. Anyway they need the fun of fairy tales. You do," he sighed, "when you live among bricks and mortar. I know."

We had now reached the main road, and with a nod and "Goodnight," we went our different ways.

That same walk taught me how differently we saw things. Bert talked about it and took all the girls he liked over the same ground. "But it wasn't the same at all," he complained one noon as we strolled to school in the heat.

I never spoke of it nor went over the same paths again, knowing that the magic of the atmosphere could never be recaptured, but only spoiled, by consciously searching for it.

.   .   .

That summer a young assistant master was appointed in his department, and D. H. L. took him home. As always with a new acquaintance whom he liked, he lionized him so that they were rarely seen apart. This newcomer was anxious to go down a mine. One of our teachers arranged it, and permission was given for a certain number. D. H. L. said his sister wanted to come, but the number had already been chosen and none of us would withdraw to make room for her. The official who had obtained our permit was very upset lest she should come and so increase the number allowed, and get him blamed.

"You'll have to tell her that she can't come," Bert ordered me, and carrying out this order turned him cold and haughty, and he said many mean things about me.

At the pit-head, Bert ignored me; but as we were five or six in the party, I hardly noticed it, except to be amused that his sister's whim should mean so much to him. We explored the pit under the guidance of a miner not at all pleased with the job, and, returning up the shaft subdued and impressed by the sight of men on their knees at the coal face, we came to the surface black and quiet. As we turned home, silenced by all we had seen of ways by which man must earn bread, Bert was the first to speak.

"Didn't it blow hard coming up the shaft! Didn't it blow up your trousers!"

And an older teacher whom we all loved said absently:

"It did!"

We looked at one another in comic dismay, and, feeling something wrong, she looked around at us.

"What did I say? What was it Bert said? Oh, come now, do tell me. Perhaps it isn't as dreadful as you make me think it is!"

The laughter that followed the telling was a great relief to the sombre thoughts produced by the miners at work, and lifted a little the ban under which I was expected to squirm.

.   .   .

That winter [1902–1903?] Bert had an opportunity to earn a few shillings on market night keeping accounts for the leading pork butcher. He shivered as he told us, dreading the publicity.

"Don't pass by when you go to science class," he begged. "Bang on the window or something to let me see you, and I shan't feel so lonely."

We promised faithfully to visit him, though he would be on the other side of the glass. So as we went to science class, we each of us singly drew his attention as he sat on a high stool at the desk in the butcher's shop just beyond the window display. As we returned, we stood arm-in-

arm the full width of the window and grinned in sympathy with him in
his prison. He wore his cap and looked cold, and smiled back anxiously
and enviously, and there we faced him and cheered him up, he assured us,
by not passing him by forgotten. Not until a customer claimed his attention did we move away, though shoved and pushed by the milling crowd.

. . .

Bert's Saturday visits were a matter of course with us but, we were
given to understand, much resented by his family. His mother often said
to my father that "Our Bert might as well pack his box" and stay with us,
but Father laughed and said Bert could come just when he liked. He was
always welcome, she would have to suit herself. So he continued. His
elder sister [Emily] came "to see what was the great attraction," and
complained unceasingly about the distance.

"I don't see why our Bert comes so far."

Bert sat beside her, polite and attentive. He insisted that it didn't seem
far to him.

"I declare we can't keep him back," said Emily. "Just as soon as he's
had his dinner, he's up and off. Never mind what we say, he's bound he's
going to the Haggs, and we can't hold him."

We all laughed, and took her to see the well in the wood, and then
she sat and rested, "ready for that awful walk back." Bert looked very
miserable sitting quietly instead of doing the things he liked. He was the
very model of a young brother, obedient to an elder sister's command
that he behave properly.

"She thinks she's got him under her thumb," we said among ourselves,
pitying him.

She took him away in the early evening, and as "Goodnights" were
called down the Warren, Bert turned and sent a flashing glance which
told us he would soon be back.

. . .

We all looked to Bert for some special delight. My mother liked his
light chat as he rested after the long walk. Then others of us would take
him into the wood which held an attraction at every season of the year;
and when he brought a paint box and sat painting a little scene, we thought
him wonderful. At the crowded tea table, we all liked to talk, and after
tea there were generally some lessons done, for my sister [Jessie], now a
pupil-teacher in the village a mile from home,[32] was his pupil. He insisted on helping her from the first, and they would pore over their books

at a side table while the evening work went on—milking, bathing the little children before the kitchen fire, finishing up some baking perhaps. And then, all being finished, we would join together again and sing songs, or sometimes we would dance, and sometimes read aloud in turn from a book we all wanted to read at once. It was a splendid time for all of us, and Bert was always the centre to whom we all looked as leader, a position he thoroughly enjoyed.

From this jollity I had to withdraw because of approaching examinations. I gave up every diversion to reserve my energy for the long day at school, the long walk, and the evening's study, and soon I was little more than an outsider in the Saturday fun. But Bert grew more popular, for now the little children were old enough to appreciate him, and they confided secrets in him, showed him their playing place in the wood, and begged for stories from him. And always there was a book we "simply must" read that Bert brought from the library. He would gather currants from the bushes in the garden, and peel apples for tea in summer or make toast in winter. Outside he found many things to do with my brothers at their work. The annual ratting, when the old staddles of the stocks were pulled away to make room for the new, was a time of great excitement, and Bert was ruddy and bright-eyed with exertion.

.　　.　　.

A different Bert was the one who sat at his table studying, four or five girls sitting about chatting with his mother who amused them by her emphatic pronouncements on persons and things, her keen eyes watching when they appealed to her son for help in some problem.

Mrs. Lawrence talked of herself: how her father, finding himself possessed of six daughters, came from Kent to Nottingham where they could earn a living in the lace trade. Her own children were often a theme of conversation.

"Aye, you're all alike. The mother can slave her heart out and you leave her. Look at my eldest. 'I shall never leave you, Mother.' Many a time he said that, and there he was, arming a girl around almost before he was out of knickerbockers. And the next one soon cast off the old one for the young ones."

" 'There's safety in numbers,' though, isn't there, Mother?" Bert would say with a wink at us.

"Aye, my lad, there is," she would return, swiftly and emphatically.

.　　.　　.

About this time [1903] changes were made in the system of tuition of pupil-teachers whereby they were to attend a Centre in the neighbouring town of Ilkeston, instead of the morning hour before school with the Head. How happily they set off to catch the train on their days at Centre, leaving those of us who were too near the final exams to be allowed to make the change lonely and longing for the stimulation numbers always bring. Though I was left to finish out my apprenticeship under the old rules, my sister [Jessie] from her school near home made the long journey to the station in all weathers. An assistant in my department came by train and was very impressed by a new face at the station.

"There's a lot of new kids going to Centre now. They were on the platform waiting for their train, and there was one new girl whose face is a perfect picture. She's the loveliest face I've ever seen."

Asked what she was like, she began to describe lovely dark eyes, rosy cheeks, dark, curly hair, and a most beautiful expression.

"What had she on?" we asked.

And the hat and coat brought a shout from us:

"It is, it is."

"Is what?" she wanted to know.

"Her sister," they told her, and she turned to me.

"No, it can't be your sister. You're not like her in the least. Why, she's like a lovely Italian picture!"

Next Centre day at the station, she inquired the name of the lovely face and proved the girls were right. It was my sister.

.   .   .

Jessie's tuition by Bert continued on Saturday afternoons or evenings, and I was learning how much this was resented by his family and that she was to be cold-shouldered. I mentioned this to Bert, but he passed it off contemptuously.

"Them! You don't think they're going to run my life!" And then very anxiously: "Don't say anything to anybody, will you? Just ignore it all."

And so when I was twitted about his regular weekly visit ("Whom did he come to see?" "Why did he come?"), I used to say:

"For his own enjoyment, the walk, the change, the farm life."

Still I was often whipped to fury by hearing intimate details of our home life, and once demanded of Bert:

"Why do you tell everything?"

"I don't tell," he said, "I'm asked."

" 'Badgered' is what you mean!"

He didn't answer, but his lips tightened, and his eyes grew hard. For he had complained how he had to tell his family everything he did while at our house.

.   .   .

Bert looked ill as his final exams approached, in spite of our frequent assurance that he could not fail. It was that modesty over his ability, which was so apparent, that won the esteem of all brought into contact with him.

"Well, you are a goat," said a fellow student. "We all know that you know more than all of us put together, and we don't expect to fail. You don't seem to know how much you do know."

And we all endorsed his words:

" 'Them's my sentiments,' as the preacher said."

"Two dots!"

At which we all laughed, for D. H. L. himself had taught us to say "Two dots" for "ditto." And he liked to say "one *d*" for one penny; any number of pennies was that number of *d's*.

.   .   .

Our long walk to Chapel on Sunday evening gave Bert a chance to show us hospitality, and he insisted on our calling at his house on our way home. Other friends would gather there, and we would sing around the piano. Then Bert would bring out cake and tarts for us who had so far to go. But his mother's cold fury at his action choked me, so I refused to eat, to his obvious annoyance, and soon found excuses for not going to his home. Anything rather than court his mother's deep aversion. She tried to hide it under witty sallies; but whether she took refuge in irony or sarcasm, it flashed from her eyes, and the bitter curl of her lip, and the turn of her head. Bert denied all these signs. I thought it a pity to call up such hatred, but the other members of my family accepted Bert's urgent invitations.

"Don't you catch it afterwards?" I asked him.

He winced and reddened, saying swiftly:

"I understand Mother."

I felt a little sorry for her, having to fill her house with young people any evening they felt like dropping in to pass the time or ask help from Bert, but he protested:

"She likes it, she says it keeps her young."

I could not be convinced. I felt she was always watching her own young in order to frustrate any theft of Bert, and that numbers gave her a feeling of protection for him and herself. It seemed to me so obvious that she dreaded the years when only she and her husband were left together, and at any cost she would fight to keep her son for herself. The harder the battle, the harder she would fight.

Because I drew away, many things came to my ears: My parents were blamed for encouraging him to spend so much time at our house. We as a family were stealing him from his mother. My sister [Jessie] was claiming his time which should be spent in the open air. She was taking far too much for granted. He came just for his health and not because of any liking for any particular one of us.

I tried to get my parents to forbid him our house, but they laughed at me and declared they enjoyed Bert's company far too much to turn him away because I had listened to gossip.

"If his mother doesn't want him to come, she must stop him," said Father. "I shan't."

So I tried to show my resentment, and Bert soon said:

"Why don't you like me to come now? I am coming anyway. I don't care what you think you know, or what you hear, or what they say. I'm coming just the same. Go on, be nice about it."

But I couldn't be nice while he let his family malign us. He assured me it was nothing, meant nothing.

"It's just claptrap. Everybody talks that way, but you out here have no neighbours and so don't know about gossip."

Well, then, I thought he should stay away if his family hated him to come, and he scolded:

"They don't hate it, really. It's just the way they carry on. If it wasn't this, it would be something else. But I shall come," he said with quiet obstinacy, "and nothing will stop me unless your father and mother say I can't come."

And he shut his lips and sauntered away, with his head high.

.   .   .

Bert had a wonderful knowledge of the wild flowers of the wood. It was a bluebell wood with violets and forget-me-nots but no yellow flowers except the celandine, and he seemed to love especially its bright, glossy petals.

"Do you know why the earliest spring flowers are mostly yellow?" he asked us.

Some of us did not know, and he explained it was because of the scarcity of insects and therefore the need of bright colours to attract. In such informal manner our family learned much we would otherwise have missed. For we were not all students, but all liked the bits of information Bert let fall because there was always the spice he imparted of its being a discovery.

But it was with books he made us most acquainted, and though I was now only on the outer fringe of his list, I thrilled with the daring of Omar Khayyám:

> Lift not thy hands to *It* for help—for It
> Rolls impotently on as Thou or I.

My mother didn't like our discussing the *Rubáiyát* before the young children:

"I won't have their faith destroyed. You grieve me by reading such things, but you shan't take the children's faith."

Later came Darwin's theories and then Schopenhauer's essays breaking into the pattern of our life, "filling our heads with rubbish," as we women put it, and it was the attitude of all outside our family. But we delighted in even merely knowing the great names of literature. We read something of all, though I, an outcast, did not join the circle around the parlour fire where passages were read aloud and sometimes plays in their entirety.

Bert was always eager to talk about books and poetry, and brought special ones we "simply must read." Maupassant, and Ibsen, Tolstoy, Anatole France, besides our English writers, were familiar names with us, but Bert was always very frigid because I couldn't whip up the enthusiasm he felt. The marital troubles of an aunt and uncle of his seemed far more important to my way of thinking than the troubles of Anna Karenina with whom he sympathized to such a point of suffering that I accused him of being foolish.

But in the midst of his living the lives about which he was reading, he could be very practical; and as I cut the bread and butter for tea, he would tell of a recent visit to an aunt.

"She must be the champion butter spreader. She can make a pound of butter go farther than any woman I know. I watched to see how she does it, and she spreads it on, then scrapes it off, and there's a smear on the bread, but most of the butter is back in her butter dish. Oh, she knows a thing or two."

.   .   .

On very rare occasions Bert and I would find ourselves alone, and then he would blurt out a question as if he had been waiting anxiously to ask it.

"What do you think life is?"

"I don't know," I said. "I don't like the way we're bundled together and can never be ourselves. Everything's like a class at school, you must go with the crowd. You as an individual must never dare to raise your head above the crowd, or it will be cracked with a club."

"You're right," he said with startling intensity.

"And yet that's all we have, isn't it?" I added. "Our individual life is our only life, isn't it?"

"That's how I see it—" he began.

But before we could thrash out the subject, some of the family came in.

.　　.　　.

There were many walks and excursions into the country around. One Sunday afternoon we went to drink from the spring that poured from a high bank and came on some old quarries and brick kilns, and excitedly explored them. Then, straying deeper into this adventurous spot, we came upon a streamlet whose banks were thick with primroses. With cries of delight we fell upon them and gathered bunches, when suddenly we saw a young girl, very well dressed and very prim, who passed us haughtily. As we were trooping out, a hoarse shout came, and looking around, we saw an angry keeper who waved a stick at us and called on us to stop. Threateningly he called upon my eldest brother [Alan] and Bert to stand apart, and drove the rest of us off. I ran back to the boys.

"No wenches! no wenches!" blustered the keeper.

"Why, I'm nearly as old as my brother, and just as responsible."

"Back wi' thee, back to t' rest," he shouted as I stood my ground.

My brother urged me to go:

"You're only making him mad."

The little group of us waited miserably and fearfully as the bully raised his stick threateningly to the two boys.

"He's going to hit them!" somebody cried.

But he did not, only separating them and asking each his name and the names of the others. When he heard my father's name, he said that my brother must tell my father to come and see the Squire.

Father tried to assure us it would be all right. But at school much was made of it, and the opinion that somebody would have to go to prison was mooted. Every morning Bert sought me out for news and was full of misgivings, for everyone blamed us for investigating the old kilns and "rackapelting about." At the very least, we should be fined for trespass, it was thought. But Father's visit cleared up the matter, for the Squire was amused at his bullying keeper, and our fears were relieved. Bert frankly admitted he felt "a lot better with that curmudgeon settled." Talking of it afterwards, we concluded it was in keeping with life—the primrose dell where we thought we could do as we liked and were pulled up by the keeper to learn of the rights of others.

For life tumbled us with questions nobody seemed able to answer. What was it? What were we? What were our relationships? There seemed too much bickering and too little sincerity. Bert was distraught when someone repeated mean things to him.

"And they said that!" he moaned. "Why should they say that? Why does everyone say such mean things about everyone else?"

He sat white and miserable, his fingers locked against his chest. Mother said we should have to get used to hearing ourselves talked about.

"I don't think I really mind so much what they say, as being told what they say," Bert answered. "They can say anything they like about me so long as I don't get to hear about it. It's when a friend tells you what he's heard that it hurts. Don't let's ever repeat what we hear of one another. We're all right, and we know we're all right. So what does it matter what they say?"

But the misery still showed in his face.

.   .   .

Instead of coming to the Haggs always trying to please, Bert now frequently brought a grievance.

"People are brutes," he announced one day, as he sat down in the kitchen on his arrival, glowering at his new discovery. "How do you fight brutes?"

Mother didn't know. I said I tried to avoid them.

"I'm going to fight them," he said in sullen anger. "There must be a way. We can't sit down and let them trample us in hobnailed boots. Surely we can make our wits work against brute strength!"

We thought we had to put up with it, but he said:

"I'm going to fight them!"

"How?" I asked.

"I don't know yet, but I shall. You see if I don't."

.   .   .

Soon after this, Bert happened to find me alone in the kitchen and, sitting down quickly, said:

"I say, what are we?"

"If you mean what do our parents think we are—we seem to be their possessions."

"You're right," he said vehemently. "Mothers are too possessive."

"Some parents think we belong to them, never to ourselves," I went on. "And I think I belong to myself, don't you?"

Bert looked dejected and wounded; but, someone coming in at that moment, the subject was changed.

The rate of pay as pupil-teacher was very low. I started at a shilling a week with a yearly increase supposed to cover the cost of books, and Bert's pay would have been similar. So when he jerked out his feet and nearly tripped me as I came in one afternoon, we didn't take it as a joke, but looked at his boots. They were different from those he usually wore, but they were not new, so I was for passing. But again he shot out his feet across my path. I looked again at his boots and then at his face. He was watching me intently and seemed to have satisfied himself on some point, for he drew back his feet and let me pass. It was done so quickly that conversation had not stopped.

But next day Mother said:

"Poor lad, he doesn't like his boots! They must have been given him, and charity stings."

Evidently friends of mine had given them to him, and he had thrust them under my nose to find out if the gift had been talked about.

Having passed my final exams, I was now a teacher drawing a salary.[33] On some errand I had to call on Mrs. Lawrence, and she said how nice it was for Mother to have my earnings.

"I shall be thankful when some of ours start," she said. "I've been helping young ones out into the world for a long time now, but I've got nothing for it yet."

"It's all yet to come, you hope?" I suggested.

"Aye, I hope, but I've had all my hopes all dashed to the ground more than once."

She rattled crockery viciously as she laid the table for tea.

Her younger daughter [Ada] appeared from school.

"Oh," she sniffed, "I can smell my tea. Mother always gets me something tasty for Friday. It's kippers today. I think they're appetizing!"

And the three of us had a friendly tea together.

One other tea I remember—a birthday, I think—when the table was set in the bay window, the lace curtains drawn aside for the sake of the splendid view. It was a happy, gay party of lively young folk, and leaves a very pleasant memory of the house in which the Lawrence children had grown up and we young friends had spent so many lively hours.

There is one more memory of that kitchen: the table littered with water-colours and autograph albums, and Bert in his shirt sleeves painting furiously, surrounded by an admiring group of half-a-dozen girls and one boy, who had presented each other with albums for Christmas. Mrs. Lawrence sat by the hearth, exchanging quips and cracks with the liveliest of the group, beaming as we praised her son's talent. Bert painted a child with a watering-can over the flower bed and an umbrella over her own head in a heavy shower on a page of my album from himself, and wrote:

> His 'prentice han' he tried on man
> And then he made the lasses 'O'.[34]

Each one of us wanted a painting done for every one in the group, and Bert ran his fingers through his hair excitedly.

"I tell you what, you'll have to have them, and I'll do them one by one. You won't mind what I choose, will you?"

He was assured his choice would satisfy everyone.

"Just so long as there's a bit of colour will suit me," said several, all of us accepting his kindness without any sense of obligation.

Bert was the centre of the gay crowd, and we took it for granted that he liked to do us such favors. All of us must remember him and the gaiety of his company and the hospitality of his home with gratitude and genuine pleasure.

"There's nobody like Bert" was the opinion of us all.[35]

.   .   .

Bert's sympathy with people's misfortunes was quick and active. When an aunt was struck with cancer, he brought a party of girls up to our fields to pick violet leaves which were considered very soothing. He pressed us into the service.

"We shall need pounds and pounds, you know. You will help, won't you? You could pick some every time you go out, and I could take them home on Saturdays."

It was the same when an orphan cousin was opening a business in our town. He solicited custom for her among all acquaintances.

"You will have a blouse made just to give her a start, won't you? You see, she's in expenses, heavy expenses, too. Having no home, she has to pay rent and lodgings and everything."

.   .   .

During Bert's last year at the teacher's training centre [1904–1905], a play was put on by the students, and he gave me a ticket, saying his mother and elder sister [Emily] were also going. He sat with me when not with the players, and excitedly pointed out a tall, fair girl taking a prominent part as the one to be most heartily applauded. She had to sing, looking very pretty, and he sang with her low in my ear till the chorus,

> Keep off the grass
> Keep off the grass in the garden,

when he sang with all his heart. He stood up and waved his arms to show her his delight; and as the applause thundered, he stood on his seat clapping and shouting "Encore." She smiled at him from the stage. His delight at her success had a childlike quality of sincerity.

"Why don't you stand up and wave?" he demanded of me, and he was not satisfied with my explanation that I did not belong to her party.

"You could show you liked her more than just clapping," he complained.

"Well, you can tell her from me that she was lovely," I said, and he was satisfied.

We climbed the long hill from the station, talking of the play and players, and at the market place Bert said:

"I could run down with you as far as the offices and be back before they get here!"

But I said no, and he asked me to wait with him until his mother and sister caught us up. We stood talking, hearing the group climbing the hill, and presently a breathless figure came alone.

"It's our Pem," he said.

She had to catch her breath before she was able to speak.

"Our Bert can't see you to your grandma's. He's got to catch his train tomorrow morning, and he's tired out now."

"Yes, I know," I said. "We were just waiting for you."

The chattering group having reached us, we said "Goodnight," and I dropped down the hill to the valley of the brook, enjoying the silence and the scent of rain in the darkness under the trees.

Next day I wrote a careful note of thanks to Mrs. Lawrence, knowing well who had directed his giving of the ticket, even though he was now nineteen years old.[36]

[Hunstanton, Norfolk, 14 July 1905]

[To Jessie Chambers]
([We've done Castle Rising & Sandringham on our way here. We passed this place ["Below Potter Heigham"] on Monday. We are having a fine time—been paddling all afternoon—now we're at tea on the sea front.

D. H. L.[37]

May Chambers Holbrook

Bert passed his final examination brilliantly, though he had worried till almost ill that he might do only poorly. He remained as an assistant master [at the British School, Eastwood, 1905–1906], and I asked him what he was going to do, now he need not study.

"Just nothing," he replied. "I'm going to take it easy before college, and that won't be till I've saved enough to take me there."

I told him it would be nice to know he was not grinding at something and worrying.

"Do I grind and worry? Is that how I seem to you?"

I told him he seemed always jingling, never serene and content, but upsetting and tiring.

"That's just because I poke holes in your complacency. You don't like prodding."

"I'd like to poke a few holes in you," I laughed, and he said there was no need, he was full of holes.

So we laughed and said we would see if a period of "nothing to do" would help.

.   .   .

"I like restful women," Bert said. "I think a man goes to a woman for rest. That's why I don't much like ———."

And he discussed a fairly new acquaintance recently come from the city who was fond of hanging on to his arm when walking between him and her husband. It made Bert furious, and some of us delighted in deliberately meeting them face to face to hear and see his anger in the snapped "hello" and blazing eyes. We would cross the street on purpose to torment him, and, next day at school, hear his biting comments on "women who act like cripples and have men drag them along."

599

For though always in the company of girls, Bert never touched or linked arms, which was the chief reason for his popularity with them.

"You can trust him anywhere" was the verdict of all.

But an ordinary boy complained:

"I walked back with Bert on Sunday night, but never again. He was pounding and profounding like a preacher for awhile. Then he began to whine about his married sister's baby being born dead or something. He carried on till I was sick of it, and I said, 'Well, can't she have another?' That shut him up."

.   .   .

It was soon apparent that Bert's thoughts had turned to writing, as well as reading, books. The actual fact was not mentioned, but the signs were many. He showed such keen interest in words and phrases.

" 'A black ousel!' " he would say. "There is such a thing. It's a blackbird. I looked *ousel* up. 'You black ousel,' our mother said to the girls. 'You black ousel.' " And he rolled it over his tongue.

He would burst out most unexpectedly:

"Mother does know a lot of old words, and they come out when she's mad. Father was sitting by the fire. Roaring it was—you'd think he'd scorch. 'You salamander you!' she suddenly cried at him. She was right: a salamander lives in fire, according to old myths." And he told us what he had read about salamanders since his mother's outcry.

"I keep my ear always cocked for the unexpected," he said. "You never know what jewel she'll drop. But she has to be mad before they leap up from where they have lain, forgotten since childhood."

These bits dropped as Bert sat in the kitchen where Mother and I were at some task. I remember he was toasting bread before a glowing fire when he told us of the salamander.

Another time he was very flushed with glittery eyes, and suddenly he said:

" 'Tears! tears thick as pipe-stails streaming! Tears dropping like peas! And neither kind will do you any good, you saucy madam!' That's what Mother said this morning to the girls."

We laughed with him, but didn't ask why the remark, knowing now the cause of his flushed face and feverish eyes. Anger and tears at home always showed in his face, though he rarely told us of family rows.

"A headache!" was his usual laconic explanation of his flush.

.   .   .

One day in our kitchen, Bert sat with a strange, deep, intense expression in his eyes, his face slightly flushed, and talked of some ancestor who wrote hymns. I felt he had discovered some power within himself that stirred him almost to confession. He recited a few lines.

"Did you compose that?" I asked.

"No," he said. "That's a hymn by Beardsall.[38] You've seen the name in the hymn book."

I suggested he at once follow his ancestor's example, and he laughed shyly and said:

"The Muse doesn't work to order. She's coy like a woman!"

After a pause, he continued gravely:

"Still, Beardsall wrote some fine hymns. Mother's name was Beardsall. Of the same family, I think. *Beardsall. Beardsall.* I like the name, don't you? Listen how nice it is when you sound the *r* and *d* distinctly. It's a good, hard name. You can wrap your tongue around it."

Bert sat on Mother's low rocking chair, his hands clasped between his knees, looking around at us with that strange glow in his eyes as if he felt it must be impossible we did not also feel the stress he laboured under. I thought the mantle of his hymn-writing ancestor had fallen wondrously upon him.

It was later, when he was away at the seaside [1907], that letters describing Robin Hood's Bay made Mother remark:

"I think he must be writing a book."

She looked grave.

"I'm afraid for him," she added. "With his ideas, he could set the world on fire."

.   .   .

Perhaps Bert dreaded the inevitable changes when he said:

"Don't you think it would be possible, if we were rich, to have a large house, really big, you know, and all the people one likes best live together? All in the one house? Oh, plenty of room inside and out, of course, but a sort of centre where one could always find those one wanted, a place all of us could come to as a home. I think it would be heaps nicer than to be all scattered and apart. Besides, there'd always be somebody one liked near at hand. I know I should love something of the sort. Haven't you often felt sad at the thought of the gradual breakup of families or groups of friends like ours? I have—and it could be avoided, if we had means. I should like to be rich and try it, shouldn't you?"

It was a beautiful thought, but it seemed impractical to me and on a par with his love of heroines like Dora and Hetty—pretty playmates, but useless wives! Besides, he found fault with those who were very kind to him like my mother, so I had no faith in his success as head of a house full of friends. He would criticize them as he criticized us, which I felt, in our house, eating our food, was unfair.

It happened that Bert dropped in as I was alone mixing a cake for tea, and he told me of a recipe his mother used "which is really very nice."

"Your mother always makes them too dry," he said. "She should mix them wetter."

I had hard work to keep from flinging a handful of flour in his face. He saw my anger and stopped abruptly, and I said quietly:

"Yes, Mother makes them so, because we like them that way!"

He agreed, rather ashamed of his criticism. But I made the rock buns very rocky, and at the tea table remarked to him:

"If they do not suit you, why trouble to eat them?"

My sister [Jessie] sometimes rebuked me, sorrowfully saying my tongue was too sharp, but I couldn't bear that he should criticize us right at home. I heard enough of what his family said about us, outside. He endeared himself to all my family, so I did not repeat what I heard, in case my parents would refuse to hold him responsible, knowing the cross-examination he underwent at home. He frequently said to me sadly:

" 'To know all is to forgive all.' "

"Well, then, tell me all, and we'll see!"

But he would only look miserable and driven, and say no more.

.　　.　　.

Discovering that people and the world could be very ugly made Bert seem to want to hurt someone in return for the hard knocks he was getting, and at Christmas he vented his spleen as we played charades. In the word *fanatic,* he went up in the attic dressed like an old crone to fetch down her lazy son. His shrill, withering vituperation made me shiver. As he played the fanatic, he was so realistic that when my little brother and sister, dressed to represent choirboys, broke into song, it was a relief to laugh at their clear piping:

> Do you know,
> Poor old Joe
> Lost a penny farthing
> In the snow.

"You acted a bit too well," we told Bert. "You *became* a fanatic."

He seemed very much pleased with his performance and said he had enjoyed it.

"Repent!" he had shouted with blazing eyes and wild gesticulations as he preached. "Judgment. The last day! Hellfire for everyone!"

"You should be a revivalist," we said. "Your forked lightning would terrify your congregation to the mercy seat."

He appeared to have worked off all his vindictiveness and became the sunny Bert we knew best—a very different Bert from the one of a later party held in the schoolroom [of the British School, Eastwood, 1905–1906] where he taught.

It was a big crowd of mixed ages, the mothers as well as sons and daughters. When things darkened and were becoming dead, Mrs. Lawrence asked Bert to do something. He quickly exerted himself and set the ball of fire rolling, and became the centre, the leader, quite naturally. But soon he left the others to carry on, and came over to me red and vexed.

"I'm not going to make a fool of myself any longer before that crowd of women."

"They don't think you're a fool," I said. "They think you are a splendid entertainer."

"Yes, till the day after tomorrow, then I shall be hearing on every side tales of my imbecility."

And he smilingly refused requests and coaxing, saying he knew no more games and had no further suggestions. His mother looked very disappointed, for Bert was a son to be proud of, tall and lithe and the centre of attraction.

"Everyone likes our Bert," Mrs. Lawrence liked to beam, "and there's safety in numbers."

But ugly aspersions were cast on a son who could be a "Jack among the Maidens," and "Summat's wrong, somewhere!" was said. Bert heard of such criticism, but held that his own ideas of behaviour were right, and carried himself proudly.

.   .   .

I saw very little of Bert, but if I happened to be at home on Saturday afternoons, it was obvious that his place in our family was as secure as ever. He made a special appeal to each one. My sister [Jessie] was studying hard, and they both seemed to become more and more absorbed in books, strolling in the sunshine with a book, or sitting by the parlour fire

603

where Father or an elder brother often joined them. Once or twice I went in the wood with Bert while he sketched a little scene. He wanted some member of our family with him in case the keepers should order him out if he were alone. On one occasion, a keeper stood behind an oak trunk, his velvet suit so merging that only his red face betrayed him. He watched till he was tired, then withdrew, perhaps thinking we never knew he was in the vicinity. Another time a mutual acquaintance so astonishingly appeared in the main riding that I thought it must be only my imagination. The lack of surprise exhibited by Bert and the guarded casualness of their greeting fired me with the notion that she had been delegated to spy out the land and that Bert had had some inkling she was coming. I was glad that dust had been thrown in inquisitive eyes.

. . .

Bert criticized his mother one day. He and his younger sister [Ada] had been romping about and broken the back or leg of a chair belonging to the front room suite.

"Mother was so mad she called in Father, and they both carried on ridiculously. It might be a crime we'd committed instead of a measly chair damaged. Oh, yes, it's spoiled the suite if it can't be repaired neatly. But even so, what's a measly chair to make such a fuss about? It's the moral attitude I mind. It shouldn't be moral! They correct us nowadays by making a misdemeanor a moral offense. It isn't the right way, I'm sure. Look at the way you've been brought up, and all of us. Always the moral aspect. We've damaged a chair. Well, what of it? We didn't do it viciously. We were larking about and must have been rougher than we thought. We were happy and at play, and that's heaps more important than a broken chair! Have it mended if possible, but don't make it a moral issue!"

He was what he called "quite ratty" about it, and looked very red and vexed because my sympathy was with his parents, the owners of the broken chair.

"They keep on saying how much they paid for that suite," Bert continued, "and what each chair cost, making out that we've destroyed so much money's worth. They don't see that the damage to the chair isn't a patch on the damage they're doing our spontaneous joy in life by harping on it. Let it drop! It's done, it can't be undone if they talk their heads off!"

. . .

Bert's family had moved about half-a-mile to a house [39] more spacious both inside and out, with a garden and a view from the living-room window, not into the black brick yard with outbuildings, but over the roofs of the town to the church tower in the distance. Now he brought roots of perennials to our farm garden, and learned many flower names and passed them on to us.

"I found out what your rock cress is really called: It is *Arabis*. And these are *primulas*."

But the name we rolled over our tongues with most pleasure was *ranunculus*. Bert planted the roots he brought and a few annual seeds left from their own flower garden.

"And the white flower all over the grotto here is *alyssum*. I like it, don't you?" And he spelled the word out.

The move was the first change to take place. The next change was his going to college.

.   .   .

Bert served as assistant master in the same school [British School, Eastwood, 1905–1906] until he had saved enough to take the teachers training course at Nottingham University College [1906–1908], travelling daily as he had done when going to High School. The Saturday visits continued, and the reading became deeper. The questions on the way of life taught by home, school, and Chapel became more revolutionary. My mother grieved, but Father treated it as growing pains.

"They'll learn sense when they go out into the world," he said.

But Mother feared much harm would be done before sense dawned, and warned that discussions on God and religion be carried on out of the hearing of the younger members of the family. In Chapel Bert sat looking straight ahead, his pale, studious face betraying nothing. His profile was turned toward the congregation because of their pew in the transept, and many must recall the well-shaped head with thick, fine, light hair, the chin firm and uplifted, the closed lips, and eyes set under a forehead that overhung them and was very full above the temples, with the ears delicate and flat to the head. There was a quiet yet alert expression on his face, a high seriousness. He did not need to gaze or even glance around for entertainment, having more than enough to occupy his thoughts. When he stood to sing, tall and slim, he was straight but easy and graceful, one hand holding the hymn book and the other resting on the top of the pew. He sang with pleasure, but always with that expression of intellectual detachment, as though his mind were analyzing the words and what they sought to convey.

Outside the big gates we stood in groups, and Bert sought out my family for the walk home. My parents drove in the morning, but those of us old enough to walk the distance attended the evening service. Bert still insisted on taking those of us who would go to his home where they sang around the piano. I heard them as I passed their window to my own home.[40]

.   .   .

Coming into my home one day after a shower, Bert exclaimed:
"Look at the mud. It has splashed on the glass from the window box!"
"I don't mind that," I declared.
"Don't you?" he said. "Our mother would."
"Oh, yes, I know," I laughed.
"Oh, yes, you know, and you laugh?"
He raised his brows questioningly.
"Why not?" I asked lightly. "It's better to laugh at people who refuse a window box because of the splashes which are so easily rubbed off. When they refuse flowers because there's a splash of mud, isn't it better to laugh at them than to copy them?"
"The flowers are worth the mud, to my thinking," Bert said.

.   .   .

On his weekly visit to the Haggs, Bert was bringing books and theories that seemed rank heresy. Right and wrong were questioned—laws that had been formulated by the church to hold us in subjection. Mother drew her younger children around her out of harm's way.

"I don't want them to hear such ideas while they are little and impressionable," she said. "They'd never know any better."

The rest of us listened and read and laughed it off, feeling that the old laws were the only practicable ones for us. Though Bert appeared to be tearing the established way of life to pieces, it was not having much effect on us.

His own kindliness did not diminish, either; for, after getting home from college, he went to read to a girl ill with consumption, and his day was a long one.

The long walk to the station required an early start.

"I have a boiled egg for breakfast," Bert explained. "Then I'm away. It's a sort of treadmill regularity."

He ate dinner in town, and my eldest brother [Alan] meeting him there, complained of the small amount served.

"They must think a fellow has no appetite," Alan said.

And Bert remarked with a slight grimace:

"One has to fit one's appetite to the plate one can afford."

"I should starve to death on such a dinner every day!" said my brother.

"It is a hungry business," admitted Bert, "unless, of course, one is a pluto and can afford another six *d* per diem for a larger plate!"

"Do you go hungry?" asked a younger member of the family in horror.

"Oh, no, no—of course not," Bert answered hurriedly. "But on a frosty, nippy day, or in a fresh March breeze the appetite is sharpened, and then you must do as I said—put it to the plate you can afford."

We all shook our heads and were glad we were not attending college and could sometimes eat a little more dinner than Bert could get.

We were very interested in college and asked many questions. The subjects we heard most about were singing and botany. Many plant names new to us came our way, and accounts of the nature study he delighted in. All this Bert shared with us through his vivid description.

The songs were also shared. We began with *Bill beans and jolly big lumps of fat* to the tune of the *Soldiers Chorus,* then the *Soldiers Chorus* proper, and *Who Is Sylvia? Ariel's Song* followed, then *Golden Slumbers,* and songs grave and gay—so many that a list of them would look like an index of a song book. We all loved singing, and Mother could take the alto part beautifully. Around the piano or in the kitchen we sang in groups, but singing also went on in the sheds and fields. Bert always beckoned me into the group if I arrived during a sing. He liked everyone to enjoy what he was enjoying. Sometimes I refused to join the singing group, resenting some criticism repeated to me of some member of our family or our way of life from Mrs. Lawrence. My mother would say:

"I know you think we listen to Bert too much, but you must admit he's worth listening to."

And I would retort:

"He's lucky to have a place to come and be listened to, and have no responsibilities. Nobody here has any claim on him, though you may expect to have when he has passed college and has a position."

"His mother won't let him," Mother said. "We never expect to claim him. In fact, though you must not repeat it, I should be exceedingly sorry to see him marry anyone I love. We love him for himself, but I think he would spoil the life of any woman who married him."

"Well, then," I said, "treat him as you would any other young man, and tell him to stay away."

"We couldn't do that," my mother asserted. "He is one of us now. Besides, he isn't an ordinary young man."

And so Bert continued his weekly visits, bringing new interests and new ideas to the farm in the valley.

. . .

I asked Bert once if now he played with men at cricket.

"No," he replied. "Why should I play cricket with men when I may play tennis with the girls? They're much nicer, don't you think?"

. . .

Bert stalked haughtily into my own home one day, and after a few preliminaries said:

"Mother hears you had a visit from your minister's wife!"

I glanced at him in surprise at his way of putting it, but he continued in a high voice:

"Well, she's never been to visit Mother, and Mother says she doesn't care if she never comes. She has nothing to say anyway when you do get in her company."

I felt ashamed that Bert should do such an errand; but, remembering how he was dominated, I took the trouble of telling him in detail the reason for the visit, and he became himself again, and ashamed of his errand.

"You know I like her, don't you?" he said earnestly.

And we praised her dark and dainty beauty, her soft Scots accent and low voice, and the fun that could leap into her eyes. But I did not tell him she had invited me to visit her, nor did I pay the visit, fearing to inflame jealousy aroused and so endanger her peace of mind. But I was disappointed not to go.

. . .

At Christmas [1907] my sister Jessie's name appeared over the winning story in a contest,[41] and word was brought to me that Bert was writing stories but letting my sister get the credit. I posted a note, asking Bert to let me have the facts. Next morning, on his way to the station, he ran in, laid a note on the chair near the door, crying, "I'm late, I'm late," and was gone.[42]

Lynn Croft/Eastwood/Notts./Wed. night [11? December 1907]

⟨ Dear May [Chambers Holbrook],

The tale is Jessie's; do not accept any such reports. Whoever can have promulgated it? The miserable cacklers in Eastwood are always so ready to jump to conclusions & bandy names.

Do not say anything to those at the Haggs, it would make them feel so uncomfortable, perhaps vexed—

I am

Yours

D. H. Lawrence [43]

May Chambers Holbrook

The note said the story was my sister's, nothing more. I showed it to the many inquirers, and the controversy got hot.

Later my sister explained that as only one entry was allowed, Bert had written three stories, using different names, and the one under her name happened to be the winner. But if she had stolen that story from him, her integrity could not have been more bitterly assailed, and I asked Bert why he allowed it. He shook his head frantically, crying despairingly:

"I have no moral courage."

.　　.　　.

Bert began to change, and I asked him if College was doing it, or was it Schopenhauer?

"Life," he said, "and it gives me spiritual dyspepsia. It's right. You can have spiritual dyspepsia. You used to say you had intelligence in your feet when you followed the bridle path in the dark. Well, I've got dyspepsia in my soul!"

He was not finding at College that for which he was always searching —"Truth and Beauty," he called it.

"Where is it?" he asked.

"Why not try 'Come day, go day, God send Sunday'?" I asked.

"Yes, live like a cabbage," he said with the quiet obstinacy of conviction. "You're trying it, but you won't be able to do it. I know you won't."

The books he introduced to the farm, my mother said sadly, she never thought to see under her roof: Darwin's *Origin of Species,* and Huxley and Haeckel.[44] Then there were also the "Realists," and my father complained:

"A bit too real for me. All they do, as I can see, is stir up the mud. What good do they do just picturing the dismal side of life? We can see that plain enough."

But Bert defended them, as he did pictures we didn't care for, as a "representation of life." I told him there was the difference in him from other people. They didn't want "representation of life," but entertainment or information.

"Oh, yes, the great unwashed," he said, witheringly. "But there are others, you know."

He tried hard to take some of us a little way along the path he was treading by talking to us about the empyrean, at the home of a mutual friend. He had some sort of sketch or diagram on a big sheet of paper pinned to a chair back. We were ashamed not to understand him and sorry for his increasing humiliation at this failure to make us understand.

"It's not you, it's us," declared a college-trained schoolmistress. "You're too clever for us."

"I'm sorry," he apologized. "I thought you would have taken this in your course."

"Well, if I did, it's evaporated," she admitted. "I don't know a thing about it now."

"I'm sorry, I'm sorry," he kept repeating, as if in distress; and though we urged him to lay the blame on our ignorance, he seemed to feel his failure keenly.

"I've been a silly ass," he said savagely on the way home.

I tried to assure him that nobody else thought so but only felt help-lessly ignorant.

"That's just it," he cried. "Don't you see it makes a gulf? It leaves me lonely."

.   .   .

There were many who began to dread the loneliness they were bound to feel as College drew to a close and the life of which Bert had been the centre would be over. The market for assistant masters seemed to be glutted; and though he passed the examinations with six distinctions,[45] he had to wait three months before obtaining a post at a salary he con-sidered fair.[46] He spent much of his time at the farm, helping with the work. The dread of his leaving hung over all, and yet he must have begun to feel that his dependence upon his family had grown irksome.

"Isn't money hell!" he exclaimed to me passionately. "I'm spending too much on stamps for applications!"

"You'll soon have money of your own," I tried to comfort him.

"I shall!" he cried vindictively, "and then I can pay them back. All of it."

Eventually in October [1908] he was appointed assistant master at a school in Croydon.[47] Why need fate have taken him so far away? we wondered. Why need he go to London? And yet it seemed right that he should go to London. He had sometimes hinted that he feared the world would drag him away its whole width from the valley he loved so deeply. Having become accustomed to the fret of his going, to us it seemed very fit that his brilliance should have a London polish. He left a blank that no other could fill, and there was envy of those who had gained him. His first letters were full of the anguish of the loss of the old life. Sorrow had to be smothered in order to cheer him. Everyone of the group watched for a letter signed with the magic initials D. H. L.[48]

William Holbrook

D. H. was a constant visitor at a cottage we were living in. Now of course the relationship with us and David was much like a brother and sister relationship, as he came and departed when the spirit moved him. I know he loved to come where he could do and say just what he pleased, even to using strong language to win his point. But he had a hard antagonist to browbeat in my wife, who insisted he was too young and inexperienced, in being so cocksure that what he knew and said was the Gospel. These ranglements would proceed all night and well into the a.m., each trying to prove himself the smarter of the two. I, of course, would fall asleep, which added more fuel to the fury, wherein D. H. would scream and shout:

"Look at that farm bumpkin, chaw bacon, hasn't the wit to keep awake. Then they say all men are equal."

I would mumble something about I'd done a day's work, when off would fly his lid:

"So have I, a damned harder day than you."

Then I would lead off with, "Yes, but I've something tangible to show for it. What have you to prove it's worth a damn or ever will be?"

I want to say that to be in D. H.'s company was a tonic. A more sincere friend one could not wish to find, with a most infectious laugh.[49]

[Dorking, Surrey, 7 November 1908]

[To May Chambers Holbrook]

⟨ *Forgive me for not sending you sooner—I thought you would have the Haggs news. I should love you to be here to ride with me through Surrey*

—it is a most sweet and lovely country. The roads are perfect—and the masses of gorgeous foliage almost dazzle one. It is exceedingly beautiful. Let me have a line from you some time, will you. My address 12 Colworth Rd Addiscombe Croydon. I think of you & Will often.

Yrs

D. H. L.[50]

12 Colworth Rd/Addiscombe/Croydon,/2 Dec. 1908

❨ My dear May [Chambers Holbrook],

I was surprised and pleased to see your handwriting, once so familiar, now so rarely received. What a quaint, serious girl you are! Do you feel like a chrysalis opening too late, when the Spring & the Summer have passed? Bless me—it is only June with you.

One does seem buried in Eastwood—but the grave is no deeper there than elsewhere. There is a cousin of mine who lives in the heart of London —not far from Picadilly [sic]. She is thirty two, and has worked in a sort of warehouse all her life (in a really nice job). She is more unlearned, and less developed than anyone I have ever met, of her years. Towns oftener swamp one than carry one out onto the big ocean of life. Townspeople are indeed glib and noisy, but there is not much at the bottom of them. They are less individual, less self-opinionated and conceited than country people, but less, far less serious. It is with them work, and after work, conscious striving after relaxation. In Eastwood, people work, and then drift into their small pleasures; here they pursue a shallow pleasure, and it leaves no room for a prolific idleness, a fruitful leisure. Do not lament a town so much. Truly, there are meetings, and, better, theatres and concerts. But meetings are places where one develops an abnormal tone, which it takes some time to soften down again, and theatres & concerts have not much staying power. The true heart of the world is a book; there are sufficient among your acquaintances to make a complete world, but you must learn from books how to know them. A book is better than a meeting. The essence of things is stored in books; in meetings & speeches the essence is diluted with hot water & sugar, and may be a dash of fire spirits. Read, my dear, read Balzac and Ibsen & Tolstoi and think about them; don't take offence at them; they were great men, all, & who are we that we should curl our lips. One thing that a townsman does less frequently than the countryman—that is to lift his head in the scorn that has never understood.

612

Pardon me for my preaching; you provoke it; you make me feel serious.

Shall I tell you something about School? Oh Davidson Rd is a fine red place—new and splendid! There is a great hall, with wood block floor; dumb-bells and Indian Clubs hang round the walls. The class rooms open off one side; large, lofty rooms, with dual desks; everything smooth and bright and neat. I have Std IV—about 50 boys now. They are queerly mixed. Six are the orphans of actors and actresses, who live in the Actors home near us. They are delightful boys, refined, manly, and amiable. The other week we had Beerbohm Tree [51] & Cyril Maude [52] & other big actresses & actors round to see them in School. Then I have eight lads from the Gordon Home: waifs and strays living by charity. They are of insolent, resentful disposition; that is only superficial, owing to training, I think. When they are forced to respect you (by the cane)—they linger round you to do little things for you. Poor devils—they make me jolly mad, but I am sorry for them. I have boys who will leave me at Christmas to go to a fairly expensive Grammar School; and I have lads whose five bare toes peep at me through their remnants of boots as they sit in the desks, boys who cannot drill, because their boots & clothing will not allow of it. We have free meals and free breakfasts now the winter is on. It is rather pitiful to see them gathered in the canteen for dinner—some sixty or seventy boys and girls. The canteen is a mission room, with pictures of the feeding of the ten thousand & Peter smiting the rock. Hélas—not much water runs from the smitten rock of charity. Some of my boys have the thin lips, and the dreadful unwrinkling of nervous brows characteristic of the underfed. Ours is a strange, incoherent school. The boss [53] is a delightful man (a bit of a fathead sometimes, but kind as an angel)—but he is a weak disciplinarian. The tone of the school is lax, and to establish oneself & to keep ones equilibrium is not easy.

As for my digs—they are fine. We have the jolliest fat baby, eight months old. You cannot tell how fond I am of her; her fine hazel eyes laugh at me so brightly, and her soft fingers wandering over my face and grasping at my cheeks speak to me so cunningly.[54] Then Freddy is a quaint, jolly maiden. I took her uptown on Saturday to see the shops; we went into a great draper's where there is a Father Christmas Cave, & bears and—and paradise all in one nook. The bairnie pays threepence, & the Real Father Christmas gives her a bundle of toys. We did enjoy ourselves, Freddy & I.

On Saturday I am going to London to see the great shops. I wish you might come too. My regards to Will

& Love to you

D. H. L.[55]

12 Colworth Rd./Addiscombe/Croydon./16 Feb. 1909

❪ My dear May [Chambers Holbrook],

I guess you have moved,[56] and I am not sure of your postal address, but I venture a little letter to you.

It seems such a short time since I came back, although it is nearly six weeks. The weeks spin round noiselessly like a balanced wheel; suddenly one realises it is Friday night, and that one has two days in which to please one's self. It is very comfortable, but not stimulating. I find my soul slowing down into comfort; it is tiresome to have even to write a letter. But I have gathered myself for a moment.

We have flitted; not from the house, but we have come to dwell in the drawing room, making it now the dining room. It is a small place, but bright; at the back, away from the little, still street. You know we are on the very edge of the town; there are great trees on the Addiscombe Rd, at the end of Colworth. Here, in this room, there is a glass door, opening onto our little garden. Beyond the grey board fence at the bottom rises the embankment, a quiet, grassy embankment of a light railway that runs from the great lines—S.E. & the London, Brighton. In the dark, as if suspended in the air, little trains pass bright and yellow across the uncurtained door. The little trains have only one carriage, something like a tram car, and often there are no passengers; sometimes two, taking the space of one, fancying themselves secure in the privacy of a corner. It is quaint, like looking out on the world from a star, to watch them jog slowly past.[57] Indoors, Hilda Mary is hanging onto my legs, laughing up at me. She has brilliant hazel eyes, so round and daring. Soon I shall take her and get her to sleep. She does not like to go to bed, but I am a good 'dustman.' I hold her tight and sing—roar away at the noisiest songs. This subdues her, she tucks her face in my neck and toddles off to 'bo', while her hair tickles my nose to a frenzy. It is very still outside; you can just hear the trams hum as they start from the terminus beyond the embankment.

I went to London a week last Saturday, to the winter exhibition at the Academy. It is very strange out West, down Piccadilly, on Saturday morning. There are women such as I have never seen before, beautiful, flowing women, with a pride and grace you never meet in the provinces. The proud, ruling air of these women of the stately West is astounding; I stand still and stare at them. In the square in front of Burlington House, carriages are trotting sumptuously round and round waiting while the ladies are walking through the gallery. There are some glorious pictures. The most notable *painter is a French Peasant, Bastien Lepage.*[58] *Ah, you should see a beautiful woman in dark velvet costume with great orange feathers flowing onto her shoulders stand looking at 'Pauvre Fauvelle.' She looks, she pouts, her mouth relaxes[.] "Too sad" she says to the gentleman[.] "But the country does desolate one like that; I have felt like it myself." She moves on to a romantic picture of Abbey,*[59] *and talks brightly about Maurice Hewlett.*[60] *'Pauvre Fauvelle' is a terrible picture of a peasant girl wrapped in a lump of sacking; you feel her face paint itself in your heart, and you turn away; the sorrow is too keen and real. The academy is full of magnificent works.*

I went in the afternoon to Hornsey, to see George Hill.[61] *On the Sunday he took me to the Alexandra Palace. It is a ghastly place, all sham, sham chalk statues, sham stone, wood and paint, sham trees, sham everything, & everything dirty, broken, the sham exposed. My heart feels sick to think of it. And there, on Sunday afternoon, in the great hall, there was an organ recital. The organ is big & good; but the gathering! There were some three or four hundred people, all that respectable class of poor city people such as one never sees in Croydon. All unhealthy, weedy, impoverished specimens. The worst of it was, there was hardly one face to look at; I shouldn't mind their figures, if their faces were interesting. There was no character, no anything; they were very much like —— —— —— —Mon Dieu!*

You will be happy now out of Moorgreen. I cannot quite understand where you are. Is it this side George's? Tell me—is it on the Moorgreen main road? I do not know Prices'. I know Renshaws, Mrs. Rollings, Cunningham's,—no more. I hope you are well. Have you heard of Emily's baby girl. Give my regards to Will and to everyone

Yrs

D. H. L.

P.S. Nelson's series of 7d modern writers is very good—get H. G. Wells' "Kipps,"—only sevenpence. Then get something of G. Gissing, & the others

D. H. L.[62]

[Shanklin, Isle of Wight, 10 August 1909]

[To May Chambers Holbrook]

([*How is the world using you? Whenever I look over the cliffs far down at the sea I think of you: you have an affection for high white cliffs, have you not? We sailed round the island yesterday, calling at Ventnor & Ryde —& Southsea on the mainland—& Sandown. It was delightful. We passed* close to the Needles—they are not a scrap like needles: they are great, ragged lumps of white rock walking out into the sea, & a lighthouse at the end. You have no idea how pretty the Solent & Spithead are—such shimmering iridescent running water. I am coming to tea with you next week—invite me.

D. H. L.[63]

May Chambers Holbrook

Bert was in his second year of teaching in Croydon when the terrible discovery was made [August, 1910] that his mother had cancer. A sister of hers had died of it already, so we were all prepared for what must somehow be endured.

Bert dropped into my home one Friday afternoon as I was dusting, when I thought he was in far-off London. There was anguish behind his smile at my astonishment.

"I'm grieved and sorry," I said. "Do you want to talk about it, or shall I finish dusting?"

"Oh, finish. Life must not wait on death."

He smiled, but I saw his lips twitch.

He talked disconnectedly about his mother, and how they had sent for him, and how awkward it was to leave school, though he expected to come every second week-end till . . . . He threw up his head and smiled bleakly.

"I hate life because of death," I burst out impulsively.

"But, girl," he said in amazement, "you wouldn't refuse life because of death? You wouldn't, would you?"

"Yes," I said.

"But don't you see that's stagnation, and pretty soon extinction," he expostulated, "and then you'd not have life with all it means, with death only at the end. You'd have death all the time. Void, that's what you'd be. No life at all. Oh, don't you see life *is*, and death must be. Both *are*. What we have to do is accept both. We can do no other."

I stood with my duster, leaning against the bureau and rejoicing that I had got him talking. That would relieve his feelings. I was contrary just to keep him excited, and declared that life was never worth death, that nothing was worth anything. He tried hard to control his exasperation but could not, and called me names and wished he could shake me.

"It's apathy," he cried, "sheer apathy. You ought to be ashamed."

When my husband lifted the latch, there were warm greetings.

"Why, hello, Bert," said Bill, halting a moment as if unbelieving. "Why, of course, you've come home. I wish it had been for a different reason."

"Hello, Bill."

There was a pause after the warm handshake, and Bill looked across at me.

"Why, what are you doing with your dress not changed?" he asked.

"Never mind her dress, Bill," said Bert. "Get her to change her outlook, her attitude towards life."

"Why, what's wrong with it?" inquired Bill.

"Wrong?" Bert spat out.

But I went to change my dress. As I was getting tea ready, Bert talked and Bill laughed, and presently Bert laughed.

.   .   .

But laughter did not play a big part in Bert's subsequent visits, although it always seemed a great relief to him to talk with Bill, who could never keep laughter out of his conversation. The shock of his own mother's death had taught him to face the inevitable.

"It is all beyond us," Bill said, "and we had better laugh for what we have, than cry for what is gone ahead of us."

Bert wished he could be that way.

"But I can't," he said. "It's no good trying. In Croydon they call me 'the egoist,' but they're wrong. I'm not an egoist."

He shook his head.

I asked Bert what he called himself.

"I call myself a man and let it go at that," Bill broke in.

"And you're right, Bill," Bert said vehemently, "damned right. This other stuff's all my eye."

"I call you a 'blunderbuss,'" I said to Bill.

"You would," said Bert, scathingly. "But he's right. Call yourself a man, be a man, live a man, and do all this cheeseparing of life later on."

"Yes," I said, "if you know what life is."

"Of course you'd say that," Bert scolded. "Of course you would! What is life, Bill?"

And Bill said to him life was just living, taking things as they come, and doing the best you can.

"All this pounding and profounding is no good to me," Bill said.

"No, and I'll tell you why," explained Bert. "It's because you are a natural gentleman. I wish my instincts led me direct, as yours do." He

617

paused, then: "I remember your mother dying. We'd be about fourteen, wouldn't we? I wonder how I'd have turned out with no hand guiding me into a groove these last eleven years. I wonder . . . ."

He flushed, opened his lips, but closed them again without speaking.

.   .   .

Bert had come home "to wait—," as he said.

"She doesn't want to die."

"No," I said. "How do you comfort her?"

"I can't, but my sisters do. They say, 'You'll see Ern and Grandmother, and all you have missed so much.' But she says, 'I've learned to do without them. I want to stay with those I have here.' And they tell her again how nice it will be to see them in heaven, and how we shall come to her. They can make believe like that, but I can't, I can't. I've nothing to offer her. No comfort at all."

He sat shaking his head slowly, sorrowfully, looking disconsolate.

"Well, she saw your book," [64] I offered. "It must comfort you to have achieved that while she could have pride in it."

But he was shaking his head.

"No, no," he said sadly.

"No?" I echoed.

"No, she didn't like it."

"Why?" I demanded.

He shook his head sadly.

"I don't know. She didn't like it. Even disliked it."

"Still," I protested, "she must be proud of you, of your ability to write a book. You've given her that. It can't help but be a source of pride."

"No," he insisted miserably, "she doesn't like what I write. Perhaps if it had been romance . . . . But I couldn't write that."

He had sat with his hands clasped loosely between his knees, his head bent. Now he glanced up at me with a piteous smile.

"Strange, isn't it, that I couldn't please her?"

I shook my head.

"What *did* she want?"

"Me," he said softly. "Just me."

.   .   .

"Death long drawn out is an awful thing," Bert said one day, trying to smile.

"It shouldn't be allowed, really," he said presently, and his voice was rough as if his throat ached. For a long time he sat looking into the fire.

"There Mother lies all day, almost silent."

"And you just watch and wait," I said.

"Just watch and wait," he echoed softly.

After a while he repeated it.

"Just watch and wait, watch and wait. There's nothing more to do. She doesn't talk to us at all now. She hardly speaks. She's hardly conscious and yet," he paused and looked at me, "at the exact right time she says, 'Have they got your father's dinner all ready for when he comes home?' " His eyes and voice were soft and questioning. "Why does she think of that? How does she know the time? If either of the girls is there, she asks, 'Is your father's dinner ready?' It's all she can do to say as much as that, and yet she makes the effort. Why is it? Is it mere habit, the habit of thirty-odd years? Or is it that she regrets, or recalls . . . ?"

His voice trailed off into silence as he looked into the fire.

· · ·

"She's barely conscious now. I doubt if she knows us."

Bert pressed his back against the high armchair and lifted his head as if bracing himself to say it:

"And Father never goes up to see her."

I said, "But he asks."

"Oh, he asks. Every day as he gets in from the pit, he asks, 'How's your mother today?' and we tell him." His voice fell to a shocked, almost horrified tone. "But he never goes up to see her."

"He knows without seeing," I said.

"But he *ought* to go up," he insisted softly. "He ought to *want* to see her. He should go up."

"He can't," I ventured. "Things have happened between them."

"But he was once her lover," he protested with wide eyes.

"That doesn't matter," I said.

"Then what does matter?" he demanded in a voice that broke as if strangled.

· · ·

"They're asking when I shall be back at school," Bert said. "They say they must put someone in my place if I'm away much longer."

"How can you tell how long?" I asked indignantly.

"Yes, but they've been very good. It stands to reason they can't manage much longer."

After a long silence, Bert said:

"It isn't Mother lying there now. Really it isn't. It's her body, but she isn't there. I don't care what anybody says, Mother is not there. There's no consciousness at all. She doesn't know any of us. She has no pain because that is killed by morphia. I tell you Mother herself is gone."

.　　　.　　　.

A day or two later [9 December 1910],[65] Bert came in with a hurt and tender expression on his face.

"She's gone," I said.

He nodded. "It's all over." He turned as the door opened. "Mother died this morning, Bill."

"Your mother's dead, eh?"

"Mother is dead," he repeated.

We all stood looking, asking with our eyes the questions that were tearing at our hearts. What is death? Where is she now? Oh, where is she now? Suddenly I said:

"Let us help you. Can we help you? Is there *anything* we can do?"

Then we all sat down to discuss immediate plans. Bill was to drive to the station for the flowers on the day of the funeral.

"I shall write little poems to her," Bert said. "She'd like that." [66]

[Lincoln, 24 August 1911]

[To May Chambers Holbrook]

❲ Last day in Lincoln—seen riot & a fire—great fun. But I'm dreading the return to school. I went to Shirebrook—wonder when I shall see you again.

Addio

D. H. Lawrence [67]

16 Colworth Rd/Addiscombe/Croydon/11 Oct 1911

❲ My dear May [Chambers Holbrook],

It was nice of you to send me the eggs—they are scarce as gold here. They are bonny ones, too. But ye should sell 'em, my dear, not waste 'em on the likes o' me.

I have had the most wearisome week end, rushing round with George.

Rush, rush[,] its one big struggle, nowadays, to get things done. It's eleven now, at night. I've been working since 7.0 at verse, getting it ready to take to Edward Garnett on Friday[.] Oh my dear Lord, I am so tired. I tell you what I should like, now. You know we're living here in the kitchen, small and bare and ugly, because the electric isn't connected up—all too poor to have it done—truth. I should like a small house of my own—small as yours —one warm, sweet room—a woman who loved me to rest me. God! And night after night one stumbles up, half blind with work or with wastefulness—ah bosh.

Jones [68] is just jawing me how to make my fortune in literature. I listen patiently, then resume my pencil. I have worked all night at verse—you don't know what that means. Life is a bit disproportionate, don't you think —either all struggle and bludgeoning and battle by oneself, or dependence, and ease, with overmuch softness of rest. This week, I am very tired. But I shall work it off.

I am wondering if I shall see you at Christmas. I may not be near Eastwood. What a long time.

I had a letter tonight, from an admirer of the White Peacock—saying Mrs. Thurston,[69] the lady novelist who died a while back, read my book a short time before her death, and thought it so beautiful, & was so much moved by it. She is dead—and she read the Peacock—and mother never read it. How funny everything is.

> I will go to bed—Goodbye
> D. H. Lawrence [70]

[16, Colworth Road, Addiscombe, Croydon] Wednesday/6 Dec 1911

⟨ My dear May [Chambers Holbrook]

The eggs have come—they are very pretty—one only cracked: that is to be made into a custard pudding. It is very good of you to take so much trouble[.]

I am much stronger—but still on my back—17th day. Neither to right nor to left can I lie, nor may I be propped up half an inch. But soon the doctor will let me be reared up.

I am pretty happy—except at evening when I always feel rotten. I can sleep fairly well. When I wake there is Nurse crocheting in the shade-light. She crochets so slowly & clumsily, I laugh at her. Sometimes she is asleep. But usually she is at me with milk or medicine, much to my disgust. At six oclock I don't pretend to sleep any more. Then Nurse draws the blind up

& we talk while it grows day. When it rains, the day won't come. I'm always glad when its eight oclock. Now Nurse brings me coffee & toast for breakfast.

I am allowed to read. I have got to review a book of German poetry & a book of Minnesinger translations. I like the German poetry, but not the translations.

It is sunny today. I envy the sparrows and the starlings. This is the most I've written since I've been ill.

My regards to Will. I will write to you again

Love

D. H. Lawrence [71]

Compton House,/St. Peter's Road,/Bournemouth./7 Jan 1912

(My dear May [Chambers Holbrook],

Isn't it scandalous that I haven't written you before. But now I'm convalescent, I am more reluctant to do my duty than ever.

I came down here yesterday. It is a big house—45 folk in now—there were 80 last week. I am still a forlorn lost lamb—but am getting used to things. I write in the billiard room, & a fellow is giving physical demonstrations, very weird, to a little Finnish chap. The latter I have chattered to. It is wonderful what chances for being interesting some people miss. He looks like a Mongol—the Finns are Mongolian—& he speaks like no one else on Earth. But he talks commonplace. It's a shame.

The place is pretty—a big town set among trees—& such heaps of pine trees, very dark. The cliffs are golden—sand-stone, quite soft. They look very nice with the sun on them: and the sea, like a great churning of milk with golden patches far off, coming in long rollers & smashing high up, the loveliest of smashed waves, white & leaping, & slewing all over the promenade. It is very pretty. Now it is moonlight—after dinner. The bay is very long, & double, like this

[rough sketch]

so we look along the surf at the moon. The white light glitters like fire on the front of each wave, just as it rears to fall. Then, in the flat wash, the foam is shadow like dark lace, & then skerts [sic] off the water like silvery grey silk—lovely. I wish you were down here to see it all.

Your cheese was so nice, by the way. I wondered however, in winter you had managed to make it. It was awfully good of you.

The Finn is waiting for me to go out. The sea has been like milk, & like *white steel, all day. I will write you a nice letter later—this is a scrawl. Write to me here—I am so forlorn[.]*

Regards to Will   I shall be home in 5 or 6 weeks—Hurray!
Love
D. H. Lawrence [72]

[Compton House, St. Peter's Road, Bournemouth, 2 February 1912]

[To May Chambers Holbrook]
(Are you wondering what has become of me? I am scandalously lax in my correspondence.

Tomorrow I leave here—& for some things am very sorry. I go for a week to Garnetts, down in Kent—then, on the 9th or 10th I shall come to Eastwood. I look forward so much to seeing you & having a bit of a razzle.

Yrs
D. H. Lawrence

Regards to Will.[73]

Worksop [Notts.]—Tuesday [5 March 1912]

[To May Chambers Holbrook]
(—Rather rum old place—snied with colliers—just been in a pub & found it crowded[?] out—Going to the Priory—Shirebrook's too slow for anything   How's Bill—

D. H. L.[74]

% Mrs Plumb/Bradnop/Leek/Staffs/28 March 1912

(My dear Toutz [May Chambers Holbrook],[75]

I am here since Monday—shall be home again—D. V. [—] on Saturday evening. It's a truly rural sort of place. Diddler and I dodge about at evening. His school has 51 kids—a girl for the infants. It's pretty—Derbyshire-ish—grey stone—fields dark green. I gave the little clods a lesson on color yesterday afternoon—they gorped like frogs. Afterwards the Vicar & I had a heart-rending discussion for an hour and a half, on the church. In the evening Diddler took me a tat-tar,[76] and of course got lost. We wriggled over a river on a rail. It's very Switzerlandish, just over the Long Shaw. Later we called at a farm, where the old woman reigns supreme in a fur shoulder-cape, and the old man, deaf as a post, blorts like a bullock occasionally, nearly making you jump out of your skin. Mrs. Titterton is the masterful sort. She gives me to understand she would mother me: manage me, that means. She mothers her own three great sons to such an extent that they will never marry. She keeps them in order, but they're very happy: live good & healthy animals. Jack runs the rig in Leek occasionally. A woman throned is really ——!

I'll bring you Man & Superman on Sunday. I suppose J[essie]. will be at the cottage. The play was very good. I said nothing to Mrs. Weekley about coming over. Will discuss it further with you.

Messages to Bill

Love

D. H. Lawrence [77]

[Brentford, Middx., 26 April 1912] [78]

[To William Holbrook]

([Oh Bill—it's ripping down here—slightly different from the cottage—Heaven on a lower plane, shall we say? By the end of this razzle, I shall sigh for peace under a pear-tree.

Love

D. H. Lawrence [79]

[Hotel Deutscher Hof, Metz, Lorraine, Germany, 4 May 1912]

[To May Chambers Holbrook]

([Here I am at last—it's a wild long journey. Everything went quite smooth however. I'm already drinking my third pint of German beer. Heaven knows what a size I shall be by the time I get back. Lord, these German mugs.

Love

D. H. Lawrence [80]

Hôtel Rheinischer Hof—Trier [Rheinprovinz, Germany, 9 May 1912]

[To May Chambers Holbrook]

([This is a most delicious place—Trier. There's a wild old cathedral, most Catholic, great black stone gateways—oh it's a sweet town. It lies right

down in the valley—like Matlock Town—like this picture. I am sitting on
a steep hill, looking between the trees at the town below, and the river.
The foot of the hills is covered with vineyards. How you would love it!
But Moorgreen seems sweet to me. There's my address till Monday.

Love & to Will

D. H. Lawrence

I had to leave Metz, because they were going to arrest me for staring at their
idiotic fortifications.

D. H. L.[81]

[Drachenfels on the Rhine River, near Bonn, Germany]

Sunday [19 May 1912]

[To May Chambers Holbrook]

❲ I write on the top of Drachenfels—high above the Rhine. The river
winds and twists till it seems climbing the sky, far off. There are steep
mountains—or hills—covered entirely with wood. There is an island right
below—with tiny steamers going by—and near at hand, on the air, two
red butterflies making love. If they can spin and kiss at this height, there
in mid-air—then why should I bother about myself. There is a faint mist
over all the Rhineland—really magical. I hope you'll come one day. We
have come down on the steamer from Bonn.

Love—& to Will

D. H. Lawrence [82]

[Gasthaus zur Post, Beuerberg im Isarthal, Bavaria, Germany, 29 May 1912]

[To May Chambers Holbrook]

❲ I am now down in the Isar Valley—30 miles from Munich. It's a lovely
place—wild valley, great blue mountains—snow capped—& masses of the
loveliest flowers. You would simply adore it. We are in the midst of this
play—it's a sort of OberAmmergau Passion business—ripping. Shall be
moving in a day or two.

Love & to Will

D. H. L.[83]

Icking/bei München/Isarthal. [Bavaria, Germany, 8 June 1912]

[To May Chambers Holbrook]

❲ Your card followed me down here. What a long way off you seem! Bavaria is lovelier than a dream, thick with flowers that even our garden would hardly grow. We have breakfast on the balcony. Below, the peasants work in the wheat—one stroke of the hoe in five minutes. Beyond, in the pine woods, the pale green glacier river, icy to look at. Beyond, a great lot of mountains, all day long changing. In the evening their snow is like flame on the dusk. I wish you could see it all. Today we are shopping in München.

Love & to Will

D. H. Lawrence [84]

[Icking bei München, Isarthal, Bavaria, Germany, 13 July 1912]

[To May Chambers Holbrook]

What an exciting letter that was! The emigration idea is, I should say, a fine one. Australia is a new country, new morals: it is not a split from England, but a new nation. But which of the States?—You don't say—N.S. Wales or Queensland? I shan't come back to England for a long time, if I can help it. Now, I want to wander. Your notes were good—rather fascinating—do go on, I should love the rest.

I think, at the end of next week I am going on a walking tour, over Innsbrück & the Austrian Tyrol to Verona. I am not sure yet. But I will let you have addresses later on. 'Haus Vogelnest'—Wolfratshausen will always find me.[85] But move, tell Will he must move. I will write to him. It is so hot here now, I want to get up to the snow.

Love

D. H. Lawrence [86]

[Sterzing am Brenner, Tirol, Austria (now Italy), 2 September 1912]

[To William Holbrook]

I'm still on the go—came over the mountains with a couple of fellows [87] on Wednesday, through the snow. Glory, but it was cold. Now it's hotter, & getting Italian in feel. I am fearfully interested about the emigration business. Tell me about your business & things. You might let me have a line to Bozen—in Tirol—(Haupt-postlagernd). It is some 70 miles on, so I shall be there next Friday or so. But write at once & tell me. I must write as soon as I get settled. How is Jont? [88]

Love

D. H. Lawrence [89]

[*Villa Igéa, Lago di Garda, Italy, ? January? 1913*]

[*To William Holbrook*]

. . . .

❨ *Now this is positively the last word I am going to say about the whole matter. I swear hereafter to keep out of the pulpit. But I only preach because it affects me about you.*

If you had 24 bob a week, what would you do? Oh God, it is a purposeless generation.

I wish you were here. We have a box at the theatre—no it's not like Teddy Rayners [90]—*and we see Amleto who is Hamlet with an Eyetalian hat on—and we nearly die.* [91] *The men and women are faithful in marriage, on the whole—but they have tribes of children. The butcher said to his wife one night "You were going to have an infant, weren't you?" "Yes, you dolt," she said. "I had it this morning. There it is in the cradle." And she went out to fetch some charcoal in. They are a spunky lot, and no soul or intellect. It's an awful relief to live among them. The theatre is quite grand. On Sunday all the men get blind drunk. I go to a pub in Bogliaco sometimes. It's a rum shop. There's a great open fireplace, about level with your knees, for the guest of honor. So I sit on one with my feet near the fire. And raised up above the company I drink my Vermouth.* [92] *And now and then the girl comes to blow up the fire with a great long blow-pipe of iron, the earliest form of bellows. Then I talk to the draper, & learn to play cards with the most awful ugly Neapolitan cards you ever saw. And one man has been in South America, & another talks German, and when they are a bit tipsy their eyes blaze. But they are gentle and awfully nice. They drink new wine—ghastly stuff. One can also get hot punch. I wish you were here —I do, with all my heart. We have an enormous flat to ourselves—& could put up a regiment. I have got wine & brandy, & the stove going, and a great room, & devil a fellow to drink with. It's sad.*

I'm not going to settle down. I shall be in England sometime in spring. Then I shall come abroad again for the winter. There's nothing like keeping on the move. I love Italy, & want to go south to Naples. I love these people. They haven't learnt not to be themselves yet. Let me hear what you are going to do. We'd better stick together.

Yours—also to a cinder (it's an oath)

D. H. Lawrence [93]

[Lucerne, Switzerland, 22 September 1913]

[To May Chambers Holbrook]

❨ I hope you got my letter from Wolfratshausen. God knows where my own letters are wandering now. I am going across Switzerland on foot. Came over the Rigi today to Lucerne, & now am going down the lake to Fluelen. When I get an address, in Italy, I will send it you. Love to both.

D. H. L.[94]

Lerici per Fiascherino/Golfo della Spezia/Italia/domenica—22 febbraio [1914]

❨ My dear May [Chambers Holbrook],

Why don't you write me a proper letter and tell me about Will's going to Canada? [95] You know right well I want to hear. Is he going anywhere definite?—is he going with the boys?—I don't like the idea of their staying at Doncaster. It is the same here, the vineyards and the terraces are falling into disuse, while the men go to America to work in the factories, or they go as stokers on board ship. Here almost every man has spent his time in America—seven years in Buenos Ayres, or in the United States. They will not stay any longer in Italy to be peasants without money. —You know that here they work the land on the 'half' system. There is no rent. The peasant takes the land, works up the olives and the wine, takes half the crop for himself, gives half to the landlord: half the wine, half the oil, half the wood, and half the maize. And the system no longer holds. In some parts the peasant only gets a third. They work and slave, they make a living, and save a little. But in ten years of America they can save as much as in a hundred years of Italy. And the men can't settle any more. They seem to have a nostalgia of restlessness. Italy is a country on the change, and suffering it acutely. Fifty years ago, almost every man was a peasant. In one generation it has all changed. So that now the conditions are strange, there is a queer lethargy among the women, and a queer, sad, gnawing restlessness among the men. They leave their wives for seven years at a time—it is a queer business altogether. It is queer how the old, unconscious carelessness and fatalism of indisposition is working rapidly, decomposing, making the nation feverish and active. There is no religion to speak of. Catholicism is in disrepute. It is a queer country. When I think how practically seven men out of ten emigrate from the villages round about, go for seven years at least—then the stability of the world seems gone. What is England and Italy and America, when they mix their populations as they do.[96]

Here it is as beautiful as ever. There is a big, big bowl of violets on the table. In the rocks by the sea the little white and yellow narcissus, such as one buys off Rowley's greengrocer cart in Eastwood, are twinkling away in the sunshine. Down the steep slopes there are many magenta coloured little anemones. —They are beating down the olives with long canes, and all the ground is sprinkled with the little black fruit like damsons. And all the mills by the little streams are grinding away, the peasant women are carrying great panniers of olives on their heads down to the village. It is all wonderful and sunny and beautiful. But it is all threaded through with this same absence and unsureness of emigration.

We have heaps of friends here. This morning early came a little priest from the Seminary at Sarzana, to bring us a little music: the schoolmistress from Tellaro will come this afternoon to tell us of her love affair with Luigi, who is the handsomest man I have ever seen handle a guitar, and who makes love very badly with the Maestra:[97] yesterday we spent the day at the Cochranes, who are rich as rich—butler and footman to serve four people at table—tomorrow we go to the Pearses[98] at Marigola, with whom the Empress Frederich stayed for a winter. It is a mixed life—and we have it pretty well both ways. I like people as people anywhere.

I think we come to England in June, when we shall be married. But I want to come back here in the autumn, to this beloved, beautiful little cottage.

The sea is rough today, no boating among the rocks. It is a sad sound, the waves all the time broken on the rocks & caves.

Please ask Will to write to me, and write to me also yourself. I am sorry you have been ill. I was hoping that there, happy again in the little country school, you would be well. —Tell me news of J[essie]. and the boys and your mother and father, will you. Tell me all about them. And if there is anything you want to know, just tell me.

Tanti, tanti saluti from us both

D. H. Lawrence[99]

APPENDIX

APPENDIX

In the following glossary, I have attempted to identify the names most frequently referred to in this third and final volume of the Lawrence biography. Starred entries mark contributors to this volume, and at the conclusion of entries I have indicated those who contributed memoirs to Volume I and/or Volume II. Additional biographical data, pertinent to an understanding of a whole career, may sometimes be found in "Notes and Sources," following initial source identifications. In this glossary, I have on occasion omitted certain nonce identifications given in "Notes and Sources."

°ACTON, HAROLD (MARIO MITCHELL) (1904———). Eng. writer long resident in Italy. Knew Lawrence at Villa Mirenda, Scandicci (1926–1928). Friend of Norman Douglas, Reggie Turner, Pino Orioli, Scott-Moncrieff in Florence.

°ALDINGTON, RICHARD (1892———). Eng. poet, novelist, biographer, critic, editor, translator. Devoted friend of Lawrence from July, 1914. Educ. Dover Coll. and London U. Marriage (18 Oct. 1913) to Hilda Doolittle ("H. D."), Amer. Imagist poet, ended in divorce. Served in World War I (1916–1918). At first a leader of the Imagists, he later refused to be identified with any movement. In Aug., 1926, Lawrence visited him at Malthouse Cottage, Padworth, Berks.; in Oct., 1926, Mr. Aldington visited the Lawrences at Villa Mirenda, Scandicci, Florence; and in Oct.–Nov., 1928, the Lawrences were his guests at La Vigie, Île de Port-Cros, Var, France. Author of *D. H. Lawrence: An Indiscretion* (1927); *Life for Life's Sake* (1941); *D. H. Lawrence: Portrait of a Genius But . . .* (1950); *Pinorman* (1954). Editor, with Giuseppe Orioli, of Lawrence's *Last Poems* (1932) and of an anthology compiled from the prose of Lawrence, *The Spirit of Place* (1935), and author of introductions to Lawrence reprints by Penguin and Heinemann. Now makes home in France. See Vol. I.

"ARABELLA." See YORKE, DOROTHY ("Arabella").

°BARR, MRS. BARBARA, nee BARBARA WEEKLEY (1904———). Daughter of Prof. Ernest and Frieda Weekley. B. at Nottm. Educ. at dame school, Bedford Park, London, and St. Paul's Girls School, London; art school, Nottm.; and

633

Slade School of Art, London. In 1923 again met Lawrence at Catherine Carswell's. Stayed with Lawrences at Spotorno (1925), at Florence (1927, 1928), at Bandol (Winter, 1928–1929, 1930). With Lawrence when he died. After return to England, lived with father at Chiswick until marriage (1934) to John Stuart Barr, journalist and politician. Daughter Ursula born in 1936. Now lives in London. See Vols. I and II.

BEVERIDGE, MILLICENT. Scottish painter. B. at Hukcaldy, Scotland, studied art at Glasgow, and thereafter lived chiefly in Paris. Knew Lawrence during Taormina period (1920–1922), and renewed friendship after Lawrence's return to Europe in 1925.

°BRETT, THE HON. DOROTHY E. ("Brett") (10 Nov. 1891———). British-born painter, since 1924 resident in Taos, N. Mex. Devoted friend of Lawrence from late 1915. Sailed from Eng. to U.S. with Lawrences in Spring, 1924, travelled with them to Oaxaca (1924–1925), neighbored at Del Monte Ranch (Summer, 1925), saw Lawrence last times in Capri and Italy (Spring, 1926). Daughter of Reginald Baliol Brett, 2nd Viscount Esher; sister of the Ranee of Sarawak. Encouraged by Gen. Sir Ian Hamilton, studied at Slade School of Art, London. Among her friends of this period were Katherine Mansfield, Virginia Woolf, Lytton Strachey, Bertrand Russell, Aldous Huxley, Mark Gertler. Since coming to U.S., has been part of a circle that has included Mabel Dodge Luhan, Alfred Stieglitz, Georgia O'Keeffe, Robinson Jeffers. Author of *Lawrence and Brett* (1933). See Vols. I and II.

°BREWSTER, MRS. ACHSAH, nee ACHSAH BARLOW. Amer. painter, long resident abroad. B. in New Haven, Conn. Married (Dec., 1910) Earl H. Brewster. Together with husband, knew Lawrences at Capri during Taormina period (1921–1922), persuaded them to follow to Ceylon (1922), continued friendship in Europe upon Lawrences' return from U.S. in 1925. Co-author (with Earl H. Brewster) of *D. H. Lawrence: Reminiscences and Correspondence* (1934), containing Lawrence letters not included in *Letters*. See Vol. II.

°BREWSTER, EARL H. (1878———). Amer. painter and student of oriental philosophy, long resident abroad—Europe, Ceylon, India. B. in Chagrin Falls, Ohio. Married (Dec., 1910) Achsah Barlow. Together with wife, knew Lawrences at Capri during Taormina period (1921–1922), persuaded them to follow to Ceylon (1922), continued friendship in Europe upon Lawrences' return from U.S. in 1925. Co-author (with Achsah Barlow Brewster) of *D. H. Lawrence: Reminiscences and Correspondence* (1934), containing Lawrence letters not included in *Letters*. Since 1935, has made his home in India. See Vol. II.

BREWSTER, HARWOOD (1913———), now Mrs. Harwood Picard of Washington, D.C. Daughter of Earl H. and Achsah Barlow Brewster.

°BROWN, CURTIS (1866–1945). Managing Director of the International Publishing Bureau, Curtis Brown, Ltd., of London, Paris, and New York. He became Lawrence's literary agent in England in 1921, and later (1923) in America. Author of *Contacts* (1935), containing Lawrence letters not included in *Letters*.

°BURROW, DR. TRIGANT (1875–1950). Amer. psychoanalyst and specialist in group-analysis; Scientific Director of The Lifwynn Foundation (1927–1950). Corresponded with Lawrence (1925–1927).

BURROWS, LOUISE ("Louie") (13 Feb. 1888——). Daughter of Alfred and Louisa Wheatley Burrows. B. at Ilkeston, Derby. Lived at Church Cottage, Cossall, near Ilkeston; later moved to Quorn, Leics. Met Lawrence while he was attending Pupil-Teacher Centre at Ilkeston (1903–1905). Lawrence proposed marriage 3 Dec. 1910; relationship ended Feb., 1912. A school-teacher.

°BYNNER, WITTER ("Hal") (1881——). Amer. poet. Knew the Lawrences during New Mexico periods (1922–1925), travelled with them and Willard ("Spud") Johnson in Mexico (Spring, 1923), neighbored at Chapala, Jalisco, Mexico (May–July, 1923). Author of *Journey with Genius* (1951), containing Lawrence letters not included in *Letters*. Divides time between homes in Santa Fe, N. Mex., and Chapala. See Vol. II.

CANNAN, MRS. MARY, nee MARY ANSELL, actress. Married James M. Barrie, then Gilbert Cannan. Friend and neighbor of the Lawrences and Mac-kenzies while all were living near Chesham, Bucks. *ca.* Aug., 1914—Jan., 1915, and thereafter during their sojourns in Europe.

°CARSWELL, MRS. CATHERINE, nee CATHERINE ROXBURGH MACFARLANE (1879–1946). Scottish writer. Devoted friend of Lawrence from Summer, 1914, seeing him last in London in Sept., 1926. Daughter of George Gray Mac-farlane, merchant of Glasgow. Married (1903) Herbert P. M. Jackson (marriage annulled, 1908); (1915) Donald Carswell (1882–1940), Scot-tish barrister, journalist, and writer. Reviewer and dramatic critic for *Glasgow Herald* (1907–1911). Author of *The Savage Pilgrimage* (1932, 1951). Son, John Carswell (1918——), edited her autobiographic *Lying Awake* (1950). See Vols. I and II.

°CARTER, FREDERICK. Eng. painter and etcher. To discuss Apocalyptic sym-bols, Lawrence visited him at Pontesbury, Salop, in early Jan., 1924; and Mr. Carter visited the dying Lawrence at Bandol in Nov., 1929. Author of *D. H. Lawrence and the Body Mystical* (1932). See Vol. II.

°CERF, BENNETT (Alfred) (1898——). Amer. book publisher, editor, colum-nist. With Norman Douglas, visited Lawrence at Villa Mirenda, Scandicci, Florence, in June, 1928.

CHAMBERS, ALAN AUBREY (2 July 1882—20 May 1946). Son of Mr. and Mrs. Edmund Chambers of The Haggs; older brother of Jessie, May, and J. D. Chambers. Friend of Lawrence. Married (15 Oct. 1910) Alvina Lawrence, D. H. Lawrence's first cousin. Emigrated to Canada.

CHAMBERS, EDMUND (10 Jan. 1863—10 May 1946). Married (? Oct. 1881) Sarah Ann Oates. Father of May, Jessie, J. D. Chambers, etc. Tenant of The Haggs.

CHAMBERS, HUBERT (23 April 1888——). Son of Mr. and Mrs. Edmund Cham-bers of The Haggs; younger brother of May and Jessie; older brother of J. D. Chambers. Emigrated to Canada.

°CHAMBERS, DR. J(ONATHAN). D(AVID). (13 Oct. 1898——). Son of Mr. and Mrs. Edmund Chambers of The Haggs; younger brother of May and Jessie

Chambers. Now a Professor in sub-department of Economic Hist., The University, Nottm. See Vol. I.

°CHAMBERS, JESSIE. See WOOD, MRS. JESSIE.

°CHAMBERS, (MURIEL) MAY. See HOLBROOK, MRS. (MURIEL) MAY.

CHAMBERS, MRS. SARAH ANN, nee SARAH ANN OATES (27 Feb. 1859—8 Jan. 1937). Married (? Oct. 1881) Edmund Chambers. Mother of May, Jessie, J. D. Chambers, etc.

°CLARKE, MRS. ADA, nee (LETTICE) ADA LAWRENCE (16 June 1887—3 July 1948). D. H. Lawrence's younger sister. Married (1913) W. Edward Clarke of Ripley, Derby. Co-author (with G. Stuart Gelder) of *Early Life of D. H. Lawrence* (1932), containing Lawrence letters not included in *Letters*. See Vol. I.

°CROSBY, CARESSE, MRS. HARRY CROSBY, nee MARY JACOB (1892——). Amer. editor and publisher. Married (1922) Harry Crosby, and with him founded (1927) Black Sun Press at 2 rue Cardinale in Paris. Published *de luxe* editions of Lawrence's *Sun* (Oct., 1928) and *The Escaped Cock* (Sept., 1929). *Ca.* March, 1929, Lawrence visited the Crosbys at Le Moulin du Soleil, Ermenonville, Oise, France.

CROSBY, HARRY (GREW) (1898–1929). Amer. poet and publisher of *de luxe* editions. Married (1922) Mary Jacob Peabody ("Caresse"). With Caresse, founded (1927) Black Sun Press at 2 rue Cardinale in Paris. Advisory editor (1928–1929) of *transition*. Published *de luxe* editions of Lawrence's *Sun* (Oct., 1928) and *The Escaped Cock* (Sept., 1929). Lawrence wrote preface for his *Chariot of the Sun* (1931). *Ca.* March, 1929, Lawrence visited the Crosbys at Le Moulin du Soleil, Ermenonville, Oise, France. Committed suicide in New York City.

°DAVIDSON, JO (1883–1952). Amer. sculptor, best known for busts of famous contemporaries. Made clay head of dying Lawrence at Ad Astra Sanatorium, Vence, late Feb., 1930.

°DAVIES, RHYS (1903——). Anglo-Welsh novelist and short-story writer. Visited Lawrence at Bandol, Dec., 1928—March, 1929; travelled with him to Paris, March, 1929.

°DAVIS, ROBERT HOBART ("Bob") (1869–1942). Amer. playwright, editor, traveller, amateur photographer, columnist for *New York Sun*. Photographed Lawrence in Orioli's bookshop at 6, Lungarno Corsini, Florence, in May, 1928.

°DOUGLAS, (GEORGE) NORMAN (1868–1952). Eng. writer. Met Lawrence during *English Review* days (*ca.* 1909), again in Florence in Nov., 1919, and thereafter during Lawrence's stays in and near Florence in 1921, 1925–1929. Introduced Lawrence to Maurice Magnus in Nov., 1919, upheld Magnus against Lawrence in *D. H. Lawrence and Maurice Magnus: A Plea for Better Manners* (1924) and elsewhere. Served as the prototype for the character James Argyle in *Aaron's Rod* (1922). Author of *Siren Land* (1911), *Old Calabria* (1915), *South Wind* (1917), *Looking Back* (1933), etc. See Vol. II.

°GARDINER, MARGARET (MRS. MARGARET GARDINER-BERNAL, 1904——). Sister of Rolf Gardiner. Visited Lawrence at Villa Mirenda, Scandicci, Florence, *ca.* April, 1928.

°GARDINER, ROLF (1902———). Eng. farmer, forester, pioneer of Land Service Camps for Youth in Northern Europe following World War I. Educ. at Cambridge. In 1927, with avowed purpose of fulfilling Lawrence's vision, founded the Springhead estate, at Fontmell Magna, Shaftesbury, Dorset. Met Lawrence in London, Aug., 1926, visited him at Les Diablerets, Feb., 1928. Now divides time between Springhead and Nyasaland.

°GERHARDI, WILLIAM (ALEXANDER) (1895———). Eng. novelist. B. in St. Petersburg (Leningrad) of Eng. parents. Met Lawrence in London, Oct., 1925.

°GHISELIN, BREWSTER (1903———). Amer. poet, scholar, educator. Visited Lawrence at Bandol, Jan., 1929.

°GOLDRING, DOUGLAS (1887———). Eng. editor, novelist, critic, travel writer. In 1908, was associated with Ford Madox Ford as sub-editor of *English Review*, at which time saw Lawrence. Renewed friendship during second Hermitage period (1919), encouraged production of *Touch and Go* and arranged for its printing (1920), interested Insel-Verlag in publishing Lawrence in Germany, Thomas Seltzer, in U.S. Author of autobiography *Odd Man Out* (1935) and *Life Interests* (1948), each containing Lawrence letters not included in *Letters*. See Vols. I and II.

HESTER, GORDON. Detective Inspector, "C" Division, Metropolitan Police District, London. On 5 July 1929, led police raid on Lawrence Exhibition at Warren Gallery, 39a, Maddox St., London, W. 1.

HILTON, MRS. ENID C., nee ENID C. HOPKIN. Daughter of Councillor William Edward Hopkin and his first wife, Sallie A., of Eastwood. Married Laurence Hilton. In the late 1920's, visited the Lawrences in Italy. In London, helped distribute banned Orioli edition of *Lady Chatterley's Lover* to subscribers in England; worked with Aldous Huxley on preparation of *Letters*. Now makes her home at Ukiah, Calif. See Vol. I.

°HOLBROOK, MRS. (MURIEL) MAY, nee (MURIEL) MAY CHAMBERS (20 Oct. 1883—8 July 1955). Daughter of Mr. and Mrs. Edmund Chambers of The Haggs; older sister of Jessie and J. D. Chambers. Schoolteacher. Married (1 Nov. 1906) William Holbrook. In 1915, emigrated to Canada.

°HOLBROOK, WILLIAM (? Dec. 1884———). B. in Smalley, Derby. General stoneworker. Married (1 Nov. 1906) (Muriel) May Chambers. In Spring, 1914, emigrated to Canada.

°HOLDEN, RALPH A(INSWORTH). (1880–1950). Member of firm of Richardson Sowerby, Holden & Co. of 5, John St., Bedford Row, London, W.C. 1, solicitors for Dorothy and Philip Trotter in Lawrence Exhibition case (1929).

°HOPKIN, COUNCILLOR WILLIAM EDWARD (12 June 1862—2 Dec. 1951). Lifelong friend of Lawrence at Eastwood. B. at Castle Donington, Leics., moved to Eastwood when very young. Married Sallie A.; Olive L. Father of Enid C. Hilton by first wife. Colliery clerk, cobbler, proprietor of bootshop in Eastwood, magistrate and member of County Council, antiquarian, local historian. Preserved valuable collection of Lawrenciana. See Vol. I.

°Hughes, Glenn Arthur (1894———). Prof. of Eng. Lit. and Dir. of School of Drama, U. of Wash. Met Lawrence in Spain in May, 1929, while a J. S. Guggenheim Memorial fellow. Author of *Imagism and Imagists* (1931), etc. See Vol. I.

Hutchinson, St. John, K.C. (1884–1942). Eng. barrister-at-law, Dorothy Warren Trotter's defense council during Lawrence Exhibition case (1929). Married (1910) Mary Barnes. Had known Lawrence personally during War Years in England.

°Huxley, Aldous (Leonard) (1894———). Eng. novelist, short-story writer, dramatist, essayist, poet, biographer. Met Lawrence in London, Dec., 1915. From 1926 was often with Lawrence (Florence, Forte dei Marmi, Les Diablerets, Bandol, Paris, Chexbres, Vence). With Lawrence when he died. Brother of Sir Julian Huxley. Educ. at Eton and at Baliol Coll., Oxford. Married (1919) Maria Nys (?–1955), a Belgian who had gone to England during World War I as refugee; (1956) Laura Archera. Associated with J. M. Murry on *Athenaeum* (1919–1920). Edited Lawrence's *Letters* (1932), to which contributed Introduction. Now lives in Calif. See Vol. I.

Huxley, Sir Julian (Sorell) (1887———). Eng. biologist and author. Older brother of Aldous Huxley. Married (1919) Marie Juliette Baillot of Neuchâtel, Switzerland. With Lawrence at Les Diablerets, Feb., 1928, and elsewhere during last years of his life.

°Jaffe-Richthofen, Dr. Else (1874———). Eldest of three daughters of Baron and Baronin Friedrich von Richthofen; Frieda's older sister. Prof. of Social Economics. German translator of Lawrence's *Sons and Lovers, Rainbow, Boy in the Bush,* "The Fox," *Woman Who Rode Away, Plumed Serpent,* etc. Married Dr. Edgar Jaffe, Prof. of Political Economy at U. of Heidelberg. Now lives in Heidelberg. *The Rainbow* is dedicated to her. See Vol. I.

°Johns, Orrick (1887–1946). Amer. poet. Visited Lawrence at Villa Mirenda, Scandicci, Florence, *ca.* July, 1927, possibly again in 1928.

King, Mrs. Emily, nee Emily Una Lawrence (21 March 1882———). D. H. Lawrence's older sister, later Mrs. Samuel King of North Muskham, Notts. See Vol. I.

Lawrence, Emily Una. See King, Mrs. Emily.

°Lawrence, Frieda. See Ravagli, Mrs. Frieda Lawrence.

°Lawrence, (Lettice) Ada. See Clarke, Mrs. Ada.

°Lindsay, Jack (1900———). Australian-born writer, long resident in England. With P. R. Stephensen, operated Fanfrolico Press with offices at 71, High Holborn, London (1926–1930). Declined to publish Lawrence's *Paintings,* encouraged Stephensen to found Mandrake Press.

°Luhan (Lujan), Mrs. Mabel Dodge, nee Mabel Ganson (1879———). Amer. autobiographer, hostess, patroness of arts, long a resident of Taos, N. Mex. Encouraged Lawrence to come to Taos in 1922 to write of Amer. Indian life, and knew him personally from Sept., 1922, to Oct., 1924, their correspondence continuing until his death. In 1923, married Antonio ("Tony") Luhan (Lujan), Pueblo Indian. Author of autobiography *Intimate Memories.* Her *Lorenzo in Taos* (1932) contains Lawrence letters not included in *Letters.* See Vol. II.

°MACKENZIE, LADY (FAITH) COMPTON, nee FAITH STONE. Eng. writer. Married (1905) (Edward Montague) Compton Mackenzie (later Sir Compton Mackenzie). (See Vols. I and II.) The Lawrences had made friends with the Mackenzies while all were living near Chesham, Bucks., *ca.* Aug., 1914 —Jan., 1915, and renewed the friendship on Capri, Dec., 1919—Feb., 1920, Mar., 1926. Author of three volumes of autobiography: *As Much as I Dare* (1938), *More Than I Should* (1940), *Always Afternoon* (1943). See Vol. II.

MEAD, FREDERICK (1847–1945). Eng. magistrate before whose Court of Summary Jurisdiction, Metropolitan Police District, sitting at Marlborough Street Police Court, London, was heard Lawrence Exhibition case (8 Aug. 1929).

°MIRENDA, SIGNOR RAUL. Lawrence's landlord at Villa Mirenda, Scandicci, Florence (May, 1926—June, 1928). An Army officer.

°MOHR, (DR.) MAX (1891–1944). German doctor and dramatist. Met Lawrence at Villa Jaffe, Irschenhausen, *ca.* Aug., 1927, visited him at Les Diablerets, Feb., 1928. In Aug.–Sept., 1929, Lawrences stayed at Kaffee Angermeir, Rottach-am-Tegernsee, Bavaria, near Mohr's farm-home *Wulfsgrube*. Visited Lawrence at Bandol, Sept.–Oct., 1929. Wife, Kathe; daughter, Eve. Emigrated from Germany in 1935, spent last years of life in Shanghai.

°MORLAND, DR. ANDREW (JOHN), M.D., F.R.C.P. (1896–1957). Eng. physician and specialist in pulmonary tuberculosis. At request of Mark Gertler, visited dying Lawrence at Bandol in Jan., 1930, for him recommended Ad Astra Sanatorium at Vence.

°MURRY, JOHN MIDDLETON (1889–1957). Eng. author, editor, critic, farmer. Met Lawrence in London, Summer, 1913. Witness at marriage (13 July 1914) of Lawrence and Frieda. Married (1918) Katherine Mansfield; (1924) Violet le Maistre; Elizabeth Cockbayne. Together with Katherine Mansfield, was neighbor of Lawrences at Chesham, Bucks., Autumn, 1914; at Higher Tregerthen, Zennor, St. Ives, Cornwall, Spring, 1916. Again knew Lawrence in London, Dec., 1923—March, 1924, Oct., 1925. Ed. of *Athenaeum* (1919–1921), of *Adelphi* (1923–1930), etc. Author of *Son of Woman* (1931, 1954), *Reminiscences of D. H. Lawrence* (1933), the autobiography *Between Two Worlds* (1934), *Love, Freedom and Society* (1957). Ed. of Katherine Mansfield. Last resided at Diss, Norfolk. See Vols. I and II.

MUSKETT, HERBERT GEORGE, C.B.E. (1864–1947). Senior partner in firm of Wontner & Sons of 40, Bedford Row, London, W.C. 1, solicitors to the Commissioner of Metropolitan Police in *Rainbow* prosecution (1915) and Lawrence Exhibition case (1929).

°NEFF, JOHN C. (1913——). Amer. free-lance writer. Wrote memoir describing visit to Ravaglis at Kiowa Ranch (pub. 1937).

NICHOLS, ROBERT (MALISE BOWYER) (1893–1944). Eng. poet and dramatist. Met Lawrence in London, Nov., 1915, and again in Majorca, April, 1929. Friend of Philip Heseltine (Peter Warlock). See Vol. I.

°ORIOLI, GIUSÈPPE ("Pino") (1884–1942). Italian antiquarian bookseller and publisher. B. at Alfonsine, Italy. Met Lawrence in Cornwall (1916–1917), renewed acquaintance in Florence (1919–1922, 1926–1928). Owned famous bookshop on Lungarno Corsini in Florence. Supervised publication of *Lady Chatterley's Lover*, published Lawrence's translation of *The Story of Doctor Manente, The Virgin and the Gipsy, Apocalypse*, co-edited, with Richard Aldington, *Last Poems.*

°PATMORE, MRS. BRIGIT. Eng. writer. B. in Ireland, but has lived all her life in England or abroad. Married grandson of Coventry Patmore. Friend of Violet Hunt at South Lodge. Met Lawrence through Ford Madox Ford prior to World War I, was part of Lawrence-Aldington circle during Mecklenburgh Square days, 1917, renewed friendship during Lawrences' visit to England in Summer, 1926. As guest of Aldingtons, was with Lawrences last at La Vigie, Île de Port-Cros, Var, Oct.–Nov., 1928.

°PEARCE, T(HOMAS). M(ATTHEWS). (1902——). Prof., Dept. of Eng., U. of N. Mex., Albuquerque. Friend of Ravaglis. Wrote memoir describing Frieda's funeral.

RAUH, IDA, actress. Married (1911) author Max Eastman (div., 1922), later Andrew Dasburg, artist. Knew Lawrence during New Mexico period (1922–1925). For her, in 1925, Lawrence wrote his Biblical play, *David*. She was with Frieda and Frieda's daughter Barbara (Mrs. Barbara Weekley Barr) in Vence at the time of Lawrence's death.

°RAVAGLI, CAPT. ANGELO ("Angelino") (1891——). Husband of Frieda. B. in Tredozio, Italy. Saw service in World War I. Met the Lawrences in Nov., 1925, when they rented Villa Bernarda, Spotorno, owned by his wife. Visited Lawrences at Villa Mirenda. In April, 1933, came with Frieda to San Cristobal, N. Mex., to help her on Kiowa Ranch. Married (Oct., 1950) Frieda, became an Amer. citizen.

°RAVAGLI, MRS. FRIEDA LAWRENCE, nee EMMA MARIA FRIEDA JOHANNA VON RICHTHOFEN (11 Aug. 1879—11 Aug. 1956). Second daughter of Baron and Baronin Friedrich von Richthofen of Germany. Married (Sept., 1899) Ernest Weekley, by whom three children: Charles Montague (1900——), Elsa (1902——), Barbara (1904——); marriage dissolved (28 May 1914). Married (13 July 1914) D. H. Lawrence; (Oct., 1950) Capt. Angelo Ravagli. Spent last years of her life at El Prado, N. Mex., and Port Isabel, Tex. Her *"Not I, But the Wind . . ."* (1934) contains Lawrence letters not included in *Letters*. See Vols. I and II.

RICHTHOFEN, BARONIN VON, nee MARQUIER (1851?–1931?). Frieda's mother. In 1920's, lived at Baden-Baden.

RICHTHOFEN, JOHANNA VON ("Nusch") (1882——). Youngest daughter of Baron and Baronin Friedrich von Richthofen; younger sister of Frieda. Later Frau Max Schreibershofen; later Frau Emil Krug.

°ROBINSON, ROLAND E. (1913——). Irish-born Australian poet. Wrote memoir of visit to Lawrence's "Wyewurk," Thirroul, N.S.W. (pub. 1953).

ROBINSON & Co., MESSRS. PERCY. London solicitors acting for Lawrence in Exhibition case (1929).

°ROWSE, A(LFRED. L(ESLIE)., F.R.S.L. (1903——). Eng. historian, now a Fellow of All Souls College, Oxford. Wrote "spirit-of-place" essay on Lawrence's Eastwood (pub. 1952).

°Schoenberner, Franz (1892———). German editor and writer, now resident in U.S. Editor of *Jugend* (1926–1929), editor-in-chief of *Simplicissimus* (1929–1933). Through Dr. Else Jaffe-Richthofen, met Lawrence at Villa Jaffe, Irschenhausen, Bavaria, Sept., 1927.

°Schorer, Mark (1908———). Amer. novelist, critic, biographer, now Prof. of Eng., U. of Calif., Berkeley. Wrote memoir describing visit to Villa Mirenda, Scandicci, Florence (pub. 1953).

°Scott, Geoffrey (1885–1929). Eng. author and editor. Toward end of his life, was employed in America by the late Col. Ralph H. Isham in editing his recently acquired Boswell papers. On brief visit to England in Summer, 1929, supported his friends Dorothy and Philip Trotter during Lawrence Exhibition troubles in London; on 17 July 1929, wrote letter to Arnold Bennett soliciting his backing of the Trotters and Lawrence. Caught chill on sea-voyage, died of pneumonia in New York.

Seaman, Mrs. Elsa, nee Elsa Weekley (1902———). Daughter of Prof. Ernest and Frieda Weekley. Married Edward Seaman. Now lives at Ham, Richmond, Surrey.

Secker, Martin (1882———). Lawrence's principal publisher in Eng. from 1921 until the 1930's when the Eng. rights to his books were bought up by Heinemann. Mr. Secker also published the early work of Sir Compton Mackenzie, Norman Douglas, Gilbert Cannan, Francis Brett Young, Viola Meynell, and others. His business was reconstructed in 1935 under the style of Martin Secker and Warburg, Ltd. In 1937, he severed his connection to become a director of The Richards Press, Ltd.

°Siebenhaar, W(illiam). (1863–1937). Holland-born W.A. writer, author of the lyrical romance *Dorothea*, translator of E. D. Dekker's *Max Havelaar* (1927) for which Lawrence wrote introduction. Met Lawrence briefly at Perth in May, 1922, again in London, Sept., 1926.

°Sitwell, Sir Osbert, Bt., C.B.E. (1892———). Eng. poet, short-story writer, autobiographer. With sister, Dame Edith Sitwell (1887———), visited the Lawrences at Villa Mirenda in May, 1927.

°Soupault, Philippe (1897———). French poet, novelist, biographer. On behalf of French publisher Kra, wrote letter of 30 June 1928 prompting Lawrence to write hitherto unpublished "Autobiography."

Stephensen, P(ercival). R(eginald). (1901———). Australian writer and editor. With Jack Lindsay, operated Fanfrolico Press in London (1926–1929); thereafter, with Edward Goldston, bookseller, The Mandrake Press, which published Lawrence's *Paintings* (June, 1929) and *A Propos of Lady Chatterley's Lover* (June, 1930). The privately printed, unexpurgated *Pansies* (Aug., 1929) carries the Stephensen imprint. Visited Lawrence at Bandol, Dec., 1928—Jan., 1929. Returned to Australia in 1930's.

°Trotter, Mrs. Dorothy, nee Dorothy Warren (1896–1954). Owner of Warren Gallery at 39a, Maddox St., London, W. 1, where Lawrence's pictures were exhibited (June–Sept., 1929). Niece of Lady Ottoline Morrell; friend of Mark Gertler, Barbara Weekley, Catherine Carswell. Knew Lawrence personally at Garsington and Hampstead, 1915. Married (1928) Philip (Coutts) Trotter.

°Trotter, Philip (Coutts). Married (1928) Dorothy Warren, and functioned as her partner in Warren Gallery, doing routine administration while she retained art direction. In World War I, served in Welsh Guards and thereafter held ADC and staff appointments in various parts of Europe. From 1926 to 1929, operated wholesale depot in Hatton Garden, London, for sale of "Styrian Jade." Now lives in Edinburgh.

°UNTERMEYER, MRS. JEAN STARR (1886———). Amer. poet, anthologist, translator. Met the Lawrences in London, Sept., 1926.

°UNTERMEYER, LOUIS (1885———). Amer. poet, editor, anthologist. Met Lawrence first in Italy, then in London, Sept., 1926.

°WARREN, DOROTHY. See TROTTER, MRS. DOROTHY.

°WATSON, JEAN. On 16 July 1928, as Manager of Foreign Department, Curtis Brown, Ltd., London, forwarded to Lawrence Philippe Soupault's letter (30 June 1928) requesting biographical information, thus prompting Lawrence's hitherto unpublished "Autobiography." Now Mrs. Spencer Curtis Brown.

°WEEKLEY, BARBARA. See BARR, MRS. BARBARA.

°WEEKLEY, (CHARLES) MONTAGUE (1900———). Son of Prof. Ernest and Frieda Weekley. Educ. at St. Paul's School, London, and Oxford. Asst. in Dept. of Circulation, Victoria and Albert Museum (1924), and Deputy Keeper (1938). General Finance Branch, Ministry of Supply (1939–1943); Southern Dept., Foreign Office (1943–1944); Ministry of Education (1944–1946). Trustee of Whitechapel Art Gallery and a Governor of Parmiter's School from 1946. Officer-in-Charge of Bethnal Green Museum, London, since 1946. Author of *William Morris* (1934), *Thomas Bewick* (1953); General Ed. of The Library of English Art. See Vol. I.

WEEKLEY, ELSA. See SEAMAN, MRS. ELSA.

°WILKINSON, WALTER. Eng. puppetmaster. With brother, Gair Wilkinson, artist, a neighbor of the Lawrences during their tenancy of the Villa Mirenda, Scandicci, Florence (May, 1926—June, 1928).

WONTNER & SONS. See MUSKETT, HERBERT GEORGE.

°WOOD, MRS. JESSIE, nee JESSIE CHAMBERS (29 Jan. 1887—3 April 1944). Devoted friend of Lawrence during Eastwood and Croydon years. Known also as "E. T.," "Miriam," "Muriel," "The Princess." Daughter of Mr. and Mrs. Edmund Chambers of The Haggs. Helped Lawrence launch his writing career (1909). Married (3 June 1915) Mr. John R. Wood of Nottm. Author of *D. H. Lawrence: A Personal Record* (1935). See Vol. I.

YORKE, DOROTHY ("Arabella") (1892———). Amer. from Reading, Pa., long (28 years) resident in England, France, Italy. Had flat at 44, Mecklenburgh Sq., London, while Lawrences lived in Aldington flat at same address after expulsion from Cornwall (Oct., 1917). Friend of the Aldingtons. Knew the Lawrences at Middleton-by-Wirksworth (1918–1919), Scandicci (1926), Île de Port-Cros (1928).

Necrology (Vols. I and II)

DALLYN, MRS. VIOLA, nee VIOLA MEYNELL (188?–1956).
GAWLER, MRS. MAY EVA (1873–1957).
McLEOD, A. W. (1884–1956).
ROSMER, MRS. IRENE ROOKE (?–1958).
WESTON, EDWARD (1886–1958).

MAJOR FIRST EDITIONS OF THE WORKS OF D. H. LAWRENCE

For the data incorporated in the following list, I am indebted to Edward D. McDonald's *A Bibliography of the Writings of D. H. Lawrence* and *The Writings of D. H. Lawrence, 1925–1930: A Bibliographical Supplement,* and to William White's *D. H. Lawrence: A Checklist, 1931–1950.* Although it includes all major first editions, the list ignores certain minor items of interest to the collector only, most contributions to books and periodicals, and selections of his work made after Lawrence's death. For additional details, the reader is referred to the authorities above.

Aaron's Rod (novel). New York: Thomas Seltzer, April, 1922; London: Martin Secker, June, 1922.

Altitude (play). *The Laughing Horse* (No. 20, Summer, 1938).

Amores (poems). London: Duckworth, July, 1916; New York: B. W. Huebsch, 1916.

Apocalypse (essay). With an Introduction by Richard Aldington. Florence: G. Orioli, May, 1931; London: Martin Secker, 1932; New York: Viking, 1932.

A Propos of Lady Chatterley's Lover (essay extended from *My Skirmish with Jolly Roger*). London: The Mandrake Press, June, 1930; London: Heinemann, 1931; in Harry T. Moore, ed., *Sex, Literature and Censorship* (New York: Twayne, 1953), pp. 89–122 [first American publication].

Assorted Articles. London: Martin Secker, April, 1930; New York: Knopf, 1930.

Bay: A Book of Poems. Cover and Decorations designed by Anne Estelle Rice. London: The Beaumont Press, November, 1919.

Birds, Beasts and Flowers (poems). New York: Thomas Seltzer, 9 October 1923; London: Martin Secker, November, 1923 [includes *Tortoises*]; London: The Cresset Press, June, 1930 [with illustrations by Blair Hughes–Stanton].

Boy in the Bush, The (novel, with M. L. Skinner). London: Martin Secker, August, 1924; New York: Thomas Seltzer, 1924.

Captain's Doll, The (short novels). New York: Thomas Seltzer, April, 1923; London: Martin Secker, March, 1923, with title: *The Ladybird.*

Cavalleria Rusticana and Other Stories (translation from Giovanni Verga). With a Translator's Preface by D. H. Lawrence. London: Jonathan Cape, March, 1928; New York: Lincoln MacVeagh, The Dial Press, 1928.

Collected Poems. 2 vols. London: Martin Secker, September, 1928; New York: Jonathan Cape and Harrison Smith, 1928.

Collier's Friday Night, A (play). With an Introduction by Edward Garnett. London: Martin Secker, 1934.

David (play). London: Martin Secker, March, 1926; New York: Knopf, 1926.

"Delilah and Mr. Bircumshaw" (short story). *Virginia Quarterly Review*, XVI (No. 2, Spring, 1940), 257–66.

D. H. Lawrence's Letters to Bertrand Russell. Edited, with an Introduction by Harry T. Moore. New York: Gotham Book Mart, 1948.

England, My England and Other Stories. New York: Thomas Seltzer, 24 October 1922; London: Martin Secker, January, 1924.

Escaped Cock, The (short novel, original title of *The Man Who Died*). Paris: The Black Sun Press, September, 1929 [with water-color decorations by D. H. Lawrence]; London: Martin Secker, March, 1931, with title: *The Man Who Died;* New York: Knopf, 1931, with title: *The Man Who Died.*

Etruscan Places (travel essays). London: Martin Secker, 1932; New York: Viking, 1932.

Fantasia of the Unconscious (essays). New York: Thomas Seltzer, 23 October 1922; London: Martin Secker, September, 1923.

Fight for Barbara (play). *Argosy* [London], December, 1933.

First Lady Chatterley, The (novel). With a MS Report by Esther Forbes, and a Foreword by Frieda Lawrence. New York: The Dial Press, 1944.

"Gentleman from San Francisco, The" (translation with S. S. Koteliansky from Ivan Bunin), in Ivan Bunin, *The Gentleman from San Francisco and Other Stories,* trans. by S. S. Koteliansky and Leonard Woolf. London: The Hogarth Press, 1922.

Glad Ghosts (short story). London: Benn, November, 1926. Included in *The Woman Who Rode Away and Other Stories.*

"Introduction," in M[aurice] M[agnus], *Memoirs of the Foreign Legion.* London: Martin Secker, September, 1924; New York: Knopf, January, 1925.

Kangaroo (novel). London: Martin Secker, September, 1923; New York: Thomas Seltzer, 1923.

Ladybird, The (short novels). London: Martin Secker, March, 1923; New York: Thomas Seltzer, April, 1923, with title: *The Captain's Doll.*

Lady Chatterley's Lover (novel). Florence: Privately Printed, July, 1928 [unexpurgated]; Paris: Privately Printed, May, 1929 [Paris Popular Edition, unexpurgated, including "My Skirmish with Jolly Roger"]; London: Martin Secker, 1932 [Authorized Abridged Edition]; New York: Knopf, 1932 [Authorized Abridged Edition].

Last Poems. Edited by Richard Aldington and Giuseppe Orioli, with an Introduction by Richard Aldington. Florence: G. Orioli, 1932; New York: Viking, 1933; London: Heinemann, 1935.

Letters. Edited and with an Introduction by Aldous Huxley. London: Heinemann, 1932; New York: Viking, 1932.

Little Novels of Sicily (translation from Giovanni Verga). With a Note on Giovanni Verga by D. H. Lawrence. New York: Thomas Seltzer, March, 1925; Oxford: Basil Blackwell, April, 1925.

Look! We Have Come Through! (poems). London: Chatto, December, 1917; New York: B. W. Huebsch, 1918.

Lost Girl, The (novel). London: Martin Secker, November, 1920; New York: Thomas Seltzer, 1921.

Love Among the Haystacks and Other Pieces (short stories). With a Reminiscence by David Garnett. London: The Nonesuch Press, December, 1930; New York: Random House, n. d. [Limited Edition]; New York: Viking, 1933.

Lovely Lady and Other Stories, The. London: Martin Secker, 1933, including "The Man Who Loved Islands"; New York: Viking, 1933.

Love Poems and Others. London: Duckworth, February, 1913; New York: Mitchell Kennerley, 1913.

Man Who Died, The (short novel). Paris: The Black Sun Press, September, 1929, with title: *The Escaped Cock;* London: Martin Secker, March, 1931; New York: Knopf, 1931.

Married Man, The (play). *Virginia Quarterly Review*, XVI (Autumn, 1940), 523–47.

Mastro-don Gesualdo (translation from Giovanni Verga). With a Biographical Note [by D. H. Lawrence]. New York: Thomas Seltzer, 1923; London: Jonathan Cape, March, 1925.

Merry-Go-Round, The (play). *Virginia Quarterly Review*, XVII (Winter, 1941), Supp., 1–44.

Mr. Noon (fragment of a novel), in *A Modern Lover*. London: Martin Secker, 1934; New York: Viking, 1934.

Modern Lover, A (short stories and an unfinished novel). London: Martin Secker, 1934; New York: Viking, 1934.

Mornings in Mexico (travel essays). London: Martin Secker, July, 1927; New York: Knopf, 1927.

"Mortal Coil, The" (short story). *The Seven Arts*, July, 1917.

Movements in European History. London: Oxford University Press, March, 1921, under pseudonyn "Lawrence H. Davison"; Oxford University Press, May, 1925 [Large paper Edition, illustrated], under "D. H. Lawrence"; Oxford University Press, May, 1925 [Regular trade Edition, illustrated], under "D. H. Lawrence."

My Skirmish with Jolly Roger (essay). "Written as an Introduction to and a Motivation of the Paris Edition of Lady Chatterley's Lover." New York: Random House, July, 1929.

Nettles (poems). Criterion Miscellany No. 11. London: Faber, March, 1930.

New Poems. London: Martin Secker, October, 1918; New York: B. W. Huebsch, 1920.

Paintings of D. H. Lawrence, The. With an Introduction by D. H. Lawrence. London: The Mandrake Press, June, 1929.

Pansies (poems). London: Martin Secker, July, 1929 [ordinary trade edition, expurgated]; London: Privately Printed for Subscribers only by P. R. Stephensen, August, 1929 [special definitive edition, unexpurgated, with an Introduction by D. H. Lawrence]; New York: Knopf, 1929 [ordinary trade edition, expurgated].

Phoenix: The Posthumous Papers. Edited and with an Introduction by Edward D. McDonald. London: Heinemann, 1936; New York: Viking, 1936.

Plays of D. H. Lawrence, The. London: Martin Secker, 1933.

Plumed Serpent, The (*Quetzalcoatl*) (novel). London: Martin Secker, January, 1926; New York: Knopf, 1926.

Pornography and Obscenity (essay). London: Faber, November, 1929 [Criterion Miscellany No. 5]; New York: Knopf, 1930.

Prelude, A. His First and Previously Unrecorded Work. With an Explanatory Foreword by P. Beaumont Wadsworth. Thames Ditton, Surrey: The Merle Press, 1949.

"Princess, The" (short story), in *St. Mawr: Together with The Princess.* London: Martin Secker, May, 1925.

Prussian Officer and Other Stories, The. London: Duckworth, December, 1914; New York: B. W. Huebsch, 1916.

Psychoanalysis and the Unconscious (essays). New York: Thomas Seltzer, May, 1921 [special issue of the first edition]; New York: Thomas Seltzer, May, 1921 [ordinary trade edition]; London: Martin Secker, July, 1923 [ordinary trade edition].

"Rachel Annand Taylor" (lecture), in Ada Lawrence and G. Stuart Gelder, *Young Lorenzo: Early Life of D. H. Lawrence, Containing Hitherto Unpublished Letters, Articles and Reproductions of Pictures.* Florence: G. Orioli, 1931.

Rainbow, The (novel). London: Methuen, 30 September 1915; New York: B. W. Huebsch, 1916 [expurgated text]; New York: Thomas Seltzer, 1924 [expurgated Huebsch text]; London: Martin Secker, 1926 ["new edition (revised)"].

Rawdon's Roof (short story). The Woburn Books No. 7. London: Elkin Mathews and Marrot, March, 1928. Included in *The Lovely Lady and Other Stories.*

Reflections on the Death of a Porcupine and Other Essays. Philadelphia: The Centaur Press, December, 1925; London: Martin Secker, 1934.

St. Mawr: Together with The Princess (short novel and short story). London: Martin Secker, May, 1925; New York: Knopf, 1925, with title: *St. Mawr* [without "The Princess"].

Sea and Sardinia (travel essays). With Eight Pictures in Color by Jan Juta. New York: Thomas Seltzer, 12 December 1921; London: Martin Secker, April, 1923.

Sex Locked Out (essay). "Reprinted, December, 1928, from the Sunday Dispatch, London, November 25, 1928." London: Privately Printed, December, 1928. Included in *Assorted Articles,* with title "Sex versus Loveliness."

Sons and Lovers (novel). London: Duckworth, May, 1913; New York: Mitchell Kennerley, 1913.

Story of Doctor Manente, The: Being the Tenth and Last Story from the Suppers of A. F. Grazzini Called Il Lasca (translation). Introduction by D. H. Lawrence. Florence: G. Orioli, March, 1929.

Studies in Classic American Literature (criticism). New York: Thomas Seltzer, August, 1923; London: Martin Secker, June, 1924.

Sun (short story). London: E. Archer, September, 1926 [first form]; Paris: The Black Sun Press, October, 1928 [authorized unexpurgated edition]; Privately Printed, 1929 [pirated, unexpurgated American edition].

Tales. London: Martin Secker, 1934.

"Thimble, The" (short story). *The Seven Arts,* March, 1917.

Tortoises (poems). New York: Thomas Seltzer, 9 December 1921. Included in the English edition of *Birds, Beasts and Flowers* [London: Martin Secker, November, 1923].

Touch and Go (play). With a Preface by D. H. Lawrence. London: C. W. Daniel, May, 1920; New York: Thomas Seltzer, 1920.

Trespasser, The (novel). London: Duckworth, May, 1912; New York: Mitchell Kennerley, 1912.

Triumph of the Machine, The (poem). With drawings by Althea Willoughby. The Ariel Poems No. 28. London: Faber, September, 1930. Included in *Last Poems*.

Twilight in Italy (travel essays). London: Duckworth, June, 1916; New York: B. W. Huebsch, 1916.

Virgin and the Gipsy, The (short novel). Florence: G. Orioli, May, 1930; London: Martin Secker, October, 1930; New York: Knopf, 1930.

White Peacock, The (novel). New York: Duffield, 19 January 1911; London: Heinemann, 20 January 1911.

Widowing of Mrs. Holroyd, The (play). With an Introduction by Edwin Björkman. New York: Mitchell Kennerley, 1 April 1914; London: Duckworth, April, 1914.

Woman Who Rode Away and Other Stories, The. London: Martin Secker, 24 May 1928; New York: Knopf, 25 May 1928, including "The Man Who Loved Islands."

Women in Love (novel). New York: Privately Printed for Subscribers Only, November, 1920 [Limited Edition]; London: Martin Secker, May, 1921 [first English edition]; New York: Privately Printed for Subscribers Only, May, 1922 [special signed edition by Thomas Seltzer for Martin Secker]; New York: Thomas Seltzer, October, 1922 [first American trade edition].

BIBLIOGRAPHY

NOTES AND SOURCES

BIBLIOGRAPHY

Included in the following two lists are the published works and identifications of MS materials to which reference is made in this third volume of the Lawrence biography. In my "Notes and Sources," I have made consistent use of shortened forms whenever possible: author or author plus abbreviated title, and, for the works by D. H. Lawrence, titles alone.

I. BOOKS AND ARTICLES

Aldington, Richard. "D. H. Lawrence," *Everyman*, III (No. 59, 13 March 1930), [193], 204–5.

——. *D. H. Lawrence: Portrait of a Genius But* . . . . New York: Duell, Sloan & Pearce, 1950.

——. *Life for Life's Sake*. New York: Viking, 1941.

——. *Pinorman: Personal Recollections of Norman Douglas, Pino Orioli and Charles Prentice*. London: Heinemann, 1954.

Anonymous. "Famous Novelist's Shameful Book: A Landmark in Evil," *John Bull*, XLIV (No. 1166, 20 October 1928), 11.

——. "Lewd Book Banned. . . ," *The Sunday Chronicle* [Manchester], 14 October 1928, p. 1d.

——. "Mr. D. H. Lawrence's Lost Will/Lawrence v. Lawrence and Others/ Before the President," *The Times* [London], 4 November 1932, p. 4.

——. "A Talk with Lawrence's 'Princess' . . . ," *The Star* [London], 9 April 1930.

Brett, Dorothy. *Lawrence and Brett: A Friendship*. Philadelphia: Lippincott, 1933. Copyright, 1933, by Miss Dorothy Brett, Taos, New Mexico.

Brewster, Earl, and Achsah. *D. H. Lawrence: Reminiscences and Correspondence*. London: Martin Secker, 1934.

Brown, Curtis. *Contacts*. New York: Harper, 1935.

Burrow, Trigant. *A Search for Man's Sanity: The Selected Letters of Trigant Burrow with Biographical Notes*. New York: Oxford University Press, 1958.

Bynner, Witter. *Journey with Genius: Recollections and Reflections Concerning the D. H. Lawrences*. New York: Day, 1951.

Carswell, Catherine. "D. H. Lawrence," *Time and Tide*, XI (No. 11, 14 March 1930), 342.

——. *The Savage Pilgrimage: A Narrative of D. H. Lawrence*. Rev. ed. London: Martin Secker, 1932; London: Secker & Warburg, 1951 (pagination the same).

Carter, Frederick. *D. H. Lawrence and the Body Mystical*. London: Denis Archer, 1932.

651

Cerf, Bennett. "Trade Winds," *The Saturday Review of Literature,* XXXV (No. 13, 29 March 1952), 6, 8. Copyright, 1952, by Bennett Cerf. Reprinted by permission from his Trade Winds column in the *Saturday Review of Literature.*

Crosby, Caresse. *The Passionate Years.* New York: Dial Press, 1953.

Davidson, Jo. *Between Sittings: An Informal Autobiography.* New York: Dial Press, 1951. Copyright, 1951, by Jo Davidson. Reprinted by permission of The Dial Press, Inc.

Davies, Rhys. "D. H. Lawrence in Bandol," *Horizon,* II (No. 10, October, 1940), 191–208.

Davis, Robert H. "D. H. Lawrence, Shy Genius, Sits for Two Camera Studies," *The New York Times Book Review,* 23 December 1928, p. 5.

Douglas, Norman. *Looking Back.* New York: Harcourt, 1933. Selections reprinted by permission of the copyright owners, Chatto and Windus, Ltd.

Fabes, Gilbert H. *D. H. Lawrence: His First Editions: Points and Values.* London: W. and G. Foyle, 1933.

G., G. S., "D. H. Lawrence and His Art . . . ," *The Nottingham Journal,* 28 August 1929.

Gardiner, Margaret. "Meeting the Master," *Horizon,* II (No. 10, October, 1940), 184–90.

Gerhardi, William. *Memoirs of a Polyglot.* New York: Knopf, 1931.

Ghiselin, Brewster. *The Nets.* New York: Dutton, 1955. Copyright, 1954, by *Poetry.* From the book *The Nets* by Brewster Ghiselin. Published by E. P. Dutton & Co., Inc., 1955. Reprinted by permission of the publishers.

———. "D. H. Lawrence in Bandol." *Western Humanities Review,* XII (No. 4, Autumn, 1958). Copyright, 1958, University of Utah.

Goldring, Douglas. *Life Interests.* London: MacDonald, 1948.

Hopkin, William Edward. "The Lawrence Pictures . . . ," *The Nottingham Journal,* 29 August 1929.

Hughes, Glenn. *Imagism and Imagists.* Stanford University, Calif.: Stanford University Press, 1931.

Johns, Orrick. *Time of Our Lives: The Story of My Father and Myself.* New York: Stackpole Sons, 1937.

Lawrence, Ada, and Gelder, G. Stuart. *Early Life of D. H. Lawrence: Together with Hitherto Unpublished Letters and Articles.* London: Martin Secker, 1932.

Lawrence, D. H. *Assorted Articles.* New York: Knopf, 1930.

———.*D. H. Lawrence's Letters to Bertrand Russell.* Edited, with an Introduction by Harry T. Moore. New York: Gotham Book Mart, 1948.

———. *Letters.* Edited and with an Introduction by Aldous Huxley. New York: Viking, 1932.

———. "Letters to S. S. Koteliansky," *Encounter 3,* I (No. 3, December, 1953), 29–35.

———. *Phoenix: The Posthumous Papers.* Edited and with an Introduction by Edward D. McDonald. New York: Viking, 1936.

———. "Seized Pictures . . . ," *The Nottingham Evening Post,* 11 July 1929.

———. "The Unpublished Letters from D. H. Lawrence to Max Mohr," *T'ien*

Hsia Monthly [Shanghai], I (No. 1, August, 1935), 7–8, 21–36; I (No. 2, September, 1935), 166–79.

Lawrence, Frieda. *"Not I, But the Wind . . . ."* New York: Viking, 1934. Copyright, 1934, by Frieda Lawrence. Selections reprinted by permission of the Viking Press, Inc., New York.

Luhan, Mabel Dodge. *Lorenzo in Taos.* New York: Knopf, 1932.

———. "The Lawrence I Knew . . . ," Supplement to *The Carmelite* [Carmel, Calif.], III (No. 6, 19 March 1930), iii–v.

McDonald, Edward D. *A Bibliography of the Writings of D. H. Lawrence.* With a Foreword by D. H. Lawrence. Philadelphia: Centaur Book Shop, 1925.

———. *The Writings of D. H. Lawrence, 1925–1930: A Bibliographical Supplement.* Philadelphia: Centaur Book Shop, 1931.

Mackenzie, Faith Compton. *More Than I Should.* London: Collins, 1940. Selections reprinted by permission of the author and of Collins.

Moore, Harry T. *The Intelligent Heart: The Story of D. H. Lawrence.* New York: Farrar, Straus & Young, 1954.

———. *The Life and Works of D. H. Lawrence.* New York: Twayne, 1951.

———. *Poste Restante: A Lawrence Travel Calendar.* With an Introduction by Mark Schorer. Berkeley and Los Angeles: University of California Press, 1956.

Murry, John Middleton. *Reminiscences of D. H. Lawrence.* London: Jonathan Cape, 1933; The Life and Letters Series No. 74: London: Jonathan Cape, 1936 (pagination the same).

Neff, John C. "A Visit to Kiowa Ranch," *The New Mexico Quarterly,* VII (No. 2, May, 1937), 116–20.

Nehls, Edward, ed. *D. H. Lawrence: A Composite Biography.* Vol. I. With a Foreword by Frieda Lawrence Ravagli. Madison: University of Wisconsin Press, 1957.

———. *D. H. Lawrence: A Composite Biography.* Vol. II. With a Foreword by Witter Bynner. Madison: University of Wisconsin Press, 1958.

Orioli, G. *Adventures of a Bookseller.* New York: McBride, 1938.

Parliamentary Debates (House of Commons), 5th Series, CCXXV (28 February 1929), cols. 2158–63.

Patmore, Brigit. "Conversations with D. H. Lawrence," *The London Magazine,* IV (No. 6, June, 1957), 31–45.

Powell, Lawrence Clark. *The Manuscripts of D. H. Lawrence: A Descriptive Catalogue.* With a Foreword by Aldous Huxley. Los Angeles: The Public Library, 1937.

Robinson, Roland E. "D. H. Lawrence in Australia," *The Bulletin* [Sydney], 8 April 1953, pp. 2, 35.

Rowse, A. L. *The English Past: Evocations of Persons and Places.* New York: Macmillan, 1952.

Schoenberner, Franz. *Confessions of a European Intellectual.* New York: Macmillan, 1946.

Schorer, Mark. "I Will Send Address: New Letters of D. H. Lawrence," *The London Magazine,* III (No. 2, February, 1956), 44–67.

Schorer, Mark. "Two Houses, Two Ways," *New World Writing* (Fourth Mentor Selection), pp. 145–54. Copyright, 1953, by The New American Library of World Literature, Inc.

Sitwell, Osbert. *Penny Foolish: A Book of Tirades & Panegyrics*. London: Macmillan, 1935.

T., E. [Jessie Chambers]. *D. H. Lawrence: A Personal Record*. London: Jonathan Cape, 1935.

———. " 'E. T.' on D. H. Lawrence: A Letter to a Common Friend," *Arena: A Literary Magazine* [London] (No. 4, [1950]), 61–65.

Tedlock, E. W., Jr. *The Frieda Lawrence Collection of D. H. Lawrence Manuscripts: A Descriptive Bibliography*. With a Foreword by Frieda Lawrence. Albuquerque: University of New Mexico Press, 1948.

Untermeyer, Louis. *From Another World: The Autobiography of Louis Untermeyer*. New York: Harcourt, [1939]. Copyright, 1939, by Harcourt, Brace and Company, Inc. Used by permission of the author and the publishers.

White, William. *D. H. Lawrence: A Checklist, 1931–1950*. With a Foreword by Frieda Lawrence. Detroit: Wayne University Press, 1950.

II. MANUSCRIPT SOURCES

Acton, Harold. Composite of extracts from two letters (5 April 1954 and 24 May 1957) to the editor.

Barr, Barbara Weekley. Final installments of a long memoir completed in 1954. The earlier installments have been published in the first and second volumes of the present work.

Burrow, Dr. Trigant. Extract from a letter (28 June 1944) to Mrs. Mary Freeman.

———. Extract from a letter (21 August 1944) to Mrs. Mary Freeman.

Bynner, Witter. Complete text of a letter (19 January 1928) to Lawrence. Excerpts have been printed in Bynner, pp. 331–32.

Chambers, Dr. J. D. Solicited memoir written in 1957.

———. Solicited note, concerning May Chambers Holbrook memoirs, written in 1957.

Gardiner, Rolf. Memoir written in 1929 and revised in 1956.

———. Solicited memoirs completed in February, 1956.

———. Letters to Lawrence (2).

———. Letter to Catherine Carswell.

Holbrook, May Chambers. Memoirs of Lawrence in typewritten MS plus concluding sections of handwritten MS, both of uncertain date.

Holbrook, William. Extract from a letter (1 February 1957) to the editor.

Hopkin, William E. "D. H. Lawrence: A Personal Memoir," a talk sponsored by the BBC and recorded by the Birmingham studios of the BBC (17 August 1949). The final installment is printed here for the first time with the permission of Mrs. Olive L. Hopkin. The earlier installments were published in the first volume of the present work.

Jaffe-Richthofen, Else. The final installment of a solicited memoir written in

March, 1954. Translated from the German by Mrs. Doreen E. Hill. The earlier installment has been published in the first volume of the present work.

Lawrence, D. H. "Autobiography," presumed written *ca.* July, 1928. From the MS in the possession of Mr. Spencer Curtis Brown.

———. Letters or postcards to Jessie Chambers (1), William Gerhardi (1), Brewster Ghiselin (4), May Chambers Holbrook (20), William Holbrook (3), Frieda Lawrence (1), Dorothy Warren Trotter (14), Jean Starr Untermeyer (1), Montague Weekley (1).

Lawrence, Frieda. Letters to Brewster Ghiselin (1), Dorothy Warren Trotter (7), Montague Weekley (1), H. G. Wells (1).

Lindsay, Jack. Solicited memoir written in February, 1958.

Mirenda, Raul. Solicited memoir completed in 1954. Translated from the Italian by F. J. Hill.

Morland, Dr. Andrew. Memoir written (1952) for Harry T. Moore, and published in part in Moore, *Intelligent Heart*, pp. 427–28.

Order. Obscene Prints. Metropolitan Police District, London, 8 August 1929.

Pearce, T. M. Solicited memoir entitled "Frieda—In Memory," written in August, 1957.

Ravagli, Capt. Angelo. Solicited memoir written in 1957.

Richardson Sowerby, Holden & Co. Letters to Philip Trotter (2).

———. Letter to Wontner & Sons.

Scott, Geoffrey. Letter to Arnold Bennett.

Siebenhaar, W. Memoir entitled "Reminiscences of D. H. Lawrence," dated "15 July 1930." From the MS in the possession of Heinemann, Ltd.

Soupault, Philippe. Letter to Mlle. Marguerite Scialtiel.

Trotter, Dorothy Warren. Letters to Lawrence (3).

Trotter, Philip. Solicited memoir completed in 1957.

Untermeyer, Jean Starr. Excerpt from a letter (28 June 1956) to the editor.

Watson, Jean. Letter to Lawrence.

Weekley, Montague. The concluding installments of a solicited memoir written in February, 1954. The first installments were published in the first volume of the present work.

Wilkinson, Walter. Solicited memoir written in 1954.

Wood, Jessie Chambers. "The Bankrupt," short story, date unknown.

———. Letters to May Chambers Holbrook (3).

NOTES AND SOURCES

CHAPTER I

1 D. H. L. postcard to J. M. Murry, from Garland's Hotel, Suffolk Street, Pall Mall, S.W. 1, dated 1 October 1925, Murry, *Reminiscences*, p. 197.

2 Lawrence's "first week-end" in England would have been that beginning Friday, 2 October 1925; and the "Sunday" mentioned by Mrs. Carswell would therefore have fallen on 4 October 1925. Elsewhere (p. 242), Mrs. Carswell wrote that Lawrence went to the Midlands "on the Wednesday following his visit to us . . . ," i.e., 7 October 1925, a date confirmed elsewhere. (See *Letters*, p. 647; Moore, *Intelligent Heart*, p. 345.) Presumably Lawrence returned to London after his visit with the Carswells at High Wycombe, Bucks., and before setting off for the Midlands. I labor the point because Prof. Harry T. Moore suggests that Lawrence paid his visit to High Wycombe *ca.* 8–9 October 1925 en route to the Midlands.— Moore, *Intelligent Heart*, p. 346; Moore, *Poste Restante*, p. 84.

3 Mrs. Carswell, her husband Donald, their young son John Patrick, and Lawrence.

4 Lawrence had left Thomas Seltzer, on the verge of bankruptcy, for Alfred A. Knopf.

5 Carswell, pp. 239–41.

6 Original publication of an installment of a long memoir completed in 1954. The preceding sections of the memoir have appeared in Vols. I and II of the present work.

7 D. H. L. letter to Mr. and Mrs. A. D. Hawk, from Garland's Hotel, London, dated 7 October 1925, Moore, *Intelligent Heart*, p. 345.

8 Unpublished D. H. L. letter to Catherine Carswell, no address given, dated "'Tuesday' [13th]," Moore, *Poste Restante*, p. 84.

9 D. H. L. letter to Martin Secker, from ℅ Mrs. W. E. Clarke, Ripley, Derby., dated "Friday" [16 October 1925], *Letters*, pp. 647–48.

10 Original publication of an installment of a long memoir completed in 1954.

11 Carswell, pp. 241–42.

12 In a letter (23 June 1953) to the editor, Margaret Kennedy (1896——), English author of *The Constant Nymph* (1924), wrote: "I have written nothing on Lawrence and never, so far as I remember, exchanged a word with him, although we were once both present at the same cocktail party and were pointed out to one another."

13 In a letter (1 May 1953) to the editor, Rose Macaulay (1889?——),

English novelist, has written: "No, I believe I never met D. H. Lawrence . . . . I think I remember a passage in D. H. Lawrence's journal [*Letters*] in which he mentions some people he met at tea somewhere, and included my name; but it turned out afterward that he had confused me with another writer."

14 D. H. L. letter to J. M. Murry, from 73, Gower St., W.C. 1, dated "Monday (Oct., 1925)," *Letters*, p. 648; dated "Monday [Oct. 27?]," Murry, *Reminiscences*, p. 198.

15 Lord Beaverbrook (1879———), British statesman and newspaper owner, born William Maxwell Aitken, in Newcastle, New Brunswick, Canada. He was the Canadian government representative at the Western Front in World War I, later took charge of Canadian war records. In 1918, he became Minister of Information under David Lloyd George, and, in 1940–1945, held several posts in Churchill's wartime cabinet. Since 1917, he has been the publisher of the London newspapers *Daily Express*, *Sunday Express*, and *Evening Standard*, all markedly Imperialist in their point of view.

16 The complete text of this D. H. L. letter to William Gerhardi is published for the first time in the text below under the date 14 November 1928.

17 Gerhardi, pp. 224–29. An abbreviated version of this memoir appeared as "Literary Vignettes—II" in *The Saturday Review* [London], 151 (No. 3947, 20 June 1931), 893–94. William (Alexander) Gerhardi (1895———), English novelist, was born in St. Petersburg (Leningrad) of English parents. His career as a "polyglot" began as a child, when he could already speak fluent English, Russian, French, and German. During World War I, he served as military attaché to the British Embassy in Petrograd (Leningrad); from 1918 to 1920, with the British Military Mission to Siberia. During World War II, he was with the European division of the BBC. He has travelled widely, but now maintains London as his permanent address. His works include *Futility* (1922), *Anton Chekhov* (1925), *The Polyglots* (1925), *Jazz and Jasper* (1928), *Memoirs of a Polyglot* (1931), *My Wife's the Least of It* (1938), *The Romanovs* (1939), etc. For a character sketch of William Gerhardi, see Ethel Mannin, *Confessions and Impressions* (London: Jarrolds, 1930), pp. 245–48.

18 D. H. L. letter to J. M. Murry, from 73, Gower St., W.C. 1, dated "Monday (Oct., 1925)," *Letters*, p. 648; dated "Monday [Oct. 27?]," Murry, *Reminiscences*, p. 198.

19 The greater portion of this D. H. L. postcard to J. M. Murry is reprinted in the text above under the date 1 October 1925. See also Murry, *Reminiscences*, p. 197.

20 See Murry's expansion of his discussion with Lawrence on the subject of Jesus in *Reminiscences*, pp. 201–3.

21 Later, Murry agreed to visit the Lawrences at the Villa Bernarda, Spotorno, for a fortnight in January, 1926. Mrs. Murry, the former Violet le Maistre, was expecting a second child. "As a simple matter of precaution, I asked the doctor whether there would be any harm in my wife's making the journey. Rather to my surprise, he peremptorily forbade it, and since I was

determined not to leave her behind, I wrote to tell Lawrence what had happened, and that we could not come."—Murry, *Reminiscences*, pp. 120–21.

22 Murry, *Reminiscences*, pp. 118–20.

23 D. H. L. letter to J. M. Murry, from % Frau von Richthofen, Ludwig-Wilhelmstift, Baden-Baden, dated 31 October [1925], *Letters*, p. 649; Murry, *Reminiscences*, p. 200.

24 D. H. L. letter to Curtis Brown, from % Signor Capellero, Villa Maria, Spotorno (Genova), Riviera Ponente, Italy, dated 16 November 1925, *Letters*, pp. 649–50.

25 Frieda Lawrence, p. 179.

26 Original publication of an installment of a solicited memoir written in 1957. In a letter (22 April 1957) to the editor, Capt. Angelo Ravagli has written: "I was born in Tredozio (at that time Province of Florence), Italy, November 27, 1891. I was in the first World War from the start—May 24, 1915 to the end. I entered as a corporal and was then promoted Lieutenant in 1916 for merit of war. I was taken prisoner of war by the German Army in October, 1917. Repatriated at the end of 1918. Wounded twice. Decorated three times. Promoted Captain in August, 1926. Left the Italian Army definitely in April, 1933, and came to America with Frieda Lawrence to help her on the Kiowa Ranch, San Cristobal, New Mexico. (I came the first time on leave without salary for six months in 1931, and then went back to my Regiment.) There I did almost anything: Farming, building the new house, the Chapel, the swimming pool, did some paintings, sculpture, and finally ceramics. In October, 1950, Frieda and I got married and I became an American citizen."

27 D. H. L. letter to J. M. Murry, from Villa Bernardo [*sic*], Spotorno (Genova), dated 19 November 1925, *Letters*, p. 650. In a letter to Earl H. Brewster from London, dated 26 October 1925, Lawrence had written: "Miss Brett said she was sailing on 24th Oct. from New York and would stay in Capri in the Hotel Webster."—Brewster, pp. 83–84.

28 D. H. L. letter to William Hawk, no address given, dated 18 December [1925], Moore, *Intelligent Heart*, p. 348.

29 D. H. L. postcard to The Hon. Dorothy Brett, from Spotorno, dated "(Dec. 7, 1925)," *Letters*, p. 651.

30 D. H. L. letter (translated from the German) to Frieda's mother, Frau Baronin von Richthofen, from Villa Bernarda, Spotorno, Prov. di Genova, dated 16 December 1925, Frieda Lawrence, p. 182.

31 D. H. L. letter to The Hon. Dorothy Brett, from Villa Bernardo [*sic*], Spotorno, Prov. di Genova, dated 29 December 1925, *Letters*, p. 651.

32 Cf. Frieda Lawrence, pp. 179–80.

33 See Prof. Harry T. Moore: "The John Lawrence who was D. H.'s grandfather was brought up in [Nottingham] . . . . He had learned the [tailor's] trade in Nottingham from his stepfather George Dooley, who—according to D. H.'s brother, George Lawrence—had married John's mother after her husband was killed at Waterloo."—Moore, *Intelligent Heart*, p. 5.

34 *Background* (1933), the first volume of Mrs. Luhan's autobiography *Intimate Memories.*—Luhan, p. 281.

35 In Rome, on 7 April 1926, the Hon. Violet Albina Gibson, sister of Lord Ashbourne, shot at Premier Mussolini, slightly wounding him in both nostrils. Mussolini's personal appeal halted rioting by Fascist mobs. See *The New York Times,* 8 April 1926, p. 1.

36 A reference to the concluding sketch, "A Little Moonshine with Lemon." In it, Lawrence noted the fact that "It is a feast day, St. Catherine's Day" —i.e., 25 November, the Feast Day of St. Catherine Virgin Martyr. The sketch was first printed in *Laughing Horse* (No. 13, D. H. Lawrence number, April, 1926), 1–3, and later reprinted as the final essay in *Mornings in Mexico.*

37 Original publication of an installment of a long memoir completed in 1954.

38 *Glad Ghosts* was published in two parts in *The Dial,* LXXXI, 1–21 (No. 1, July, 1926), and 123–41 (No. 2, August, 1926), and in a limited edition (London: Ernest Benn, Ltd., November, 1926); it was later (1928) included in *The Woman Who Rode Away.*—McDonald, *Supplement,* pp. 95, 33, 37–39.

39 In its first form, *Sun* was published in London by E. Archer, September, 1926 (one hundred copies); in its later, expanded form, in Paris by the Black Sun Press, October, 1928. A pirated edition, following the Black Sun authorized unexpurgated edition, was privately printed in New York (?) in 1929. In its first form, *Sun* was also included in *The Woman Who Rode Away.*—McDonald, *Supplement,* pp. 32–33, 43–46; Tedlock, pp. 58–59.

40 D. H. L. letter to The Hon. Dorothy Brett, from Villa Bernardo [*sic*], Spotorno, Genova, dated "Saturday (Jan. 10th, 1926)" [Saturday, 9 January 1926], *Letters,* p. 654.

41 D. H. L. letter to Earl H. and Achsah Barlow Brewster, from Villa Bernardo [*sic*], Spotorno (Genova), dated 9 January 1926, Brewster, p. 91.

42 In January, 1926, Lawrence was working on three MSS: (a) *Glad Ghosts,* (b) *Sun,* and (c) *The Virgin and the Gipsy.* Cf. Catherine Carswell: "I came to take it as a sign, when Lawrence wrote to say he was writing nothing, that even as I read his letter he would be deep in some new undertaking."—Carswell, pp. 79–80.

43 D. H. L. letter to The Hon. Dorothy Brett, from Villa Bernardo [*sic*], Spotorno (Genova), dated 25 January 1926, *Letters,* p. 656.

44 Dedicated "To Frieda," *The Virgin and the Gipsy* was not published until 1930. The short novel's initial situation of a married woman running off with a "young and penniless man" may owe something to Lawrence's own elopement with Frieda in 1912. Lawrence's acquaintance with Frieda's now grown daughters, Elsa and Barbara, may have provided an additional stimulus. His recent trip to the Midlands may have revived his interest in the bleak Derbyshire hills for the novel's setting, as they had once provided him with the background for "The Wintry Peacock." Ada Lawrence Clarke confirms the latter: "In *The Virgin and the Gypsy* [Lawrence] varied one or two names, Woodlinkin being Wirksworth and Amberdale,

Ambergate in the Derbyshire hills."—Ada Lawrence and Gelder, p. 217. While living at Chapel Farm Cottage, Hermitage, Berks., Lawrence wrote on 12 March 1918: "There is a gipsy camp near here—and how I envy them—down a sandy lane under some pine trees."—*Letters*, p. 439.

45 D. H. L. letter to Miss Nancy Pearn, from Villa Bernardo [*sic*], Spotorno, Genova, Italy, dated 29 January 1926, *Letters*, p. 658. (The late Miss Nancy Pearn was, in the 1920's, a staff member of Curtis Brown, Ltd., of London. Later, she was one of the directors of the literary agency of Pearn, Pollinger and Higham, Ltd., of London.)

46 D. H. L. letter to The Hon. Dorothy Brett, from Spotorno, mistakenly dated "Thursday, Feb. 9th, 1926" [Thursday, 11 February 1926], *Letters*, pp. 659–60.

47 Original publication of an installment of a long memoir completed in 1954.

48 Original publication of an installment of a memoir written in 1957.

49 D. H. L. letter to William Hawk [from Villa Bernarda, Spotorno, Italy], dated 19 February [1926], Moore, *Intelligent Heart*, p. 351.

50 D. H. L. letter to G. R. G. Conway, from Monte Carlo, dated 24 February [1926], Moore, *Intelligent Heart*, p. 351.

51 D. H. L. letter to Catherine Carswell, with the permanent address "Villa Bernardo [*sic*], Spotorno, Prov. di Genova, Italy," dated 4 March 1926, *Letters*, p. 662.

52 While the Lawrences and she were living in New Mexico, in the summer of 1925, Lawrence had persuaded The Hon. Dorothy Brett to go to Capri, and had written a letter to introduce her to Earl and Achsah Brewster.— Brett, pp. 236–37. On 26 October 1925, Lawrence wrote to Earl Brewster from London: "Miss Brett said she was sailing on 24 Oct. from New York, and would stop in Capri in the Hotel Webster. Look her up if you hear nothing of her, will you?"—Brewster, pp. 83–84. On 25 November 1925, Lawrence, by then just settled in the Villa Bernarda, Spotorno, again wrote to Earl Brewster: "Now I hear from Miss Brett that she is in Capri." —Brewster, p. 84.

53 Frederick Victor Branford (1892――), English poet, editor, soldier; founder of the magazine *Voices;* author of *Titans and Gods* (1922), *Five Poems* (1923), *The White Stallion* (1924). Wife, Martha.

54 Miss Brett's entire *Lawrence and Brett* is written *to* Lawrence. In her writings, the pronoun *you* therefore is to be read as *Lawrence.*

55 Prince, Azul, Aaron: horses belonging to the Lawrences at Kiowa Ranch, San Cristobal, New Mexico.

56 Brett, pp. 267–76.

57 Presumably a reference to "The Man Who Loved Islands," first printed in *The Dial,* LXXXIII (No. 1, July, 1927), 1–25, then in *The London Mercury,* XVI (No. 94, August, 1927), 370–88, and included in the American (but not the English) edition of *The Woman Who Rode Away.* —McDonald, *Supplement,* p. 96. (In 1933, the story was included in the English edition of *The Lovely Lady.*) Or possibly to "Two Blue Birds," first printed in *The Dial,* LXXXII (No. 4, April, 1927), 287–301, and included in *The Woman Who Rode Away.*—McDonald, *Supplement,* p. 96. In an

interview (1950) with Prof. Harry T. Moore, Sir Compton Mackenzie said that "Lawrence's fiction often gives a distorted view of his acquaintances because 'he had a trick of describing a person's setting or background vividly, and then putting into the setting an ectoplasm entirely of his own creation.' "—Moore, *Intelligent Heart,* p. 187. See Vol. II, p. 454 n44, of the present work.

58 See Murry, *Reminiscences,* p. 166.

59 The memoirs concerning the Café Royal supper (December, 1923) are collected in Vol. II, pp. 295–305, of the present work.

60 Faith Compton Mackenzie, *More Than I Should,* pp. 32–35.

61 John Ellingham Brooks, Greek scholar, translator, long a resident of Capri, whom Lawrence first met during his brief sojourn there, December, 1919 —February, 1920. See Vol. II, p. 454 n39, of the present work.

62 Mary Cannan?

63 A reference to William Ernest ("Ern"), second oldest of the Lawrence brothers.

64 Francis Brett Young (1884–1954), English novelist and poet, and his wife, Jessica. Friends on Capri, December, 1919—February, 1920, they had helped the Lawrences locate Fontana Vecchia at Taormina, Sicily, in March, 1920. See Vol. II, pp. 20, 30–31, of the present work.

65 Brett, pp. 276–88.

66 "The Rocking-Horse Winner" was first published in Lady Cynthia Asquith's *The Ghost-Book: Sixteen New Stories of the Uncanny* (London: Hutchinson, October, 1926).—McDonald, *Supplement,* pp. 82–83. It was later included in the posthumous *Lovely Lady* (1933). To date "The Rocking-Horse Winner" is the only Lawrence short story to have been filmed. Produced by John Mills, and written and directed by Anthony Pelissier, the film was made in England in 1949 with a cast that included John Mills as Bassett; Valerie Hobson as the mother; and John Howard Davies as Paul.

67 Brewster, pp. 265–67.

68 Brewster, pp. 93–94.

69 Lawrence had known the Scots painter Millicent Beveridge during his Taormina period (1920–1922). *Ca.* April–May, 1921, she had painted Lawrence's portrait. (See frontispiece to Vol. II of the present work; *Letters,* pp. 520–21.) See Vol. II, p. 461 n140, of the present work. Prof. Harry T. Moore has identified Mabel Harrison only as a friend of Millicent Beveridge.—Moore, *Intelligent Heart,* p. 352.

70 Brett, pp. 288–96.

71 D. H. L. letter to Mabel Dodge Luhan, from Ravello, dated 18 March 1926, Luhan, pp. 291–92.

72 Brett, pp. 296–99. In a letter to Mrs. Mabel Dodge Luhan, written from Spotorno on 19 April 1926, Lawrence wrote: "I heard from Brett that she is landing in Boston about May 16th: she sails from Naples on May 2nd. She wants to go back to Del Monte."—Luhan, p. 297. See also Brewster, pp. 97–98.

73 D. H. L. letter to Earl H. and Achsah Barlow Brewster, from Spotorno,

dated 11 April [1926], Brewster, p. 94. At Ravenna, Lawrence was briefly glimpsed by the English biographer, critic, and editor Peter Quennell (1905——). "He was with two solid-looking, middle-aged Englishwomen; and I did my best to overhear his conversation at the hotel dinnertable." Mr. Quennell was "impressed by the rather provincial twang of his voice—the odd loofah-ish consistency of his beard—and a look of fragility and a kind of tearing schoolboyish slyness in his attitude towards his two large and motherly companions."—Moore, *Intelligent Heart*, p. 353.

74 D. H. L. letter (translated from the German) to Frieda's mother, Frau Baronin von Richthofen, from Villa Bernarda, Spotorno, Riviera di Ponente, dated Easter Sunday [4 April 1926], Frieda Lawrence, p. 183.

75 D. H. L. letter to Frieda's sister Dr. Else Jaffe-Richthofen, from Villa Bernarda, Spotorno, Genoa, mistakenly dated "7 March 1926" [7 April 1926], Frieda Lawrence, p. 184.

76 Original publication of an installment of a long memoir completed in 1954.

77 D. H. L. letter (postcard?) to Ada Lawrence Clarke, from Spotorno, Italy, dated 19 April 1926, Ada Lawrence and Gelder, p. 108.

78 See Frieda Lawrence, p. 181.

79 Original publication of an installment of a solicited memoir written in 1957.

CHAPTER II

1 D. H. L. letter to Jan Juta, from Pensione Lucchesi, Florence, dated " '24 April' [1926]," Moore, *Intelligent Heart*, pp. 353–54.

2 See Aldous Huxley's Introduction to *Letters*, p. xxviii. The brief memoir describing the first meeting of Aldous Huxley and Lawrence (1915) is reprinted in Vol. I, pp. 339–40, of the present work.

3 Original publication of an installment of a long memoir completed in 1954.

4 D. H. L. letter to Earl H. Brewster, from Pensione Zucchesi [Lucchesi], Lungarno Zecca, Florence, dated 25 April 1926, Brewster, p. 97.

5 D. H. L. letter to The Hon. Dorothy Brett, from Villa Mirenda, S. Paolo Mosciano, Scandicci, Florence, dated 15 May 1926, *Letters*, p. 667. On the problem of dating Lawrence's move to the Villa Mirenda, see Moore, *Poste Restante*, p. 87.

6 In a letter (18 April 1954) to the editor, Sig. Raul Mirenda has written: "This villa [i.e., the Wilkinsons'] was then the property of some people called Poggi, who resided at Florence and used to let the villa for periods."

7 In a letter (18 April 1954) to the editor, Sig. Raul Mirenda has written: "The villa of my family where the writer Lawrence was entertained is situated on a little hill, which rises 159 metres above sea level. This hill takes its name, the hill of Saint Paul at Mosciano, from a little church dedicated to Saint Paul and erected on the same hill, a short distance from my villa. Through a distortion of the name in dialect, which in time has become accepted usage, the name Saint Paul has become San Polo."

8 In a letter (18 April 1954) to the editor, Sig. Raul Mirenda has written:

"Neither I nor my family had previously let the country house, which has now belonged to us for four generations. An exception was made in the case of Lawrence, because when I became acquainted with him I was struck by his personality, his intelligence, and his courteous good nature. After the departure of the Lawrences, our country house was not let again to anybody, either as a whole, or in part."

9 For the publishing history of *Lady Chatterley's Lover,* see the entry under "Major First Editions."

10 I am unable to identify the Lawrence painting to which Sig. Mirenda refers. Neither can I trace it as one of the paintings exhibited in London.

11 Possibly a reference to *Contadini.* See Chap. III, Note 185, below.

12 See *Letters,* pp. 684, 704; Ada Lawrence and Gelder, pp. 115–17, 134–35.

13 See Frieda Lawrence, p. 244.

14 For two of Lawrence's letters to Signorina Giulia Pini, see *Letters,* pp. 762, 805–7. See also *Letters,* p. 753.

15 See *Letters,* p. 806.

16 Original publication of a solicited memoir completed in 1954. Translated from the Italian by F. J. Hill. The quotations from Sig. Mirenda's correspondence with the editor (Notes 6–8, above) were also translated by Mr. Hill. In a letter (18 April 1954) to the editor, Sig. Mirenda has described himself as "an Army officer, at present on the reserve, passionately devoted to history and literature."

17 Lawrence's oil painting *Boccaccio Story.*

18 See Note 6, above. Mr. Walter Wilkinson's brother, Gair Wilkinson, English painter, now makes his home at Bridgewater, Somerset.

19 Original publication of a solicited memoir written in 1954. The concluding lines are from "Wedlock," Part II, in *Look! We Have Come Through!* and *Collected Poems,* II. Walter Wilkinson, English puppetmaster, is the author of *The Peep Show* (1927, 1932), *Vagabonds and Puppets* (1930), *Puppets in Yorkshire* (1931), *Puppets into Scotland* (1935), *A Sussex Peep Show* (1934), *Puppets Through Lancashire* (1936), *Puppets Through America* (1938), *Puppets in Wales* (1948), etc. For Lawrence's review of *The Peep Show* (London: G. Bles, April, 1927; new ed., February, 1932), see *The Calendar: A Quarterly Review* [London], IV (No. 2, July, 1927), 164–68; reprinted in *Phoenix,* pp. 372–76.—*Phoenix,* p. 841.

20 The "Holograph Manuscript of the translation into German by Frieda Lawrence of the play—'David' " (Item 33) was offered for sale by Melvin Rare Books, 156, St. John's Road, Edinburgh, 12, in *A Catalogue of Valuable Books by D. H. Lawrence Comprising Some of the Author's Own and Frieda Lawrence's Inscribed Copies[,] Manuscripts[,] Proof and Association Copies[,] Rare Editions and English Editions* in the summer of 1949.

21 D. H. L. letter to The Hon. Dorothy Brett, from Villa Mirenda, Scandicci, Florence, dated 23 June 1926, *Letters,* pp. 669–70.

22 Angelo Ravagli.

23 D. H. L. letter to Martin Secker, from Villa Mirenda, Scandicci, Florence, dated 5 July 1926, *Letters,* pp. 670–71.

24 D. H. L. letter to Catherine Carswell, from Baden-Baden, dated 18 July [1926], Moore, *Intelligent Heart*, p. 356.

25 D. H. L. letter to The Hon. Dorothy Brett, from Baden-Baden, dated 29 July 1926, *Letters*, p. 675.

26 Cf. D. H. L. letter to Giusèppe (Pino) Orioli, from Sutton-on-Sea, Lincs., dated 11 September [1926]: "Aldous Huxley came to see me in London— he has gone off to Cortina, in the Dolomites, to take a house there. He seemed no brisker than ever."—Moore, *Intelligent Heart*, pp. 356–57.

27 Indians, man and wife, employed by the Lawrences at Kiowa Ranch, San Cristobal, New Mexico.

28 Adapted into journal form from a letter written by Frieda Lawrence Ravagli to Mabel Dodge Luhan, from 25 Rossetti Mansions, Flood Street, Chelsea, London, dated 8 August 1926, Luhan, pp. 307–8.

29 Mr. Weekley had last seen Lawrence in the summer of 1913. See Vol. I, pp. 197–98, of the present work.

30 Original publication of an installment of a solicited memoir written in February, 1954.

31 Goldsworthy Lowes Dickinson (1862–1932), Fellow, King's College, Cambridge; humanist, historian, and philosophical writer.

32 For Lawrence on Cambridge University, see Vol. I, pp. 282–85 (Bertrand Russell), 286–88 (John Maynard Keynes), 290, 302, of the present work; Moore, *Letters to Russell*, p. 43; Moore, *Intelligent Heart*, pp. 182–86.

33 See, for examples, I. A. Richards, *Science and Poetry* (1925) and *Practical Criticism* (1929). See also his articles "A Background for Contemporary Poetry," *The Criterion: A Quarterly Review* [London], III (No. 12, July, 1925), 511–28, and "Lawrence as a Poet," *New Verse* (No. 1, January, 1933), 15–17.

34 Joachim of Floris (1145–1202), Italian mystic, who divided all time into three ages, of the Father, the Son (from 1 to 1260 A.D.), and the Holy Spirit.

35 See the essays "The Lemon Gardens" and "The Theatre" in *Twilight in Italy*.

36 See the introduction to F. R. Leavis' *D. H. Lawrence: Novelist* (1955).

37 See "A Spiritual Woman" in *Amores*. Considerably revised, the poem was retitled "These Clever Women" for *Collected Poems*, I.

38 Ludwig Wittgenstein (1889–1951), author of *Tractatus Logico-Philosophicus* (1922).

39 See John Maynard Keynes, *Two Memoirs: Dr. Melchior: A Defeated Enemy and My Early Beliefs*, introduced by David Garnett (New York: August M. Kelley, 1949), p. 103. The pertinent section appears in Vol. I, p. 288, of the present work.

40 Anthony Mario Ludovici (1882–––), English writer; author of *Who Is to Be Master of the World?* (1909), *Nietzsche: His Life and Works* (1910), *Nietzsche and Art* (1911), *A Defence of Aristocracy* (1915), *Man's Descent from the Gods* (1921), *The False Assumptions of Democracy* (1921), etc.

41 In 1919, the Hon. Violet Douglas-Pennant was dismissed from the office

of Commandant of the Women's Royal Air Force. The inquiry by a Select Committee of the House of Lords into her dismissal was ended on 11 November 1919. See *The New York Times,* 29 October 1919, p. 2, col. 5; 12 November 1919, p. 17, col. 6; 9 December 1919, p. 19, col. 3.

M.I. 5: Military Intelligence, Section Five, i.e., the counterintelligence section of the British War Office.

42 Cecil James Sharp (1859–1924), British musician, music teacher, anthologist; compiler of *A Book of British Song* (1902), *English Folk-Carols* (1911), etc.

43 Ernest Thompson Seton (1860–1946), American writer and artist, originally named Ernest Seton Thompson. Born in England, he lived in the backwoods of Canada (1866–1870) and on the western plains (1882–1887). Author of many nature stories, usually illustrated by himself, including *Wild Animals I Have Known* (1898), *The Biography of a Grizzly* (1900), etc. He founded Woodcraft Indians (1902), precursor of Boy Scouts.

Sir Robert Stephenson Smyth (1857–1941), 1st Baron Baden-Powell, British soldier. He inaugurated the Boy Scout movement (1908) and, with his sister Agnes, the Girl Guides (1910).

44 Sir Oswald (Ernald) Mosley (1896————), English politician. In 1932, he organized the British Union of Fascists, known as Blackshirts. From 1940 to 1943, he was interned by the British government. After World War II he attempted to revive the movement.

45 See *Letters,* p. 708.

46 See *Letters,* p. 708.

47 See *Letters,* pp. 707–8.

48 See *Letters,* p. 708.

49 Annie Besant, nee Wood (1847–1933), English theosophist and Indian political leader. She joined the Theosophist Society (1889), became a devoted pupil of Madame Blavatsky, was president of the society (1907–1933). She organized the India Home Rule League, was president of the Indian National Congress (1917). Author of many publications on theosophy.

50 See *Letters,* pp. 712–13.

51 See *Letters,* p. 692.

52 A reference to the Gurdjieff Institute at Fontainebleau, where Katherine Mansfield had died (9 January 1923).

53 See *Letters,* pp. 705–7 (where the letter is dated 7 January 1928).

54 Springhead, Fontmell Magna, Shaftesbury, Dorset, seat of Mr. Gardiner's agricultural estate, originally Gore Farm.

55 Sixteen of these nineteen letters are printed in *Letters.*

56 Original publication of a solicited memoir completed in February, 1956.

57 Mrs. Catherine Carswell states that the Chelsea flat belonged to Millicent Beveridge.—Carswell, p. 253.

58 See *Letters,* pp. 674–75.

59 Lady Gertrude Helena Bone, wife of Sir Muirhead Bone (1876–1953), Scottish etcher and painter.

60 Original publication of a memoir written in 1929 and revised in 1956.

"Born in 1902, [Rolf Gardiner] worked after the first World War for the union of youth in northern Europe. He started the first volunteer work service camps in Germany and Yorkshire, and helped to found in Germany and Holland centres for the training of young people in regional reconstruction, including the unique Musikheim at Frankfort-on-Oder, a centre of social therapy through music, art and husbandry. In 1927 he founded the Springhead estate where Land Service Camps for students and unemployed were held from 1929 to 1939.

"He was a member of the Dorset County Council from 1937 to 1946, organised the revival of flax production in Wessex (1938–43), was from 1941–47 convenor of 'a Kinship in Husbandry,' and helped to found the Council for the Church and Countryside. He is chairman of the Cranborne Chase Co-operative (forestry) group, president of the S.W. Woodlands Association, became president of the Dorset Federation of Young Farmers' Clubs, and chairman of the Dorset Rural Industries Committee. He has extensive interests in Africa and is part-owner of an island in Finland. He has served on the Council of the Soil Association since inauguration . . . ." —*Wessex Letters from Springhead* [Shaftesbury, Dorset] (Advent, 1957), p. 2.

See Rolf Gardiner, ed. (with Heinz Rocholl), *Britain and Germany: A Frank Discussion Instigated by Members of the Younger Generation* (London: Williams and Norgate, 1928); Rolf Gardiner, ed., *In Northern Europe, 1930: Activities by Some Members of the Younger Generation in Britain and Germany* (London: Anglo-German Academic Bureau, 1931); Rolf Gardiner, *World without End: British Politics and the Younger Generation* (London: Cobden-Sanderson, 1932); Rolf Gardiner, *North Sea and Baltic, 1932–1936* (first series), *North Sea and Baltic, 1937–1941* (new series); Rolf Gardiner, *Wessex Letters from Springhead* (continuing series, from 1942); *England Herself: Ventures in Rural Restoration* (London: Faber, 1943), of particular interest to the Lawrence student; Anon., *The German Singers: An Account of Some British-German Activities, 1928–1930* (National Union of Students); Virginia Coit, *Recent Developments in German Adult Education* (World Association of Adult Education, 1932).

In a letter (28 February 1956) to the editor, Mr. Gardiner has written: "The point about Lawrence surely was that his real life was the life projected out of the raw materials of his daily living into the imaginative greater world of his novels and poems. A man is greater than a man. He is overshadowed by his inspiration, his demon, his guardian-angel, his guides. It is these who really write his books, use him, play through him. Most modern writers are pot-bound by their intellectual egos, by their personal wills, by their social views, or scientific brains, or aptitudes as entertainers. Lawrence was the work-man priest of his imagination, the disciple of his genius, that Genius being something, or some Forces, far greater than himself. So it is surely with all the really great genii, artists. But, as so often happens, there is an inconsistency: the small petulant ego inserts itself into the stream of inspiration, the wilful self ceases to

666

serve and starts to shout, spit or kick. That was Lawrence's tragedy and dilemma. I told him myself that, wise though much of *Lady Chatterley* was, it was weak in so far as Lawrence damn-well wanted to fling it in the teeth of the obscene, squeamish, mealy-mouthed, hypocritical loveless public. *Épater les bourgeois* was not entirely absent from Lawrence's temperament; he wanted to have his revenge, and I sympathised with his mood. But this . . . was the smaller, less likeable Lawrence, human enough, but not worthy of his greatness."

61 See David Garnett, *The Golden Echo* (New York: Harcourt, 1954), p. 245; Vol. I, p. 176, of the present work. Mr. Aldington would have read the phrase in Mr. Garnett's "Reminiscence," which originally prefaced Lawrence's posthumous *Love Among the Haystacks* (1930), and which was revised for *The Golden Echo.*

62 See the concluding three paragraphs of *Apocalypse.*

63 See Shelley's "Adonais," xxxii.

64 On this point, Mr. Aldington is mistaken. Frieda remained in London while Lawrence went to the Midlands and Scotland. Together they left London on 28 September 1926 for Paris and thence to Florence.

65 Millicent Beveridge and Mabel Harrison?

66 Richard Aldington, *D. H. Lawrence: An Indiscretion* (Seattle: University of Washington Book Store, 1927). The English edition of this pamphlet, *D. H. Lawrence* (London: Chatto & Windus, 1930), differs slightly from the earlier American form. See McDonald, *Supplement,* pp. 105, 106.

67 Aldington, *Life for Life's Sake,* pp. 301–7.

68 Lawrence went to Newtonmore to visit Millicent Beveridge's family.— Carswell, p. 253.

69 D. H. L. letter to Mabel Dodge Luhan, no address given, dated 14 August 1926, Luhan, p. 309.

70 Cf. Lawrence's short story "The Man Who Loved Islands." See Chap. I, Note 57, above.

71 D. H. L. letter to Frieda's sister Dr. Else Jaffe-Richthofen, from the address "At Bailhathadan [Bailabhadan], Newtonmore, Inverness," dated 20 August 1926, Frieda Lawrence, pp. 212–13.

72 D. H. L. letter to The Hon. Dorothy Brett, from Mablethorpe, Lincolnshire, dated 26 August 1926, *Letters,* pp. 676–77.

73 D. H. L. letter to Earl H. Brewster, from Sutton-on-Sea, Lincs., dated 29 August 1926, Brewster, p. 103. See Moore, *Poste Restante,* p. 89.

74 D. H. L. letter to Earl H. Brewster, from Sutton-on-Sea, Lincs., dated 30 August 1926, Brewster, pp. 104–5.

75 D. H. L. letter to Rolf Gardiner, from Sutton-on-Sea, dated 12 September 1926, *Letters,* p. 677.

76 D. H. L. letter to Rolf Gardiner, from Villa Mirenda, Scandicci, Florence, dated 3 December 1926, *Letters,* p. 682.

77 "Autobiographical Fragment," in *Phoenix,* pp. 822–24. Within the text the date of the narrator's sleep is given as October, 1927. See Tedlock, pp. 64–65.

78 Hopkin, "D. H. Lawrence: A Personal Memoir." Original publication of a

portion of a BBC recording (17 August 1949). For the earlier portions, see
Vol. I, pp. 21–25, 70–75, of the present work. See also the late Councillor
Hopkin's letter (16 October 1949) to Prof. Harry T. Moore, quoted in
Moore, *Intelligent Heart*, p. 357.

79 During World War I, Lawrence had projected a series of platform lectures
with Bertrand Russell. See Harry T. Moore, ed., *D. H. Lawrence's Letters
to Bertrand Russell* (New York: Gotham Book Mart, 1948).

80 Carswell, pp. 254–56.

81 See Rebecca West, "Elegy," in *The New Adelphi*, III (No. 4, June–August,
1930), 301; *D. H. Lawrence* (London: Martin Secker, 1930), p. 17;
Ending in Earnest: A Literary Log (Garden City, New York: Doubleday,
Doran, 1931), p. 264.

82 The source of this oft-repeated charade may be traced to the evening
Lawrence heard Florence Farr (Mrs. Edward Emery) perform upon the
psaltery at the home of Ernest Rhys *ca.* 1910. See Vol. I, pp. 129–32, of
the present work.

83 See Keats's letter to Benjamin Bailey, dated 22 November 1817.

84 It is likely that this section of Mrs. Patmore's memoir belongs to the Lawrences' visit to England in the summer of 1926, during a part of which
time they lived at Carlingford House, 30, Willoughby Road, Hampstead,
and were seeing Dorothy Richardson. If this be the case, then Mrs. Patmore's Sunday visit would have fallen on either 19 or 26 September 1926.

85 Dorothy M. Richardson (Mrs. Alan Odle, 1882–1957), English novelist,
sometimes credited with having introduced the stream-of-consciousness
technique into English fiction. Her magnum opus, *Pilgrimage,* began with
Pointed Roofs (1915) and concluded with the twelfth novel of the series,
Dimple Hill (1938).

86 Patmore, "Conversations with Lawrence," *The London Magazine,* 4 (No. 6,
June, 1957), 31–37. In a letter (22 June 1957) to the editor, Mrs. Patmore has written of herself: "Brigit Patmore was born in Ireland but has
lived all her life in England or abroad. A novel [*No Tomorrow* (1929)]
of hers has been published in America and a book of short stories [*This
Impassioned Onlooker* (1926)] in England: also two translations: *Mar-
montel's Memoirs,* and Constantin de Grunwald's *Nicholas I.* After marrying a grandson of Coventry Patmore, she became a friend of Violet Hunt
and a constant frequenter of the circle of famous writers meeting at
South Lodge. She has two sons, Derek Patmore, author, journalist, playwright and impressario of art, and Michael Patmore, a director of J. Walter
Thompson and specialist in commercial television."

87 D. H. L. letter to Mabel Dodge Luhan, from 30 Willoughby Rd., Hampstead, N.W. 3, dated 23 September 1926, Luhan, pp. 310–11.

88 The relevant passage is quoted in the text immediately above under the
date 23 September 1926.

89 Louis Untermeyer, pp. 319–20. Louis Untermeyer (1885——), American
poet, editor, anthologist. His *Moses* (1928) he considers the "best of his
fiction . . . a combination of historical reconstruction and poetic fantasia."

His marriage (1907) to Jean Starr Untermeyer was dissolved. See also Mr. Untermeyer's chapter on Lawrence in *Makers of the Modern World* (New York: Simon and Schuster, 1955), pp. 632–42.

90 From a letter (28 June 1956) to the editor. Jean Starr Untermeyer (1886——), American poet, anthologist, and translator, was born in Zanesville, Ohio. Except for sojourns abroad, she has lived most of her life in New York City. She is the author of *Growing Pains* (1918), *Dreams Out of Darkness* (1921), *Steep Ascent* (1927), *Wingèd Child* (1936), and *Love and Need* (1940), her collected poems; and the translator of Oscar Bie's *Franz Schubert* (1928) and Hermann Broch's *The Death of Virgil* (1945). Her marriage (1907) to Louis Untermeyer was dissolved.

On 2 February 1922, Lawrence had written to Mrs. Untermeyer from "Fontana Vecchia/Taormina/Sicilia":

Dear Mrs. Untermeyer

I received your two books of poems, also your letter. The poems I have read—most of them aloud to my wife. I think the greatest achievement is when pure speech goes straight into poetry, without having to put on Sunday clothes. One is so weary weary of affectations and showing off. But as for the "struggle"—heavens where is it going to land us? Where is it going to land you? We shall see the next step in your next book of poems.

My best wishes to Louis Untermeyer. We *were* coming to America, my wife & I. Now we are going to Ceylon—This month I hope. They say Paradise was once in Ceylon. Was it ever in America? Or will it be? Or is America where Paradise is perfectly lost? Even that's an achievement.

Hope I may meet you & your husband one day.

Yours very sincerely
D. H. Lawrence

(Original publication)

91 From November, 1918, through June, 1919, Lawrence had published in *The English Review* several of the essays later to be revised for *Studies in Classic American Literature*. For details, see McDonald, pp. 121–22.

92 See Vol. II, p. 475 n37, of the present work.

93 For memoirs by Mrs. A. L. Jenkins (as told by H. E. L. Priday), see Vol. II, pp. 115–17, 131–33, 150–52, of the present work.

94 See *Kangaroo*, Chap. I, "Torestin."

95 For memoirs by and notes on the late Miss Mollie L. Skinner, see Vol. II, pp. 136–39, 271–74, 476 n47, of the present work. Miss Skinner's partner at "Holiday House," Leithdale, Darlington, W.A., was her Quaker friend, Miss Ellen Beakbane. *Letters of a V.A.D.* had been released (1918) under the *nom de plume* R. E. Leake.

96 London's famous "Poetry Bookshop," in Devonshire Street, Theobalds Road, London, under the management of the poet Harold Munro (1879–1932), was a rendezvous for poets. *Poetry Review* (1912) and *The Chapbook* (1919–1921) were issued there. See Douglas Goldring, *Life Interests*

(London: MacDonald, 1948), pp. 232–38; *The Nineteen Twenties: A General Survey and some Personal Memories* (London: Nicholson & Watson, 1945), pp. 152–59.

97 Louis (Marie Anne) Couperus (1863–1923), Dutch fiction writer. His *De Boeken der kleine Zielen* (1901–1903), containing *Small Souls, The Later Life, The Twilight of the Souls,* and *Dr. Adriaan,* has been translated into English as *The Book of the Small Souls* (1932).

98 Eduard Douwes Dekker (1820–1887), pseudonym Multatuli, Dutch writer. He served in the Dutch colonial civil service in the Dutch East Indies (1838–1857), protested against abuses in the Dutch colonial system, resigned when threatened with dismissal. His *Max Havelaar* (1859) was written to expose the evils of Dutch administration in Java.

99 Presumably a reference to Victor Desmond Courtney (1894———), managing editor of *The Sunday Times* of Perth, director of the Western Press, Ltd., and of *Call* and *Mirror* Newspapers, Ltd.

100 See Mollie Skinner, "Correspondence: D. H. Lawrence," *Southerly* [Sydney, Australia], 13 (No. 4, 1952), 233–35, reprinted in Vol. II, pp. 136–39, of the present work.

101 See Mollie Skinner, "D. H. Lawrence and *The Boy in the Bush,*" *Meanjin: A Literary Magazine* [Melbourne, Australia], 9 (No. 4, Summer, 1950), 260–63, reprinted in Vol. II, pp. 271–74, of the present work.

102 See D. H. L. letter to Mrs. A. L. Jenkins, from Darlington, dated Wednesday [17 May 1922], Vol. II, p. 132, of the present work.

103 Jacob Thomas Grein (1862–1935), English dramatic critic. Born in Amsterdam, he emigrated to England as a young man and became a naturalized citizen of England (1895). He served on the staffs of *Life* (1889–1891), *The Sunday Times* (1897–1918), *The Illustrated London News* (1920–1935); founded the Independent Theatre (1891) and the People's Theatre (1923).

104 See Note 106, below.

105 G[ladys]. B[ronwyn]. Stern (1890———), English novelist; author of *Pantomime* (1914), *The Black Seat* (1923), *Tents of Israel* [*The Matriarch*] (1924), *Thunderstorm* (1925), *Debonair* (1928), *Mosaic* (1930), *Monogram* (1936), *The Woman in the Hall* (1939), *Another Part of the Forest* (1941), *The Young Matriarch* (1942), *Trumpet Voluntary* (1944), *Benefits Forgot* (1949), etc.

106 See *Letters,* pp. 559–60, 565.

107 Gustave Aimard, pseudonym of Olivier Gloux (1818–1883), French traveler and writer, author of novels of adventure, including *The Trappers of Arkansas* (1858), *Arizona Bandits* (1882), etc.

108 (Thomas) Mayne Reid (1818–1883), Irish writer. He came to the U.S. (*ca.* 1838), served in the Mexican War, established himself in England (1849), where he devoted himself to writing. Among his adventure stories are *The Rifle Rangers* (1850), *The War Trail* (1857), *Afloat in the Forest* (1865), *The Castaways* (1870), *Free Lances* (1881). His *The Quadroon* (1856) formed the basis of Boucicault's play *The Octoroon.* See "The Fox."

109 See *Letters,* p. 583; Note 101, above.

110 Edward Garnett? See Vol. II, p. 510 n201, of the present work.

111 Lawrence's sister Mrs. Ada Lawrence Clarke and her friend Mrs. Booth. See *Letters*, pp. 659–60.

112 See *Letters*, pp. 666–67.

113 For Lawrence's introduction to W. Siebenhaar's translation of E. D. Dekker's *Max Havelaar*, see the original edition (New York: Knopf, 1927) or *Phoenix*, pp. 236–39.

114 In a sequence of unpublished letters, Lawrence wrote to W. Siebenhaar from Sutton, Lincs., on 7 September 1926, saying he would be in London in about a week and asking Siebenhaar if he knew an inexpensive, good hotel. Again from Sutton, 10 September 1926, Lawrence thanked Siebenhaar for a telegram about rooms, and explained that friends had already arranged for the Lawrences to stay in Hampstead. From 30, Willoughby Rd., Hampstead, Lawrence wrote on 22 September 1926, saying that he was sorry he and Frieda were out when Siebenhaar called, that they were leaving for Paris on the following Tuesday [28 September 1926]; could Siebenhaar come to tea tomorrow (Thursday) [23 September 1926]? Again from 30, Willoughby Rd., Hampstead, on 24 September 1926, Lawrence asked what happens to letters addressed to Siebenhaar, and suggested that on the following Monday [27 September 1926], the day before the Lawrences were scheduled to leave for Paris, he and Siebenhaar meet on the steps of the National Gallery; but he would have to go on to lunch soon after.

115 Sir John Collings Squire (1884——), early pseudonym Solomon Eagle, English poet, journalist, and editor; founder and editor (1919–1934) of *The London Mercury*. Mr. Siebenhaar's reference is probably to J. C. Squire, "D. H. Lawrence," *The Observer* [London], 9 March 1930. For a spirited rebuttal, see John Arrow, *J. C. Squire v. D. H. Lawrence*, Blue Moon Booklet No. 4 (London: E. Lahr, [1930]).

116 Original publication of a memoir entitled "Reminiscences of D. H. Lawrence," dated "15 July 1930." William Siebenhaar (1863–1937) was born in Holland and emigrated to Western Australia as a young man. For several years he taught at the Perth High School, and then entered the Government Service. In the 1930's, he took up residence in England, where he died. He translated Pelsart's *Journal* (*Western Mail*, Christmas Number, 1897), and in 1910 produced *Dorothea*, a lyrical romance of over 3,000 lines, said to be the most ambitious poetical work ever to come from Western Australia.

117 See Catherine Carswell: "Recently I reminded Koteliansky of this conversation, adding that I was now completely removed from the state of alienation which he had deplored. He had forgotten the discussion, but admitted that he had once held such views, though he had since found reason to change them."—Carswell, p. 256, note.

118 As Prof. Harry T. Moore has pointed out, Lawrence's attitudes as reflected in this recalled dialogue are "a kind of restatement of the theme of 'The Rocking-Horse Winner,' the story which Cynthia Asquith published later that year [October, 1926] in her collection *The Ghost Book*."—Moore,

671

Intelligent Heart, p. 357. See McDonald, *Supplement,* pp. 82–83. See also Brewster, pp. 265–66.

119 Carswell, pp. 256–57.

120 Original publication of the concluding installment of a solicited memoir written in February, 1954.

121 D. H. L. letter to Miss [Gertrude] Cooper, from Villa Mirenda, Scandicci, Florence, dated 5 October 1926, Ada Lawrence and Gelder, pp. 109–10.

122 See *Letters,* p. 678.

123 Aldington, *Portrait of a Genius,* pp. 373–74.

124 D. H. L. letter to Miss [Gertrude] Cooper, from "Mirenda," dated 18 October 1926, Ada Lawrence and Gelder, pp. 111–12.

125 The interpolations (given in the text within brackets) were written in by Lawrence.

126 Original publication.

127 Original publication.

128 Aldous and Maria Huxley were living at the Villa Ino Colli, Cortina d'Ampezzo, Italy. "It's in the Trento region, north of Padua, in the Mountains." —Luhan, p. 318.

129 D. H. L. letter to Miss [Gertrude] Cooper, from Villa Mirenda, Florence, dated 28 October 1926, Ada Lawrence and Gelder, pp. 112–13.

130 "Making Pictures," in *Assorted Articles,* pp. 195–96.

131 D. H. L. letter to Mabel Dodge Luhan, from Villa Mirenda, Scandicci, (Florence), dated 30 October 1926, Luhan, p. 313.

132 D. H. L. letter to Maria and Aldous Huxley, from Villa Mirenda, Scandicci, Firenze, dated 11 November 1926, *Letters,* p. 680. The reference is to Lawrence's oil painting *A Holy Family.*

133 D. H. L. letter to Miss [Gertrude] Cooper, from Villa Mirenda, dated 23 November 1926, Ada Lawrence and Gelder, pp. 113–15.

134 "Lawrence had written from Villa Mirenda (11 Oct. 1926) asking about the singing tour and the Schleswig camp. He said: 'I am sympathetic fundamentally, but I feel how very hard it is to get anything *real* going. Until a few men have an active feeling that the world, the social world, can offer little or nothing any more; and until there can be some tangible desire for a new sort of relationship between people; one is bound to beat about the bush. It is difficult not to fall into preciosity and a sort of faddism.' "—Rolf Gardiner (March, 1956). See *Letters,* pp. 678–80.

135 "The Rendsburg meeting was an attempt to convene leaders of youth groups in Germany, Britain and Scandinavia. It was held at Rendsburg through the good offices of Theodor Steltzer who in 1944–45 was one of the Kreisauer Resistance group led by Helmut von Moltke against the Nazi tyranny. Steltzer was one of the few survivors and became premier of Schleswig-Holstein under the British occupation. In 1926 I was the initiator of the meeting together with Götsch and Heinrich Rocholl. From this gathering proceeded plans which came to fruition during the succeeding seven years."—Rolf Gardiner (March, 1956).

136 "The 'singing tour' by the Märkische Spielgemeinde I organized in southern England. It was the first concert tour by a group of the German youth

movement in England since the war, and made a profound impression. Georg Götsch, later director of the Musikheim at Frankfurt on the Oder, conducted the music."—Rolf Gardiner (March, 1956).

137 Charles Edward Montague (1867–1928), British journalist and man of letters. He was a member of the staff of the *Manchester Guardian* (1890–1914, 1919–1925), author of the novels *A Hind Let Loose* (1910), *Disenchantment* (1922), *Rough Justice* (1926), etc.

138 Martin Schlensog (1897——), composer of folksong settings and chorus and instrumental pieces, was born in Silesia, now makes his home near Hamburg.

139 "Lawrence's criticism of the impression I made on him contained some marvellous words: 'You see one cannot suddenly decapitate oneself. If barren idealism and intellectualism are the cause, it's not the head's fault. The head is really a quite sensible member, which knows what's what: or *must* know. One needs to establish a fuller relationship between oneself and the universe, and between oneself and one's fellow man and fellow woman. It doesn't mean cutting out the "brothers in Christ" business simply: it means expanding it into a full relationship, where there can be also physical and passional meeting, as there used to be in the old dances and rituals. We have to know how to go out and meet one another, upon the third ground, the holy ground.' I was deeply in agreement with Lawrence's view and under its influence, in spite of his impression of my 'fighting, passionate part' never issuing from its shell."—Rolf Gardiner (March, 1956). See *Letters*, p. 679.

140 Cf. the dream motif employed by Lawrence in "Autobiographical Fragment," in *Phoenix*, pp. 817–36.

141 Original publication. For Lawrence's reply, see his letter to Rolf Gardiner, from Villa Mirenda, Scandicci, Florence, dated 3 December 1926, *Letters*, pp. 680–83.

142 D. H. L. letter to Mabel Dodge Luhan, from Villa Mirenda, Scandicci, Firenze, dated 6 December 1926, Luhan, p. 316. The reference is to Lawrence's oil painting *Boccaccio Story*.

143 "*The Widowing of Mrs. Holroyd* was produced under the auspices of the Three Hundred Club, under the direction of Mrs. Geoffrey Whitworth (who was a friend of my family) at the Kingsway Theatre, London, on December 12, 13 and 19, 1926. 'Mrs. Holroyd' was played by Marda Vanne who was at that time the wife of J. G. Strydom, now Afrikaner Nationalist prime minister of the Union of South Africa. She wrote to me about her performance, which I thought magnificent: 'I felt all the time that I was failing Lawrence . . . . My own country, South Africa, has in it something of the doom-like quality you speak of. Perhaps that is why Mrs. Holroyd is so very real to me.' Blackmore was played by Colin Keith-Johnston. The producer S. Esmé Percy had helped me in 1922 when I started a tour, showing English folk dances, in Germany at the Deutsches Theater in Cologne, then in occupation of the British Army of the Rhine."—Rolf Gardiner (March, 1956).

For professional reviews of the production of *The Widowing of Mrs.*

Holroyd, see Desmond MacCarthy in *The New Statesman,* XXVIII (No. 712, 18 December 1926), 310; Ivor Brown in *The Saturday Review,* 142 (No. 3712, 18 December 1926), 767; H. H. in *The Outlook* [London], LVIII (No. 1508, 24 December 1926), 629; Horace Shipp, *The English Review,* XLIV (No. 1, January, 1927), 119–21.—McDonald, *Supplement,* p. 113. See also *The Times* [London], 14 December 1926, p. 12*b;* James Agate in *The Sunday Times* [London], 19 December 1926. See also Vol. I, p. 598 n537, of the present work.

144 (S.) Esmé Percy (1887–1957), English actor and producer.

145 Frederick Hazleton's *Sweeney Todd, the Barber of Fleet Street, or, The String of Pearls* (produced *ca.* 1865).

146 See *Letters,* pp. 680–83.

147 "The farmstead in the Cotswolds became, of course, Gore Farm on the Dorset downs. For a long while I hankered after the Cotswolds with the Shakespearian rural traditions of which I always had a deep bond. But eventually it was Wessex that claimed me, not Saxon Mercia."—Rolf Gardiner (March, 1956).

148 "*Wisdom and Action in Northern Europe* seems to have accumulated throughout my life. The first draft, of which the letter speaks, was lost (together with large parts of the novel *David's Sling*) when a cleptomaniac stole my luggage at Graz in January 1927 and threw it into the River Mur. A compendious and expanded version was finally written in 1944–46, but was never published as a whole. A number of chapters were printed in my *Wessex Letters from Springhead* (1946–48) and some of this material appeared in a German version on the Continent."—Rolf Gardiner (March, 1956).

149 "Of the programme outlined to Lawrence for 1927 quite a lot was fulfilled, particularly the Northumbrian expedition in September which was one of the most ambitious and large-scale efforts of my youth. An account of it written in 1938 was included in the material from *Wisdom and Action in Northern Europe* published in the *Wessex Letters from Springhead.* It was a turning point in the story of the German Buende."—Rolf Gardiner (March, 1956).

150 Original publication.

151 D. H. L. letter to Miss [Gertrude] Cooper, from Villa Mirenda, Florence, dated 21 December 1926, Ada Lawrence and Gelder, pp. 115–17.

152 D. H. L. letter to M[aria] Huxley, from Villa Mirenda, Scandicci, Firenze, dated 28 December 1926, *Letters,* pp. 684–85.

153 D. H. L. letter to Frieda's sister Dr. Else Jaffe-Richthofen, from Villa Mirenda, Scandicci, Florence, dated 10 January 1927, Frieda Lawrence, p. 220.

154 D. H. L. letter to Mabel Dodge Luhan, from Villa Mirenda, Scandicci (Florence), dated 17 January 1927, Luhan, p. 322.

155 Brewster, pp. 112–13.

156 D. H. L. letter to Achsah Barlow Brewster, from Villa Mirenda, Scandicci (Florence), dated 19 January 1927, Brewster, p. 113.

157 D. H. L. letter to Miss [Gertrude] Cooper, from Villa Mirenda, dated 23 January 1927, Ada Lawrence and Gelder, pp. 118–19.

158 D. H. L. letter to Earl H. Brewster, from Villa Mirenda, Scandicci, Florence, dated 6 February 1927, Brewster, p. 116.

159 D. H. L. letter to The Hon. Dorothy Brett, from Villa Mirenda, Scandicci, Florence, dated 9 February 1927, *Letters,* p. 686.

160 D. H. L. letter to Miss [Gertrude] Cooper, from Mirenda, dated 16 February 1927, Ada Lawrence and Gelder, p. 121.

161 D. H. L. letter to Earl H. Brewster, from Villa Mirenda, Scandicci, Florence, dated 27 February 1927, Brewster, pp. 117–18.

162 Lawrence's critical essay "John Galsworthy" originally appeared in *Scrutinies,* by various writers, collected by Edgell Richword (London: Wishart, 1928), pp. 51–72.—McDonald, *Supplement,* pp. 84–85. It is reprinted in *Phoenix,* pp. 539–50. See also McDonald in *Phoenix,* pp. xxi–xxii. For mention of an unpublished Galsworthy letter on Lawrence concerning *The Rainbow,* see Moore, *Intelligent Heart,* pp. 204–5.

163 D. H. L. letter to Miss [Nancy] Pearn, from Villa Mirenda, Scandicci, Florence, dated 28 February 1927, *Letters,* p. 687.

164 D. H. L. letter to The Hon. Dorothy Brett, from Villa Mirenda, Scandicci, Florence, dated 8 March 1927, *Letters,* pp. 688–89.

165 "The Lovely Lady" was originally published in Lady Cynthia Asquith's "Murder book" *The Black Cap* (London: Hutchinson, 1927), and later included as the title story in *The Lovely Lady and Other Stories.*

166 D. H. L. letter to Miss [Nancy] Pearn, from Villa Mirenda, Scandicci, Florence, dated 11 March 1927, *Letters,* p. 689.

167 Unpublished D. H. L. letter to Enid Hilton [from Villa Mirenda, Scandicci, Florence, Italy], dated 17 March [1927], Moore, *Poste Restante,* p. 90.

168 Possibly a reference to Lawrence's Aunt Emma (Mrs. Emma Saxton), a sister of Arthur John Lawrence, and to her donkey Jack. See Ada Lawrence and Gelder, pp. 38–40; reprinted in Vol. I, pp. 18–19, of the present work.

169 Presumably a son of Lawrence's eldest brother, George Arthur.

170 Cf. Lawrence's essay "Pictures on the Wall," originally published as "Dead Pictures on the Wall" in *Vanity Fair,* 33 (No. 4, December, 1929), 88, 108, 140, and as "Pictures on the Wall" in *The Architectural Review* [London], LXVII (No. 2, February, 1930), 55–57, and later included in *Assorted Articles.*—McDonald, *Supplement,* pp. 100–101.

171 See Lawrence in a letter to Harwood Brewster, from Hotel Fischer, Villach, Karnten, Austria, dated 17 August 1927: "[Give] the blue Venus a kiss for me, and wipe young Mercury's nose. As for the rest of the statues, I refuse to have any communication with them."—Brewster, p. 145.

172 Probably a reference to Lawrence's essay "Flowery Tuscany," originally published in monthly installments in *The Monthly Criterion: A Literary Review* [London], VI, 305–10 (No. 4, October, 1927), 403–8 (No. 5, November, 1927), and 516–22 (No. 6, December, 1927); and as "A Year in Flowery Tuscany," in *Travel,* LIII (No. 6, April, 1929), 25–29, 56, 58, 60; and reprinted in *Phoenix,* pp. 45–58.—McDonald, *Supplement,* pp. 97, 99. In February, 1927, Millicent Beveridge had taken a villa in the neighborhood of the Villa Mirenda. She told Catherine Carswell "how she went walking with [Lawrence] once in the hills near Florence at the height of the Tuscan spring, and how as they went he named and discoursed upon at least thirty

varieties. It was out of that walk that he wrote the three fragrant, categorical and joyous essays on 'Flowers in Tuscany' [*sic*] which appeared in the *Criterion*."—Carswell, pp. 267, 106–7.

173 Brewster, pp. 271–78.

174 D. H. L. letter to Miss [Nancy] Pearn, from Palazzo Cimbrone, Ravello (Salerno), dated 22 March 1927, *Letters*, p. 690.

175 See *Etruscan Places*, Chap. V, "Vulci."

176 Mr. Brewster appears to have been mistaken as to both the date and the place of that glimpse into the little shop window. The date: Palm Sunday, 10 April 1927.—Moore, *Poste Restante*, pp. 91–92. The place: Volterra. See Lawrence's letter of 3 May 1927, quoted in text below (Brewster, p. 128); see also D. H. L. letter of 21 October 1927, Brewster, p. 151.

177 Only the Black Sun Press edition of this story carries the original title *The Escaped Cock*. For both the London (Martin Secker) and the New York (Knopf) editions, the title was changed to *The Man Who Died*. See also Note 247, below.

178 Brewster, pp. 120–24. For a detailed itinerary of the Etruscan tour, see Moore, *Poste Restante*, pp. 91–92; for Lawrence's own record, see *Etruscan Places*.

179 D. H. L. letter to Miss [Nancy] Pearn, from Villa Mirenda, Scandicci, Florence, dated 12 April 1927, *Letters*, pp. 690–91.

180 Not to be confused with Frieda's older daughter Elsa, later Mrs. Edward Seaman.

181 D. H. L. letter (translated from the German) to Frieda's mother, Frau Baronin von Richthofen, from Villa Mirenda, Scandicci, Florence, dated 14 April 1927, Frieda Lawrence, pp. 223–24.

182 *Nuns with the Gardener* is better known as *Boccaccio Story*. The "picture of naked men among autumn willows" is probably a reference to the oil painting *Red Willow Trees*.

183 Original publication of an installment of a long memoir completed in 1954.

184 D. H. L. letter to Mabel Dodge Luhan, from Scandicci (Florence), Villa Mirenda, dated 14 April 1927, Luhan, pp. 325–26.

185 D. H. L. letter to Earl H. Brewster, from Villa Mirenda, Scandicci (Firenze), dated 28 April 1927, Brewster, p. 126. The reference is to Lawrence's first attempt at the story later entitled *The Escaped Cock* (*The Man Who Died*).

186 D. H. L. letter to Martin Secker, from Villa Mirenda, Scandicci, Firenze, dated 29 April 1927, *Letters*, p. 691. Possibly Lawrence was writing the sketch "The Nightingale," originally published in *The Forum*, LXXVIII (No. 3, September, 1927), 382–87, and *The Spectator*, 139 (No. 5176, 10 September 1927), 377–78.—McDonald, *Supplement*, p. 96. It has been reprinted in Frieda Lawrence, pp. 201–7, and in *Phoenix*, pp. 40–44.

187 D. H. L. letter to Earl H. Brewster, from Villa Mirenda, Scandicci, Firenze, dated 3 May 1927, Brewster, pp. 127–28.

188 D. H. L. letter to Earl H. Brewster, from Villa Mirenda, Scandicci (Firenze), dated 13 May 1927, Brewster, pp. 129–30.

189 D. H. L. letter to Miss [Gertrude] Cooper, from "Mirenda," dated 19 May 1927, Ada Lawrence and Gelder, pp. 124–25.

190 For reviews of the production of *David* at the Regent Theatre, London, 22 May 1927, see Richard Jennings, "The Theatre," *The Spectator* (No. 5161, 28 May 1927), 939–40; *The Times* [London], 24 May 1927, p. 14*b*.

191 D. H. L. letter to Mabel Dodge Luhan, from Scandicci, Florence, Villa Mirenda, dated 28 May 1927, Luhan, p. 330.

192 Sitwell, *Penny Foolish,* pp. 295–97. See Note 312, below. Sir Osbert Sitwell, Bt., C.B.E. (1892———), distinguished English poet, short-story writer, autobiographer. Brother of Dame Edith Sitwell (1887———) and Sacheverell Sitwell (1897———).

There are other glimpses of Lawrence and Frieda at Montegufoni, Tuscan home of the late Sir George Sitwell, Sir Osbert's father: "Many of the visitors were distinguished in the arts, but my father and mother never knew who they were. Sometimes, therefore, when I was in England, my mother would, if she remembered the names, write to me, to make inquiries concerning the identity of her guests, or to give me a description of them. And I found that my mother's pen pictures were always more vibrant and full of point than my father's. 'A Mr. D. H. Lawrence came over the other day,' she wrote, 'a funny little petit-maître of a man with flat features and a beard. He says he is a writer, and seems to know all of you. His wife is a large German. She went round the house with your father, and when he showed her anything, would look at him, lean against one of the gilded beds, and breathe heavily.' "—Sir Osbert Sitwell, *Laughter in the Next Room* (Boston: Little, Brown, 1948), pp. 310–11.

Perhaps it was during this same visit to Montegufoni that Lawrence told Sir George that he wished (Dame) Edith Sitwell "would consult him about rhythm." See Sitwell, *Laughter in the Next Room,* pp. 356–57. See also Frieda Lawrence, pp. 195–96.

193 D. H. L. letter to Frieda's sister Dr. Else Jaffe-Richthofen, from Villa Mirenda, Scandicci, Florence, dated 1 June 1927, Frieda Lawrence, p. 225.

194 See Frieda Lawrence Ravagli: "People came to see us at the Mirenda. Capitano Ravagli had come to Florence for a military case—he came to see us and showed Lawrence his military travel-pass. When Lawrence saw it: *Capitano Ravagli* deve *partire* (must *leave*) *at such and such a time* . . . he shook his head and said resentfully: 'Why must? why must? there shouldn't be any *must.* . . .' "—Frieda Lawrence, p. 195.

195 Original publication of an installment of a solicited memoir written in 1957. I am unable to date with any certainty Capt. Ravagli's visit to the Villa Mirenda.

196 Lawrence's essay on Cerveteri appeared originally as "City of the Dead at Cerveteri," in *Travel,* L (No. 1, November, 1927), 12–16, 50; as "Sketches of Etruscan Places (i) Cerveteri," in *World To-day,* February, 1928.— McDonald, *Supplement,* p. 97. His essay on Tarquinia appeared originally as "Ancient Metropolis of the Etruscans," in *Travel,* L (No. 2, December, 1927), 20–25, 55; as "Sketches of Etruscan Places (ii) Tarquinia," in *World To-day,* March, 1928.—McDonald, *Supplement,* p. 97. As Cerveteri" and "Tarquinia," both were included in *Etruscan Places.*

197 D. H. L. letter to Earl H. Brewster, from Villa Mirenda, Scandicci (Firenze), dated 9 June [1927], Brewster, p. 137.

198 D. H. L. letter to Ada Lawrence Clarke, from "Mirenda," dated 11 June 1927, Ada Lawrence and Gelder, p. 125.

199 D. H. L. letter to S. S. Koteliansky, from Villa Mirenda, Scandicci, Florence, dated 13 June 1927, *Encounter 3*, I (No. 3, December, 1953), 33.

200 D. H. L. letter to Miss [Gertrude] Cooper, from "Mirenda," dated 21 June 1927, Ada Lawrence and Gelder, pp. 126–27.

201 Cf. Lawrence's essay "Fireworks in Florence," in *Phoenix*, pp. 123–27. The sketch was apparently written on 25 June of the previous year, 1926: "Yesterday being St. John's Day, the 24th June . . . ." See Tedlock, pp. 192–93; *Phoenix*, p. 839. As "Fireworks," the sketch was originally published in *The Nation and Athenaeum*, XLI (No. 2, 16 April 1927), 47–49, and in *The Forum*, LXXVII (No. 5, May, 1927), 648–54.—McDonald, *Supplement*, p. 96.

202 D. H. L. letter to Earl H. Brewster, from Villa Mirenda, Scandicci (Firenze), undated, Brewster, p. 138. Lawrence's essay on Volterra was originally published as "The Wind-swept Strongholds of Volterra," in *Travel*, L (No. 4, February, 1928), 31–35, 44, and, as "Sketches of Etruscan Places (iv) Volterra," in *World To-day*, May, 1928.—McDonald, *Supplement*, pp. 97–98. As "Volterra," the essay was later included in *Etruscan Places*.

203 Frieda Lawrence, pp. 194–95.

204 D. H. L. letter (translated from the German) to Frieda's mother, Frau Baronin von Richthofen, from Villa Mirenda, Scandicci, Florence, dated 11 July 1927, Frieda Lawrence, p. 228.

205 D. H. L. letter to Dr. Trigant Burrow, from Villa Mirenda, Scandicci, Florence, dated 13 July 1927, *Letters*, p. 693.

206 Extract from a letter (28 June 1944) to Mrs. Mary Freeman.

207 In a letter (20 August 1957) to the editor, Miss Aimée Guggenheimer, Office Secretary at The Lifwynn Foundation, Westport, Conn., has written: "In 1920 at the time Dr. Burrow sent this paper ["Psychoanalysis in Theory and in Life"] to Mr. Rosenberg, he had only copies that had been privately printed, and they bore no reference. Later on it was revised and published in *The Journal of Nervous and Mental Disease*, LXIV (No. 3, 1926), 209–24." (For Mr. Max Rosenberg, see text below.) Lawrence acknowledged receipt of the paper in a letter to Dr. Trigant Burrow, from the Villa Mirenda, Scandicci, Florence, Italy, dated "Christmas Day, 1926." See *Letters*, pp. 683–84.

208 At this point, Dr. Burrow listed in reverse order "the eight papers whose dates of publication are closest to 'Psychoanalysis in Theory and in Life' ":

"The Origin of the Incest-Awe," *The Psychoanalytic Review*, V (1918), 243–54.

"Notes with Reference to Freud, Jung and Adler," *The Journal of Abnormal Psychology*, XII (1917), 161–67.

"The Genesis and Meaning of 'Homosexuality' and its Relation to the Problem of Introverted Mental States," *The Psychoanalytic Review*, IV (1917), 272–84. (See *Letters*, p. 694.)

"The Meaning of Psychoanalysis," *The Journal of Abnormal Psychology*, XII (1917), 56–68.

"Conceptions and Misconceptions in Psychoanalysis," *The Journal of the American Medical Association,* LXVIII (1917), 355–60; reprinted in Benjamin Harrow, ed., *Contemporary Science* (New York: Boni & Liveright, 1921), pp. 211–29.

"Permutations within the Sphere of Consciousness, or The Factor of Repression and its Influence upon Education," *The Journal of Abnormal Psychology,* XI (1916), 178–88.

"The Philology of Hysteria—An A Priori Study of the Neuroses in the Light of Freudian Psychology," *The Journal of the American Medical Association,* LXVI (1916), 783–87.

"The Psychanalyst and the Community," *The Journal of the American Medical Association,* LXIII (1914), 1876–78.

209 See also a letter (2 October 1942) from Dr. Trigant Burrow to Prof. Frederick J. Hoffman: "With regard to Lawrence there was no 'association' between us, as it happens that I never met him. A student of mine interested him in some of my earlier writings, and through them he was prompted to put out the little volume he called *Psychoanalysis and the Unconscious.* Lawrence was very sympathetic to my trend at that time and showed an uncommon insight into it. But unless I am greatly mistaken, he would have made short shrift of my later work as it bears upon the organism's disordered patterns of tension in their relation to neurotic conditions." See also Burrow, pp. 442–43.

210 Trigant Burrow, "Social Images versus Reality," *The Journal of Abnormal Psychology and Social Psychology,* XIX (1924), 230–35.

211 Trigant Burrow, "Character and the Neuroses," *The Psychoanalytic Review,* I (No. 2, 1914), 121–28.

212 The above four paragraphs of text are extracted from a letter (21 August 1944) to Mrs. Mary Freeman.

213 Extract from a letter (11 July 1930) to Mrs. Trigant Burrow.—Burrow, p. 230. In a letter (20 August 1957) to the editor, Miss Aimée Guggenheimer has furnished the following biography of the late Dr. Trigant Burrow:

"Trigant Burrow was born in Norfolk, Virginia, on September 7, 1875, the son of John W. and Anastasia Devereux Burrow. He attended private schools in Norfolk and New York City, and had his academic training at Fordham University. He studied medicine at the University of Virginia, taking his M.D. in 1899. Following a year abroad devoted largely to postgraduate medical work, he returned to America and settled in Baltimore where he pursued medical and other studies at The Johns Hopkins University. In 1904 he married Emily Sherwood Bryan of Cambridge, Maryland, and they had two children. He took his Ph.D. in psychology at Hopkins in 1909, and he spent the following year in Zurich where he studied psychoanalysis with Carl G. Jung.

"After his return to Baltimore Burrow developed a large and successful practice as a psychoanalyst. He was one of the founders of the American Psychoanalytic Association (1911) and its president during 1925–1926. Gradually he came to sense the wider social implications of individual neurotic disorders, and developed a method of research which he first called group-analysis and later phyloanalysis. Lawrence was greatly impressed by what he called the 'subjective honesty' underlying Burrow's approach. [See *Phoenix*, p. 377.]

"In order to provide the needed community setting for his work, Burrow and several of his associates organized The Lifwynn Foundation for Laboratory Research in Analytic and Social Psychiatry [now located at Westport, Conn.] of which he was Scientific Director from the time of its incorporation in 1927 until his death on May 24, 1950.

"Following years of systematic observation of social reactions in daily group sessions, Burrow found evidence that a 'social neurosis' distorts human relationships and institutions and pervades so-called 'normal' behavior. His investigations came eventually to centre upon internal tensional patterns correlated with man's varying behavior expressions, and he developed a technique that would aid in the establishment of behavioral health.

"Burrow's researches are reported in a large number of papers that appeared in various technical journals and in five books. These are *The Social Basis of Consciousness* (1927), *The Structure of Insanity* (1932), *The Biology of Human Conflict* (1937), *The Neurosis of Man* (1949) and *Science and Man's Behavior* (1953)."

For Lawrence's review of Dr. Trigant Burrow's *The Social Basis of Consciousness* (New York: Harcourt, 1927; London: Kegan Paul, June, 1927), see the (American) *Bookman*, LXVI (No. 3, November, 1927), 314–17, reprinted in *Phoenix*, pp. 377–82. See also *Letters*, pp. 695–97.

Seven letters from Dr. Burrow to Lawrence follow. Three have been extracted from *A Search for Man's Sanity: The Selected Letters of Trigant Burrow with Biographical Notes* (New York: Oxford University Press, 1958); the remaining four are published here for the first time.

The Tuscany Apartments/Baltimore, Maryland/January 28, 1925
[To:] Mr. D. H. Lawrence,/ c/o Curtis Brown Ltd.,/6 Henrietta St., W. C. 2,/London, England.

Dear Mr. Lawrence:

You were so good as to be interested in some earlier writings of mine and I have thought many times to write you of my appreciation and to say how much I have enjoyed your own delightful essays on psychoanalysis. Knowing your feeling for the subject I am prompted to send you reprints of two recent papers of mine. They are part of a larger thesis that is the outcome of intensive research of the last years with groups of students involving the social reactions of "the unconscious." I had hoped that this work would have found its way to publication, but it is evident that American publishers are very chary of scientific trends whose basis lacks the accustomed precedents.

I should be very glad if these essays may be of interest to you. With appreciations and good wishes,

[Original publication]

Very sincerely yours,
Trigant Burrow

The Tuscany Apartments/Baltimore, Maryland/May 6, 1926
Dear Mr. Lawrence:

I have been long in replying to your very thoughtful and interesting letter from New Mexico. [See *Letters,* pp. 642–43.] I had hoped your travels might bring you nearer our doors and that there might have been the opportunity of meeting you.

Remembering your interest in some earlier things of mine, I am sending to you, separately, reprints of more recent material. I feel naturally the futility of hoping for any wide acceptance of formulations which rest, as these do, upon a technique in which my colleagues in general have as yet not had the opportunity of participation. I hope it may seem to you that they indicate at least the right direction of approach.

With my kind regards,

Very sincerely yours,
[Trigant Burrow]

Mr. D. H. Lawrence,/c/o Curtis Brown, Ltd.,/6 Henrietta Street, W.C. 2,/London, England. [Original publication]

The Tuscany Apartments/Baltimore, Maryland/October 25, 1926
Dear Mr. Lawrence:

I am sending off to you today offprints of some recent writings. You have always been good about reading my things and I hope sometime you will find the leisure to run through these.

With the conclusion of the arduous years of researches in the development of a social technique of analysis I am hoping to be able to formulate our position in clearer terms than I have hitherto been able to do. Certainly it has broadened my approach to private analysis to a degree that is not to be measured.

I am looking forward to spending much of my winter in New York and to the prospect of very interesting contacts there in connection with my work. I wish it were sometime possible to meet you. Or are you not planning to be in this country again for some time?

With my kind regards,

Very sincerely yours,
Trigant Burrow

Mr. D. H. Lawrence,/c/o Curtis Brown Ltd.,/6 Henrietta Street,/London W.C. 2,/England. [See *Letters,* pp. 683–84. Original publication]

16 Park Avenue/New York City/February 7, 1927.
Dear D. H. Lawrence:

Many thanks for your good letter from Florence of January 12th ["Christmas Day, 1926," *Letters,* p. 683]. I am very glad you felt with me in my paper, "Psychoanalysis in Theory and in Life." What you say of my involved sentences is too terribly true. See if my language is not improving in this essay I am sending you today, "The Reabsorbed Affect and Its Elimination" [*The British Journal of Medical Psychology,* VI (Part 3, 1926), 209–18].

No, nobody listens to me. But I do not expect them to. I didn't listen myself. Circumstances, very unusual circumstances, *compelled* my mood to listen whether or no. And now and then I have the opportunity of compelling by extension this same mood acknowledgment in others. But it is only by compulsion that our willful mood is touched, not by persuasion. Intellectualism simply does not figure for a moment in the process.

No, I am not a Jew. I like them and they like me, but racially I am not one of them. My ancestry is chiefly French, though in recent generations depleted with English and Irish strains.

Your letters and their sympathetic encouragement have meant very much to me. You should have stopped to see me on your way from Mexico to England. This winter I am in New York in response to the group interest there on the part of several people. It has been an interesting experience, this fresh contact with a totally new environment and the opportunity to approach it from an entirely fresh mood basis. The response there has been more than I had had any expectation of. New York also has its soberness and its pain.

You are so fortunate to travel as much as you do. I think each year I shall set out but each year there are interests that stand momentarily in the way.

With my good wishes,   Sincerely yours,
Trigant Burrow

Mr. D. H. Lawrence,/Villa Mirenda,/Scandicci,/Florence, Italy. [See Burrow, pp. 163–64.]

Lifwynn Camp/Merrill, New York/July 12, 1927

Dear Mr. Lawrence:

It has been ages since I have heard from you. [See letter of 13 July 1927 in *Letters*, pp. 693–94.] I am writing to tell you that I have taken the liberty of asking Kegan Paul who have brought out the English edition of my book —"The Social Basis of Consciousness"—to send a copy of it to you. It is a relief to have this book completed. It was first written some four years ago, and has been on my hands all this while.

I have just come up to these hills for my summer's work, and things are as yet in much disarray, but I wanted to send you just this line and have you know of my pleasure in placing your name among the first to whom my book should go. I have always appreciated your sympathetic understanding of my endeavors.

With my kind regards,   Sincerely yours,
Trigant Burrow

Mr. D. H. Lawrence,/c/o Curtis Brown Ltd.,/6 Henrietta Street, W.C. 2/London,/England. [Original publication]

Lifwynn Camp/Merrill/Clinton County/New York/September 9, 1927
My dear Lawrence:

It seems good to have at last a moment when I may write you. You have been very much in my thought. Your letter [See *Letters,* pp. 695–97.] was so heartening and so very kind. I want to say to you first, though, how sorry I am that you have been ill—that you were born ill, born protesting at being born. I, myself, howled about it for one mortal year, they tell me, but the insult did not get deeper into my organism than that. I have been whimpering softly to myself, though, ever since, and I mean to go on whimpering until Man is born (even if only some small bit of the occiput presents) and there is an end of his image and of unconsciousness.

When people are ill, who should be well, I feel I must go to them and do something. As a matter of fact nobody could do less than I if he went to you. I have always disliked medicine—that is medicine as pathology. What knowledge I acquired in the long years of my apprenticeship in laboratory and clinic has left me today with little more than a futile tenderness. Do they take your clothes off and put you in the sun? That's the first thing. But I am sure your own instinct has seen to that. Or perhaps, like myself, you are making a living? That is very bad for you. Not even the sun can reach a man who is making a living. This enforced over-concentration of interest upon the nutritional instinct sets up such rigidities, such artificial tensions in us, there is no breathing right, no right rhythm anywhere, and the scalp binds till the head would break.

Sometime we must feel into these things together—that is all group-analysis is anyway. It is breaking up old adhesions and unnatural contractions within the organism of man. How can men be well if Man is not? And Man is so well essentially. There are just the contractions (habituated now throughout the centuries) with which he shrinks in fear from the anomaly of his own image, his stupid purpose in life apart from the purpose that is life. I do not know why we need permit God to do to us what he did to Adam. Adam had nothing approaching our educational advantages.

I do know what you mean, and I am heartily with you, I think, in your feeling about religion. But isn't it with religion as it is with love—love that cannot endure to hear its own name so much as whispered? "They put their finger on their lip, the powers above. They love but name not love." What man can adore and call it adoring!

Yes I am married, very much so. I have also a son, 22, who is this summer with me in camp, and a daughter, 18. Mrs. Burrow and Emily have lately been not far distant neighbors of yours, I think. They were in Italy for a while on their tour of Europe this summer.

But about marriage. What I said of marriage, I said of marriage as ownership. And marriage *is* ownership—let's face it. I think no two people were ever more stupid and reluctant to face this unsavory actuality in their lives than my wife and myself, but we have kept at it, and the deeper understanding and sympathy and confidence that have come of it, I count among the richest meanings of the many rich meanings that life has brought to me.

About the "cut-offness"—I do not want to be tedious and seem to talk to you, as people so often feel that I do, with teasing paradox—but really it is not you who are cut off, but the image *you* have of "you." So that your question as to what one is to do about the cut-offness, I can only answer, as far as my experience goes, by saying that this image that is socially reciprocated everywhere must, it seems to me, be dissolved in the common pool of social images that now make for those differentiae among us that are really the projected image of each. If it is not your organism that is cut off—your organism with its feelings and instincts and its unending joy of life—but some purely artificial image, superstitiously sponsored under the traditional mood-protectorate of a primitive fear-ridden society, what avails it to look to the organism for one's mending? Our mental pathology does not really *touch* our organism. Think of it! All our pathology boiled down reveals at last that there was nothing there. Only images mutually supported by images socially begotten and socially sustained. This social distemper is a social obligation to remedy, and we psychiatrists (myself included) have been all this while but standing in the way.

You are right—one cannot forgive. All our forgivingness is spiritual snobbery. But then for us to say with our minds that forgivingness is stupid leads us from the actuality of a mood that does in fact cherish (as a mood based upon the parent-image must) a deep-seated sense of guilt, of self-blame. If I am stupid enough to blame myself, it is up to me to be stupid enough to forgive myself. A stupid equation, but not so stupid as an equation left unresolved.

I love what you say about my excruciating style. It *is* awful, and you have diagnosed me in no imprecise manner. The as yet unresolved conflict within me between science and art is the thunderous noise one hears on every page as I come laboring along. It seemed to me that in some of my later things my breathing was less stertorous. I hope so.

It is good of you to have in mind the thought of possibly writing a review of my book [*The Social Basis of Consciousness*]. It would mean much to me to have your very understanding comment upon it. And I, too, hope very earnestly that we shall meet. After October first my head-quarters will be at 67 Park Avenue, New York City.

My daughter is making her debut this winter (she would not miss it) and I shall be much in Baltimore, but my work will be in New York, and I am looking forward with real zest to the winter's interests and to newer and, I hope, saner adjustments.

I do hope you will be well soon and that you will keep in mind how much I enjoy having your good letters.

Sincerely yours,
Trigant Burrow

P.S. Won't you reserve your verdict and not say quite yet that "men were never fully societal"? Do you know Kropotkin's "Mutual Aid," and do you know the passages in "The Origin of Species" from which Kropotkin really fashioned his thesis? It is the subjective sense of this societal and organic interconnection or continuum among us as a species that is really the whole meaning of my position, and group analysis but the clearing away of the manifold image differentiae that have so separated man from himself.

Mr. D. H. Lawrence/Villa Mirenda/Scandicci/Florence/Italy. [See Burrow, pp. 184–88.]

67 Park Avenue/New York, N.Y./December 21, 1927
Dear Mr. Lawrence:

I am ashamed of myself that I have not written you before this to tell you how deeply I appreciated the very kind and sympathetic review of my book that you sent to the "Bookman." It was such a generous recognition on your part and has, I am sure, stimulated no little recognition among readers generally. It was very good of you and I have appreciated deeply your thoughtfulness in this.

You will be glad to know, and perhaps as surprised as I am, that the book is really being read and finding not a few favorable reviews. I had no idea it would be so. In the last weeks I have been trying to make amends for the obscurities and difficulties in "The Social Basis of Consciousness" by putting together material from some more recent notes.

A small group of us is enjoying immensely the winter in the country about Greenwich, Connecticut. I believe I wrote you of our plan in my reply to your good letter to me of last summer.° By the way, I sent my letter to Scandicci and hope it found its way to you. For closer acquaintance sake I tried to enter into the questions suggested in your letter to me.

I hope that you have entirely recovered from the illness that was so great a distress to you at the time you wrote me.

This is to-day no more than a word to acknowledge your kindness in giving so much helpful impetus to a thoughtful reception of my book. I assure you it has meant very much.

With my very cordial greetings for Christmas and the New Year, believe me

Gratefully and sincerely,
Trigant Burrow

Mr. D. H. Lawrence,/Villa Mirenda,/Scandicci,/Florence, Italy. [See Burrow, pp. 195–96.]

214 Frieda Lawrence letter to Mabel Dodge Luhan, from Villa Mirenda, dated "Thursday, 21. VII. 27," Luhan, p. 332.

215 See text below under date 18 November 1927. See also Note 260, below.

216 In the first version of his memoir, published in 1930 (see Note 219, below), the late Mr. Johns had written: "I saw D. H. Lawrence twice in Italy, once in 1927 and again in 1928." He wrote of his "first visit in summer, 1927" and again: "At that first visit, Lawrence had looked like a very sick man. . . . Before and after that August of 1927, if I remember rightly, he had rushed off to Switzerland . . . ." In *Time of Our Lives,*

° "We have been unable to locate the reply Dr. Burrows refers to, and assume it was hand-written."—Aimée Guggenheimer.

however, the text reprinted here, he wrote: "At that second visit, Lawrence had looked like a very sick man. . . . Before and after that August of 1927, if I remember rightly, he had rushed off to Switzerland . . . ." (pp. 272–73). I take it, on the basis of Frieda's letter to Mabel Dodge Luhan dated 21 July 1927, quoted in text above (see Luhan, p. 332), that Mr. Johns was right, or clearer, the first time: that his first visit took place in July (not August), 1927. Lawrence "rushed off" to Villach, Austria, in August, 1927; to Switzerland in January and June, 1928.

217 Zoë Akins (1886———), American poet and playwright; author of poetry, as *Interpretations* (1911), *The Hills Grow Smaller* (1937); and plays, as *Déclassée* (1919), *Daddy's Gone a-Hunting* (1921), *A Royal Fandango* (1924), *The Greeks Had a Word for It* (1929), *The Old Maid* (1935), *The Little Miracle* (1936); a novel, *Forever Young* (1941). Recipient of the Pulitzer drama prize (1934–1935).

218 I am unable to trace this letter in *Lorenzo in Taos*.

219 Johns, pp. 270–74. With slight variations, this excerpt had appeared as "Lawrence in Italy," in Supplement to *The Carmelite*, III (No. 6, 19 March 1930), vi–viii. Orrick Johns (1887–1946), American poet, was born in St. Louis, Mo., and studied at the University of Missouri and Washington University. He helped to found the Players' Club of St. Louis. An early contributor to *Poetry,* he continued to publish verse and prose while writing advertising copy. From 1926 to 1929, he lived in Capri, Naples, Florence, Venice, Sicily, and then settled in Carmel, Calif. He became an associate editor of *New Masses,* co-organizer of the first American Writers' Congress and the League of American Writers, Director of the Federal Writers Project of the WPA in New York City (1935–1936). He married (1929) Caroline Blackman, (1937) Doria Berton. On 8 July 1946, he ended his own life by taking poison at his home in Danbury, Conn. He was the author of three volumes of poetry: *Asphalt* (1919), *Black Branches* (1920), *Wild Plum* (1926); a novel, *Blindfold* (1923); an autobiography, *Time of Our Lives* (1937).

220 D. H. L. letter to Frieda's sister Dr. Else Jaffe-Richthofen, from Villa Mirenda, Scandicci, Firenze, dated only "Montag" [?25 July 1927], Frieda Lawrence, p. 262.

221 D. H. L. letter to Mark Gertler, from Villa Mirenda, Scandicci, Italy, dated 31 July 1927, Moore, *Intelligent Heart,* pp. 366–67.

222 D. H. L. letter to Ada Lawrence Clarke, from Villach, Karuten [Kärnten], Austria, dated 8 August 1927, Ada Lawrence and Gelder, pp. 128–30.

223 In 1923, Frieda's younger sister, Johanna ("Nusch"), then Frau Max Schreibershofen, had married Emil Krug. See Lawrence's letter of 13 or 20 August 1927 to Giusèppe (Pino) Orioli: "She, my cognata, is not very contented, having got a newish bourgeoisie banker husband, ten years older than herself, instead of a neer-do-well ex-army officer—she changed them four years ago—the husbands, I mean—and the good bourgeois bores and oppresses her, and she is in a bad humour, having always lived a gay life; and altogether I think the female of a species is a trial nowadays."—Moore, *Intelligent Heart,* p. 368. In May, 1949, after a separation

of fifteen years, Johanna visited Frieda at Taos.—*El Crepusculo* [Taos, N. Mex.], 16 August 1956.

224 D. H. L. letter to Dorothy Yorke, from Hotel Fischer, Villach, Austria, dated 11 August 1927, Moore, *Intelligent Heart*, pp. 367–68.

225 D. H. L. letter to Harwood Brewster, from Hotel Fischer, Villach, Karnten, Austria, dated 17 August 1927, Brewster, pp. 144–45.

226 D. H. L. letter to Mabel Dodge Luhan, from Hotel Fischer, Villach, Austria, dated 25 August 1927, Luhan, p. 333.

227 Lawrence and Frieda had stayed at the Villa Jaffe as long ago as 1912.

228 D. H. L. letter (postcard?) to Ada Lawrence Clarke, from "Nr. Munich," dated 4 September 1927, Ada Lawrence and Gelder, p. 131.

229 D. H. L. letter to Ada Lawrence Clarke, from "Nr. Munich," dated 7 September 1927, Ada Lawrence and Gelder, pp. 131–32.

230 D. H. L. letter to Frieda's sister Dr. Else Jaffe-Richthofen, no address given [Villa Jaffe, Irschenhausen, Bavaria], dated only "Saturday Morning" [17 September 1927], Frieda Lawrence, p. 232.

231 Apparently Lawrence received a payment of M.180 from *Jugend* for "Rex." See Frieda Lawrence, pp. 255, 271.

232 Hans Carossa (1878——), German prose writer, poet, and physician, born in Tölz, Bavaria. He is the author of *Doktor Bürgers Ende* (1913), *Der Arzt Gion* (1931; *Doctor Gion*, 1933), *Geheimnisse des reiferen Lebens* (1936); several volumes of autobiographical works: *Eine Kindheit* (1922; *A Childhood*, 1930), *Rumänisches Tagebuch* (1924; *A Roumanian Diary*, 1929), *Verwandlungen einer Jugend* (1928; *Boyhood and Youth*, 1930), *Führung und Geleit* (1933), and *Das Jahr der schönen Täuschungen* (1941); *Gesammelte Gedichte* (poems, 1938), etc.

233 Lawrence's sketch "Rex" was published in *Jugend* [Munich], 33 (No. 43, 20 October 1928), 678–81, 691, in an authorized translation into German by Else Jaffe-Richthofen. For the original, see *Phoenix*, pp. 14–21.

234 Knut Hamsun (1859–1952), Norwegian novelist. Among his best-known novels are *Hunger* (1890), *Pan* (1894), and *The Growth of the Soil* (1917). Winner of the Nobel Prize in Literature (1920). In World War II, he sympathized with the Germans in Norway.

235 Cf. Mary Freeman, *D. H. Lawrence: A Basic Study of His Ideas* (Gainesville: University of Florida Press, 1955), Chap. XVIII: "Lawrence and Fascism," pp. 189–207. See also S. H. Nulle, "D. H. Lawrence and the Fascist Movement," *New Mexico Quarterly*, February, 1940; and Mrs. Mary Freeman's rejoinder to Mr. Nulle, "D. H. Lawrence in Valhalla?" *New Mexico Quarterly*, November, 1940.

236 In a letter (8 August 1951) to the editor, Frieda Lawrence Ravagli wrote of Lawrence as being "almost symbolical the miner's son, who worked & delved in the darkness and underground of the human being—."

237 Schoenberner, pp. 282–90. With slight variations, printed as "When D. H. Lawrence Was Shocked," in *The Saturday Review of Literature*, XXIX (No. 8, 23 February 1946), 18–19. Franz Schoenberner (1892——), German editor and writer, now resident in the U.S. Born in Berlin, he was the son of a Protestant minister. After seeing military service in World War I, he became editor of *Auslandspost* and occasional editor of *Neue Merkur*

(1923–1924) of Munich, editor of *Jugend* (1926–1929), then editor-in-chief of *Simplicissimus* (1929–1933), both of Munich. He left Germany in 1933, lived in France for eight years, came to U.S. in 1941. He now lives in New York City. Author of *Confessions of a European Intellectual* (1946), *Inside Story of an Outsider* (1949), *You Still Have Your Head: Excursions from Immobility* (1957).

238 D. H. L. letter to Earl H. and Achsah Barlow Brewster, from Irschenhausen, Post Ebenhausen, bei München, dated 17 September 1927, Brewster, p. 149.

239 Dr. Else Jaffe-Richthofen translated Lawrence's *Sons and Lovers, The Boy in the Bush*, "The Fox," *The Woman Who Rode Away*, and *The Plumed Serpent* into German. See also Note 233, above.

240 Original publication of an installment of a long memoir completed in 1954.

241 D. H. L. letter to Frieda's sister Dr. Else Jaffe-Richthofen, from Irschenhausen, dated only "Sunday," Frieda Lawrence, pp. 218–19.

242 D. H. L. letter (translated from the German) to Frieda's mother, Frau Baronin von Richthofen, from Irschenhausen, Isartal, dated "Wednesday/ 29 September 1927" [Wednesday, 28 September 1927, or Thursday, 29 September 1927], Frieda Lawrence, p. 233.

243 D. H. L. letter (translated from the German) to Frieda's sister Dr. Else Jaffe-Richthofen, from Hotel Eden, Baden-Baden, dated only "Friday," Frieda Lawrence, pp. 234–35.

244 D. H. L. letter to Max Mohr, from Kurhaus Eden, Baden Baden, dated 10 October 1927, in *T'ien Hsia Monthly* [Shanghai], I (No. 1, August, 1935), 23–24.

245 D. H. L. letter (translated from the German) to Frieda's mother, Frau Baronin von Richthofen, from Villa Mirenda, Scandicci, Florence, dated only "Thursday," Frieda Lawrence, p. 249.

246 Probably a reference to *The Woman Who Rode Away*, the publication of which was postponed, both in London and New York, until May, 1928.

247 "The Escaped Cock," later to be expanded for separate publication under the title *The Man Who Died*, was published in *The Forum*, LXXIX (No. 2, February, 1928), 286–96.—McDonald, *Supplement*, p. 97.

248 For Lawrence's sketch "The Nightingale," see Note 186, above.

249 D. H. L. letter to Earl H. and Achsah Barlow Brewster, from Villa Mirenda, Scandicci, Firenze, dated 21 October 1927, Brewster, p. 151.

250 D. H. L. letter to Frieda's mother, Frau Baronin von Richthofen, from Villa Mirenda, Scandicci, Florence, dated only "Sunday," Frieda Lawrence, p. 252. Lawrence's oil painting *The Tiger* (so-called) is now in the possession of the editor.

251 D. H. L. letter to Earl H. Brewster, from Villa Mirenda, Scandicci, Firenze, dated 8 November [1927], Brewster, pp. 152–53.

252 D. H. L. letter to Frieda's sister Dr. Else Jaffe-Richthofen, from Villa Mirenda, Scandicci, Firenze, dated 14 November 1927, Frieda Lawrence, pp. 236–37.

253 Reginald ("Reggie") Turner (1869–1938), English novelist, author of *Castles in Kensington* (1904), *Davray's Affairs* (1906), *Uncle Peaceable*

(1906), *Samson Unshorn* (1909), *Count Florio and Phyllis K.* (1910), *King Philip the Gay* (1911), etc. Harold Acton has called Reggie Turner "a conversationalist in the delicately manicured tradition of the eighteen nineties."—Nancy Cunard, *Grand Man* (London: Secker & Warburg, 1954), pp. 237–38. He probably served as the original of Algy Constable in Lawrence's *Aaron's Rod.*—Moore, *Intelligent Heart*, p. 258. Long a resident of Florence, he died in 1938, having willed £20,000 to Giusèppe ("Pino") Orioli. For glimpses of Reggie Turner, see Richard Aldington, *Pinorman* (London: Heinemann, 1954).

254 Charles Kenneth Michael Scott-Moncrieff (1889–1930), Scottish translator of Stendhal's works, the authorized translator of Proust (*Remembrance of Things Past*) and Pirandello.

255 D. H. L. letter to Aldous Huxley, from Mirenda, dated only "Monday," *Letters*, p. 701.

256 Extracts from two letters (5 April 1954 and 24 May 1957) to the editor. Harold (Mario Mitchell) Acton (1904——), English writer long resident in Italy. Author of *Humdrum* (1929), *This Chaos* (1930), *Last Medici* (1932), *Peonies and Ponies* (novel, 1941), *Memoirs of an Aesthete* (1948), *Prince Isidore* (1951), *Bourbons of Naples* (1956), etc.

257 D. H. L. letter to Curtis Brown, from Villa Mirenda, Scandicci, Florence, dated 18 November 1927, Brown, pp. 82–83.

258 May Sinclair (1870?–1946), English novelist; author of *The Divine Fire* (1904), *The Tree of Heaven* (1917), *Mary Olivier: A Life* (1919), *Mr. Waddington of Wyck* (1921), *A Cure of Souls* (1923), *The Rector of Wyck* (1925), *The Intercessor and Other Stories* (1931), etc. For Miss Sinclair's protest against the suppression of *The Rainbow*, see McDonald, pp. 38–39, reprinted in Vol. I, p. 579 n195, of the present work.

259 Brown, pp. 81–82, 86. Curtis Brown (1866–1945), American literary agent, long resident in England. He was born in Lisle, New York, the son of Lewis H. and Ellen Curtis Brown, and educated in the public schools of Buffalo. He worked for the Buffalo *Express* (1884–1894); as Sunday editor for the New York *Press* (1894–1898); as London representative of the *Press* (1898–1910). He was the proprietor of the Curtis Brown Newspaper Syndicate of London (1898–1915); founder and managing director of the International Publishing Bureau (1900–1945); managing director of Curtis Brown, Ltd., of New York, London, and Paris (1916–1945). (In 1941, he sold the controlling interest in the New York branch of Curtis Brown, Ltd., to Alan C. Collins, now its president, but remained vice-president and director of the New York organization.) Although most of his career as an agent was spent in England, he retained his American citizenship. He acted as distributor for the writings of Woodrow Wilson, Sir Winston Churchill, David Lloyd George, General Mark W. Clark, Sumner Welles, George Bernard Shaw, H. G. Wells, Eve Curie, A. A. Milne, John Galsworthy, etc. In 1890, he married Caroline Louise Lord. Their son, Spencer Brown, is now the general manager of Curtis Brown, Ltd., London; their daughter is Mrs. A. D. V. Horton. He died at his home, Peck Farm, Whitney Point, New York. He wrote the

autobiography *Contacts* (1935). See *The Times* [London], 25 September 1945, p. 6f; *The Publishers' Weekly*, 148 (No. 13, 29 September 1945), 1566.

260 Lawrence had known Michael Arlen as Dikran Kouyoumdjian in England during the War Years. See Vol. I of the present work.

261 D. H. L. letter to Mabel Dodge Luhan, from Scandicci, Firenze, Villa Mirenda, dated 18 November 1927, Luhan, pp. 334–35.

262 D. H. L. letter to Frieda's sister Dr. Else Jaffe-Richthofen, from Villa Mirenda, Scandicci, Firenze, dated 12 December 1927, Frieda Lawrence, p. 240.

263 For the first version of *Lady Chatterley's Lover*, see *The First Lady Chatterley* (New York: Dial, 1944), and Tedlock, pp. 20–21; for a note on the MS of the second version (as yet unpublished), see Tedlock, pp. 23–24. See also "The Three Versions of *Lady Chatterley's Lover*," Tedlock, pp. 279–316.

264 D. H. L. letter to Max Mohr, from Villa Mirenda, Scandicci, Florence, dated "Sunday/17 December" [Sunday, 18 December 1927, or Saturday, 17 December 1927], *T'ien Hsia Monthly* [Shanghai], I (No. 1, August, 1935), 26.

265 D. H. L. letter to Max Mohr, from Villa Mirenda, Scandicci, Florence, dated 23 December 1927, *T'ien Hsia Monthly* [Shanghai], I (No. 1, August, 1935), 27–28.

266 For Dino Bandelli, see the memoir of Signor Raul Mirenda, above.

267 D. H. L. letter (translated from the German) to Frieda's mother, Frau Baronin von Richthofen, from Villa Mirenda, Scandicci, Florence, dated only "Sunday" [25 December 1927], Frieda Lawrence, p. 242.

268 See Note 2, above.

269 On 10 January 1926, Lawrence had written to The Hon. Dorothy Brett, from the Villa Bernarda, Spotorno: "I read Aldous Huxley's *Along the Road*. . . . It's little essays about Italy—very nice in its way."—*Letters*, p. 655.

270 Vernon Lee, pseudonym of Violet Paget (1856–1935), English essayist and art critic, from 1871 resident in Italy. Her books include *Studies of the Eighteenth Century in Italy* (1880), *Limbo* (essays, 1897), *Ariadne in Mantua* (play, 1903), *Satan the Waster* (1920), *Music and Its Lovers* (1932).

271 Huxley, "Introduction," *Letters*, pp. xxix–xxxii. Under the title "D. H. Lawrence," the Introduction to *Letters* is also included in Mr. Huxley's collection *The Olive Tree* (1936).

272 D. H. L. letter (translated from the German) to Frieda's mother, Frau Baronin von Richthofen, from Villa Mirenda, Scandicci, dated only "Wednesday" [28 December 1927], Frieda Lawrence, p. 244.

273 D. H. L. letter to The Hon. Dorothy Brett, from Villa Mirenda, Scandicci, Florence, dated 6 January 1928, *Letters*, pp. 704–5.

274 D. H. L. letter to Earl H. and Achsah Barlow Brewster, from Villa Mirenda, Scandicci, Firenze, dated 11 January 1928, Brewster, p. 159.

275 D. H. L. letter to Rolf Gardiner, from Villa Mirenda, Scandicci, Firenze,

dated "Monday, 17. I. 28" [Monday, 16 January 1928, or Tuesday, 17 January 1928], *Letters*, p. 708.

276 D. H. L. letter (postcard?) to Ada Lawrence Clarke, from Chalet Beau Site, Les Diablerets (Vaud), dated only "1928," Ada Lawrence and Gelder, p. 138.

277 Alfred Richard Orage (1873–1934), English journalist, psychologist, exponent of social credit, and editor of the Fabian *The New Age* (1907–1922), to which Shaw, Wells, Chesterton, Bennett, Belloc, and Havelock Ellis contributed, and in which younger writers such as Katherine Mansfield, J. C. Squire, Ezra Pound, Richard Aldington, and Michael Arlen were encouraged. He later became a disciple first of the occultist P. D. Ouspensky, and then of the mystic George Gurdjieff at Fontainebleau. "[He] constantly pursued an ideal, the lineaments of which he saw, at different times, in guild socialism, the philosophy of Nietzsche . . . , the mysticism of Gurdjieff, and the economic doctrine of social credit."— *D.N.B.*, 1931–1940. Author of *Nietzsche in Outline and Aphorism* (1907), *Frederick Nietzsche: The Dionysian Spirit of the Age* (1911), *Readers and Writers* (1922), *The Art of Reading* (1930), *Selected Essays and Critical Writings* (1935), *Social Credit and the Fear of Leisure* (1935), *Political and Economic Writings* (1935).

278 Original publication in full. See also Bynner, pp. 331–32. For Lawrence's now famous reply (13 March 1928) to Witter Bynner, see *Letters*, pp. 719–20.

279 D. H. L. letter to Earl H. Brewster, from Chalet Beau Site, Les Diablerets (Vaud) Suisse, dated 3 February 1928, Brewster, pp. 160–61.

280 Sir Julian (Sorell) Huxley (1887————), English biologist and author; older brother of Aldous Huxley. Married (1919) Marie Juliette Baillot of Neuchâtel, Switzerland. Professor (1925–1927) and honorary lecturer (1927–1935), King's College, London; onetime director general of UNESCO. Author of *The Individual in the Animal Kingdom* (1911), *Essays of a Biologist* (1923), *The Stream of Life* (1926), *The Science of Life* (with H. G. and G. P. Wells, 1929), *Ants* (1929), *What Dare I Think?* (1930), *If I Were Dictator* (1934), *At the Zoo* (1936), *Evolution Restated* (1940), *Evolution: The Modern Synthesis* (1942), *Heredity East and West* (1949), etc.

281 The first half of the MS of *Lady Chatterley's Lover* had been typed by Catherine Carswell in London. Lawrence had a complete typed copy of the novel in his hands on 2 March 1928. See Moore, *Intelligent Heart*, p. 376.

282 D. H. L. letter to Giusèppe ("Pino") Orioli, from Châlet Beau Site, Diablerets, Switz., dated 6 February 1928, Moore, *Intelligent Heart*, p. 375.

283 See *Letters*, p. 710.

284 For a brief memoir by Prof. Alfred Weber, see Vol. I, p. 166, of the present work.

285 See Note 54, above.

286 See *Letters*, pp. 680–81.

287 See *Letters,* p. 711.

288 Original publication of a memoir completed in 1956. The dates of Mr. Gardiner's visit to Les Diablerets were apparently 10, 11, and 12 February 1928. See *Letters,* p. 710.

289 D. H. L. letter to Earl H. and Achsah Barlow Brewster, from Chalet Beau Site, Les Diablerets (Vaud), dated 27 February 1928, Brewster, pp. 161–62.

290 D. H. L. letter to Giusèppe ("Pino") Orioli [from Châlet Beau Site, Les Diablerets], dated 3 March 1928, Moore, *Intelligent Heart,* p. 376.

291 In 1928, a member of Curtis Brown, Ltd., London; later a director of Pearn, Pollinger & Higham, Ltd., London, authors' agents. Now director of Lawrence Pollinger, Ltd., London, authors' agent.

292 D. H. L. letter to Martin Secker, from Diablerets, dated 5 March 1928, *Letters,* pp. 713–14.

293 D. H. L. letter to Juliette Huxley, from Villa Mirenda, Scandicci, Florence, dated 8 March 1928, *Letters,* p. 714. The reference is to Lawrence's water color *Fire-Dance.*

294 D. H. L. letter to Aldous and Maria Huxley, from Villa Mirenda, Scandicci, Firenze, dated 9 March [1928], *Letters,* p. 715.

295 See Note 254, above.

296 See *Letters,* p. 119.

297 See *Letters,* p. 216.

298 Cf. *Letters,* p. 384. But the reference is to *Women in Love,* not "The Miracle" ("The Horse-Dealer's Daughter").

299 Cf. *Letters,* p. 274. The actual quotation: "[*The Rainbow* is] one of the important novels in the language."

300 Cf. Aldington, *Pinorman,* p. 195.

301 Cf. Aldington, *Pinorman,* pp. 195–97.

302 Cf. Aldington, *Pinorman,* pp. 197–98.

303 Cf. Aldington, *Pinorman,* p. 194.

304 Several of these hitherto unpublished Lawrence letters to Orioli have been printed in Prof. Moore's *The Intelligent Heart.*

305 In her memoir "D. H. Lawrence, 1885–1930," Lady Ottoline Morrell had written: "[Lawrence's] favourite device of the Phoenix suits him well. He has plucked from himself his own life, and has given it courageously, generously to all who know how to read him aright, with unprejudiced eyes."—*The Nation and Athenaeum,* XLVI (No. 25, 22 March 1930), 860. To this, Norman Douglas took exception: "Your contributor O. M. . . . confuses the Phoenix with the Pelican. I am not trying to be professorial, and I only point out this little slip in case he should be tempted, as I hope he will, to reprint elsewhere his impression of D. H. L."—*The Nation and Athenaeum,* XLVII (No. 1, 5 April 1930), 11–12.

306 Cf. Cecil Gray: "I remember one evening during the last war when Norman Douglas and I were comparing notes and exchanging reminiscences concerning [Lawrence] and Norman said: 'Do you realize that no one who knew Lawrence well, as we know him, was sorry when he died?'" —Cecil Gray, *Musical Chairs* (London: Home & Van Thal, 1948), p. 139.

307 Orioli, pp. 232–34. Giusèppe ("Pino") Orioli (1884–1942), Italian antiquarian bookseller and publisher, was born at Alfonsine, Italy. Between
the ages 14–20, he worked in a barber's shop in Florence. From 1904 to
1907, he fulfilled his military service as Sanitary Corporal of an infantry
regiment at Como. Thereafter, he went to London, where he gave lessons
in Italian to private pupils. He became a partner with J. I. Davis in "The
Polyglot Library" on Charing Cross Rd., London. Then, in 1910, Davis
and Orioli opened a bookshop in the Via dei Vecchietti in Florence, both
returning to London in 1913 where they opened a bookshop at 24 Museum
St. (Orioli met Lawrence in Cornwall in 1916–1917). He saw military
duty in World War I, first in Bologna, then with the Italian Military
Mission in London. In April, 1920, Orioli went to Florence, opening a
bookshop in the Lungarno Acciaiuoli, later at 6 Lungarno Corsini, then at
14 Lungarno delle Grazie. He met Norman Douglas in June, 1922. In
1929, he began publication of the "Lungarno Series." He died in Lisbon
in 1942. Author of *Moving Along: Just a Diary* (1934) and *Adventures of
a Bookseller* (1937). Richard Aldington has warned that Norman Douglas
may well have written or rewritten Sig. Orioli's memoirs on Lawrence. See
Aldington, *Pinorman*, pp. 194, 212, etc.

308 D. H. L. letter to Curtis Brown, from Villa Mirenda, Scandicci, Florence,
dated 15 March 1928, *Letters*, p. 717.

309 D. H. L. letter to Maria Huxley, from Villa Mirenda, Scandicci, Firenze,
dated only "Friday," *Letters*, p. 723.

310 Not to be confused with the Holland-born W.A. writer, William Siebenhaar.

311 See Note 192, above.

312 In a letter (6 June 1957) to the editor, Sir Osbert Sitwell has confirmed
this telegram.

    See Frieda Lawrence Ravagli: "One Sunday afternoon [May, 1927]
Osbert and Edith Sitwell came [to the Villa Mirenda]. They moved us
strangely. They seemed so oversensitive, as if something had hurt them
too much, as if they had to keep up a brave front to the world, to pretend
they didn't care and yet they only cared much too much. When they left,
we went for a long walk, disturbed by them. But how afterwards they
could think that *Lady Chatterley* had anything to do with them, is beyond
me. *Lady Chatterley* was written and finished before Lawrence ever set
eyes on any Sitwell."—Frieda Lawrence, pp. 195–96.

    In his letter (6 June 1957) to the editor, Sir Osbert has written: "No
one ever said that Lawrence's book was written after meeting us, but he
claimed, I understood, to have known the place [Renishaw] and to have
used it as a background. He certainly had never entered the house, as his
descriptions of it prove. He may, of course, have trespassed in the park.
Nevertheless, since Renishaw is some twenty miles from where he lived,
I think it unlikely."

313 A film version of *Lady Chatterley's Lover*, with Danielle Darrieux as Lady
Chatterley, Leo Genn as Chatterley, and Erno Crisa as Mellors, directed by
the French director Marc Allegret and produced by an Englishman, Daniel
Angel, was released in 1956.

314 Original publication of an installment of a long memoir completed in 1954.
315 D. H. L. letter to Maria Huxley, from Villa Mirenda, Scandicci, Firenze, dated only "Friday," *Letters,* p. 723.
316 See "Making Pictures," in *Assorted Articles,* pp. 196–97.
317 *Creative Art,* July, 1929, and *The Studio,* July, 1929.—McDonald, *Supplement,* p. 100.
318 Lawrence's introduction to *The Paintings of D. H. Lawrence* (London: Mandrake, June, 1929) is reprinted in *Phoenix,* pp. 551–84.
319 See "Making Pictures," in *Assorted Articles,* p. 206.
320 See "Making Pictures," in *Assorted Articles,* p. 200.
321 See Frieda Lawrence, pp. 191, 193.
322 See Brewster, pp. 123–24 (Volterra visit), 112–13 (on Lawrence's pictures). See also Brewster, p. 281 (Achsah on pictures).
323 See Aldington, *Portrait of a Genius,* pp. 379–80.
324 See Carswell, p. 272.
325 "For a brilliant exposition of Philistine strategy and objectives, see Roger Fry's essay 'London Sculptors and Sculptures' in his *Transformations* (London: Chatto & Windus, 1926)."—Philip Trotter.
326 See Charles Marriott's critical notice of the Warren Gallery's opening exhibition in *The Times* [London], 26 May 1927.
327 "A tattered, bescribbled catalogue of this memorable event, described by *The Times* [London, 15 June 1925, p. 16c] as 'a most entertaining exhibition' is in my hands. Its title was 'Etchings by/Her Majesty the late Queen Victoria/and the Prince Consort/also/Victorian Pictures and Objets d'art/June 12th until July 3rd, 1925.' The royal exhibits were largely a complete collaboration, either drawn by the Queen and etched by the Prince or vice versa; but *The Times* finds the Queen's individual work 'far superior' to the Prince Consort's or to those 'by him and the Queen in collaboration,' and praises her 'selection from the facts according to the nature of the medium, and clear and decisive statement . . . distinctly "modernist" in flavour.' Mr. (now Sir) Osbert Sitwell's preface—one of his miniature masterpieces in its delicious blend of satire with wistful appreciation—gives the prize to *Islay,* a poignant drawing of a shaggy dog with uplifted paw, as 'perhaps the most eloquent of her works,' with its 'intensity of feeling,' and proclaims her 'an artistic pioneer.' A fine muster of XIX Century masters, Wilkie, Cruikshank, Leech, etc. surround and support their sovereign on the walls."—Philip Trotter.
328 See "A New Gallery," in the *Westminster Gazette,* 25 April 1927.
329 "See 'The Air of Bloomsbury,' a review of J. K. Johnstone's *The Bloomsbury Group,* in *The Times Literary Supplement* (20 August 1954), 1."—Philip Trotter. See also Clive Bell's essay "Bloomsbury" in *Old Friends* (New York: Harcourt, 1957).
330 See *The Nation and Athenaeum,* XLII (No. 3, 22 October 1927), 116.
331 Evan Walters (1893———), Welsh water-color painter, was born at Llangyfelach, near Swansea. He studied art at the Swansea School of Art and the Royal Academy, London; exhibited at the Royal Academy (1921–1926).
332 Augustus John, "Art: The Paintings of Evan Walters," *Vogue* [London],

LXXI (No. 1, 11 January 1928), 40–41, 62. "Perhaps Augustus John's greatest service to the Warren Gallery in its early days (for he will figure again in this history) was the racy and entertaining foreword he contributed to Dorothy Warren's Christmas exhibition of 'seasonable gifts.' Here, for a maximum price of 25/–, her own exhibitors and famous artists and craftsmen threw in every form of decorative work. The exhibition filled both floors of her premises, was superbly arranged and had a brilliant press."—Philip Trotter. See Chap. III, Note 256, below.

333 Henry Moore (1898———), English sculptor, whose works are notable "for balancing of mass with vacant spaces that emphasize three-dimensionality." In 1940 he was commissioned by the British government to make a series of drawings in underground bomb shelters.

334 See *The Times* [London], 26 January 1928.

335 From a personal letter to Mr. Philip Trotter, written by Mr. Hubert Wellington, in the late 1920's Principal of the Royal College of Art, Edinburgh. In a recent letter (10 September 1957) to Mr. Trotter, Mr. Wellington added: "One result of Dorothy's crusade for Henry Moore in Germany was the purchase of three works by the Hamburg Gallery, before any official recognition had been given to him in this country."

336 On 27 January 1916, Lawrence suggested to Dollie Radford that she invite Dorothy Warren ("She is beautiful.") and Dikran Kouyoumdjian (later Michael Arlen) to tea. See Vol. I, p. 357, of the present work.

337 Original publication of an installment of a solicited memoir completed in 1957. Of the late Dorothy Warren Trotter (1896–1954), Mr. Philip Trotter has written (23 August 1957): "Dorothy Cecil Wynter Warren, only daughter and eldest child of the late Edward Prioleau Warren, F.S.A., and niece of Sir Herbert Warren, president of Magdalen College, Oxford. The family is Norman. She was a goddaughter of Henry James. Educated Queens College, London. Apart from gallery-owning her principal activities were interior decoration and designing, a notable success being Studio 3D, Broadcasting House, London, designed in the character of a Regency library. These activities were interrupted when, in 1935, a speculative building outrage perpetrated on our semi-detached house in Maida Vale (the other half of the building was demolished) inspired the idea of creating the Londoners' League, the first of the preservation societies to champion the cause of small domestic architecture and working class development of good period and planning. After the destruction of our house in the second World War, we moved to Scotland, where she devoted herself mainly to the interests of East European refugees of the Orthodox Church. She died in February, 1954."

Of himself, Mr. Trotter has written (23 August and 11 September 1957): "Philip Coutts Trotter, son of Col. Sir Philip Trotter; a Scottish Border family. Educated Charterhouse. Served World War I Welsh Guards, thereafter held ADC & staff appointments in various parts of Europe. Married Dorothy Warren 1928.

"My last duty in the British Military Mission (on which it closed down) was to bring the Austrian Gendarmerie into the West strip of Hungary, to which was given the bogus name *Burgenland* for the purpose. In the course of my service there I strayed into one of the loveliest castles in Europe, owned by an enchanting Hungarian. In his mountain is a green translucent stone. We gave it the bogus name of 'Styrian Jade,' started quarrying, installed a turnery, & began business in 1923. In 1926 I opened a wholesale depot in Hatton Garden, London, which I retained for nearly a year after marrying, as my retail dealers did not like my stock being in a gallery frequented regularly by the whole art world. I closed Hatton Garden after the Lawrence Exhibition [1929]; and the two businesses ran side by side but separate. From immediately after my marriage I functioned as Dorothy's partner in the Gallery, doing most of the routine administration, she retaining the art direction."

338 Original publication.

339 D. H. L. letter to Aldous Huxley, from Villa Mirenda, dated 27 March 1928, *Letters*, p. 725.

340 Harry (Grew) Crosby (1898–1929) was born in Boston, the son of Stephen Van Rensselaer Crosby, a banker, and the former Henrietta M. Grew, a sister of Mrs. J. Pierpont Morgan. In 1919, after service with an American ambulance unit in France, he entered Harvard, being graduated in 1922. He married Mary Jacob Peabody ("Caresse") in 1922. Having worked briefly in banks in New York City and Paris, in 1927, together with his wife Caresse, he founded the Black Sun Press at 2 rue Cardinale, in Paris. From 1928 to 1929, he was an advisory editor of *transition*. On 10 December 1929, he committed suicide in New York City. (See Chap. III, Note 387, below.) He was the author of *Shadow of the Sun* (1922), *Sonnets for Caresse* (1926), *Chariot of the Sun* (1927), *Transit of Venus* (1928), *Torch Bearer* (1929), *Aphrodite in Flight* (1929), etc. (For Lawrence's preface to Harry Crosby's *Chariot of the Sun*, see *Phoenix*, pp. 255–62.) See "In Memoriam: Harry Crosby," *transition* (No. 19–20, Spring-Summer, June, 1930), 221–32, for tributes by Kay Boyle, Hart Crane, Stuart Gilbert, Eugene Jolas, Archibald MacLeish, Philippe Soupault. See also Malcolm Cowley, *Exile's Return: A Literary Odyssey of the 1920's* (New York: Viking, 1951), pp. 246–88. See also Caresse Crosby, *The Passionate Years* (New York: Dial Press, 1953).

341 See Chap. I, Note 39, above.

342 D. H. L. letter to Miss Nancy Pearn, from Villa Mirenda, Scandicci, Florence, dated 1 April 1928, *Letters*, pp. 725–26.

343 The Black Sun Press (1927–1939) was located at 2 rue Cardinale, Paris. Among the editions de luxe published by Harry and Caresse Crosby were Poe's *Fall of the House of Usher*, *47 Lettres inédites de Marcel Proust à Walter Berry*, Hart Crane's *The Bridge*, as well as Lawrence's *Sun* and *The Escaped Cock*.

344 See Lawrence's answer (26 February 1928), *Letters*, pp. 710–11.

345 Roger Lescaret, master-printer for the Black Sun Press. See Caresse Crosby, pp. 146 ff.

346 Lawrence apparently sent Harry Crosby the MS of *Sun* on 30 April 1928. See *Letters*, pp. 726, 738.

347 For the authorized unexpurgated edition of *Sun*, published by the Black
Sun Press in October, 1928, see McDonald, *Supplement*, pp. 43–44.

348 For a short time after his graduation from Harvard in 1922, Harry Crosby
had worked at the State Street Trust, New York; he was later transferred
to the Morgan Bank in Paris. J. P. Morgan was his uncle by marriage.

349 "Steve" Crosby, Harry Crosby's father.

350 In a letter (25 June 1956) to the editor, Mr. Edward Weeks has written:
"[The] truth is that I never met D. H. Lawrence and to the best of my
remembrance never had any correspondence with him either.

"Harry Crosby, on the other hand, was an intimate friend of mine, and I
have always regretted that my apprenticeship in Boston on the *Atlantic*
tied me down and prevented me from visiting him and Caresse as I had
hoped to do."

351 On 1 April 1928, Lawrence wrote to Harry Crosby: "That was very nice
of you to send me that little pseudo-book full of red gold. How beautiful
the gold is!—such a pity it ever became currency. One should love it for
its yellow life, answering the sun. I shan't spend it if I can help it."—
Letters, p. 726. Again, on "Friday, 26 May, 1928" [Friday, 25 May 1928,
or Saturday, 26 May 1928], almost a month after he had sent him the
bound MS of *Sun* (see *Letters*, p. 738), Lawrence again wrote to Harry
Crosby: "My wife went to Florence yesterday and brought the Queen of
Naples' snuff-box and three pieces of gold, from Orioli, to my utter amazement."—*Letters*, pp. 742–43. Apparently the Crosbys sent Lawrence at
least two shipments of gold pieces in the spring of 1928. In November–
December, 1928, Lawrence was at Île de Port-Cros and Bandol, not
Florence. I am unable to reconcile the dates supplied by Lawrence's letters
with those remembered by Caresse Crosby in the memoirs that follow.

352 See Note 353, below.

353 Narcisse Noir, a whippet, and Zulu: dogs belonging to the Crosbys and
Powells, respectively. Peter and Gretchen Powell: American friends of the
Crosbys. See Caresse Crosby, pp. 118, 136–37. Frans and Mai de Geeteres:
Dutch artist and his wife, who lived on a houseboat, *Le Vert Gallant*, on
the Seine; friends of the Crosbys. See Caresse Crosby, pp. 151–55. Compte
Armand de la Rochefoucauld, from whom the Crosbys purchased Le
Moulin du Soleil at Ermenonville, Oise, France. See Caresse Crosby, pp.
164–67.

354 The books of Harry Crosby's cousin Walter Van Rensselaer Berry, who
died in October, 1928, leaving to him "my entire library except such items
as my good friend, Edith Wharton, may care to choose . . . ." See Caresse
Crosby, pp. 106, 212.

355 See Note 351, above.

356 Caresse Crosby, pp. 190–91, 218–22. Caresse Crosby (1892——), nee
Mary Jacob, American editor and publisher, born in New York City. She
married (1915) Richard R. Peabody, by whom two children (div. 1922);
(1922) Harry Crosby; (1937?) Selbert Saffold Young (div.). Known as
"Polly" to her oldest friends, she was named "Caresse" by Harry Crosby.
With Harry Crosby, she founded the Black Sun Press at 2 rue Cardinale,

in Paris (1927–1939); edited the Crosby Continental Editions (the imprint still occasionally appears). She was a leading spirit in the Women Against War group, and head of the World Citizenship Movement. Since 1945, she has edited *Portfolio: An International Review* (Washington and Paris: The Black Sun Press), of which Henry Miller, Selden Rodman, and Harry T. Moore were associate editors. She is the author of three volumes of poetry: *Graven Images* (1926), *Painted Shores* (1927), *Poems for Harry Crosby* (1931); with Harry Crosby, joint editor of *47 Lettres inédites de Marcel Proust à Walter Berry* (1930); illustrator of Harry Crosby's *Mad Queen* (verse, B.S.P., n.d.) and his *Sun* (verse, B.S.P., n.d.); designer and editor of George Grosz' *Interregnum* (B.S.P., 1936); author of the autobiography *The Passionate Years* (1953), etc.

357 D. H. L. letter to Aldous Huxley, from Villa Mirenda, dated 2 April [1928], *Letters*, pp. 729–30.

358 Prince Leopold of Loewenstein-Wertheim (1903———), in full Felician Leopold Friedrich Ludwig Hubertus Prinz zu Loewenstein-Wertheim-Freudenberg; also Graf von Loewenstein-Scharffeneck. He was born at Salzburg, Austria, the second son of the late Prince Maximilian of Loewenstein-Wertheim-Freudenberg (Count of Loewenstein-Scharffeneck). His mother is the daughter of the late Henry, Lord Pirbright, P.C., at one time Under Secretary of State for the Colonies. Educated at Munich and at the University of Vienna, he came to England in 1926, and after the advent of the Nazi regime, became a voluntary exile and a British subject. He has been connected with publishing and literary work all his life. With William Gerhardi, he is the co-author of *Meet Yourself As You Really Were* (1936), adapted by Victor Rosen as *Analyze Yourself: How to See Yourself as You Really Are* (1955); translator of Adalbert von Chamisso, *Peter Schlemihl* (1957) and Eduard Mörike, *Mozart's Journey to Prague* (1957), etc.

359 Lawrence had known the English painter Mark Gertler (1892–1939) during the War Years, their friendship dating from the Lawrences' Chesham period (late 1914). Gertler was a friend of the Gilbert Cannans and The Hon. Dorothy Brett. See Vol. I of the present work.

360 Original publication.

361 D. H. L. letter to Earl H. and Achsah Barlow Brewster, from Villa Mirenda, Scandicci, Florence, dated 13 April 1928, Brewster, pp. 167–68.

362 A reference to the original form of "The Escaped Cock," which had been published in *The Forum*, LXXIX (No. 2, February, 1928), 286–96.— McDonald, *Supplement*, p. 97.

363 See D. H. L. letter to Maria Huxley, from Villa Mirenda, Scandicci, Firenze, dated "Tuesday, 16 April, 1928" [Tuesday, 17 April 1928, or Monday, 16 April 1928]: "And a woman who's been my friend for years told me on Saturday that my pictures were disgusting and unnecessary, and even old-fashioned. Really, I shall have to buy a weapon of some sort. Wish I had the skunk's."—*Letters*, p. 732.

364 Margaret Gardiner, in *Horizon*, II (No. 10, October, 1940), 184–90. Margaret (Emilia) Gardiner (1904———), sister of Rolf Gardiner, is now Mrs. Margaret Gardiner-Bernal of Hampstead, London, N.W. 3.

365 D. H. L. letter to Earl H. Brewster, from Villa Mirenda, Scandicci (Florence), dated 25 April 1928, Brewster, pp. 169–70.

366 D. H. L. letter to Frieda's sister Dr. Else Jaffe-Richthofen, from Villa Mirenda, Scandicci, Florence, dated 4 May 1928, Frieda Lawrence, p. 258.

367 Davis, in *The New York Times Book Review,* 23 December 1928, p. 5. Robert Hobart ("Bob") Davis (1869–1942), American writer, editor, traveller, photographer, was born at Brownsville, Neb. He was a member of the executive board of the *New York Sun,* and world correspondent and columnist ("Bob Davis Reveals") for the same paper; the author of many plays, travel books, etc. As an amateur photographer, he made more than 3,000 portraits of prominent people and published *Man Makes His Own Mask* (1932), a collection of portraits, with biographical notes, of 130 notable subjects.

368 D. H. L. letter to Lady Ottoline Morrell, from Villa Mirenda, Scandicci, Florence, dated 24 May 1928, *Letters,* pp. 741–42.

369 Mistakenly given as 1929 in the original printing of the article in *The Saturday Review of Literature,* 29 March 1952, and corrected to 6 June 1928 in the issue of 10 May 1952. See Note 371, below.

370 And, in New York, by Knopf, January, 1925.

371 Cerf, in *The Saturday Review of Literature,* XXXV (No. 13, 29 March 1952), 6, 8. For Frieda Lawrence Ravagli's spirited response to this reminiscence, and for Mr. Cerf's rebuttal, see *The Saturday Review of Literature,* XXXV (No. 19, 10 May 1952), 25. See also Brewster, p. 282, reprinted in text, below.

    Bennett (Alfred) Cerf (1898——), American book publisher, founded the Modern Library, Inc. (1925) and Random House, Inc. (1927). He has been a contributing editor of *This Week* and the *Saturday Review,* and of late has become widely known as a television personality.

    On 27 March 1928, Lawrence wrote to Aldous Huxley: "Was in Florence yesterday—saw Douglas—looking very old—off in a week's time to Aleppo —or so he says—by Orient Express—do you remember its time-table in Diablerets? From Aleppo he wants to go to Baalbeck—and then presumably, to rise into heaven. He's terribly at an end of everything."— *Letters,* p. 724.

    This meeting of Lawrence and Douglas on 26 March 1928 may have been the occasion of the reconciliation after the Magnus quarrel recorded by Richard Aldington: "It would never have done for those two rare spirits to remain estranged, and fortunately dear Pino [Orioli] was there to reconcile them. He talked them both over to a recognition of their sins, and staged a meeting at his book shop on the Lungarno. It was done admirably. Lawrence and Frieda were there talking to Pino, and in came Norman as arranged. There was a moment of embarrassed silence, and then Norman made a gesture which with him means he accepts you as a friend—he offered Lawrence his snuff box:

    " 'Have a pinch of snuff, dearie.'

    "Lawrence took it.

" 'Isn't it curious'—sniff—'only Norman and my father'—sniff—'ever gave me snuff?'

"That was all, and they were as good friends as ever."—Aldington, *Life for Life's Sake,* p. 376.

See also Frieda Lawrence Ravagli: "I was thrilled at the fireworks of wit that went off between Lawrence and Douglas. They never quarreled. I understood that Douglas had to stand up for his friend Magnus and to Lawrence's logical puritanical mind Magnus presented a problem of human relations."—Frieda Lawrence, pp. 98–99.

372 D. H. L. letter to Giusèppe ("Pino") Orioli [from Villa Mirenda, Scandicci, Florence], dated 7 June [1928], Moore, *Intelligent Heart,* p. 380.

373 D. H. L. letter (postcard?) to Ada Lawrence Clarke, from Florence, dated only "1928," Ada Lawrence and Gelder, p. 142.

374 One of the two men with Norman Douglas may have been Bennett Cerf, in which event the date of the Brewsters' visit would have been 5–6 June 1928. See Mr. Cerf's memoir, above.

375 Brewster, pp. 281–85.

376 D. H. L. letter to Giusèppe ("Pino") Orioli, from Chexbres-sur-Vevey, Switz., dated " 'Thursday' [June 21, 1928]," Moore, *Intelligent Heart,* pp. 380–81.

377 Brewster, pp. 285–86.

378 "Insouciance" was not published until its inclusion in *Assorted Articles.* See Tedlock, pp. 220–21.

379 On this point, Mr. Brewster is mistaken. Although Lawrence himself received an advance copy of the Orioli edition of *Lady Chatterley's Lover* at Chexbres-sur-Vevey on 28 June 1928, the novel was not officially released until July, 1928. See D. H. L. letter (28 June 1928) in Moore, *Intelligent Heart,* p. 381, reprinted in part in text below. See also McDonald, *Supplement,* pp. 39–40.

380 Brewster, pp. 170–72.

381 These pictures had been taken to London by the Lawrences' friend Mrs. Enid C. Hilton, following her visit to Florence. See Moore, *Intelligent Heart,* p. 381.

382 Original publication.

383 "Dorothy Warren's exhibitions of contemporary British art in Berlin and elsewhere were a first pioneer step in a movement that is now part of the stock-in-trade of the British Council, working on a Foreign Office grant and advised by high officials of the state machinery of aesthetics. For a young woman with no capital, presenting her own selection of artists— some (like Sickert) already famous, but mostly known in London only through her efforts, they were a *tour de force.* Lord Dabernon, as British Ambassador at Berlin, opening the first of these exhibitions, paid tribute to their contribution to international understanding."—Philip Trotter.

384 "Mrs. Ena Mathias, one of the two sisters in the famous Sargent portrait, *The Wyndham Sisters."*—Philip Trotter.

385 Lawrence's copy of Fra Angelico's *Flight into Egypt.* See "Making Pictures," in *Assorted Articles,* p. 204.

386 "The German sculptor mentioned in the letter was the late Georg Kolbe, sculptor of the Heine Memorial at Frankfurt."—Philip Trotter.

387 Presumably the address of Mrs. Enid C. Hilton. See D. H. L. letter of 20 July 1928, in text below.

388 "The Hon. Lucille Beckett, daughter of Lord Grimthorpe; by her first marriage wife of Count Czernin, Austrian Chancellor in the first war."—Philip Trotter. In 1927, the Brewsters had lived in the Palazzo Cimbrone, Lord Grimthorpe's place at Ravello.

389 Original publication.

390 D. H. L. letter to Giusèppe ("Pino") Orioli, from Chexbres-sur-Vevey, Switz., dated 28 June 1928, Moore, *Intelligent Heart*, p. 381.

391 Original publication.

392 Brewster, pp. 286–87.

393 D. H. L. letter to Earl H. and Achsah Barlow Brewster, from Hotel National, Gstaad, dated "Sunday evening" [8 July 1928], Brewster, pp. 172–73.

394 D. H. L. letter to Enid C. Hilton, from Gsteig b. Gstaad, Switz., dated 20 July 1928, Moore, *Intelligent Heart*, pp. 382–83.

395 See *Phoenix*, pp. 780–98. "Unpublished heretofore."—*Phoenix*, p. 841.

396 "Cocksure Women and Hensure Men" was first published in *The Forum,* LXXXI (No. 1, January, 1929), L, and later included in *Assorted Articles* —McDonald, *Supplement*, p. 99.

397 See Tedlock, pp. 69–70.

398 "The Blue Moccasins" was originally published in *Plain Talk,* IV (No. 2, February, 1929), 138–48, and later included in *The Lovely Lady.*—McDonald, *Supplement*, p. 99.

399 See Tedlock, pp. 69–71.

400 Mrs. T. Needham, nee Margaret E. King, now of Shipley, Derby.

401 Brewster, pp. 287–93. "Hymns in a Man's Life" was first published in *The Evening News* [London], 13 October 1928, later included in *Assorted Articles.*—McDonald, *Supplement*, p. 98.

402 Dr. Ananda Kentish Coomaraswamy (1877–1947), East Indian scholar, long resident in U.S. Author of books on Buddhism and the art and literature of India, including *The Dance of Siva* (1918). He was the editor of East Indian terms for *Webster's New International Dictionary,* 2nd ed.; Keeper of Indian and Mohammedan Art in the Museum of Fine Arts, Boston.

403 J. C. Chatterji, *Kashmir Shaivism: Being a Brief Introduction to the History, Literature, and Doctrines of the Advaita Shaiva Philosophy of Kashmir, Specifically Called the Trika System* (Vol. 2, Fasc. I, of the Kashmir Series of Texts and Studies; London: Luzac, 1914).

404 Dhan Gopal Mukerji (1890–1936), writer, born in Calcutta, India. He is best remembered for such children's books as *Kari the Elephant* (1923) and *Gay Neck* (1927); he was also the author of *Caste and Outcast* (1923), *A Son of Mother India Answers* (1928), *Path of Prayer* (1934), etc.

405 Brewster, pp. 172, 173–75.

406 Alfred Stieglitz (1864–1946), American photographer and art exhibitor, promoted photography as a fine art, and edited photography magazines (1892–1917). In 1905 he opened the famous gallery "291" at 291 Fifth Avenue, New York City, where he exhibited photographic art and introduced Cézanne, Picasso, and other modern French masters to the American public. Married (1924) Georgia O'Keeffe (1887———), American muralist and landscape painter. See *Letters,* pp. 750, 757, 760.

407 Original publication.

408 Original publication. Melle. Marguerite Scialtiel: literary agent in Paris, now of 14 rue Chanoinesse. Melle. Denise Clairouin: originally a translator, then a literary agent in Paris, deceased. Philippe Soupault: in 1928, the *directeur litteraire* of the French publishing house Kra. Philippe Soupault (1897———), French poet, novelist, and biographer, began writing under the influence of Guillaume Apollinaire and other surrealists. With Louis Aragon and André Breton, he founded the review *Littérature;* in 1920, he collaborated on Paul Elouard's dadaist publication, *Proverbe.* In 1926, he was excluded from the surrealist movement. He is the author of several collections of poems: *Aquarium* (1917), *Rose des vents* (1920), *Westwego* (1924), *Wang-Wang* (1924), *Georgia* (1926), *Poésies complète* (1939); novels, such as *Le Bon Apôtre* (1923), *En joue* (1925), *Le Nègre* (1927), *Les Dernières nuits de Paris* (1928); biographical studies, such as *Henri Rousseau, le douanier* (1927), *William Blake* (1928), *Charlot* (1931, on Charles Chaplin), *Baudelaire* (1931), *Debussy* (1932), *Souvenirs de James Joyce* (1944); plays, such as *La fille qui faisait des miracles* (1951), *Le Parasite* (1952), *Comment Dresser une Garce* (1954), *Tous ensemble au bout du monde* (1955), etc.

409 See Chap. I, Note 45, above.

410 Original publication. In 1928 the Manager of the Foreign Department of Curtis Brown, Ltd., London, Jean Watson is now Mrs. Spencer Curtis Brown.

411 Original publication. Lawrence wrote this biographical note on the backs of the letters written by Mr. Philippe Soupault and Miss Jean Watson (printed in text immediately above), to which he added a small sheet, measuring 6¾" x 8¾", numbered by him 3 and 4. For a glimpse at another, unpublished, autobiographical fragment (now in the library of the University of Cincinnati), see Stephen Spender, *The Creative Element* (New York: British Book Center, 1954), p. 97. See also "Autobiographical Sketch," in *Assorted Articles,* pp. 172–82.

412 D. H. L. letter to Aldous and Maria Huxley, from Kesselmatte, Gsteig b. Gstaad, dated 31 July 1928, *Letters,* pp. 746–47.

413 D. H. L. letter to Mabel Dodge Luhan, from Kesselmatte, Gsteig b. Gstaad, (Berne) Switzerland, dated 9 August 1928, Luhan, pp. 337–38.

414 D. H. L. letter to Maria and Aldous Huxley, from Kesselmatte, Gsteig b. Gstaad (Bern), dated 15 August 1928, *Letters,* pp. 749–50.

415 D. H. L. letter to Alfred Stieglitz, from Kesselmatte, Gsteig b. Gstaad (Bern), Switzerland, dated 15 August 1928, *Letters,* p. 751.

416 D. H. L. letter to Ada Lawrence Clarke, from Kesselmatte, (Bern) Switzerland, dated 16 August 1928, Ada Lawrence and Gelder, pp. 139–40.

417 Original publication.

418 D. H. L. letter to Laurence E. Pollinger, from Kesselmatte, Gsteig b. Gstaad (Bern), Switzerland, dated 27 August 1928, *Letters,* pp. 756–57.

419 Original publication.

420 Original publication.

421 See *Letters,* pp. 757–58.

422 Original publication.

423 D. H. L. letter to Aldous Huxley, from Kesselmatte, Gsteig b. Gstaad, dated "Sunday, after Tea" [?2 September 1928], *Letters,* pp. 752–54.

424 The "panels," one of which was *Finding of Moses,* were taken to London by Lawrence's sister Mrs. Emily King, and transferred to Mrs. Enid C. Hilton for delivery to Dorothy Warren Trotter. See *Letters,* pp. 758–59.

425 See *Letters,* p. 760.

426 Original publication.

427 D. H. L. letter to Ada Lawrence Clarke, from Switzerland, dated 10 September 1928, Ada Lawrence and Gelder, p. 141.

428 D. H. L. letter to Maria Huxley, from Hôtel Löwen, Lichtenthal, Baden-Baden, dated 22 September 1928, *Letters,* p. 761.

429 The "X." reference here is identified as "obviously Norman Douglas" by Richard Aldington in *Portrait of a Genius,* p. 391.

430 For Lawrence's "beautiful allegory," see "Mercury," in *Phoenix,* pp. 35–39. The essay was originally published in *The Atlantic Monthly,* 139 (No. 2, February, 1927), 197–200, and *The Nation and Athenaeum,* XL (No. 18, 5 February 1927), 622–23.—McDonald, *Supplement,* p. 96. Prof. E. W. Tedlock, Jr., has conjectured the date July, 1926, for its composition, or between that date and publication. See Tedlock, pp. 193–94; *Letters,* p. 675.

431 Brewster, pp. 293–98.

432 Brewster, pp. 179–80.

433 D. H. L. letter to Maria Huxley, from Hôtel Löwen, Lichtenthal b. Baden-Baden, dated 25 September 1928, *Letters,* p. 763.

434 Brewster, pp. 298–99.

CHAPTER III

1 D. H. L. postcard to Ada Lawrence Clarke, from Le Levandou [*sic*], dated only "1928," Ada Lawrence and Gelder, pp. 142–43. See Moore, *Poste Restante,* p. 97.

2 See Richard Aldington: "[I] arranged to come up by ship from Naples to Marseille, meeting another friend at Toulon, and the Lawrences at Toulon or les Salins d'Hyères. As I might have expected, they failed to keep their rendezvous . . . . I now regret very much the money I spent in sending telegrams from Port-Cros with prepaid answers to Lawrence (whose reply always was 'Waiting for Frieda') only to find his letters to other people

reporting blandly that there was 'no sign' of me!"—Aldington, *Portrait of a Genius*, pp. 393–94.

3 D. H. L. postcard to Earl H. and Achsah Barlow Brewster, from Le Lavandou, undated, Brewster, p. 182. See Moore, *Poste Restante*, p. 97.

4 D. H. L. postcard to Earl H. and Achsah Barlow Brewster, from Le Lavandou, undated, Brewster, p. 181. See Moore, *Poste Restante*, p. 97.

5 D. H. L. postcard to Earl H. and Achsah Barlow Brewster, from Le Lavandou, undated, Brewster, p. 181. See Moore, *Poste Restante*, p. 97.

6 D. H. L. letter to Earl H. and Achsah Barlow Brewster, from La Vigie, Ile de Port-Cros, Var, dated 20 October 1928, Brewster, pp. 182–83.

7 Morris L. Ernst (1888——), American lawyer and representative of British and American authors, particularly on censorship cases such as Radclyffe Hall's *The Well of Loneliness* and James Joyce's *Ulysses*. (See Mr. Ernst's Foreword to *Ulysses*.) During World War II, he became the personal representative to President Roosevelt on various missions to England, and later served on President Truman's Committee on Civil Rights. With William Seagle, he was the co-author of *To the Pure* (1928). I am unable to trace Lawrence's article on *To the Pure*, but for Lawrence's letter to Mr. Ernst, dated 10 November 1928, see *Letters*, pp. 768–69.

8 For Lawrence's reactions to Aldous Huxley's *Point Counter Point*, see his poem "I am in a Novel—" in *Pansies*, and his letter to Aldous Huxley dated only "Sunday" in *Letters*, pp. 765–66. (See also *Letters*, p. 791.) For Lawrence's poem on Attila, see "Attila" in *Pansies*. See also index to *Movements in European History* for Lawrence's earlier interpretation of Attila.

9 Aldington, *Life for Life's Sake*, pp. 329–31, 333.

10 *The Story of Doctor Manente Being the Tenth and Last Story from the Suppers of A. F. Grazzini Called Il Lasca*, translated and with an introduction by Lawrence, was published by G. Orioli at 6 Lungarno Corsini, Florence, in March, 1929, as one of the translations in Orioli's Lungarno Series. See McDonald, *Supplement*, pp. 75–76. See Lawrence's letter to Orioli from Île de Port-Cros, dated " 'Sunday' [21 October 1928]," in Moore, *Intelligent Heart*, p. 391. See also Richard Aldington: "Orioli had a story that Lawrence wrote the whole of the introduction to his translation of *The Story of Doctor Manente* in the bookshop on the Lung' Arno. He was dissatisfied by the Introduction written by someone else, turned over the galleys, and produced his own, quite indifferent to the people coming in and out of the shop and all the resonant Italian voices."—Aldington, *Portrait of a Genius*, p. 118.

11 The final page of text (p. 108) of *The Story of Doctor Manente* retains the inverted pyramid of type.

12 I am unable to identify the "short essay" referred to. Cf. Note 7, above.

13 See Powell, pp. 75–76; Tedlock, pp. 143–49.

14 *Rawdon's Roof* was first published as No. 7 of the Woburn Books, by Elkin Mathews & Marrot, London, March, 1928.—McDonald, *Supplement*, pp. 35–36. It was later included in the posthumous *Lovely Lady* (1933).

15 Patmore, in *The London Magazine,* 4 (No. 6, June, 1957), 38–44.

16 D. H. L. letter to Earl H. and Achsah Barlow Brewster, from La Vigie, Ile de Port-Cros, Var, dated 8 November [1928], Brewster, pp. 184–85.

17 Anonymous, "Famous Novelist's Shameful Book: A Landmark in Evil," *John Bull,* XLIV (No. 1166, 20 October 1928), 11.

19 Anonymous, "Lewd Book Banned . . . ," *The Sunday Chronicle* [Manchester], 14 October 1928, p. 1*d.*

19 In a letter (17 August 1954) to the editor, Mr. William Gerhardi has written: "The background of this letter should be more interesting to a Lawrence scholar if I explain that it was in answer to my letter in which I pulled Lawrence's leg at the expense of Lord Beaverbrook, with whom my long friendship was clouded intermittently by his failure to live up to my conception of an unilateral friendship: which is to differ from oneself only in the friend's superior capacity to further one's own interests. The occasion was the inauguration of the Scottish *Daily Express* which carried in the Beaverbrook Press a full-page manifesto over the signature of Lord Beaverbrook, in which he claimed to have created his newspapers by invoking not his brain alone but other organs as well. I charged Lawrence with Beaverbrook's conversion to the Lawrence creed of the 'complete man.' That he should not see that work so humourless must invalidate its seriousness, prompted me at the same time to pull his leg at the expense of Aldous Huxley, whose flights into vicarious erudition for the purpose of arriving at platitudinous conclusions, struck me (in the absence, in Huxley's case, of any sense of ecstasy, as the prerequisite to all art) as even more preposterous. Hence the wary but pathetic attempt on the part of D. H. Lawrence to be humorous at all cost, to dissociate himself from Huxley's portrait [as Rampion in *Point Counter Point*] and from his own involuntary caricature in the Beaverbrook manifesto."

20 Original publication of this letter in full. A fragment has been published in Hugh Kingsmill's *D. H. Lawrence* (London: Methuen, 1938), p. 224.

21 Aldington, *Life for Life's Sake,* pp. 333–34.

22 Patmore, in *The London Magazine,* 4 (No. 6, June, 1957), 44–45. For a D. H. L. letter (11 January 1929) to Brigit Patmore, see Patmore, p. 45, and Moore, *Intelligent Heart,* p. 397.

23 D. H. L. letter to Achsah Barlow Brewster, from Hotel Beau Rivage, Bandol, Var, dated "Sunday" [18 November 1928], Brewster, p. 185.

24 D. H. L. letter to Maria Huxley, from Beau Rivage, Bandol, Var, dated only "Wednesday" [21? November 1928], *Letters,* p. 770. For Lawrence's translation of Il Lasca, see Note 10, above.

25 For Lawrence's "little newspaper articles" in *The Evening News* [London] and *The Sunday Dispatch* [London], see McDonald, *Supplement,* pp. 98–99. Many of them were to be collected in *Assorted Articles.* I have been unable to trace a contribution to *The Daily Express* [London].

26 D. H. L. letter to The Hon. Dorothy Brett, from Hôtel Beau Rivage, Bandol, Var, France, dated 24 November 1928, *Letters,* p. 771. Lawrence's story "None of That," never published in magazine form, was included in *The Woman Who Rode Away* (1928).

27 D. H. L. letter to Mrs. Enid C. Hilton, from Hôtel Beau Rivage, Bandol, Var, dated 7 December 1928, *Letters*, pp. 772–73.

28 D. H. L. letter to Aldous and Maria Huxley, from Hôtel Beau Rivage, Bandol, dated 15 December 1928, *Letters*, pp. 773–74.

29 See Dorothy Warren Trotter's letter to Lawrence dated 29 August 1928 in text, above.

30 Original publication of an installment of a solicited memoir completed in 1957.

31 See Note 75, below.

32 Original publication.

33 D. H. L. letter (translated from the German) to Frieda's mother, Frau Baronin von Richthofen, from Hôtel Beau Rivage, Bandol, Var, dated 19 December 1928, Frieda Lawrence, p. 270.

34 A more complete text of this letter is provided in Moore, *Intelligent Heart*, p. 393. Prof. Moore has conjectured "November 28, 1928?" as the date of the "Monday" provided by the original; but Monday fell on 26 November 1928. The letter adds the fact that the London bookseller, Charles Lahr of 68, Red Lion Street, Holborn, London, had sent Lawrence Mr. Davies' address.

35 *Withered Root* (1927).

36 See Lawrence's letter to Rhys Davies, from Bandol, France, dated " 'Sunday' [Dec. 9, 1928]," in Moore, *Intelligent Heart,* pp. 394–95.

37 From "Give Me a Sponge," in *Nettles.*

38 A reference to Lawrence's water color *Spring.*

39 See No. 11, "Tranquillity," of Lawrence's creed in the essay "Benjamin Franklin," Chapter II of *Studies in Classic American Literature.*

40 See "November by the Sea—" in *Pansies.*

41 In a letter to Aldous Huxley, from Beau Rivage, Bandol, dated only "Sunday" [23? December 1928], Lawrence thanked him for a copy of *Rasputin:* "Frieda got wildly thrilled" over it. See *Letters*, p. 776.

42 Davies, in *Horizon*, II (No. 10, October, 1940), 191–202. Rhys Davies (1903———), Anglo-Welsh novelist and short-story writer, was born in the Rhondda Valley of Wales. As a young man, he worked at various jobs in offices and stores in London until his first novel, *The Withered Root,* was published in 1927. Then he left for France. He has since lived in London, with frequent trips to Wales, France, Italy, and Germany. During World War II, he worked in the London War Office. His novels include *The Withered Root* (1927), *Count Your Blessings* (1932), *The Red Hills* (1932), *A Time to Laugh* (1937), *Jubilee Blues* (1938), *Under the Rose* (1940), *Tomorrow to Fresh Woods* (1941), *The Black Venus* (1944), *The Dark Daughters* (1947), *Marianne* (1951), *The Painted King* (1954); his collections of short stories, *A Pig in a Poke* (1931), *Love Provoked* (1933), *The Things Men Do* (1936), *A Finger in Every Pie* (1942), *The Trip to London* (1946), *Boy With a Trumpet* (1949), etc.

43 "New Mexico" was originally published in *Survey Graphic*, LXVI (1 May 1931), 153–55.—McDonald, *Supplement,* p. 102. It was later reprinted in *Phoenix*, pp. 141–47.

44 D. H. L. letter to Mabel Dodge Luhan, from Hotel Beau Rivage, Bandol, Var, dated 25 December 1928, Luhan, p. 339.

45 D. H. L. letter to Earl H., Achsah Barlow, and Harwood Brewster, from Hotel Beau Rivage, Bandol, Var, dated 28 December 1928, Brewster, p. 190.

46 D. H. L. letter to Aldous Huxley, from Hôtel Beau Rivage, Bandol, dated "Sat. 30 Dec." [Saturday, 29 December 1928, or Sunday, 30 December 1928], *Letters*, pp. 782–83.

47 D. H. L. letter to Aldous Huxley, from Hôtel Beau Rivage, Bandol, Var, dated 6 January 1929, *Letters*, p. 785.

48 See Lawrence's poem "Ultimate Reality," in *Last Poems*.

49 Original publication of an installment of a long memoir completed in 1954.

50 D. H. L. letter to Laurence E. Pollinger, from Hôtel Beau Rivage, Var, dated 7 January 1929, *Letters*, pp. 786–87.

51 D. H. L. letter to Rhys Davies, from Hôtel Beau Rivage, Bandol, Var, dated 11 January 1929, *Letters*, p. 789.

52 See Notes 108 and 109, below.

53 Mary Austin, nee Hunter (1868–1934), American author, who lived for many years in California and New Mexico, and who "did much to introduce Indian and Spanish elements of U.S. culture into American literature." She was the author of the novels *The Land of Little Rain* (1903), *Lost Borders* (1909), *The Lovely Lady* (1913), *The Man Jesus* (1915), *The Land of Journeys' Ending* (1924), *Starry Adventure* (1931); an autobiography, *Earth Horizon* (1932), the plays *The Arrow Maker* (1911) and *The Man Who Didn't Believe in Christmas* (1916), etc.

54 A reference to either "Indians and Entertainment," "Dance of the Sprouting Corn," or "The Hopi Snake Dance," three essays included in *Mornings in Mexico*.

55 See Chap. II, Note 186, above.

56 See Powell, p. 36; Tedlock, pp. 103–4.

57 Adolph Francis Alphonse Bandelier (1840–1914), American archaeologist, was born in Switzerland. He carried on field researches in New Mexico (1880–1889) and explored Peru and Bolivia (1892–1902), and served on the staff of the Museum of Natural History, New York City (1903 ff.). He wrote on archaeology of southwestern United States, Mexico, and Central and South America, as well as *The Delight Makers* (1890) and *The Golden Man* (1893). In his essay "Indians and Entertainment" (included in *Mornings in Mexico*), Lawrence mentions Bandelier; see also *Phoenix*, pp. 336, 359.

58 As "American Heroes," Lawrence's review of William Carlos Williams' *In the American Grain* was originally published in *The Nation*, 122 (No. 3171, 14 April 1926), pp. 413–14. See McDonald, *Supplement*, pp. 94–95. The review is reprinted in *Phoenix*, pp. 334–36.

59 See Note 8, above.

60 See the black and white cut above the colophon (p. 145) of *The Paintings of D. H. Lawrence*.

61 See "Introduction to These Paintings," in *Phoenix*, pp. 567 ff.

62 Cf. Frieda Lawrence, p. 69.

63 Ghiselin, "D. H. Lawrence in Bandol," in *Western Humanities Review*, XII (No. 4, Autumn, 1958). Brewster Ghiselin (1903——), American poet, scholar, educator, was born in Webster Groves, Mo. He took his A.B. (1927) and his M.A. (1928) at the University of California. He has been an instructor in English at the University of Utah (1929–1931, 1934–1938), an assistant at the University of California (1931–1933), lecturer (1938–1939), assistant professor (1939–1946), associate professor (1946–1950), professor (1950——), and Director of the Annual Writers' Conference (1947——) at the University of Utah. He is the author of two volumes of poetry: *Against the Circle* (1946) and *The Nets* (1955); the editor of *The Creative Process* (1952).

In a letter (14 December 1957) to the editor, Mr. Ghiselin has written concerning his memoir: "[This] memoir represents my attempt to give the truth about Lawrence in full accord with my impressions recorded in 1929 —only shaped with more skill than I had then. I have used much of my old material word for word and have checked every bit of information against one or another dependable ground. When notes and memory failed me I have not invented anything about Lawrence. Fortunately, I have been able to make a portrait with available materials that seems to me true and full, within the limitations of the perspective that I had when I was with Lawrence. I believe the thing is of the same validity as if I had written it all in Bandol in 1929. My own speeches, not always derived from notes, are sometimes only approximately exact, however." See also Brewster Ghiselin, "D. H. Lawrence and a New World," *Western Review*, 11 (Spring, 1947), 150–59.

64 Ghiselin, "The Nets," from *The Nets*, pp. 15–16.

65 D. H. L. letter to Rhys Davies, from Hôtel Beau Rivage, Bandol, Var, dated 11 January 1929, *Letters*, p. 788.

66 *The Daily News* [London], 24 January 1929.

67 Original publication of an installment of a solicited memoir completed in 1957.

68 Norman Alfred William Lindsay (1879——), Australian cartoonist, black-and-white artist, and novelist.

69 See Frederick J. Hoffman, Charles Allen, and Carolyn F. Ulrich, *The Little Magazine: A History and Bibliography* (Princeton, N.J.: Princeton University Press, 1946), pp. 5, 74–75, 288–89.

70 See Chap. II, Note 115, above.

71 James Douglas (1867–1940), when editor of the London *Star*, had written a review of Lawrence's *The Rainbow*, which was at least partially responsible for the police proceedings against the book in late 1915. See *Letters*, p. 502.

72 See Note 94, below.

73 Percival Reginald Stephensen (1901——) was born at Biggenden, Queensland, Australia. Having received his B.A. at the University of Queensland, he became the Queensland Rhodes Scholar (1924) and took his B.A. degree with honors at Oxford. Thereafter he worked in the Fanfrolico

and Mandrake Presses in London, and as joint editor with Jack Lindsay of *The London Aphrodite*. After his return to Australia in the early 1930's, he became managing director of the Endeavour Press in Sydney (1932–1933). He is the author of prose and verse accompanying collections of satirical drawings, namely, *The Sink of Solitude* (1928), *Policeman of the Lord* (1928), and *The Well of Sleevelessness: A Tale for the Least of These Little Ones* (1929). He is the author also of *The Bushwhackers: Sketches of Life in the Australian Outback* (1929), *The Legend of Aleister Crowley* (1930), *The Life Story of Harry Buckland, Master of Hounds* (1931), *Pavlova* (with H. Hyden, 1931), *The Foundations of Culture in Australia: An Essay Towards National Self Respect* (1936), *Sail Ho!* (with Sir James Bisset, 1958). See also his *Kookaburras and Satyrs: Some Recollections of the Fanfrolico Press* (Cremorne, N.S.W.: Talkarra Press, 1954).

74 Radclyffe Hall (1866–1943), English novelist and poet, author of the controversial *The Well of Loneliness* (1928).

75 See Lawrence's letter to Giusèppe ("Pino") Orioli, from Palma de Majorca, "Ascensión," mistakenly dated "[May 9, 1929]" and later corrected to "[18 April 1929]": "The Fanfrolico Press has more or less dissolved. The *working* partner was always Stephensen—Lindsay was the literary side of it. Stephensen has joined with Edward Goldston the Jew bookseller of Museum St. to make the Mandrake Press, of which my pictures are the first thing done."—Moore, *Intelligent Heart*, p. 403. For the correction of the date, see Moore, *Poste Restante*, p. 100.

In about March, 1929, Mr. P. R. Stephensen wrote in *Kookaburras and Satyrs*, he left the Fanfrolico Press. "I had other plans. In January [1929], on a visit to the South of France, I had met D. H. Lawrence and offered to publish a book of reproductions of his paintings; but Lawrence did not want to be associated with the Fanfrolico Press, as he disagreed with the Lindsay Aesthetic. I therefore (in partnership with a bookseller named Edward Goldston) founded The Mandrake Press . . . ."—P. R. Stephensen, *Kookaburras and Satyrs: Some Recollections of the Fanfrolico Press* (Cremorne, N.S.W.: Talkarra Press, 1954), p. 31.

76 See Charles MacLaurin, *Post Mortem: Essays, Historical and Medical* (New York: George H. Doran, [?1922]; New York: George H. Doran, 1923; London: Jonathan Cape, March, 1923). The preface of the book is dated "Sydney, 1922." The text of *Post Mortem* is also available in *Post Mortems of Mere Mortals: Essays, Historical and Medical* (New York: Sun Dial Press, 1940). In his acknowledgments (p. viii) to this edition, Dr. MacLaurin has written: "The first drafts of these essays appeared in the *Australasian Medical Journal, The Sydney Bulletin,* the Australian *Home, Art in Australia,* and the Australian *Forum.*"

77 See D. H. L. letter to Rhys Davies, dated "Christmas Day, 1928": "Lindsay sent me this morning *another* copy of his Dionysos book!"—*Letters,* p. 778.

78 For Edgell Richword, see Chap. II, Note 162, above.

79 Original publication of a solicited memoir written in February, 1958. Jack Lindsay (1900———), Australian-born writer long resident in England, was born John Lindsay, at Melbourne, Australia, son of Norman Lindsay (see

Note 68, above), Australian artist and writer; and brother of Philip Lindsay (1906–1958), historical novelist and film story writer. Graduated B.A. with first-class honours in Latin and Greek at the University of Queensland, he then became a free-lance writer in Sydney. The printing of his first books on a hand press led to his departure to London "to invade the area of the fine book at its British fountainhead." There he operated the Fanfrolico Press (1926–1930) with P. R. Stephensen (see Note 73, above), and edited the anthology *The London Aphrodite: A Miscellany of Poems, Stories, and Essays by Various Hands Eminent or Rebellious* (six sections, August, 1928—June, 1929). He is a prolific translator and the author of many volumes of biography, history, and criticism, as well as novels with both historical and contemporary settings.

80 D. H. L. letter to Curtis Brown, from Hôtel Beau Rivage, Bandol, Var, France, dated 24 January 1929, *Letters,* p. 790.

81 Possibly a reference to "Swan" or "Give Us Gods," in *Pansies.*

82 This "Special Definitive Edition" of *Pansies,* limited to 500 copies, was printed for subscribers only by P. R. Stephensen of 41 Museum Street, London, W.C. 1. Although specifically dated June, 1929, distribution did not really begin until August, 1929. See McDonald, *Supplement,* pp. 52–54.

83 Davies, in *Horizon,* II (No. 10, October, 1940), 202–3.

84 See Van Wyck Brooks, Alfred Kreymborg, Lewis Mumford, and Paul Rosenfield, eds., *The American Caravan: A Yearbook of American Literature* (1927); or possibly Alfred Kreymborg, Lewis Mumford, and Paul Rosenfield, eds., *The Second American Caravan* (1928).

85 Lawrence's introduction to Edward Dahlberg's *Bottom Dogs* (London: G. P. Putnam's Sons, November, 1929; New York: Simon and Schuster, 1930) is reprinted in *Phoenix,* pp. 267–73. See McDonald, *Supplement,* p. 86.

Edward Dahlberg (1900——), American novelist, poet, and critic, was born in Boston. He spent his childhood with his mother, an itinerant hairdresser, in Louisville, Memphis, New Orleans, Dallas, and Denver before settling in Kansas City, where the mother opened a ladies' barber shop. "The shop, the cowboys and politicians and big horse and mule traders that came to it, are the basis of my first novel, *Bottom Dogs* . . . ." His greatest teachers were "my mother, Kansas City, the Cleveland orphanage, where I was an inmate until my seventeenth year, and the roving boxcars in which I hutted and slept as a hobo in 1919." He later lived for some time in Paris, London, Florence, and Brussels, but eventually returned to the U.S. His principal works include *Bottom Dogs* (1929), *From Flushing to Calvary* (1932), *Those Who Perish* (1934), *Do These Bones Live* (1941), *Sing, O Barren* (1947), *The Flea of Sodom* (1950), etc.

86 Original publication.

87 D. H. L. letter to Lady Ottoline Morrell, from Hôtel Beau Rivage, Bandol, Var, dated 5 February 1929, *Letters,* pp. 792–93.

88 D. H. L. letter to Earl H. and Achsah Barlow Brewster, from Hotel Beau Rivage, Bandol, Var, dated 7 February 1929, Brewster, pp. 194–96.

89 In a letter (26 August 1957) to the editor, Mr. Ghiselin has written: "The little African instrument referred to was a fragile sounding box of wood with steel tines. The tip of one had evidently been broken recently, and for this reason I judged that it ought to be packed in a strong wooden box to make sure it would travel. A box of the right size was hard to find. I had been ill, as I told Lawrence in my letter responding to this one, and I had also been deeply preoccupied with writing, as I did not tell him."

90 Jack Clarke, son of Ada and W. E. Clarke of Ripley, Derby., was destined to die in a German prison camp in World War II. See Moore, *Intelligent Heart*, p. 438.

91 Original publication.

92 D. H. L. letter to Maria Huxley, from Hôtel Beau Rivage, Bandol, Var, dated 18 February 1929, *Letters*, pp. 794–95.

93 Colonel Harry Day (1880–1939), M.P. (Labour) Southwark Central (1924–1931, 1935–1939).

94 Sir William Joynson-Hicks ("Jix"), 1st Viscount Brentford (1865–1932), Home Secretary (1924–1929).

95 Morgan Jones (1885–1939), M.P. (Labour) Caerphilly Division (1921–1939).

96 Sir Frank Cecil Meyer, 2nd Bt. (1886–1935), M.P. (Conservative) Great Yarmouth (1924–1929).

97 Norah C. James, *The Sleeveless Errand* (New York: Morrow, 1929; Toronto: McClelland, 1929; London: The Scholartis Press, 1929).

98 Rt. Hon. Ellen Cicely Wilkinson (1891–1947), M.P. (Labour) Middlesbrough E. (1924–1931).

99 Frederick William Pethick-Lawrence, 1st Baron of Peaslake (1871——), M.P. (Labour) West Leicester (1923–1931).

100 Capt. Rt. Hon. Edward A. Fitzroy (1869–1943), Speaker of the House of Commons (1928–1943).

101 "Lord Campbell's Obscene Publications Act. This dated from 1857."— Moore, *Intelligent Heart*, p. 204.

102 Rt. Hon. James Ramsay MacDonald (1866–1937), M.P. (Labour) Aberavon Division of Glamorganshire (1922–1929).

103 Lieut.-Comm. Joseph Montague Kenworthy, R.N., 10th Baron Strabolgi of England (1886–1953), M.P. (Labour) Central Hull (1926–1931).

104 Charles George Ammon, 1st Baron of Camberwell, M.P. (Labour) North Camberwell (1922–1931).

105 *The Parliamentary Debates,* House of Commons, 5th Series, CCXXV (28 February 1929), cols. 2158–63.

106 D. H. L. letter to Mabel Dodge Luhan, from Hotel Beau Rivage, Bandol, Var, dated 2 March 1929, Luhan, p. 342.

107 D. H. L. letter to Aldous and Maria Huxley, from Bandol, Var, undated, *Letters*, p. 797. See Moore, *Poste Restante*, pp. 98–99.

108 Miss Sylvia Beach published under the imprint Shakespeare and Co. at her bookshop first located in the rue Dupuytren, then at 12, rue de l'Odéon, Paris.

109 Sylvia Beach had failed to answer Lawrence's letter of mid-December,

1928, suggesting that she "look after" a stock edition of *Lady Chatterley's Lover*. See *Letters*, pp. 774, 782, 784, 785.

110 For Lawrence on James Joyce, see *Letters*, pp. 750, 759; "Surgery for the Novel—or a Bomb," in *Phoenix*, pp. 517–18. See also William Deakin, "D. H. Lawrence's Attacks on Proust and Joyce," *Essays in Criticism*, VII (No. 4, October, 1957), 383–403. On 17 December 1931, Joyce wrote to Harriet Shaw Weaver: "I read the first 15 pages of the usual sloppy English [of *Lady Chatterley's Lover*] which is a piece of propaganda in favour of something which, outside of D. H. L.'s country at any rate, makes all the propaganda for itself."—Stuart Gilbert, ed., *Letters of James Joyce* (New York: Viking, 1957), p. 309.

111 The "Paris Popular Edition" of *Lady Chatterley's Lover* (including "My Skirmish With Jolly Roger"), "Privately Printed," was published in May, 1929, by Edward Titus. See Moore, *Intelligent Heart*, pp. 402, 405; McDonald, *Supplement*, pp. 47–48.

112 For the projected *Squib*, see *Letters*, pp. 827–28, 840; Moore, *Intelligent Heart*, pp. 415, 421–22; Mark Schorer, "I Will Send Address: New Letters of D. H. Lawrence," in *The London Magazine*, III (No. 2, February, 1956), 66–67.

113 Davies, in *Horizon*, II (No. 10, October, 1940), 203–7.

114 Unpublished D. H. L. letter to Giusèppe ("Pino") Orioli, from Suresnes, Seine (3 rue de Bac), dated 18 March [1929], Moore, *Poste Restante*, p. 99.

115 D. H. L. letter to Earl H. and Achsah Barlow Brewster, from 3 rue de Bac, Suresnes, Seine, dated "Sat." [23? March 1929], Brewster, p. 199.

116 Unpublished D. H. L. letter to Giusèppe ("Pino") Orioli, from Paris (Hôtel de Versailles), dated 26 March 1929, Moore, *Poste Restante*, p. 99.

117 Original publication.

118 See Moore, *Poste Restante*, p. 99.

119 Jean Varda, collagist and mosaicist in glass, mirror, painted concrete, etc., now living in California.

120 Constance Crowninshield Coolidge Atherton of Boston, the "C. C. C." of Harry Crosby's *Diary* (Paris: Black Sun Press, 1932). See Caresse Crosby, pp. 112–13. Her portrait has been painted by Augustus John.

121 Caresse Crosby, pp. 222–23.

122 See Note 111, above.

123 D. H. L. letter to Max Mohr, from Hotel de Versailles, 60 Bvd Montparnasse, Paris 15, dated 5 April 1929, Mohr, *T'ien Hsia Monthly* [Shanghai], I (No. 1, August, 1935), 34.

124 D. H. L. letter to Earl H. and Achsah Barlow Brewster, from [c/o] Thomas Cook and Son, Calle Fontanella 19, Barcelona, Spain, dated 15 April 1929, Brewster, pp. 200–201.

125 D. H. L. letter to Giusèppe ("Pino") Orioli, from [Hotel Royal] Palma de Majorca, incorrectly dated " 'Ascensión' [May 9, 1929]," Moore, *Intelligent Heart*, pp. 403–4, the conjectured date corrected to 18 April 1929 in Moore, *Poste Restante*, p. 100.

126 For memoirs by Robert Nichols (1893–1944), English poet and dramatist,

whom Lawrence had known in England during the War Years, see Cecil Gray and Others, *Peter Warlock: A Memoir of Philip Heseltine*, The Life and Letters Series No. 84 (London: Jonathan Cape, 1938), pp. 89–92, reprinted in Vol. I, pp. 331–32, 450–51, of the present work.

127 D. H. L. letter to Rhys Davies, from Hôtel Príncipe Alfonso, Palma de Mallorca, Spain, incorrectly dated "25 April, 1929," *Letters*, pp. 801–2, and corrected to 24 April 1929 in Moore, *Poste Restante*, p. 100.

128 Original publication.

129 D. H. L. letter to The Hon. Dorothy Brett, from Hôtel Príncipe Alfonso, Palma de Mallorca, Spain, dated 27 April 1929, *Letters*, p. 803.

130 D. H. L. letter to Maria and Aldous Huxley, from Hôtel Príncipe Alfonso, Palma de Mallorca, dated "Ascension Day (May 9th, 1929)," *Letters*, pp. 804–5. Possibly the letter should be dated 18 April 1929. See Note 125, above.

131 Hughes, pp. 190–91.

132 D. H. L. letter to Earl H. and Achsah Barlow Brewster, from Hotel Principe Alfonso, Palma de Mallorca, Spain, dated 17 May 1929, Brewster, pp. 201–2.

133 D. H. L. letter to Rhys Davies, from Hôtel Príncipe Alfonso, Palma de Mallorca, Spain, dated 26 May 1929, *Letters*, p. 814.

134 D. H. L. letter to Ada Lawrence Clarke, from Palma de Mallorca, Spain, dated 2 June 1929, Ada Lawrence and Gelder, pp. 149–50.

135 See Frieda Lawrence, p. 198.

136 *The Paintings of D. H. Lawrence*, with an Introduction by D. H. Lawrence (London: The Mandrake Press, June, 1929). There has been no American edition of this book.—McDonald, *Supplement*, pp. 48–50. Lawrence's "Introduction to These Paintings" is reprinted in *Phoenix*, pp. 551–84. See Hubert Crehan, "Lady Chatterley's Painter: The Banned Pictures of D. H. Lawrence," *Art News*, LV (No. 10, February, 1957), 38–41, 63–64, 66.

137 D. H. L. letter to Frieda's sister Dr. Else Jaffe-Richthofen, from Hotel Príncipe Alfonso, Palma de Mallorca, Spain, dated 12 June 1929, Frieda Lawrence, pp. 272–73.

138 D. H. L. letter to The Hon. Dorothy Brett, from Forte dei Marmi, Italy, c/o Curtis Brown, Ltd., 6, Henrietta St., Covent Garden, London, W.C. 2, dated 23 June 1929, *Letters*, pp. 815–16.

139 Original publication.

140 I am unable to explain the reference to Billy Nell. But see *Letters*, p. 808.

141 See Note 111, above.

142 Charles Lahr, bookseller, of 68, Red Lion Street, Holborn, London. See Note 34, above.

143 Probably a reference to the Lawrence self-portrait used in the P. R. Stephensen edition of *Pansies* (August, 1929), later reproduced in Stephen Potter, *D. H. Lawrence: A First Study* (1930); Murry, *Son of Woman* (1931 ed.); Father William Tiverton, *D. H. Lawrence and Human Existence* (1951).

144 S. S. Koteliansky ("Kot") (1882–1955), Ukrainian-born translator, in England from *ca.* 1914. Lawrence and he had met in the summer of 1914. See Vols. I and II of the present work.

145 Georgia O'Keeffe (1887———), American painter, wife of Alfred Stieglitz. (See Chap. II, Note 406, above.) She is known especially for her paintings of New Mexican desert scenes, and for her stylized flower studies.

146 See *Letters,* p. 815.

147 For Costanza, see *Letters,* pp. 824, 826. Otherwise, I am unable to identify the name.

148 Possibly "Peterich" is the "Ekkie" referred to in *Letters,* p. 824. Otherwise, I am unable to identify the name.

149 Original publication.

150 Original publication.

151 From the first draft of the form letter appeal to the public sent out by the Warren Gallery ("We have recourse to you . . ."). See text, pp. 368–69.

152 See *Letters,* p. 859.

153 "In view of the continued agitation over *Lady Chatterley's Lover,* invitations had been sent out on a revised and abridged mailing list."—Philip Trotter.

154 See Frieda Lawrence, p. 191.

155 See Huxley, Introduction to *Letters,* p. ix. "Though applying ostensibly to the writer the assessment cannot exclude Lawrence's paintings, whose companionship often meant more to him than human society."—Philip Trotter.

156 See *Letters,* p. 729; Carswell, p. 160, note 1.

157 See "Making Pictures," in *Assorted Articles,* p. 201.

158 See Carswell, p. 273.

159 From "Our London Art Critic," "D. H. Lawrence's Paintings: A Novelist as Artist," *The Scotsman* [Edinburgh], 17 June 1929.

160 See *Sea and Sardinia,* Chap. V, "To Sorgono."

161 See *Sea and Sardinia,* Chap. V, "To Sorgono."

162 See *Sea and Sardinia,* Chap. VI, "To Nuoro."

163 "As a composition *Boccaccio Story* was the undisputed masterpiece; it was the only painting that we might legitimately have been asked to withdraw from exhibition. It illustrates a moment in the *Decameron,* 1st Story of the 3rd Day: 'Massetto di Lamporechio feigns to be dumb, and obtains a gardener's place in a convent of women, who with one accord make haste to lie with him.' The judgment on the picture as a work of art came from the police-court cells at Gt. Marlborough St. after the raid. The story must wait its turn; it is too good to take out of its context."—Philip Trotter.

164 See *Letters,* p. 689.

165 See Brewster, p. 135.

166 See Brewster, pp. 123–24. See also Chap. II, Note 176, above.

167 " 'Making Pictures' first appeared in the July, 1929, issue of *Creative Art,* with a reproduction of *The Finding of Moses,* and in the July, 1929, issue of *The Studio* as well—but in the middle of the month, about a week after the police raid."—Philip Trotter. See McDonald, *Supplement,* p. 100.

168 See Carswell, p. 273.

169 See Brewster, p. 118.

170 See Note 136, above.

171 Thomas Wade Earp (1892–1958), English art critic, author of *The Gate of Bronze* (1918), *Still Life and Flower Painting* (1930), *Augustus John* (1934), *Van Gogh* (1934), *The Modern Movement in Painting* (1935), *French Painting* (1945); translator of Stendhal.

172 See T. W. Earp, "Mr. Lawrence on Painting," *The New Statesman*, XXXIII (No. 851, 17 August 1929), 578.

173 See "Introduction to These Paintings," in *Phoenix*, p. 561.

174 See *Sea and Sardinia*, Chap. II, "The Sea."

175 See *Letters*, p. 697.

176 From the poem "Paradise Re-entered," included in *Look! We Have Come Through!* and again in *Collected Poems*, II.

177 See *Letters*, p. 686.

178 See Brewster, p. 151.

179 See *Letters*, p. 696.

180 Gwen John, free-lance art critic and author (not to be confused with the sister of Augustus John). Author of *Luck of War* (play, 1922), *The Prince* (1923), *Queen Elizabeth* (1924), *Plays of Innocence* (1925), *Mr. Jardyne* (1928), *Mere Immortals* (1930), etc.

181 "Cherry Robbers" was included in *Love Poems and Others* and again in *Collected Poems*, I.

182 Gwen John, "Paintings by D. H. Lawrence: The Eye of a Poet's Mind," *Everyman*, I (No. 22, 27 June 1929), 27.

183 See "When I Went to the Film," in *Pansies*.

184 "Frank Rutter (1876–1937), English art critic and prolific writer on art. Curator of the Leeds Art Gallery (1912–1917). European editor of *International Studio* (New York). For twenty-five years, the art critic for *The Sunday Times* (London)."—Philip Trotter.

185 "This fine painting [*Contadini*] disappeared with several others from a half-way house between our London home and the wartime sanctuary of Thomas Agnew & Son. It was, I believe, the only picture drawn from a living model."—Philip Trotter.

186 Frank Rutter, *The Sunday Times* [London], 23 June 1929.

187 From "Our London Art Critic," "D. H. Lawrence's Paintings: A Novelist as Artist," *The Scotsman* [Edinburgh], 17 June 1929. See Note 159, above.

188 Evelyn Herbert, "From the Pen to the Brush: Rude Force of Mr. Lawrence," *Western Mail* [Cardiff], 26 June 1929.

189 Earp, in *The New Statesman*, XXXIII (No. 851, 17 August 1929), 578. For Lawrence on Mr. Earp, see the untitled poem in *Last Poems* beginning "I heard a little chicken chirp . . . ." In a letter (9 August 1957) to the editor, Mr. Philip Trotter has written, concerning Lawrence's "silly little doggerel": "Lawrence's spleen has here played havoc with his judgment or intuition. Mr. Earp is the most un-chirpy-chickeny personality in contemporary English letters. He is an accomplished writer of critical prose; his grave demeanour and few words, always chosen for their direct simplicity, add value to his rare humour. His *Who's Who* entry, against the heading *Recreations*, is 'Silence.'"

190 See *Letters*, p. 740.

191 See Brewster, pp. 116, 112.

192 See the colophon page of *The Paintings of D. H. Lawrence.*

193 "Paul Konody (1872–1933), born in Budapest, was the art critic for *The Daily Mail* and *The Observer.* A prolific writer on art, he published numerous biographies of British, Italian, French, and Flemish painters."—Philip Trotter.

194 See Notes 159 and 187, above.

195 Paul Konody, in *The Observer* [London], 16 June 1929.

196 "Charles Marriott (1869——), born in Bristol, has written fiction as well as art criticism and art history."—Philip Trotter. See Chap. II, Note 326, above.

197 See Brewster, p. 118.

198 "Lawrence's only published reference to this picture [*Family on a Verandah*] gives no support to this theory. See his letter to Aldous Huxley, dated 25 April 1928, in which he writes of doing a 'Family in Garden,' *Letters,* p. 736."—Philip Trotter.

199 "Gwen John also took exception to this picture [*Spring*]. '[It] will be avoided by sensitive people,' she wrote. [See Note 182, above.] The boys are playing in conventional schoolboy manner. Lawrence has merely stripped them in pursuance of his quest for 'phallic beauty.' The picture has no erotic intention; but the dull bareness of the inadequate hillock they are playing on, and the total lack of background, make it—in contrast to the woodland *Dance-Sketch*—a dreary little picture."—Philip Trotter.

200 "Achsah Brewster called this large canvas [*Fight with an Amazon*] 'the hounds of heaven.' [See Brewster, p. 281.] Because the massive woman was standing full front view with her legs wide apart I too found it shocking to the eye, but was not otherwise embittered or corrupted. As for 'dripping jaws,' one only of the four animals (? wolves, hounds, or dogs) had a red aura round its mouth."—Philip Trotter.

201 See *The Daily Express* [London], 17 June 1929.

202 "Lest this irrelevance should point to lack of letters in its editorial office, the same paper returned to the charge next day protesting against the exhibition of an illustration of Boccaccio's story of the nuns and the gardener."—Philip Trotter.

203 *The Daily Telegraph* [London], 27 June 1929, leader page.

204 See "Indecent Pictures," in *The Morning Post* [London], 18 June 1929, p. 11e: "There is on view in a West End gallery (writes our Art Critic) a collection of paintings and drawings by Mr. D. H. Lawrence, the novelist, of the most distasteful character. Even readers of his novels could not have expected anything quite like some of the pictures on the walls.

"What may be to some extent masked in literature by innuendo, in painted representations such as some of these by Mr. Lawrence becomes naked and ashamed.

"One cannot understand the mentality of the man who will produce works of this description. The worst of Señor Beltran-Masses' paintings were chaste compared with several of those by Mr. Lawrence."

For subsequent notices of the Lawrence Exhibition in *The Morning Post,* see the issues of 6 July 1929, p. 11*c;* 8 July 1929, p. 12*b;* 12 July 1929, p. 4*b.*

205 "Sales records are no longer to hand. Inevitably many people got in without buying a catalogue, or entered on that of another visitor."—Philip Trotter.

206 "Some years after the Lawrence exhibition, a local councillor was brought before a magistrate on a Common Informer's complaint, on a charge of non-attendance in church. The magistrate, in reluctantly imposing the minimum penalty, observed that the Law, in its zeal for the detection of crime, had 'enlisted the motive of personal gain.' There seems no reason to suppose that Jaundice was actuated by any motive other than meddling." —Philip Trotter.

207 Original publication of an installment of a solicited memoir completed in 1957.

208 D. H. L. letter to Max Mohr, from Forte dei Marmi (Lucca), dated 2 July 1929, Mohr, *T'ien Hsia Monthly* [Shanghai], I (No. 2, September, 1935), 167.

209 D. H. L. letter to Frieda, from 6 Lungarno Corsini, Florence, dated 7 July [1929], Frieda Lawrence, p. 274.

210 D. H. L. letter to Frieda, from Florence, dated only "Monday night" [8 July 1929], Frieda Lawrence, p. 276.

211 "This is a mistake. *'Eve'* was not seized. D. H. L. is quite clearly referring to *Flight Back into Paradise,* by far the biggest picture in the exhibition. He would never have singled out a water-colour [*Throwing Back the Apple*]. Of course neither of these was seized."—Philip Trotter.

212 Original publication.

213 See Carswell, p. 297.

214 "Geoffrey Scott (1885–1929), author of *The Architecture of Humanism* (1914, rev. 1924), *A Box of Paints* (1923), *The Portrait of Zélide* (1925), *Poems* (1931), etc., was then at the end of a brief visit home from America, where he was employed by the late Col. Ralph H. Isham in editing his recently-acquired Boswell papers, preparatory to writing his life."—Philip Trotter.

215 For Arnold Bennett on Lawrence, see *The Evening Standard* [London], 10 April 1930, or *The Manchester Evening News,* 10 April 1930. The Bennett text is reprinted in part in Vol. I, p. 458, of the present work.

216 See Carswell, p. 298.

217 "We learned later that Mr. Hester attained the eminence entitling him to dismantle a picture gallery as the protective shadow of Prime Minister Asquith during the suffragette persecution before the first war. He was a tall, fine-looking man, and his manners, after the initial shots, were impeccable."—Philip Trotter.

218 "St. John Hutchinson, K.C., scholar and collector. As a barrister he had made a name in defence of individuals whose civil liberties were in any way threatened."—Philip Trotter. Lawrence had known St. John Hutchinson personally during the War Years in England. His wife, Mary, was a cousin of the Stracheys. Mark Gertler had painted his portrait.

219 Aga Khan (1877–1957), Indian leader, the hereditary head of the Mohammedan Ismaili sect; founder of the All-India Moslem League in 1906; representative of India at the League of Nations in the 1930's.

220 In a letter (8 February 1952) to the editor, Mr. Richard Aldington recalled that in 1930 the Aga Khan offered to buy the Lawrence paintings from Frieda. The offer was withdrawn when Frieda asked £20,000— about $100,000 in those days.

221 "Sir Geoffrey Keynes [1887——], Eng. surgeon and literary critic. A consulting surgeon of St. Bartholomew's Hospital, London; Hon. Librarian of the Royal College of Surgeons; a prolific writer on surgery, the circulation of the blood, etc. In the literary field, he has written on Sir Thomas Browne, William Hazlitt, Jane Austen, and, above all, Blake."—Philip Trotter.

222 Geoffrey Keynes, ed., *Pencil Drawings of William Blake* (London: Nonesuch Press, 1927), Introduction, "Blake's Pencil Drawings," p. ix.

223 Geoffrey Keynes, p. x.

224 Lewis Carroll, *La chasse au snark, une agonie en huit crises*, traduit pour la première fois en français par Louis Aragon (Chapelle-Réanville, Eure: Hours Press, 1929).

225 George Grosz (1893——), German painter, once a leader in the school of German expressionism known as "The New Objectivity." His work expressed hatred of the bourgeoisie, militarism, and capitalism; satirized World War I and postwar conditions in Germany. In 1932, he emigrated to the United States, and established a studio near New York City. His paintings were among those condemned as "degenerate" by the Nazi regime.

226 See *The Daily Chronicle* [London], 6 July 1929.

227 See Chap. II, Note 328, above.

228 Angna Enters (1907——), American dancer, painter, and author. Combining the arts of dance, pantomime, music, and costume, she has created new theater forms.

229 See *The Daily Dispatch* [London], 6 July 1929.

230 Frederick Mead (1847–1945), English magistrate before whose Court of Summary Jurisdiction, Metropolitan Police District, sitting at Marlborough Street Police Court, London, was heard the Lawrence Exhibition case (8 August 1929). See text, below.

231 See C. G. L. Ducann, "Obscene Libel," *John O'London's Weekly*, LXIII (No. 1557, 14 May 1954), 477–78.

232 "The periodical publishing the article printed my correction of the alleged closing of the exhibition by Mr. Mead; but informed me that the barrister maintained that, in the matter of the Blake book, 'this was exactly as Mr. Mead put it.' It is for others to defend the late magistrate's memory; but I submit that historical truth has claims in its own rights."—Philip Trotter. See Mr. Trotter's letter in *John O'London's Weekly*, LXIII (No. 1559, 28 May 1954), 528.

233 See *The Nottinghamshire Evening News*, 8 July 1929.

234 Richardson Sowerby, Holden & Co., solicitors for the Warren Gallery. The firm's address remains 5, John Street, London, W.C. 1.

235 Wontner & Sons, solicitors for the Commissioner of Police. Current address: 125, High Holborn, London, W.C. 1.

236 Original publication. On 15 August 1929, Messrs. Wontner & Sons acknowledged receipt of this communication, and on 29 August 1929, reported that, after an investigation by his officers, the Commissioner of Police could not accept any responsibility for the damage done to *Boccaccio Story*.

237 Original publication of an installment of a solicited memoir completed in 1957.

238 D. H. L. letter to Max Mohr, from 6 Lungarno Corsini, Firenze, dated 10 July 1929, Mohr, *T'ien Hsia Monthly* [Shanghai], I (No. 2, September, 1935), 168.

239 Frieda Lawrence, p. 199.

240 See Aldington, *Portrait of a Genius,* p. 405.

241 See Frieda Lawrence, p. 199, and text, above.

242 See Aldington, *Portrait of a Genius,* p. 405.

243 See Aldington, *Portrait of a Genius,* p. 407.

244 One of the "victims" of the Marlborough Street Police Court (though not of Mr. Mead) was Sir Basil Thomson (1861–1939), English police commissioner, prison warden, and author. He was Prime Minister of Tonga, Governor of Dartmoor Prison (to 1907), Assistant Commissioner of Metropolitan Police (1913–1919), Director of Intelligence at Scotland Yard (1919–1921). "In 1925 Thomson and a woman with whom he had been sitting were arrested in Hyde Park. He was found guilty of committing an act in violation of public decency and was fined £5 and £5 costs, also forfeiting his original recognisances of £5. This finding was upheld on appeal. Thomson's defence was that he had gone to the Park to find a certain Communist speaker, and to gain firsthand material for a book he was writing, called *The Police and the Public*. Character witnesses included Vice-Admiral Sir William Hall, M.P. and Mr. Reginald McKenna, a former Home Secretary. The Magistrate rendered his verdict 'with regret.'"—René MacColl, *Roger Casement: A New Judgment* (New York: Norton, 1957), p. 315. See also *The Times* [London], 17 December 1925, p. 16*f*; 5 January 1926, p. 7*a*; 6 January 1926, p. 7*a*; 5 February 1926, p. 11*b*; 6 February 1926, p. 4*f*.

245 "The 'vetoes' run right through the correspondence from 4th July, 1928: 'I'm not anxious at all to sell the big ones. I have only those seven . . . .' But the letters are never unequivocal except in respect of the three that were no longer Lawrence's to sell. These were: *Dance-Sketch* to Elsa Weekley, *North Sea* to the Huxleys, and our selection, *Contadini*. Our claim would be further weakened by the sale of some 12,000 catalogues."—Philip Trotter.

246 Original publication. The late Mr. Ralph A. Holden (1880–1950) was the head of the Gray's Inn firm of Richardson Sowerby, Holden & Co., solicitors for the Warren Gallery.

247 See D. H. L. letter to Giusèppe ("Pino") Orioli, from Bühl (Baden), Germany, dated 29 July 1929: "I can't be bothered with the Victor Cunard nonsense of telephones."—Moore, *Intelligent Heart,* p. 410.

248 Original publication of a long installment of a solicited memoir completed in 1957.

249 Original publication.

250 Original publication of an installment of a solicited memoir completed in 1957.

251 Dorothy Warren Trotter's "long and senseless letter" mentioned by Lawrence in a letter to Giusèppe ("Pino") Orioli, from Bühl (Baden), Germany, dated 29 July 1929. See Moore, *Intelligent Heart,* p. 410. "Mrs. Trotter's letter is now lost."—Philip Trotter.

252 "[In her 'long and senseless letter'] presumably Dorothy mentioned that should things go wrong at Gt. Marlborough St. we should appeal to Quarter Sessions."—Philip Trotter.

253 Original publication. Quotations from this letter have been published in Moore, *Intelligent Heart,* p. 409.

254 Original publication.

255 Original publication of an installment of a solicited memoir completed in 1957.

256 Augustus (Edwin) John (1878———), British portrait and mural painter. Through Lady Cynthia Asquith, he had met Lawrence in London in Autumn, 1917(?). For a memoir, see Augustus John, *Chiaroscuro: Fragments of Autobiography* (New York: Pellegrini & Cudahy, 1952), p. 85, reprinted in Vol. I, p. 440, of the present work. See also Chap. II, Note 332, above.

257 "I presume 'lack of' is a typist's blunder."—Philip Trotter.

258 See Note 263, below.

259 See Note 264, below.

260 Original publication. "This letter was among Geoffrey Scott's last: returning to America a fortnight later he caught a chill on the voyage and died of pneumonia in New York on the 14th August 1929, age 46. The letter was dictated onto the typewriter in great haste and in no way reflects the chiseled perfection of Scott's published prose."—Philip Trotter. For Arnold Bennett, see Note 215, above.

261 "The history of this great picture is confused, some authorities alleging that it was destroyed by order of the church under Louis XII. But the eminent French authority M. Reiset held the version in the National Gallery to be authentic."—Philip Trotter.

262 No. III B 77 of The Wallace Collection.

263 "[Geoffrey Scott] is wrong; there is not a trace."—Philip Trotter.

264 "The remark, of course, ignores the 'sale and gain' clause of the Act."— Philip Trotter.

265 "Cf. the lack of melody and rhythm with which Verdi was charged by his first reviewers, and the 'cockney school' article on Keats (*Blackwood's Magazine,* August, 1818), followed by *The Quarterly Review* (dated April, 1818, but published September, 1818), with its 'savage and tartarly stuff.' " —Philip Trotter.

266 Havelock Ellis, *Studies in the Psychology of Sex,* Vol. VI, p. 94. The quotation is given as a footnote in Frederick Hallis, *The Law and Ob-*

scenity (London: Desmond Harmsworth, 1932), p. 18, "an excellent brochure based mainly on the Lawrence Exhibition case."—Philip Trotter.

267 Dr. Tancred Borenius (?–1948). "In his dual devotion to art and his native Finland, recalls Paderewski. Is said to have taught himself English by writing in English a history of English art. With many artistic poets his preferred designation was Professor of History of Art, University College, London. 'To the general public his name was most familiar in connection with the excavations at Clarendon Palace near Salisbury, and as that of an ardent pleader for . . . Finland. By a smaller circle of students he was highly esteemed as an art historian with a wide range of knowledge, unconventional in his views, and suggestive in his observations.' (*The Times* [London], 4 September 1948.)"—Philip Trotter.

268 Glyn Philpot (1884–1937). "Prolific portrait painter in Britain and U.S.A., 1913 and 1930. His *Marble Workers* gained 1st prize gold medal and £300 at Pittsburgh, 1912. Painted in Paris and Spain. 'Sense of integrity, awareness that hackwork leads to sterility militated against his brilliant prospects as a portrait painter' (*D.N.B.*)."—Philip Trotter.

269 Sir William Orpen (1878–1931). "The 'prodigy' of Dublin Met. Art School at 11; fellow-student of Augustus John. Famous portrait and conversation piece painter; but from 1917 was official war painter in France and Belgium. Most of this great collection was presented to nation after 1918 exhibition at Agnew's. 'Then followed nine months of intense activity at the peace conferences in Paris and Versailles' (*D.N.B.*)."—Philip Trotter.

270 "Lady Orpen and Lady Rothenstein were both daughters of the artist W. J. Knewstub, Rossetti's only pupil."—Philip Trotter.

271 *Ca.* November, 1915, Lytton Strachey and Lawrence had met, and Strachey had taken steps to protest the suppression of *The Rainbow*. See David Garnett, *The Flowers of the Forest* (New York: Harcourt, 1956), pp. 95–96, reprinted in Vol. I, pp. 342–43, of the present work.

272 Roger (Eliot) Fry (1866–1934), English painter and critic, educated at Cambridge. Author of *Sir Joshua Reynolds' Discourses* (1905), *Vision and Design* (1920), *Transformations* (1926), *Henri Matisse* (1930), *Reflections on British Painting* (1934), *Last Lectures* (1939). A member of the so-called "Bloomsbury Group."

273 See Garnett, *Flowers of the Forest*, p. 95. "Earlier in this work [*Flowers of the Forest*, pp. 34–36], Mr. Garnett may have thrown light on Bloomsbury's hesitant support of anything to do with Lawrence as painter. The incident, one of the most lamentable manifestations of Lawrence's darker self, was in 1915, at a small tea party in Duncan Grant's studio, Lawrence having applied to see his pictures. Grant, a rising star of Bloomsbury, was then at the beginning of a brilliant career. Lawrence dismissed each picture, as Grant produced it, in a crescendo of unrestrained disapproval. Garnett concludes the terrible episode: 'Duncan himself appeared to have developed toothache and sat with his hands on his knees, rocking himself gently in his chair, not attempting a word in defence of his works. Everything, however, has an end, and at last Lawrence, feeling he had done his good deed for the day, said that they must be going.' Lawrence wrote next

day to Ottoline Morrell [*Letters,* pp. 219–20], passing on to her the duty of admonishing Duncan Grant."—Philip Trotter. Mr. Garnett's account of Lawrence's visit to Duncan Grant's studio is reprinted in Vol. I, pp. 266–69, of the present work.

274 See Roger Fry, "London Sculptors and Sculptures" in *Transformations: Critical and Speculative Essays on Art* (London: Chatto & Windus, 1926), pp. 136–56.

275 Sir Jacob Epstein (1880———), American sculptor of Russo-Polish descent, born in New York City. He studied under Rodin. Since 1905, he has worked chiefly in England. His massive creations done in startlingly unconventional style have caused much controversy. Some of his best work is bronze portraiture.

276 See Fry, *Transformations,* p. 141.

277 (Arthur) Clive (Howard) Bell (1881———), English critic in art and literature, had met Lawrence during the War Years. See Vol. I, p. 343, of the present work.

278 See Roger Fry, *Cézanne: A Study of His Development* (New York: Macmillan, 1927), p. 10.

279 See "Introduction to These Paintings," in *Phoenix,* pp. 571–72.

280 See Fry, *Cézanne,* p. 1.

281 See Note 172, above.

282 See "Introduction to These Paintings," in *Phoenix,* p. 569.

283 See "Introduction to These Paintings," in *Phoenix,* pp. 568, 577, 569, 573.

284 See "Introduction to These Paintings," in *Phoenix,* pp. 580–81.

285 See Clive Bell, *Landmarks in Nineteenth Century Painting* (London: Chatto & Windus, 1927), Preface, p. vi.

286 Sir Desmond MacCarthy (1878–1952), English journalist and critic; literary editor of *The New Statesman* (1920 ff.), later dramatic critic; editor of *Life and Letters.* His principal works include *Experience* (1935), *Drama* (collected essays, 1940), *Shaw* (1951), *Shaw's Plays in Review* (1951), *Memories* (1953), *Portraits* (1954), *Humanities* (1954), *Theatre* (1955). See Desmond MacCarthy, "Notes on D. H. Lawrence," in *Life and Letters,* IV (No. 24, May, 1930), 384–95. See also *The Sunday Times* [London], 11 August 1929.

287 "See *The Times* [London], 15 August 1929."—Philip Trotter.

288 See Note 184, above.

289 Albert Daniel Rutherston (1881–1953), English painter, illustrator, stage designer; Ruskin Master of Drawing, University of Oxford (1929–1949).

290 Edmund Henry Hynman, 1st Viscount Allenby (1861–1936), English field marshal.

291 Sir William Sefton Brancker (1877–1930), English air vice-marshal (1924), who perished in the disaster of the airship *R. 101.*

292 Charles Prestwich Scott (1846–1932), English journalist, editor (from 1872) of the *Manchester Guardian.*

293 Mansfield Duval Forbes (1889–1936), English writer and Fellow of Clare College, University of Cambridge (1913–1936); Lecturer, etc., the Faculty of English and Member of the Faculty of Fine Arts and Architecture, University of Cambridge.

294 Nancy Mitford (1904——), English novelist, author of *The Pursuit of Love* (1945), *Love in a Cold Climate* (1949), *The Blessing* (1951), etc.; wife of The Hon. Peter Rodd.

295 Vita Sackville-West (1892——), English poet and novelist; Lady Nicolson, wife of Sir Harold Nicolson.

296 The Rt. Hon. Harold Baker (1877——), M.P. (Labour), representing Accrington Division, Lancs. (1910–1918); Financial Secretary to the War Office (1912–1913); Member of H.M.'s Army Council, European War (1914); Inspector of Quartermaster-General Services (1916); Fellow of Winchester College (1933), Warden (1936–1946).

297 Sir (Hubert Miles) Gladwyn Jebb (1900——), British Ambassador to France since 1954. In 1929–1931, he was Private Secretary to the Parliamentary Under-Secretary of State. Married (1929) Cynthia, daughter of Sir Saxton Noble.

298 See Notes 180 and 182, above.

299 Maurice Baring (1874–1945), English journalist and author of poems, plays, novels, and books on Russia and Russian literature.

300 See "Making Pictures," in *Assorted Articles*, pp. 203–4.

301 See "Making Pictures," in *Assorted Articles*, pp. 199–200.

302 For reproductions of several of these early Lawrence pictures, see Ada Lawrence and G. Stuart Gelder, *Young Lorenzo: Early Life of D. H. Lawrence: Containing Hitherto Unpublished Letters, Articles and Reproductions of Pictures* (Florence: G. Orioli, 1931). The pictures are *not* reproduced in Ada Lawrence and G. Stuart Gelder, *Early Life of D. H. Lawrence: Together with Hitherto Unpublished Letters and Articles* (London: Martin Secker, 1932).

303 See " 'News' Man's Notebook: D. H. Lawrence's Pictures: Mr. A. J. Statham's Opinion," *The Evening News* [London], 16 August 1929.

304 The excerpts are taken from *Pornography and Obscenity*, first printed in *This Quarter* [Paris], II (No. 1, July–September, 1929), 17–27, later published separately by Faber, London, November, 1929 (Criterion Miscellany No. 5), and Knopf, New York, 1930.—McDonald, *Supplement*, pp. 100, 57–58.

305 See "Seized Pictures . . . ," *The Nottingham Evening Post*, 11 July 1929. See the same text in *The Daily Express* [London], 11 July 1929.

306 F. G. Stone, "D. H. Lawrence and Art," *The New Leader* [London], 7 July 1929.

307 S. Hilton, in *The New Leader* [London], 20 July 1929.

308 See "Art for Dirt's Sake," *John Bull*, XLVI (No. 1205, 20 July 1929), 8.

309 Anonymous, "Censoring Art," *The Bazaar* [London], CXXI (No. 28, 13 July 1929), 9.

310 See "From Our Own Correspondent," "Artist of Ideas," *The Glasgow Bulletin*, 15 July 1929.

311 Original publication of an installment of a solicited memoir completed in 1957.

312 Unpublished D. H. L. letter to Charles Lahr, from Florence, dated "Tuesday evening" [16 July 1929], Moore, *Poste Restante*, p. 101.

313 Douglas, pp. 287–89.

314 D. H. L. letter to Laurence E. Pollinger, from Hôtel Goldner Löwen, Lichtenthal, Baden-Baden, dated 20 July 1929, *Letters*, p. 817.

315 Original publication.

316 D. H. L. letter to Laurence E. Pollinger, from Kurhaus Plättig, Bei Bühl (Baden), dated 25 July 1929, *Letters*, p. 818.

317 Cf. "13,000 People," in *Nettles*.

318 Mrs. Grover, former secretary of the Warren Gallery, and Miss Young, the current secretary. Both were helping Dorothy Warren Trotter during the Lawrence exhibition.

319 Original publication.

320 Concerning Lawrence and the Baronin von Richthofen, Frieda Lawrence has written: "Happy was their relationship. Only the last time, when my mother was so frail and old herself, being with Lawrence who was so very ill, they got on each other's nerves, and when she saw him often so irritable with me, she said: 'He isn't grateful to you for all you do for him.' But I did not feel like that myself; I was glad to do everything for him I possibly could. It seemed little enough."—Frieda Lawrence, pp. 94–95.

321 D. H. L. letter to Giusèppe ("Pino") Orioli, from Bühl (Baden), Germany, dated 2 August 1929, Moore, *Intelligent Heart*, pp. 412–13.

322 Original publication.

323 Original publication.

324 The gardener in Lawrence's painting *Boccaccio Story*. See Note 163, above.

325 *The Daily Sketch* [London], 9 August 1929.

326 *The Evening Standard* [London], 8 August 1929.

327 *The Star* [London], 8 August 1929.

328 "The essential facts have been given, with varying degrees of accuracy, in many books, the best authority (among those I have read) being Mr. Richard Aldington's *D. H. Lawrence: Portrait of a Genius But* . . . [pp. 400–401]. My purpose here is to trace the path of broad farce and incongruity by which the final anticlimax was reached. Press quotations are from *The Daily Telegraph*, except for one from *The Daily Express*, two from Frederick Hallis' *The Law and Obscenity* (London: Desmond Harmsworth, 1932), who worked from our verbatim report, no longer extant; and, for the Magistrate's closing words, from *The Times*. Incidental colouring matter is drawn from personal memories or from hilarious comment current that evening in Boulestin's restaurant. The long passage relating to *Ecce Homo* by George Grosz is here omitted. The Magistrate ordered it to be restored, since it was not for sale."—Philip Trotter.

329 Herbert G. Muskett, head of Wontner & Sons, solicitors for the police. In 1915, he had appeared as the solicitor for the Commissioner of Police in the suppression of *The Rainbow*.

330 "Mr. Muskett's felicitous choice of language is happily preserved in a thousand press reports. His tonetic resources, since he was not a broadcaster and they were probably never recorded, are presumably lost. For instance, as one walks down Bond Street everything that catches the eye does so *for purposes of sale and gain*. Yet, as Mr. Muskett fixed this indict-

ment on the exhibits of the Warren Gallery, a slight but perceptible shudder gripped the Court. The phrase was not reported."—Philip Trotter. See Hallis, pp. 16–17.

331 "Cf. p. 344 of text above, for the exact words that passed between us on the 5th July."—Philip Trotter.

332 Hallis, p. 15.

333 *The Daily Telegraph* [London], 8 August 1929.

334 *The Daily Express* [London], 8 August 1929.

335 "In specifying my 'Big Five' [John, Agnew, Borenius, Philpot, Orpen] as our eminent sponsors I was keeping strictly to evidence in documents under my hand. From different press reports it is evident that we had furnished Hutchinson with more names than these, notably that of Sir William Rothenstein, Principal of the Royal College, and a very eminent figure of his day."—Philip Trotter.

336 "No newspaper recorded this observation; but I recall it vividly and the suppressed laughter that it evoked."—Philip Trotter.

337 "If my memory is correct this was linked with the Magistrate's approval of the lengthy hearing."—Philip Trotter. See *The Times* [London], 9 August 1929, p. 9.

338 "Geoffrey Scott had completed the first six volumes of the Boswell papers." —Philip Trotter.

339 *The Times* [London], 15 August 1929.

340 Original publication of an installment of a solicited memoir completed in 1957.

341 D. H. L. letter to Maria Huxley, from Hôtel Löwen, Lichtenthal, Baden-Baden, dated 12 August 1929, *Letters,* pp. 823–24.

342 Original publication.

343 D. H. L. letter to Frieda's sister Dr. Else Jaffe-Richthofen, from Löwen, Lichtental, Baden-Baden, dated 21 August 1929, Frieda Lawrence, p. 279.

344 See V. de S. Pinto, "D. H. Lawrence: Letter Writer and Craftsman in Verse. Some Hitherto Unpublished Material," *Renaissance and Modern Studies* [University of Nottingham], I (1957), 5–34.

345 *The Nottingham Journal,* 28 August 1929. The interview is signed with the initials "G. S. G."

346 *The Nottingham Journal,* 29 August 1929. To the late Councillor Hopkin's article, the Editor appended the following note: "Our correspondent is in error in assuming that by publishing an interview with Mr. Lawrence's sister we associated ourselves with the views therein expressed. It is obvious that some of the passages in *Pansies,* at any rate, were open to grave disapprobation."

347 D. H. L. letter to W. E. Hopkin, from Kaffee Angermaier, Rottach-am-Tegernsee, Oberbayern, dated 30 August 1929, *Letters,* p. 829.

348 D. H. L. letter to Achsah Barlow and Harwood Brewster, from Kaffee Angermaier, Rottach-am-Tegernsee, Oberbayern, dated 5 September 1929, Brewster, pp. 211–12.

349 D. H. L. letter to Enid C. Hilton, from Kaffee Angermaier, Rottach-am-

Tegernsee, Oberbayern, dated "Friday (Sept., 1929)" [6 September 1929], *Letters*, p. 831.

350 I am unable to trace this poem among Lawrence's published poetry.

351 From a letter (13 June 1935) by Mohr, written from Shanghai, to Mr. Wen Yuan-ning, Editor-in-Chief of *T'ien Hsia Monthly* [Shanghai], I (No. 1, August, 1935), 21–22. Max Mohr (1891–1944), German doctor and writer. He emigrated from Germany in 1935: "He was neither a Jew nor a socialist, and yet the time came when he had to tell his wife and child: 'Let me go. I cannot endure this Third Reich. For me it is hell.'" He arrived in Shanghai with ten dollars in his pocket, "my instruments, my medical training, a few photos of the family I had left behind in Germany, the Letters of D. H. Lawrence, and the glorious feeling that I had finished with Germany." He died in Shanghai of "one of the deadly diseases it was his onerous mission to heal." See Erika and Klaus Mann, *Escape to Life* (Boston: Houghton Mifflin, 1939), pp. 219–21. Max Mohr was the author of *Frau Maries Gast* (novel, 1919), *Tarras* (play, 1919), *Gregor Rosso* (play, 1920), *Dadakratie* (play, 1920), *Molow* (1920), *Improvisationen im Juni* (play, 1920), *Das gelbe Zelt* (play, 1921), *Sirill am Wrack* (play, 1922), *Der Arbeiter Esau* (play, 1923), *Die Karawane* (play, 1924), *Ramper* (play, 1925), *Platingruben in Tulpin* (play, 1926), *Pimpus und Caxa* (play, 1927), *Venus in den Fischen* (novel, 1928), *Die Heidin* (novel, 1929), *Die Welt der Enkel* (play, 1930), *Die Freundschaft von Ladiz* (novel, 1931), *Frau ohne Reue* (novel, 1933), etc.

352 Original publication. Frieda's letter is headed simply "Monday," and my dating of it is highly conjectural. Geoffrey Scott died in New York on 14 August 1929. In mid-September, Lawrence was writing to his friends of the possibility of moving on to Cassis. (See *Letters*, p. 835; Brewster, pp. 215, 216.) I have taken this as a clue to the dating of Frieda's letter, and have assigned to it the date ?9 September 1929, in which event it would have been written from Rottach.

353 D. H. L. letter to Giusèppe ("Pino") Orioli, from Rottach-am-Tegernsee, Germany, dated 13 September 1929, Moore, *Intelligent Heart*, pp. 416–17.

354 See the article reprinted from *The Times* [London], 4 November 1932, in Chap. IV, below.

355 See Harry T. Moore, ed., *D. H. Lawrence's Letters to Bertrand Russell* (New York: Gotham Book Mart, 1948), pp. 59–60.

356 See Katherine Mansfield, *Letters to John Middleton Murry: 1913–1922*, edited by John Middleton Murry (New York: Knopf, 1951), p. 470. The pertinent passage of the letter is reprinted in Vol. II, p. 23, of the present work.

357 See Moore, *Intelligent Heart*, pp. 418–19. See also *Letters*, p. 835.

358 Original publication of the concluding installment of a solicited memoir completed in 1957.

359 D. H. L. letter to Achsah Barlow Brewster, from Rottach, dated only "Saturday" [14 September 1929], Brewster, p. 215.

360 D. H. L. letter to Earl H. Brewster, from Hotel Beau Rivage, Bandol, Var,

mistakenly dated "17 Sept. 1929" [27 September 1929], Brewster, pp. 219–20. For dating, see Moore, *Poste Restante,* p. 102.

361 D. H. L. letter to Frieda's sister Dr. Else Jaffe-Richthofen, from Villa Beau Soleil, Bandol, Var, France, dated 4 October 1929, Frieda Lawrence, p. 281.

362 D. H. L. letter to Aldous and Maria Huxley, from Villa Beau Soleil, Bandol, Var, dated 23 October 1929, *Letters,* pp. 842–43.

363 William Ralph Inge, *The Philosophy of Plotinus* (1918).

364 Gilbert Murray, *Five Stages of Greek Religion* (1925).

365 Brewster, pp. 303–6. For the "poem to fire," see Tedlock, pp. 213–14.

366 D. H. L. letter to Mabel Dodge Luhan, from Villa Beau Soleil, Bandol, Var, France, dated 29 October 1929, Luhan, pp. 348–49.

367 See Brewster, p. 175; reprinted in text, p. 230, above.

368 Brewster, pp. 223, 224–28.

369 Original publication.

370 D. H. L. letter to Aldous and Maria Huxley, from Beau Soleil, Bandol, dated 9 November 1929, *Letters,* p. 845.

371 Harry and Caresse Crosby had sent Frieda the gramophone. See *Letters,* pp. 822, 826.

372 D. H. L. letter to Max and Kathe Mohr, from Villa Beau Soleil, Bandol, Var, dated 14 November 1929, Mohr, *T'ien Hsia Monthly* [Shanghai], I (No. 2, September, 1935), 174–75.

373 D. H. L. letter to Max Mohr, from Bandol, Var, dated "Thursday/20 November 1929" [Thursday, 21 November 1929, or Wednesday, 20 November 1929], Mohr, *T'ien Hsia Monthly* [Shanghai], I (No. 2, September, 1935), 175–76.

374 Lawrence had visited Frederick Carter at Pontesbury, Shropshire, in early January, 1924, to discuss Apocalyptic symbols. See Carter, pp. 5, 33–42, reprinted in Vol. II, pp. 313–19, of the present work.

375 D. H. L. letter to Max Mohr, from Bandol, Var, dated "Thursday/20 November 1929" [Thursday, 21 November 1929, or Wednesday, 20 November 1929], Mohr, *T'ien Hsia Monthly* [Shanghai], I (No. 2, September, 1935), 175.

376 *Dragon of Revelation,* for which see text below, and Note 378, below.

377 Charles François Dupuis (1742–1809), author of *L'Origine de Tous les Cultes ou Religion Universelle* (1795).

378 This shorter introduction to *The Dragon of the Apocalypse* was originally printed as "Introduction" in *The London Mercury,* XXII (No. 129, July, 1930), 217–26, and was then reprinted in *Phoenix,* pp. 292–303. See Mr. Carter's letter to the Editor, *The London Mercury,* XXII (No. 131, September, 1930), 451; Edward D. McDonald in Introduction to *Phoenix,* pp. xviii–xix; Tedlock, pp. 141–49; Moore, *Intelligent Heart,* pp. 423–25. Lawrence's original introduction, or contribution, to *The Dragon of the Apocalypse* became the posthumous *Apocalypse.*

379 The contents of this D. H. L. postcard to Frederick Carter are given more fully in Moore, *Intelligent Heart,* p. 425.

380 Carter, pp. 43–53, 55, 61–63. Frederick Carter, English painter and etcher, was born near Bradford, Yorks., and was educated as a civil engineer and surveyor. At the age of nineteen, he went to Paris to continue his studies and turned to drawing. Upon his return to England, he worked for poster printers, and then resumed his studies, gaining three successive gold medals in the National Competition, South Kensington, for book illustrations. His published drawings and etchings decorate books by Cyril Tourneur, Byron's *Manfred,* and Heine's *Florentine Nights.* He is the author of *Gold Like Glass* (1932); *The Dragon of Revelation* (1932), revised as *Symbols of Revelation* (1934), etc.

381 I.e., *Pornography and Obscenity.* See Note 304, above. Prof. Harry T. Moore has written that by 9 December 1929, Lawrence could report to Orioli that the pamphlet was selling 12,000 copies a week.—Moore, *Intelligent Heart,* p. 420.

382 D. H. L. letter to Ada Lawrence Clarke, from Bandol, Var, dated 10 December 1929, Ada Lawrence and Gelder, p. 155.

383 Anna di Chiara, an American, and her husband, old friends of the Lawrences from Capri.

384 The former actress, Ida Rauh. After her divorce from the author Max Eastman (1922), she had married Andrew Dasburg. The Lawrences had known her in their New Mexico years (1922–1925). For her, in 1925, Lawrence had written his Biblical play, *David.* Ida Rauh's sister, Blanche, married the French painter Louis de Kerstrat, brother of Jo Davidson's first wife, Yvonne. See Note 428, below.

385 D. H. L. letter to Frederick Carter, from Beau Soleil, Bandol, France, dated 15 December 1929, Moore, *Intelligent Heart,* p. 424.

386 See Note 384, above.

387 "Henry Grew Crosby, 32 years old, member of a socially prominent Boston family, who registered a few days ago with his wife at the Savoy Plaza Hotel, and Mrs. Josephine Rotch Bigelow, the wife of Albert S. Bigelow, a Harvard student, were found shot dead in the bedroom of a studio apartment in the Hotel Des Artistes, 1 West Sixty-seventh Street [New York City], about 10 o'clock last night [10 December 1929].

"The couple had died in what Dr. Charles Norris, medical examiner, described as a suicide compact. Crosby and Mrs. Bigelow lay fully dressed in bed in the apartment of Crosby's friend, Stanley Mortimer Jr., a portrait painter, on the ninth floor of the hotel."—*The New York Times,* 11 December 1929, p. 1.

388 D. H. L. letter to Max and Kathe Mohr, from Beau Soleil, Bandol, Var, France, dated 19 December 1929, Mohr, *T'ien Hsia Monthly* [Shanghai], I (No. 2, September, 1935), 177–78.

389 D. H. L. letter to Maria Huxley, from Beau Soleil, Var, Bandol, dated "Thursday, Dec., 1929" [19 December 1929], *Letters,* pp. 849–50.

390 D. H. L. letter to Mark Gertler, from Beau Soleil, Bandol, Var, dated 23 December 1929, *Letters,* p. 850.

391 With an introduction by Richard Aldington, Lawrence's posthumous *Apocalypse* was published by G. Orioli, Florence, 1931; Martin Secker,

London, 1932; Viking, New York, 1932; The Albatross, Hamburg, Paris, Bologna, 1932.—White, p. 9. See Note 378, above.

392 Brewster, pp. 307–9.

393 D. H. L. letter to Maria and Aldous Huxley, from Beau Soleil, Bandol, dated 6 January 1930, *Letters*, pp. 852–53.

394 Douglas, pp. 289–90.

395 D. H. L. letter to Mabel Dodge Luhan, from Villa Beau Soleil, Bandol, Var, France, dated 6 January 1930, Luhan, pp. 350–51.

396 D. H. L. letter to Mabel Dodge Luhan, from Villa Beau Soleil, Bandol, France, dated 21 January 1930, Luhan, p. 351.

397 Among others, Mark Gertler. See *Letters*, p. 850. See also Chap II, Note 359.

398 In a letter (12 September 1952) to Prof. Harry T. Moore, Dr. Morland wrote: "It is very hard to say when [Lawrence's] tuberculosis began. I do not think the childhood illnesses or the pneumonia at sixteen had any bearing on his tuberculosis. The onset of this probably predated his first attack of haemorrhage by at least a few months or possibly considerably longer."—Moore, *Intelligent Heart*, p. 33.

399 Cf. George Godwin, "Fascinating Problem of Genius and Disease: Does the Mind Bloom as the Body Decays?" in *The Manchester Dispatch* [Withy Grove, Manchester], 10 March 1930.

400 From a memoir written (1952) for Prof. Harry T. Moore, and published in part in Moore, *Intelligent Heart*, pp. 427–28. Dr. Andrew (John) Morland, M.D., F.RC.P. (1896–1957), English physician. From 1928 to 1935, he was a member of the staff of Mundesley Sanatorium, Mundesley, Norfolk. In 1935, he joined the staff of French Hospital, London; in 1937, that of University College Hospital, London, where he became head of the department of chest diseases. See *The Times* [London], 15 July 1957, p. 14a; 22 July 1957, p. 14a. In 1928, he married Dorothy Saunders. He is the author of *Pulmonary Tuberculosis in General Practice* (1932).

401 D. H. L. letter to Lady Ottoline Morrell, from Villa Beau Soleil, Bandol, Var, dated 21 January 1930, *Letters*, p. 855.

402 See Chap. II, Note 284, above.

403 See Lawrence's poem "Bavarian Gentians," in *Last Poems*.

404 For Lawrence on Thomas Hardy, see "Study of Thomas Hardy," written in 1914–1915, and first published in full in *Phoenix*, pp. 398–516. The third chapter had been published in *The Book-Collector's Quarterly* [London], II (No. V, Jan.–Mar., 1932), 44–61, and in *John O'London's Weekly*, XXVI (No. 674, 12 March 1932), 897–98, 916, and XXVI (No. 675, 19 March 1932), 960, 966.—*Phoenix*, p. 841.

405 See Chap. II, Note 162, above.

406 Original publication of the final installment of a solicited memoir written in March, 1954. Translated from the German by Mrs. Doreen E. Hill. For the first installment of the memoir, see Vol. I, p. 165, of the present work. For Herbert E. Herlitschka, see Frieda Lawrence, p. 283.

407 Campbell Dixon's dramatization of Aldous Huxley's *Point Counter Point* was entitled *This Way to Paradise*.

408 D. H. L. letter to Max Mohr, from Beau Soleil, Bandol, Var, France, dated 30 January 1930, Mohr, *T'ien Hsia Monthly* [Shanghai], I (No. 2, September, 1935), 178–79.

409 Original publication of an installment of a long memoir completed in 1954.

410 D. H. L. letter to Frieda's sister Dr. Else Jaffe-Richthofen, from Beau Soliel, Bandol, Var, dated 30 January 1930, Frieda Lawrence, p. 285.

411 Original publication.

412 D. H. L. letter to Ada Lawrence Clarke, from Beau Soleil, Bandol, dated 3 February 1930, Ada Lawrence and Gelder, pp. 157–58.

413 See Brewster, pp. 28, 230.

414 Brewster, pp. 309–10.

415 Brewster, pp. 228–29.

416 D. H. L. letter to Maria Huxley, from Ad Astra, Vence, A.M., dated only "Friday" [7 February 1930], *Letters*, p. 858.

417 Brewster, pp. 229, 231.

418 D. H. L. letter to Maria Huxley, from Ad Astra, Vence, dated only "Wed." [12? February 1930], *Letters*, pp. 858–59.

419 The Lawrences, together with Katherine Mansfield and John Middleton Murry, had attended a party at the Wellses' home in Hampstead *ca.* mid-August, 1914. And Mrs. Wells, Violet Hunt, and Ford Madox Ford had motored to Greatham in March, 1915, to see the Lawrences. (Lawrence was at Cambridge visiting Bertrand Russell.) See Vol. I, pp. 237–40, 288–89, of the present work.

420 Original publication.

421 Possibly Evelyn Thorogood, subsequently of 12, Lloyd's Square, London, W.C. 1. See "From D. H. Lawrence's Death-Bed," in *The Evening Standard* [London], 6 October 1937, p. 26, reproduced on p. 440.

422 See Note 220, above.

423 D. H. L. letter to Earl H. Brewster, from Ad Astra, Vence A.M., dated only "Thursday" [27 February 1930], Brewster, pp. 232–33.

424 The first Mrs. Jo Davidson, the former Yvonne de Kerstrat. See Note 384, above.

425 See Lawrence's letter to Rhys Davies [from Hôtel Beau Rivage, Bandol, Var], dated "Christmas Day, 1928": "The dressing-gown came this morning as I sat in bed at coffee—very resplendent and I look as if I was just going to utter the unutterable name of God in it."—*Letters*, p. 778.

426 For photographs of his bust of Lawrence, see Jo Davidson's *Between Sittings,* facing p. 215; *The New York Times Book Review,* 2 January 1955, p. 1, etc.

427 Mrs. Harry Payne Whitney (1877?–1942), nee Gertrude Vanderbilt, daughter of Cornelius Vanderbilt. Herself a sculptor, she carved the Aztec fountain in the Pan-American building and the *Titanic* memorial in Washington, D.C. In 1931, she opened the Whitney Museum of American Art in New York City, later (1943) consolidated with the Metropolitan Museum of Art.

428 Davidson, pp. 251–52. I have corrected the mistaken *Venice* of the original text to *Vence.* Jo Davidson (1883–1952), American sculptor, was born in New York City. He is best known for busts of such famous contemporaries

as Franklin Delano Roosevelt, Woodrow Wilson, Albert Einstein, Gandhi, Charlie Chaplin, Joseph Conrad, James Joyce, etc. See Note 384, above.

429 Blair (Rowlands) Hughes-Stanton (1902——), English painter and engraver. See Mr. Hughes-Stanton's wood engravings for the illustrated edition of *Birds, Beasts and Flowers* (London: Cresset Press, 1930), and for *The Ship of Death and Other Poems* (London: Martin Secker, 1933), the latter a selection from Lawrence's *Last Poems*.

430 Now the Villa Aurella. See Moore, *Intelligent Heart*, p. 436.

431 See Note 421, above.

432 Original publication of an installment of a long memoir completed in 1954.

433 Frieda Lawrence, pp. 287–96.

CHAPTER IV

1 Cf. British United Press item, "Funeral of D. H. Lawrence," with the dateline "Monte Carlo, Tuesday [4 March 1930]": "Only a few intimate friends were at the graveside when Mr. D. H. Lawrence, the novelist, was buried in the cemetery of the Riviera mountain village of Vence to-day. Headed by Mrs. Lawrence, the author's wife, the small group followed the coffin from the Villa Roberment [*sic*] to the cemetery, where the Rev. Cecil conducted a simple graveside ceremony."—*Notts Journal* [Nottingham], 5 March 1930.

2 See Prof. Harry T. Moore: "According to legend, Lawrence's personal symbol, the phoenix, was patterned in colored pebbles on his gravestone by a peasant who was devoted to him: the story has both annoyed and amused the designer, Dominique Matteucci, who considers himself not a peasant, but a capitalist. The stone was finally removed in 1935, when at Frieda's behest Angelo Ravagli went to Vence and arranged to have Lawrence's body disinterred and cremated."—Moore, *Intelligent Heart*, pp. 440–41. Lawrence's body was cremated on 13 March 1935 at the Crématoire du Cimetière Saint-Pierre in Marseille.—E. W. Tedlock, Jr. In 1954, Lawrence's tombstone was in the possession of Mrs. Martha Gordon-Crotch of 6 Blvd. Paul André, Vence.

3 Louise ("Louie") Burrows, to whom Lawrence had been engaged from December, 1910, to February, 1912. See Vol. I, p. 556 n97, of the present work.

4 Original publication of an installment of a memoir completed in 1954.

5 Brewster, pp. 310–11.

6 Original publication of the concluding installment of a solicited memoir written in 1957.

7 *The Star* [London], 11 March 1930.

8 *The Sheffield Independent*, ? March 1930.

9 Goldring, *Life Interests*, pp. 97–99. See also Douglas Goldring, *Odd Man Out: The Autobiography of a "Propaganda Novelist"* (London: Chapman and Hall, 1935), pp. 262–64; Douglas Goldring, *The Nineteen Twenties: A General Survey and some Personal Memories* (London: Nicholson & Watson, 1945), pp. 241–43.

10 Gerhardi, p. 229.

11 See *Letters,* pp. 769–70. Lawrence's letter to J. D. Chambers was written from Ile de Port-Cros, Var, France, and dated 14 November 1928.

12 Original publication.

13 See *Letters,* p. 851. The letter, written from Beau Soleil, Bandol, Var, is dated 23 December 1929.

14 Signed "A Correspondent," the obituary notice in *The Times Literary Supplement,* 13 March 1930, p. 208, was written by John Middleton Murry, and is reprinted in Murry, *Reminiscences,* pp. 277–81, and in text, below. For its unsigned obituary notice, see *The Manchester Guardian,* 4 March 1930.

15 Davies, in *Horizon,* II (No. 10, October, 1940), 207–8.

16 See "Pomegranate," in *Birds, Beasts and Flowers,* and in *Collected Poems,* II.

17 See *The Lost Girl,* Chap. XVI, "Suspense."

18 See D. H. Lawrence, *The Spirit of Place: An Anthology Compiled from the Prose of D. H. Lawrence,* edited and with an Introduction by Richard Aldington (London: Heinemann, 1935).

19 Richard Aldington, "D. H. Lawrence," in *Everyman,* III (No. 59, 13 March 1930), [193], 204–5.

20 Cf. Frieda Lawrence, p. 81.

21 Cf. D. H. L. letter to J. M. Murry, from Zennor, St. Ives, Cornwall, dated 23 May 1917: "There is no writing and publishing news. Philosophy interests me most now—not novels or stories. I find people ultimately boring: and you can't have fiction without people. So fiction does not, at the bottom, interest me any more. I am weary of humanity and human things. One is happy in the thoughts only that transcend humanity."— *Letters,* p. 413.

22 Murry [signed "A Correspondent"], in *The Times Literary Supplement,* 13 March 1930, p. 208; reprinted in Murry, *Reminiscences,* pp. 277–81.

23 Carswell, "D. H. Lawrence" [a letter to the editor], *Time and Tide,* XI (No. 11, 14 March 1930), 342.

24 See Edwin Arlington Robinson's "Eros Turannos."

25 Dirk Coster, *The Living and the Lifeless: Marginalia,* trans. from the Dutch with an Introduction by Beatrice M. Hinkle (New York: Harcourt, Brace, 1929).

26 Luhan, "The Lawrence I Knew . . . ," in Supplement to *The Carmelite* [Carmel, Calif.], III (No. 6, 19 March 1930), iii–v.

27 Original publication of an installment of a long memoir completed in 1954.

28 Original publication. Mr. Ghiselin has noted the fact that Frieda's letter, undated, was postmarked 31 March 1930, and mailed in *London.*

29 See "Autobiographical Sketch," in *Assorted Articles,* p. 175.

30 Lawrence's posthumous *Assorted Articles* (London: Martin Secker, April, 1930; New York: Knopf, 1930).—McDonald, *Supplement,* pp. 59–60.

31 Anonymous ["From Our Special Correspondent"], "A Talk with Lawrence's 'Princess,'" in *The Star* [London], 9 April 1930. The interview is headed "Near Croydon, Wednesday [?9 April 1930]." Jessie Chambers Wood's home address was 43, Breck Hill Road, Woodthorpe, Nottingham.

32 *The Times* [London], 12 June 1930, p. 16*d.*

33 A reference to the special D. H. Lawrence number of *The New Adelphi,* III (No. 4, June-August, 1930). "The portrait is from a photograph taken in Mallorca last year." The essay, "Nottingham and the Mining Country-side," is reprinted in *Phoenix,* pp. 133–40.

34 Original publication.

35 Mrs. Hamilton Eames, for whom see *Letters,* pp. 700–701, 720.

36 Original publication.

37 Mrs. Carswell's "Reminiscences of D. H. Lawrence," subsequently expanded into the book *The Savage Pilgrimage* (1932; rev. ed., 1932, 1951), appeared originally in five installments in *The New Adelphi,* November, 1931—March, 1932.

38 On Tuesday, 8 July 1930, there appeared in *The Times* [London] a letter from Aldous Huxley to the Editor: "Sir,—I shall be most grateful if you will give publicity to the following communication, addressed to all those who may have any letters from the late D. H. Lawrence in their possession. The administrators of Mr. Lawrence's estate have asked me to collect his letters, and arrangements have been made for having them copied and filed. May I therefore ask all those of Lawrence's correspondents to whom I have not already written personally to send their letters to Mrs. Hilton, 44, Mecklenburgh-square, London, W.C. 1? The originals will be copied and returned as soon as possible. If it should be decided to publish any of the letters (the copyright in which vests exclusively in the estate) correspondents will be informed, which of their letters or parts of letters have been selected. I am, Sir, yours, &c., Aldous Huxley. La Gorguette, Sanary (Var), France."—*The Times* [London], 8 July 1930, p. 10*d*.

39 "Perhaps my conviction of Lawrence's capacity and desire for 'practical leadership' was rather a case of the wish being father to the thought on my part. The value of my correspondence with him, however, may lie in stressing this hitherto neglected aspect of his nature and purpose. I still think *The Plumed Serpent* was a daringly courageous *tour de force*, though Harry Moore and Professor Leavis seem to believe that Lawrence's convictions faltered before he finished the book. I wonder. Mexico certainly developed a potential capacity for ruthless justice and constructual definiteness in him. It was the *extreme* point of his development. After that he regressed, and came back to his home in Europe and even to the background of Christian theology and mythology."—Rolf Gardiner (March, 1956).

40 See *Studies in Classic American Literature,* Chap. I, "The Spirit of Place."

41 "Christopher Henry Oldham Scaife, one of my closest friends, himself a poet (President of the Union of Oxford, 1923, assistant professor of English Literature, University of Egypt, now professor at the American University of Beirut). His exposition of the novels and poems was rather along the lines of Leavis's later work."—Rolf Gardiner (March, 1956). Professor Scaife is the author of *The Poetry of Alfred Tennyson* (1930), *Towards Corinth, O Englishman* (poems, 1934), *Latter Day Athenian* (poems, 1937), etc.

42 "Adrian Stokes [1854–1935], another contemporary, writer on aesthetic and cultural problems (*Sunrise in the West* [1927], *Stones of Rimini*

733

[1934], etc.). I rather believe that he met Lawrence in Italy. But I don't think there was much rapport between them."—Rolf Gardiner (March, 1956).

43 A Dr. Dege, "a medical doctor, the head of a *Klinik* at Frankfurt-on-Oder which specialized in lung cases." As Christmas, 1927, approached, he and his German wife, a friend of Mrs. Carswell, had offered to "treat Lawrence for nothing, or for what he could afford without a strain." But Lawrence, at the Villa Mirenda, "though greatly attracted by our descriptions of the place and of the doctor, wrote that it was 'too far, too far.' "—Carswell, pp. 274–75.

44 Original publication. See also Mr. Gardiner's later (1952) statement on Lawrence in Moore, *Intelligent Heart*, pp. 395–96.

45 See Witter Bynner: "Mrs. Lawrence's attorney made his final plea, his summing-up, drew an eloquent picture of the long years of poverty, of the couple's unfailing devotion to each other, of their idyllic life together with never a quarrel, at which his client, unable to contain herself longer, fountained to her feet protesting, 'Oh, but no! That's not true! We fought like hell!' After a moment of shock the room burst into laughter, with Frieda finally joining. Laughter, as usual with her, was a following wave of her heated sincerity. The wig of the judge bent forward, while his hand hid his lips. Then, recovering, he solemnly announced himself to be persuaded of the plaintiff's 'obvious honesty' and decided in her favor."—Bynner, p. 347.

46 Anonymous, "Mr. D. H. Lawrence's Lost Will/Lawrence v. Lawrence and Others/Before the President," in *The Times* [London], 4 November 1932, p. 4. See Frieda Lawrence Ravagli in an undated, unpublished letter: "I wasn't sure of winning[,] not until the case came on: a severe old judge Lord Merrivale, but I pulled all my forces together in the witnessbox, just went ahead, felt I could convince crocodiles that Lawrence wanted me to have his inheritance—They say I was convincing—But the triumph was Lorenzo's—And the way Lawrence is pervading this England now is just surprising, I am full of the deepest satisfaction for *his* sake—I have not lived in vain—So there's a song of triumph for you."—Moore, *Intelligent Heart*, p. 438.

47 See Helen Corke, "Not L[awrence]. and 'A[pocalypse].' "—Helen Corke, *D. H. Lawrence's "Princess": A Memory of Jessie Chambers* (Thames Ditton, Surrey: The Merle Press, 1951), p. 39, note.

48 Helen Corke, *Lawrence and "Apocalypse"* (London: Heinemann, 1933).

49 "The End," "The Bride," and "The Virgin Mother." See E. T. [Jessie Chambers], *D. H. Lawrence: A Personal Record* (London: Jonathan Cape, 1935), p. 184. The three poems were included in *Amores*, and again in *Collected Poems*, I.

50 See Helen Corke, *Lawrence and "Apocalypse,"* pp. 90–93.

51 See Note 11, above.

52 The word *earnest* was indicated by the marks "———(?)" in the *Arena* transcription of the MS letter, but supplied by the Helen Corke transcription. See Note 55, below.

53 Possibly Jessie Chambers Wood may also have been reading Lawrence's essay "Aristocracy," included in *Reflections on the Death of a Porcupine*.

54 Frederick Carter, *D. H. Lawrence and the Body Mystical* (London: Denis Archer, 1932).

55 [Jessie Chambers Wood], " 'E. T.' on D. H. Lawrence: A Letter to a Common Friend [Helen Corke]," *Arena: A Literary Magazine* [London], I (No. 4, [1950]), 61–65. (With John Davenport and Randall Swingler, Jack Lindsay was a co-editor of *Arena*.) In a somewhat shortened form, the letter is also available in Helen Corke, *D. H. Lawrence's "Princess": A Memory of Jessie Chambers*, pp. 39–46.

56 Emile Delavenay (1905———) is now Chief of the Service of Documents and Publications at UNESCO, Paris. See E. Delavenay, "Sur un examplaire de Schopenhauer annoté par D. H. Lawrence," *Revue Anglo-Américaine*, XIII (February, 1936), 234–38, reprinted in Vol. I, pp. 66–70, of the present work.

57 Janko Lavrin (1887———), Professor of Slavonic Languages, The University, Nottingham (1923); Emeritus Professor (1953). Author of *Aspects of Modernism* (1935), *An Introduction to the Russian Novel* (1942), *Dostoevsky* (1943), *Tolstoy* (1944), *Pushkin and Russian Literature* (1947), *Nietzsche* (1948), *From Pushkin to Mayakovsky* (1948), *Ibsen* (1950), *Nikolai Gogol* (1951), *Goncharov* (1954), *Russian Writers* (1954), etc. With Edwin Muir, co-editor of the short-lived (May, 1934—Feb., 1935) *European Quarterly: A Review of Modern Literature, Art and Life* [London]. See Janko Lavrin, "Sex and Eros (On Rozanov, Weininger, and D. H. Lawrence)," *The European Quarterly*, I (No. 2, August, 1934), 88–96; reprinted in *Aspects of Modernism, from Wilde to Pirandello* (London: Stanley Nott, 1935), pp. 141–59.

58 See Jessie Chambers Wood: "Parts of the chapters on Student Days, Literary Formation, and Literary Début have appeared in *The European Quarterly* . . . ."—E. T., p. [11]. See E. T. [Jessie Chambers Wood], "The Literary Formation of D. H. Lawrence: Some Personal Reminiscences," *The European Quarterly: A Review of Modern Literature, Art and Life* [London], I (No. 1, May, 1934), 36–45; "D. H. Lawrence's Student Days: Personal Reminiscences," *The European Quarterly*, I (No. 2, August, 1934), 106–14; "D. H. Lawrence's Literary Debut: Personal Reminiscences," *The European Quarterly*, I (No. 3, November, 1934), 159–68.

59 Original publication.

60 Bynner, p. 348. See also Moore, *Intelligent Heart*, pp. 440–41.

61 Merrill Moore (1903———), American poet, author of *The Noise That Time Makes* (1929), *Six Sides to a Man* (1935), *M* (1938), etc.

62 Louis Untermeyer, p. 325.

63 Original publication of the concluding installment of a long memoir completed in 1954.

64 Cf. "New Mexico," in *Phoenix*, pp. 141–47.

65 In a letter (13 March 1957) to the editor, Mr. Witter Bynner identified Frieda's gift as a copy of Lawrence's *Bay*.

66 In a postscript to a letter (13 August 1956) to the editor, Mr. Witter Bynner has written: "Since dictating this I have had a 75th birthday to which Frieda was coming. We had several times celebrated our birthdays together—mine the 10th, hers the 11th. They did not tell me on the 10th that she had had a stroke; but on the morning of the 11th it was broken to me that she had died. Better of course than to have survived paralyzed —but a sad blow, from which I am still dazed."

67 "The pallbearers at the services on Monday [13 August 1956] were: William Goyen, Joseph Glasco, Chilton Anderson, William Hawk, Joseph Montoya, and Saki Karavas. The honorary pallbearers were Tony Lujan, Thomas Benrimo, Eric Hausner, Joseph Fleck, Ward Lockwood, Witter Bynner, Claude Anderson, Spud Johnson, Ted Mackie, William James, John Yaple, Louis Cottam, Richard Dicus, Theodore Hutton, and Matt Pearce."—T. M. Pearce.

68 See *Letters,* p. 803.

69 See *Letters,* pp. 856–57.

70 "Letter to the author, sent from Taos, October 17, 1956. The grave for Frieda Lawrence is in front of the chapel and to the left."—T. M. Pearce.

71 William Goyen (1918———), American novelist and short-story writer; author of *The House of Breath* (novel, 1950), *Ghost and Flesh* (short stories, 1952), etc.

72 Included in *Look! We Have Come Through!,* and again in *Collected Poems,* II.

73 Original publication of a solicited memoir entitled "Frieda—In Memory," written in August, 1957. T(homas). M(atthews). Pearce (1902———), Prof., Dept. of English, University of New Mexico, Albuquerque, N. Mex. See also T. M. Pearce, "Pilgrimage to Taos," in the *New Mexico Magazine* [Santa Fe], July, 1955, pp. 18, 52–53.

CHAPTER V

1 See the three versions of the unfinished "The Ship of Death" in *Last Poems.*

2 See Thomas Hardy, "When I Set Out for Lyonnesse."

3 See *Sons and Lovers,* Chap. I, "The Early Married Life of the Morels."

4 I am unable to supply the name of the Lawrence work referred to here.

5 See A. E. Housman, *A Shropshire Lad,* LII: "Far in a western brookland . . . ."

6 See "The Virgin Mother," in *Collected Poems,* I. An earlier version had appeared in *Amores.*

7 In "Hymns in a Man's Life," Lawrence remembered that over the organ-loft of the Congregational chapel in Eastwood were inscribed the words "O worship the Lord in the beauty of holiness."—*Assorted Articles,* p. 191. See also Brewster, p. 274.

8 See "Hymns in a Man's Life," in *Assorted Articles,* pp. 183–93. Cf. E. T., pp. 16–17.

9 See E. T., p. 31.

10 See *The White Peacock,* Part II, Chap. VIII, "A Poem of Friendship."

11 See Ada Lawrence and Gelder, p. 19.

12 See *Sons and Lovers*, Chap. IV, "The Young Life of Paul."
13 See *Sons and Lovers*, Chap. IV, "The Young Life of Paul."
14 See "Discord in Childhood" in *Amores* and *Collected Poems*, I.
15 See *Sons and Lovers*, Chap. IV, "The Young Life of Paul."
16 See E. T., pp. 54–55. See also *Aaron's Rod*, Chap. IV, "The Pillar of Salt," and Chap. XI, "More Pillar of Salt."
17 See E. T., p. 36.
18 See E. T., p. 54.
19 See E. T., p. 56.
20 See E. T., p. 138.
21 See E. T., p. 143.
22 See E. T., p. 196.
23 See E. T., p. 200.
24 See E. T., p. 204.
25 See E. T., p. 198.
26 See E. T., p. 199.
27 See E. T., p. 30.
28 See Ada Lawrence and Gelder, pp. 23, 25.
29 See E. T., p. 130.
30 See E. T., p. 217.
31 See E. T., p. 147.
32 See E. T., p. 153.
33 See E. T., p. 187.
34 See E. T., pp. 31, 47.
35 See E. T., pp. 222–23.
36 See E. T., p. 49.
37 Rowse, pp. 217–37. A(lfred). L(eslie). Rowse (1903——), F.R.S.L., English historian, now a Fellow of All Souls College, Oxford. See also Ken Gay, "Lawrence's Birthplace," *Tribune* [London], 26 May 1950, pp. 23–24.
38 Bynner, pp. xiv–xv.
39 See *Kangaroo*, Chap. V, "Coo-ee."
40 See *Kangaroo*, Chap. V, "Coo-ee."
41 See *Kangaroo*, Chap. V, "Coo-ee."
42 See *Kangaroo*, Chap. V, "Coo-ee."
43 See *Kangaroo*, Chap. V, "Coo-ee."
44 See *Kangaroo*, Chap. V, "Coo-ee."
45 See *Kangaroo*, Chap. V, "Coo-ee."
46 See *Kangaroo*, Chap. X, "Diggers."
47 See *Kangaroo*, Chap. VIII, "Volcanic Evidence."
48 See *Kangaroo*, Chap. XVIII, "Adieu Australia."
49 See *Kangaroo*, Chap. XVIII, "Adieu Australia."
50 See *Kangaroo*, Chap. XVIII, "Adieu Australia."
51 I am unable to supply the source of this quotation.
52 See "Flowery Tuscany," in *Phoenix*, p. 45. (The reference to *Twilight in Italy* is an error.)
53 See Richard Aldington, *D. H. Lawrence: An Appreciation* (Harmondsworth, Middlesex: Penguin, 1950), p. 21.

54 Robinson, in *The Bulletin* [Sydney], 8 April 1953, pp. 2, 35. In a letter (23 December 1953) to the editor, Mr. Roland E. Robinson has written: "Although I was born in Ireland [1913], I lived with my parents at Nottingham, England until I was nine among a lot of the Lawrence country of *The White Peacock.* But I did not read, or know of, Lawrence until about fifteen years ago." Mr. Robinson emigrated to Australia at the age of fourteen. He has worked on stations in western N.S.W., and, during World War II, served as clerk, storeman, and timekeeper with the Allied Works Council in the Northern Territory. He is the author of *Beyond the Grass-tree Spears* (poems, 1944), *Language of the Sand* (poems, 1949), *Legend and Dreaming* (legends of the Australian aborigines, 1952), *Tumult of the Swans* (poems, 1953), etc. He now makes his home at Rose Bay, N.S.W.

55 See "New Mexico," in *Phoenix*, p. 142.

56 Neff, in *The New Mexico Quarterly*, VII (No. 2, May, 1937), 116–20. In a letter (22 February 1958) to the editor, Mr. John C. Neff has written: "I am a free lance writer and have lived here in New York since the end of the war. I was born in Cleveland in 1913 and attended public schools there. I attended Kenyon College (where, indeed, I met J. M. Murry and, through him, Frieda and the others) and graduated *cum laude* in English in 1936. Then, a large and leisurely and inexpensive tour of Europe. Before all this, during the summertime, I spent about six or seven seasons on cattle ranches in New Mexico—in the Jemez Mountains close to what is now the Los Alamos atomic center and in the Sangre de Cristo Mountains and the flat country southward toward Santa Rosa. I mention this merely because my first published novel is about that country . . . it's called *Maria* and was published by Ives Washburn in 1951. I have also published short stories and articles in national magazines and have frequently reviewed fiction for the Sunday *New York Times.* I served in the army for six years during the war, fought in all the campaigns in Europe from Omaha Beach to the fall of Berlin. I have continued active, since then, in the Army Reserve and am at this time Chief of Staff of the 77th Infantry Division (Reserve) here in New York City. It is a job which vastly hampers my writing but I am literally so glad to be living in freedom that I really don't mind spending long hours with things military."

For another visit with Frieda, see Chap. IV, Note 73, above.

57 See *Letters*, p. 665.

58 See *Letters*, p. 721.

59 See Brewster, p. 140.

60 See *Letters*, p. 698.

61 See "Forte dei Marmi," in *Last Poems.*

62 See *Letters*, pp. 669, 684.

63 See "Furniture," in *Last Poems.*

64 See Brewster, p. 106.

65 See *Letters*, p. 722.

66 See *Letters*, p. 667.

67 See *Letters*, p. 667.

68 See "The Ship of Death," in *Last Poems.*

69 See *Letters*, p. 685.

70 See *Letters,* p. 689.
71 See *Letters,* p. 695.
72 See *Letters,* p. 702.
73 See "Loneliness," in *Last Poems.*
74 See "Nothing to Save," in *Last Poems.*
75 See *Letters,* p. 694.
76 See Brewster, p. 129.
77 See Brewster, pp. 152–53.
78 See *Letters,* p. 671.
79 See *Letters,* p. 691.
80 See *Letters,* p. 691.
81 See *Letters,* p. 678.
82 See *Letters,* p. 714.
83 See *Letters,* p. 672.
84 See *Letters,* p. 670.
85 See Frieda Lawrence Ravagli: "Then [Lawrence] wrote *Lady Chatterley.* After breakfast—we had it at seven or so—he would take his book and pen and a cushion, followed by John the dog, and go into the woods behind the Mirenda and come back to lunch with what he had written." —Frieda Lawrence, p. 193.
86 See *Letters,* p. 712.
87 See *Letters,* p. 777.
88 See *Letters,* pp. 709–10.
89 See *Letters,* p. 746.
90 Schorer, in *New World Writing* (Fourth Mentor Selection), pp. 145–54. Mark Schorer (1908———), American novelist, critic, and biographer, now Professor of English, University of California, Berkeley. In 1952, he lived in Italy, working on a critical study of Lawrence.

CHAPTER VI

1 See Moore, *Intelligent Heart,* p. 27; Vol. I, p. 544 n51, of the present work. In a letter (10 September 1957) to the editor, Dr. J. D. Chambers has supplied the birth, marriage, and death dates for his mother, father, sisters, and brothers, his source being the Chambers family Bible:

[Name	Birth	Marriage	Death]	
Sarah Ann [Oates] Chambers	27 Feb. 1859	? Oct. 1881	8 Jan.	1937
Edmund Chambers	10 Jan. 1863	? Oct. 1881	10 May	1946
Alan Aubrey Chambers	2 July 1882	15 Oct. 1910	20 May	1946
Muriel May Chambers	20 Oct. 1883	1 Nov. 1906	[8 July	1955]
John Oates Chambers	21 Nov. 1885		15 May	1886
Jessie Chambers	29 Jan. 1887	3 June 1915	[3 Apr.	1944]
Hubert Chambers	23 Apr. 1888			
Bernard Oates Chambers	4 Feb. 1890	10 Mar. 1921		
Emily Chambers	25 Aug. 1892		22 Sep.	1892
Mary ["Mollie"] Chambers	15 Jan. 1896	27 Nov. 1916		
Jonathan David Chambers	13 Oct. 1898	[8 Apr. 1926]		

2 *The Rathe Primrose,* begun *ca.* 1910, revised in early 1911, later entitled *Eunice Temple,* and ultimately destroyed. See Corke, *D. H. Lawrence's "Princess,"* p. 25.

3 "Later in life my father was a great reader of novels, including those of Henry James. His favourite was *The Golden Bowl* on the flyleaf of which he wrote 'From David. The finest constructed novel I have ever read.' He liked it so much he thought I must have intended him to keep it! He wrote a very good letter and had a passion for reading aloud. He read aloud *Tess of the D'Urbervilles* when it came out in serial form, and I remember in particular the speeches of Lloyd George and the tales of Eden Phillpotts."—J. D. Chambers.

4 "Edmund Chambers' mother, Mrs. Elizabeth Chambers, nee Hodgkinson; wife of Jonathan Chambers, a pawnbroker known locally as 'Pawny,' and later the owner of an off-license in The Breach, Eastwood."—J. D. Chambers. See Note 88, below. Lawrence's acqaintance with this Grandmother Chambers may have contributed to his conception of Meg's grandmother (George Saxton's great-aunt) at the Ram Inn of *The White Peacock,* Part II, Chap. I, "Strange Blossoms and Strange New Budding."

5 "This, of course, is only my impression. They certainly had a different attitude to Lawrence. They became very good friends later in life."—J. D. Chambers.

6 See Note 4, above.

7 See Chap. IV, Note 57, above.

8 Mark (Max) Plowman (1883–1941), Editor of *The Adelphi* (Oct., 1930—June, 1931; Oct., 1938—May, 1941).

9 Original publication of a solicited memoir written in 1957.

10 Original publication. I have been unable to determine the date of composition of "The Bankrupt."

11 Original publication of a solicited memoir written in 1957. Of the two May Chambers Holbrook MSS recovered by Dr. J. D. Chambers, one is a water-soaked, handwritten memoir of thirty-four pages; the other, the carbon copy of a typed memoir of sixty-three pages. Neither appears to contain Mrs. Holbrook's final revisions, and I have been obliged, in preparing the memoirs for publication, to divide the long paragraphs into shorter ones, to supply name tags for dialogue, to add an occasional date and footnote. The typewritten memoir ends abruptly with Lawrence's departure for Croydon in 1908; the handwritten memoir gives a much less detailed picture of Lawrence up to that date, but adds several scenes describing the Lawrence who returned home to Eastwood in the early winter of 1910–1911 to attend his dying mother. I have, therefore, added these scenes to the fuller, typewritten memoir.

Dr. Chambers is unable to supply me with more than a conjectured dating for the memoirs. But in a letter (6 May 1957) to the editor, Mr. William Holbrook has written: "I have been mystified where, how, and when these papers were being written. This is how it all came about, so far as I am concerned. Mrs. Holbrook left the farm in Saskatchewan, Canada, to take possession of a piece of property here in B.C., and I stayed behind to get things cleared away, which held me back a year or more. So as one usually does at such times, a last minute rush through all the rooms, and then I remember seeing the handwritten papers, scattered here and yon. At that time I figured by their abandoned appearance, musty and discolored, they were considered of little account, but nevertheless I stuffed them into a library box and from there they got to her brother Bernard. Then along comes Dr. Chambers . . . .

"I am so very sure in my own mind that Mrs. Holbrook had given up all thoughts of bringing them before the public. She never at any time said a word about them, and I can only imagine they were written, when Mrs. Holbrook was residing in Saskatchewan: the date could be around 1916 on."

In another letter (18 June 1957) to the editor, Mr. Holbrook wrote: "I still think that Mrs. Holbrook had given up the idea of publishing these memoirs as I know they lay around as you can see by the stained appearance, then too I eight years ago came across them lying around loosely in a carton along with reams of other MS. Now I am satisfied in my mind that these memoirs of D. H. were being written at the time Mrs. Holbrook was away in Saskatchewan: teaching school, therefore I would not be around. This seclusion is much appreciated among writers as you will know. I know she preferred early morning for this duty.

"The date would be around 1918 or thereabouts. To my knowledge I never remember her to have received any correspondence from D. H. L. after she came to live permanently on the Farm. That would be around 1920. And of course we know that D. H. had got to where he could not abide very long any place, hence his globe trotting."

In the opening lines of the *handwritten* MS, Mrs. Holbrook wrote that Lawrence was "not quite twenty-seven" when she saw him last, i.e., 1912, and that she had not heard his name mentioned in twenty years. Lawrence's last known letter to Mrs. Holbrook is dated 22 February 1914 (see text, pp. 628–29): it is therefore possible that the handwritten MS may have been written in 1934, i.e., twenty years after Mrs. Holbrook had last heard Lawrence's name mentioned, and that the typewritten MS was written thereafter. Such conjectures may in turn lead to another—that it was Jessie Chambers Wood's letter of 21 June 1935 (see Chap. IV, above) and/or the arrival of her *D. H. Lawrence: A Personal Record* (1935) that prompted Mrs. Holbrook to begin Lawrence memoirs of her own.

Concerning the May Chambers Holbrook MSS, two facts are remarkable: (a) the restraint with which she treated the complex relationship of Lawrence and her sister Jessie; (b) the lack of emphasis upon Lawrence's friendship for her older brother Alan, whom Dr. Chambers has spoken of as "Bert's best friend among the boys."

12 See Note 4, above.

13 *Snobs:* "A game played with five cubes, usually made of china. The cubes are tossed and then caught on the back of an open-fingered hand."—J. D. Chambers.

14 Emily Una Lawrence, later Mrs. Samuel King, whose family nickname, among others, was Pamela, or Virtue Rewarded.

15 3 Walker Street (third house from Nottingham Road end), Eastwood.

16 Possibly a reference to the photograph of the Lawrence family reproduced in Ada Lawrence and Gelder; Moore, *Intelligent Heart;* Aldington, *Portrait of a Genius.*

17 The Reverend Mr. Robert Reid, Scottish minister of the Congregational chapel, Eastwood, from 1898.

18 Gypsy Dennis, a stenographer in London, prototype of Louisa Lily Denys Western of *Sons and Lovers.*

19 A reference to George Arthur Lawrence.

20 *Clatting:* chattering, gossiping, telling tales.

21 "Strictly, High Park Wood, not a part of Sherwood Forest."—J. D. Chambers.

22 Beauvale Priory, southeast of Haggs Farm in the High Park Wood area, the setting of Lawrence's early story "A Fragment of Stained Glass."

23 *Wigging:* reprimand, telling-off.

24 Although the typewritten MS clearly has *tethes,* it is likely that the intended word was *tether,* a rough game played by miners' children in the Eastwood area when Lawrence was a boy. In March, 1958, the County Librarian at Eastwood described the game *tether* as follows: "One 'gang' of children would secure a rival 'gang' of children, bind their hands together with rope, and rope them to each other. One end of the rope would be tied to one door knob, and the other end to someone else's door knob. Both doors would be knocked at, at the same time, and then the children secured by the rope would be pulled in opposite directions as the respective owners tried to open their doors."

25 See Note 17, above.

26 *Tantafflin:* fancy little cake or tart. See *The White Peacock,* Part I, Chap. III, "A Vendor of Visions." See also "Her Turn."

27 More likely, another photograph of Gypsy Dennis, less décolleté than the first. See *Sons and Lovers,* Chap. V, "Paul Launches into Life."

28 J. H. Haywood, Ltd., of 9, Castle Gate, Nottingham.

29 Mrs. John Berry, nee Lettice Beardsall, Mrs. Lawrence's sister. She kept a boardinghouse at Skegness, Lincs.

30 In 1909, Barrie's wife, the actress Mary Ansell, left him for Gilbert Cannan, the novelist. In late 1914, Lawrence and Frieda were friends and neighbors of the Cannans at Chesham, Bucks., and after 1919 Mary Cannan was often with the Lawrences during their sojourns in Europe.

31 The British School, Albert Street, Eastwood.

32 "Jessie started her teaching at Underwood School."—J. D. Chambers.

33 "May Chambers began her career as a teacher at Beauvale School, Eastwood."—J. D. Chambers.

34 See Robert Burns, "Green Grow the Rashes," Stanza 5.

35 Cf. D. H. L. letter to Miss Gertrude Cooper, from Villa Mirenda, dated 23 January 1927: "Do you remember in Lynn Croft, when we used to have

autograph albums, and put verses and little paintings in them? I can remember Frances [Cooper] chose for somebody's:

> 'But human bodies are such fools
> For all their colleges and schools
> That when no *real* ills perplex 'em
> They make enough themselves to vex 'em.' "

—Ada Lawrence and Gelder, pp. 119–20.

36 Original publication of the first installment of the typewritten May Chambers Holbrook MS.

37 Original publication. Legend on face of postcard: "Below Potter Heigham." Postmark: Hunstanton,/Norfolk/JU 14 05. Address: Miss J. Chambers/ Haggs Farm/Underwood/Jacksdale/Notts.

38 Prof. Harry T. Moore has recorded the fact that D. H. Lawrence's great-grandfather, the grandfather of Lydia Beardsall Lawrence, John Newton (1802–1886) of Nottingham, was a hymn writer, and that his *Sovereignty* is one of the great Nonconformist tunes.—Moore, *Intelligent Heart*, p. 6.

39 In 1902 or 1903, the Lawrence family moved from No. 3 Walker Street to No. 97 Lynn Croft, Eastwood.

40 On 1 November 1906, the Rev. Robert Reid had performed the marriage ceremony for May Chambers and William Holbrook at the Congregational Church, Eastwood, and the young couple had made their first home in Barber Street, Lynn Croft, Eastwood.

41 Lawrence's short story "A Prelude" was printed in *The Nottinghamshire Guardian,* 7 December 1907, and signed "Rosalind"—the pseudonym under which it had been submitted for Jessie Chambers. See E. T., pp. 113–14. See also D. H. Lawrence, *A Prelude: His First and Previously Unpublished Work,* with an Explanatory Foreword by P. Beaumont Wadsworth (Thames Ditton, Surrey: The Merle Press, 1949).

42 Original publication of the second installment of the typewritten MS by May Chambers Holbrook.

43 Original publication. Envelope address: Mrs. W. Holbrook/Barber St.

44 Jessie Chambers Wood noted: "The materialist philosophy came in full blast with T. H. Huxley's *Man's Place in Nature,* Darwin's *Origin of Species,* and Haeckel's *Riddle of the Universe.* This rationalistic teaching impressed Lawrence deeply."—E. T., p. 112.

45 Jessie Chambers Wood has recorded: "In the final examination of the Board of Education Lawrence had six distinctions: Education, French, Botany, History, Geography, and Mathematics. Ironically, he had no distinction in English."—E. T., p. 82.

46 In his "Autobiographical Sketch," Lawrence himself recorded the fact that his salary was "a hundred pounds a year."—*Assorted Articles*, p. 175.

47 The Davidson Road School, now the Davidson Secondary School, Croydon, Surrey, near London. Lawrence was carried on the faculty roster from 12 October 1908 to 9 March 1912.

48 Original publication of the third and final installment of the typewritten

MS by May Chambers Holbrook. Fortunately, I have been able to carry forward the memoirs by excerpting the last pages of the *handwritten* MS. See Note 11, above.

49 Original publication of an extract from a letter (1 February 1957) to the editor.

50 Original publication. Legend on face of postcard: "Dorking, Glory Woods." Postmark: Dorking/NO 7 08. Address: Mrs. W. Holbrook/Barber St./Eastwood/Notts.

51 Sir Herbert Beerbohm Tree (1853–1917), English actor-manager.

52 Cyril Maude (1861–1951), English actor; co-manager of the Haymarket Theatre, London (1896–1905); builder and manager of The Playhouse (to 1915).

53 Philip F. T. Smith, Lawrence's headmaster at Davidson Road School, Croydon (1908–1912). See Vol. I, pp. 84–89, 141–42, 150–51, of the present work.

54 Lawrence's landlord, first at 12, Colworth Rd., then, after Sept., 1911, at 16, Colworth Road, Addiscombe, Croydon, was John William ("Super") Jones, the school attendance officer of Davidson Road School, Croydon. For Lawrence's poems on the "jolliest fat baby, eight months old," see "A Baby Running Barefoot" and "A Baby Asleep After Pain" in *Amores* and *Collected Poems*, I. See also "The Old Adam" in *A Modern Lover* and "Delilah and Mr. Bircumshaw" in *Virginia Quarterly Review*, XVI (No. 2, Spring, 1940), 257–66. See also Vol. I, pp. 82–84, of the present work.

55 Original publication.

56 See Note 62, below.

57 Cf. "The Old Adam" in *A Modern Lover*.

58 Jules Bastien-Lepage (1848–1884), French painter, noted for his peasant scenes.

59 Edwin Austin Abbey (1852–1911), American painter.

60 Maurice Henry Hewlett (1861–1923), English essayist, novelist, and poet.

61 In a letter (14 March 1957) to the editor, Mr. William Holbrook has described George Hill as "a very worthy and upright citizen." And he added: "How, and in what way, he came into D. H. L.'s life, I have no idea, as he was old enough to be his parent."

62 Original publication. Address on envelope: Mrs. Will Holbrook/Moorgreen/Newthorpe/Notts. Another hand: Try Barber St./Hill Top/Eastwood.

63 Original publication. Legend on face of postcard: "View from Chine Hill, Shanklin—Isle of Wight." Postmark: Shanklin S.O., Isle of Wight/AU 10 09[.] Address: Mrs. W. Holbrook/Moorgreen/Newthorpe/Notts.

64 Lawrence had asked for, and Heinemann had sent, a special advance copy of *The White Peacock* so that Mrs. Lawrence might see it. See *Letters*, p. 7. Although Mrs. Lawrence held this copy in her hands on 2 December 1910, the novel was not officially published until January, 1911.

65 The exact date of Lydia Beardsall Lawrence's death had remained uncertain until the researches of Prof. Majl Ewing of the University of California,

Los Angeles. In a letter (7 September 1956) to the editor, Prof. Ewing wrote: "I got a 'certified' copy of an 'Entry of a Death' at Somerset House [London] for Lydia Lawrence. She died December 9 [1910]—cause listed as 1) Carcinoma of the stomach, 2) Exhaustion. D. H. made the report (his signature) and the cause of death was certified by H. M. Gillespie, M.B."

66 Original publication of the concluding sections of the handwritten May Chambers Holbrook MSS. See Note 11, above.

67 Original publication. Legend on face of postcard: "Lincoln Cathedral, South Porch." Postmark: Lincoln, AU 24 11[?]. Address: Mrs. Will Holbrook/Moorgreen/Newthorpe/Notts.

68 See Note 54, above.

69 Katherine Cecil Thurston, nee Madden (1875–1911), English novelist, author of *John Chilcote, M.P.* (1904). See *Letters,* p. 14.

70 Original publication.

71 Original publication.

72 Original publication.

73 Original publication. Legend on face of postcard: "Compton House, St. Peter's Road, Bournemouth." Postmark: Bournemouth, FE 2 12. Address: Mrs. Will Holbrook/Moorgreen/Newthorpe/Notts.

74 Original publication. Legend on face of postcard: "Clumber Terrace Steps." Postmark: Worksop, MR 5 12[?]. Address: Mrs. W[.] Holbrook/Moorgreen/Newthorpe/Notts.

75 *Toutz:* "Well, this was an endearing term to address one's Ladylove, and often used as Toots or Tootsy, a word used mostly by the young of that day . . . ."—William Holbrook (14 March 1957).

76 *Took me a tat-tar [?tat-tah]:* " 'Took me for a walk,' strictly for young children."—William Holbrook (14 March 1957). " 'Took baby for a *ta-ta'*—outing or walk."—J. D. Chambers (22 February 1958).

77 Original publication.

78 Lawrence was to spend the weekend of 27–28 April 1912 at the Cearne, home of Edward Garnett at Edenbridge, Kent, where Frieda was also to be a guest. See *Letters,* pp. 36–37.

79 Original publication. Legend on face of postcard: "Temple of the Sun, Kew Gardens." Postmark: Brentford, AP 26 12. Address: Will Holbrook Esq./Moorgreen/Newthorpe/Notts.

80 Original publication. Legend on face of postcard: "Metz.—Totenbrüche/Pont des Mort." Postmark: Metz 4 5 12. Address: Mrs. W. Holbrook/Moorgreen/Newthorpe/Notts./England.

81 Original publication. Legend on face of postcard: "Berncastel-Cues, Burg Landshut." Postmark: Trier, 9 5 12. Address: Mrs. Will Holbrook/Moorgreen/Newthorpe/Notts./England.

82 Original publication. Legend on face of postcard: "Rolandseck, Nonnenwert und Siebengebirge." Postmark: Drachenfels[?]. Address: Mrs. W. Holbrook/Moorgreen/Newthorpe/Notts./England.

83 Original publication. Legend on face of postcard: "Oktober 1741 Pfingsten 1912 Beyrberg unter dem Schutze der Rosenkranzkönigin." Postmark:

Beuerberg, 29 5 12. Address. Mrs. W. Holbrook/Moorgreen/Newthorpe/
Notts./England.

84 Original publication. Legend on face of postcard: "Die Quelle. La source."
Postmark: München 8 Jun 12. Address: Mrs. Will Holbrook/Moorgreen/
Newthorpe/Notts./England.

85 A temporary home of Dr. Else Jaffe-Richthofen, Frieda's sister. See Moore,
Intelligent Heart, p. 126.

86 Original publication. Legend on face of postcard: "Wolfratshausen, Isartal-
bahn." Postmark: Indecipherable, but stamped "Nottingham JY 15 12."
Address: Mrs. Will Holbrook/Moorgreen/Newthorpe/Notts./England.

87 David Garnett and Harold Hobson. See *Letters,* p. 58.

88 "Now this calls for a lot of explaining. 'Jonty' and 'Pawnie' were nicknames
tagged onto my wife, as she was belonging to a very old Family whose
name was Chambers. This name and the offsprings from them were very
extensive in the Village, where they had lived for hundreds of years, and
so had, one might say, become a permanent institution, grown into the
land, and never questioned their prior rights to everything pertaining
thereof.

"So now when one married into this numerous clan it was required that
you define which branch of the Chambers you came from. Now Mrs. Holbrook's grandfather's name was Jonathan and he kept a Pawnshop so was
locally designated as either Jonty or Pawnie. . . . I am afraid I am somewhat to blame too, as I mostly spoke of her as Pawnie, the old people called
her Jonty."—William Holbrook (14 March 1957). See Note 4, above.

89 Original publication. Legend on face of postcard: "Blick von der Rosskopf-
hütte (2191 m) auf Wildekreuzsplitze." Postmark: —rzing, ? 2 12. Address: Will Holbrook Esq./Moorgreen/Newthorpe/Notts[.]/England.

90 In a letter (1 February 1957) to the editor, Mr. William Holbrook wrote:
"Here I must explain who this Rayner outfit were. They were travelling
showmen, one night stand of actors which visited the hamlets around
England. The price was 2 pence. Planks (rough seats) were provided,
but the wealthy Tycoons could be accommodated with a strip of carpet,
but this luxury cost 6 pence or half a bob, known by the public as a Tan-
ner. The cast included all the Rayner family, two or three generations of
them. This tribe of Yemen got so carried away with their blood-and-thunder
performance that they staged a real blood-letting performance on each
other, much to our delight. Then we were getting 2 pennyworth. This,
needless to say, was super de luxe to the intended play, which was *Sweenie
Todd the Barber* or *The Murder in the Red Barn.* All this was enacted in a
much worn old tent, and was lighted by coal oil flares." See also Moore,
Intelligent Heart, p. 12. See also Lawrence: "It was Saturday . . . , and
the lads ran off to the little travelling theatre that had halted at West-
wold. . . . [They] sat open-mouthed in the theatre, gloriously nicknamed
the 'Blood-Tub,' watching heroes die with much writhing, and heaving,
and struggling up to say a word, and collapsing without having said
it . . . ."—*The White Peacock,* Part I, Chap. 6, "The Education of
George."

91 See "On the Lago di Garda," Part III, "The Theatre," in *Twilight in Italy*.

92 Cf. the raised platform in the pub scene of the *Burns Novel,* on which Lawrence was working at this time. See Vol. I, pp. 193–94, of the present work.

93 Original publication.

94 Original publication. Legend on face of postcard: "Luzern mit dem Pilatus." Postmark: Luzern, 22 IX 1913. Address: Mrs. Will Holbrook/ Woldsway/Plumtree Park/Nr. Nottingham/England.

95 In a letter (18 June 1957) to the editor, Mr. William Holbrook wrote: "I came to Canada one year ahead of Mrs. Holbrook. This was March 21st 1914. Mrs. Holbrook came the year after, 1915. On the Christmas of 1916 I along with two of Mrs. Holbrook's brothers were batching in a dilapidated log shack far north in Saskatchewan. The temperature was registering 63° below zero and the warm air in this shack melted the frozen dirt floor. So I that night decided to write of this unusual experience to D. H. whose address was in Sunny Italy [Cornwall]. I told him our conditions and that the legs of my chair had sunk into the floor down to the staves and before my letter could be finished I too would be sitting on the dirt. He answered me by saying nobody but a Bloody fool would put up with that, when he could be like himself sitting in a pub drinking good beer, so come along we've lots of room in a big rambling house, with only him and Frieda to hear the echoes. The things that passed through my mind were, why should two men who knew the company of nice, interesting people back in a snug cottage in England, I in a frigid zone and he, D. H., in a sunny clime. Why oh why? men destined never to meet again. We truly drank from different cups and continued to do so. Oh yes, also in his reply he commenced by telling me he had received my trash while crossing a moon-lit lagoon. Then he commenced to do as he often did, get abusive by word vehemently."

96 Cf. "On the Lago di Garda," Part IV, "San Gaudenzio," and Part VII, "John," in *Twilight in Italy*.

97 Signorina Eva Rainusso, schoolmistress, at Lerici, per Tellaro, Sarzana. See *Letters,* p. 298; Frieda Lawrence, p. 72.

98 See *Letters,* p. 175.

99 Original publication.

INDEX

Italic numerals indicate memoirs, letters, fiction, and articles reproduced in the text.